History and Jewish Historians

HISTORY AND JEWISH HISTORIANS

Essays and Addresses

By Salo W. Baron

Compiled with a Foreword by
Arthur Hertzberg *and* Leon A. Feldman

The Jewish Publication Society of America
5725   PHILADELPHIA   1964

In honor of the seventieth birthday of
Professor Salo Wittmayer Baron
Professor Emeritus of Jewish History,
Literature, and Institutions
on the Miller Foundation, Columbia University

Foreword

ON THE OCCASION of his sixtieth birthday, which occurred in 1955, a group of Salo Wittmayer Baron's former students joined together in publishing a *Festschrift*. The essays which appeared in that volume dealt with aspects of the whole range of Jewish history, from biblical times to the modern era. Such testimony to the variety of fields to which Professor Baron's students are contributing was a tribute to the depth and catholicity of his teaching.

Baron is continuing with undiminished vigor to labor on his *magnum opus,* the many-volumed new presentation of his *A Social and Religious History of the Jews.* Other books are coming from his pen, and his scholarly and communal leadership continues at its accustomed pace. Only the calendar is evidence for the fact that his seventieth birthday is now approaching.

A number of informal conversations among some of his disciples and admirers has resulted in the idea that one way of paying homage to a scholar is to study his work. The many printed volumes of Salo Baron's large productivity are quite readily available, but there are hundreds of articles, some of them of the length of monographs, which are scattered in journals and periodicals. Most of these are relatively unknown. More important still, to gather them together in an organized form amounts to a journey of discovery. To have the reprints arranged by topic means that you are suddenly aware that many, perhaps most, of these essays do not stand separately. In a number of areas Baron has really been writing books, even though the various parts have appeared, with lapses of time, in scattered journals and in several languages.

In the course of the next few years, it is our hope that several such volumes of collected essays will appear. This book is the first. There is very good reason why it should be devoted entirely to theoretical questions in the understanding of history. It is an open secret that the world of scholarship has been hoping for many years that Professor Baron would publish an extended statement, in book form, of his historic vision and theory. To the present he has preferred to let his outlook be more implicit in his narrative and analytic writing than explicit in a book on historiography. He has, nonetheless, through the years commented on the work of most of his major predecessors. In several essays he has outlined, synthetically, his views of major periods of the Jewish past. Together these hundreds of pages come close to providing us with the hoped-for connected account of Baron's theoretical views.

It would be impertinent, as well as impossible, for disciples of a master to attempt, even in a few brief paragraphs, to assess his work in the field of historical theory. We have neither the distance nor the knowledge. Salo Baron has himself taught us that all conclusions are constantly subject to revision, and that his own views are not revelation. We are therefore certain that even this formidable polyhistor has left room for scholars yet to come to see things which he has not seen. A tentative answer can however begin to be given to the question: what characterizes Baron's vision of Jewish history?

It is central to his outlook that Jewish experience through the ages has not happened in isolation. The Jews have lived within a larger world. In some versions of Jewish history this world has been imagined as either non-existent, in any important sense, or as the unchanging enemy. Jewish history thus became an account of the inner life of the Jews and of the ways that they could find of resisting hostility (*Leidens- und Gelehrtengeschichte*). Such an approach required of the Jewish historian no great insight into the history of the various gentile worlds, for, by definition, such knowledge was of little importance to understanding Jewish history. Baron has insisted that at no point in the whole of their experience have the Jews failed to come into serious encounter with other cultures. The image of a sealed community is not true even for the most closed of ghettos. Secondly, these influences have not always been of one kind. The multi-national Austro-Hungarian empire and the multi-cultural late Roman empire are much different contexts for Jewish history than the religious and cultural monism of the generation of Muhammed. In each of the changing ages and climes within which the Jews have lived, their history can be understood only as part of human history, in general.

This view has important consequences. As a theory it reflects an outlook which refuses to regard the Jews as pariahs, always in a position of otherness and over-againstness. Baron is no Pollyanna. He is keenly aware of the tragic dimensions of Jewish history. At the very apex of his public career, when he appeared as witness in Jerusalem at the Eichmann trial, he reached heights of eloquence and passion in describing the long history of Jewish suffering. Nonetheless, Baron is no Cassandra, either. He has been pre-eminent in calling attention to the ages of quiet and even cooperation between Jews and Gentiles. He has labored to prove that all of Jewish history is not a vale of tears. In essence, he has brought forward into the twentieth century, into an age marked by man's loss of faith in his own goodness, the more spacious hopes of the earlier century in which he was born. Rooted as he also is in classic Jewish thought and feeling, Baron continues to believe that man is not irretrievably evil and that the human past is not a tale of unrelieved wickedness.

This view also has important technical consequences for defining the field of Jewish historical research. It increases enormously the burden upon the Jewish historian. To work in the manner of Baron, one must be a first-class general historian, who is able to write in an original way, as Baron has, on such subjects as Lassalle's political theory and on the interrelations between modern nationalism and religion. The task is all the more onerous if the field of a historian's research is not limited to one period but extends over the whole of Jewish history. This people has lived among many cultures. To describe it in all these contexts requires an adequate knowledge of current research in all the aspects of Western and Middle-Eastern history. The protean intellectual and linguistic equipment that is required for such scholarship, the sheer industry that it takes and the capacity to maintain independent critical judgment in so many fields is a phenomenon of the greatest rarity.

Having asserted that Jewish history is part of general history, Baron has inevitably had to confront the question: What is different about the Jews? His answer stands in a line of classic Jewish thought that is rooted in the Bible itself. In his view, the Jews are a peculiar people because they have been the bearers, from their beginnings, of a Messianic religion of universal import. The meaning of the career of Jewry in history is to live in the dimension of time, as a people which exemplifies, through its particular way of life, universal moral ideas. Other peoples are created in space, on their lands. Their sense of community is rooted in geography, and it tends to die when such a people is exiled. The encounters of the Jews with Palestine are indeed the apexes of Jewish historic creativity, but Baron sees more to Jewish experience, even in those periods, than the simple fact of a people living on its land. Even during the First Commonwealth, and certainly during the Second, the Jews were characterized by the presence of an influential diaspora. When the complete Exile began, they were prepared by prior experience to exist without a base on their own land. This people yearned always to be restored to Palestine, but it could cope with the fact of landlessness.

Baron thus affirms the importance for Jewish history both of Zion and of the Jewish communities outside the homeland, and he passes no judgment on the merit of one as over against the other. In its totality, this international people, retaining its spiritual and communal identity in changing ages and places, is the harbinger of the human future, when all identities will be historical rather than geographical.

As a stance out of which to conduct the work of historical research and of synthesis, this outlook has the great virtue that it enables him to see value in every kind of Jewish community, idea, personality, or age. Characteristically, Baron neither praises or blames, but understands and sympathizes.

The roots of Baron's views are in philosophical idealism, as applied to history. Among modern Jewish thinkers, his explanation of Jewish uniqueness is related to the thought of Nahman Krochmal, among others. What is new, and characteristic, in his religiously oriented idealism is Baron's insistence on studying the hard facts of communal life within which Jewish ideals have been embedded. For him, scholars and men of the spirit are not alone the major bearers of Judaism. Peddlers, economic innovators and factions struggling with each other for the control of Jewish communal organization—all the many kinds of people who go to make up a society are of consequence in his depiction of the career of Jewry. If Israel, the people, is the bearer of its spirit, Baron's vision is broad enough to see that that spirit has expressed itself in the most mundane social facts.

It is our hope that, by collecting these essays on historiography, we will be making a contribution to furthering the understanding of Salo Baron's method and of his conception of Jewish history. We are certain that his work has implications which extend beyond his many fields of research to the crucial questions of this age.

ARTHUR HERTZBERG
LEON A. FELDMAN

Preface

A HISTORY OF history is an excellent mirror of the changing attitudes of human societies. Even if dealing with the same events and historical trends, successive historians have differed in their evaluation not only because of their different personal philosophies and attitudes, but also because they shared the dominant values and approaches of their respective generations. Most fascinating has been especially the transition from the full or partial acceptance of old legends by the medieval writers to the critical, sometimes overcritical, separation of fact from folklore by the nineteenth-century historians and to the ultimate, more tempered acceptance of both as significant phenomena of human experience, characteristic of our own time. One need not share Goethe's extreme criticism of the new critical approaches which, in his opinion, "through some pedantic truth had displaced something great and of superior value for us," and yet embrace ancient legends as an independent source of understanding of the human or Jewish appreciation of the past. That is why the mixture of history and legend characteristic of "The Historical Outlook of Maimonides" is as much part of the Jewish views of history as are the interpretations of the more critical schools of the nineteenth and twentieth centuries.

It has long been felt, therefore, that a comprehensive history of Jewish historiography would fill an important lacuna in Jewish learning. Thus far Moritz Steinschneider's *Geschichtsliteratur der Juden* is the only available full-length study. But as mentioned below (Essay 12) this volume offers in the main a bibliographical survey rather than a comprehensive historical analysis. Otherwise we are still limited to a few critical studies of individual historians, such as are included in the present collection which, it is hoped, may furnish some of the brick and mortar needed for the erection of that major historiographic structure.

It is a somewhat melancholy experience for any author to review a selection of his essays published over a period of nearly half a century. The oldest of these articles (Essay 11, Part 2) was written in 1917 on the occasion of Heinrich Graetz's hundredth anniversary. Another (Essay 8) was the first study published by me in English after my arrival in the United States in 1926. Still another presents one of my latest publications (Essay 5) written but a few months ago for the twenty-fifth anniversary number of the quarterly, *Jewish Social Studies,* of which I have had the honor of serving as an editor from its inception.

The rereading of the first of these essays reminded me of Thomas Babington Macaulay's experience when his study of Milton was to be reprinted in his *Critical and Historical Essays* in 1856. Like Macaulay, I could no longer fully agree with the contents and form of that first scholarly study which I had written "fresh from college." In contrast to Macaulay, however, who allowed his study of Milton to be reprinted without change, I first had to translate my article from German and hence had the opportunity of introducing numerous stylistic changes and condensations. Not that my admiration for Graetz had diminished in the intervening years. In fact, not only had I the satisfaction of seeing this essay appear in Graetz's own *Monatsschrift* in January, 1918, but some ten years later I was invited to fill Graetz's chair at the Breslau Theological Seminary. Subsequent historic events have shown that I had no reason to regret my inability to accept that honoring invitation. Yet such admiration never hampered my critical approach which, I am confident, comes to the fore also with respect to all other historians included in this collection.

Understandably, these essays, written over many years and originally appearing in different journals with their differing editorial policies, have shown great divergences in spelling, punctuation, and other technical details. An effort was made to achieve here as much uniformity as was possible, without making a fetish of it and without unduly delaying the publication of this collection. Understanding readers, it is hoped, will prove indulgent.

It is with real pleasure that I express my heartfelt thanks to my pupils, Professor Leon Feldman and Rabbi Arthur Hertzberg, for having taken the initiative to cull from my numerous articles those pertaining to the specific methodological and historiographic aspects of Jewish history. They have also arranged for the publication of this volume and for the preparation of its Index. I am also grateful to my secretary, Mrs. Rebecca Fischer, for her assistance in proof-reading and in the preparation of some manuscripts, especially of the four essays (included in Nos. 7, 8, 11) which appear here for the first time in an English translation. Above all I am indebted here, as in almost everything I have written over the last thirty years, to the devoted cooperation of my wife, Mrs. Jeannette Meisel Baron, who has been a genuine helpmate to me in the entire process of research, writing and publication.

SALO W. BARON

Yifat Shalom
Canaan, Conn.
May 19, 1964

Contents

Acknowledgements

We are grateful to the publishers of the books and periodicals listed below for their generosity in granting permission for the republication of articles written by Professor Salo W. Baron:

American Academy for Jewish Research for *Proceedings* and *Ginzberg Jubilee Volume*

The Leo Baeck Institute for *Monatsschrift für Geschichte und Wissenschaft des Judentums*

Encyclopedia Judaica

Hebrew Union College-Jewish Institute of Religion for *Abrahams Memorial Volume*

Jewish Social Studies

Jewish Theological Seminary of America for the *Marx Jubilee Volume*

The Menorah Journal

Midstream

Revue des Etudes Juives

World Jewish Congress, British Section, for *Simon Dubnow*

History and Jewish Historians

PART I

Essays in History

I

Who Is a Jew*

No more ironical situation can be envisaged than for a people to be of several minds about the nature of its own identity. And yet such a sharp division of opinion was recently demonstrated by the changing attitudes of the government of Israel concerning the definition of a Jew. This definition is a practical necessity inasmuch as, in the absence of a written constitution, the "fundamental" laws passed by the Knesset include the so-called Law of Return which pledges the country for all future times to admit Jews to its borders. But that the definition of who is a Jew under the terms of that law should become a matter of political controversy, and that a changing coalition of parties composing the government should force a total reversal of a position taken by a previous cabinet is but another illustration of the extraordinary nature of Jewish life and the general impossibility to apply to it the prevailing criteria of religious allegiance.

Not that one need necessarily look for a generally acceptable clear-cut definition. Definitions are sometimes the most awkward means of reaching substantive agreements and understanding; they have more often than not generated endless controversies. Without looking for definitions we all have a fairly clear understanding of, for instance, who is an American, although opinions have diverged widely about who, or what, is "un-American." In the case of the Jews, however, there is indeed room not only for different formulations, but also for genuine differences of opinion on the underlying assumptions. In fact, the controversy over who is a Jew has had many facets throughout the history of the Jewish dispersion.

* Reprinted from *Midstream,* vol. VI, no. 2, spring, 1960.

Originally, of course, the term Jew was a derivative from the country of Judah, the southern of the two kingdoms of ancient Israel. With the disappearance of Northern Israel after the fall of Samaria in 721 B.C.E., Judah remained as the sole Jewish state which guarded its independence for another 135 years. The descendants of these ancient Judeans became the Jews of all following generations.

However, the controversy begins at this very point. Modern biblical scholars, particularly the adherents of the long-regnant Wellhausenian theories concerning the dating of "documents" in the Bible, have long ago begun calling the religion of ancient Israel before the fall of Jerusalem the Israelite or Hebrew religion. These scholars have claimed that only after the return from the Babylonian Exile, and the establishment of the new "theocracy" of the Second Commonwealth did the new priestly and law-centered religion of "Judaism" emerge under the leadership of Ezra the Scribe and his associates and disciples.

Characteristic of this entire school of biblical criticism was a distinguished work published in 1896 by Eduard Meyer, one of the leading ancient historians at the turn of the century. The very title of the book formulated a program. By calling it *Die Entstehung des Judentums* (The Origin of Judaism), Meyer clearly indicated that the period of Ezra had marked a complete break with the past of prophetic Judaism which had now been replaced by the new law and ritualism of the Priestly Code. As an historian, moreover, Meyer attributed the rise of that new "Jewish" religion and civilization to the new position of the Jews as a subject people of the Persian empire. It was, indeed, in the interest of Persia's Achaemenid dynasty which ruled, as the Book of Esther informs us, over one hundred and twenty-seven provinces, to keep its multifarious racial, ethnic and religious groups under effective control with the aid of their own leaders. Under that policy, the early Achaemenid empire builders, including Cyrus and Darius I, endowed also the new theocracy of Jerusalem with much authority and thus helped to mold the new "Judaism." With complete abandon, Meyer exclaimed that post-exilic Judaism had thus been created "in the name of the Persian king and on the strength of the authority of his empire.

6

The effects of the Achaemenid Empire thus extend directly to our day with a power equalled by few contemporary phenomena."

Few biblical critics, to be sure, will subscribe today to this sweeping assertion, or even to its underlying theories concerning the chronological sequence of the relevant biblical documents. Yet Meyer's general outlook still dominates the minds of Bible students, particularly in the Christian world, and post-exilic "Judaism" still is frequently differentiated from the pre-exilic "Israelitic" faith. "Jewish" history has thus artificially been foreshortened by at least a millennium.

Nor is this concept entirely the result of modern critical approaches. In many ways it is but a variant of the old Christian concept which saw in the Jewish people and its religion a mere *praeparatio evangelica,* a preliminary phase before the advent of the Christian "redeemer." Eusebius, who wrote an entire book under this very title, and other Church Fathers untiringly underscored the difference between the old and the new dispensations. They taught that the Jew had indeed formerly belonged to the "chosen people" but, by repudiating Jesus, he had forfeited his chosenness which had been transferred to the Christian community. The new Jew might still be Israel in the flesh, but it is the Christian who had become Israel in the spirit. The term "Jew" thus gradually became among Christians a term of opprobrium. In discussing, for instance, the ceremony of circumcision, the Christian apologist Justin Martyr, a native of Palestinian Shechem-Nablus living after the Roman suppression of the Bar Kocheba revolt, exclaimed: "[It] was given for a sign that you may be separated from other nations, and from us; and that you alone may suffer that which you now justly suffer; and that your land may be desolate, and your cities burned with fire; and that strangers may eat your food in your presence, and not one of you may go up to Jerusalem."

So convinced had the Christians become that they were the genuine spiritual descendants of Abraham that no lesser a thinker than St. Augustine expressed the fear that, through this constant emphasis on the spiritual kinship between the two faiths, the distinction between Christian and Jew might be completely blurred.

7

To uphold this difference, Christian teachers began using the term Jew more and more in a pejorative sense. As early as the second century, Melito of Sardis used some fanciful Hebrew etymologies, in part borrowed from the Jewish philosopher Philo, to explain that the term Israel means a man who "saw God," and hence refers to a Christian. Judah, on the other hand, means an adherent of the synagogue of Satan, while finally Ishmael, who was later to play a great role as the alleged progenitor of the Arab world and the Muslim religion, really meant "one who obeys," that is obeys his own lust. Before long some Christian thinkers began denying the very indebtedness of their faith to Judaism. Invoking the accepted Christian doctrine that, as a son of God, Jesus was pre-existent and that, hence, Christianity and its teachings really antedated the very creation of the world, St. Ignatius of Antioch by a mental tour de force indulged the paradox that "Christianity did not believe in Judaism, but Judaism believed in Christianity."

Not surprisingly, the term Jew began losing some of its ethnic-religious connotations and served more and more as a means of name calling of any opponent. Just as today people indiscriminately label adversaries communists or fascists without necessarily attributing to them the belief in the specific doctrines of either totalitarian movement, so did many Christians classify any deviationist from their accepted dogmas a Jew. It is truly remarkable to find even in the measured legal terminology of Roman imperial decrees, in which every word and term were weighed with great care and juristic precision, the reiterated designation of "Nestorius, the Jew." This condemnation of the famous heresiarch, whose Nestorian sect quickly penetrated Iran and from there paved the way for Christianity's entrance into central Asia and the Far East, was ultimately incorporated in the Code of Justinian, one of the classical compilations of Roman law. A sixth-century patriarch of Antioch who, to the best of our knowledge, had no drop of Jewish blood in his veins and betrayed no friendly feelings towards Jews, was likewise recklessly dubbed by his enemies: Severus, the Jew.

With somewhat greater justice were those Christian sectarians who steadily invoked the Old Testament in support of their doc-

8

trines styled Jews, especially by those of their antagonists who had been imbued with the Gnostic-Marcionite hostility toward the old dispensation. But in the heat of their arguments polemists often forsook this distinction and dismissed as "Jews" even such adversaries of the Old Testament as the medieval French Catharists. This tradition continued into modern times when Charles Maurras, the well-known French anti-Semite and fascist sympathizer, condemned in one breath Judaism, the Bible-minded Protestantism, and Free Masonry as the three manifestations of the Jewish spirit diametrically opposed to the genuinely "Roman," and hence "Aryan" spirit of Roman Catholicism.

When during the Middle Ages the Jewish people was gradually alienated from the soil and had to turn more and more to commerce and moneylending as sources of its livelihood, the term Jew began assuming also a new socio-economic connotation. At first the identification of a Jew with a merchant was done without any animus. In an early German toll ordinance of 906 we find the matter-of-fact provision that "Jews and other merchants" should pay such and such a toll. Before long, however, the widespread Jewish credit transactions aroused sharp animosities not only among the borrowers, who readily took loans when they needed the money but heartily disliked the lenders when they had to repay their debts with interest. The very charging of any interest, however small, was generally condemned by the Church and public opinion. If an exception was made for Jews in their capacity of "infidels," this certainly did not enhance their reputation. Under the impact of the general religious fanaticism accompanying the Crusades, a leading French churchman, Peter "the Venerable" of Cluny, advised his king drastically to suppress Jewish usury by forcing the Jews into manual labor and, preferably, by eliminating them altogether. His far more distinguished and humane contemporary, St. Bernard of Clairvaux, successfully intervened in behalf of the German Jews then threatened by crusading mobs, but he did not hesitate to agitate against the newly elected Pope Anacletus II, the great-grandson of a Jewish convert, for the "Jewish offspring now occupies the see of St. Peter to the injury of Christ." At the same time, perhaps unconsciously, he also coined a new memorable phrase. He declared that Christian usurers are wont *peius judaizare* (to judaize in a worse fashion) than Jewish moneylenders themselves. Phrases like "Jews and other usurers" (found, for instance, in a municipal ordinance of Forli, Italy, adopted in 1359), were employed as a matter of course. Thenceforth the term "judaizing," without altogether losing its original meaning of practicing Jewish rites or converting someone to Judaism, was increasingly used as the equivalent of charging usurious rates of interest and, more broadly, of economically exploiting the weak masses of the population.

For centuries thereafter the term "Jew" appeared in all western literatures, even in some dictionaries, as a synonym for usurer, exploiter, and swindler. It even was used as a verb, "to jew," in the same objectionable sense. No lesser a leader of French Enlightenment than François Marie Arouet de Voltaire allowed himself the following intemperate outburst in the article "Juif" in his *Philosophic Dictionary*:

> In short, we find them [the Jews] only an ignorant and barbarous people, who have long united the most sordid avarice with the most detestable superstition and the most invincible hatred for every people by whom they are tolerated and enriched. Still, we ought not to burn them.

All these debates affected the Jews to but a minor extent. Unperturbedly, the Jewish people considered itself part of an unbroken chain of evolution going back to Abraham, Isaac and Jacob. The distinction between Israel and Judah appeared to it as but a reflection of the ancient purely political divisions between the two co-existing Palestinian kingdoms. Religiously and ethnically the whole people was a single unit, Amos the Judean preaching freely in the northern sanctuary in the name of their common God and their common sense of justice. Although he was expelled by the northern king as an undesirable alien, the people of Northern Israel felt such a deep kinship to the people of Judah that even today it is difficult for scholars to trace the actual boundaries between the two Jewish states. After the fall of Samaria, the Judeans laid claim to the northern areas and, under Josiah, actually succeeded in recapturing much of the territory lost to the foreign invaders. Nor was the people ever mentally reconciled to any such permanent division; even when Jerusalem was occupied by enemies, prophet after prophet predicted the speedy reunification of the two branches during the forthcoming redemption. In the people's memory the fall of Samaria played but a relatively minor role, while that of Jerusalem assumed an almost cosmic significance. Permanently thereafter the destruction and rebuilding of the Temple loomed as major events within the general historic continuity of the entire people.

Forever after the Jews of the now growing dispersion considered themselves as but offshoots of the same united Palestinian community. They were prone to forget that there had existed a large Diaspora even before the fall of Jerusalem. True, the Babylonians prided themselves on the antiquity of their settlements and pointed to such monuments as a synagogue in Nehardea which had allegedly been founded by the exiled Judean king, Jehoiachin. During the Middle Ages they still made pilgrimages to the tomb of the prophet Ezekiel and boasted of other reputed survivals of their uninterrupted life in the Euphrates Valley since the Babylonian Exile. But they were prepared to overlook any evidence of still older vestiges of pre-exilic life. Egyptian Jewry, too, which had embraced far-flung communities from the Mediterranean to the borders of Ethiopia before the destruction of the First Temple and included the well-known Jewish military colony of Elephantine, placed there to defend Egypt against Ethiopian raids, forgot its early origins and considered itself as originating primarily from the Second Jewish Commonwealth.

It was this generally shared assumption of a constant stream of emigration from the Second Commonwealth which alone enabled the aforementioned biblical critics to reconcile the allegedly late post-exilic origin of the biblical canon with the fact of its universal acceptance by the Jewish people throughout its dispersion. In any case, the Diaspora's physical links with the Jerusalem community were reinforced by the frequent pilgrimages of its members to the

Holy Land and its annual collections of half shekels and other gifts for the Second Temple. In its own consciousness these historical and practical links were so strong that the unity of the whole people and the unbroken community of its descent and destiny were never subject to doubt.

This feeling of unity, wholly independent of changing political constellations and the subjection of important segments of the people to different local and imperial sovereignties, helped the Jews overcome the greatest crisis of their history, including the second fall of Jerusalem. In those centuries they became inured to living in a world divided between Rome and Parthia, and later between the Roman and the Persian empires. Nor were these sentiments of integral unity in any way affected by the large-scale influx of non-Jewish proselytes and semiproselytes in the period before the rise of Christianity. Anyone born to Jewish parents, or rather because of the biological certainty, born to a Jewish mother, was considered a Jew; a Jew remained a Jew even if he sinned and converted himself to another faith but subsequently repented. The proselyte, on the other hand, was by legal fiction declared a newly born child who, through the performance of prescribed rituals, was transformed into a member of the Jewish community not only spiritually but also physically. To underscore this total transformation, the rabbis emphasized that a proselyte automatically divested himself of all his family ties and hence had no blood relatives whatsoever. In pure theory he should be allowed to marry his own mother without committing incest. In practice, of course, the rabbis outlawed such incestuous unions, but they had to use the subterfuge that outsiders, unfamiliar with this legal fiction, might otherwise consider Judaism less inimical to incest than it really was. Because of this total rebirth, the proselyte has been technically considered a physical descendant of the Jewish patriarchs, and in his prayers, at least according to the majority opinion, he was supposed to recite the respective benedictions referring to "our forefathers Abraham, Isaac, and Jacob" on a par with a born Jew. Although in his own lifetime he still faced some minor discriminatory provisions of a social character retained on the statute books—a woman proselyte, for instance, could not marry a "priest"—all knew that such distinctions would be wiped out with respect to the proselytes' offspring. In short, in Jewish eyes, a Jew was a member of the community by virtue of both faith and descent; he was permanently linked together with other Jews in a community of destiny as willed by God.

In the Emancipation era, however, this singleness of purpose was deeply undermined through the acceptance by the Jews themselves of the views regnant in their environment. Emancipation meant not only equality of rights, but also the integration of the Jewish minority into the fabric of the majority peoples. With that integration went also a greater or lesser surrender by Jews of their own attitudes to those dominant among their neighbors. The more "progressive" Jews were, the more emotionally they had become involved in the struggle for emancipation and integration, and the more likely they were to accept the judgment of their Christian neighbors in all matters, including the latter's low appreciation of Jews and Judaism. One of the first manifestations of that inferiority feeling was the avoidance by many champions of Jewish equality, both Christian and Jewish, of the term "Jew" which had, as we recall, become in the Christian world an objectionable term. It now became customary to describe the Jewish minority by the less noxious terms of Hebrews or Israelites. Even in free America, we have had such journals as the *American Hebrew* or the *American Israelite*. It was a sign of the growing Jewish self-assertion and pride when, as early as 1830, Gabriel Riesser, the then leading protagonist in the struggle for Jewish equality, defiantly called his new magazine *Der Jude* (The Jew).

More significantly, many Jews were prepared to accept from their liberal neighbors certain basic assumptions concerning Judaism. Over a period of several centuries and through a series of sanguinary wars of religion between Catholicism and Protestantism, the Western world reached a concept of nationality and statehood as divorced from religious allegiance. Religion now began to be treated more and more as a private affair of each individual, to whom complete liberty of conscience was guaranteed by states which often embraced a variety of religious groups. In extreme cases the state divorced itself completely from the Church. In this era of an ever more rampant secular nationalism the nations demanded total subservience of all their citizens in the cultural-ethnic sense, regardless of their religious denominations. Under these new conditions of the Western world—they did not fully apply outside the Western sphere even in the twentieth century—Jews, too, began to be viewed as but one of the many religious communities, sharing with their fellow Americans, Englishmen, Germans, and so forth, not only a political and civic allegiance to their country but also the same national culture. In short, the Jews were to become, if they had not yet so turned, merely Germans or Frenchmen of the "Mosaic persuasion," different from their fellow nationals only by their religious observance.

This formula, largely subscribed to even by some of the most loyal Jews in the early decades of the nineteenth century, did not stand up under the harsh realities of the contemporary world. To begin with, even as a religion Judaism had always embraced a great many ethnic ingredients. If, after centuries of struggle between State and Church and between various religious denominations within each country, Christendom itself could not entirely suppress the link between nationality and religion, this was doubly true in the case of Judaism, whose ethnicism had always been deeply rooted in religion and vice versa. The very attempt of extreme Reform to suppress these ethnic elements of the Jewish faith proved ineffectual and of relatively short duration. More, the realities of millions of Jews living in East-Central Europe, in their overwhelming majority speaking Yiddish and living their own cultural life, rendered illusory any declaration, however well-meaning and sincere, concerning the Jewish faith being a "pure" denationalized religion. Before long the new Jewish nationalism and Zionism defiantly took up the cudgels in behalf of the existing Jewish national group.

Simultaneously, the rise of the modern anti-Semitic movements proved that Jews, whether believers or unbelievers, were victimized alike by their assailants. Ultimately, racial anti-Semitism proclaimed the permanence and immutability of the Jewish group by virtue of blood and descent regardless of individual religious beliefs and observances; indeed even regardless of conversion to a non-Jewish faith. In 1933, many thousands of born Christians, including hundreds of Catholic priests and Protestant pastors, discovered to their chagrin that, because genealogical research had detected that they had a single Jewish grandparent, they were officially stamped as members of the "non-Aryan" group.

Under these circumstances, the term "Jew" achieved many new connotations. To the racial anti-Semite a Jew was a person of Jewish descent, wholly or partially. To the spokesmen of the religious groups, the Jew remained principally, if not exclusively, the believer, however nominal, in the tenets of the Jewish faith. This was particularly true in the western countries where the majority of Jews were genuinely assimilated to the cultures of their environment. To the secular nationalists, especially in Eastern Europe, a Jew was primarily a member of his national group.

Logically, such national spokesmen would have to consider a Jew any member of their community who had turned Christian or Muslim. It was rather inconsistent on the part of Zionist leaders when, under the pressure of public opinion, they withheld admission to the Zionist organization from Jewish converts to another faith. They rationalized this refusal by arguing that in the contemporary world relatively few conversions were taking place because of genuine spiritual convictions; most of them were undergone for careerist or amorous reasons. An embattled minority like the Jewish could indeed view all religious "renegades" for such external, secular reasons as deserters with whom it wished to have no dealings whatsoever. But there were not lacking voices which demanded the recognition of genuine religious differences within the Jewish camp, just as they had long been recognized within other national groups.

Matters became further complicated by the lack of universally accepted objective criteria for national allegiance. In the Western countries the term nationality was used largely as a political synonym for citizenship, and being of French nationality, for example, meant being a citizen of the French Republic; but in East-Central Europe, the Balkans, and other areas of mixed nationalities, it became perfectly manifest that, for instance, a Pole by nationality could be, and usually was before 1914, a perfectly good Austrian, Russian, or Prussian citizen. Since all other criteria, such as territorial concentration, use of a common language, racial descent, and community of religious beliefs had broken down as the clear differentiating elements of nationality, leading nationalist thinkers of the late nineteenth century came to the conclusion that objective criteria must be abandoned in favor of some such subjective concepts as that of a nationality being merely a group linked together by a community of descent and destiny. This definition of a *Schicksals- und Kulturgemeinschaft,* first propagated by the Austrian Social-Democrats in order to secure peace within the nationalistically riven Austro-Hungarian Empire, fit the Jewish situation in many lands quite well, and was enthusiastically adopted by both proletarian and bourgeois nationalists. With this new definition, the accent was laid not on such objective ascertainable facts as one's ancestry, speech habits, or religious observance, but rather on the emotional feelings of each individual and his subjective sense of belonging to a particular group.

It is small wonder, then, that the term "Jew" now meant many things to many different people. I still remember how many of us awoke with a start when we read in the press the first reports concerning the results of the census conducted in 1921 by the newly created Republic of Czechoslovakia. In accordance with the peace treaties, as well as with the long professed desires of its leaders Masaryk and Beneš, the new Republic recognized the rights of its several national, as well as religious, minorities to full cultural self-determination without in any way restricting the equal rights of all citizens. From the outset Jews were recognized as both a national and a religious minority and answered, in this vein, the pertinent queries of the census enumerators.

The results were truly surprising. The official figures showed that there were 336,520 Czechoslovak nationals (in addition to 17,822 foreigners) professing the "Israelitic" religion. Their majority, 180,616, declared themselves to be members of the Jewish nationality (this majority was larger in Slovakia and Carpatho-Ruthenia but it turned into a minority in the main provinces of Moravia,

Bohemia, and Silesia). Of the rest 73,371 signed up as members of the Czech nationality, 49,123 as Germans, 29,473 as Magyars, 3,751 as Russians, 74 as Poles and 112 as belonging to other nationalities. In addition, there were 100 persons who professed no religion but were members of the Jewish nationality. More astonishingly, there also were some members of the Jewish nationality who professed the Roman-Catholic faith (74), Greek Catholicism (23), Greek Orthodoxy (12), Protestantism (19), and one, a woman, who was an adherent of the new Czechoslovak national faith. Thus the 180,616 members of the Jewish nationality who also professed the Jewish faith were joined by 229 co-nationals who professed other religions or none. There probably were many more thousands of Jews who never signed up as Jews by either nationality or religion and thus did not appear as such in the census.

Nevertheless, some of these unrecorded, and hence statistically non-existent Jews, probably contributed to one or another Jewish cause and perhaps were ultimately buried in a Jewish cemetery. Certainly a great many were considered as Jews by their neighbors, Jewish as well as Christian. What happened in Czechoslovakia in 1921 was multiplied several times over in other censuses of the newly created or enlarged states from the Baltic to the Aegean.

Even more radical was the transformation in the Soviet Union. Almost immediately after its seizure of power, the Soviet regime proclaimed the principle of national minority rights for the entire Union. New nationalities were actually discovered and alphabets created for them by the Soviet leaders. From the outset, Jews were treated as such a nationality and Yiddish was recognized as an official language in some local town councils, courts, and particularly in schools. At the same time, religion in general was now denounced as a mere opiate for the people. The law of July, 1918, subsequently rephrased in 1929 and ultimately taken over into the Soviet Constitution of 1936 (Art. 124), provided: "Freedom for the conduct of religious worship and freedom for anti-religious propaganda is recognized for all citizens." With full government support the Godless Societies were spreading their anti-religious gospel, especially among the youth. The latter, unable to receive religious instruction in any school—such instruction to children under eighteen was prohibited by law—grew up without any knowledge of religion except as inadequately imparted by some parents at home under great difficulties.

Not surprisingly, Jews were now counted primarily as members of the Jewish nationality, rather than as adherents of the Jewish faith. As early as 1926, the first Soviet census listed some 2,750,000 "Jews" among the Soviet residents, but it used this term as an exclusively national designation. In the ultimate sense, of course, the decision as to whether he was a Jew had to be left to each individual. For instance, Leon Trotsky seems from the outset to have changed not only his Jewish name, Bronstein, to the Russian Trotsky, but also to have abandoned completely both his Jewish faith and his Jewish nationality. His passport probably always read "Russian" in the rubric assigned to nationality. On the other hand, I was told on good authority, although I could never authenticate it, that upon his arrival in this country as Soviet ambassador, Maxim Litvinoff carried with him a passport showing his "Jewish" nationality. It appears that in the latest census of 1959, too, the approximately 2,250,000 who registered as Jews thus styled themselves only by virtue of their nationality, although no more than one-fifth still declared Yiddish as their spoken language. By a curious inconsistency, however, it may be noted, the leaders of the Soviet Jewish communities—whatever the meaning of this term may be—refused the invitation to the World Jewish Congress meeting in Stockholm in the summer of 1959 under the remarkable excuse that, being in charge of purely religious congregations, they had nothing to do with the political affairs which were to be discussed at the Congress sessions.

With the rise of the state of Israel a further element was introduced into this conceptual confusion. One can, of course, be an Israeli citizen without being a Jew by either nationality or religion. There are, indeed, some 200,000 Muslim and Christian Arabs who enjoy the status of Israeli citizens. Most Christian wives of Jewish citizens are also Israeli citizens without being counted as either members of the synagogue or the Jewish ethnic group. On the other hand, many a young Israeli has become impatient with the Jewish heritage of the last two millennia which, as he has usually been taught in school, has mainly consisted of the nightmare of unremitting persecutions. In his eagerness to start a new life, he is prepared to consider the history of his people as relevant only insofar as it relates to the First and Second Jewish Commonwealths and then start it over again in 1948. At best he may allow the preceding half century as a sort of prehistory of his new state. At the same time the Law of Return specifically admits all "Jews" to free immigration, thus opening to them also the gates for speedy naturalization. It is the difficulty of defining a Jew under the terms of this law that has played havoc with the country's domestic policies and led to the aforementioned divergent interpretations by the Israeli ministries during the last two years.

One may see, therefore, how complicated the conceptual situation has become. Let us, for the sake of argument, assume that three Jewish brothers, identical triplets, were born early in this century in Odessa and they are still alive today. One of them has settled in New York, another in Tel Aviv, while the third has remained in Odessa. Under the prevailing environmental concepts, the New York Jew is primarily a Jew by religion; the one living in Odessa is likely to disclaim any religious allegiance, but to consider himself a Jew by nationality; the resident of Tel Aviv, finally, may be neither religious nor particularly interested in national problems, but be completely satisfied with his Israeli citizenship. Under exceptional circumstances he may even have joined the fringe movement of so-called "Canaanites" who demand that the Israelis develop their own native Palestinian culture at total variance with the "Jewish" cultures of the dispersion. And yet the three brothers still are essentially the same persons and it is a sheer accident as to which of them resides in which country.

What then is a Jew today? Evidently theory cannot be imposed upon realities but it must adjust itself to them. Since the Jewish realities are such that they make Jewishness differently meaningful to different people, the concept Jew must become wide enough to embrace all these variations. Clearly, in this country a Jew will be so regarded by both himself and most of his neighbors so long as he was born a Jew and has never formally joined another religion. He may be a total agnostic or atheist, he may participate in no Jewish communal endeavor and yet, short of his public declaration of a change of faith, he will be universally considered a Jew. Even after his conversion some Christians, particularly of the unfriendly variety, will still style him a Jew. In Israel, on the other hand, his religious allegiance will play a relatively minor role, but his Jewish descent and cultural conformity, superimposed upon his Israeli citizenship, will be the decisive criterion. In the Soviet Union, finally, he will still be considered a Jew primarily by nationality.

True, under the oppressive system of the post-war years, the Soviet Jew finds but few avenues open to his national self-expression. The Yiddish elementary and secondary schools, which thirty years ago had accommodated 250,000 Jewish children, are now closed. The once flourishing Yiddish press and theater have disappeared, with the exception of a very tiny provincial paper in Birobidjan. Even in Russia, therefore, the main avenue for self-realization as a Jew still is the synagogue, however anemic an institution it may appear to us. In general, too, national minority rights, once the white hope of the non-Zionist secular Jewish nationalists, have been losing ground since the Second World War. Unless supported by strong territorial and linguistic buttresses, they have not proved genuinely viable under the conflicting imperial and nationalist systems of our age. Deprived of such territorial and linguistic concentration, the Jews outside of Israel can, indeed, entertain little hope for the adequate development of their culture in divorcement from religion. Outside of Israel, therefore, even the definition of a Jew seems to be veering back somewhat toward the traditional concept of the pre-Emancipation era, but with the strong modification that today there are millions of Jewish "sinners" who are yet considered religious Jews.

All of this is not intended to deny the right of the Israel Cabinet to decide upon its own definition. One of the prime prerogatives of national sovereignty is for any state to regulate immigration to its territory. Having in a most generous vein decided to curtail somewhat its own sovereignty and to bind itself for all future time (or at least so long as the fundamental law is not abrogated) freely to admit all Jews who seek admission, the State of Israel is entitled, in fact obliged, clearly to define the category of persons who are thus to be admitted. The more clarity in definition, the less equivocation there is in the administration of the law, and the less it is subject to arbitrary decisions. However, such a definition adopted for practical, legal, and administrative purposes does not necessarily have to cover all possible variations in the existing realities nor does it necessarily have to be accepted, on theoretical grounds, by a majority of the Israelis themselves. Outside Israel such a declaration may with equal freedom be accepted or rejected by Jews and non-Jews, according to their own experiences and the dictates of their own consciences.

In short, in the present situation of the Jewish people, whether one calls it history-made or God-willed, objective criteria are no longer exclusively valid. In our age of Emancipation, there are indeed profound differences among various segments of Jews living in different lands and even among those who share the same citizenship. The Jewish people is nevertheless held together by such intangibles as its basically common heritage, the positive will to survive on the part of a large number, probably the majority of its members, the realistic observation that there exists a genuine interdependence of fate among the Jews throughout the world, and last but not least, the outward pressures of discrimination and anti-Semitic attacks which draw no line of demarcation between one kind of Jew and another.

Under these circumstances Jews may have to abandon, at least for a long while, the quest for an all-inclusive objective formula. As a permanent minority outside of Israel, we are insisting upon the right of Jews and other minorities freely to pursue their own religious and cultural aims in a pluralistic society. We shall similarly have to learn to get along with much cultural pluralism in our own midst. I for one am prepared, therefore, to recognize, even for practical purposes, everyone as a Jew who (1) is born of Jewish parents and has not been converted to another faith; (2) is born of mixed parentage but declares himself a Jew and is so considered by the majority of his neighbors; and (3) one who by conscious will has adopted Judaism and joined the membership of the Jewish community. In the ultimate sense, it is thus the subjective decision of the individual concerned and the equally subjective opinion of his neighbors which is almost as important as the objective facts of descent and religious commitment.

2

World Dimensions
of Jewish History*

BOTH JEWISH AND WORLD SCHOLARSHIP have long recognized that
Jewish history, particularly during the two and a half millennia of
the dispersion, cannot be fully understood without the background
of the various civilizations under which Jews happened to live. By
giving his ten-volume Jewish history the telling title, *Weltgeschichte
des jüdischen Volkes,* Simon M. Dubnow announced that he wished
to treat his subject within the framework of world history. Referring
to this title which he had undoubtedly chosen in cooperation with
his German translator, Aaron Steinberg, Dubnow wrote in his
Introduction:

> *World History of the Jewish People* is perhaps an unusual
> title, but it corresponds fully to the content and scope of this
> unusual segment of the history of mankind. It is customary
> to speak of "World History" in conjunction with the general
> history of highly developed nations, as distinguished from the
> history of single countries and peoples. The destiny of the
> Jewish people, however, has unfolded in such a way that it
> possesses a world history of its own in the literal sense of the
> word. It embraces in a physical sense almost the entire civilized
> world (except India and China) and it coincides chronolog-
> ically with the whole course of the historical existence of
> mankind. Judaism represents a true historical microcosm, and
> thus there is excellent justification for speaking of world his-
> tory of the Jewish people.[1]

* Reprinted from *Simon Dubnow—The Man and His Work,* ed. by Aaron
Steinberg (Paris, 1963), pp. 26-40. First published without notes as The Leo
Baeck Memorial Lecture 5 (New York, 1962).

Of course, we have now come to realize that world history is not quite tantamount to the history of the western world. Since Dubnow wrote these lines, there was a tremendous upsurge not only of the ancient civilized nations of China and India but also of the newly developing nations of Africa. All of them clamor for a place in the sun, and wish to assume their rightful place in the history of mankind. After all, the five Asiatic countries of Japan, China, Indonesia, India and Pakistan alone embrace between them one half of the world's population. From this perspective the Jewish rôle in world history is somewhat more limited in area, but not necessarily in intensity. The very re-emergence of the far eastern nations and the re-entry of the other Afro-Asian peoples upon the scene of world history has largely been the effect of their progressive westernization. Hence, directly or indirectly, the Jewish factor in the rise and evolution of the western world has considerable bearing also on the historic destinies of these nations.

In practice, however, neither Dubnow nor most of his contemporaries have greatly advanced in this respect beyond their predecessors, including Graetz. This older treatment of Jewish history which may, perhaps uncharitably, be designated "the isolationist approach to Jewish history" still had a modicum of justification at the time when Graetz and the other nineteenth-century historians were chiefly interested in the intellectual history of the Jewish people. Although here, too, any keen student of thought and literature realized that there were deep interrelations between certain ideas advanced by Jewish and non-Jewish thinkers and that linguistic media and literary formulations depended, to a very large extent, on environmental factors. Certainly, no one, even in Graetz's time, ventured to analyze medieval Jewish religious philosophy without reference to the Arab schools of religious thought. With the development of Near Eastern archaeology no one could venture to discuss even biblical doctrines and literary forms without reference to Babylonian, Canaanite or Egyptian culture. Yet even the Babylonian Talmud has until now been treated as if Babylonian Jewry under the Parthian and Sassanian empires had lived in total isolation from its neighbors. Similarly, medieval and early modern Jewish history both in the

East and the West have been treated as if the environment only occasionally encroached on Jewish life with some specific "influences," while Jewish "contributions to civilization" were limited to some specialized fields of philosophic and scientific "transmission."

Of course, modern life has taught the Jews a lesson to the contrary. Certainly, in the Emancipation era Jewish history has become an integral part of the history of the countries in which Jews happened to live, since the Jewish people itself had become integrated into the fabric of the national lives of the host peoples. But even before these integrative processes could achieve full amalgamation of Jewish and world currents, it became manifest that, throughout history, there was a profound interrelation between the Jewish and the general strains of evolution. More and more have twentieth-century scholars, dealing with individual countries (for instance, Yitzhak Fritz Baer in his treatment of the Jews of Spain), come to the realization that only a fuller understanding of the interplay of Jewish and general societal factors could pave the way for a better understanding of many vital historic developments. Much more, however, has yet to be done before a deeper penetration into this interplay of forces can shed new light on the history of both.

I

In some respects, these world dimensions of the Jewish people's career on earth had been adumbrated already at its cradle. According to the biblical tradition, Patriarch Abraham was born and bred in Ur of Chaldaea but, having discovered his new religion, he emigrated to the land of Canaan. From there he proceeded to Egypt and returned to Canaan. The historicity of this great figure, long doubted by extreme biblical critics, is now almost generally accepted by scholars. Certainly, after the excavations of Ur had brought to light many testimonies of an intensive moon worship in that ancient Babylonian city, the biblical names of Abraham's family, beginning with his father, Terah (reminiscent of *yerah, yareah* = moon), his own original name Abram (High Father), often used for the moon

25

deity, his wife's name Sarah (a frequent appellative of Astarte), his relative Laban (related to *lebanah* = moon), all having some bearing on the moon and its worship, had become much more revealing. An Old Testament writer, imaginatively describing the lifetime of the great patriarch centuries after the event, could not possibly have been so familiar with Abraham's religious background as to invent these names. In any case, according to the biblical narrative, Abraham had, in his own career and thought, combined the fruits of the three leading civilizations of his time, those of the Fertile Crescent, Egypt and Canaan. Even Palestine and northern Syria which, however politically divided, were united by their common Canaanite speech and religion, had behind them by the time of Abraham, as we now increasingly realize, a history of civilized life of a millennium or two, or as long as that of most European countries today. The patriarch thus set in motion an historic evolution which, ultimately, led to the formation of a people and a religious group whose world historical functions were far to transcend its numerical strength.

True, in recent times, the term "international Jew" has become a fighting word for German and other anti-Semites. On the other hand, the designation of *Weltvolk* was long used by European Jewish socialists of the Bund variety to buttress their particular brand of anti-Zionist Diaspora nationalism. Yet even these biased misapplications could not controvert the basic historic truth that, by the mere fact of its interterritorial dispersion, the Jewish people has always had a direct stake in international developments. Willy-nilly it also often developed in the various countries of its settlement certain basic attitudes to national affairs which may have proved irksome, not only to the local one-hundred per cent nationalists, but, more recently, also to the professedly internationally minded communist assailants of Jewish "cosmopolitanism." Moreover, whatever one's personal leanings in these controversial matters may be, the historic fact of deep Jewish involvement in many world-wide trends and movements can hardly be denied. It is, indeed, from the vantage point of such world movements that Jewish history must be re-examined.

One aspect of Jewish history which seems particularly pertinent in our day is the Jewish people's more or less constant life in divided worlds. To some extent this factor operated already during the First Commonwealth when ancient Israel, whether tribally divided or united under one or two kingdoms, lived in a period of unceasing tension between the two great empires of the Euphrates and the Nile Valleys. In fact, it was fortunate for both Jewish and mankind's history that between 1200 and 900 B.C.E., world history took, so to speak, time out in that region, because the conflict between Egypt and Assyria-Babylonia had become quiescent. Although Egypt still nominally claimed overlordship over Palestine, it did not prevent ancient Israel from taking, during these crucial three centuries, deep roots in the country, and from laying there firm foundations for its own religion and culture. With the resumption of these imperial struggles in the ninth century, to be sure, Israel was again drawn into the vortex of world politics, but by that time its national life and thought had become so well grounded that it could maintain itself even in the face of recurrent catastrophes. Subsequently the entire people was united for a relatively short time within the vast Persian empire but, soon after Alexander, the Jews again began living between such rival empires as Egypt and Syria, later Rome and Parthia or Persia, and, finally, between Christendom and Islam.

Jewish intellectual leaders were not oblivious of both the challenges and the opportunities arising for their people from such permanent divisions. While in many ways complicating Jewish communal exchanges—there was a time when Parthia actually prohibited pilgrimages to Roman Palestine, a prohibition which some pious pilgrims succeeded in evading—such divisions also guaranteed the survival of at least some segments of Jewry when either general upheavals or specific outbursts of religious intolerance endangered it under one civilization. The author of *Seder Eliyahu Rabbah* used the form of an ancient rabbinic homily for his astute observation that God had purposely divided the world "in order to preserve Israel."[2] Whether this statement was made in the third or in the ninth century (scholars are still divided on the date of that famous midrash), it well reflected the existing reality that the general insecurity of Jewish life was, in part, remedied by the lack of simultaneity in the hostile actions of overwhelmingly powerful neighbors.

Needless to say, such a position between two worlds often was very uncomfortable, indeed dangerous. During wars between world powers many Jews located at the frontiers suffered severely. Moreover, if ever the people tried to play one power against the other, particularly in the political and military spheres, it came to grief. Its uprising, for example, against Trajan, in 115-17, held out more promise than the other Jewish revolts against Rome precisely because the Roman armies were then engaged in a sharp struggle with Parthia. The leaders of Egyptian, Cypriot and other "rebellious" Jewish armies could cherish the hope that, by cutting the lifeline between Rome and Mesopotamia, they might help the Parthians to destroy the Roman legions and thus open the way for the liberation of the entire Near East from the Roman yoke. They miscalculated and, as a result, Cypriot Jewry was totally eliminated from the island for centuries, while that of Egypt was so disastrously weakened that, until the Arab conquest, it never recovered even a shred of its former glory. Similarly, the last sustained effort of Palestinian Jewry to shake off Byzantine domination, by helping the Persian armies to conquer and administer the Holy Land five centuries after Trajan, ended with an equally profound reversal when the victorious Emperor Heraclius re-entered Jerusalem in 628. Here the effects might have been more enduringly catastrophic, inasmuch as four years later the emperor, for reasons which have not yet been fully clarified, decided to suppress Judaism in the whole length and breadth of his empire. Allegedly under his direct inspiration, but probably not without the contributory impact of the news arriving from the Near-Eastern area of conflict, Jewish settlements were almost totally wiped out by the decrees of Visigothic, Gallic, and Langobard kings. That this first large-scale outlawry of Judaism, covering practically all Mediterranean lands, did not quite cut short the historic career of the Jewish people in those areas was mainly owing to the sudden emergence of a third force, the expansion of Islam.

Even where Jews as such were not politically or militarily involved, the subsequent struggles between Islam and Christendom frequently raised the spectre of their annihilation. To begin with, there was no end of rumors about Jewish disloyalty. When the Moors invaded Spain in 712 they, indeed, found allies among the Jews decimated under the last Visigothic kings. Such a fifth column was perfectly natural in a world which placed religious allegiance and even class interests far above patriotic loyalty to a state. But suspicions were rampant even where they had no basis in fact. For example, according to contemporary chroniclers, Jews opened the gates of Bordeaux to Moorish conquerors. The only difficulty with this story is that the Moors never entered Bordeaux. No less absurd were the later rumors spreading throughout Germany that Jews tried to help the terrifying Mongolian invaders of 1241 with camouflaged shipments of arms. The era of Crusades flooded the western world with such a wave of religious fanaticism, combined with self-sacrificial devotion to one's ideals, that the Jews in both parts of the world were bound to suffer. The story of the Christian Crusaders' massacres of Jews has long been known. But the reaction of the Muslim side was no less explosive. If in the entire history of Islam we hear of only one radical suppression of Judaism as well as Christianity, namely that proclaimed by the Almohade kings of Morocco and Spain in the twelfth century, we must remember that the very rise of that extremist sect was largely conditioned by Islam's counteraction to the western Crusading challenge.

At the same time, these world divisions also created new opportunities for the Jewish people. In an earlier paper[3] I have tried to show that Yehudah Halevi's remarkable nationalistic reformulation of Judaism in both his philosophic and poetic works can be understood only as "an answer to an historic challenge," namely, to the challenge of the Crusades. More permanently, the world division after the rise of Islam opened to Jews the opportunity of serving as the great mediators between East and West. They alone happened to be a tolerated religious minority under western Christendom. Their ubiquity, interterritorial solidarity, the availability to them of a common language, Hebrew, and of a common law and institutions derived from the Talmud—all that made them the natural inter-mediaries in world trade, in which by the ninth century they had largely displaced the Syriac Christians. They also could help bridge the intellectual gap by first acquainting the newly nascent Arab world with the fruits of ancient science and philosophy and, subse-quently, on a much larger scale, by assisting in the transmission of that combined heritage of the Graeco-Roman, Indo-Persian and Islamic civilizations to the upsurging western nations. Moreover, by their very persistence in the adherence to their ideals and ways of life, they set the example of dissent from the established verities which could serve as a source of inspiration for any disaffected group. Not surprisingly, almost every heretical movement in the West was blamed by its opponents on the Jews and their Scriptures.

New adjustments were needed when the western world was again divided between Christendom and a rejuvenated Islam under the aegis of the Ottoman Empire. Not by coincidence did Joseph ha-Kohen, the Jewish historian of the mid-sixteenth century, attempt to rewrite the history of the world in terms of the perennial conflict between East and West, or what he called the "Frankish" and the "Ottoman" kings. Once again Jews were in both parts of the world, sharing in their glories and defeats alike. The inherent dangers of such a division were magnified, at least in the short run, by the inner divisions within Christendom itself as a result of the Reforma-tion, Catholic Restoration and the sanguinary Wars of Religion. At first Bohemian Jewry was sharply assailed because of its allegedly pro-Hussite position. Soon thereafter the very survival of all Central-European Jewry was threatened by Martin Luther's *volte face* from a fairly sympathetic to a rabidly hostile attitude. Yet during the great wars, when Catholics and Protestants sought to destroy one another, both parties sometimes spared the Jews as the much-needed neutralist third force. Viewed from all these and many other angles, Jewish history from ancient times to the emancipation era assumes new significance as a factor in world history at large.

Nor is the task over today. Once again, the Jewish people finds itself on the brink of a deep clash between a new East and a new West, and is right in the middle of that world vortex. The largest and the second-largest agglomerations of Jews at this moment are located in the United States and the Soviet Union, the two protagonists in that world drama. Without venturing into the realm of prophecy, one may nevertheless, on the basis of this long historic record, expect that this particular position in both worlds, however exposed and perilous to the Jewish people, is also fraught with challenges which may indeed stimulate it to perform once again some major pioneering functions on behalf of human civilization.

II

Pioneering has indeed been a major keynote of all Jewish history. It was natural for a permanent minority entering any new area to find that all normal positions in the economy and social structure of that area had already been occupied. Simply to make a living, it was absolutely necessary for these new arrivals to find new openings by exploiting certain hitherto undetected possibilities, and to widen, so to say, the crevices in the body politic of the host nations into regular fields of endeavor. Socially, too, they had to expand into uncharted areas and to create new niches for themselves. Facing these challenges, a generally gifted people which, through its great emphasis on education and learning was constantly sharpening its mental abilities, succeeded in opening up for itself new, unprecedented avenues.

It is not generally known that even in antiquity Jews belonged to the pioneering nations. I need not expatiate on their towering new discoveries in the fields of religion and ethics. But less is known about their economic contributions. The cryptic references in the Bible give us but a bare inkling of what Israel's conquest of the Edomite lands in the Negev and its access to the Red Sea in Elath has meant to human civilization. However short-lived, this experiment of navigating the Red Sea and the Indian Ocean opened up to the Israelites and their Phoenician allies the old civilizations of southern Arabia, East Africa and, probably, also of the Indian subcontinent and the East Indies, bringing them for the first time into direct contact with the Mediterranean world. More enduring was the Jewish impact on the various countries of the dispersion after the fall of Samaria and Jerusalem. It appears that Jewish exiles made a major contribution to Babylonian banking at a time when the neo-Babylonian civilization was generally taking on many semi-capitalistic hues. Later on, it was they who seem to have brought the olive tree into the Euphrates Valley and thus helped introduce there a new type of oil production to replace the inferior sesame oil. We must bear in mind that in antiquity oil performed the combined functions of an important foodstuff, drug, cosmetic and lighting fuel. Nor did the Jews carry coals to Newcastle when they introduced a new type of viticulture into the ancient Nile Valley. From Josephus and other sources we learn that some of the Palestinian fruits were considered delicacies at the imperial tables of Rome, although these had at their disposal the best produce of the whole Mediterranean world. The balsam of Gilead, we are told, was so precious in the eyes of the Romans that not only did they pay for its weight in gold but, during the great Roman-Jewish war of 66-70, their soldiers tried to salvage every bush. The Jewish army, on the other hand, pursuing a sort of "scorched earth" policy, attempted to destroy these bushes rather than surrender them to the enemy, and, according to Pliny, "there have been pitched battles in defense of a shrub."

Nor is it widely known that, before the days of Muhammed, arid and unproductive southern Arabia had been turned into a flourishing area of agriculture under the domination of Jewish tribesmen. But once the new "Messenger" succeeded in destroying most of these north Arabian communities and in turning the entire area into the homeland of an ever vaster Islamic empire, the agricultural production began declining sharply. Although supported by a never ending wave of pilgrims, revered as the cradle of Islam and sanctified by the two holy cities of Mecca and Medina, that part of the peninsula, in fact all of it, reverted to its natural aridity, from whose backwardness it has begun to recover only during the last decades of oil exploitation.

Such pioneering efforts continued in many other countries. To mention only a few more facets of agricultural production, it has been stated that southern Russia had rice cultivation exclusively during the period of Khazar domination. Only after a lapse of centuries was rice produced there during the last generations. The stimulation of silk production through the planting of mulberry trees and the spread of silk weaving in Sicily and elsewhere; the introduction into that island of the cultivation of henna and indigo by North African Jews settled there by the Hohenstaufen emperor, Frederick II; and the contracting for the cultivation of the kermes bush in southern France to supply a much-needed raw material for dyeing, are other well-known instances of the impact of Jewish "know-how" on European agriculture and industry during the early stages of their emergence from the backwardness of the "dark ages." In Germany's under-developed areas Jews contributed mightily to the upbuilding of the nascent urban centers in their progression from the Rhinelands to the Elbe, the Oder and the Vistula. This story of pioneering has continued in many areas down to the present day. Without subscribing to Werner Sombart's much discussed exaggerations, one must nevertheless admit that the Jews played in the rise and evolution of modern capitalism in central Europe and elsewhere a role wholly disproportionate to their numerical strength. Nor may we discount the impact of these economic contributions on the political life of the modern nations. Again Sombart may have gone too far in stating that the prince and the Jew went hand in hand in building up the modern German state. But the significant part played by the court Jew in this vital transformation has been emerging with increasing clarity from the researches of Selma Stern-Täubler and Heinrich Schnee. In more recent times Jewish financiers were particularly active in the construction of railroads, in all sorts of real estate transactions which helped to build up the European and American metropolises and, in the last decades, in the astounding development of suburban settlements. Jewish contributions to the labor union movements throughout the world just as readily transcended the people's numerical ratio to the population. Nor should one neglect in this context the important contributions made by humble Jewish peddlers in many lands, both by creating new wants and thus preparing the ground for mass markets and mass production, and as factors in the otherwise rather tenuous lines of communication between the city and the countryside. The recent Jewish contributions to the film, radio and television industries, on the one hand, and the development of nuclear energy on the other hand, are too well known to require further discussion.

At the same time the people's vital energies were also turned inward. To make Jewish life bearable in ever-changing environments, Jews had to pioneer along new organizational and intellectual lines and to adjust their own religious and communal structures to the varying needs of the moment. The very formation of Diaspora communities enjoying considerable self-determination and maintaining unbroken continuity through the ages was an historic feat unparalleled in depth and duration. With it went the introduction of such new, indeed revolutionary, institutions as the synagogue, an informal place of worship substituting for the ancient temples with their sacrificial worship. Today, when a large part of mankind worships in churches, mosques and similar institutions, the revolutionary character of that ancient Jewish invention is readily obscured. Jews also had to pioneer along new communal lines whenever their migrations removed them from sheltered ghetto conditions to countries of emancipation, especially wherever separation of State and Church had weakened the governmental underpinnings of their communal structure. In a Presidential Address,[4] delivered before the American Jewish Historical Society in 1954, I had occasion to cite a number of illustrations of such intensive "American Jewish Communal Pioneering," a process which is still continuing today. Yet many of these innovations, and particularly their ideological rationales, were clearly paced by similar earlier efforts of European, especially German Jewry. Palestinian, and later Israeli, Jews, have likewise demonstrated an unprecedented vigor in building their new state, which is now actually able to serve in many ways as mentor and example to the other seven hundred million human beings, or a quarter of all mankind, who have achieved national independence during the last two decades.

In all these pioneering ventures there was, of course, a constant

34

interplay of Jewish and world history. On their migrations from country to country and continent to continent, Jews met recurrent challenges, not by any preconceived plans, but rather by their sheer will to survive in defiance of the natural forces of either violent annihilation or total absorption by neighbors under more subtle pressures. To maintain this inner continuity and yet to be flexible enough to adjust its living conditions to the ever-changing external conditions was not only a living testimony to the vitality and perseverance of the people, but also to the integral nexus between its own history and that of the nations among whom it lived.

III

At times, however, these external forces assumed dimensions with which the Jewish people was not able to cope. Certainly, in periods of greatest tension, widespread massacres often wiped out hundreds or thousands of communities (for instance, during the Black Death period in Germany), Jews being able to salvage only a few remnants of communal life in those countries. Relatively few survived by fleeing to more hospitable lands. Similarly, when large-scale expulsions were decreed by hostile governments such as those from England in 1290, from France in 1394, from Spain in 1492, and many Central-European states and cities during the fifteenth and sixteenth centuries, there was no alternative for the staunchly loyal Jews but to tear up their roots in their centuries-old habitations and to turn to other countries. In these cases the impact of world historical developments upon the very fundamentals of Jewish history is quite obvious.

On another occasion I have even proposed a regular formula to explain these alternating outbursts of intolerance and toleration through the inner evolution of the host countries. I have suggested that, in addition to the more or less constant religious antagonisms and some basic economic rivalries, one must pay close attention to the growth of nationalism as a major factor in changing Jewish destinies at all times, but especially in the medieval and early modern periods. One may almost speak of an "historical law" that before the Emancipation era, national states, that is states in which the population was nationally homogeneous, sooner or later turned against their Jewish "subjects" and sought to eliminate this "alien" ingredient. At the other extreme were the multi-national states which actually considered their Jews as a valuable cementing force in helping to maintain their overall imperial unity. Such states were usually not only quite tolerant toward their resident Jews, but also tried to attract new Jewish settlers, endowing them with many privileges. In between these two extremes there were intermediate forms such as what, for lack of a better expression, I called the "part of nationality states," which shared with the national states their intolerant tendencies but lacked their power and simultaneity of action. Early modern Germany and Italy are typical examples of such states, each of which constituted only a portion of the whole German or Italian nation, but which, whether fully sovereign as in Italy, or paying more or less nominal allegiance to the emperor, followed its own needs, desires, even whims, in keeping or ejecting its Jewry. I need not elaborate here this recurrent phenomenon except for saying that in the Emancipation era the new forms of nationalism, as divorced from religion, tried to achieve substantially the same aim of national homogeneity by assimilating their Jews without religious conversion—a process quite unthinkable during the Middle Ages when religion played a most integral part in the entire fabric of national politics and culture. Nevertheless, even in the latest phase of history, extreme nationalism, which reached its climax in Fascism and Nazism, unavoidably operated to the detriment of the Jewish community.

Such outside influences have so deeply affected the career of the Jewish people that the question could be raised about the extent to which it could still appear as the subject, rather than the object, of its history. This query was heard with particular urgency among German scholars during the Nazi era. Struck by a tempest totally out of their control, realizing that the catastrophe which had befallen German Jewry seemed so completely unrelated to what the Jews themselves had done or failed to do, one could draw the ready generalization that Diaspora Jewry has always been tossed about on the waves of history beyond its own volition. This was, of course, an overstatement. Certainly, the manifold Jewish pioneering contributions of which we have spoken clearly controverted this allegedly passive historical role of the Jewish people. On the contrary, one could contend with equal ease that, without its inner resources and firm determination to survive, the people would long ago have been submerged by the hostile waves about them. Yet no one could deny the deep impact of such external factors not only on the economic and political life of the Jews but also on their minds. In fact, during the very Hitler era a great many Jews became more conscious of their Jewish heritage and more loyal to their own tradition than they had ever been before, causing—I think, unjustifiably—some patriotic Jews to speak with scorn of these "Hitler Jews" who included also children of mixed marriages and some relapsed converts. But all that debate could only highlight the deeper inter-relations between world history and Jewish history.

As a matter of fact, however, this external impact on the history of the Jews should not have come as a surprise to any student of history. More than a century ago, Leopold von Ranke spent a lifetime of research and writing and published volume after volume of significant historic contributions, stressing in particular his doctrine of the primacy of foreign relations over domestic affairs in the history of every nation. Subsequent researches have borne out his thesis. Surely even naturally isolationist America has learned to its chagrin that its foreign relations, as exemplified by the hot and cold wars of the twentieth century, have had a far greater impact on its destinies than the most dramatic internal changes. Today it is easy to predict that the daily life of most Americans over the next decade or two may be more deeply affected by actions and words of Russian and Chinese dictators than by the very will and conscious design of the American Congress and Executive. In the case of Jews, we must remember, anti-Semitism or philo-Semitism has always played the role of the people's foreign relations, parallel to those affecting states in their relations with one another. Just as Pearl Harbor created almost overnight an unprecedented feeling of solidarity among Americans hitherto divided on almost all international issues, so did any major anti-Semitic onslaught unite Jews who, in more leisurely periods, could indulge in an enormous diversity of opinion or in profound indifference toward the fate of their people. It was in such a leisurely period that the ironic designation of anti-Semitism as an "international benevolent society for the preservation of Judaism" could be coined. Racial anti-Semitism, in particular, with its implacability and the shutting off of all avenues of escape, indubitably served as a potent force in recementing the unity of a people broken asunder under the wheels of the powerful Emancipation movement. On the other hand, the very ability of Jews to resist such overwhelming hostile forces, time and again reappearing in their history, and to maintain in spite of them a measure of unbroken continuity in their communal and cultural life, offers the best testimony for the survivalist urge and great creative adaptability of a vigorous people marching onward through all its historic trials and tribulations.

IV

Such integral treatment of Jewish history, as a peculiar segment of and in constant interrelations with world history, as postulated here, raises, however, many methodological problems. Most significant, doubtless, is the question of how to treat divergent biases appearing in the sources relating to the same events. This has, in fact, been one of the stumbling blocks confronting UNESCO's Scientific and Cultural History of Mankind. Even in this generally less controversial area, the editors have experienced considerable difficulty in overcoming the different approaches and interpretations placed on the same historical developments by different nations. This disparity is doubly noticeable, of course, in the more embattled domains of political and economic history. Scholars have long deplored the fact that, for instance, the descriptions of the Napoleonic Wars in German and French textbooks bore so little resemblance to one another. To some extent the same held true for a long time for the descriptions of the American Civil War presented by northern or southern authors. In Jewish history, too, such divergences must be expected and an attempt must be made to bridge them in some dispassionate way.

To cite only a few well-known examples: the Talmud and Midrash hardly ever mention the name Titus, the Flavian general, later emperor, without adding the epithet *ha-rasha'* (the evildoer). From the Jewish point of view he was, of course, the man most responsible for the fall of Jerusalem and the burning of the Temple, controversial as his personal role in the latter event may have been even in antiquity. If one reads, on the other hand, descriptions by Roman authors, Titus appears as an extremely good-natured man who allegedly considered any day wasted if he was unable to perform on it some very good deed. Similarly, Emperor Hadrian is roundly condemned by the rabbis as the man responsible for prohibition of public assemblies for Jewish study, and the outlawry of circumcision, both part of his general plan to submerge Judaism in the pagan civilization. Viewed from the vantage point of Roman policies, this Spanish-born emperor was evidently only a loyal and far-sighted Roman patriot who genuinely believed in the merits of what we like to call the "melting pot" ideology. He simply could not comprehend why Jews should insist upon their segregated mode of living, and resist that total integration into the magnificent Graeco-Roman civilization which he staunchly believed to be a blessing for both the Empire and all its subject peoples. Nor could he understand why his enlightened administration should continue to tolerate a "barbaric" custom like the circumcision of infants as practiced by Jews or that of older boys performed among Arab tribes and Egyptian priests. Moreover, it appears that he and his associates became aware of some incipient signs of biological decay in Roman society, which not long thereafter led to widespread birth-control and an actual decline of the imperial population. To stem that incipient trend, the Empire sharply prohibited castration, Hadrian viewing circumcision as something very much akin to this dangerous practice. On their part, of course, the Jews could not submit to these imperial decrees. It may still be controversial as to whether the prohibition of circumcision preceded or followed the outbreak of the Bar Kokhba revolt, but there is no question that Hadrian's approach to full integration of Jews and the rabbinic teachings about the fundamentals of the Jewish faith were utterly irreconcilable and had to result in bloody conflict. At the same time, it must not be forgotten that neither Titus nor Hadrian were vulgar anti-Semites. As a matter of record, Titus as well as his father, Vespasian, in the very midst of the Great War, resisted all attempts of the Antiochian and Alexandrian citizens to use this Jewish "rebellion" as an excuse for the curtailment of Jewish rights and the withdrawal of what, according to Josephus, was Jewish *isonomia,* or complete equality of rights. Nor did Hadrian, despite his sharp attacks on Jewish religious autonomy, ever attempt to restrict Jewish civil and political rights.

In short, in the clash of these two outlooks on life, we have the makings of a modern tragedy in which unexpected concatenations of circumstances lead individuals, fully justified from their own standpoints, into insoluble conflicts with one another. The old historiography, Jewish and non-Jewish, with its recognized preference for treating history along the lines of the old-type tragedy, with its heroes and villains, could afford to disregard contrary evidence, and also treat the Jewish historic evolution from the viewpoint of the Jewish sources alone. Such one-sided treatment is simply no longer possible today.

On the other hand, world history may likewise look different from the perspective and from data furnished by Jewish history. Edward I of England, Philip Augustus, Saint Louis and Philip the Fair of France may loom as distinguished monarchs who performed major functions in the unification and reorganization of their respective kingdoms. Their personalities and governmental methods acquire new coloring, however, when placed alongside their ruthless treatment of their Jewish subjects. In other cases, Jewish sources and events may merely confirm the impressions gathered from other records. The three Fredericks who bore the titles of Roman emperors are a case in point. The image of the great Frederick I Barbarossa, so extolled in German sagas and chronicles, is certainly not dimmed by the preamble to his privilege in favor of Regensburg Jewry of 1182 which read:[5]

> It is the duty of Our Imperial Majesty, as well as a requirement of justice and a demand of reason, that We rightly preserve his due to every one of Our loyal subjects, not only the adherents of the Christian faith, but also to those who differ from Our faith and live in accordance with the rites of their ancestral traditions. We must provide for their persevering in their customs and secure peace for their persons and property. For this reason We announce to all faithful subjects of the Empire, present and future, that, deeply concerned with the welfare of all Jews living in Our Empire who are known to belong to the imperial Chamber by virtue of a special prerogative of Our dignity, We concede to Our Regensburg Jews and confirm with Our imperial authority their good customs which their ancestors had secured through the grace and favor of Our predecessors until Our time.

Similarly, the split personality of Frederick II is also fully reflected in his treatment of Jews. On the one hand, this *stupor mundi,* who astounded contemporaries by the vastness of his learning and the variety of his intellectual interests, maintained at his court in Naples a number of distinguished Jewish scholars and effectively used Jewish assistance in his attempt to erect in his Italian possessions "the first modern state in Europe." On the other hand, he was driven by his conflict with the Papacy, as I have tried to show in a recent paper,[6] to assert his overlordship over Jews in so extreme a fashion as to lay the foundations for the institution of medieval Jewish "serfdom," a term he was the first to use in official secular legislation. The weak and oscillating Frederick III, finally, revealed no less inconsistency in his dealings with Jews. While his rapacity placed him alongside some of the worst exploiters of medieval Jewry, he nevertheless staunchly protected them against some, if not all, of their enemies; for instance, the burghers of Regensburg. This protective attitude was to earn for him the exclamation by a Jew-baiting contemporary chronicler that "he was popularly called the king of

Jews, rather than the king of Romans."[7] Such examples, whether in confirmation or in rectification of historically accepted general facts and views, can readily be multiplied.

In conclusion, we may perhaps understand these new, more integral approaches as part of the growing trend in contemporary historiography to try to comprehend world-wide historic movements from world-wide, as well as national, perspectives. Similarly, Jewish history will have to be better understood in terms of its world dimensions and from the combined broader vantage point of Jewish and world history. That such an approach will require new, often unprecedented, methods, and that it is beset with innumerable technical difficulties, goes without saying. One of the greatest handicaps for every historian is, of course, the fact that "world history" itself is a combination of many regional, national and local histories, which often have marked peculiarities of their own. Any student of Jewish history must, of course, be cognizant of these important variations as well. But just as the Jewish people, whenever confronted with unprecedented challenges, was resourceful enough to meet them in some new pioneering ways, so am I confident that the historians of that people will also find some creative answers to the new challenges facing them, and thus perhaps help to blaze some new paths for the general re-evaluation of the human past.

3

Modern Capitalism
and Jewish Fate*

MUCH ADO HAS BEEN MADE IN RECENT YEARS about the "unavoidable" passing of our capitalist civilization. Not only socialists of all wings but members of the capitalist class themselves have often preached, or at least uneasily conceded, that the old social order is doomed and is soon going to be replaced by another order based upon some form of powerful social control. When applied to the future of the Jews, the question has often been raised, with either glee or anxiety, as to whether the Jewish people, as such, was likely to survive the passing of the present civilization and the rise of a new, wholly unprecedented order.

The "Ultimate" Solution of the Jewish Question

Hitler and his satellites constantly shouted from the housetops that the speedy downfall of "Jewish pluto-democracy" would soon bring about the "ultimate solution of the Jewish question," that is, the final disappearance of the Jew from the world scene. Unperturbedly lumping communism together with capitalism, they declared both to be mere instruments of Jewish world domination, which allegedly they had set out to destroy. This line of reasoning, silenced during the two years of official "non-aggression," was resumed with increasing vigor since the German attack on Russia in June, 1941. In his secret order to the German troops at the beginning of the offensive against the Soviet capital on October 2nd, Hitler sharply attacked the poverty of the Russian people, which

* Reprinted from *The Menorah Journal*, vol. XXX, no. 2, Summer, 1942.

43

"does not consist of soldiers but a majority of beasts," and placed the responsibility for it upon the Jews. "This is a result of nearly a twenty-five-year-long Jewish rule that, as bolshevism, is basically similar to the general form of capitalism. The bearers of this system in both cases are the same: Jews and only Jews." (From the translation published in *The New York Times* of Oct. 10, 1941, page 2.)

Curiously, as in its many other doctrines, this degenerate brand of socialism, Hitler's National Socialism, stole a leaf out of Marxism, giving it a peculiar, unconscionable twist. In his only considered public utterance on the Jewish question, his essay *Zur Judenfrage*, published in 1844, Karl Marx, viewing Jewish realities from the narrow angle of contemporary western German Jewry, readily identified the Jewish people with the existing civil society (*bürgerliche Gesellschaft*), and to all intents and purposes predicted the simultaneous disappearance of both in the new social order. Referring to the problem of Jewish emancipation which was then most heatedly debated, he harped on the theme, often decried since as a classical instance of Jewish self-hatred, that what the world at large needed was not the emancipation of the Jew but mankind's release from the shackles of the "Jewish" spirit of capitalism. "The social emancipation of the Jew is the emancipation of society from Judaism"—so runs the climactic sentence of Marx's essay. In other words, once capitalism is replaced by socialism, the Jewish question will resolve itself by the complete absorption of the Jews as individuals in western society, their thorough amalgamation with the non-Jews, the total disappearance of the Jewish group.

To be sure, these irate remarks did not remain unchallenged in the subsequent evolution of Marxism. Jewish disciples in particular, such as Ber Borochov and Chaim Zhitlovsky, evolved theories of Jewish nationalism which postulated the survival of the Jews, as a national if not as a religious group, even within the new Marxian internationalist order. However, the main exponents of official Marxism, especially the western social-democrats of the school of Karl Kautsky and Otto Bauer, long declined to recognize the Jews as a national group at all. In their definition of nationality, emphasizing the linguistic element above all others, they held that the

Jews, particularly those outside the Yiddish-speaking areas, lacked the essential characteristics of a nationality. As social-democrats they did concede that, religion being a private affair of the individual, the Jewish religion might continue to attract many worshipers. But as Marxian socialists, confronted by the European reality of a strong alliance between the churches and states or, worse yet, the states' ruling classes, they also nurtured the belief that before long all religious "opiates" would vanish and give way to a truly secular, "scientific," socialist society. Thus, devoid of both national and religious links, the Jewish people could confidently be expected sooner or later to submerge its identity and disappear in the vast sea of humanity.

Lenin, too—although, unlike his German confrères, he lived in the milieu of the East-European mass settlement with its pulsating, distinctly Jewish ethnic and cultural life—long denied the existence of a Jewish nationality. In his protracted struggle with the Bund he even disputed the need of a special Jewish socialist group the better to propagandize socialism among the Jews. In two noteworthy essays, written as late as 1913, he declared:

> The Jews in the civilized world are not a nation, they have become most of all assimilated . . . . The Jews in Galicia and Russia are not a nation, they unfortunately (and not through their fault, but owing to the Purishkeviches) are still a *caste*. . . . [These facts] indicate that "assimilation" can be denounced only by the Jewish reactionary petty bourgeois, who wish to turn back the wheel of history, and to force it to move, not from the conditions of Russia and Galicia to the conditions of Paris and New York, but in the opposite direction . . . .
>
> Whoever directly or otherwise puts forward the slogan of Jewish national culture (however well intentioned he may be) is the enemy of the proletariat, the defender of the *old* and *caste* element in Jewry, the tool of the rabbis and of the bourgeoisie. (Quoted from the English translation, *Lenin on the Jewish Question,* New York, 1934, pages 13, 15.)

Since Lenin's opposition to the established religions, reinforced as it was by the interlocking of State and Church in tsarist Russia, was even more vigorous than that of his western comrades, there was nothing in his doctrine to hold out any promise for the continued existence of the Jewish group in a communist society. To be sure, under the stress of an overwhelming Jewish national sentiment in the Russia of 1917, which was clearly demonstrated also in the elections to the Constituent Assembly then held, Lenin apparently reversed his earlier views. He included the Jewish national minority in the provisions for "the free development of the national minorities and ethnographic groups living within the confines of Russia," enunciated as one of the Soviet Union's basic policies on November 15, 1917. But he and Stalin often made it perfectly clear that they had accepted minority safeguards merely as the best means of eliminating those sharp nationalist clashes which had torn asunder many capitalist societies in Europe, and they looked forward to a time when all nationalities would disappear from the earth. Just as State supremacy under the dictatorship of the proletariat, they taught, is indispensable in the transitional stage of the social revolution—which is to lead, in accordance with Marxian predictions, to the ultimate "withering away" of the State—so are nationalities to be given free rein until such time as they, too, shall wither away in the great single socialist culture of mankind.

Western Jewish communists, adhering more closely and consistently to the traditional line of reasoning, anticipated a much speedier extinction of the Jewish group. In a book published in 1931, the Austrian communist, Otto Heller, while extolling the pro-Jewish measures of the Soviet regime, nevertheless proclaimed the forthcoming "decline of Judaism" as the immediate result of the new order. Judaism having always been, in his opinion, but a function of "merchandise," it would find absolutely no room in a socialist society, where merchandise and trade would disappear as a significant social factor. Similar sentiments were voiced by German communists, such as Alfred Kantorowicz in his essay in *Die Klärung,* on the very eve of the Hitler revolution. While conceding that the "liquidation" of the Jewish question does not necessarily involve the liquidation of Judaism, and leaving open the question whether the Jewish nationality (like dozens of other nationalities) should be maintained "for the time being," Kantorowicz clearly indicated his belief that its "social assimilation" would fairly soon lead also to its "national assimilation."

Confronted by such dire forebodings on the part of avowed friends, as well as professed enemies, many young Jews have begun asking anxious questions as to the future of their people in the new world order. Those of them who decline to subscribe to any totalitarian ideology, who believe in the continued force of the democratic order, have been puzzled by the traditional demands of complete Jewish assimilation to the surrounding cultures preached alike by friends and foes ever since the beginning of the Emancipation era. They have been especially perplexed by the oft-repeated assertions concerning the great Jewish contributions to the rise of modern capitalism and the enormous strides made by the Jewish people under the system of free enterprise and rugged individualism. Would not all these achievements be nullified in a system of greater social control? Are not the Jews bound to lose out with every weakening of the capitalist system of production, even if such weakening be not necessarily combined with the disappearance of civil liberties, civic equality and, generally, of political democracy?

An answer to these questions can be given only through a dispassionate examination of the historic relationships between modern captialism and the Jews.

We are not referring here to the old and much-debated problem of Jewish influences on the evolution of modern capitalism. This problem, heatedly discussed many years ago after the publication of Werner Sombart's brilliant, though undisciplined, treatise (*Die Juden und das Wirtschaftsleben,* Leipzig, 1911), has been reduced to its proper proportions through the more detailed researches of Waetjen, Herbert Bloom and others. Much is yet to be done to ascertain the basic facts of modern Jewish economic history in various lands, and to correlate them with the general economic trends of the respective periods and areas. But it appears more and more certain that, though the Jews have contributed to the development of modern capitalism in most of its focal areas—Holland, England, France, Germany and the United States—much beyond their numerical strength which for the most part was very slight, they were neither the originators of modern capitalism nor in any way its decisive protagonists. Nor is there any conclusive evidence for the oft-asserted great influence of post-biblical Judaism on the emergence of the "capitalist spirit" and the modern commercial techniques. The affinities between the "capitalist" attitude to life and the rational ingredients of Jewish tradition may have exceeded those between capitalism and otherworldly early Christianity, or between capitalism and the feudalist social hierarchy of the medieval Church. But they certainly are not greater than capitalism's affinities with the "spirit" of the Hellenistic civilization or of the Islamic Renaissance, both of which vitally influenced the transition from medieval to modern Europe. In any case, the nearly total absence of Jews from the greatest foci of incipient capitalism, such as Florence and Genoa in the thirteenth and fourteenth centuries, and from such important sources of leadership in advanced capitalist thinking and living as modern Scotland, precludes all such rash generalizations.

Far more relevant to our present inquiry is the opposite aspect, hitherto almost totally ignored, of the influence of modern capitalism on the Jew and his destiny. Only by a clearer understanding of what capitalism has meant to the Jews in the past may we obtain a glimpse of what its passing or radical readjustment may have in store for the Jewish people in the future.

Early and Advanced Capitalism

A sharp distinction should be drawn between the different stages in the evolution of modern capitalism. Following Werner Sombart, the author of several standard works on modern capitalism, most contemporary students divide this evolution into three distinct phases: (1) early capitalism (*Frühkapitalismus*), which roughly corresponds to the period of the Commercial Revolution; (2) advanced capitalism (*Hochkapitalismus*), established as a result of the Industrial Revolution; and (3) late capitalism (*Spätkapitalis-*

mus), the socio-economic symbol for our present-day mechanized civilization. We need not necessarily subscribe to Sombart's analysis of the salient features of each of these stages. In particular, we may dislike the implication of senility and forthcoming doom in this three-fold division with the term "late capitalism." Nevertheless, it provides us a point of departure for the discussion of our problem. Despite gradual transitions from one form to another and despite the great differences in geographic areas, it may be asserted that in the West early capitalism grew slowly from the fourteenth to the middle of the eighteenth century, advanced capitalism was firmly established in the years 1750-1914, while late capitalism represents the economic developments of the last several decades. This evolution was greatly retarded in most areas of Central Europe; and the bulk of Eastern Europe, main reservoir of Jewish strength, was just emerging from the initial stages of advanced capitalism when its further growth was cut short by the Communist Revolution. On the other hand, late capitalism, adumbrated in England, France and Germany before World War I, reached its climax in the United States in the expansive 1920's.

Both early and advanced capitalism undoubtedly had a great many beneficial aspects for the Jews as well as the world at large. By speeding up the process of production and throwing an ever-increasing number of goods upon the markets, it forced the Western man greatly to enlarge the economic basis of his subsistence, both horizontally and vertically. New areas were opened for human settlement and exploitation. New intensified methods of production helped to develop ever-new resources and to utilize them most efficaciously. The Jews could only benefit from both these lines of expansion. By the middle of the sixteenth century, excluded from all of western, northern and northeastern Europe and reduced to a relatively small area in the Mediterranean Basin (except the Iberian Peninsula) and its extension into Germany and Poland, the Jewish people badly needed new outlets for migration. Early capitalism paved the way for an unprecedented transplantation of Jewish masses. Before long, often following a vanguard of Marranos, Jews found their way into all new countries, and, often through them, breached the walls of many old countries previously closed to them. Within three centuries they spread to almost all the lands of the world, establishing increasingly vigorous communities from San Francisco to Shanghai. The new methods of production, too, opened up to them new occupational avenues, while at the same time helping to batter down the numerous restrictions placed upon their former productive capacity by the medieval guild system and antagonistic state legislation.

Early capitalism greatly stimulated also the growth of population. At a time when machinery had not yet extensively replaced human labor as the main factor in production, increasing numbers of workers were needed to produce the necessary goods for ever-growing consumption. Although afflicted by the concomitant evils of the sweatshop, child labor, periodic unemployment and so forth, early capitalism placed a new economic emphasis upon human numbers, thoroughly revolutionizing the social estimate of population movements. Under the influence of the mercantilist school of economics and despite subsequent Malthusian warnings, in themselves perhaps a reflection of the incipient industrial revolution, governments shared with industrial management the belief in the great advantages of ever-expanding numbers. The opening of new areas for colonization, constituting a steady drain on European manpower, further sustained this belief in the basic benefits of population increase. Combined with the constant progress in public hygiene and medical arts, which speedily reduced mortality rates to an unprecedented low level, the century of relative peace and prosperity after the Napoleonic Wars witnessed a numerical expansion of the European man unparalleled in history for an area so vast.

The Jewish population, too, multiplied with amazing rapidity. In fact, if the present author's estimates are at all correct, in the two and a half centuries from 1660 to 1914 the Jewish people grew numerically some fifteen times over (approximately from 850,000 to 12,500,000), while mankind at large increased only by some 250 per cent, Europe by some 350 per cent, and the white or Caucasian population as a whole in not much higher a ratio. It was indubitably under the stimulus of early capitalism that a downward trend of many centuries—which, after the Thirty Years' War and the Cossack massacres, had reduced the Jewish population to the lowest point in its history during the Christian era—was now completely reversed. The ever-growing concentration of the western populations in urban and metropolitan areas also admirably fitted into the scheme of Jewish experience. The urbanization of the Jewish people, begun in antiquity, had run counter to the trends of the age, progressing rather than diminishing during the medieval period. Now, in the new western centers of population, which began to embrace ever-increasing majorities of the respective countries, the Jews could deploy their training and skills, acquired over numberless generations, much more effectively than in the predominantly rural economies of the medieval and early modern times.

If the Jews thus shared with the western world as a whole the opportunities for numerical and geographic expansion and, despite their stupendous growth in numbers, enjoyed on the average an increasingly higher standard of life, other basic factors in early and advanced capitalism seemed even more favorable to them. In the new economic conditions money replaced land as the main factor of economic, social and even political life. To finance the newer methods of production, to help exploit the newer countries, to set in motion the vastly greater flow of commerce as well as to supply the life-blood for the increasingly ambitious state ventures requiring large standing armies of soldiers and bureaucrats, capital—or its temporary equivalent, credit—was badly needed. The Jews, who through long processes of medieval discrimination, had been practically forced off the land and driven into trade—in particular, the money trade—now saw themselves suddenly placed in a strategic position. The bulk of their fortunes had long been concentrated in money, or goods readily convertible into money. They also had an age-old experience in the field of credit transactions which, for all practical purposes, multiplied the available cash resources many times over. In the heyday of finance capital, Central European Jews in particular found themselves, through historical circumstances, in the possession of a relatively larger share of floating capital and in better command of newer techniques for its most effective utilization. The story of the Central European "Court Jew," of his part in the struggle of the modern state against the vested interests of the privileged "estates," has only begun to be told in illuminating detail, distortions of Nazi pseudo-science notwithstanding. The great role played by the Rothschilds in helping to finance some of the most important political and industrial ventures of the nineteenth century, even leaving aside the enormous exaggerations by biased or gullible contemporaries, was possible only because of the relative shortage of capital in an expansive economy and governmental system. The new emphasis upon international commerce, too, opened to dispersed Jewry new avenues for establishing international relations. Their business and family contacts transcended the innumerable state boundaries; for a time their juridical self-government united them under a single system of laws generally more advanced than that of their neighbors; thus they were enabled to spread a network of export and import firms throughout the western world. These factors made them welcome accessions to the national power even of states where religious prejudice still operated against their free admission.

Most important of all was the new emphasis upon individualism. Combined with a new appreciation of the individual man through the Renaissance, Enlightenment and modern science, combined also with the new stress upon individual responsibility in the religions of the Reformation, early capitalism paved the way for the substitution of an individualistic economy and society for the controlled economy and closed society of the Catholic Middle Ages. In the economic sense, particularly, private enterprise began to be appreciated as never before. The individual entrepreneur, fighting his way through an increasingly competitive world, now became the main bearer of the new economic system.

The Jew, too, began to be viewed more and more as an individual, rather than as a member of his group. Whereas in preceding generations his entire political, economic and even cultural situation had been predetermined by his membership in a corporate body enjoying a special legal status, highly restricted in its economic endeavors and bound together by a uniform world outlook and communal control, now he saw himself increasingly evaluated on the basis of personal merit and achievement. His economic emancipation as a private entrepreneur, making his way in the new world of competitive liberties, was soon accompanied by his intellectual release from the overwhelming control of Jewish communal tradition, and finally by his political emancipation and admission to the status of full-fledged and equal citizenship in democratic societies. While still suffering from many atavistic prejudices and social discrimination, he found the new world so vastly more liberal and so much more open to the display of his energies that he readily began to view the old ghetto world as a frightful experience of bygone "dark ages." He even looked forward, with semi-religious fervor, to the "Messianic Era" of universal emancipation and the brotherhood of man, to be brought about by the untrammeled progress of political democracy and the capitalist intensification of production.

As against these indubitably great benefits bestowed upon the Jews by early and advanced capitalism—population increase, better geographic distribution, new economic opportunity, higher standard of life, political equality and complete intellectual freedom—stand out many equally serious shortcomings. In fact, it was capitalism, operating from its inception in the direction of political emancipation and cultural assimilation, that began to threaten the very survival of the Jewish people even more menacingly than had the antagonism and large-scale exclusion of the previous feudal system.

The new emphasis upon individualism seriously undermined the Jewish group life. Gone was the overpowering control of the ghetto community. Particularly in those countries where individualism, and with it political democracy, reached their highest degree of fruition, the Jewish community began to labor under the prevailing separation of State and Church. Instead of being, as previously, a powerful organ of public law, it became a purely voluntary association of individuals following their own wishes and desires, however inconsistent and whimsical. The ensuing disorganization of Jewish communal life often undermined the Jewishness of even those members who still paid it formal allegiance. Countless thousands left the

53

Jewish fold and joined other churches, or, after intermarrying with other ethnic groups, raised their children in other faiths. Among those who continued formally to profess the Jewish religion, numberless individuals have, more or less consistently, refused to participate in the general life of Jewry. Today, not only is the number of unsynagogued Jews high, especially in America, the inner cohesion of even those who partake of synagogue or some other organized forms of Jewish life has often diminished to a vanishing point. Such cohesion often depends on the assistance of the purely negative forces of anti-Jewish persecution or discrimination. Apart from the insecurity and superficiality of these negative loyalties, the ensuing concentration of communal efforts upon defense and relief has tended to exhaust the few remaining communal energies and, in all cases, to divert them from more constructive tasks.

Worst of all, there are in all western Jewish communities innumerable Jews whom I have frequently ventured to style the "inverted Marranos." Those appear and act outwardly as Jews; they are recognized as Jews by themselves and their environment. But they deeply resent this fact which, for one reason or another, they cannot alter. Such inverted Marranos, hating their Jewish heritage and involuntary allegiance, usually become self-haters of a pathological kind. They not only destroy their own peace of mind; they are a menace to the equilibrium of the general as well as Jewish society around them.

In short, much as the Jew as an individual may have benefited by early and advanced capitalism, he undoubtedly lost a great deal *qua* Jew, that is, as a member of his group and faith.

The dangers of individualism were heightened by the new and related forces of materialism in life. With the shift in emphasis from the traditional medieval values to the all-pervading force of money as the main instrument of production and political power, nearly all walks of human endeavor were permeated with a new spirit of materialism. This affected the Jew no less than his neighbors. Within the medieval Jewish community—largely formed in non-feudal antiquity and influenced by the Jewries of Muslim lands, it had never fully been reduced to a typical "estate" in medieval society—wealth

54

always played a pre-eminent role. But, as a rule, wealth was effectively counterbalanced—indeed, more often than not far outweighed —by the influence and social dignity of descent (*yihus*), piety, and especially learning. It was not that prominent lineage granted Jews any special legal prerogatives such as were given to Christians born into the estate of nobility. Nor did piety and learning create any distinct, superior class of charismatic priests such as existed in the contemporary privileged Catholic clergy. None the less, men claiming any one of these three distinctions, and still more those who combined all three (as was often the case), easily overshadowed their rich coreligionists in the social estimation of their fellow-Jews and even in the actual exercise of communal power and leadership. We may readily discount some of the widespread exaggerated notions of the rabbi's position in the ghetto community, as fostered by both the predominantly rabbinic orientation of extant sources and the romanticizing modern scholarship. We must nevertheless admit that at least until the rise of the early modern *parnasim,* who ruled the communities of Holland, Germany and Poland with an iron hand, the leadership rested principally with scholars and men distinguished by good deeds or renowned ancestry, which itself was largely esti mated on the basis of scholarly or pious deserts. In modern life leadership shifted entirely to the moneyed classes—we all know with what disastrous results.

Combined with both individualism and materialism there went on also a progressive rationalization and secularization of Jewish life. The new reliance on human reason, rather than on supernatural revelation or socially controlled tradition, increasingly led to the concentration upon a modern, rational, "scientific" culture. The Jews felt the impact of these new forces even more strongly than their Christian neighbors, not only because of the shorter span of time allowed them for their readjustment but also because of the double pressure of rationalization and outward assimilation. What western civilization gradually accomplished from the days of the Italian Renaissance to those of modern liberalism, the bulk of Jewry living in East-Central Europe or under Islam had to achieve within a few generations. At the same time, the distance traversed was even greater. A medieval European became, in the course of five centuries, a modern European. The medieval Jew was to become a modern European or American within two or three generations. Little wonder he was overwhelmed by the new forces of transformation, which much too often became for him forces of disintegration.

Rationalization and secularization, moreover, began to threaten the very foundation of Jewish life—the Jewish religion. Whereas the secularized European and American nations could easily fall back upon powerful national traditions and cultures for their continued existence, the Jews—in their own eyes as well as in those of their neighbors a religious group, principally, if not exclusively—could only view with alarm the progressive weakening of religious sanctions. Despite the rise of strong nationalist, "cultural," and secular trends in Jewry, it is still a debatable question whether there is any chance of long-term survival for a Jewish people stripped of its religious function.

In any case, the combined forces of individualism, materialism, rationalism and secularism have placed so many question marks upon the future destinies of Jewry as to outweigh the benefits of early and advanced capitalism in the minds of many patriotic Jews, who consider the survival of Judaism and the Jewish people a matter of supreme importance to themselves and the world at large.

Late Capitalism

The more recent developments in capitalism have, on the whole, tended to aggravate these adverse factors in the evolution of early and advanced capitalism, while, at the same time, its advantageous features have been greatly weakened. This has resulted in a considerable sharpening of the Jewish crisis in recent years.

Rationalization and secularization have reached a climax in the latest period of extreme mechanization. Not only has high-pressure production and distribution presupposed the most efficient planning along strictly rational lines; the psychological readjustments to the recurrent business cycles, with their intermittent crises, have become powerful vehicles of secularization. Thorstein Veblen once rightly pointed out that the great dependence of workers and entrepreneurs on uncontrollable business constellations has tended to undermine man's trust in the divine guidance of social and individual destinies, and to replace it by an awesome reverence for the inscrutable operation of economic laws. With ever greater stress laid upon the production and circulation of goods, materialism, too, gained further ground. The economic functions, always important, now assumed a focal position in the consciousness of man. The economic interpretation of history, whether or not in its extreme Marxian formulation, has now left the restricted domain of academic discussion in scholarly circles and sunk deeply into the popular mind.

Little wonder that the Jewish people, too, came under the sway of these new trends. Combined with its geographic redistribution during the last half century—shifting its center of gravity from Eastern Europe, with its pre-capitalist or early capitalist structure, to the focal centers of capitalism in the United States, the British Empire, and other parts west—the forces of materialism, rationalism, and secularism became ever more powerful foes of Jewish tradition and mores.

Even more significant is the progressive reversal of the original trends that were beneficial to Jews. Late capitalism, based upon the marvelous exploitation of mechanized means of production, has tended to diminish the early capitalist appreciation of population strength. No longer were ever-growing masses of labor needed to satisfy the increasing appetites of mankind. On the contrary, technological unemployment became a permanent factor; and, apart from the extraordinary periods of emergency such as during the total World War II, shortages of labor often appeared as a remote threat indeed. While a variety of other social and cultural factors undoubtedly contributed to the constant retardation in the growth of western populations, the declining birthrate before 1940 was a reflection of the new low economic evaluation of human numbers.

The Jews, doubly sensitive to the operation of these new factors through their extreme urbanization and peculiar economic stratification, responded even more quickly than their neighbors. If before 1914 world Jewry as a whole revealed a stupendous biological power of regeneration, its retardation in the inter-war period has exceeded the corresponding ratios among most non-Jewish groups in their respective countries. In Germany where, as a result of rapid capitalist expansion in the Hohenzollern era and due also to the greater availability of Jewish statistical data, the newer trends in Jewish population were clearly revealed even before 1914, the seriousness of the situation inspired Dr. Felix Teilhaber to publish his much-discussed work, *Der Untergang der deutschen Juden* (1911). On the basis of available sociological and statistical materials as well as his own manifold experiences as a gynecological practitioner, the author reached the conclusion that, unless reinforced by immigrants, German Jewry would not continue to reproduce itself, and before long would entirely vanish from the German scene. In historic reality, German Jewry did not live in such complete isolation; its diminishing ranks were constantly replenished by ever new waves of migration, which were in part forcibly set in motion by the German military occupation of Russo-Polish areas during World War I. Nevertheless the symptoms were sufficiently threatening; and when the basic trend began to spread to more and more countries, gradually penetrating even the East European fountain of Jewish biological strength, a real menace to world Jewry was revealed. Even American Jewry, according to recent estimates, had become biologically stationary, thus anticipating the general movement in American population by several decades. The numerical retardation of the Jews in this country may have been temporarily checked by the stream of refugees and the general wave of marriages brought on by the war (no reliable Jewish data concerning the latter aspect are as yet available); but there is no denying that the Jewish world population, the ultimate source of all Jewish migrations, which as late as the 1920's had still been increasing at the rate of about 150,000 annually, witnessed a progressive diminution of that increase to one-half or less within a single decade. In 1939-45 the enormous numerical losses sustained by Jewry in war-stricken and Nazi-dominated areas resulted in an actual decrease of population for the first time since the catastrophic decade of 1648-57.

Decreasing shortages of labor also inspired a changed attitude towards immigration. Not only the older countries with their population surpluses, but also the more recently settled areas previously open to large-scale colonization and migration, now increasingly abandoned their open door policy. The United States, before 1914 the classical haven for migrants, became by 1930 a country of emigration rather than immigration. To be sure, this temporary excess of emigrants over immigrants ceased after the depression and under the stimulus of the great world unrest. Nevertheless, within the quota system, the opportunities for immigrating into this country are so slight that any appreciable number of Jewish re-emigrants would easily tip the scale in favor of emigration. In the United States the contemporaneous closing of the frontier was no doubt a major contributing factor; but in the vast open spaces of Latin America, Canada and Australia the reduced facilities for immigration are entirely due to the rise of economic nationalism. This type of nationalism is in many ways merely a reflection of the late capitalist depreciation of population growth and of the ever sharper struggle for world markets, as the necessary but shrinking safety valves for mechanical overproduction.

The Jewish people, probably more in need of migratory outlets than any other people in the world, was bound to suffer severely from the new hostility toward migration. Before Hitler's rise to power but few Jews succeeded in penetrating the closed gates. For a time Palestine alone seemed to hold out real promise for Jewish mass immigration. After 1936, however, for both local and imperial reasons, Palestine's opportunities had been dwindling, politically, if not economically, while the concurrent expansion of such facilities in the western hemisphere, likewise political rather than economic, remained far behind the minimum needs. The problem of Jewish migration was, indeed, one of the major aspects of the Jewish question awaiting solution at the conclusion of World War II. But if the Evian Conference could be considered an adumbration of the future conflicts between the humanitarian drive for expansion and the late capitalist trend toward contraction, the prospects did not seem to be very bright; at least until after the rise of the State of Israel.

Despite further growth of economic materialism, banking has recently been losing much of the ground it had gained under early and advanced capitalism. In his fine treatise on "Finance Capital" published in 1910, the late Rudolf Hilferding, a victim of Nazi barbarism, showed that even before World War I the growing concentration of industrial capital tended to make industrial management ever more independent of banking. This process, before 1914 more marked in England than in either Germany or the United States, became well-nigh irresistible after 1920. In our country the famous hearings at the Temporary National Economic Committee's "investigation of concentration of economic power" in 1939-40 demonstrated that since 1921 the largest American corporations were able to finance all their outlay not only for upkeep, but also for considerable plant expansion, from their own capital reserves. This is not a purely accidental or temporary phenomenon; it is intimately tied up with late capitalist economy. Depreciation reserves alone, if conservatively computed, often prove sufficient to allow for replacements of outworn machinery by newer, more productive and less expensive models, and hence for a considerable expansion of the plant's productive capacity. Little wonder that the banker, especially the private banker, previously the dominant figure in the directorates of industrial corporations, has been losing his hold on them during the last forty years. His formerly great role in negotiating public loans—a role which, throughout the nineteenth century, had made him an indispensable complement to the governmental structure—has likewise sharply declined since World War I. That war made such enormous demands upon public treasuries that, outstripping the resources of any banker or group of bankers, it forced the governments to turn directly, even though with the technical assistance of bankers, to the public at large. To be sure, in the 1920's many international loans were still negotiated by banking syndicates, and even today banks still serve as the main agencies for the distribution of public debentures; but since the collapse of 1929, banking as a whole, and private banking in particular, has lost much of its commanding position and prestige and has become subject to ever stricter governmental control even in non-totalitarian countries.

Obviously the Jews could not remain unaffected. Having made their greatest contributions to the earlier stages of capitalism and, reciprocally, having obtained their largest share in socio-political influence through their part in western banking and allied endeavors, they could not but suffer from this loss of status by the profession. They suffered, in fact, not only insofar as they happened to be members of that profession but, also indirectly, as members of the Jewish group as a whole. The simultaneous concentration of banking in the hands of ever more powerful corporations—such as the Big Five in London and the Chase National, National City, and other banks in New York, where few, if any, Jews have been admitted to leading positions—has further helped to undermine the position of the private banker, formerly the main protagonist in the drama of capitalism and the most influential leader of the emancipated Jewish community.

The rise of corporations has deeply affected also the most basic principle of early capitalism, economic individualism. Much as "rugged individualism" is still superficially identified with capitalist leadership, there is no denying that in recent decades the trend toward corporate concentration has tended to create monopolies or near-monopolies which have greatly curtailed competitive opportunities and weakened the individualistic basis of all western economies. The private entrepreneur has seen himself increasingly converted into an employee of a vast corporation with a largely self-perpetuating hierarchy of officialdom, at best controlled by a small minority of large stockholders. It seemed altogether ridiculous to speak of "private initiative" in the case of the ever growing mass of white-collar workers and petty shareholders whose voice carried less weight in the most crucial managerial decisions than that of the manual workers operating through their increasingly powerful unions. Not only in industry, moreover, but even in trade, the growth of the chain stores has tended greatly to reduce competition as the basis for free and unshackled private enterprise.

The Jews long ago began to bear the brunt of these new develop-

ments. Whether or not, as is often asserted, the Jew is natively predisposed to serve as master of his machine rather than as a cog in it,
there is little doubt that his age-old training and previous experience
prepared him for greater effectiveness as a private entrepreneur, however small, than as a member of an economic bureaucracy. This is,
of course, by no means an immutable natural phenomenon; it may
easily disappear in time. For the present, however, the adverse effects
of corporate growth upon the mass of Jewish traders and artisans
are undeniable. Corporate control, moreover, has often tended to
introduce into personnel policies social prejudices springing from
entirely unrelated, non-economic sources. It is common knowledge
that Jews find it extremely difficult to obtain employment in a great
many corporations, and their share in the industrial, and even
commercial, bureaucracy is often far below their proportion in the
population. The Jewish shopkeepers, in particular, the backbone of
the Jewish middle class and hence of the entire people, are now
confronted by the overwhelming competition of the chain store,
while their attempts to give up their independence and become
chain store employees may be thwarted by anti-Jewish discrimination. This is true even in the field of banking, which has often been
considered a particularly Jewish preserve. Most banking corporations
in this country and in England have but a slight percentage of
Jewish employees.

In short, late capitalism, while further deepening the menace to
the survival of the Jewish people arising from growing secularization and materialism, has greatly weakened the beneficial effects
on Jewry of the earlier capitalist era in regard to its numerical and
geographic expansion, the importance of its share in banking, and
the egalitarian leveling of all groups by the operation of the individualistic principle.

Future Possibilities

For these reasons, analyzed here along somewhat oversimplified
lines, the much publicized passing away of the present form of

capitalism—should it, indeed, occur in the near future—would not necessarily be deplored by the majority of Jews. Individual Jews undoubtedly would suffer in the transition from this to another order. As individuals, acting as members of their class endangered by the new evolution, they may, and undoubtedly will, undertake everything in their power to stem the tide. But there will be many other Jews whose self-interest will undoubtedly drive them into the opposite camp, and these may, with equal legitimacy, try to hasten the transition to some new order. Since the matter is not primarily of Jewish concern and is in no way dependent on the will of Jews, or on common Jewish action even if one could conceive such a Jewish unity in purpose, the freedom of disparate individual action could scarcely be denied even by the most devoted Jews. The very extremists among them, and they are few, who place the interests of the Jewish people above all other interests, could not gainsay such individual freedom of action in a domain which is not peculiarly Jewish.

On the other hand, it would be dangerous, perhaps fatal, to accept unreservedly the assertion, become fashionable in recent years among German Jews overwhelmed by an external catastrophe, that the Jewish people has always been but the "object" of its history. In this sweeping formulation the assertion is demonstrably untrue, since it can easily be shown that Jewish history in the dispersion has always consisted of a remarkable interplay of external and internal factors. While the Jewish people's ability to survive has greatly depended on environmental variations in religious toleration and on its socio-ethnic acceptability to various nations and governments, the fact of its long survival must ultimately be credited to its own inner will to live and its power to adjust itself to such changing environments. That is why one may readily concede that in such matters as the future of capitalism the interests and desires of the Jewish people, even were they unanimous, would be of little avail, and yet believe in the efficacy of intelligent communal planning, to smooth the path and diminish the inevitable sufferings during the period of transition. It is certainly not enough to become pathetically eloquent on the subject of these sufferings, even though such eloquence and pathos are hallowed by a long and venerable tradition of the "lachrymose" conception of Jewish history. Neither will it do to throw up hands in despair and fatalistically bend one's head before the inscrutable future. At this critical juncture of our history it is the duty of all thoughtful Jews to analyze as calmly as possible the future prospects of the Jewish people, and to consider alternative courses of action which might facilitate its adjustment to whatever new civilization will emerge from our turbulent era.

Whatever their point of view, however, Jews need not be seriously concerned about the reputed indissoluble nexus between the fate of capitalism and the fate of Judaism. Just as we know that the Jewish people existed long before the rise of modern capitalism, and reached great heights of cultural achievement under semi-feudal Persia and in medieval Europe, so we may rest assured that the survival of the Jewish people is by no means contingent on the survival of the present structure of our civilization. The identification of modern capitalism with "the spirit of Judaism," false and profoundly misleading even in the heyday of early or advanced capitalism, has become a tragic irony during the recent critical decades. We should also constantly bear in mind that the great crisis of Jewish life did not begin in 1933, and has not automatically resolved itself by the defeat of Hitler. Even if out of the ruins of contemporary Europe and Asia there emerges a new type of social democracy—in some respects adumbrated by the American New Deal and the social transformation of England, but in many other ways as yet wholly unpredictable —there will remain the insistent need of constant creative readjustment of the Jewish economic, social and cultural structure. The measure of its success or failure, however, will ultimately depend not only on the strength of the continued will of the Jewish masses to survive, but on the creativeness and efficacy of their leadership.

4

Emphases in Jewish History*

EVERY GENERATION WRITES ITS OWN HISTORY OF PAST GENERATIONS. This truism has served as a means of disparaging historical research and writing. If history is so pliable, it has been argued, as to serve the needs of every generation; if the same objective facts lend themselves to different, often contradictory interpretations, what then is the value of history as an objective review of these facts? Others, however, have maintained that the main purpose of history is not to restate isolated facts and correlate them into a consecutive narrative, but to serve as a *magistra vitae,* as a teacher and guide in meeting contemporary situations. It is this elasticity of history which makes it so easily applicable to new situations and establishes its position not only in the realm of theoretical studies intended for the satisfaction of intellectual curiosity or amusement, but as an applied social science which is of practical significance to statesmen, men of affairs, and the intelligent public at large.

For a long time, too, there has been a controversy over the question of whether history is a science or an art; whether it is primarily based upon a restatement of objective, coolly analyzed non-controversial facts, or whether its aim consists above all in the artistic, often intuitive recreating of the totality of human destiny upon earth or of that of any of its significant parts. Few historians today will agree whole-heartedly with Macaulay's definition of history as "a compound of poetry and philosophy," which "impresses general truths

* Reprinted from *Jewish Social Studies,* vol. 1, no. 1, 1939. The substance of this article was also presented in a paper read at the annual session of the National Council for Jewish Education, in Washington, D. C. on May 28, 1938. The author used this occasion to explain certain fundamental views which are implied in and illustrated by the first edition of his *Social and Religious History of the Jews.*

on the mind by a vivid representation of particular characters and incidents." But hardly any other definition of the mutual relationships between history, poetry, and philosophy will meet more universal and whole-hearted approval among the teachers and practitioners of these three branches of human endeavor.

I

There are several specific approaches to general and Jewish history, however, which merit more general attention. In the first place, present-day scholarship is confronted anew by the problem of the relations between history and chronology. Evidently the most important single factor in history is that of chronological sequence. If one searches for a fundamental concept which would be as germane to history as is, for example, the idea of justice to the domain of law, one can hardly find, it appears, any better concept than that of "development." Development does not necessarily mean "evolution," and still less does it imply the idea of "progress." Both latter terms introduce an element of evaluation in that they involve an assumption that history reveals a progression from the lower to the higher, which may or may not have been the meaning of human history. But no historian, however detached he may be, can visualize the past of man or of any group of men without conceiving it in terms of a certain line of development from one stage to another, from one peculiar form to another.

Such development naturally takes place in time, and chronology, therefore, has become an integral part of all historical treatment. This might also help to explain how the writing of history originally grew out of historical chronicles, which handed down to posterity the record of events in strict chronological sequence. Even the chroniclers could not always avoid completing the description of a certain chain of events before proceeding to the narration of some other development which took place simultaneously. The more historiography emancipated itself from the mere registering of events into an interpretation of past developments, the more were the rigid chronological shackles cast off in favor of a consecutive analysis or relation of events and trends which, for one reason or another, appeared to the historian as belonging to the same whole.

In the historical annal a compromise was struck between the dictates of chronology and the necessity of grouping intrinsic developments in their respective units. The annalists of ancient Rome and Renaissance Italy described, often with great brilliancy, the events of each particular year. Within that year, any series of happenings which showed a certain inner relationship to one another and which could be explained in the light of the particular author's philosophy of history was brought together in one consecutive account. But each narrative had to stop at the end of the year, giving way to another, often unrelated, series of happenings, until all the developments which appeared significant within the framework of that particular year were exhausted. Only then could a thread of an earlier description be resumed insofar as any of these specific series of happenings found its continuation in the subsequent year or years. A military campaign or international negotiations, a court intrigue or a love affair, biographical incidents in the careers of kings, writers, generals or artists all had to be interrupted, for instance, at the end of December and resumed after a long interval in another chapter dealing with a subsequent year.

With the progress of historical thinking and writing the annalistic chains became too heavy to bear. It was one of the great achievements of modern historiography to have thrown off the shackles of this type of approach. Historians have come to lengthen more and more the periods under discussion in each particular section of their works, as the underlying currents which they attempt to describe happen to be of longer duration. In this respect, too, the progress of recent historiography from a primarily biographical and military-diplomatic to a preponderantly social orientation has tended to lengthen the periods reviewed in their inner relationships. As long as the biographies of leading individuals, as long as dramatic turns in military campaigns, or diplomatic exchanges of notes occupied the focal position in the historic narrative, so long could historians adhere to the chronological sequence of these happenings with somewhat greater consistency. When the emphasis was shifted, however, to underlying social events, it was easily recognized that certain basic movements took decades, if not centuries, to generate, grow, and decay. The analysis of each such movement often had to be isolated in treatment and completed before one could try to interpret another contemporary development in a similar narrative extending over a period of many generations.

In the field of Jewish historiography this general scheme of development is revealed in the evolution from the annals of Zacuto, Ibn Verga, and Joseph ha-Kohen through Jost's and Graetz's more chronological, and therefore briefer, periods to Dubnow's more extended epochs of the successive hegemonies of distinctive Jewish centers. From their respective points of view both Graetz and Dubnow were right: the former in adhering to a close chronological scheme, and Dubnow in severely criticizing him for the "confusion" arising from the "synchronistic" treatment of political, socio-economic, and literary developments in various countries within the confines of the same chapter.[1] The writers on social history, on the other hand, such as Güdemann, Berliner, and Abrahams, were forced largely to abandon the chronological pattern and to choose a topical division for their chapters. Topical discussion naturally has its dangers. Medieval Jewish history, particularly, presents an enormous multitude of local variations of a basically uniform universal theme, and must be viewed against an ever-changing background in the Christian societies of the Mediterranean and the northern lands. A treatment such as that found in Abrahams' *Jewish Life in the Middle Ages,* therefore, is likely to blur the contours of a multicolored, sordid reality and to offer instead an over-simplified and hence somewhat distorted and idealized generalization. With greater skill and lesser bias, but unfortunately also at the expense of brevity and lucidity, Abrahams might have been able to avoid some of the pitfalls of the topical arrangement. But all the genuine merits of his fine presentation would have been completely lost if he had chosen the other extreme of closely adhering to a chronological or geographic sequence.

It was because of the realization of this trend in modern historiography that the author, not without hesitation, chose the title "History" for his particular analysis of the social and religious experiences of the Jewish people. In trying to describe the interaction of social and economic developments and the Jewish religion, attention had to be paid primarily to those basic forces in both society and religion which, operating over a period of countless generations, influenced one another in a demonstrable form. The history of the Jewish people along these broad lines had to be divided into three main epochs. Without reference to the otherwise noteworthy Krochmal-Graetzian scheme of the successive cycles of growth and decay in Jewish history, three major phases stood out in the historical evolution of the Jewish people: (1) that of ancient Israel, from its beginnings to the Hellenistic period; (2) that of Pharisaic-rabbinic Judaism, from Alexander the Great or the Maccabees to the seventeenth century; (3) that of modern Judaism during the last three centuries.

In the history of ancient Israel, the periods of the socio-religious developments roughly coincide with the chronological sequence of Israel's origins, the era of the monarchy and the crisis of exile and restoration. After that time the chronological sequence became less and less important and, for example, the history of the Jews under Islam, medieval as well as modern, had to be separately treated from medieval and early modern Christendom. The story of the rise and development of Hasidism had to be told in conjunction with the evolution of the Kabbalah and popular ethics within the general make-up of the medieval and early modern ghetto. At the same time the chronologically preceding influences of the Protestant Reformation upon Jewish history had to be treated in a subsequent chapter as an integral factor in the transformation of modern Europe and in the ensuing emancipation of the Jews.

II

More important than the chronological problem, the solution of which, under the exigencies of each particular type of inquiry, will necessarily be left to the more or less arbitrary decision of the individual historian, are the problems arising from the divergent approaches to history. One such approach emphasizes the natural foundations and limitations of human history, a point of view exemplified in Buckle's *History of Civilization in England*. It cannot be denied of course that history, occurring in space as well as in time, is definitely bound to certain limited areas and therefore influenced by climatic, meteorological, hydrographic, geological, and other natural phenomena associated with the physical environment of the particular area. No one, however, thus far has attempted to write a history of the Jews from the exclusive point of view of the influences emanating from their habitat in various periods. Such an attempt as undertaken by Buckle for English civilization would evidently fail to help reconstruct the history of a people which for millennia has been divorced from its own soil, and which has tried, with varying success, to acclimatize itself to changing geographic environments. It can definitely be shown, however, that the geography of Palestine played a very decisive role in the shaping of the destinies of the Jews in antiquity and thus also influenced profoundly the succeeding generations. One certainly cannot complain of a dearth of either geographic or historical material. A mere glance at the large volumes of Peter Thomsen's bibliography of Palestine[2] will easily convince one that within the last several decades more books and articles have been written on Palestine than on any other area comparable in size. Certain basic geographic phenomena have also been examined with respect to their possible influences upon history. The contrast between the sea and the eastern desert, it is now generally conceded, was undoubtedly coresponsible for the millennial conflicts between the sedentary and the Bedouin populations. The natural division of the country into some forty single geographic units certainly was a contributory cause to the rise of tribalism, provincialism, and separatism which so largely determined the course of Palestinian life after the establishment of the Canaanite city states, as it now seems, under the impact of the Hyksos domination. The curious socio-economic and political phenomena resulting from the geological preponderance of limestone, the effects of the frequent deficiency of rainfall and the ensuing excess of evaporation over precipitation upon agriculture and population density, the irretrievable damages inflicted upon Palestine by the constant process of deforestation and soil erosion (in particular under the mismanagement of the successive Muslim administrations), the losses of life and property sustained during the recurrent earthquakes—these and other elements of the eternal interplay of geographic and historic factors have been rather well scrutinized. It appears, nevertheless, that a closer examination of the available archaeological material would help to clarify further the interrelations between man and nature within the confines of ancient and medieval Palestine.

The influence of geography upon Jewish history in the Diaspora offers a much more difficult and altogether unique problem; as unique, indeed, as is the history of Jewish dispersion. A thorough investigation of the Jewish settlements in various periods and of the forces emanating from their respective natural environments would undoubtedly help elucidate a number of otherwise unexplainable phenomena in the history of many Jewish communities. Such topographical studies are unfortunately available only for a few countries and, while having undoubted pioneering merits, can hardly be classified as sufficiently comprehensive and searching. Ancient Babylonia, the cradle of the Talmud, has found investigators such as Neubauer and Obermayer who have at least tried to identify the place names mentioned in the Talmud and establish a few bare geographical essentials. Certain western lands have produced works of the type of the *Gallia Judaica* and *Germania Judaica,* which give a general description of the recorded Jewish settlements in these countries. A few topographical studies have analyzed the location and other physical characteristics of various Jewish quarters in the Middle Ages and early modern times.[3] But much more will have to be accomplished before any intelligent attempt can be undertaken to correlate the geographic and historical data in these and other regions and to deduce from them any tentatively valid general conclusions.

Of course, the individual scholar's philosophy of history and perhaps his contemporary biases will color his ultimate decision even with respect to this problem. Those, for example, who are extremely

Palestinocentric, who believe that the Jews have never had any real history outside of Palestine and that, except for the remnant which will be saved in Zion, Diaspora Jewry is doomed to extinction,[4] will naturally focus their attention upon the geography of Palestine as the primary factor, and disparage the influence of the physical background of Diaspora history. Others will argue, from an opposite angle, that the significant historical developments of the Jews on Palestinian soil were limited to but a few centuries, that the Jews had had a Diaspora even before Moses, and once more began to settle in foreign lands not later than the eighth century B.C.E. Throughout the Second Commonwealth, it can hardly be denied, the Palestinian center was confronted by Jewish communities extending over a vast area from Egypt to Persia, the aggregate population of which consistently outnumbered the Jewish settlements in the mother country. Most scholars and teachers will undoubtedly take the middle position that a clear analysis of every facet of physical life affecting both Palestinian and Diaspora Jewry is of supreme significance for the understanding of Jewish history in its entirety.

These remarks are not to be construed as an advocacy of the extremist Bucklean views on the influence of the geographic factor in Jewish history. On the contrary, in the present author's opinion, the history of the Jewish people offers a supreme example of a group attempting (and to a certain extent succeeding) to live on despite nature; of a nationality gradually divorced from state and territory, which has consequently become somewhat immune from the influences emanating from the soil and its derivatives. It is no mere accident, indeed, that no Jewish historian has ever attempted to write a Bucklean history of the Jews. Such an attempt, opposed to the very core of Jewish history, would naturally have been doomed to utter failure. Nevertheless, a better understanding of the influences emanating from the physical factors, which have consistently threatened to submerge the people's conscious endeavor to emancipate itself from the forces of nature, will greatly help to clarify the successive relapses of various groups of Jews into a state of acquiescence with the dictates of nature, and the serious handicaps encountered by the people as a whole in its main historic procession.

72

III

In recent years the *economic* approach has become much more important for Jewish history. In the first place students of Marxism and exponents of socialist ideologies have tried to interpret the history of the Jews in terms of basic changes in economic structure and the class struggle within the Jewish community. Quite a few bourgeois economists, Jewish and non-Jewish, have explained the main contributions of the Jews to western civilization along certain lines of economic endeavor. Werner Sombart and his disciples as well as opponents, following the example set by Wilhelm Roscher, Max Weber, Lujo Brentano and a good many others, have paid special attention to the alleged or real affinities between capitalism and the Jewish spirit. Others, beginning with Levi Herzfeld, the unduly forgotten founder of modern Jewish economic historiography, began to collate the available facts concerning the economic activities of the Jews in various periods and to correlate them with the non-economic aspects of Jewish life in the past.

It must be borne in mind, however, that so far neither the Marxist nor the other economic interpreters of Jewish history have succeeded in producing a general synthetic work on the entirety of Jewish experience. The contributions of these schools, some of them undoubtedly of great value, are limited to fragmentary explanations of certain phases of Jewish history. The periods most extensively discussed are either that of ancient Israel, in which the Soviet scholars N. M. Nicolsky and M. Lurie (more recently "purged"), as well as Abram Menes in Germany and France have made significant contributions; that of Jewry in medieval Europe, in which the comprehensive works of Caro and Schipper have been effectively supplemented by many monographic writings; or else the last two or three centuries in the life of the Jewish communities in Russia and Poland. While many of these studies have shed new and illuminating light on certain stages in the history of the Jewish people, no attempts have as yet been made to extend these researches into other equally important phases of Jewish history, and to correlate their findings into a continuous historical account of the career of the people as it unfolded itself under the stimulus of preponderantly economic factors, if not altogether under the dictates of economic determinism. The few generalizations found, for instance, in Karl Marx's essay on the Jewish question; the investigations of one of his outstanding disciples, Karl Kautsky, on the Jewish "race" and the "foundations of Christianity," or the recent dire prophecies of the forthcoming "decline of Judaism" by Otto Heller,[5] have been clearly controverted by the facts of Jewish history with which the authors were not familiar.

Even more sadly neglected has been the history of the changing Jewish views on economic behavior from antiquity to the present. Besides illuminating a significant element in the world outlook of the successive generations, such a history would shed new light upon the changing economic realities, both in their conformity and non-conformity with the prevailing economic theory. It would also furnish the relatively most solid bridge to cover the gap between these economic realities and the dominant ideologies of the various periods, and thus open new vistas for the understanding of the economic factor in the entire evolution of the Jewish people. In writing the section on "Rabbinic Social Philosophy" the present author was, none the less, at a loss to indicate any scholarly literature on the subject. There is really none deserving this name. Most investigations thus far have been carried on in conjunction with the examination of certain juridical elements in the Talmud or in medieval law, in which the purely economic factors were but incidentally treated. Such studies, dealing with the normative, with what ought to be, cannot satisfactorily answer the main economic inquiry of what is or what was. Nor can they really explain attitudes toward domains of economic life which are not regulated by law, indeed, which are frequently devised to evade and, hence, to co-exist with the contemporaneous law. It is, for instance, well known today that not only in medieval Europe, but also in the countries of Islam, many pious Jews, often leaders of the Jewish community, engaged in extensive moneylending activities and charged interest to Jews as well as to non-Jews. Some of them charged interest to their own heavily burdened communities. At the same time the actual law prohibited, as verbal usury, even expressing thanks for the extension of a loan. Many new types of business transactions had been devised to circumvent the law, thus making it possible to obtain perfectly legitimate unearned income from capital. A few economic data are given also in the none-too-rich and none-too-profound literature on Jewish ethics. But hardly any extensive researches have ever been undertaken to study Jewish economic teachings as such either from the standpoint of economic theory or economic history.[6]

The present shortcomings need not be discouraging to future researchers of and writers on Jewish economic history, nor do they, by themselves, disprove the validity of an economic approach to all history. Much new information is yet to be expected not only from the lifting out of obscurity of the large mass of relevant economic-historical material hidden away in libraries and archives, but also from the elucidation of the influences exercised by the economic forces upon the totality of Jewish life in each particular period and country. We feel, however, no less strongly that among the histories of the different human groups, that of the Jews will most stubbornly resist any full explanation which may be advanced for it exclusively on the basis of the progressive changes in the means of production or of any other economic transformations.

IV

It is no mere accident that it is the *idealistic* type of historiography which has dominated Jewish historical writing for centuries, in fact, for millennia. There is really no vital distinction between the ancient theistic view of history and some of the modern idealistic approaches. For the biblical historians, those marvellous writers of history who may lay claim to the title of "fathers" of historiography, it was God's will, humanly comprehensible even though supernatural, which guided the destinies of mankind and of Israel. Under this scheme almost all happenings could be interpreted in the light of the moral-religious behavior of the Jewish group, however small its

75

numbers. This theocratic view of history was carried on, with minor or major modifications, by the ancient and medieval authors for whom, of course, the experience of exile and the ensuing need for apologetics became of paramount importance. With Messianism looming large as the ultimate goal for Jewish as well as human history, the Jewish writers on historical themes were long satisfied with this generic explanation.

In modern historiography it was the more humanistic type of the "spirit of Judaism" which took the place of God as the determining factor. With all its variations, from Krochmal and Zunz to Geiger, Graetz and Güdemann, the underlying concept, nurtured from the overpowering forces of Hegelianism and the German idealistic philosophy in general, was in more than one respect but a continuation of the old doctrine. Did not Hegel himself still visualize all history as a gradual unfolding of a divine plan? "God lets men direct their particular passions and interests as they please; but the result is the accomplishment of His plans, and these differ from the ends sought by those whom He employs."[7] The basic outlook of the nineteenth century *Wissenschaft des Judentums* was to see in Jewish history the gradual progression of the Jewish religious or national spirit in its various vicissitudes and adjustments to the changing environments. To be sure, the accusation frequently heard that Graetz, for example, had placed exclusive stress upon the biographies of rabbis and the story of anti-Jewish persecutions is clearly contradicted by his own programmatic formulation of the "national character" of the entire history of the post-talmudic period. "As the history of a national entity [*Volksstamm*] Jewish history is far from being merely a history of literature or of individual scholars into which it is turned by the nature of the records and the one-sidedness [of the investigators]. On the contrary, literature and the religious evolution, as well as the extremely tragic martyrology of this nationality or community, are but single incidents in its historic evolution. They are by no means its root essentials."[8] Notwithstanding this clear-cut reservation, the distinguished historian could not himself escape the impact of those records and of that one-sidedness in his own treatment of history.

Even the positivists among the Jewish thinkers, such as Ahad Ha-am and Dubnow, essentially accepted the primacy of such "inner" factors. They set up a sort of autonomous national will which was the driving force in shaping the destinies of the people and which, in the supreme interest of national self-preservation, made all the necessary adjustments required in the different periods and regions. Today, too, a great many Jewish historians still follow one or another of these "idealistic" methods of interpretation. Some will perhaps concede the shortcomings of such an approach to the history of any other nation, but will none the less insist that in the case of the Jews, whose general psychological and social make-up throughout history was so largely determined by their own religion and by the religious attitudes of their neighbors, no other explanation can do equal justice to the specific nature of the subject. Some will, somewhat more reluctantly, adopt one or another idealistic approach out of the practical consideration that the principal records left behind by Jewish leadership throughout the ages are of an almost exclusively religious and literary nature. If one wishes to remain true to the spirit of the authors of these records, such scholars might argue, one cannot avoid accepting, in some degree, the underlying philosophy of these writings which is outspokenly idealistic. In short, the Jewish people, having been at least until the last two or three generations primarily a religious body of men—there never having been any empiric Jewish group which would have proved its ability to survive without religion; the position of the Jews outside of the mass settlements of Eastern Europe down to the World War still having been visualized by Jews and non-Jews alike as that of an exclusively religious group—the preponderance of the idealistic type of historiography, whether or not it substituted nationality for religion, becomes self-explanatory. It is, moreover, to this general approach to Jewish history that we are deeply indebted for the most extensive as well as intensive investigations of the Jewish past in both its totality and its larger or smaller subdivisions.

It cannot be denied, however, that the idealistic approach no longer satisfies our present generation of scholars and students. There is a growing feeling that the historical explanations of the Jewish past

77

must not fundamentally deviate from the general patterns of history which we accept for mankind at large or for any other particular national group. To be sure, every unbiased investigator will admit that general methods necessarily must be adapted to the requirements of each particular subject and that, for instance, no one can deal with the history of the United States in exactly the same way as he would investigate the history of China. There is, nevertheless, a growing sentiment that the differences in methods must needs remain limited to such an indispensable adaptation of one and the same fundamental approach.

V

The *sociological* approach to Jewish history has, therefore, become very fashionable in our day. Unfortunately the term sociology itself has, from its inception, been so ambiguous as to cover an endless multitude of sins. There probably are nowadays as many "sociologies" in the world as there are distinguished sociologists. When applied to history this term has become even more equivocal. Simon Dubnow in his *Weltgeschichte,* up till now the only major professed attempt to explain the history of the Jews in sociological terms, has programmatically proclaimed the need for a sociological interpretation in the introduction to his work. But in his actual description of the Jewish past he has no more succeeded in realizing his program than had Graetz in avoiding the pitfalls of the *Leidens- und Gelehrtengeschichte* which he himself had so bluntly denounced. Except for his artificial attempts at periodization, his forced quest for hegemony centers in various periods and, due to his own political "autonomism," his special attention to Jewish self-government, one finds in Dubnow's otherwise remarkable attempt at a new synthesis of Jewish history little that is a substantial advance over Graetz's still unsurpassed Jewish history. Other sociological approaches to Jewish history have likewise been tried. But with the exception of Max Weber's *Religionssoziologie,* with its very suggestive analysis of the ancient Israelitic religion in the author's own sociological terms, we have but a few monographs on specific subjects which really deserve the attention of modern scholarship.

The following remarks are intended neither as a full definition of, nor as a program for, a new sociological approach to Jewish history; they merely wish to suggest a few integral elements for such an approach which seem to hold out great promise for the near future. Much specialized research as well as analytical thinking will yet be needed before these issues will be sufficiently clarified for a more definitive systematic treatment.

The importance of the *biological* approach to history can hardly be overestimated. No reference is here made to the racial ideologies, propagated especially by the German national socialist historians, who view the history of mankind primarily as the perennial battleground of warring races. One need not altogether deny the importance of racial characteristics for human history, and nevertheless admit that our knowledge of what constitutes a race is still in its prescientific stage. Unceasing racial mixtures, moreover, have been so preponderant upon the historic scene, and the peculiarities of each race in the physical and psychological sense are so arbitrarily defined, that an attempt to construe basic historical developments on this foundation is like building skyscrapers on quicksand. Anthropology will have greatly to improve its own methods of research, to accumulate and sift infinitely more material and to obtain at least some tentative agreement among its leading exponents, before it can become a valid instrument for general or Jewish historical research. So far we must be satisfied with a few interesting sidelights thrown by anthropology and comparative ethnology upon the life of ancient Israel in the early stages of its evolution and upon the complex problems of contemporary Jewish readjustment.

Much greater promise is held out by an analysis of the important population developments and their bearing upon the general history of the Jewish people. It must be admitted that this aspect of human history has been sadly neglected, and the history of the Jewish population has naturally suffered from this general neglect. The present author hopes, some day, to write an extensive work on "Jewish history in the light of numbers." A small installment of this work was published in Hebrew some years ago in the form of a preliminary essay on "The Israelitic Population under the Kings." No one is more fully aware of the enormous difficulties confronting such an undertaking which probably vastly exceeds the resources of present-day scholarship. Nevertheless, an attempt must sooner or later be made to find out the various stages in the growth and decay of the numerical strength of the Jews throughout their recorded history. The rates of Jewish natality and mortality in different periods; the varying age and sex distribution in each generation; the numerical division between the urban and the rural groups; the extent and the biological effects of polygamy in various Jewish settlements; the frequency and effects of intermarriage, whether officially more or less tolerated or outlawed—are all problems of vital significance for the understanding of the economic structure, the social relationships, and even of certain cultural and religious developments of the Jewish, as of any other, people. Undoubtedly there are long stretches of Jewish history in which the evidence concerning these basic facts is either too limited or altogether non-existent. Even where extant sources have preserved some sort of statistical material, their reliability is subject to grave doubts. The predilection of many ancient and medieval authors for exaggeratingly high numbers, the total indifference of many others to the factual background of their figures, and the greater likelihood of errors in the transmission of numbers than almost any other part of ancient texts present tremendous obstacles to detached investigation. On the other hand, population and other censuses and compilations of lists of taxpayers were much more frequent and searching in antiquity and in certain medieval countries than is generally known today. In any case the time seems overdue for the marshalling of all the available information and for its utmost exploitation by statisticians, sociologists, and historians. That is why the present author has felt justified in his *History* to call briefly, and in many ways tentatively, the attention of the public to the great influence exercised by these biological factors on the other phases of Jewish social and religious life in the crucial periods of ancient Israel, before and after the second fall of Jerusalem, and during the last three centuries.

Another significant approach may perhaps be styled the *normative-factual approach*. Thereby we mean an examination of the predominantly legal and ethical sources and a contrast of them with the known facts of the Jews' socio-economic and cultural life. The importance of law and ethics, especially for Jewish history, has long been recognized. Was not law the very core of the Jewish religion and culture? Was not "ethical montheism" Judaism's major contribution to civilization, on which modern Jews have frequently prided themselves, not without apologetic exaggeration? However, we must realize that even in such a generally law-abiding and ethically-minded community as that of the Jews, actuality never fully corresponded to the norm.

In fact the norm itself changed its significance with the changing realities. One characteristic illustration will suffice here. Judaism may pride itself on having introduced for the first time into the history of legal systems the protective principle of *ona'ah,* whereby both parties to a contract were protected against over-reaching and misrepresentation if the price exceeded its normal level by but one-sixth. The Roman *laesio enormis,* enacted several centuries later probably under the direct or indirect influence of Jewish law, more reluctantly granted such protection in the case of damages reaching to some 50-100 percent. It should be noted, however, that under the original conditions of agricultural Palestine, transactions involving the sale of land, slaves and deeds were exempted from the operation of this law. The reason for these exemptions is clear. Land was anything but a sheer commodity in ancient Palestine. It was held for many generations by the same family. Voluntary transfers were so exceptional and so much the result of a particular farmer's urgent need to dispose of his property that a severe limitation of the permissible price range would, as a rule, have handicapped rather than protected the person in whose behalf it had been enacted. Slaves, too, were primarily acquired for domestic service with a view toward their permanent association with the households of their respective masters. The sale of a slave by a Palestinian farmer or artisan was likewise in the nature of an exceptional, more or less forced disposal of property, which called for no stringent limitation of the right of free contractual price fixing. Deeds served at that time merely as instruments of evidence and had by themselves practically no commercial value.

Centuries later the Jews found themselves increasingly transformed into a mercantile nation, living under the advanced semi-capitalistic civilization of the medieval Caliphate. Commercial transactions involving the sale of land or urban real estate became a prominent feature of Jewish commerce. Jews were frequently found among the leading slave merchants of the period. The transfer of deeds and negotiable instruments of all kinds became a primary branch of business of the Jewish bankers and merchants in the Orient. Evidently the retention of the three exemptions from the protective laws against misrepresentations at that period simply meant that three large domains of economic endeavor were exempted from legal regimentation and placed under the full operation of the liberalistic laws of supply and demand.

It is evidently not enough to know the text of the law, and even to learn that over a period of many centuries it was neither repealed nor modified. In order to know what it actually meant we must place it within the framework of changing reality. We must come to learn that there is not only a constant transmutation of meaning in words and concepts, but also in the superficially unchanged legal and ethical norms, legal and ethical constitutions. Frequently Jewish law was "adjusted" to life simply by *not* having undergone any formal change. Only a full analysis of both theory and practice may enable the historian to comprehend the institutional growth of any civilization, and especially of such an intrinsically "normative" civilization as the Jewish, marching under the flag of its eternal and divine, but nevertheless profoundly adjustable, Torah.

Another integral element of historic sociology ought to be the *communal* approach to Jewish history. By that term we wish to designate an analysis of the changing aspects of Jewish communal co-existence in different environments and of their influence upon the daily life of the masses as well as upon the conscious formula-

82

tions of the leaders. Even in the period of Israelitic monarchy, it appears, the life of the great mass of Israelites was much more affected by the happenings in the numerous towns, hamlets, and villages and by the municipal administration, judiciary, and priesthood than by the events which took place at the royal courts, the high army commands, or the temples of either Jerusalem or Samaria. Undoubtedly due to the inherent weakness of the Israelitic monarchy and the small size of the two capitals, which between them never seem to have harbored more than 5 or 6 percent of the Israelitic population, the local forces far transcended in importance those of the central agencies of both state and religion. We must guard ourselves against being misled by the sources, mostly written in these central points, into overestimating the significance of the centers as against that of the local agencies, the recorded history of which unfortunately is very meager.

This experience of the ancient Israelites was duplicated on a worldwide scale in the Jewish communities of the dispersion. Here the control was further divided between the central and local powers of the non-Jewish state and the central and local management of the Jewish community. Only a proper balance between these centripetal and centrifugal forces, between the influences of the non-Jewish monarchs or cities and of the interterritorial, provincial, and local Jewish leadership (exemplified in the Palestinian patriarchate, the Babylonian exilarchate and gaonate, the provincial ethnarchate, *negidut,* synod or council and the individual Jewish community) can furnish the proper perspective for the understanding of the most vital developments in Jewish life.

The need for refining the peculiar methods required for the investigation of Jewish communal history may perhaps best be illustrated by the age-old problem of "democracy" in the Jewish communal structure. While there undoubtedly existed certain democratic forms in many Jewish communities, a great many others possessed decidedly aristocratic, if not monarchial, features. On the one hand, we possess records of communities with direct elections, in the case of Leghorn during a brief period in the eighteenth century even of the extremely democratic election by lot; on the other hand, we find

83

innumerable communities whose officials were appointed by an exilarch, a *nagid* or another provincial leader. The local *dayyanim* appointed by the exilarchs in many communities of the Near East over a period of several centuries were not only the official administrators of justice, but as the main tax collectors for the benefit of the community as well as of the state they wielded enormous power in all communal affairs. The rabbinate, as a permanent salaried office, was not yet developed and the local elders, even where such were elected, hardly counterbalanced the accumulation of power in the hands of these appointed officials. The *hakham-bashis* of the Ottoman empire likewise were powerful executives exercising vast control over the life of the bulk of Sephardic and Oriental Jewry in modern times. However, their life-long tenure of office at least depended on their election by the communal leaders in Constantinople (often with the collaboration of representatives from other communities), and was not hereditary for countless generations as was the office of the Babylonian exilarchs. Even those western communities which could boast of theoretically democratic forms of government were frequently dependent, politically as well as economically, upon a leading Court Jew. His whimsical desires had to be respected by his fellow members, because the residential rights of the entire community frequently depended on the privileges granted to him personally or at best upon those of a small coterie of such influential chiefs.

In almost all communities, moreover, the non-taxpaying members were excluded from the exercise of electoral rights. One might argue that such restriction became necessary to prevent the numerous Jews supported by the community from influencing the elections in a spirit of excessive liberality towards themselves. This argument has become familiar to the American newspaper readers in connection with the alleged abuses of relief and WPA funds to influence elections in the United States. Whatever the reason, it cannot be denied that substantial sections of the community were thus barred from voting. In some communities only the taxpayers of a higher than average tax were allowed to vote. More important still, according to the traditional concepts of Orthodox Jewry, women

84

were always excluded from voting and from taking any other part
in the public life of the community. The rabbinic interpretation of
Psalms 45.14 operated, like the Catholic *mulier taceat in ecclesia,*
as an insurmountable bar to women's active participation in communal boards.

On the other hand, a much more profound type of "democracy"
was achieved through the common ideals and practice of education.
Every father was obliged to provide education for his sons, and the
community was responsible for the education of all, especially the
poor. Through education one could attain the highest position of
power and eminence in Jewry. There was also an inherent solidarity
in the life of a struggling minority which transcended the class
differences and, still more, the relatively minor distinctions in electoral rights. In short, democracy in the Jewish community is not a
myth. But to understand its role properly one must bear in mind
that no strictly political form can correspond to the essentially non-
political type of organization as represented by the ancient or
medieval *kehillah.* The Jewish people had in its millennial evolution
progressed so far along the road of emancipation from both state
and territory, had developed even in its substitutes for a state so
many new non-political features, that it is quite erroneous to look
in its communal structure for organizational forms taken from the
strictly political fields of state power.[9]

We may be permitted, finally, to make mention of the *socio-
religious* approach to Jewish history, which a good many readers
seem to have detected in our recent presentation. It will be well to
bear in mind the fact to which the reader's attention has repeatedly
been called, that this social and religious treatment of Jewish history
arose out of a specific interest in the interrelations between society
and religion in the entire historic experience of the Jewish people.
The author's warnings against the generalization of this approach,
primarily determined by the theme, seem to have remained un-
heeded even by quite a few critics. It is evident, moreover, that
religion could generally be classified as just another social force,
and that a socio-religious approach would only be the equivalent of
a general sociological approach with some specific emphasis upon

religion. Such specific emphasis, it must be admitted, is entirely warranted in the case of the Jews. There is no doubt that among the various social factors, population, economics, community, secular culture, and religion, the latter has held the most conspicuous place at least in the consciousness of the Jews throughout the three and a half millennia of their existence. In no other people's history has the impact of religion been so strong, continuous, and comprehensive as in the history of the Jews, especially in post-biblical times. It is consequently but the unavoidable and intrinsically justified adaptation of the general method of sociological interpretation to the peculiar problems of Jewish history when the element of religious experience is given its due large share within the totality of the social forces. In this sense, and in this alone, we may agree to calling this particular variation of the general sociological method a "socioreligious" approach to Jewish history.

VI

In conclusion we may be allowed to add a few remarks on the application of these methods to the *teaching* of Jewish history. The effects of any change in approach and methodology upon the higher education and the professional training of young historians is self-evident. However, one must never lose sight of the warning, sounded by Theodor Mommsen,[10] that "it is a dangerous and pernicious illusion when a professor of history believes he is able to train historians in the same fashion as one would train philologists or mathematicians at a university. With greater justification than in the case of the latter, one must say of the historian that he is not being trained but born, not being educated but educates himself." And Mommsen undoubtedly was one of the greatest teachers of history, who succeeded in instilling in his students both a reverence for and a critical attitude toward the ancient sources, and in teaching them to correlate disparate incidents into a great whole. Nevertheless, the recurrent raising of such methodological issues, the discussion of their general aspects and, even more fruitfully, the pointing out of their specific application to particular subjects under discussion in an advanced seminar, will undoubtedly help the younger adept of the historical sciences to clarify these issues in his own mind and to make those vital decisions for which he may or may not have been "born" in the ultimate sense.

Such methodological clarification is of no lesser significance for the teacher of history to the non-professional mass of students. Whatever one's personal opinion may be about the desirability of the school functioning as an indoctrinating agency, one must admit that the viewpoints impressed upon youth in its formative age have lasting effects. Not only the totalitarian governments, communist as well as fascist, have recognized the extreme importance of indoctrination in the primary and secondary schools, but also a democratic country, such as France, has raised generations of citizens upon a *Weltanschauung* deeply colored by an historical tradition nurtured from the springs of French nationalism and the new democratic institutions. The newspapers recently reported that, after prolonged negotiations between representative groups of French and German teachers of history, an agreement was tentatively reached concerning many controversial issues of historical tradition and a closer harmonization of the French and German textbooks in history. A widely accepted, though frequently exploded, view of the American Revolution has similarly colored the outlook of generations of school children and adults throughout the United States.

Such type of indoctrination has undoubtedly been one of the essentials of Jewish education throughout the ages. The forces of survival of the Jewish people were greatly strengthened by the prevailing view of general and Jewish history which, instilled in the early years of childhood, was steadily reimpressed upon the minds of the adults through oral and written preachments. One wonders whether the Jews could have altogether survived the medieval persecutions without the philosophy of history which emphasized the temporary as well as purifying character of the Exile, and its ultimate disappearance in the Messianic age. It cannot be denied that some of the vitality of the Jewish people has been sapped in recent generations by the loss of such a comprehensive, generally accepted philosophy of history, and the ensuing lack of indoctrination of the entire people in a common interpretation of its past.

We all realize, therefore, the practical dangers of historical iconoclasm. The undermining of traditional beliefs effected in the minds of many pious young Jews, as well as Christians, through the historical "higher" criticism of the Bible may serve as a warning with respect to the removal of other "idols in history." It was, consequently, not without hesitation that the present author undertook some years back and has ever since continued to reveal the historical foundations as well as the inadequacies of "the lachrymose conception of Jewish history." He still recalls the shock he received when after the publication of a preliminary essay on this subject, the representative of a leading publishing house in New York suggested that he write a book "debunking" the Jewish Middle Ages. Time and again he also had the perhaps tragi-comic experience of finding the Jewish public sort of enamored with the tales of ancient and modern persecutions. Denying, for example, that any large-scale pogroms had taken place in the territories of ethnographic Poland before 1936 evoked an instantaneous storm of protests not against the alleged perpetrators of such massacres, but against himself for venturing to deny them. Quite evidently this lachrymose conception of Jewish history has served as an eminent means of social control from the days of the ancient rabbis, and its repudiation now might help further to weaken the authority of Jewish communal leadership.

On closer analysis, however, we can easily perceive that such weakening is the cause rather than the effect of the new historical orientation. The generations which have become ripe for biblical criticism have long before begun to cast off in practice the "shackles" of the biblical tradition. We now see more and more clearly that the great transformations in religious history usually begin with changes in ritual and religious observance rather than with those in dogma and religious theory. As a result of the economic, social, intellectual, and ultimately also political emancipation, there had started a complete disintegration of Jewish communal control long before the nineteenth century, when the "science of Judaism" began its memorable process of "cutting down the plantations" of the accepted theory. So, too, in our own days the absence of a common interpretation of Judaism and of an agreement as to the essential criteria of Jewishness, brought about by the disparate socio-economic interests, cultural backgrounds, and factional struggles within the various groups of Jewry, militates against the very possibility of indoctrinating Jewish youth in a convincing, because uniform, view of the Jewish past. That is why, it seems, the removal of outworn historical conceptions is not only dictated by the scientific conscience of the investigator and by the quest for truth of the genuinely interested public, but may also, in the long run, pave the way towards the formulation of a new philosophy of Jewish history which would more closely correspond to our own modern social needs and our new intellectual requirements. A comprehensive, generally accepted emphasis in and explanation of Jewish history will, in any case, have to await the return of a certain stability in the social and cultural structure of the Jewish people. The new effective social control of the community, confidently to be expected in that new "universalist" age, would easily devise its own new full-fledged philosophy of history and the means of instilling it in its own youth.

5

Newer Emphases
in Jewish History*

SMALL TWENTY-FIVE YEARS AGO I HAD THE HONOR of preparing an essay on "Emphases in Jewish History" for the inaugural issue of this journal.[1] This essay began by quoting the truism that "every generation writes its own history of past generations." Now a quarter century later, a new generation of historians has arisen which, of course, views history from some novel angles. Twenty-five years may not ordinarily be regarded as a full generation. But, according to the old adage that "war years count double," this particular quarter century, which witnessed such tremendous transformations in both world history and Jewish history, may definitely be considered more than a generation. Certainly, the destruction of European Jewry and the rise of the State of Israel have opened the eyes of our contemporaries to many heretofore neglected facets and nuances in the lives of earlier generations. Together with the abandonment of some old, and the adoption of new, values, these events have forced many scholars to revise their historical approaches.

Broadened Geographic Horizons

The decline of Ashkenazi Jewry, resulting from the Great Catastrophe, and the reawakening of many old Sephardi and Oriental communities have aroused renewed interest in the past destinies of these Jewries. The physical dispersal of many scholars would by itself have weakened their traditional concentration on

* Reprinted from *Jewish Social Studies,* vol. XXV, no. 4, 1963.

the history of Jews in the German-speaking and East European areas. A few decades ago the output of East-Central European historians far outstripped, both quantitatively and qualitatively, that of all other Jewish scholars combined. Though not entirely oblivious of what happened in other lands—in fact, the histories of the Jews in France, England, the United States and in the Middle Eastern countries owed a great deal to their researches— the German, Polish and Russian Jewish historians, not surprisingly, viewed all late medieval and modern Jewish history from a Germano-centric or East-European-centered orientation. These characteristic approaches were transplanted even to other countries by those scholars who had been born and trained in that old reservoir of Jewish intellectual manpower and who, upon settling in a new country, began writing the history of the local Jewish communities.

All that has changed in the last twenty-five years. True, the history of the East-Central European Jewries has not completely lost its attraction for the older and younger scholars of our time, although the number of historians intimately familiar with the East European languages and cultures has greatly diminished. The intensive research into the Great Catastrophe, now being conducted especially under the auspices of the Yad Washem in Jerusalem, the Yivo Institute for Jewish Research in New York and related groups in other countries, has by itself not only kept alive Jewish scholarly interest in the events of the years 1933-45, but has also brought forth a multitude of more or less valuable monographs dealing with the whole history of the destroyed local and regional communities. Other scholars, particularly those grouped around the Leo Baeck Institute in New York, London and Jerusalem, have helped revive the former concern for the history of the German-speaking communities.[2]

However, the histories of other communities, too, have begun to come into their own. American Jewish history, for instance, has emerged during the last quarter century as an independent, respectable discipline. Formerly written almost exclusively by amateur historians, principally lawyers and rabbis, it revealed the characteristic filiopietistic attitude toward the early generations of American

Jews. Now it is widely recognized that the last century since the Civil War is historically even more significant, and that its far greater complexities can be studied only with the more refined techniques of modern historiography. The last quarter century has indeed witnessed the publication of a considerable number of histories of American Jewish communities, a detailed examination of population and other sociological trends within American Jewry, more advanced approaches toward American Jewish biography, and so forth.[3] American Jewish historical research has thus finally come of age. Not quite on the same level yet, but nevertheless truly encouraging, have been the incipient efforts to write carefully balanced histories, general as well as monographic, of Jewish life in Latin America, Canada, and other British Commonwealth countries.

Most dramatic has been the reversal of the traditional attitude toward the more peripheral Middle Eastern and North African Jewish settlements. In part, this new concern for the smaller and long-isolated communities was owing to the growing interest of anthropologists and students of religion in some "exotic" offshoots of world Jewry. To a larger extent, however, this transformation came as a result of the new position attained by the Sephardi and Oriental Jews within the totality of Jewish life today and particularly within the rapidly expanding Yishuv in Israel. The ingathering of exiles, which had begun long before the establishment of the new state, but had received unprecedented momentum in the last fifteen years, has brought together within the boundaries of Israel descendants of the far-flung communities of both East and West. Today almost balanced numerically, these major groups have had to live together and to understand one another also with respect to their historically deep-rooted mores and outlook.

Quite early, some Israeli scholars, particularly the former president of Israel, Yitzhak Ben-Zvi, had evinced deep interest in Jewish minority cultures. Starting with the oldest, and in some respects, the most exotic minority, the Samaritans, to whom he dedicated a number of important monographs, Ben-Zvi enlarged the scope of his investigations to cover the various distant branches of the

Jewish people. Many of his essays relating to such distant groups appeared under the title of *Nidhe Yisrael* (The Dispersed of Israel) both in Hebrew and in English.⁴ It was quite appropriate, therefore, that a special Institute for Research on Jewish Communities in the East, affiliated with the Hebrew University in Jerusalem, came to be known as the Ben-Zvi Institute. Directed by him, with the able assistance of its present director, Meir Benayahu, the Institute had set for itself the task of gathering the scattered documentation, publishing a journal and numerous monographs in all fields pertaining to the Oriental Jewries. The publications hitherto issued have already greatly enriched our knowledge of the history not only of these remote communities but, indirectly, also of world Jewry.⁵ One may indeed look forward to further studies of this kind helping to evaluate anew the whole course of medieval and modern Jewish history.

More recently there has also been an awakened interest in the history of Jews on the African continent, especially south of the Arabic-speaking area which has long been part and parcel of the Mediterranean world and thus an intrinsic ingredient of Jewish history. Until recently, scholarly interest in African Jews was limited to a few travelers or anthropologists. Only the sizable community of Ethiopian Falashas has attracted the attention of scholars like Joseph Halévy and Abraham Faitlovitch, the latter being more interested in "redeeming" the contemporary Falashas from their "backwardness" than in general historical studies of their past. Even today Jewish historical research with respect to the entire area south of the Sahara desert still is in its infancy, except for the history of South African Jewry which is more European than African in character. But at least some beginnings have been made for a more intensive investigation of the historic connections between the Jewish people and religion and the awakening African nations.⁶

In short, a mere glance at the histories written by Graetz, Jawitz, Dubnow or Margolis and Marx suffices to show how relatively "parochial" Jewish historiography had been even during the interwar period. Such history writing is simply no longer feasible today. Just as world history can no longer be written, as it used to be, principally in terms of the western evolution, so has Jewish historiography begun gradually to abandon its exclusive concentration on the traditionally narrow geographic areas in Europe and the adjoining Mediterranean lands.

New Meaning of Heroism

Perhaps an even more far-reaching change in the appreciation of historic facts has come about through the new evaluation of the meaning of heroism. Since ancient times, Judaism, and following it its daughter religions of Christianity and Islam, glorified religious martyrdom. Essentially introduced into human history by the Maccabean revolt, this emphasis was further strengthened by the growing opposition of the Pharisees and the talmudic sages to the Maccabean dynasty. Not the Maccabean warrior, but rather the Maccabean martyr for the faith, was now remembered in Jewish and Christian circles. The apocryphal story of Hannah and her seven sons outperformed in the memory of men the warlike exploits of Mattathias and his sons. Ultimately, when the Talmud briefly discussed the festival of Hanukkah, the original national liberation movement was almost forgotten and its place was taken by the religious miracle of a small pitcher of oil which kept the flame burning for eight days.

Similarly, the Christian faith originated with the crucifixion of Jesus and the martyrdom of several apostles. What would have happened to the memory of the Nazarene if, instead of meekly marching toward his doom bearing the cross, he had stood up fighting and killed two or three Roman legionnaires before being slain by a Roman spear? It was only because he demonstrated the force of his own doctrine of the meek inheriting the earth through his own excruciating martyrdom that he became the founder of a great world religion. This fundamental difference between such readiness for "meek" religious martyrdom and the Roman principle of *dulce et decorum est pro patria mori,* which stressed patri-

94

otic self-sacrifice on the battlefield, was well understood by the outstanding medieval Jewish philosopher of history, the great poet Yehudah Halevi, who wrote:

> Christians do not glory in kings, heroes and rich people, but in those who followed Jesus all the time before his faith had taken firm root among them. They wandered away, or hid themselves, or were killed wherever one of them was found, suffered disgrace and slaughter for the sake of their belief. . . . The light of God rests only upon the souls of the humble![7]

Halevi's contemporaries demonstrated by deeds what the poet-philosopher taught in theory. Living in the age of the Crusades, with its first large-scale massacres of Jews in Christian Europe, these contemporaries outdid their predecessors in their readiness to sacrifice their lives for their religious ideals. When the Crusader mobs appeared before the Rhineland cities and besieged the Jewish quarters or the castles in which Jews had found refuge, many of the latter, in order to avoid the temptation of saving their lives through conversion, introduced the system of preventive self-immolation as a testimony to their staunch adherence to their faith. While such mass suicide had already been performed by the last defenders of Judean independence in the aftermath of the war with the Romans, the medieval elders and rabbis who performed the ritualistic slaughter on their friends and relatives and finally on themselves were hardly cognizant of that military prototype but considered themselves as performing a purely religious sacrifice before the Lord. Curiously, the chroniclers of that period, who through their epic narratives of these sufferings tried to build the morale of the surviving Jews, hardly had an eye for the occasional armed resistance offered by their coreligionists to the assailants. In fact, the remarkable episode of a local Jewish community resisting the attackers, slaying two hundred of them, and thus averting the catastrophe, was deemed worthy of no more than a casual reference in the midst of these horror recitals. The very name of the city, given in the sources as *SLA,* has not yet been fully identified.[8]

What a contrast to our present day! Many of us have so completely lost the feeling for religious martyrdom that we evince total lack of comprehension for the meek surrender of most of the six million Jewish victims of the Nazi "final solution." We glorify, above every other phase of the great tragedy, the uprising in the Warsaw ghetto. To a lesser extent we praise similar uprisings in other communities and sing with deep emotional dedication the songs of partisans. Why have the millions of others failed to resist? Knowing well enough that their end had come, why did they not kill in the process some of their barbarian assailants? These questions are so universally repeated and they so basically underlie much of the literature relating to the Jewish tragedy of the Nazi era that all sorts of explanations have been offered for this passive submission. To that extent not only public opinion, Jewish and Gentile alike, but also Jewish historiography have veered away from the traditional Jewish acceptance of the divine will and the emphasis on the ultimate victory of meekness and passive resistance.

Not that I wish to minimize the heroism of the Warsaw rebels, fighting hopelessly against tremendous odds. Nor must one underestimate the role of the Jewish partisans during World War II who not only had to combat an overwhelmingly powerful enemy, but also frequently found only lukewarm support from their fellow partisans among the East European nations. Clearly, I too am a child of this age. All my life I have been struggling against the hitherto dominant "lachrymose conception of Jewish history"— a term which I have been using for more than forty years—because I have felt that an overemphasis on Jewish sufferings distorted the total picture of the Jewish historic evolution and, at the same time, badly served a generation which had become impatient with the nightmare of endless persecutions and massacres.

However, just as we must not misunderstand the true realities of life and psychology among the still predominant Orthodox and traditionalist East European Jewish masses during the Nazi era, so must we not overlook the inherent tragedies of Jewish life during the two millennia of the dispersion. Our generation may celebrate annually the Hanukkah festival essentially as the feast of national liberation and see in Judah Maccabee and his brothers the heroic fighters for national independence, and yet we must recognize that for two thousand years the Jewish people has kindled its Hanukkah lights mainly in memory of the great miracle and the epochal religious event of the "rededication" of the Temple in Jerusalem.

A more balanced view must also be taken by Jewish historians with respect to concerted Jewish political action. In the past, neither the need nor the possibility of such action was fully understood. No crasser illustration need be adduced than the earlier generations' lack of historic appreciation of the few political actions of this type which had taken place in their lifetime. We may recall how Ottoman Jewry, led by the distinguished members of the House of Mendes, Doña Gracia and Don Joseph, attempted to retaliate for the burning of twenty-four Marranos in the city of Ancona in 1556. This tragedy, occurring in clear violation of earlier privileges granted that community by the reigning popes, called forth not only the traditional poetic elegies, some recited for generations thereafter in the local community on the Ninth of Ab, but also a concerted effort to set an example that such barbarity should not go unpunished. Since Ancona happened to be the main harbor of the Papal States, through which flowed much of that country's vital Levant trade, the Turkish Jewish leaders proclaimed a boycott on that harbor and began diverting all shipping under their control to the neighboring port city of Pesaro. This daring excommunication of the papal regime by Turkish Jewry failed, partly because economic realities proved stronger than ideological devotion, and partly because of the lack of unity characteristic of world Jewry then and later with respect to united political actions.

Equally significant, however, is the reaction to these events on the part of contemporary Jewish enlightened opinion and of later historians both in Italy and in Turkey. A contemporary chronicler and eye-witness of the events, who devoted his remarkable Hebrew chronicle to the history of the various persecutions inflicted by Pope Paul IV on the Jewish communities of the Papal States, and particularly Ancona and Civitanova, went into great detail in describing the legislative and administrative measures taken against his coreligionists. He even departed from the accepted approach of Jewish historians before the Renaissance age and tried to understand the mechanics of the papal administration and its background in the international relations of the period. But in interpreting the cause of Jewish sufferings in Ancona, he fell back on the traditional Jewish self-accusation, going back to the days of the Israeli prophets. He wrote:

> Because of our numerous sins he [the pope] suceeded in trampling under his feet the remnant of Israel living in exile under his reign, for the Lord has been contemplating its numerous sins and His heart had turned to hating His people. The latter's behavior had become overbearing in exile because of its wealth while it lived securely in its beautiful dwellings, courts and palaces, everyone going to his vineyard or field and carrying his gold and silver with him. But they forgot the Lord and did not set aside time for study; because of their wealth they neglected the Torah.

This eyewitness and fellow sufferer has nothing to say about the Turkish boycott. Similarly, the historian Joseph ha-Kohen devotes but three lines to the intervention of the sultan with the pope, brought about by the good offices of Doña Gracia whom he admires, but assigns two pages to a description of the Jewish sufferings.[9]

Most remarkably, Joshua Soncino, a distinguished Constantinople rabbi, who opposed the continuation of the boycott, argued against the preference being given to Pesaro, then under the duke of Urbino. He claimed that far "more serious" than the death of the twenty-four Marranos and the condemnation of scores of others to galley slavery and total ruination was a prank played by the duke's brother in the synagogue in Pesaro. Together with a few other reckless Jew-baiters, the young man had captured a scroll of law, dressed a pig in its mantle, and placed the latter in the synagogue Ark. Since the duke had apparently allowed this outrage to go unpunished, he was worse than the persecutors of the Ancona Marranos for, Soncino insisted, "there is no greater insult to all of Israel [than the Pesaro incident], for in all localities it is the custom of the whole world to respect the scrolls of law."[10]

Could one imagine in our own days the desecration of a synagogue or a cemetery to be considered a greater tragedy than the slaying of a large number of Jews? If I may indulge in a personal recollection, I remember that after the Jewish Cultural Reconstruction had salvaged some eleven hundred Hebrew scrolls of the Law from the Nazi holocaust and brought some of them to New York, I happened to attend the ceremonial burying of numerous fragments of the scrolls no longer usable for worship. Such a burial would have been considered a major event in earlier centuries. Several years ago it was hardly recorded in the daily papers and never, to the best of my knowledge, was it stressed again in the ramified literature on the "final solution."

Of course, this transformation has taken place because of the general secularization of modern life and the specific assimilation of non-Jewish patterns of thought by Jews which is characteristic of the Emancipation era. In contrast to Halevi's days, the Christian world now glorifies its statesmen, conquerors and men of wealth above its saints and martyrs. The Roman concept of the supreme sacrifice for patriotic and nationalistic causes has displaced the ideal of religious martyrdom among Christians and Jews alike. Historiography could only follow suit. The heroic fighter for Israel's independence in 1948 has taken the place of the great religious martyr of former ages in the consciousness not only of the Israeli population, but also of the majority of Jewish youth the world over. Not surprisingly, therefore, the Israeli historians have turned their main attention to the heroes of the First and Second Commonwealths at the expense of the previously much more intensively studied Jewish Middle Ages and early modern times. Historians in the countries of the dispersion have likewise taken up the Jewish role in their countries' revolutionary armies, their political struggles for civil rights, their endeavors to ameliorate the fate of the workingman and other phases of political and economic Jewish life. Yet it is to be hoped that this newer emphasis on politics, economics and military affairs, however justifiable on objective as well as psychological grounds, will not totally displace the understanding for the *Leidens- und Gelehrtengeschichte* which had so completely dominated Jewish historical writing of the nineteenth and early twentieth centuries.

Jewish and General History

Another result of the expanding Emancipation has been the growing recognition that Jewish history cannot be understood without its intimate tie-up with general history. Long familiar to historians of ancient Israel and the Second Jewish Commonwealth, who realized that the historic evolution of a small country wedged in between the large empires of Egypt and the Fertile Crescent and later part of the Hellenistic and Roman imperial systems could not be understood without that broader background of Middle Eastern or Graeco-Roman history, this approach has long been neglected by students of medieval and early modern Jewish developments. Clearly, because of their minority status, the fate of the dispersed Jewish communities depended to an even larger extent on the propelling historic forces within the neighboring civilizations or even on some developments within each region or locality.

In part, to be sure, this "isolationist" approach to Jewish history was occasioned by the practical consideration that the large majority of Jewish historians had been thoroughly versed in Hebrew letters and, at best, possessed some additional training in Semitic philology or general philosophy. Everybody believed that once he could read a text correctly, he was fully equipped for any historical or biographical reconstruction. Moreover, in the early pioneering stages of the nineteenth-century "science of Judaism," much preliminary work had to be done in uncovering the numerous manuscripts still hidden in archives and libraries, publishing them in careful critical editions, and subjecting them to a thorough scholarly analysis. The work of synthesis, when attempted by men like Heinrich Graetz, of necessity largely summarized these newly detected sources and presented a comprehensive picture of the inner Jewish developments as reflected in them. Only after this preliminary ingathering of materials had been accomplished in the course of two or three generations—of course, much extant documentation still remains unexplored—was it possible to start integrating the information thus gained into the fabric of the general western evolution, independently clarified by generations of outstanding historians.

During the last few decades, these earlier trends were actually reversed. To begin with, more and more students of Jewish history were now recruited from professionally trained historians or social scientists, rather than theologians or philologists. Some of the shortcomings of modern Jewish historiography stem, in fact, from the relative unfamiliarity of some newer students of the Jewish past with the Hebraic tradition and source materials. Many of them resemble, at least in part, those numerous non-Jewish historians, going back to Jacques Basnage, the great Huguenot pioneer historian of the Jewish people of the early eighteenth century, who look at Jewish history from the outside, rather than (like most of their predecessors) as insiders with that unconscious "feeling" for what was historically relevant to the past generations.

More fundamentally, the developments of the last three decades have clearly demonstrated to Jews and non-Jews alike how dependent Jewish history has been on external developments. Going to the other extreme, some German-Jewish scholars of the 1930's suggested that the Jews have always been objects, rather than subjects, of their history. Their own overwhelming experience of the tragic fate of European Jewry for reasons entirely beyond its control taught them, they believed, that Jewish destinies throughout the history of the dispersion have in the ultimate sense been controlled by such external forces. They readily overlooked the fact that, were the Jews mere objects of the general historical evolution, they could not possibly have survived the successive waves of hostility throughout the ages. It seems indubitable that a proper understanding of Jewish history presupposes the close interchange of external and internal factors. One could indeed suggest that all Jewish history, particularly during the last two millennia of the dispersion, was essentially the resultant of conflicting internal and external pressures. In cases of great emergency, such as enforced exiles, mass conversions or massacres, the resultant hewed more closely to the external line. More normal and pacific times gave far more room for the display of inner drives, and thus the resultant line came closer to the manifestations of the people's will to survive and the development of those intellectual and religious forces which were to secure that survival. It has indeed become the task of the recent generations of historians and those of the future to balance these external and internal pressures against one another and thus to promote the deeper understanding of the entire Jewish past. An incidental gain of this new approach will be the light which the specific Jewish evolution is able to shed on general history as well, if viewed not from the traditional angle of the majority peoples, but rather from the vantage point of a permanent minority.

In a recent paper,[11] I have tried to illustrate the considerable difficulties accruing to historians from this novel integrated treatment. This is a problem not peculiar to Jewish history, but to all histories of individual peoples or groups. One of the great difficulties confronting any genuine attempt to write a universal history of mankind arises from the heretofore disparate interpretations of the various national histories by specialists in their respective fields. It is a matter of record that when one studies, for example, the history of the Napoleonic Wars from German and French textbooks, one can hardly recognize that one is dealing with the same facts. Russian history since the Revolution of 1917, as described by Soviet scholars, bears little resemblance to the same story narrated by western historians. In fact, sometimes the history of even so recent an event as World War II written by communist authors in Russia greatly differs, depending on the time of its writing and publication.[12] A mere glance at the two editions of the *Large Russian Encyclopedia* will clearly reflect the changing biases of the Communist Party during the four and a half decades of its regime. For one example, the story of Jews and Judaism, given in its first edition of 1932 some one hundred and ten columns of space with a fairly detailed review of many historic developments, even if forced into the straightjacket of the materialistic conception of history, was reduced twenty years later to but four columns of rather hostile generalizations in the second edition.[13]

It is small wonder, then, that when the UNESCO undertook to publish *A Scientific and Cultural History of Mankind*—it did not dare to tackle the far more controversial areas of political and economic history—it ran up against such strongly conflicting nationalist and ideological biases, that the project has taken many more years than had been planned. Having had the honor of serving as Corresponding Member of that undertaking from its inception, I can testify to the editors' sincere desire to produce an impartial over-all history of human culture; but the resistance of opposing traditions could be overcome only by endless negotiations and compromises.

Even more disconcerting are the conflicting biases in the original sources themselves. Everyone knows of the only partially true official communiqués which emanated from the Headquarters of the Allied and the Nazi armies during World War II or, for that matter, from the headquarters of opposing armies during any war. Apart from occasional outright lies, these announcements often consisted of half-truths; they sinned particularly on the side of omission in periods of defeat. In a paper[14] mentioned earlier, I adduced the example of the sharp contrast between the Roman and the Jewish sources relating to the Great War of 66-70 c.e. and the Bar Kokhba Revolt. From the Roman standpoint, there hardly ever was a more gentle emperor than Titus. Yet in the rabbinic sources this destroyer of the Jewish Temple is rarely mentioned without the epithet *ha-rasha* (the Evil-Doer) and the legend about his unnatural death is reported with great relish. Similarly, Hadrian, who, from the standpoint of the Roman Empire's melting pot was the great unifier and promoter of the advanced form of Graeco-Roman civilization, appears in the Jewish sources as a ruthless oppressor. His outlawry of circumcision, which he, however mistakenly, considered both an obstacle to the unity of Roman civilization and a barbaric act likely to contribute to the incipient biological decline of the Roman population, was legitimately viewed in Jewish circles as an extreme attempt at undermining the survival of the Jewish people and an instance of ruthless religious intolerance.

At the same time, the Jewish sources other than Josephus, who addressed himself to Gentile rather than Jewish audiences, completely ignore the fact that in the midst of these protracted and for them unexpectedly difficult wars, these very emperors (including Titus' father, Vespasian) insisted upon the preservation of the equality of rights of the Jews throughout the Empire. The only punitive infringement of that equality was that the half-shekel tax previously paid by all adult male Jews to the Temple in Jerusalem was now to be delivered to the Temple of Jupiter Capitolinus, then in the throes of reconstruction after a fire. But both Vespasian and Titus, in the very midst of the Great War, rejected the requests of Alexandrine and Antiochian delegations that they use the opportunity of the Jewish "rebellion" to suspend the equality of their Jewish compatriots. Nor did Hadrian make any effort to restrict the rights of Jews *qua* citizens, whatever that term may have connoted in the then highly checkered constitutional structure of the various parts of the Empire.

A conscientious historian will, of course, try to balance such original reports in the sources and offer a fairly impartial resolution of the difficulties which may never satisfy a partisan, but which will approach objective historical truths a little more closely. This is no mean task. No such attempt is ever likely to achieve unanimous acceptance. But this is unfortunately the general difficulty of all humanities and social sciences; they can never achieve perfect objectivity. Nonetheless a serious effort in this direction is imperative, if history is not to be turned into mere propaganda.

Rising Antihistorical Trends

It is this very attempt at historical objectivity which has often militated against the full acceptance of historical studies by Jewish thinkers and the masses alike. Quite early in the development of the "science of Judaism," a patriotic scholar like Samuel David Luzzatto complained that his German confrères had been treating the Jewish past "as other students investigate the antiquities of Egypt or Assyria, Babylonia or Persia."[15] But it was precisely this conscious endeavor by Zunz, Geiger, and particularly Jost, to write more dispassionately on Jewish history, approximating the way they would write the history of other ancient or modern nations, which marked the great advance in the science of Judaism. Needless to say, none of them achieved this ideal fully, but the very attempt at doing it was a rather revolutionary and, in the long run, healthy reaction to past precedents.

We witness today a resurgence of Luzzatto's complaint which received new nourishment from the general, more practical reaction against the "historicism" of the nineteenth century. Some philosophers and sociologists, particularly of the pragmatic schools, have felt that the overemphasis on history often yielded fruits of little value to contemporary action, which seemed to them the main purpose of all studies. This approach found even more outspoken partisans among exponents of pure science, who often stated that the history of science had little relation to their contemporary pursuit of knowledge. They argued that since theories regnant but ten years before were frequently thrown into limbo, one need not bother to find out what happened in scientific research hundreds or thousands of years ago. True, even scientists and pragmatic philosophers have become somewhat more modest in recent years; they have come to realize that their present verities are no more perennial than those of their predecessors. Hence some of them have come around to the recognition that, by studying the various trials and errors of earlier generations and the gradual progress in the acquisition of human knowledge, they themselves might also achieve a more balanced view of their own findings at least in their broader universal implications.

Anti-historicism has been aggravated in the study of religion by the peculiar aspects of that discipline. We need not go into great length in discussing these aspects, for they have thus far affected historians and, therefore, also the newer emphases on history to but a minor extent. Suffice it to say, therefore, that the problem of history versus faith, which has so deeply agitated Christian theologians in recent generations, has also affected some thinking of Jewish students. True, the issue is not as burning in Jewish theology as it is in the theology of the New Testament. But the quest of some religious thinkers to distinguish between pure historical truths and "meta-historical" religious truths could play havoc with even a modicum of historical objectivity in future researches.[16]

More immediately threatening, however, has been the return of some groups to the type of thinking dominating Jewish life in the period before the rise of the science of Judaism. That thinking, characterized by the constant reiteration of the old talmudic adage, *Mai de-hava hava* (What was, was), now again questions the practical good which one might expect to derive from the ascertainment of historical facts. A return to the study of the classical sources of either Judaism or Christianity, purportedly yielding the more absolute truths of divine revelation in contrast to the more relativistic truths of any historical research, has become the conscious or unconscious watchword of many neo-orthodox trends which are now fighting for supremacy within Jewish, as well as Christian, theology. That they appeal also to a generation despondent over the breakdown of its older relativistic values and hence urgently engaged in the quest for certainty makes this type of anti-historicism doubly meaningful. However, since it is not likely to generate any new emphasis on history as such, it need not be elaborated in the present context.

PART II

Maimonides

6

The Historical Outlook
of Maimonides*

WE ARE NOT CONCERNED HERE WITH THE QUESTION of how much
history Maimonides knew or how accurate was the historical information he was able to obtain. It would be wholly presumptuous
to judge the amount of knowledge of any medieval writer from
the vantage point of modern historical scholarship based upon
centuries of untiring critical research and the application of historical methods unknown to the medieval mind.

Neither is it a question of how much relevant information
for the history of Maimonides' own time we may be able to
gather from his writings. Especially his responsa and epistles contain numerous incidents of historical value which have not been
fully utilized by modern research. A careful examination or
re-examination of these incidents in connection with other sources
available today would throw new light on certain phases of
twelfth century history. But this task, however alluring, has been
excluded from the scope of the present investigation.

Nor is its objective to inquire into the extent to which history
and dogma appeared as conflicting entities in the mind of Maimonides. The entire problem of *Glaube und Geschichte,* so troublesome to many modern Protestant theologians, loses much of its
acuteness in Judaism through the absence of the conflict between
the historical and the eternal Christ. The comparatively slight
antinomy between the historical Torah, given to the Israelitic
people at a particular historical juncture, and its eternal validity
—even if one failed to subscribe to the aggadic doctrine of its
pre-existence[1]—caused no misgivings in the mind of the medieval
Jew, steeped in the tradition of the sudden revelation on Mt. Sinai.[2]

* Reprinted from the *Proceedings of the American Academy for Jewish
Research,* vol. VI (1935), 5-113.

Our main concern here is to find out from the innumerable, mostly incidental, utterances of Maimonides what were his general as well as specific views on the past of mankind and of the Jewish people. These utterances naturally render only a fraction of what he really thought about human and Jewish history. But they happen to cover such a variety of episodes extending over so vast a range of generations that one may really regard them as a cross-section of all of Maimonides' historical views. At any rate, they appear sufficiently comprehensive and meaningful to allow for a reconstruction of their author's historical *Weltbild*. If we shall discover that the Maimonidean outlook on history was but typical of that of a twelfth-century educated Jew, this will be no reflection upon the profundity of the contributions of the jurist and philosopher, but serve as an even more illuminating example of the basic attitudes of medieval men.[3]

Needless to say, the ancient history of the Jews was seen by Maimonides and his contemporaries through the spectacle of the talmudic and post-talmudic Aggadah. Critical as some of the Geonim and Maimonides himself were of numerous aggadic teachings which ran counter to scientific fact or philosophic reasoning, they rather uncritically accepted any semilegendary reconstructions of the Jewish past. However, they not only had to be selective in the choice of their historic *aggadot,* but they also often had to adjust them to the outlook of their own time. Their view of the post-talmudic period was necessarily based upon events and traditions which had interveningly accumulated in the Mediterranean communities. In this respect Maimonides' outlook on history is a combination of widely accepted talmudic-rabbinic concepts and of medieval adjustments made either by the intervening generations or by Maimonides himself.

Jewish and Arab Historiography

Maimonides was not a historian. The logical bent of his mind was frequently impatient with the accidental turns of historical events. Even his philosophic master, Aristotle, had not developed a philosophy of history and had claimed that epic poetry "is more philosophical and earnest than history." Nevertheless, Aristotle himself could not refrain from applying the historical method to his investigations in the field of political theory. As is well known, he collected constitutions enacted in various Greek city-states over a period of several generations and examined them critically before proceeding to derive general conclusions from them. For Maimonides the urge to engage in similar researches existed to an even greater degree. His most significant contribution consisted in the recodification of traditional law. Such law being bound up with tradition and tradition being a primary historical factor, the nexus between law and history was easily given. Indeed, the Arab chronicler Ṭabari, for one example, devoted his prolific literary output to the two major fields, his interpretation of the Koran in the light of tradition and his famous historical work. That is why Maimuni's general repudiation of historical literature as found in the following statement calls for a specific explanation: "It is sheer waste of time; as in the case of books found among the Arabs describing historical events, the government of kings and Arab genealogy, or books of songs and similar works which neither possess wisdom nor yield profit for the body, but are merely a waste of time."[4]

We can no longer be satisfied with the reason advanced by Geiger that "Arabian historiography of that time with its anecdotes and tales appeared to him as worthless." Geiger, writing in 1850, was familiar with only a few, rather inferior Arabian historical writings, and shared the general prejudice against them voiced by European scholars from the days of Gibbon. It was after 1850 that most of the significant historical contributions of the Arabs before and after Maimonides became available to the western public in editions and translations. Maimonides may have looked down with contempt upon the anecdotal type of history which filled many volumes with lurid tales of intrigues and love affairs of prominent caliphs and viziers, such as were included in Ibn Miskaiwaihi's *The Experiences of Nations*. But he must have recognized the profound quest for truth and honest philosophic attitude of an all-embracing historian such as Al-Mas'udi. He must also have known of Al-Biruni's attempt to develop a scientific, almost "mathematical method of historiography." Neither could he have wished to deprecate the works of the great Arabian historians of religion, beginning with Al-Mas'udi's disciple Mutahdar al-Maqdasi who around 966 wrote his *Book of Creation and of History*. It is not unlikely that Maimuni knew of the Spaniard Ibn Hazm and of his own older contemporary Al-Shahrastani.[5]

Nor were Jewish historians altogether lacking. In Abraham ibn Daud, his distinguished philosophical predecessor, he could have found a guide also to historical investigations. While by no means measuring up to the standards of the classical Arabian historians, the *Book of Tradition* furnished a careful historical survey of the literary leaders of the people. In Abraham bar Hiyya and Yehudah Halevi, whose works he undoubtedly knew, Maimuni also had before him significant attempts at reshaping the Jewish conception of history in accordance with the new demands. Abraham bar Hiyya especially, confronted in Spain not only with Arabian but Christian historical reconstructions, developed a theory of Jewish history which adapted Augustinian and Isidorian teachings to Jewish needs. His philosophy of history might have stimulated further historical thinking were it not perhaps for the transcending influence of the "unhistorical" Maimonidean thought.[6]

The peculiarity of Abraham bar Hiyya's method may offer us a partial explanation for Maimonides' reticence. Abraham bar Hiyya, following numerous Arabian historians, combined the study of astrology with that of history and tried to explain many historical developments through the positive or negative influence of stars.[7] Maimonides, a harsh opponent of that "lie against reason," sharply condemned all attempts not only to prognosticate the future, but also to project such astrological prognostications into the past.[8] He may also have felt a certain aversion to the Arabic historical writings because, no matter how universalist in compass, they were dogmatically restricted by the teachings of Islam and contained many a derogatory utterance on the subject of Judaism. In some instances the glowing descriptions of the lives of Muhammed and the other heroes of Islam and the glorification of Muslim political and cultural power undermined the belief of Jewish youth. Samau'al ibn Yahya al-Maghribi actually tells us that in his early youth he had first read many historical novels and then proceeded to study the more reliable historical chronicles of Al-Miskaiwaihi and Tabari which eventually led him to apostasy. We have reason to believe that Maimonides was familiar with the polemical work of his older contemporary.[9]

Other more fundamental factors contributed to checking the influence of the Arabian historians on the Jews. True to the basically political orientation of Islam and the needs of the Caliphate, the Arab historical literature was essentially political. Not only those works which dealt with political history as such —and these were the majority—but also the various biographical collections or those dealing with the history of philosophers, physicians and sectarians had a decidedly political tinge. Careful genealogical investigations were imperative under the system of state grants extended to the descendants of Muhammed and his closest companions. Since Omar I the subsidies varied in accordance with the degree of relationship. Not until Ibn Khaldun's sociological interpretation of history, moreover, did Arab historiography fully emancipate itself from the tradition of the early chronicles to write history in terms of the deeds of individual monarchs, generals and religious leaders. Non-political Judaism lacked such incentives. It, too, was prone to record a few acts of outstanding individuals, but these were so deeply imbedded in the general flow of tradition that they hardly lent themselves to extensive biographical and still less to comprehensive historical treatment. Although on the whole still as insistent upon family purity and noble descent (*yihus*) as it had been in the Sassanian age, Judaism under Islam had few vested interests in genealogy. Neither did it have the stimuli given by the dynastic-religious struggle over the legitimacy of succession to the prophet, which so long dominated all public affairs of the Muslim world.

Whatever the reasons, Maimonides undoubtedly was consciously "unhistorical." Unconsciously, however, he could not help referring to the history of his people when he wished to explain certain contemporary phenomena. Sometimes he construed new historical hypotheses, in order to elucidate obscure phases in Jewish law, the oppressed position of his people or perplexing features in the outside world. The following summary of his historical views and opinions, arranged in a more or less chronological order, may give us an inkling of his type of historical approach.[10]

The Early History of Mankind

The early days of humanity before Abraham were of interest to Maimonides only from the point of view of the origins of the various religions and their influence on the subsequent legislation in ancient Israel. Although he acknowledged, as is well known, that by strictly philosophic arguments the creation of the world can neither be proved nor disproved, he believed that creation *ex nihilo* at a certain date was an indubitable historical fact. He even followed the rabbinic chronology that about 2500 years elapsed from Adam to Moses.

It is characteristic that the personality of the first man attracted his attention only to a slight degree. He pays little attention to the innumerable legends found in the Talmud and the Midrashim concerning Adam and Eve. He only mentions the court's injunction to witnesses in the case of capital prosecution concerning the purpose of the creation of a single man and the continuous basic similarity of the shape of all men, which nevertheless leaves room for endless facial variations. God wanted to demonstrate that he who destroys one person should be placed on a par with one who destroys the entire world, and that everyone should be entitled to claim that the world was created for his sake.[11] Maimuni also gives the following very interesting explanation for the sanctity of the Temple in Jerusalem. "It is a tradition accepted by everyone," he states, "that the place where David and Solomon built the altar on the threshing floor of Araunah is the place on which

Abraham had erected his altar and offered Isaac, and where Noah had built his when he left the ark. This is the very altar on which Cain and Abel had offered and on which Adam, too, had brought a sacrifice when he was created; and this was precisely the spot from which he was created. As the sages said, Adam was created from the place of his atonement."[12]

It is evident that Maimonides believed that Adam was a monotheist worshipping the God of Israel. He speaks in another connection of the six commandments which God imposed upon Adam, namely the five prohibitions of idolatry, blasphemy, murder, incest, robbery and the obligation to preserve the law and order. Thereafter Noah received the additional commandment forbidding the consumption of a part cut off from a living animal (אבר מן החי). Through this historical hypothesis, Maimonides, following the Aggadah,[13] evades the difficulty arising from the frequently contradictory talmudic computations concerning the six or seven commandments of the sons of Noah.

If idolatry was thus outlawed from the very beginning, how can we explain the rise of the pagan religions? This question engaged Maimonides' attention throughout his life and he tried to obtain as much information as possible on the early history of religion. "I have also read," he says, "on the subject of all idolatry; it seems to me that there has not remained a work on this topic written in Arabic [or] translated from other languages, which I have not read, examined its contents and grasped its full meaning."[14] Unfortunately, he does not seem to have read this literature very critically and most of his assumptions seem to be based upon spurious or otherwise unreliable writings. Among these the *Nabatean Agriculture* occupies a most prominent place. In his systematic fashion he sifted the data supplied by these sources and organized them into a full theory concerning the origin of paganism, which he repeated in various formulations in his *Commentary* on the Mishnah, his *Code* and most extensively in his *Guide*.[15]

In its briefest form, as given in the introduction to the laws pertaining to idolaters, this theory runs as follows: In the days of Enosh[16] the people committed a grievous error. Enosh and his associates among the sages of that generation reasoned that, since God had created the stars and the spheres to guide the world and placed them in a high position as servants doing his will, they must be worthy of praise and reverence. It undoubtedly is his will that people pay homage to those whom He had elevated, just as an earthly king regards it as a tribute to himself when his counselors are honored. Thereupon they began building temples to the stars, offered to them and exalted them in prayers, all in order to comply with what they erroneously thought to be the will of God. "And this was the very core of idolatry." After a time there arose among them false prophets, who demanded in the name of God that there be erected an image and that the entire people with its women and children worship in front of it. So they invented images of stars, caused their erection in temples, under trees and on mountain tops, and persuaded the people that these idols were capable of helping or harming them. Still later, there began arising other liars who announced that that very star, sphere or angel[17] had spoken to them and asked that it be worshipped in such and such a fashion. In the course of time different rituals devoted to the worship of many such idols originated in various parts of the world. Soon the name of God himself was forgotten and the populace knew only those images of wood and stone and those temples built of stone in whose worship it had grown up. Its scholars and priests finally believed that there actually was no god but the stars and spheres for whose sake those images had been made. There remained but a few select individuals, such as Enoch,[18] Methuselah, Noah, Shem and Eber, who still recognized the one and only God. These men, although not prophets in the technical sense, because never recipients of direct orders from God, served as teachers and guides for their few associates.[19]

The idolatrous majority, in Maimonides' opinion, was greatly steeped in magic and astrology. Its entire worship was based upon magically conjuring the celestial bodies to comply with its will. Magic rites and astrology were widespread among the

Sabaeans, Chaldeans, Egyptians, Canaanites and the other nations, but found place neither in the works of the Greek philosophers, "who were unquestionably wise men," nor in those of the Persians.[20] Sabean worship frequently included orgiastic cults, sacrifices of children and special prerogatives as well as costumes for their priests, all of which were found objectionable by the restorers of purified monotheism from Abraham to Moses. It is especially the Sabean cult which prevailed in the environment of both the patriarch and the lawgiver and against which both of them took a firm stand.[21] In fact, Maimonides thinks that this opposition of the founders of Judaism to the Sabean ritual explains many obscure points in Jewish law. In his daring attempt to find rational explanations for each and every detail of Mosaic law, Maimonides frequently refers to that intentional contrast. For example, shaving the ends of one's head and beard was prohibited because the idolatrous priests used to do so. Also the biblical taboos of *kilaim* and *shu'atnez* arose from the suppression of both Sabean priestly costumes and orgiastic rites which accompanied the grafting of one plant upon another. The distasteful sensuous cults, such as hinted at in the Bible in connection with the worship of Baal Peor, influenced the lawgiver to insist upon the wearing of trousers by officiating priests and certain requirements of abstinence.[22] The Sabeans also had an unholy reverence for blood. On the one hand, they regarded it as extremely impure and, on the other, they consumed it because they regarded it as the food of demons whose friendship they wanted to conjure by such conviviality.[23] In pursuing this hypothesis, Maimuni occasionally realizes that he can submit no evidence from the sources. Thus when he tries to explain the otherwise irrational prohibition of mixing meat with milk, he advances first the medical reason that it causes overfullness, then immediately reverts to his general theory that it was intended to counteract a Sabean custom and adds significantly: "This I consider the best reason for this prohibition, although in the books on Sabean rites which I have read there is no mention of this custom."[24] He justifies such assumptions on the ground that the pagan priests of the pre-

Abrahamic days composed many writings which were known to the early Jewish legislators but have since largely been lost. "If we knew all the particulars of this [the Sabean] worship and were informed of all the details of those doctrines, we would clearly see the wisdom of every detail in the sacrificial service, in the laws concerning impurity and in other laws the objective of which I am unable to state."[25]

The change came when Abraham, the "pillar of the world," arose among the Sabeans. Hardly weaned from the breast, he began speculating day and night on the motions of the spheres and the necessary existence of a supreme power determining those motions. Maimonides finds evidence for the story of Abraham not only in the biblical records and the Aggadah, but also in the distorted accounts contained in the Sabean writings. Eventually, at the age of forty, the patriarch, inspired by God's word and distinguished by excellent qualities of mind and character, arose against the superstitious creed of his environment and destroyed the idols.[26] He soon began propagandizing his faith with great success.[27] After enduring severe persecutions on the part of the king (Nimrod), he went to Palestine where he erected an altar on Mount Moriah because it was the highest among the mountains in the country. In this respect he simply followed a custom prevalent among the pagans of his day. However, to counteract the prevailing worship of the sun in which the worshippers usually turned east, he placed his altar in the western direction, thus adumbrating the position of the future Holy of Holies in the Temple of Jerusalem.[28] In his very death he exemplified the doctrine of immortality, inasmuch as his soul joined the righteous ones among his forefathers, while his body was buried with those of his descendants.[29] On the whole, he was an outstanding prophet in his own right, although he did not appear, as did Moses after him, with an express message from God. One can easily perceive the Maimonidean emphasis upon the superiority of Moses over Abraham as against the notions current among the Muslims concerning the fuller revelation in the days of "Ibrahim." Nevertheless, as the first believer in the one and only God, Abraham really deserves that "most people, as we see at present, agree in praising him and in being proud of him; so that even those who are not his descendants call themselves by his name."[30]

In the careers of the other patriarchs Maimonides sees primarily examples of moral behavior. For instance, when he enjoins his readers to be reticent in matters of sex and wherever possible not to speak of them at all, he quotes the aggadic reference to the extreme innocence of Jacob.[31] In another connection, in trying to prove that a prophet must be of a serene mind and mood, he quotes the example of Jacob who at the time when he feared the encounter with Esau or when he mourned for Joseph was abandoned by the spirit of prophecy.[32] Jacob is also held up as a shining example of a conscientious laborer who devotes all his energy to the task assigned to him by his employer.[33] At the same time Esau, generally pictured as an evildoer, was nevertheless rewarded for honoring his father. That is why he not only became the founder of the kingdom of Edom, but his descendants were to hold a high position in the world thereafter. In part, as Amalekites, they were to be destroyed and their name blotted out, but other sections were to survive in Edom and later to achieve greatness through Rome and the Catholic Church which will last until the days of the Messiah.[34] For that purpose the Torah enumerates in great detail the chieftains of Seir so as to enable Israelitic readers to distinguish between the Amalekites and the other Edomites who were to be allowed to live as Israel's neighbors. It also intends to illustrate by a specific example the precarious position of a people which chooses to be governed by kings of alien stock.[35]

In the days of Jacob and his sons the claim of the Jews to Palestine was already well established. Setting an example for a later custom, Jacob and Joseph, at their death in Egypt, commanded that their bones be buried in the sacred soil of Palestine.[36] More, Jacob and his sons, while occupying Canaanite territories, could already demand from the natives, as did their successors in the days of Joshua, not only complete submission and annual tribute, but also the observance of the seven Noahide command-

ments. With the violation of one such commandment, namely
the prohibition of robbery by Shechem, Maimonides motivates the
punitive measures taken by Simon and Levi, since according to
the law, as codified by himself, the conquered natives who violate
one of the commandments are subject to extinction by the force
of arms.[37]

In the meantime the body of commandments imposed upon
the Jews was steadily growing. To the seven Noahide commandments was added in the days of Abraham that of circumcision.
Abraham was particularly fit to be the initiator of that custom,
because he was a man of great moral restraint, and the major
aim of circumcision consisted in counteracting the sexual appe-
tite. From that time on this commandment became obligatory
for all true descendants of Abraham, which excluded Ishmael
and Esau, but included the sons of Keturah. As the descendants
of Keturah, Maimonides argues, had since been absorbed by
the other Arab tribes, the Arabs are likewise bound to observe
this rite on the eighth day after birth—evidently a recognition
of contemporary practice with a polemical point in regard to the
age.[38] Abraham has also added the morning prayer as an obligatory performance. Isaac followed his example by imposing the
segregation of the tithe and an afternoon prayer. Jacob finally
added the prohibition of the nervus ischiaticus (*gid ha-nasheh*)
and instituted an evening prayer.[39] On his deathbed he specifically
enjoined his sons to adhere strictly to the unity of God.[40] He also
appointed one of them, Levi, head of an academy to teach the
way of God and the observance of the Abrahamitic law.[41]

In the following generations, the Israelites, then in Egyptian
bondage, were nonetheless frequently derelict in the observance
of the laws. The majority abandoned even the practice of circumcision and wholly relapsed into idolatry by adopting the
Egyptian mode of life. Only the tribe of Levi maintained the
original purity of the patriarchal creed and Amram became the
recipient of additional divine commandments.[42] Through the
Levitical tribe the patriarchal age was thus linked with the great
work of Moses.

The Law of Moses

In Moses the history of Israel and of mankind reaches its climactic achievement. Moses was not only a great leader—Maimonides calls him "king"[43]—and lawgiver from whom the entire system of written and oral law had sprung, but most of all a great prophet. In the well-known Maimonidean theory of prophecy there are eleven degrees of prophetic gifts, the lowest of which were occasionally shared by non-Jews, but the highest being reserved for the ancient Israelitic prophets. Above all these, however, stood Moses who had come nearer the divine presence than any mortal before or after. In four fundamental aspects the prophetic gifts of Moses so radically differed from those of other prophets that we apply the term prophet to him only as a homonym. Moses was also the only man who performed miracles and received the revelation "publicly in the presence of friend and enemy, his followers and his opponents."[44] This made the Mosaic miracles distinguished from those of all other prophets, including even Joshua and Elijah, who performed them in the presence of a large part of the people.[45] Neither will there ever be a prophet of the same rank; even the Messiah will be only second in greatness after him. In this sense he was the true "seal of prophecy."[46] Little wonder that the Jewish people swears in the name of Moses to the present day.[47]

Personally Moses was distinguished by many traits of character. Most of all he was extremely humble. Like his talmudic predecessors, Maimonides takes pains to point to Moses's humility—the only virtue whose very exaggeration is meritorious—as a shining example for all judges and leaders of Israel.[48] Moses was also ready to take the part of an oppressed against his oppressor regardless of personal danger. He and his brother Aaron were early forewarned by God that they were chosen to leadership not for their personal aggrandizement but to be cursed and stoned by their own people. When Moses occasionally lost his patience he was severely rebuked by God. In his interesting polemic on the radical condemnation of mass conversion under compulsion in his *Epistle on Conversion,* he cites the example of Moses who was severely reprimanded by God for doubting that the people of Israel would believe in his mission. This reprimand is the more remarkable the lower the Israelites had sunk in Egyptian bond-age. In retaliation he was himself to be found guilty of disbelief in God's power to produce water out of a stone. Apart from being thereafter forced to abandon his leadership before the con-quest of Palestine, he was temporarily stricken with leprosy at the time of uttering his doubts.[49]

As a leader he proceeded to reform his coreligionists while still in Egypt. In the first place, the masses of the non-Levitical Israelites had to undergo circumcision which Moses, assisted by Aaron and Joshua, personally performed. To complete the require-ments established by law for the adoption of Judaism by prose-lytes, the Israelites after entering the desert had also to go through the ritual of baptism and to offer sacrifices.[50] Through the Exodus from Egypt the subsequent work of Moses and the entire legisla-tion became possible. That is why any infringement upon law and morality (for instance, the use of unjust scales or usury) is an implied denial of the historicity of the Exodus. To commemorate it, the Sabbath—otherwise a weekly reminder of the creation *ex nihilo*—was given to the Jewish people.[51] Upon leaving Egypt the Israelites were repeatedly warned never to settle there again. Mai-monides, although writing on Egyptian soil, has no scruples in declaring it a strict legal prohibition of eternal validity.[52]

In the desert Moses undertook to organize the unwieldy mass. In the first place, he separated the general group of Israelites from that of the Levites, placing the sanctuary in the vanguard of the marchers.[53] In constructing the Tabernacle he laid the foundations and established a prototype for the subsequent temples in Jerusalem. Indeed, his ultimate goal was the Temple in Zion whose location, previously selected by Abraham, was known to him and toward which he enjoined the Israelites to turn in their prayers.[54] Fearing to impose upon the Jews a ritual whose exalted purity they could not possibly grasp, he included animal sacrifices in the worship at the tabernacle. Only to counteract the Egyptian reverence for the ram and the Sabean "preference" for sacrificing beasts of prey, he instituted the sacrifice of household cattle and, for the sake of the poor, of certain domesticated birds. On account of the bad odors connected with the slaughtering of numerous animals, he added the various forms of incense and the oil of ointment.[55] He was also the only one to prepare the sacred oil which was afterwards deposited in the containers held throughout the period of the first Temple. No oil other than that prepared by Moses himself was ever used for anointing kings and high priests. Once the original Mosaic oil was gone, the Second Commonwealth had to get along without ointment even for the high priests who had to substitute special vestments as an outward form of consecration. The first vessels in the tabernacle were prepared for sacred use through that consecrated oil, but this practice was not repeated thereafter in the Temple.[56] Moses erected an altar whose dimensions remained exemplary for the subsequent altars erected by Solomon and the returning Babylonian exiles, and which was to serve as a model also for the fourth altar to be erected in the days of the Messiah. However, the material was different: "hollow" instead of "beaten work." Among the decorative arts employed by Moses the use of "cherubim" is especially worthy of notice because thereby "Moses clearly proclaimed the theory of the existence of a number of angels" which leads us to believe in prophecy and in the law and opposes idolatry. Maimonides professes inability, however, to produce any reason for the use of a table and showbread.[57]

Moses gave his people a political organization headed by a council of seventy elders. He, as the head of the council, was not included in that number. From that time on such a "sanhedrin" was a permanent feature of Jewish public law and every chairman, called *nasi,* was a deputy of the lawgiver himself.[58] Moses also laid down for all future generations the fundamentals of warfare which, under God's direction, he had tried to humanize. For example, when he laid siege on Midian he was told to leave a path open for refugees that they might escape from the city.[59]

While he was ordered ruthlessly to exterminate the seven Palestinian nations and to swear vengeance on Amalek, he could deal more mildly with the Ammonites and Moabites. Although the Israelites were not to offer them peace—the legal preliminary of a declaration of war against other peoples—a spontaneous offer on their part was to be readily accepted.[60] Moses was so anxious to see all the laws applicable for the subsequent settlement in Palestine realized as soon as possible, that he hastened to choose personally the three cities of refuge which were to be located in Transjordan, although he was perfectly aware that they would begin to function only after the allocation of additional three cities in western Palestine.[61]

Moses' greatest work naturally consisted in his giving the law to Israel. In the first place, there were the six hundred and thirteen commandments of the written law. Of these six hundred and eleven were transmitted to Israel through Moses, while the first two of the ten commandments were addressed directly to the people. Even in the Decalogue, however, although it was proclaimed in the presence of the entire people, Moses was apostrophized as the main recipient. That is why the singular form is used. As a matter of fact, Moses alone heard the created voice distinctly, whereas to the rest of the people it was an inarticulate murmur.[62] These six hundred and thirteen commandments were then amplified by an extensive divine interpretation given to Moses. Moses in turn ordained Joshua and his associates and instructed them in all these oral commandments. From that time on an unbroken chain of tradition brought down this oral law to the days of the Mishnah and Talmud.[63]

Some of these oral instructions are exemplified by occurrences in Moses' own lifetime. For example, family life, that "basic unit of society," was not thoroughly organized before Moses. In that primitive age "one met a woman in the market; if both agreed to marry, he took her into his house and informally made her his wife," or else "if they both agreed, he paid her a certain amount, cohabited with her on the road and went away." With the giving of the Torah marriage was attached to a ceremony of acquisition in the presence of witnesses, while free intercourse without marriage was outlawed and punishable by flagellation.[64] The Israelites, present during the Sinaitic revelation, realized the far-reaching effects of this transformation and, aware of the peculiar human weaknesses in all matters of sex, greeted it with plaints and wails.[65] In fact, intercourse with a Gentile woman (with the exception of a single sexual act with a prisoner of war for which not even a priest was to be punished) was altogether prohibited. Although not encouraged, popular lynching rather than regular court procedure was to dispose of such offenders. That this is true Mosaic law, Maimonides argues, is proved by the incident of Zimri whose assassination by Phinehas was countenanced by the great leader himself.[66] Maimonides admits, however, that such confirmatory evidence of Mosaic traditions is rarely available. In discussing, for example, the law permitting formal release from oaths and vows he admits that "this matter has no foundation at all in the written law. But Moses our teacher learned it from tradition."[67] Realizing the arbitrariness of such a statement and fearing that it might vitiate the much controverted claim to authenticity of the oral law, Maimonides tries to lay down a rule whereby true Mosaic traditions might be distinguished. He bars from that category all matters subjected to controversy in the talmudic literature, as well as those derived through logical reasoning or introduced later by special enactments and the force of custom. True traditions are only those which are so designated expressly in the authoritative documents of Judaism.[68] On the other hand, not all laws given to Moses, even if recorded in Scripture, are to be regarded as permanent legislation. Some of them were intended to meet only temporary emergencies. Maimonides counts more than three hundred laws in addition to the six hundred and thirteen commandments that are found in the Pentateuch but have no permanent validity.[69]

All the laws, moreover, were given by Moses exclusively to the Jews, as well as to those who thereafter would wish to become Jews. Non-Jews need observe only the seven Noahide commandments which would make them "the pious ones of the Gentile nations" and as such eligible for the world to come. Neither can Gentiles attain the higher degrees of prophecy. Even Balaam, Moses' contemporary, who had succeeded in foretelling both the advent of the house of David and the final redemption by the Messiah, reached only to the second of the eleven degrees of prophecy.[70] Although generally deprecating Balaam as an evil-doer, Maimuni nevertheless uses his date in support of a "family tradition" that the revival of prophecy ushering in the messianic era was due in the year 1216.[71]

All his life Moses enjoyed the cooperation of Aaron and his sons Eleazar and Ittamar. Like Joshua and the seventy elders, Eleazar and Phinehas were specially ordained to help him instruct the people in the oral interpretations of Scripture. The number of priests was at first very small so that during the desert migrations non-priestly Levites also had to be drafted to carry the tabernacle. For the subsequent generations, however, the law demanded that only full-fledged priests should bear the sanctuary upon their shoulders. To adumbrate the future divisions Moses organized the priestly class into eight groups, selecting four each from the descendants of Eleazar and Ittamar. This number was later increased by King David in cooperation with Samuel to twenty-four posts (ma'amadot) which were to be permanently in charge of the services in the sanctuary.[72] Since the leadership of Moses and Aaron was the only legitimate one in Israel, the revolt of Korah and his associates is called by Scripture a rebellion against God.[73] Among Aaron's outstanding characteristics was his pursuit of peace. Maimonides describes a psychological subterfuge frequently used by the first high priest to reform sinners. As soon as Aaron recognized that a man was naturally evil-minded, he began treating him like a decent and honorable citizen, thus inducing him to justify this attitude.[74]

Only toward the end of his life did Moses begin writing down the Torah for posterity. He used the square Hebrew characters, because of their sacred nature, leaving the "Transjordan" (old Hebrew) alphabet for profane usage, such as inscribing coins. He prepared thirteen different copies on scrolls and gave a copy each to every tribe including the Levites. Only through their inclusion in the Law of Moses did even the pre-Mosaic commandments (e.g., circumcision) become obligatory for later generations.[75] Moses died at noon of the seventh day of Adar.[76]

From Joshua to the Exile

The major task of Moses' disciple, Joshua, was to conquer Palestine, to destroy the seven peoples and to distribute the land among the Israelites. Like his master he, too, tried to proceed as humanely as was possible under the divine injunctions to eliminate the Palestinian natives. Before entering the country, says Maimonides, Joshua despatched three messages to the natives. In the first he told them that anyone wishing to escape may do so by leaving Palestine instantly. In the second he offered peace after complete surrender. In the third he declared war upon those who would resist. How then is it to be explained, one may ask, that the Gibeonites took recourse to a subterfuge? Maimonides ascribes it to their unfamiliarity with Jewish legal procedure. They thought that after rejecting the terms of Joshua's first message they had no alternative but war. Their ruse, although in itself unnecessary, aroused the ire of the Jewish commanders who refrained from exterminating them only because of the fear of desecrating the name of God.[77] Since, according to Mosaic law, converts from among the indigenous seven peoples were to be admitted to the community of the Lord, Joshua decreed the exclusion of the Gibeonites only for the duration of the Temple. David, however, in punishment of their pitiless thirst for revenge on the family of Saul, excluded them forever, and this injunction was later upheld by Ezra.[78] Neither did Joshua succeed in eradicating completely the other natives. This being a divine injunction valid as long as there remained a single member of the seven tribes, the completion of this task, too, was left to David. The few who had survived David's reign mingled with the rest of the population and totally lost their identity.[79]

In distributing the land Joshua assigned a portion to every male that participated in the Exodus. Since both Zelophehad and his father Hepher were among those who left Egypt, Zelo-phehad was entitled to his own portion and, as first-born son, to two-thirds of his father's portion. All that was the patrimony of his daughters.[80] More significantly, from the outset Joshua made certain reservations which curtailed the unrestricted private ownership of Palestinian land. According to tradition, he and his court imposed ten conditions upon the recipients of the land grants and their future heirs. He insisted, for example, that everyone be allowed to pasture sheep and goats in forests with large trees, but for the pasturage of oxen and cows there, or of sheep and goats in a young forest, the permission of the owner was to be required. The water supply of a newly arisen spring was to belong to the city regardless of the position of its main artery, and the neighbors were forbidden to interfere with the city's use thereof. Everybody was to be allowed to fish in the lake of Tiberias by hook, while only the adjacent tribe [of Naphtali] was entitled to spread out large nets obstructing navigation. Trav-ellers finding the road impassable on account of mud were to be permitted to walk alongside the roads even though they had to trespass on private grounds. These and similar reservations were enacted from the outset in order to safeguard the rights of society and its members against unrestricted private ownership.[81] Joshua also surrounded certain cities with walls, and down to the fall of Jerusalem only those cities enjoyed the specific privileges granted by the Bible to walled cities; they enjoyed them even if they no longer had any walls. But cities subsequently built or enlarged so as to require walls were not legally recognized. The same procedure was repeated immediately after the return from the Exile and would be repeated once more in the Messianic era.[82]

The conquest of Palestine by Joshua and again its occupancy by the returning exiles lent a certain sanctity to the territories occupied by them. From the legal point of view every conquest similar to that of Joshua, i.e., accomplished by a prophet or king with the concurrence of a sanhedrin, sanctified the conquered territory, provided all of Palestine had already been under Jewish domination. David's memorable conquests in Syria did not establish the same degree of sanctity, because he had acted improperly in not waiting with this expansion beyond Palestine's natural boundaries until after his occupation of Jerusalem. Forever after, Syria was to remain in Jewish law the "conquest of an individual" as against Palestine which belonged to the people as a whole. Syria thus occupied an intermediate position between the full sanctity of Palestine and the non-sanctity of foreign lands. Neither was, on the other hand, the sanctity of Palestinian soil of equal permanence in all respects. Insofar as it was concerned with the Temple and its worship, it has had eternal validity, because God's presence has been continuous. In other aspects, such as the obligatory payment of tithes, priestly dues and the observance of the year of fallowness, all of which were based upon the Jewish character of Palestinian agriculture, the underlying sanctity depended upon Jewish domination. After the first fall of Jerusalem it ceased, and was renewed by the returning exiles only for such territories as were occupied by them. After the second fall of Jerusalem, however, it continued unabated, because the second occupation, not having been accomplished by the force of arms, could not be stamped out by sheer loss of political power. At the same time the sanctity of the Palestinian regions which were not resettled by Ezra remained in abeyance throughout the Second Commonwealth, and is not to be restored until their reoccupancy by the Messianic hosts.[83]

In the days of Joshua mosaic law remained unchallenged. Under the stress of war, to be sure, Joshua himself had to take recourse to certain extralegal actions. For example, in his prosecution of Achan he disregarded the legal requirements of evidence and accepted the confession of the defendant as sufficient ground for condemnation. But this was an extraordinary measure, not intended to change the law but to meet a temporary emergency. He may also have acted in conformity with his special royal prerogatives. The same holds true of David's execution of the Amalekite slave.[84] In the early days of mourning after Moses, moreover, oblivion began to engulf many of his oral interpretations. Fortunately the first judge to follow Joshua, Othniel the son of Kenaz, was a very ingenious dialectician and succeeded in restoring them to their pristine glory.[85]

Maimonides has little to say about the Judges. He realizes that theirs was a very long period. According to the chronology accepted by him, the Tabernacle brought from the desert was first placed in Gilgal during the fourteen years of conquest and land distribution. Afterwards it was erected in Shilo where it remained for three hundred and sixty-nine years until the death of Eli. Then it was transferred to Nob and finally to Gideon, in which localities it remained for fifty-seven years until the erection of the Temple in Jerusalem.[86] In his occasional remarks concerning the events during these four centuries Maimonides mentions Mahlon and Chilion as instances of divine wrath affecting those who leave the Holy Land. Even though they were among the "great men of their generation" and had emigrated under the stress of a great famine, they deserved to perish on this score. Ruth, on the other hand, is an illustration of divine rewards coming even to unbelievers. Through her and her descendants, the royal house of David, her father Eglon, king of Moab, was rewarded for an act of reverence for the Israelitic God.[87] Samson's numerous love affairs with Gentile women appeared particularly objectionable. Maimonides on more than one occasion takes pains to explain that neither he nor Solomon, a king of Israel, could have been guilty of the grievous sin of intermarriage. What they actually did was only to dismiss lightly certain legal requirements for proselytism. According to law, no one is to be allowed to adopt Judaism for a worldly purpose such as marrying a Jew, or because of fear. Under Samson and, more, under David and Solomon, Israel's power inspired fear and the prosperity of the country opened vast opportunities. Consequently, many joined the Jewish creed not out of conviction, but for the sake of safety or other worldly advantages. Samson and Solomon accepted some of these converts as thoroughgoing proselytes and married them. As was to be expected these insincere newcomers frequently relapsed

into their idolatrous practices, so that the biblical historian felt
justified in ascribing to Solomon himself the erection of temples
for foreign gods.[88] Samuel finally is held out as an example of a
pious, learned, truly prophetic leader. Unlike Samson, who was
separated from impurity not through his own vow, but by an
angel, Samuel was a full-fledged *nazir,* as was Absalom after
him. His incorruptibility ought to serve as a model for all subsequent judges. Even his sons, who were less scrupulous, were
blamed only because they had tried unlawfully to increase the
revenue of their scribes and court sergeants rather than to derive
profit for themselves.[89]

The period of the first kings looms large in Maimonides' mind.
He believes that upon their entry into Palestine the Israelites
assumed three basic obligations in the following succession: to
elect a king, to exterminate Amalek, and to build a temple. He
also tries to interpret away the anti-monarchical passages in the
narrative of I Samuel, by stating that the great "Seer" did not
object to the wish of the people to have a king, but to the way
in which it was expressed and also because of his legitimate
suspicion that their major objective was not to fulfill the commandment but to get rid of his leadership.[90]

David appears to Maimuni as the ideal Jewish king. He was
not only a powerful king and a poet by divine grace, but also
an inspired prophet and the greatest teacher among the seventy
elders of his generation. He had been preordained by Moses
as the star that shall step forth out of Jacob.[91] As the author of
the Psalms he expressed many fundamental teachings of Judaism.
He stood out, for instance, through his desire to achieve the
world to come. He also meditated on the meaning of the particular historical experience of Israel and of its survival under
so many foreign rulers.[92] His wars were mostly of the kind
classified as "holy wars," and the soldiers participating therein
may all be assumed to have been righteous persons.[93] To increase
the study of the law he personally ordained numerous students;
once, indeed, as many as thirty thousand in a single day. He
frequently defended the law against the attacks and importunities

of skeptics and Gentiles, and the more he was annoyed by them, the stauncher grew his attachment to the Torah.[94] To prepare the ground for the Temple in Jerusalem he not only reorganized the priesthood, but also the entire levitical body and divided it likewise into twenty-four posts.[95]

For all these reasons David became the founder of a dynasty which was to endure forever and from which the redeemer would ultimately rise. David's descendants alone among the laymen were entitled to occupy seats in the court (*'azarah*) of the Temple. In contrast, the kings of Israel were not to last beyond a few generations, and their disregard of Jewish law was to make them ineligible for serving as judges or appearing as witnesses before a Jewish court.[96] No anointment of a Davidide to royal office was required, his eligibility being determined exclusively on grounds of heredity. Only in controversial cases, such as at the accession of Solomon, Joash, Jehoahaz, the oil conferred an outward sign distinguishing the legitimate from the illegitimate ruler. On the other hand, Elisha, while anointing Jehu in Northern Israel, did not use the sacred oil originally prepared by Moses, but oil of a balsam tree. The consecration of a Davidic king took place in front of a spring and followed a prescribed ritual of spreading oil, in the shape of a wreath, upon his forehead, whereas the high priest was anointed upon his brow with oil forming a Greek X.[97]

Before his death, David enjoined Solomon to make every effort to obtain an intellectual perception of God and to worship him in accordance with this perception.[98] Solomon took the advice and became not only the wisest of kings and the author of three celebrated biblical books, but also a distinguished prophet and lawgiver.[99] He received his call to prophecy in Gideon. As a lawgiver he enacted various laws with the assistance of his sanhedrin. Among these of particular significance for the future were: the introduction of the *Erub,* the declaration that hands touching impure objects acquire impurity and consequently require ablution, and the extension of the right of pedestrians to tread upon private grounds from the end of the harvest to the second half of Marheshvan.[100] In his great wisdom the king tried to penetrate behind the hidden meanings of the biblical commandments, and actually succeeded in finding the rational basis of them all except of that of the red heifer.[101] The location once selected by Abraham had been kept in strict secrecy throughout the centuries for fear that, if divulged to the public, it would strengthen the resistance of the natives to the Israelite conquest, enable the Gentile people to do harm to the place and, what is most important, give rise to disputes over its possession among the Israelitic tribes. In erecting the building he followed closely the example set by Moses and, on his part, set another example for his successors. The Second Commonwealth merely followed the Solomonic model with a few amplifications in the prophecy of Ezekiel. As soon as the Temple was erected, all other places of sacrificial worship were outlawed.[102] In building the Temple Solomon knew in advance that it was going to be destroyed in the future. To save the ark, he constructed a special hiding place deep under ground where it could be preserved in such an emergency. Indeed, King Josiah, realizing the approaching downfall, ordered the ark to be removed to that secret chamber. Along with it he also put away Aaron's rod, the bottle of the manna and the oil of ointment.[103] The size of the Temple and its precincts was also definitely laid down, and any extension beyond its original confines was contingent upon a joint decision of a king, prophet and sanhedrin and the concurrence of the divine oracles.[104]

Solomon's administration appeared to Maimonides in many ways as the ideal type of monarchy. Much of what is recorded about its acts of government furnishes substantial elements for his codification of the laws governing kings in all ages. He glosses over the shortcomings of that reign, especially with respect to the burden of taxation and enforced labor which eventually led to the disruption of the kingdom.

Solomon's successors on the thrones of Jerusalem and Samaria offer less opportunity for comments. The kings of Israel are frequently pointed out as high-handed sinners with few redeeming features. Maimuni does not dispute the legitimacy of their reign. Since Jeroboam I had been duly appointed by the prophet Ahijah, he and his successors would have ruled over Israel for a very long time, although their dynasty could not rival that of David in either significance or permanence.[105]

To emphasize the cumulative effect of major and minor sins, Maimonides cites the example of Jeroboam. Although the earthly court inflicts punishment only for the major crimes (*ḳim lei bideraba minei*), before God even the slightest transgressions add their weight to the balance. That is why Jeroboam was punished not only for the basic offense of voluntarily worshipping calves and inciting Israel to accept his idolatrous practice, but also for his neglect in the observances of the Feast of Tabernacles.[106] King Ahab was another typical sinner who misled the entire people, with the exception of only 7,000 Israelites, to the worship of Baal. Nevertheless, his greatest transgression and one which loomed largest in the denunciations of the prophet consisted in his lawless appropriation of Naboth's vineyard. He had, however, a few redeeming features and his long fasting for an additional two and a half hours was properly rewarded.[107]

Among the kings of Judah, Jehoshaphat, Hezekiah and Josiah stand out by virtue of their piety, while Manasseh is branded as a sinner of prime magnitude. Jehoshaphat's reverence for Jewish learning was so great that whenever he received a scholar he disregarded the court etiquette, descended from his throne and embraced the learned man.[108] Hezekiah did all in his power to purify the Jewish religion. Sensing that a popular medical work of the day was based upon older magic rites and the invocation of astral powers, he decided to suppress its public circulation. This move met with the approval of the scholars of that generation. They disapproved, however, of Hezekiah's declaration of a leap year on Adar 30, because the month of Adar preceding Nisan ought to have only twenty-nine days, and with the thirtieth, consequently, Nisan had already begun.[109] Manasseh appeared to Maimonides as a forerunner of the radical Bible critics of his own time who had especially assailed the inclusion of the allegedly inconsequential narratives in Scripture. Manesseh and his successors failed to comprehend that every story in the Bible has deep moral significance.[110]

Throughout the period of the kings there appeared the great prophets of Israel. The records of their lives and utterances serve as primary material for the Maimonidean theory of prophecy. Speaking, for example, of the characterological prerequisites for prophecy he emphasizes the shortcomings of even the greatest among prophets. Elijah sinned because of his short temper and was punished therefore. Elisha, although undoubtedly innocent of the offense of accepting "gifts" from the Shunammite woman frequently ascribed to him by judges and teachers who wished to exonerate their own acceptance of remuneration for public service, was likewise guilty of excessive irascibility. Their punishment—like that of Jacob when he had temporarily failed on account of his fear of Esau or his mourning for Joseph, that of Samuel when he was afraid of Saul, or of Solomon when he committed acts of cruelty—consisted in the suspension of their prophetic calling. Isaiah, too, was severely punished, because of his wholesale condemnation of the entire people of Israel, even though it really happened to be plunged in idolatry.[111] In addition to being prophets, these great masters were also the main transmitters of Jewish law. The chain of tradition was maintained by them in unbroken continuity to the days of Jeremiah who handed it over to his disciple Baruch—a typically potential but not actual prophet—and through him to the leaders in Exile, especially Ezra. As prophets these men were entitled to alter temporarily the Mosaic law, with the understanding that, with the passing of the particular emergency, the old law would be automatically restored. So we may understand Elijah's offering sacrifices outside Jerusalem or Elisha's order to cut down the trees during the Moabite war.[112]

Besides these great and true prophets there always appeared some pretenders who either uttered wholly false prophecies or, like Hananiah b. Azzur, plagiarized others to whom the true will of God had been revealed. A major characteristic of these false prophets is their sensuality, particularly in matters of sex.[113] On the other hand, there are true prophets among the Gentiles, such as Job and his friends. But the Israelites have been forewarned to give credence only to prophets who arise from their own midst.[114]

The Assyro-Babylonian invasions into Palestine had many lasting effects. Sennacherib's conquest of all adjoining territories caused a general amalgamation of the peoples and tribes adjoining Israel. The Egyptians, Edomites, Ammonites and Moabites, in particular, lost their identity, and the biblical regulations concerning the endogamous exclusion of these races could no longer be applied.[115] In the days of Sennacherib there also arose the Samaritan sect. The Cutheans, settled by the Assyrians in the cities of Samaria, gradually learned the Torah and began interpreting it in a literal sense. Although this literalism naturally led to the denial of oral law, the Samaritans were long regarded as true believers in all other respects. In fact, the rabbis acknowledged that they strictly observed all commandments accepted by them. At one time, however, the Jewish leaders grew suspicious of their worship at Mt. Gerizim and a thorough investigation brought to light that they had worshiped there an idol in the shape of a dove. All the passages in the Mishnah, says Maimonides, which declare the Samaritans to be inferior to Israel but superior to the Gentiles belong to a period before that investigation. Since that time they ought to be treated much worse than sheer idolaters.[116]

The destruction of the Temple and the ensuing Exile brought about mass apostasy. In fact all the exiles in Babylonia, with the exception of a few individuals, began worshiping foreign gods. Even "the craftsmen and the smiths," before Jerusalem's fall distinguished by their piety, now apparently surrendered to the general forces of assimilation. Among the individuals who preserved staunch orthodoxy stand out the three youngsters, Hananiah, Mishael and Azariah.[117] Daniel, otherwise a distinguished martyr, committed the grievous error of giving uncalled-for advice to Nebuchadnezzar to distribute charity.[118] The Chaldean king, on the other hand, through a few acts of piety, such as placing the name of God before that of the Jewish king, deserved a great reward. Although guilty of the burning of the Temple and the massacre of a multitude of Israelites "like the sand of the sea," he was rewarded by God with a long reign of forty years, similar in duration to that of king Solomon.[119]

From Ezra to the Talmud

The return from the Exile is always associated in Maimonides' mind with Ezra. The preceding developments under Zerubbabel appeared to him as essentially belonging to the Exilic age. Ezra was for him the recipient of the whole body of tradition from Baruch the son of Neriah, the rebuilder of the Temple and the initiator of the work of the Great Synagogue and its successors among the sages.

Before departing from Babylonia the great scribe decided to leave behind him a community of indubitably pure descent. Fearing that without a supreme court, such as was to be re-established in Jerusalem, the Babylonian sector could not permanently stave off the danger of mixing with ethnically suspicious elements, he took along with him all the ten categories enumerated in the Mishnah, including the seven lower ones, trusting that in Palestine the great court would prevent them from mingling with the rest of the people. In this fashion there remained in Babylonia only members of the first three groups, i.e., priests, Levites and Israelites of good stock.[120]

Those who returned to Palestine occupied a territory smaller than that held by the first conquerors. The sacred character of the reoccupied territories, however, exceeded in many ways that of the previous occupation. As mentioned above, the sanctity of the Second Commonwealth, because established without force, was to last forever. With respect to the Sabbatical year, for example, its full observance was imposed only upon the country up to Kezib. Between Kezib and the River or Omna, one must not perform any work during that year but the plants which grew up by themselves could be consumed by their rightful owners. Beyond these boundaries even work was permitted. In Transjordan the observance of the year of fallowness was introduced later by the rabbis without scriptural authority. But there as well as in Syria they prohibited only work, but not the consumption of spontaneous growths. On the other hand, they insisted upon the payment of the Levitical and the poor man's tithes during that year from the adjacent regions of Ammon and Moab, which were allowed to cultivate their soil. The sages were mainly prompted by the desire to see the poor man's tithe forthcoming from these less severely taxed regions to support the suffering masses of the Jewish settlement around Jerusalem during the difficult years of fallowness. This obligation was soon extended to all neighboring districts including Egypt, but did not apply to the more distant Babylonia, where the seventh year differed in no respect from all other years. Since Maimonides regarded the Sabbatical year as obligatory also after the loss of national independence, he went into great detail to delineate the boundaries of the reoccupation as against those of the First Commonwealth.[121]

Haggai, Zechariah and Malachi accompanied the returning Exiles. One gave testimony concerning the place for an altar, another added its dimensions, and the third testified that they may offer sacrifices on that altar, although the Temple had not yet been re-erected.[122] Soon after they proceeded to build a sanctuary in accordance with the architectural plans preserved from the Mosaic Tabernacle and the Solomonic Temple with certain modifications suggested by Ezekiel and the second of the above prophets. This temple lasted throughout the Second Commonwealth. Maimonides tries to reconstruct the blueprint of the sanctuary, as described in the Mishnah Middot, without realizing that there was a substantial difference between the magnificent Herodian structure described in that tractate and the much humbler house of worship erected by the poor resettlers from Babylonia. Among the noteworthy innovations he mentions the image of Susa, the Persian capital, which was engraved on the eastern gate under the government's strict orders. This engraving was to impress upon the mind of the Jewish subjects the power of their Persian sovereign and help hold them in perpetual submission.[123] In this Temple the priests achieved pre-eminence even over their Levitical confrères. The Levites, having refused to join in large numbers Ezra's expedition, were penalized by the great "Scribe" through the loss of their exclusive right to the tithe, which was now transferred to the priests.[124]

Ezra, who served as both high priest and leader of the Great Synagogue of one hundred and twenty distinguished members,[125] introduced also other significant reforms. Apart from renewing the age-old prohibition of intermarriage he decreed that for purposes of chastity even at home every Jewish woman should constantly wear a *sinar* (a kind of petticoat). More significantly, Ezra and his court inalterably laid down for all future generations the formulae of the various benedictions and the reading of the Torah in the Synagogue, and instituted that it be followed by a translation through a specifically appointed interpreter, in order that the entire people understand its content.[126]

About the three centuries between Ezra and the Maccabean upheaval Maimonides has very little to say. The later years of the Persian domination seem to have almost completely disappeared from his historical vision. Neither has he much to say about Alexander's conquest except to identify the reign of Alexander with the beginning of the Seleucid era. The spread of Hellenism and the establishment of large hellenistic communities in the dispersion as well as the growth of hellenistic literature are hardly referred to at all.[127] At most he is concerned with the talmudic laws relating to the Greek language and science. He seeks an explanation for the enactment that Scripture may not be written in foreign languages except in Greek. He finds in the Septuagint the main reason for this exceptional position of Greek, which had also found expression in the well-known exclamation of Judah the Patriarch concerning the use of either Hebrew or Greek. Prepared in order to explain the Torah to King Ptolemy, he states that the Greek translation soon became very popular among "them," so that the Greek language occupied for them the position of *ashurit*. On the other hand, the prohibition of studying Greek "science"—which he explains to connote a certain type of Greek mystery and allegory—had merely the accidental origin of a ruse used by a contemporary to mislead the Jews in their sacrificial worship in Jerusalem. Evidently this student of Aristotle could not simply reconcile himself with the idea of complete suppression of Greek science.[128]

The Maccabean revolt is likewise completely shrouded for him in the mist of legends. He has some information concerning the persecution under Antiochus Epiphanes and the restoration of a Jewish Kingdom under the Hasmoneans which, he says, lasted for two hundred years until the destruction of the Second Temple.

> Similarly during the Second Commonwealth [he relates], when the wicked Greek kingdom gained control of Palestine, they instituted severe persecutions against Israel in order to abolish the Torah. The Jews were compelled to profane the Sabbath, and were forbidden to observe the rite of circumcision. Every Jew was forced to write on his garment the words, "we have no portion in the Lord God of Israel," and to engrave upon his ox before he ploughed with it, the words, "we have no portion in Israel." This state of affairs lasted about fifty-two years. Finally, God brought to an end simultaneously their empire and their laws.

In order to prevent secret observance of Jewish law, he reports in another connection, the Greeks forbade the Jews to shut the doors of their houses.[129] At the same time he relates the story of the miraculous inexhaustibility of the oil which, in the opinion of the rabbis, was the real reason for the celebration of Hanukkah.[130] Also the story of Onias; his appointment to high priestly office, although he was the younger son of Simon the Pious, Ezra's immediate successor; his intrigue to instigate the assassination of his brother Shimi; its complete failure; his subsequent flight to Egypt and the ensuing erection of the Onias temple there—are all narrated in accordance with the talmudic legends amplified by several noteworthy details. He knows that that temple lasted for two centuries.[131]

Neither has he much to say about the individual Maccabean and

Herodian rulers. He speaks of a Johanan the high priest in whose day an investigation was made in regard to the observance of the laws of the heave-offering and the various tithes, but classifies him vaguely as holding office some time after Simon the Pious. Since that investigation discovered, he says, that in contrast to the scrupulously observed great *terumah* the segregation of the first, second and the poor man's tithes was taken lightly, a regulation was enacted that only reliable persons were entitled to testify that such segregation had taken place, whereas the fruits of an *'Am ha-Areṣ* had the dubious character of *demai*.[132] King Agrippa was for Maimuni a noble and powerful, but nonetheless illegitimate ruler. If, as Maimuni apparently assumed, he had had no Jewish mother, he was under no circumstances eligible to royal office in Israel. Maimuni dismisses briefly the talmudic story concerning the fraternization of the king with an assembly of Jews as a gesture for the sake of peace.[133] In general, he says, "it is well known that the state of affairs under the Second Temple was unsatisfactory, that the kings did not go the right way and appointed high priests by force, regardless of personal merits."[134]

He knows that at that age there appeared various religious currents, which called for specific emergency measures. For example, when Simon ben Shetah executed in Ascalon eighty women in one day without due process of law, he did not mean to establish thereby a legal precedent, but merely to meet a temporary emergency. Similarly a man was stoned for riding on horseback on the Sabbath, otherwise a minor transgression rather than a capital crime.[135] It was also the period of the rise of Sadduceeism. In accordance with the well-known talmudic narrative, Maimuni relates how Zadok and Boethus, two students of Antigonus, misunderstood their master's apophthegm that one must not serve God because of an expected reward. These disciples understood this to be an implied denial of a world to come. They soon proceeded to organize sects of their own and, in order to justify themselves before public opinion, declared that they believed in scriptural law but not in tradition. Through this subterfuge they got rid of many accepted commandments.[136] They also added an erroneous interpretation of the biblical injunction concerning the observance of the Feast of Weeks "from the morrow after the day of rest" (Lev. 23.15), and differed in many other detailed regulations. In contrast to the traditional observance, for example, to place the incense on fire before the ark in the Holy of Holies on the Day of Atonement, they demanded that it be prepared on the fire before. That is why the rabbis introduced an elaborate annual ceremony to test the orthodoxy of the officiating high priest. Sadducees differed also in the ritual of burning the red heifer.[137] Notwithstanding their numerous divisions, they found successors throughout the ages, such as those known under the name Karaites in Egypt. Maimuni insists that these sectarians be strictly segregated from the Jews and that the majority of rabbis rightly dissented from R. Jose when he taught that a Sadokite woman usually observed the laws of menstrual impurity on a par with a Jewess.[138]

Another sectarian leader was Jesus. He is to be regarded as a Jew because his mother was a Jewess. He contended that he was sent by God to clarify perplexities in the Torah and that he was the Messiah predicted by all preceding prophets. His interpretations were frequently tantamount to the annulment of the law and the instigation to defy biblical prohibitions.[139] On account of their trinitarian doctrine the Christians are legally in the category of heathens with whom one must not have any dealings on Sunday or, in Palestine, even during the preceding three days. Evidently living in a Muslim environment, Maimuni could only indulge in the luxury of prohibiting commercial intercourse with the Christian minority during one to four days of each week. On the other hand, in view of their qualified approval of Jewish Scripture, they may be given instruction in its Jewish interpretation, in the hope that they may realize their error and join the ranks of full-fledged Jews.[140] After Jesus there appeared another reformer, a descendant of Esau. Because of his glaring inconsistencies, however, he turned out to be much less harmful.[141]

The orthodox majority was throughout that period secure under the leadership of its rabbinic teachers. At first there was a Sanhedrin in Jerusalem consisting of seventy-one distinguished members of noble descent. The selection was very rigid, inasmuch as representatives of this highest tribunal traversed all of Palestine, selected the best members of every community and appointed them to serve as local judges. (From among these were very likely selected the members of the little sanhedrins placed in cities of one hundred and twenty adult male Jews or over.) The best were drafted successively for service in the two little sanhedrins in Jerusalem, placed at the entrance of the Temple mountain and that of the Temple court, until finally they appeared as candidates for office in the Great Sanhedrin itself. The wisest among them served as chairman and was called by the sages *nasi* (patriarch), taking the place of Moses.[142] The lineage of each member appears so much above any possibility of doubt that even today, by merely tracing a priest's descent through a series of pure-blooded ancestors to a member of the Sanhedrin, one proves conclusively his indubitable Aaronide extraction.[143] This Sanhedrin was first placed in the chamber *Gazit* of the Temple itself until, under the stress of foreign domination, it had to go through ten migrations. After the fall of Jerusalem it was transferred to Yabneh and, ultimately, to Tiberias.[144] As long as this high court existed, says Maimonides, there was no possibility for controversy, because all matters of dubious interpretation were brought to it for final decision. A court could reverse an action of its predecessors only if it was "larger in wisdom and numbers," even in cases where the cause underlying the original decision had disappeared. To meet the objection that all the high tribunals were of equal size and consisted of seventy-one judges—which was incidentally also true of the geonic court—Maimuni introduces the characteristic distinction that a court supported by a more numerous sector of enlightened public opinions is to be regarded as superior in numbers.[145] Apart from civil matters the Sanhedrins enjoyed also the privilege of criminal jurisdiction. Capital punishment, however, was restricted to the time when the Sanhedrins were stationed in the Temple, i.e., until forty years before its destruction.[146]

At first the "pairs" (*zugot*) stood at the head of the Sanhedrin. Maimonides mentions the five generations of Jose b. Yoezer and Jose b. Johanan; Joshua b. Perahiah and Nittai of Arbela; Judah

b. Tabbai and Simon b. Shetah; Shemaiah and Abtalion; Hillel and Shammai.[147] The number of the adherents of the two schools of Hillel and Shammai varied from time to time. During the meeting in the upper chamber of Hananiah b. Hezekiah, a profound student of Ezekiel, there were assembled all the ordained students of Jewish law in that generation. It happened that the Shammaites were then in the majority and so they passed the so-called eighteen (controversial) enactments.[148] On the whole, however, Hillel's authority was superior. He was both through learning and Davidic descent so widely revered by his contemporaries that out of deference for him they decided not to ordain any candidate without his permission or that of his successors in the patriarchal office. Under his authority, the *prosbol* was instituted, which had permanent validity because it abrogated merely a rabbinic regulation. With the revival of the full Sabbatical law according to the Torah in the Messianic age, the *prosbol* would no longer be practiced.[149] In the days of R. Gamaliel the Elder it became customary to study the Torah standing, but after his death the bodies grew weaker and they reverted to sitting during the study of the law.[150] After the fall of Jerusalem the rabbis gathered under R. Johanan b. Zakkai in the "vineyard" of Yabneh, so styled because every gathering of the sages resembles a "vineyard." There many new ordinances were issued which would automatically expire in the Messianic era.[151] Among his disciples stood out R. Eliezer, regardless of the semblance of heresy attributed to him because of his reply to an atheist judge. Maimuni has no hesitancy in ascribing to him the "famous Chapters of R. Eliezer the Great," even though he found there strange anthropomorphic concepts.[152] His disciple in turn was R. Akiba, distinguished both as scholar and martyr. He believed in Bar Kokhba as the King-Messiah and suffered death with the innumerable thousands killed after the fall of Bethar. In those emergency years he even exercised the right of proclaiming a leap year outside of Palestine, a right otherwise reserved exclusively to the high court in Jerusalem and its president.[153] This Palestinian prerogative could be maintained until the days of Abbaye and Raba, when it had to be discarded under the pressure of the Romans.[154] Maimuni also cites a story to prove the validity of a certain law even after the fall of Jerusalem and in the dispersion by arguing that R. Tarfon lived after the destruction of the Temple, and that that particular event had taken place in a country other than Palestine. Like R. Eliezer, R. Meir may serve as a living illustration of one who paid lip service to non-Jewish beliefs under constraint without in the slightest betraying his staunch orthodoxy.[155]

Throughout that period the process of progressive interpretation of the law was steadily going on. Maimuni enumerates ninety-one rabbis in whose name traditions are handed down in the Mishnah, in addition to twenty-seven others, recorded there in conjunction with some historical illustration.[156] Finally Judah the Patriarch, whose authority was such as to enable him, for example, to exempt Scythopolis (Bet Shan) from the obligation of paying tithes, compiled the Mishnah,[157] which was followed by similar compilations of *Baraitot*. All these collections, however, are merely part of a vaster body of tannaitic traditions. For example, a controversy between R. Judah and R. Simon cannot be traced back to any of the tannaitic sources, and must have originally been part of such an unwritten Baraita. Both Hai Gaon and Rabbenu Nissim failed to locate the source of that controversy.[158] Later on R. Johanan compiled the Palestinian, R. Ashi and Rabina the Babylonian Talmud about three and four hundred years, respectively, after the fall of Jerusalem. Around that time other sages compiled various Midrashim.[159]

The center of gravity gradually moved to Babylonia. To be sure, down to the days of Rabbah and Abbaye Palestinian law reigned supreme. But this was due to the persecutions suffered at that time by Babylonian Jewry.[160] Otherwise the Babylonian exilarchs were the legitimate substitutes for the ancient Judean kings to exercise dominion over all Israel. That is why an authorization obtained by a judge from the exilarch frees him from personal liability for misjudgment in any Jewish community, whereas the same authorization by the Palestinian patriarch has this effect only with respect to the Holy Land. On the other hand, Maimuni realizes that the exilarchs of the talmudic period frequently failed to live up to the requirements of righteous government. Some of them were, in fact, such ruthless despots that, in contrast to the ordinary citizens, their possession of a certain piece of property over a period of years was no proof of its legal acquisition.[161]

In that period appeared also many translations of Scripture. Maimonides speaks of Syriac, Greek, Persian and Latin (Arabic) versions in existence a long time before Muhammed. He seems personally to have been familiar only with the Aramaic versions, especially with that of Onkelos whom, following tradition, he revered as the disciple of R. Eliezer and R. Joshua.[162]

Under Islam

Maimonides has little to say about the five centuries which had elapsed from the rise of Muhammed to his own birth. Following an apparently prevalent usage he calls the founder of Islam a "madman," with both religious and political aspirations, who failed to formulate any new religious idea, but merely restated well-known concepts. Nevertheless, he attracted a large following and inflicted many wrongs upon the Jews, being himself responsible for the massacre of 24,000.[163] Following his example the Muslims of the subsequent generations oppressed the Jews and debased them even more harshly than any other nation. This statement is an obvious reflection of Maimuni's own earlier experiences in Spain and Morocco. He admits, however, that the persecution to which he had fallen victim had no parallel in history inasmuch as the enforced profession of faith consisted exclusively in lip service. The Almohades were perfectly aware of the insincerity of these professions, and did not mind it. But we hear from Maimonides himself what dangers were attached to such a verbal declaration, if one returned publicly to Judaism in a more tolerant country. He also mentions that the Christians resisted more staunchly than the Jews, and more frequently chose the alternative of martyrdom. In this rebuke to his coreligionists, he fails to take cognizance of the mass conversions of the Christian peoples of western Asia and northern Africa which in the preceding centuries had been the main cause of Islam's rapid expansion. At that time, at least, the Jews must have been more persevering.[164]

The bitter experiences of his youth failed to nurture in Maimonides rabid anti-Muslim feelings. Although frequently reiterating that the Arabs, as descendants of Ishmael are not really "the seed of Abraham" referred to in Scripture, because only in Isaac and Jacob "shall seed be called to thee" (Gen. 21.12), he consistently declines to classify Islam as a pagan religion. Even the heathen memories and practices connected with the Kaaba stone in Mecca did not in his opinion detract from the essentially monotheistic doctrine. This contention is put into bolder relief when one considers Maimuni's acceptance of the notions prevalent among the Muslims concerning Christian trinitarianism as equivalent with polytheism.[165]

This moderate attitude finds expression also with respect to the Karaites. Viewing their schism as but a direct continuation of Sadduceeism he, nevertheless, enjoins his coreligionists to treat them in a friendly fashion and to persuade them to return to Judaism. Such toleration is to be extended only to those who refrain from abusing the rabbinic sages, however.[166] As long as they profess their heresy, they must not be invited to join the quorum of three or ten Jews for benedictions and prayers, nor are their divorces legally valid. Nonetheless a woman married in accordance with the Karaite ritual requires a regular Jewish writ of divorce.[167]

Among his geonic predecessors Maimonides mentions only Saadia and Hai by name. In one connection he even speaks of the phylacteries used by the latter gaon, about which he had heard from a reliable source. His references to Saadia are mostly of a philosophical nature. Only with respect to Saadia's computation of the date of the Messiah he cites extenuating personal circumstances. More frequently he refers to Alfasi and Isaac ibn Migash. But in general he names an author primarily when he wishes to combat that author's opinion, whereas in the case of agreement he confines himself to such generic terms as "the Geonim have taught," "the Geonim have enacted," "the majority of the Geonim think so," etc. Occasionally he distinguishes between the "former" and the "latter" Geonim. But even under the first Geonim, the decline in learning was very marked, because "Israel's dispersion was greatly increased and they reached to the distant corners and islands; wars ravaged the world, armed bands obstructed the roads and the study of the Torah diminished; no longer did the Jews enter their academies in thousands and myriads, as they used to do before, but a small remnant of individuals, with God's call in their hearts, gathered in every city and country to expound the Torah."[168]

The title "gaon" had by that time lost its technical meaning as due only to the heads of the two Babylonian academies, and is here used freely with respect to any outstanding scholar. Maimuni frequently speaks of the "western Geonim," referring principally to those of Morocco and Kairowan. In fact, his relations with the contemporary Babylonian gaon, Samuel b. Ali of Baghdad, although outwardly courteous, were frequently strained. At the same time, he voices deep admiration for the learning of the younger communities of Christian France.[169] On the whole, he gives precedence to teachings and customs prevalent in Spain and Morocco as opposed to those of his adopted country, Egypt. However, he has few direct references to Spanish-Jewish letters. In many of these he is decidedly polemical, as when he mentions a monograph on *tefillin* composed by Moses of Cordova "which has misled me and all the western people before me."[170] He also sharply deprecates the numerous poetic-didactic *azharot* written in Spain, such as those by Ibn Gabirol. He only finds an extenuating circumstance in the fact that "their authors were poets and not rabbis."[171] He has still less use for the gnostic writings prevalent in his days such as the *She'ur Komah*. Once asked as to whether this work contained true mysteries of the sages, he replied sharply, "God beware that such a matter should have come out of their hands. It is merely the work of one of the Greek preachers without any doubt. In short, the scrapping of this book and the blotting out of its subject matter is a meritorious deed."[172]

Sometimes he adduces contemporary usage in explanation of historical developments. Speaking, for example, of the talmudic legislation concerning the recitation of *hallel* on Hanukkah he states, "In these days I have observed totally divergent customs in different places with respect to its reading and congregational response." In discussing the laws of charity he declares that he had never heard of a Jewish community which did not possess a *kuppah,* although there are communities which dispense with the talmudic *tamhui.* The prevalent custom today, he continues, is that the officers of the *kuppah* collect the donations every day and distribute them on Friday. Taking cognizance of the numerous conversions of Jews to Islam (and also Christianity) he mentions the daily practice and theory of both the eastern and western geonim to allow the wife of a convert to collect her marriage settlement from his property. Although such practice is evidently against talmudic law, he approves of it as a legitimate penalty for apostasy. The contemporary usage of calling a Kohen to the Torah first, regardless of the superior learning or piety of an "Israelite" present, has, in his opinion, no historical foundation in either the biblical or talmudic legislation. It has merely arisen out of the wish to avoid controversies in the community. "It has been daily practice in Spain," he asserts, "to force a defendant to follow the plaintiff to a higher court of distinguished scholars in another city, although we have no Great Tribunal similar to that of the talmudic age." The Sabbatical year is to be observed today and "the judge who, knowing of its binding force, fails to apply the law does not fear the Lord and robs the poor."[173]

Curious sidelights are frequently found in his references to the non-Jewish world. In the case of damages inflicted by an animal on the property of a Gentile, Maimuni absolves the Jewish owner from any liability on the ground of reciprocity, because Gentile courts refuse to acknowledge such claims of Jewish victims.[174] Among the reasons for the prohibition of the use of pigs, Maimuni enumerates also the native uncleanliness of that animal. "Should pork be permitted for consumption, the market places and the houses would be dirtier than privies, as you may see it today in the Frankish countries." In other words, the superiority of the Islamic civilization over that of medieval Europe also in respect to order and tidiness appears to Maimuni as beyond any doubt.[175] He also believes that there are primitive tribes possessing no religion whatsoever. Among these he enumerates "the extreme Turks that wander about in the north, the Kushites who live in the south and those in our clime who are like these."[176]

At the end of his *Epistle to Yemen,* Maimuni gives a brief sketch of several messianic movements, mostly within the living memory of his generation. This sketch is historically remarkable not only because it supplies historical information, otherwise unavailable, but also because it shows Maimuni's attempt to dissuade his Yemenite correspondents from believing in their messianic pretender by arguments taken from history. Little wonder that to his wholly non-historically-minded Hebrew translators these historical parallels seemed of less consequence than the theological argument and that, finding that these messianic currents reflected little glory upon the Jews, they omitted them altogether.[177]

Historical Chronology

In all historical considerations Maimuni shows a decidedly chronological bent. Not only does he place personalities and events in their proper historical sequence and carefully avoids confusing dates, but he has frequent discussions on the topic of chronology. Of course, this is not detached historical curiosity; in each case, he attempts primarily to clarify some legal or moral issue involved. Nevertheless, he sifts all available sources of information with the view of establishing a proper chronological order.[178]

Such an occasion arose especially in connection with the year of fallowness which even today, Maimuni insists, ought to be fully observed in Palestine and, with respect to the Sabbatical cancellation of debts, also everywhere else. In order to establish the actual seventh year during which the law is to be enforced, he develops a computation of his own. The beginning of the *shemiṭṭah* series is to be dated back to the fifteenth year after Joshua's conquest of Palestine which corresponds to the year 2504 in the era of Creation.[179] Every fiftieth year they celebrated a jubilee which thus followed closely upon every seventh sabbatical year. Each fifty-first year they started both a new jubilee and sabbatical cycle. There were altogether seventeen jubilee cycles from the entrance into Palestine to the Fall of Jerusalem. These 850 years were about evenly divided into 440 years from Joshua to the construction of the Temple, and 410 years during the period of the Temple's duration. Discounting the first fourteen years of conquest and distribution, the fall of the first Temple occurred in the thirty-sixth year of the seventeenth jubilee cycle.[180] During the seventy years of the Babylonian Exile no sabbatical year was observed, whereas the actual observance of the jubilee was permanently discontinued after the fall of Samaria, since its observance was contingent upon the settlement of all the tribes of Israel in Palestine.[181] The second Temple lasted for 420 years, but it was not before the seventh year of its existence that Ezra arrived from the Exile. In that year the series of sabbatical and jubilee cycles was resumed, although the jubilee as such was never observed again. Hence the second fall of Jerusalem (counting the year of the Tishre following that eventful ninth of Ab) was the first year of the fourth sabbatical cycle of the ninth jubilee. Computing it on the basis of the Seleucid era it suffices to add thirty-four years to the Seleucid date and divide it by fifty to find the corresponding jubilee cycle. This computation is based upon the rabbinical chronology that the Seleucid era began in the forty-first year after the return from the Exile.[182] That is why, says Maimonides, the date 1486 Sel. era (1175 C. E.) should have been the sixth in the sabbatical and the twentieth in the jubilee cycle, but the geonim, especially Hai, have a different computation, buttressed by tradition. They contend that during the Second Commonwealth the jubilee year was not counted separately, since it was not observed. The eighth sabbatical cycle consequently began in the fiftieth and not in the fifty-first year. This would also account for their different dating with regard to the actual *shemiṭṭah*. In 1175, for instance, the Jews were to observe the year of fallowness according to the Maimonidean computation, whereas according to both geonic theory and actual practice this was the first year of a subsequent sabbatical cycle. Maimonides, although theoretically adhering to his own chronology, bowed before the authority of the age-old tradition.[183] When asked many years later about the date of the Sabbatical observance, he repudiated the opinion of one of his students who tried to follow his computation, and decided in accordance with the geonim.[184]

Chronologically even more remarkable is his famous enumeration of forty generations of teachers from Moses to R. Ashi, who had carried the burden of tradition from the days of the Sinaitic revelation of the Oral Law to the conclusion of the Babylonian Talmud. While basically an elaboration of the well-known chain of tradition in M. Abot I, it contains so many new links, independently and sometimes arbitrarily derived by Maimuni from scattered rabbinic sources, that it has ever since perplexed numerous interpreters.

The difficulty begins with the very first generations. Moses taught the oral law, says Maimonides, to the elders and especially to Eleazar, Phinehas and Joshua, "all three of whom received it from Moses." Many elders received it from Joshua until Eli received it from the elders and Phinehas. Considering that in Maimuni's view at least three and a half centuries must have passed between Joshua's death and Eli's assumption of the high priestly office, one intervening link seems very disturbing. He evidently bridges over the gap by suggesting several generations of elders, but only one miraculously longeval Phinehas as representing this (third) link.[185] Eli transmitted the law to Samuel who taught it in turn to David. Maimuni does not hesitate to include the king in his list of "prophets," because he always regarded David as endowed with the gift of prophecy in a lower degree. Solomon, although also a prophet, did not continue this series, but the task fell to Ahijah the Shilonite whom Maimuni, parenthetically, calls one of Moses' direct students, who in his childhood had known the great lawgiver while still in Egypt.[186] Elijah, Ahijah's successor, is the eighth in the series. He is followed by Elisha, Jehoiada and (his son) Zechariah. Hosea, Amos, Isaiah, and Micah hold the twelfth to the fifteenth places, followed by Joel, Nahum, Habakkuk, Zephaniah and, finally, Jeremiah. Through the latter's disciple, Baruch, the chain reaches Ezra, the twenty-second in the series.[187]

Ezra's court (the men of the Great Synagogue) included, as we have seen, the post-exilic prophets, Haggai, Zechariah, Malachi and Daniel, and in the brief span of one generation we reach Simon the Just. From now on Maimuni follows the list in Abot by counting: 24) Antigonus; 25) Jose b. Yoezer and Joseph b. Johanan; 26) Joshua b. Perahiah and Nittai of Arbela; 27) Judah b. Tabbai and Simon b. Sheṭaḥ; 28) Shemayah and Abtalion; 29) Hillel and Shammai.[188] Here Maimuni inserts 30) Simon, Hillel's son and Johanan b. Zakkai and reverts in part to the list in Abot by enumerating 31) Gamaliel the Elder; 32) his son Simon; 33) his son Gamaliel [II]; 34) Simon b. Gamaliel [II]; 35) Judah the Patriarch.[189] The following generation was divided between 36) R. Johanan, the Palestinian and Rab and Samuel, the Babylonians; but they were followed only by the four Babylonian generations of 37) R. Huna; 38) Rabbah; 39) Raba; 40) R. Ashi.[190]

In addition to these great leaders, there were other scholars in every generation who constituted their "court" and cooperated with them in interpreting the Torah and issuing ordinances. Maimuni goes to great length in both Introductions to enumerate some of the leading Tannaim and Amoraim who served simultaneously with the respective protagonists.[191]

Historically, this chain of tradition—similar to the *isnad,* so popular among Arabian historians—has several remarkable features. The round number, forty, which always fascinated the Oriental mind, is here divided into equal halves for the periods before and after the first fall of Jerusalem. Jeremiah, the twentieth, concludes the first; his disciple, Baruch, opens the second series. This corresponds to the approximately equal length of the two periods in Maimuni's view. The concentration of the first five centuries in the hands of six bearers, as against fourteen (many of them contemporaries) for the following four hundred years, is undoubtedly due to the author's wish to enumerate all the great pre-exilic prophets, with the exception of Obadiah and Jonah, against whose inclusion special reasons could be advanced. The post-exilic prophets, on the other hand, had to give way to the men of the Great Synagogue, to whom they also belonged, because these were the official bearers of tradition, according to M. Abot I. This second period is about evenly divided into two periods of 445 years each, if Simon b. Hillel and his son, Gamaliel the Elder, are to be dated at approximately fifty years before the second fall of Jerusalem. A generation thus averages forty-five years which makes the contraction of the Babylonian Amoraim to five generations less strained.[192]

General Views and Method

Into this general chronological scheme of Jewish history Maimuni fits the entire history of mankind. He realizes, of course, that the Jews in his day were a minority, and probably also that they had always been a minority. In a remarkable passage of his *Code* he invokes Jer. 10.7-8 to proclaim the fundamental unity of mankind even in matters of belief. Speaking of the origin of idolatrous practices, he declares, "All the nations know that Thou art alone, and it is only their error and foolishness to believe that this vanity springs from Thy will."[193] On many occasions he professes admiration for cultures and languages other than Hebrew. In quoting, for example, Alfarabi's theory of the intellectual and physical superiority of the peoples inhabiting the middle climates, as against the Nordics and Southerners, he not only approves of these racial distinctions, which then seemed to be fully borne out by the previous history of the Mediterranean world, but also finds that the languages spoken by these nations are physiologically and logically more perfect. Among the five main languages of this group Arabic is almost identical with Hebrew, of which it is but a slight corruption, Aramean is closely related to either, while Greek is related to Aramean. Only Persian is further apart. Maimuni also takes pains to defend the beauty of the Greek speech against the facile generalizations of those who listen to the distorted Greek spoken in Muslim countries far from Byzantium by pointing out the dialectal corruptions of Hebrews and Arabs settled in distant regions of the North and South (the Yemen?).[194]

Nevertheless, world history is for him primarily the history of the Jewish people, with the other nations furnishing, so to speak, the general background. This will appear less astonishing, when one realizes that Christian historiography from Eusebius and Augustine to the days of the Renaissance treated ancient history before Jesus as an adjunct to the "sacred" history of the Hebrews, and that even Muslim historiography could not fully escape the impact of the Bible's particularist historical outlook. Of course, for Maimuni, the Jew, not even the appearance of Jesus or Muhammed caused any break in the historical continuity of the perennial dialogue between the Jews and the "nations of the world." For him the great periods of history run: 1) from Adam to Abraham and the establishment of monotheism; 2) from Abraham to Moses and the "giving of the Torah"; 3) from Moses to the building of the Solomonian Temple; 4) the duration of that Temple; 5) The Exile and Second Commonwealth; 6) the full-fledged Galut. The latter two periods are not sharply distinguished, because only a minority of Jews returned to Palestine under Ezra and because of the continuity of the talmudic tradition from Ezra to R. Ashi. The greatest event of all these was the "giving of the Torah," and the period preceding it represents a kind of human pre-history. On the other hand, Maimuni fails to draw any conclusions (except, as we shall see, indirectly through Balaam) from the coincidence that, according to his chronological views, the pre- and post-Sinaitic periods to his own day were of about equal length (of less than 2500 years each.)[195]

In this historical dialogue between Israel and the nations, which will not be concluded until the arrival of the Messiah, there arises the great problem of, one may call it, the national theodicy: the sufferings of the Jews and the relative prosperity of the other nations. The general course of Jewish history appears to Maimonides as to all medieval writers as an uninterrupted series of persecutions. When Israel received the Torah, he says, not through its own merit, but by divine grace and in recognition of the good deeds of its forefathers, all the nations became very envious and sought a quarrel with it and its God. "In every period from the time of the Sinaitic Revelation to the present there arose tyrannical and despotic Gentile Kings, such as Amalek, Sisera, Sennacherib, Nebuchadnezzar, Titus, Hadrian and many others whose first intention and purpose was to destroy our Law and suppress our religion at sword's point." The answer to this national theodicy is not only like that to the individual theodicy, namely that Israel will eventually reap the reward both in the hereafter and in the Messianic Age, but also in its indestructibility in this world. In reference to Is. 66.22 Maimuni emphasizes that—in contrast to such great nations as the Greeks and Persians, whose descendants, though physically undoubtedly still in existence, have lost their national identity—Israel's seed and name have both survived. In fulfillment of God's blessing to Jacob, Israel has always been like "the dust of the earth," trod upon by everybody, but like the dust it has also outlasted them all. That is why, in admitting a proselyte to the Jewish fold, one ought to teach him, "Know ye, that the world to come is preserved only for the pious ones, i.e., Israel. If thou seest Israel's suffering in this world, it is for the sake of the future good, for they cannot receive much well-being in this world as do the other nations, because they may become haughty, err and lose the reward of the hereafter . . . However the Holy blessed be He does not bring upon them too severe punishment, lest they completely disappear. But the other nations vanish, while they last forever."[196] Notwithstanding the endless persecutions, foreseen already by King David, the Jewish people remains a "Kingdom of priests," leader and pace-setter for all nations. It is, in fact, so beloved by God that even warranted criticism thereof may bring upon the critic dire punishment. Maimonides invokes Moses, Elijah, Isaiah and the angel who addressed Joshua, son of Jehozadak, as examples of preachers who, however justified were their reprimands of the idolatrous practices of the entire people or the marital transgressions of the priesthood, nevertheless provoked God's anger by the harshness of their condemnation.[197]

In this his apologia for the destiny of his people, Maimuni merely carried on a tradition well laid down in the talmudic age and re-enforced in the constant Judeo-Muslim polemics, where the inferiority of contemporary Jewry in political power was frequently stressed. This argument (so plausible under Islam's political orientation and fully in consonance with a deep-rooted conviction), carried over from the ancient Orient, that a victorious country is in itself a proof for the superiority of its god, had to be disproved by reference to another type of "success" in Israel's historic career. Another argument which had to be met by Jewish apologists was the evident superiority, in quantity even more than in quality, of the Muslim scientific and literary achievements. Samau'al ibn Yahia, for one example, attaches great significance to this line of reasoning. Maimonides replies with the increasingly standardized argument that the most distinguished writings of ancient Jewry, the fountain-head of ancient Greek and, consequently, also of Arabian wisdom, had been lost in the process of exile and migration. Especially the highly developed philosophic studies, which had been restricted to an intellectual minority in ancient Israel and carried on in oral tradition for generations, suffered great decline under the rule of ignorant nations.[198] All that will be remedied, however, in the future Messianic Age. The past as well as the future history of the Jews within the framework of human history is well prefigured in Daniel's vision concerning the image and the beasts. The four beasts as well as the four words "return" are allusions to the four empires of Greece, Rome,

Persia and Islam which were to exercise domination over the Jews before the advent of the Messiah. The comparatively long duration of the fourth empire indicates that the day of redemption is speedily approaching. This interpretation of Daniel's vision, Maimonides reiterates, cannot be controverted. While he refuses to derive from it an actual date and frowns upon all those who had tried "to hasten the end," he cannot refrain from referring to the above mentioned old family tradition.[199]

Although in all essentials a continuation of our earthly existence, the Messianic Era will restore both the prophecy and the monarchy of Israel. Indeed, shortly before the actual advent of the Redeemer, the Sanhedrin will be re-established. The Messiah will not abrogate any of the existing laws, but on the contrary renew the entire biblical and tannaitic legislation and reinforce all those laws which had been discarded after the destruction of the Temple. In many details the final lawgiver will even surpass his predecessors as, for example, in the case of the cities of refuge. Only six such cities were founded by Moses and Joshua, whereas the Messianic king will set apart nine. Apparently Maimuni did not believe in a miraculous elimination of accidental manslaughter in the Messianic Age! Perhaps the greatest achievement of that age may be seen in the possibilities it will offer Israel to devote itself wholeheartedly and without outside interference to the study and practice of Jewish law.[200]

This optimistic view of the ultimate future should not be mistaken for a belief in the idea of progress, even in its moderate, medieval form, such as found expression in the writings of Hugo of St. Victor, Thomas Aquinas and, especially, Roger Bacon. There were enough elements of scientific and cultural progress in Maimuni's Muslim environment to stimulate the belief in the constant forward procession of humanity. But there were at that time also sufficiently serious signs of political and social decay to tone down exuberant hopes and to produce, within two centuries, an historic thinker of Ibn Khaldun's caliber possessing the full realization of the ups and downs in human history. For Maimonides, the Jew, the contemporary situation of his people must have appeared the less encouraging, the more it was contrasted with the splendor of ancient Israel—which appeared to him in an exaggerated light—and the glory of the messianic future, to be brought about by a sudden, miraculous redemption. In the distant past, there was Moses, the greatest of all past and future men—including even the Messiah—indeed, a man of his own kind, a true superman. Neither were the other Israelitic prophets ever since rivalled in divine inspiration. Out of these conflicting impulses grew Maimuni's somewhat hazy conception that "there has never been a time in which speculation and the discovery of new matters were amiss; the sages of every generation placed great stock in the words of their predecessors and learned from them, and then discovered new things. Only in the basic principles of tradition opinions were never divided." Although speaking in connection with the early transmission of Oral Law, he undoubtedly had also the subsequent ages in mind. After all such a combination of unreserved adherence to the basic elements of Jewish tradition and of independent original variation in many details was the main characteristic of his own work. This combination—fairly typical of the medieval mind—made it possible for him, when he undertook the writing of his most daring work, to assert almost in one breath,

> "I adjure any reader of this book by God the Most High not to comment on a single word nor to explain to another any portion of it except such passages as are found clearly explained in the words of my predecessors among the illustrious teachers of our Law," and, "God the Most High knows that I have always been very much afraid to deal with the subjects which I propose to treat in this work, because they are profound mysteries which have not been treated in any extant work during the period of this captivity."[201]

From the traditional outlook on history as well as from Maimuni's own systematic-ethical bent of mind springs also his frequent reference to the history of Israel as a moral lesson for the intelligent observer. It was not without purpose, he asserts, that the Bible devoted so many chapters to the discussion of historical events and episodes. The genealogies recorded in Genesis, for example, have the advantage of eradicating doubts concerning the distribution of the peoples and the division of languages in the pre-Mosaic age. The stories of the deluge and Sodom point to the obvious moral that God is a judge. The struggle of the nine kings in Gen. 14 demonstrates the victory of a minority without a king, if assisted by God, and also serves as an example of family love (Abraham's for Lot) and of deprecation of money.[202]

In his critical attitude Maimonides reminds us distinctly of the limitations of scholastic philosophy. He realizes that facts cannot be derived through sheer reason. In fact, he bitterly reproaches those Christianized Syrians and Muslims who first develop a theory and then try to force reality to agree with it. Neither does he fully accept the testimony of majority opinion. Although in his legal writings he frequently invokes the adoption of a certain law by all Israel as an argument in favor of its validity and insists that a court which had issued an enactment, subsequently disregarded by the people, may not try to enforce its acceptance, he limits this principle—which incidentally reveals many analogies to the Islamic *ijma'*—to the application of legal precepts. In questions of scientific fact the truth does not cease to be truth even if all men should happen unanimously to disagree with it. This argument was the more important for Maimonides, the more both Islam and Christendom invoked the acceptance by large majorities as conclusive proof for the truth of their respective religions.[203] However, the truth of an historical fact is for him, as for every true scholastic, based chiefly upon reasoning rather than documentary evidence. While in problems of natural science he always gives a certain consideration to empirical evidence as against logical derivation, and to either of these against opinions voiced by the Aggadah, in point of history he leans heavily upon the authority of the legendary sources. His respect for tradition goes so far that he does not even attempt to disprove the contentions of Christian and Muslim opponents, inasmuch as they are based upon their own traditions. He merely argues against what, he thinks, are false conclusions derived from these traditional premises. For example, he does not deny the historical fact of Jesus' crucifixion by Jews, but is satisfied with the contention that the Jews simply exercised their legal right to punish an instigator to heresy.[204]

Among the other methodical problems his rejection of the astrological method stands out. Generally an opponent of astrology as a science, he objects to the utilization of horoscopes for the explanation of past events, such as applied by many Muslims and Abraham bar Hiyya. Even when he tries to prove that Abraham, Isaac, Jacob and David lived during the so-called earthly Trigon, he does it for the purpose of disproving the general misconception that such trigons exercise influence on historical events. He is, of course, particularly wrought up over those non-Jewish astrologers who denied, on astrological grounds, the future restoration of Israel.[205]

Summary

Viewing the Maimonidean outlook on history as a whole, one easily perceives that his major interests center around the Old Testament history from Moses to Ezra, and the talmudic history from Hillel to R. Ashi. The pre-Mosaic age, to which he concedes one-half of human history in point of time, is for him little more than the world's pre-history, of real interest only with respect to the origin of the pagan religions and the restoration of monotheism by Abraham. The centuries from Ezra to Hillel not only shrink in duration, because pre-Maccabean Judaism had failed to preserve lasting records of the Persian and early Hellenistic periods, but seem to Maimuni practically meaningless, as far as Palestinian Jewry is concerned, and almost non-existent in regard to the Persian-Parthian-Hellenistic dispersion. The half millenium from R. Ashi to Sherira Gaon appears to him of significance only through the rise of the "fourth" empire

(Islam), the intensification of anti-Jewish persecutions and a few geonic modifications of talmudic law. Only his own period (from about 1000 C. E.) arouses his curiosity more frequently, but this is hardly historical curiosity even in the limited sense revealed by his interest in biblical and talmudic developments.

This limitation is easily undestandable in view of his main preoccupation with Scripture and Talmud, these two basic sources of Judaism. They blend in his mind into one indistinguishable whole, and he views, as a matter of course, biblical history through the spectacles of rabbinic legend. To be sure, his mind revolts against rationally incongruous and logically untenable aggadic amplifications of scriptural narratives. Notwithstanding his frequently accentuated belief in "miracles," he often removes the edge of supernaturalism from otherwise accepted aggadic records. But the fundamental historicity of the events, so recorded, appears to him indubitable. This is not merely an "uncritical" historical approach—shared with minor variations by all his Jewish and non-Jewish contemporaries—but it is based upon a premise, legitimate in itself, that the Aggadah has retained many traditions of historical events and developments which undoubtedly took place, but which for some reason happened not to be recorded in any older source, or rather in any of those which had been earlier divulged to the public. Once this premise is accepted, one may only admire Maimuni's discretion and his, one may style it, historical instinct in selecting as a rule only such traditions which could not be controverted on chronological or other objective grounds.

From this belief in the general reliability of the ancient historical records springs also the harmonistic method of Maimuni's approach. In fact, some of his most "original" historical contributions consist in attempts to systematize and reconcile the widely scattered and frequently contradictory records. He sometimes takes recourse to a new historical hypothesis to elucidate obscure or controversial points, and, especially, in order to satisfy his own desire for an orderly, well-balanced succession of historical events. A most famous instance may be found in his theory of the transmission of tradition through forty generations, in two or four periods of almost equal duration. In this and other such instances one may perceive the meaningful guidance of human and Jewish destinies by the Creator of all.

Maimuni's historical outlook thus fits well into his general geo-, anthropo-, Judeocentric outlook on life. With all its evident shortcomings it is a well-rounded entity, fairly consistent in itself and truly representative of the outlook of the medieval Jew. Although in many details dependent on the Muslim environment and the social needs of the struggling Jewish minority, it has so well preserved the general continuity of rabbinic historical thought that, buttressed by Maimonides' growing authority in law and philosophy, it has exercised considerable influence even on the European thinkers, Kimhi, Gersonides, Meiri, Zacuto, and a host of others.[206]

PART III

Jewish Historians
and Their Viewpoints

7

Azariah de' Rossi:
A Biographical Sketch*

BORN IN MANTUA BETWEEN THE YEARS 1511 AND 1514, Azariah de'
Rossi was the scion of an ancient family which claimed descent
from the Judean exiles brought to Rome in the days of Titus. Very
few data have reached us about his life and family. In his books
there are only occasional references to his father Moses, his wife,
daughter, and the daughter's son, Benjamin. He had no sons of
his own. For a time he served as a censor of books, but it is
unclear whether he did it for the government or as an appointee
of the Jewish community in accordance with the resolution passed
by the rabbinical synod in Ferrara in 1554 which had introduced
a precensorship of all Jewish books to forestall anti-Jewish attacks.
Nor do we know whether he exercised this occupation on a salaried
basis. In any case, it appears that he was not in straitened
circumstances, for he was usually able to acquire books, including
expensive manuscripts. Toward the end of his life, however, he
found it difficult to have his large work printed; after its publication his royalties were small because, as he complains, of "the
persecutions by hypocritical and envious men." Nor do we know
for certain where he permanently resided. For a time he lived in
Venice, Ancona and Bologna. He left Bologna in 1569 after Pius
V's decree of expulsion of Jews from the Papal States.[1] He settled
in Ferrara, where he established close friendships with Jewish
and Christian scholars who influenced him greatly.

It was the earthquake in Ferrara on November 18, 1570, when
he was almost sixty years old, which undermined his and his

* Revised translation from the Hebrew published in *Eshkol, Hebrew Encyclopedia*, I (Berlin, 1929), cols. 689-93.

family's economic well-being, but also gave the impetus to his literary career. At first a Christian friend suggested to him during the catastrophe that he translate the *Letter of Aristeas* into Hebrew. He completed that rendition in twenty days, not from the Greek, of which he had insufficient command, but rather from the Latin translation by Mathias Garbitius.[2] De' Rossi gave his version the picturesque Hebrew title of *Hadrat zeqenim* (The Elders' Glory), because the *Letter* told the story of the origin of the Septuagint prepared by seventy elders. During the same period he also published a booklet on the earthquake itself and how it affected him and his family. In this essay he was greatly helped by the Italian study of the Ferrara earthquake published in that very year by the local physician, Buoni. Azariah called this little tract *Qol Elohim* (The Voice of God) because Pythagoras had thus designated all earthquakes.

A few months after this unsettling event (on the eve of Passover, 1571), he conceived the idea of his larger and far more important book which he called *Imre binah* (Words of Wisdom) because it embraced quotations of "many words of sages truly worthy of contemplation." The work is divided into four sections and sixty chapters. Section III, including chapters 29-44, bore a special heading, *Yeme 'olam* (Days of the World), because it dealt mainly with the problem of how many years had elapsed since Creation.[3] Azariah worked on this book for about a year and then spent six more months on its revision. These three tracts were then combined into a comprehensive work entitled *Me'or 'Eynaim* (Light of the Eyes) because it was "the light of my eyes and the joy of my heart." He wanted to print it immediately in Mantua which had a large Hebrew press, but the matter was delayed because of financial difficulties. In the meantime, on the advice of his friend, Leone da Sommi, the famous playwright and theatrical expert, he continued the work and finally saw it published on November 18, 1573. Subsequently, he spent another year preparing a revised edition and a list of observations found in his book on "some of the Geonim" such as Rashi, the Tosafists and Yehudah Halevi. Altogether he worked on this book for fully four years. Nor did he cease correcting it in the short span of life remaining to him, adding notes on the margins. To answer many dogmatically colored strictures by critics, he published a rejoinder called *Maṣref le-kḥesef* (Refinement of the Silver) which he completed in the days of Purim (February 24-25), 1575. He finally added a small tract entitled *Ṣedeq 'olamim* (Eternal Justice), a reply to the thirteen pointed questions raised by R. Isaac Finzi of Pesaro. But these latter-day writings remained unpublished for some three hundred years.

Like other authors of that period, Azariah also wrote poetry, mainly occasional poems of the type then usually inserted at a book's beginning and end, and in introductions to chapters. He prepared the verses used on the tombstone inscriptions of his pre-maturely deceased grandson and, ultimately, on his own funerary stone (according to legend, he had learned about the day of his death through a dream three years in advance) He also composed a few liturgical poems. One, beginning *Mizmor le-yom Shabbat* (A Song for the Sabbath Day, Holy to the Awesome God), was recited in regular synagogue services in Ferrara and in the "four communities" of the Comtat Venaissin, then under papal domina-tion. Another was included in the Roman *Maḥzor* for the seventh day of Passover. On one occasion, at least, Azariah tried his hand at foreign language poetry, composing in 1576 poems in Hebrew, Aramaic, Italian and Latin in honor of Duchess Margaritha of Savoy, who passed away at that time. His knowledge of languages is attested to also by his Italian translation of the main chronological chapter (XXXV) of his large work, as well as by his Italian epistle to the Abbot of Monte Cassino, who had paid him three scudi for his book.

De' Rossi intended to prepare a comprehensive reply to the strictures of R. David Provençali of Mantua against his defense of statements by Philo of Alexandria. He further planned to trans-late into Hebrew the *Poemander* and *Aesculapius* by Hermes Trismegistus, and to provide them with introductions and notes. Additional plans included the collection and translation of sayings by 'Aqilas cited by Jerome and Eugubinus, the near-contemporary author of the *Pentateuchi recognitio*. He had hoped that in this way "they would be combined with the work of 'Aqilas quoted by our ancient sages." All these plans, however, failed to be realized because he fell ill and died in Kislev (November-December, 1577); he was apparently buried in the vicinity of Mantua.

De' Rossi's scholarly work was a great innovation in Jewish literature. Just as general Renaissance historiography had departed from the patterns established by the medieval chroniclers, so the literary creativity of de' Rossi greatly differed from the work of Joseph ha-Kohen and the other Jewish historians of his time. Yet he was not a follower of Lionardo Bruni, as were the great Italian historians of the period, Machiavelli and Guicciardini. He may rather be counted among the school of Flavius Blondus (Biondi), who emphasized content above form. Great erudition and the effort to go back to the original sources are the outstanding characteristics of the pupils of that school, although Azariah is not always completely accurate, particularly when citing sources from memory. Unlike most contemporary chroniclers he also selected as his main subject of inquiry not events from a more recent past, but rather intriguing problems of ancient history, such as the Essenes and Philo, or else some puzzling statements in the Talmud. He also dealt with such general questions as the chronology based upon the Jewish era of Creation and Hebrew poetry. With the exception of the chronological problems, however, he did not deal at length with any particular subject but rather deliberately moved from one issue to another. We shall deal more fully with the vast scope of his interests and his historical outlook and methods in the next two essays.

Probably his greatest difficulty consisted in dealing with conflicting Hebrew and Gentile sources. Obviously, it did not occur to him to doubt any biblical text, since in that period few scholars dared to question even the classical Graeco-Roman sources. But he could not with equal ease disregard contradictions between statements of ancient and medieval rabbis and of Gentile authorities, particularly in the field of natural science. On principle, he drew the following line of demarcation:

Everything, large and small, which they handed to us as given by a tradition from Moses on Sinai, as having learned it through one of the hermeneutic rules from the Torah, or as having extended it in order to make a fence around the Torah—in all such cases far be it from us to enter any demurrer and contradict them, as if their testimony were not reliable and as if our ways were better than theirs. ... However, [we must deal differently with] matters which, by their very nature, could not have been announced to them on Sinai, such as events which happened thereafter, and with other data about which we are certain that they stated them as their own opinion without the backing of Scripture. Wherever it is possible for us to harmonize them with what has been established as true by later scholars we should do so.... But when this is impossible, we must assume that they [the sages] did not report a tradition from the Prophets but merely heard it from the scholars of their own time. ... We ought not to flatter them against their will by stating with our lips what we do not believe in our hearts.[4]

Understandably, this approach created much resentment among his Orthodox contemporaries. His practical attempt, in particular, through source criticism to clarify the complex Hebrew chronology and his computation that the actual number of years which had elapsed since Creation exceeded the computation underlying the era of Creation accepted by the Jewish people for many centuries, aroused much opposition even among his friends, including the famous Mantuan rabbis, Moses Provençali and Yehudah Leone Muscato. Nevertheless, in their public utterances, the latter seem to have defended him and it was their influence which saved him from serious embarrassment, since immediately after the publication of his *Me'or 'Eynaim* some Italian rabbis and elders (from Venice, Pesaro, Ancona, Cremona, Padua, Verona, Rome, Ferrara and Siena) decided to proclaim a mild ban, not on the author, whose way of life admittedly was beyond reproach, but on the book. Because this work had brought forth "many new interpretations not thought of by our holy forefathers," they wrote in their manifesto, "no one whatsoever shall have in his possession the aforementioned book neither in *toto* nor in part, nor to study it, unless he personally first obtains a special written permit from the rabbis of his locality." For many years after Azariah's death this ordinance was still being observed. Even his adherents considered the book as "a good thing only for informed persons" but not for ordinary readers.[5]

If this was the attitude of the Italian leaders, how much more hostile must have been the attitude of communities untouched by Renaissance culture. In Safed, in particular, that great center of sixteenth-century Halakhah and Kabbalah, many sharp opponents clamored that "there is no question that he who keeps it [de' Rossi's book] sins gravely." According to later reports, Joseph Karo (for the printing of whose extensive commentary on the Maimonidean code Azariah had greatly exerted himself a few years before) wished to put him under excommunication and only his last illness had prevented the great codifier from proclaiming the ban. Another distinguished Jewish leader, R. Loew b. Bezaleel ("Der hohe R. Loew") of Prague voiced his confidence "that this book will not be allowed to retain a name and remnant in Israel." R. Jacob Emden had heard about other scholars of that generation who had demanded the obliteration of Azariah's work, and added on his own that this book "deserves to be renamed *Me'avver 'Eynaim* [Blinding the Eye]" and that it was to be expected only from "a fool like himself." Later, however, Emden retracted and, punning on Azariah's Hebrew name *Min ha-Adummim* (de' Rossi), quoted the biblical phrase *Lo teta'ev Adomi* (Thou shalt not abhor an Edomite: Deut. 23.8).[6]

On the other hand, in the enlightened circles of that and, still more, of later generations, Azariah's work was greeted with much acclaim. Southern scholars from Amato Lusitano to Leon da Modena who wrote comments on the *Me'or 'Eynaim,* and Joseph Salomon del Medigo of Candia, as well as such northerners as Menasseh b. Israel in Amsterdam, David Gans and Yom Tob Lippmann Heller of Prague, praised it and approvingly cited some of its passages. Some statements were quoted even by opponents, especially Gedaliah ibn Yaḥya; of course, without acknowledgment.

Numerous Christian scholars, too, particularly Johannes Buxtorf, father and son, Jean Morin and Joseph de Voisin, held him in high esteem, quoted him extensively and even translated entire chapters from his book. The founders of modern Jewish scholarship, too, such as Nachman Krochmal, Leopold Zunz and others, considered de' Rossi as the most influential forerunner of the modern science of Judaism.[7]

8

Azariah de' Rossi's
Attitude to Life*

AZARIAH DE' ROSSI AS A MAN is not important for us moderns, whose world is so different from his, but as a type he evokes considerable interest. As a personality he seems—from the little we know about him[1]—not to have been of commanding power. He was not a man of strong passions in love or hatred; we do not see him constantly struggling and making his way in the ups and downs of life. He was not brilliant in wit, in spirit, in courage or in keenness of thought, like many of the outstanding characters of Renaissance Italy. Nor was he one of those creative geniuses— also quite numerous in the Italy of that time—who, compelled by an inner force, found new ways in art or thought, in trade or statesmanship. His best qualities were thorough erudition and a sincere, although rather timid, love for the truth. And so unconsciously, and rather blindly and timidly, he stumbled into a kind of immortality, when he began, at the age of sixty, to write his important historical work. But the fact that the *Me'or 'Eynaim* became so important, rendering its author one of the greatest, or perhaps the very greatest, of Jewish historians who had flourished in the seventeen centuries between Josephus and Jost, was certainly not entirely due to his own merits. It is enough to compare him with such historians as Guicciardini and Machiavelli in order to see clearly how much he falls short of the achievable standards of his time and country.

But if not unique and original, he is the more typical and representative of Italian Jewry in the sixteenth century at its best.

* Reprinted from *Jewish Studies in Memory of Israel Abrahams* (New York, 1927), pp. 12-52.

As compared with their coreligionists elsewhere, the Jews of Italy, because of their peculiar political and economic conditions and their closer social and intellectual relations with the Gentile world, had developed a somewhat distinctive cultural life of their own— an interesting synthesis of the medieval Jewish and classic Italian Renaissance spirit—so that a short survey of the fundamental views expressed by a representative man like Azariah upon life in all its aspects will throw light, I think, on a curious chapter in the neglected history of the Jewish *Weltanschauung*.

I

In the most basic questions of religion, philosophy and science, Azariah was certainly able to reconcile rather easily the views of his contemporaries with the established creed of medieval Judaism. The universal revival of the classical spirit had not yet caused any profound changes in natural science, and most of the speculations, derived from Greek philosophy, had long since been brought into a kind of agreement with traditional religious beliefs by the thinkers of Islamic, Jewish and Christian Scholasticism. And although Azariah supports his opinions by citations from Christian Fathers and Teachers to a degree as yet unheard of in Hebrew literature, as well as by references to the ancient Greek, the contemporary Italian and the usual Jewish sources, he is by no means compelled to give up any of the acknowledged principles of the older Jewish authorities.

For him the universe is like one Big Man (the inverted notion of the macrocosm and microcosm)[2] created by one immaterial[3] God out of absolutely nothing.[4] The *tohu-bohu* of the Bible, previous to Creation, explained by so many authoritative thinkers in different ways, is, according to Azariah, just this absolute nought.[5] And in reality, even the expression "previous to Creation" is not the right one, because Time itself is one of the works of Creation,[6] like Space and its derivatives, so that there was no *before* at all.

Also, after the Creation God has not left the world to itself, but it always was and always will be guided by His higher will.[7] This guidance may be indirect, as God has created Nature and its laws to perform in an established order all the different tasks which He has purposed. Therefore, such occurrences in the world as rain, winds, pestilence, famine, and premature death have no moral significance in themselves, being merely the accidental consequences of natural causes.[8] Even so, they are, as is Nature in general, only the instruments of God's general will.[9] On the other hand, if He wishes, He may sometimes use these events for a special purpose and then, although apparently unchanged, they cease to be accidental and become moral phenomena. Furthermore, there are extraordinary cases when God, either to punish evildoers or to give a warning to the perceiving world, changes the ordinary course of Nature and does things which cannot be explained by natural causes. So is, for instance, the earthquake not merely a "disease in the element of earth" or any other result of purely natural causes, as the Greek philosophers tried to make us believe, but the effect of God's special will, as had been frequently emphasized by the Teachers in the Talmud. Or at least, says Azariah— and here his harmonizing attitude toward Jewish and Greek thought appears clearly[10]—let us admit that earthquakes come sometimes from God and sometimes only from Nature. In this latter case, of course, they are merely accidents without meaning.[11] The obvious objection that many earthquakes and other natural evils would be inflicted upon the world undeservedly, is met by Azariah with a quotation from Philo[12]—that God, when creating the world, disregarded the little evil connected with the elements for the sake of the much greater good they bring. But how can Azariah reconcile this Philonic theory with his own entirely different notion of the immediate Creation and the continual direct control by God of everything that happens in the world? Is there not rather a limitation of God's omnipotence in His inability to create more perfect elements and even afterwards to alter them according to His will? This inconsistency, as many others, Azariah must leave unexplained.[13]

At any rate these elements, four in all,[14] once created by God are invested with certain qualities which in a natural way make up the construction of the sublunar world, and determine by their different combinations the infinite variety in the physical world. By reason of their weight, the things composed out of the heavier elements are placed in strata below those substances built up from the lighter ones. Therefore the terrestrial globe, composed chiefly of earth and water, the heaviest of the four elements, is at the bottom, and, as the same conditions are prevailing all around, it is also in the center of the universe.[15] It is surrounded by the lighter elements, air and fire, and their compounds. Above those, in the lunar and the higher spheres, there is a fifth element—the ether.[16] Here below we find man, the most earthly creature, made chiefly from earth, the heaviest element, as is implied by his very name, Adam, in accordance with the old biblical etymology.[17] Man is, therefore, the very core and center of life, for whose sake everything has been created to serve his needs. Was Azariah aware how deep a meaning lay in this simultaneity of bottom and center? We do not know, for even the things hitherto mentioned must be guessed from general considerations rather than read in clear statements of the author. Azariah only deals with these problems incidentally in connection with discussions on other subjects.

Being thus situated in the center of the universe, the earth as well as mankind on it is subject to the different influences of the animated[18] celestial bodies which are situated in the spheres encompassing the globe. Although Azariah by no means expresses clearly his views about the nature and the function of the heavenly spheres, we shall not err if we assume that for the most part he accepts the dominant theories of the medieval scholastics. Accordingly, the earth is encompassed by the spheres in the following order: Moon, Mercury, Venus, Sun, Mars, Jupiter, Saturn, the fixed stars and the *primum mobile*,[19] the latter by its motion influencing all the others and especially the motion of the single planets. These last, although fixed within their own spheres, have a so-called גלגל הקפה (epicycle)[20] apart, thus rotating round their axes and at the same time participating in the general movement of their spheres.[21] To support this view, Azariah quotes (against Aristotle and some talmudic authorities) not only the official Ptolemaic astronomy, but the elucidation given to it by Thomas Aquinas. Although the Bible calls the moon "the lesser light," which seems to imply that it is second only to the sun and far superior to all the stars, Azariah explains, in full accord with medieval astronomy, that the brightness of the moon is a mere result of its lesser distance from the earth, and that it shines only by light reflected from the sun.[22]

The highest authorities taught that the spheres exercise an enormous influence upon the earth and its inhabitants and Azariah sees no reason to doubt it. The tides of the seas, for instance, are directed by the movement of the *primum mobile* as well as (here he quotes from Maimonides) by the general influence of the moon upon the element of water.[23] Azariah does not hesitate to ascribe to the celestial bodies a lucky or sinister influence on the fate of mankind and of single nations. He does not tell us whether or not he accepts all the doctrines of that "classical age" (Olgiati) of judicial astrology concerning the influence of the stars on the destinies of individuals and the ability of man to foretell the future by a close observation of the different movements in the universe.[24] But he does not doubt in the least that such extraordinary changes as eclipses (although they, too, can be explained by natural reasons) imply a kind of warning for the peoples of the earth, the Jews, as we shall see, being the only exception to the rule.[25]

As a matter of fact, however, we never can really tell what is natural and what is preter- and supernatural. Our knowledge of nature is so small and so uncertain, that we can hardly deduce from it any consequences in matters of belief. Despite all his rationalistic views, despite his ironic refusal to accept poetical narratives about natural phenomena as scientifically true,[26] and despite—what is more important—the preference given by him to the experience of the senses as compared with merely logical proofs and considerations,[27] he is still extremely skeptical of the absolute value of any human science.[28] Against those doubtful achievements of the human mind the religious creeds, originating in divine revelation, stand as firm rocks of absolute certainty. Therefore, the supernatural is not less real, but perhaps even more real than the natural. Hence, Azariah does not deny the existence of demons at all.[29] On the contrary, he so firmly believes in the interference of spirits in human affairs, caused sometimes by all kinds of sorcery—no exceptional occurrence in a period when thousands of "witches" were burned at the stake— that he makes out of it an argument against a certain theory of the Pythagoreans as promoting witchcraft.[30] Still more firmly does Azariah believe in miracles. We have already seen that he was convinced that God sometimes changes the ordinary course of Nature for moral reasons. So little does he doubt that miracles are performed for the sake of Israel, that he apologizes when it occurs to him to give a natural reason for an unexpected recovery of his wife, and to compare it with an undoubted miracle of Elishah.[31] The immortality of the individual soul being a perfect certainty,[32] the religious creed in the resurrection of the dead is for him doubtful only in so far as he cannot definitely decide whether all without distinction or only those who were righteous in their lives will arise from the dust.[33] The world hereafter is for him not only as certain a reality as anything in the natural world, but in fact the ultimate goal and purpose of man and, therefore, of all Creation.[34]

II

However, this natural world was at least one reality out of many. And what he saw in it was merely a reflection of the common opinions of his contemporaries. Although his *Me'or 'Eynaim* was published thirty years after Copernicus' *De revolutionibus* and in the lifetime of Giordano Bruno, his geocentric and anthropocentric view[35] so clearly represents the general belief of the age, that such a distinguished astronomer as Tyho de Brahe[36] could still endeavor to sustain it with scientific proofs many years later. And as for the four elements, no man besides the alchemistic dreamers in that period before Joachim Jung and Robert Boyle thought of a larger number. Consequently, Azariah had only to accept the achievements of the Greek and Arabic astronomers and physicists, as acknowledged by the whole Western world. Even the more difficult task of reconciling these ruling theories with the many different opinions expressed by the Talmud, or even by the Bible itself, had been performed long before Azariah by his greater philosophic predecessors.

In one respect, however, he was facing a problem, new yet unsolved. The wonderful travels and discoveries which had taken place in the century before the composition of the *Me'or 'Eynaim* had widened the geographical horizon of mankind in an unprecedented manner, and abolished some of the most established creeds of centuries. Not to accept these new results was impossible for a man like Azariah. But how to accept them if they were so much in contradiction to what was taught by the Talmud and the Midrashim?

Even here Azariah did not have to be an extreme innovator. He merely had to apply the same method which was used by his predecessors in regard to many other remarkable utterances of the rabbis in which they were in open contradiction with the achievements of Greek and Arabian science. Azariah emphasizes again and again, while quoting many of the highest authorities in medieval Judaism (notably the last Geonim and Maimonides), that not everything uttered by the Teachers in the Talmud represents an old tradition reaching back to Moses on Sinai—which would be an unmistakable truth[37]—but that many sayings simply express the personal and possibly erroneous opinion of a single rabbi (or of a single period). It is useless, according to Azariah, to explain away those divergencies, as the honor of the Talmud is better safeguarded by admitting the possibility of a few erroneous personal statements than by violating the truth.[38] Certainly, that was in Azariah's time, although less in Italy than elsewhere, a rather daring point of view which required no little courage. It is enough to compare with it the similar, almost simultaneous attempt of R. Moses Isserles in his *Torat ha-'olah,* where all the devices of pilpulistic interpretation are used in order to reconcile traditional views with new ones, especially in regard to geographical facts. Any admission of a possible error in the Talmud is thus avoided. Azariah peremptorily declines to follow him in this course.[39]

To be sure, the method of Azariah was more in accord with historical truth, but Isserles, in reinterpreting the old documents so that they might seem to correspond with newly discovered facts, followed the traditional method of Judaism more than did Azariah. The latter, while leaving the firm ground of tradition, and yet not daring to go to the other extreme of denying the incontestable reliability of every word in the Bible, came into new difficulties. Thus while trying to reconcile the obvious fact of the new discoveries with the old *nil novi,* as well as with his conviction of the superiority of the ancient times, he wants to prove that all the new worlds were known in remote antiquity and merely forgotten later. He, therefore, maintains that the voyage of King Solomon's fleet to Ophir was a circumnavigation of the world, like that of Del Cano, the surviving captain of Magellan's expedition (1519-1522),[40] and that it was performed in the same period of three years.[41]

In this connection Azariah shows a considerable knowledge of geography, a science then already highly developed in his country. It is true that in many fundamental questions he still clings to obsolete conceptions. His chief source, for instance, for geographic distances is still Ptolemy, with only a few corrections or additions made by some of his famous contemporaries. So the inhabitable eastern hemisphere, in his opinion, extends over 180 degrees longitude, from the Canary Islands to the eastern coast of China (Canton).[42] Notwithstanding all the new explorations—which, as is well known, were facilitated to a large extent by just this illusion —the world was still convinced that the distance between those two points was equal in either direction. Accordingly, the distance between any given two points in the eastern hemisphere, reckoned by degrees of geographical longitude, must have covered more degrees than in our modern geography. No wonder, therefore, that Azariah, referring exclusively to the data of the Ptolemaic geography, places Jerusalem at 66° long. (from the Canary Islands), Jaffa at 65° 40', Cairo at 62° and Seville on the other end of the Mediterranean at 7° 15'.[43] This is based entirely upon the measurement of Ptolemy, according to which the total distance from Gibraltar (7° 30') to Iskanderun on the Syrian coast (69° 30') amounted to 62 degrees, while we count it nowadays as 41° 41'. This necessarily led to many further mistakes in detail.[44] Azariah adhered to this erroneous supposition as did all his contemporaries.[45] They disregarded entirely not only the previous measurements of Eratosthenes and Strabo and the later ones of a few Arab geographers[46] (all of whom came much nearer to the truth, and one of whom came close to one of the highest achievements of European medieval geography, the "Alphosine Tables," although composed, as is well known, under the direction of a Jew, Isaac ibn Said, in the thirteenth century), which had reduced the maximum length of the Mediterranean to 52 degrees.[47] Azariah's measurements in geographic latitude, however, are, as are those of the Ptolemaic geography in general, nearly correct. Thus he locates Jerusalem at 31° 40' latitude, Jaffa at 32° 6', Cairo at 30° and Seville at 37° 50'. Only in regard to the site of ancient Carthage (32° 26') is he curiously mistaken. He also follows Maurus and the other contemporary commentators of Ptolemy's *Geography* in their overestimate of the earth's circumference, as contrasted with the underestimate of the great Alexandrian himself.[48]

Needless to say, Azariah believes firmly in the rotundity of the earth. That idea might still have been doubted by a man like Columbus, but it could by no means be contested after Magellan. He knows also that the globe is inhabited on both hemispheres, and consequently has no doubt as to the existence of the so-called "antipodes"; while in the Middle Ages even those who were inclined to see the earth as a globe mostly believed that the inhabitable land was plunged in an enormous ocean, although they differed greatly as to the relative proportions of land and water. Furthermore, Azariah is quite sure that the *oikumene* extends to the South far beyond the tropic of Cancer, and to the North beyond the northern polar circle; these regions previously were regarded as unfit for human settlement on account of their temperature.[49] As a result of these considerations, he sees clearly that the ancient belief of the Aggadah that Jerusalem was at the very center of the earth ("the navel of the earth." Ez. 38.12) was not to be understood literally.[50] He is also aware of the obvious difficulty that, even with regard to the old *oikumene* (which, at any rate, included the bulk of the human race), this assumption could not be literally maintained. For in the supposed general extension of 0°-180° long. and 24°-66° lat. of the inhabitable land, Jerusalem, said to be situated at 66° long. and about 32° lat., was by no means in the center. In order to find some kind of scientific justification, Azariah introduces the ancient divisions of "climates." According to the differences in insolation due to the inclination of the earth's axis, medieval geography, disregarding the modifying influences of the air and ocean currents, defined 24 "climates" of different width between the Equator and the North Pole. Each "climate" represented, as we approached the Pole, an increase of half an hour in the longest day.[51] Azariah, accepting this Ptolemaic division, states that among the seven "climates" covering the bound‑ aries of the *oikumene* (here between 16° and 48° lat.), Jerusalem is placed in the fourth or middle one.[52] But how many other coun‑ tries were situated in the same "climate"!

On the other hand, in stating that the inhabitable region extends northwards to about 10° south of the North Pole, Azariah merely follows an hypothesis accepted in his time, because even if he knew of the recent discoveries of the English travellers Chan‑ cellor (1553) and Borrough (1556), who had reached Novaya Zemlya, there still remained a considerable distance to be covered before the above mentioned polar region was reached. In discuss‑ ing these problems, he is also able to rectify many rather confused notions of the medieval Jewish scholars, especially in the Franco‑ German countries, as regards geographic conditions in distant Pal‑ estine and Babylonia.[53] But this does not prevent him from making a few mistakes of his own. He assumes that Parvaim, mentioned in the Bible, is none other than Peru (an opinion shared also by a few non-Jewish scholars of that time), and that Ezion Geber near Elath on the Red Sea was also near the shore of the Mediter‑ ranean, or at least connected to it by rivers.[54] Like almost all of his contemporaries, he believed in the existence of the mythical country of Prester John of Ethiopia, identical with our Abyssinia,[55] as well as in that of the lost ten tribes of Israel.[56]

III

Of Nature outside of man, of its greatness and essential beauty, Azariah had little understanding. No wonder! If even the medieval Gentiles, the overwhelming majority of whom lived outside of the not numerous and uncrowded towns, had, until the thirteenth century[57]—as a result of their exclusively religious orientation—scarcely eyes for natural beauty, we cannot expect such appreciation from a Jew, who probably lived all his life in a relatively crowded Jewish street in Mantua or even in the comparatively spacious Ferrara, that first "modern city" in Europe, a few decades before the institution of the official ghetto. If Azariah happens to speak at all about natural phenomena, he obviously does so out of books, rather than from his own personal experience.[58] When he uses poetic comparisons, one feels instantly that these are not things seen in life, but very common, almost standardized literary similes. And when a thing occurs in his life which upsets it entirely, like the earthquake in Ferrara, he devotes a special investigation to speculations about the origin of earthquakes in general as contained in different Jewish and non-Jewish writings, but does not even try to give his own picture of this disastrous experience. It is not Nature by itself that matters. It is only Nature in relation to man. The earthquake is only a "voice of God" to warn or to punish man. Unusual cosmic phenomena are mainly signs given by God to man.

In this extremely anthropocentric world, however, there is a place apart for one people: Israel. Although, as we have seen, Azariah is ready to give up the ancient belief, cherished also by many Christian authorities whom he eagerly quotes,[59] that Palestine is the center of the earth, he does not see any reason to abandon the corresponding theory that Israel is the center of humanity. If man is the chief aim of creation, this aim is best accomplished in Israel with its supreme tasks. Therefore, Israel is under the direct guidance of God and far less dependent on Nature. Consequently, as long as the Jews are faithful to God, natural signs even of cosmic dimensions have no meaning for them. For they neither need warning by such signs, as they have other means to recognize God's will, nor are they always subjected to the ordinary course of Nature, because for them, and for them only, God performs miracles.[60]

This central position of the Jewish people in mankind is not temporary, but has to be traced back to the very origins of the world, and it will last as long as the world itself. Hebrew is not just one language among many, but it is the only language created by God himself. It was also the only one in existence until the period of the Tower of Babel, when the other languages came into use, having been invented by man. Thus all other languages are merely of human origin, Hebrew alone being of a divine source. No wonder, therefore, that it is by far the most beautiful and perfect of all spoken tongues that have ever existed.[61] As old as the language itself are also both the alphabet (*Ashshurit*), in which, declares Azariah, the Torah was written originally,[62] and the vowel points which since have been forgotten and rediscovered many times.[63] Arabic and Aramaic[64] are nothing but corrupt derivatives from the original pure Hebrew.[65] When, for example, Galen prides himself on the beauty of his own Greek—which Azariah, as he once confesses,[66] never knew satisfactorily—in comparison with which all the others are like the bleating of cattle or the twitter of birds, Azariah declares this to be mere self-praise and racial complacency.[67] That he might be guilty of the same actions never strikes Azariah's mind.[68]

However, not for its language alone is all mankind indebted to Israel. In fact, all wisdom and science, all culture and civilization, have their common source in the past of the Jewish people. And as King Solomon was the wisest of all men that ever walked on the surface of the earth, so all the main elements of knowledge came to the peoples of the earth from and through Jewish sources.[69]

Azariah quotes Maimonides here as authority for this ancient widespread belief among the Jews and partly also non-Jews, already emphasized perhaps in its extreme form in the Hellenistic period. Azariah had to admit that the Gentile world had proved itself superior to the Jews in many respects and especially in the field of natural science when he abandoned some of the most accepted views of talmudic astronomy and geography. But Azariah, like many of his predecessors, meets this objection with the argument that when the Jews went into Exile, the dominant peoples captured their Scriptures. Thus afterwards the Jews could not help learning from their neighbors in turn.[70]

Notwithstanding this catastrophe, Azariah does not doubt that the Jewish people, the oldest of all existing nations, will also survive them all and endure in Jerusalem and outside it[71] until the time of the Messiah, when it will gain uncontested supremacy. The belief in the speedy coming of the Redeemer, who would usher in the new age both for Israel and the nations, was certainly an important element in the *Weltanschauung* of Azariah as well as of the entire people.[72] Not that Azariah stresses this point very often, or that he seems to have reflected very much about it or had distinct notions as to the details involved therein. On the contrary, the problem is, in Azariah's eyes, one of those unbroachable subjects on which there is no use speculating. He sees a real danger in arguing this question, notably in the tendency of some of his contemporaries to fix in advance—by using all the different means of interpreting the Holy Scriptures—the date of the arrival of the Messiah. At the time of the composition of the *Me'or 'Eynaim* there was in many circles of Italian Jewry a very strong belief in the immediate imminence of the end of the days. It was generally expected to occur in the year 5335 (1575).[73] Azariah not only declines to accept this date as more probable than any other, but he raises his voice to caution his brethren against such prognostications, which might end, as often before, in painful disappointment.[74] Moreover the "days of the Messiah" are—in Azariah's opinion— by no means the final aim of a real Jew. They only mean freedom from external oppression and the opportunity for the faithful to accomplish more exactly all their duties, notably those applicable to Palestine alone, and to be nearer to an understanding of God. In addition, universal peace and a considerable extension of human life[75] may be regarded as important improvements. All of these advantages are confined within the natural limits of life on earth. Really final, because it is supernatural, is and remains only the world to come.[76]

IV

Belief in the superiority of the Jewish people and the Messianic hope have, in the opinion of Azariah, no practical consequences as regards the relations between Israel and the nations, as long as the Jews are actually living among them. On the contrary, Azariah devotes a special chapter (55) in his book to proving that the Jews in the dispersion are in duty bound to pray for the welfare of the country in which they live. Now Israel is spread all over the world, and it follows, therefore, that they must pray for the welfare of all nations. This result again cannot be achieved if nation wars with nation. Thus the welfare of each country and peace among nations, both notions being expressed in Hebrew by the word *Shalom,* not only correspond with the real interests of the Jews, but have also become almost religious ideals, sanctioned by a tradition which reaches back to the first dispersion in Bible times.[77]

To be sure, Azariah writes thus with the ardent hope of influencing the public opinion of the Gentiles. Nor was this an impossible undertaking at that time. Azariah could rightly expect his book to be read also by Christian scholars,[78] for many Italians were acquainted with Hebrew. There is little doubt that the abbot of the famous Monastery of Monte Cassino was not the only Christian to whom Azariah had sent his book, as a welcome gift.[79] Furthermore, the later numerous translations of single chapters of Azariah's work into different European languages prove sufficiently how much the Gentile world was interested in it long after the author's death. Nevertheless, we may take it for granted that most of the views expressed by Azariah render his firm convictions. Only occasionally may his apologetic tendency have induced him to lay stress upon a point not essentially connected with his innermost beliefs. So when he speaks about the old Jewish custom to pray for all nations alike, as already practiced by the high priest in Jerusalem, he does not mention that he knew it only from sources—Philo, Josephus, Eusebius—which he did not regard as authoritative for Jewish law. (It is not a mere coincidence that these sources are also obviously apologetic.) But still he is able to interpret many of the traditional Jewish sources in the same way without forcing them too much.[80] And when he declares that the Gentile ruler may expect from his Jewish subjects not only prayer on his behalf, but also complete obedience to the laws of the state,[81] he is entirely in the traditional line. At the same time, he may overlook many important historical facts, and he may avoid discussing the difficult topic of occasional conflicts between duties toward the state and those imposed by religion. In such cases it cannot be doubted that Azariah—like almost all of his Jewish and a large part of his non-Jewish contemporaries, notwithstanding all the theories of the supremacy of the State over the Church from Marsiglio of Padua to Machiavelli—would give preference to religious duties in all fundamental questions which could not be reconciled by the famous adage of "the law of the Kingdom is law." Nonetheless he is essentially right when he emphasizes that traditional Judaism had long ago compromised with existing facts.

On one point, however, Azariah had to be more cautious: on the question of the political constitution of the state. The Jewish tradition based upon the Bible as well as upon the later developments was not much in favor of the monarchical system. It is known how much in the discussions of the sixteenth and seventeenth centuries about the best form of government the adherents of a republican constitution always referred to the Jewish Bible, while the advocates of monarchy looked for support to the New Testament. In reality, later Judaism had to compromise here also. Jewish history in the Middle Ages has shown, with special force, that the condition of the Jews was more stable and therefore relatively better

in monarchical states than under most of the shifting popular governments. The more so because republics were to be found mostly
in city-states, where the ruling merchant class had important reasons
to impede Jewish economic competition. Hence the political theory
of the Jews became more favorable to monarchical government.

However, in Azariah's Italy, matters were not quite settled: old
republican traditions clashed with new monarchical forces. In
Mantua and Ferrara where, so far as we know, Azariah spent
much of his life, a strong, rather absolute monarchy had been long
established. No wonder, therefore, that Azariah seems to advocate
a monarchical system, although a moderate one, for the Gentile
world. He first discusses—quoting Josephus—the fundamental question: what are the ends of the state? and he reaches the conclusion
that there are two chief purposes to be distinguished. One is
internal jurisdiction, which implies the maintenance of public order,
while the second is defense against external enemies. For the first
aim the most appropriate constitution seems to be the republican,
for division of power may be a preventive against abuses. On the
other hand, the second aim is best achieved under the guidance
of one man. Consequently, the best way out of the difficulty is
that already suggested by Plato—a king who observes the fundamental laws of the country.[82]

We thus see Azariah reaching a conclusion similar to what was
to become one of the chief theories of Jean Bodin, the profoundest
political thinker of the age. But was Azariah aware of the intricate
difficulties involved in the notion of fundamental laws? While
Bodin could easily refer to Natural (and Divine) Law, then generally accepted as binding on all men including kings,[83] would
Azariah, too, acknowledge, that the Gentile State was founded on
Divine Law and hence was of divine origin? Obviously not. On
the contrary, he says immediately afterwards that the Jews alone
are guided by God in all external wars and indeed need a king
for no purpose whatever, because their jurisdiction, too, is based
upon laws divine.[84] It is true that Azariah seems to contradict
himself here. Shortly before, he cited with approval views expressed
by Philo and the Talmud, where the hostility of the Bible to

monarchy in Israel was explained away by the hypothesis that their demand for a king angered God because the way it had been voiced showed lack of faith, and because it was untimely, for God had willed that the kingdom should be established later in the time of David. Yet Azariah would hardly have admitted any Natural Law common to all mankind except the seven Noahide commands, which are certainly no protection against abuses of political power by monarchs.

At any rate in practice—this is doubtless the opinion of Azariah—the Jews should not interfere with the form of government in the different countries in which they are living. The less so, as their sojourn there is only temporary, their own real home being the Palestine of the future. So long, however, as they are staying in a country, they must remain faithful and obedient to its rulers, whoever they may be.[85] This notion, so remote from modern ideas of citizenship, that Jews were mere temporary sojourners in the countries of their dispersion, was very widely spread even in Renaissance Italy, and here we see again how much Azariah is representative of the dominant opinions of his time. The idea was strengthened not only by the reality—as elsewhere—of the strong Jewish autonomy which made of the Jews a state within a state, as was afterwards charged against them, but especially by the fundamental fact—the importance of which cannot easily be overestimated—that the political life of the Jews in most Italian cities of that period was based upon temporary *condottas,* the validity of which expired every ten years or so and had to be expressly renewed. Under such conditions the Jews could hardly be expected to regard themselves as more than a class of temporarily tolerated foreigners, and so indeed they actually were according to legal theory, if not altogether in point of fact. And this, of course, also intensified the old Messianic hopes of Italian Jewry.

Yet even this same legal theory made of the Jews legal contra-hents with the different states, who thus acknowledged them to possess a certain degree of equality and independence far removed from the contemporary juridical theory of the *servi cameratus* in Germany. And facts were even more expressive. In Italy, at least until the Counter-Reformation changed the position of the Jews entirely, their general social standing was comparatively high, and their relations with their Christian neighbors, especially in the educated circles, where interest in Jewish cultural values had increased considerably, had many elements of equality and mutual respect to a degree unparalleled in other European countries.[86]

So we understand why Azariah could go further in his appreciation of Gentile culture than the most advanced of his predecessors living in somewhat similar conditions under the rule of Islam, or in the earlier Christian Spain. He quotes in his works in an unprecedented manner from classical and Hellenistic literature— as was not surprising in Italy in the age of the Renaissance—and he also introduces, as mentioned above, many writings of the Fathers and teachers of the Church. Thus he speaks with the highest esteem of Augustine, whom he calls "the head of Christian sages,"[87] of Eusebius, Jerome, Aquinas and even of contemporary Christian theological scholars such as Eugubinus, Samotheus and many others. He goes even so far as to admit that the Jewish Teachers had sometimes learned from the Gentiles, as when R. Gamliel accepted a certain astronomic theory from Hipparchos and R. Ada ben Ahava took over another one from the famous Ptolemy, both of these theories relating to the calendar and, therefore, having some influence on the religious observance of the Jewish festivals.[88] And again Azariah accepts the chronology of Ficino, who supposes that Moses was a contemporary of Atalantes, the head of the Egyptian astronomers, and of his brother Prometheus, the head of the scholars in natural science, both of whom he regards as belonging to the biblical *ḥarṭumim,* forgetting his own theory that Moses was the fountain-head from which the Gentiles derived the chief elements of knowledge. Only in the fourth generation afterwards, in the writings of Hermes Trismegistus, does he discover the undoubted influence of Mosaic thought.[89] Even when the views of Christian scholars could by no means be reconciled with Jewish beliefs, as when Augustine interpreted some sentences of Hermes, or Gelenius expounded some passages in Philo so as to give support to the Christian dogma of the Son of

God, Azariah praises them for doing their best in the defense of their own religion.[90]

On this one point Azariah felt that he was in some regards an innovator. Other Jewish writers, especially among the Italians, had studied Gentile languages and literatures and had used them extensively in their own researches. Even in Azariah's native town, and among his own friends, such men were not exceptional. But Azariah used this material more abundantly than anyone else and he used it when discussing subjects of vital importance to Judaism. In so doing he risked opposition, for there was always a vivid current of hostility to Gentile studies, even in Italian Jewry. Such a letter as that written in 1490 by Jacob ben David Provençali from Naples to Messer Leon,[91] certainly expressed more than an individual view. Here we see a money-lover, of obscurantist tendencies, who barely approves of medicine as a profession, who praises alchemy as the art of easy money-making, and who rejects peremptorily any study of philosophy, especially Aristotle's.[92] No wonder, therefore, that Azariah incurred the enmity of some Jewish scholars, who charged him with abandoning the fundamentals of religion.[93]

As if to exculpate himself before the bar of Jewish opinion in Italy, and above all in other countries where Jews were more rigidly excluded from Gentile society and the distance between Jewish and non-Jewish culture was felt more strongly, Azariah devotes a special chapter (2) to proving that there is no sin in using sources of Gentile origin in order to clear up some obscure point and to establish some historical or scientific truth. He hardly misses a single occasion to repeat this justification. At the same time he denies any intention to introduce those *Kittim ve-Dodanim* where there is the slightest danger of conflict with Jewish Law or Tradition.[94] Gentile sources of information about the Bible can only be considered when supported by the Holy Scriptures themselves.[95] Furthermore, the evidence of the entire Gentile world is not strong enough to induce us to doubt the truthfulness and reliability of a Jewish tradition which reaches back to Moses on Sinai or to the inspired prophets.[96] For—says Azariah—if you doubt tradition, you must also doubt the Scriptures which have been handed down to us by the same kind of tradition.[97] This argument, in support of which Azariah quotes equally the Talmud and Augustine, was destined to play an important part in the "chief work of the Counter-Reformation,"[98] the *Disputationes* (1576-1588) of Cardinal Bellarmine, a younger contemporary of Azariah, who wrote to confute the Protestant denial of Catholic tradition. The Jewish sages, according to Azariah, were capable of error only when they spoke out of their own human reason and knowledge. Even in such cases, Gentile sources are only reliable when they are written without a special tendency, just as the evidence of a Gentile cannot be accepted by a rabbinic court unless it be an incidental statement, made in ignorance of its legal bearing.[99]

This constitutes Azariah's theory. In practice, however, it certainly was very difficult to distinguish between what was real tradition and what was human judgment in the rabbinical literature, where these two elements are steadily intermingled. Furthermore, however much he may have tried to avoid discussions which possibly involved practical issues, he never could tell what consequences would ultimately be drawn from his supposedly theoretical statements. While he was convinced that he was not touching upon a practical problem when he disproved the acknowledged system of Jewish chronology, his theory, if accepted throughout the Jewish world, might actually have involved unforeseen conclusions. Besides this, it is always dangerous to destroy the illusion of a people; it often happens that disillusionment weakens the national force, which was nourished by the untrue conception. This was what many of the Italian Jews felt. They would not have resisted Azariah's extensive use of non-Jewish sources, but they were revolted by some of his unorthodox conclusions and they afterwards forbade the reading of his work by Jews without the special permission of a rabbinic court. The large masses of the Jews in the North and East went a step further. They resented not only his conclusions, but also the way in which these were reached. In fact, Azariah's justification of the study of foreign languages and of the reading of non-Jewish books[100] was in itself a sufficient reason to prevent his books from being read by a majority of the Jews living in Poland, Germany and Turkey under quite different social conditions. The few favorable voices, such as those of R. David Gans and R. Yom-Tob Lippmann Heller, could not overcome the express disapproval of R. Joseph Karo, MHRL and R. Jacob Emden as well as the quiet, more effective ignoring of his work by the general reading public in the following generations until the nineteenth century. Even in Italy itself, the altered social conditions of the Jews resulting from the Counter-Reformation changed their attitude towards the Gentile world so that they were no longer in sympathy with Azariah's methods of thought. In his own environment, however, the views of Azariah seemed far from revolutionary and he remains the typical Jew of Renaissance Italy.

V

In some respects Azariah belonged rather to the conservative section of Italian Jewry. All his important works are written in Hebrew. For the rest, he confined himself, so far as we know, to the aforementioned verses written in honor of Duchess Margaritha of Savoy in four languages (Hebrew, Aramaic, Latin and Italian).[101] By contrast, there were among his contemporaries a considerable number of good Jews who published their most important works in Italian (e.g., his personal friend Leone da Sommi). For him social intercourse with the Gentiles and acknowledgment of the cultural values of non-Jewish literature had merely a theoretical importance. In life, especially in relation to Jewish Law, not the slightest change was to take place. Jewish Law and the performance of all the legal duties by every single Jew are so much the central point in Judaism, according to Azariah, that we must be grateful to the old Sages whose teachings have preserved Judaism and saved us from becoming like the other peoples of the world, "God forbid."[102] Those legal prescriptions, whether they be based upon the written or oral law, or whether they be precautionary regulations made by the talmudic teachers, are all eternal and cannot be changed, whatever the result of scientific investigation.[103] Even customary laws, based upon mere popular beliefs and usages, are valid and unchangeable. Respect for the Torah must be strictly maintained among the masses of the population and, therefore, nobody is permitted to preach in public against the slightest custom in Israel. And even in pure theory, whenever a conclusion may seem dangerous to some established popular belief, you may discuss it in writing, but never in speech before the whole people.[104]

This rather unusual distinction between the written and the spoken word will appear less strange in view of the fact that even in Italy of the Renaissance, the Jewish masses were regarded as too illiterate to follow a serious literary discussion. Moreover, Azariah, in his often expressed contempt for the uneducated, is again only a representative of that later stage of Italian Humanism which started as a lay, popular and democratic movement but ended by raising a new class of literati, whose haughtiness surpassed even that of the contemporary nobles. Azariah, personally rather modest, could not help being influenced by the prevailing prejudices of his class.[105]

Azariah goes so far in his acceptance of Jewish legislation in being, that he declares, in strict conformity with traditional Judaism, that every single interpretation of the earthly Sanhedrin is without doubt in agreement with the will of the Court in heaven.[106] Hence his anger against the Karaites who reject so many fundamental laws in Judaism.[107]

So extremely legalistic is Azariah's conception of Judaism, that he finds it a matter of course that the most serious men in past ages showed very little interest in purely theoretical questions, and least of all in historical ones.[108] Indeed, he finds it necessary to excuse himself for devoting so much of his own time and energy to the solution of scientific problems which could contribute nothing to the knowledge of the Halakhah. It is not without piquancy that we hear the most distinguished Jewish historian for many centuries apologizing for the time he wasted in studying history—a subject of no practical benefit. His excuses are also characteristic. He first points out that the human mind is moved by natural curiosity to find out the truth about everything. Secondly—and this Azariah considers to be more important—historical investigations enable us to clear up a few obscure points in the interpretation of the Bible and some apparent discrepancies in the statements of the talmudic sages.[109]

To be sure, not everything said in this way sounds quite sincere, and indeed much may have been written in order to conciliate popular opinion. But for us it is enough that Azariah felt obliged to make such allowances for current beliefs. He even goes a step further and develops a theory that the knowledge of history is far less important for the Jews than for the rest of the world. He quotes the famous passage from Livy—the passage so often used and abused in the time of the Renaissance—in which the Roman historian recommends the study of the past, which teaches us by examples how to seek the useful and to avoid the harmful. With all the exaggerated admiration which he, in common with his contemporaries, has for Livy,[110] Azariah declares the study of history to possess this didactic value for the Gentile world but not for the Jews. The latter have in their divine laws a sure guide for individuals as well as for the whole people. Every further investigation into the facts of the past ages for enlightenment in actual practical needs is, therefore, entirely superfluous and a mere loss of time.[111]

Such being his conviction, it was natural that his fundamental conception of history should still be based upon the traditional *theocratic* theory, once held by Jews and Christians alike,[112] while the Renaissance historiographers had already long[113] emancipated themselves from this basic conception. Whatever may be said in favor of the one view or the other, we may safely say that whilst Italian historiography of the fifteenth and sixteenth centuries in its most representative figures was laying foundations for secular, purely scientific, and, therefore, "modern" historical research, the leading Jewish historian of the period remained in his fundamental views typically "medieval."

Azariah's legalistic conception of Judaism, however, did not induce him to undervalue the Aggadic element in it which, as he tells us, brings a man nearer to the knowledge and love of God.[114] As a zealous student of Jewish ethical philosophy, he realized also that the *Miṣvot* include, above all, the "duties of the heart." Not that his philosophic concepts with regard to the subject were entirely clear. On the contrary, he was here again an eclectic who took over from the prevailing ideas of his age whatever was best suited to the most popular creeds of the day. Moreover, his opinions on fundamental ethical questions are sometimes very naive. Thus when he wants to disprove the chronology of the Persian kings as given by the Talmud, he stresses the argument that the same king who had done so much for the construction of the Second Temple could not have been delivered by God into the hands of his enemies.[115] Again, he takes it for granted that those among the high priests who were just and had not acquired their office by bribery, like their successors in the years of the decline, must have enjoyed a long life.[116] Also his solution for the problem of determinism versus free will is rather weak if compared with those of many of his medieval predecessors.[117]

It is also not strange that he fails to draw the necessary line between the Talmud and philosophy on the one hand, and the Kabbalah on the other. Although he was himself very little of a mystic, he still accepts this secret lore of Judaism as containing the real truth. (He quotes it almost exclusively by the then current expression *ḥokhmat ha-emet*.)[118] He does not even hesitate to give preference to the kabbalists over Maimonides, whom he himself so highly esteemed.[119] This was natural enough, for he was convinced, as were almost all of his contemporaries, that the chief kabbalistic books were really composed by the Tannaim to whom they have been ascribed,[120] albeit he confesses that there are later interpolations in the *Zohar*. But this does not hinder him from absolutely rejecting the well-known suspicions entertained against Moses de Leon, as then already voiced by Abraham Zacuto.[121] So high is his esteem for Kabbalah that he does not entirely reject even practical Kabbalah, and while quoting the sharp expressions of Maimonides against the writers of amulets, he merely demands caution against misuse of these magic spells by incompetent persons, but he does not object to them altogether.[122]

In his relation to mysticism Azariah was a child of his age. He had no taste for kabbalistic speculation and certainly not for kabbalistic practice. But this was the period of the climax in the development of the secret science, and the time when Luria and his admirers in Palestine exercised their highest influence upon the whole Jewish world and especially upon Italian Jewry. Even the Gentile world in that country had shown for a long time a deep interest in the mysteries of this Jewish occult wisdom; it is enough to mention, in this connection, the glorious youth, Giovanni Pico della Mirandola, whom Azariah quotes a few times with the highest esteem.[123] In fact, Kabbalah was in the air and there was no reason for Azariah to stand aloof. When he writes about Kabbalah he voices the regnant views of his time rather than his own original inclinations.

VI

This high esteem of the Kabbalah chiefly depended, no doubt, upon its supposed antiquity, at a time when all works of ancient origin, regardless of their intrinsic literary value, inspired such an exaggerated reverence. Moreover, one of the fundamental points in the philosophy of life of the period was the thought that the best things belong to the past. In modern times, our watchword is progress and we instinctively regard human history, notwithstanding its ebbs and flows, as a development from lower to higher forms. This idea of evolution and progress was entirely strange to the mind of a Renaissance man. On the contrary, since the Middle Ages the dominant idea in this regard had been rather of continual degeneration. This fundamental conception was so much strengthened by the Renaissance worship of everything antique, that it could even be generally believed that the body of a woman in ancient times must have been far superior in beauty to that of any modern lady.[124]

No matter whether the general innate psychological tendency to be *laudatores temporis acti*[125] is to be made responsible for this belief, or whether it is rather due to the religious supposition that the further away from Creation the more distant the world becomes from the Creator and, therefore, the more imperfect, Jew and Christian were equally certain that past ages were incontestably superior to their own. Christendom certainly was highly influenced by the dogma of original sin which involved the steady decline of mankind, only partly checked by its supernatural redemption. Its picture of the world, consequently, was essentially pessimistic; the earth was but a vale of tears stumbling down the ages towards a deplorable end on the day of the Last Judgment. Judaism, to be sure, laid far less stress on the idea of Adam's sin and looked forward in a spirit of decided optimism to the Messianic age, but it was so dependent upon Bible and Talmud that it could not help admitting as pre-eminent the epochs to which these great documents belonged. Revelation, God's words to Moses and to the prophets, whether written down in the Holy Scriptures or handed down through oral tradition, are the immovable foundations, and how can later generations be compared with that age of giants? As for the Jews' radiant hopes for the Messianic future, may not the advent of the Messiah be expected just as readily when things are at their worst? We have seen also that Azariah—in conformity with some high medieval authorities—minimizes the importance of the Messianic age as compared with the really final end, the world to come. If Eduard von Hartmann's famous statement is correct, that antiquity looked for happiness in this world, the Middle Ages in the world hereafter, and we modern men in the world hereafter as realized in this world (through the process of evolution), we see here medieval Judaism following the general trend of the period and neglecting the more modern ideal of Messianism in this world for the sake of the medieval ideal of the life to come. Furthermore, if the Western world in general had real historical reasons, in addition to these theoretical ones, to acknowledge the superiority of classical culture, how much more reason had the Jew to glorify the age of his national freedom and power? The less he actually knew about the real conditions of life in those remote ages, the more light he saw and the less shadow.

No wonder that Azariah viewed the past as a son of his age. Thus he accepts the explanation given by Naḥmanides for the abridgment of human life after the Deluge as caused chiefly by the weakening of the air.[126] So strongly does he believe in the superiority of ancient times that he uses it as an argument to prove his theory on chronology, because otherwise we should be led to the obviously impossible conclusion that the Reform of the calendar by Hillel II enabled the Jews to live more directly under the guidance of God than before.[127] Azariah holds, as we have seen, that the customary laws in Israel, derived from the wisdom of their ancestors, have to survive even when their original raison d'être is lost. Going further, he feels himself in duty bound to find an explanation, not only for everything handed down by tradition which, being divine in origin, needs no further defense, but also for all the occasional mistakes made by the sages when they spoke for themselves alone. To admit the possibility of such mistakes was in itself daring, and Azariah devotes more than one argument— as we have seen—to excusing himself for doing so. But even to him it seemed obvious that the later commentators of the Bible could not have "seen more" than the talmudic authorities.[128]

On the other hand, the scientific investigations of Azariah must have shown him that the later authorities often came nearer the truth than their predecessors.[129] Indeed, the basis for all his life's work was a firm conviction that thorough investigation into the original sources or facts would enable him to correct some erroneous views of the Talmud about chronology, about some geographic data, and other topics. Moreover, he saw quite clearly from his own practical experience that for the investigation of almost all sources it is preferable to use the latest available edition. In that period of the awakening scientific spirit, many new editions of classical works—almost critical editions in our sense—were constantly appearing. Especially in the case of Greek authors, almost all editors had begun to cite the original texts first, instead of the Latin translations exclusively in use until that time in the Western countries. It was such an edition, for instance, that Azariah himself had to use for his translation of the Letter of Aristeas.[130]

How was he to reconcile this apparent contradiction? Azariah uses for this purpose an old simile: that of the pygmies, who are seated on the shoulders of giants and, therefore, enjoy the wider outlook.[131] But was not this already a somewhat dangerous concession? The next step would be to conclude that the later generations, notwithstanding their inferior capacity, were enabled to reach a higher intellectual level than the ancients, whose accumulated knowledge was at their disposal, and finally one might be led to question that inferior capacity itself. What would remain then of the dogma of the progressive deterioration of humanity throughout the ages? In the last statement, which we have quoted from Azariah, he appears almost to have abandoned this dogma. Here again he was not conscious of his inconsistency.

However, all these inconsistencies are due not so much to Azariah's lack of capacity as to his essential method. They are intrinsically connected with his whole syncretistic attitude toward the different manifestations of the human mind. In this respect Azariah genuinely belonged to the Italian Renaissance, although only in its earlier stage, when people like Pico proclaimed the unity of the human spirit expressing itself through ancient and medieval philosophy, through Kabbalah and science, through Christianity, Judaism and Islam. But even here Azariah would not have dared to follow such a syncretist as Ficino, who declared that it is of less consequence to God how he is worshiped, than that he be indeed worshiped. Moreover, the essential content of Azariah's thought can hardly be described as an expression of the spirit of the Renaissance.

"It was in general," says Giovanni Gentile,[132] "the esthetic conception of human reality, which Humanism upheld against the medieval outlook." In Azariah there is not the slightest sign of such a conception. Indeed, just as the Jews in general had only little part in Renaissance art, the finest and profoundest manifestations of that age, or in the calling into existence of the new State as a work of art, so also Azariah's conception of life is anything but esthetic. In all essentials he still belongs to the Middle Ages. His cosmology is Ptolemaic medieval, his physical world is explained entirely by the Aristotelian medieval physics, his conception of history, the chief field of his activity, is theocratically medieval to an extreme. In the field of geography he was bound to acknowledge the new facts, but he was able to do so without giving up the fundamental conceptions of the old Ptolemaic lore. Above all, philosophy together with science is for him, as it was for the good old Middle Ages, a "handmaiden of theology."

In one point, however, there is in Azariah's teaching an important element of progress. He was not essentially a man of the Renaissance (there were few such among the Jews, except for Leone Ebreo) but neither were his ideas ultimately dependent upon the Islamic Middle Ages. What he undertook was an attempt (not the first but certainly the ablest) to reconcile Judaism with the Christian Middle Ages as well as with the early Renaissance in its newer, although not yet revolutionary, reinterpretation of classical antiquity. Azariah tried to do with Christendom what the great Spanish Jews had done with the Arabian world. As the Jews were destined to live more and more in Christian surroundings, and as the Christian nations were about to assume leadership in the further progress of mankind, his attempted synthesis, however backward-looking, contained a large promise for the future. Furthermore, it was of the highest importance that he acknowledged new discoveries in the natural world, that he tried to bring them into agreement with Judaism and not to explain them away. This was the only attitude which augured well for the time to come in a world where the volume of scientifically known facts had just begun to increase in an unprecedented degree.

These promises had to remain unfulfilled, however. By a tragic coincidence Azariah lived to witness in the course of his adult life the rise and growth of the Catholic Counter-Reformation. Twenty years before his death, he witnessed the sudden change of the Church's policy toward the Jews from that of relative kindness, often even of protection, to open antagonism. Catholicism, endangered in its very existence, struggled with renewed force against everything non-Catholic within and without. How difficult it was under these conditions to persevere in the attempt to reconcile the Christian with the Jewish worlds! The more difficult because the next and most hopeful step led towards reconciliation with Catholic scholasticism—a step pursued by Azariah. But the renewed vigor of Catholic scholastic thought, which found expression in the neo-Scholastic movement of a Bellarmine and a Suárez, was in fact a product as well as a tool of the Counter-Reformation, and its general hostile attitude toward Judaism was a formidable obstacle to mutual understanding.

Furthermore, this neo-Scholastic movement itself was doomed to failure. All the new influences of the time were against it. The modern state, early capitalism, the dissolution of the medieval society, the amazing progress in natural science, the development of rationalism—all these broke up the monumental structure raised by the medieval Church. The combination of the super-rational elements of religion with the rationalism of science, attempted by both Jewish and Christian Scholasticism, could not withstand the destructive forces which abolished all the scientific conceptions in these closed uniform systems. Thus the Church withdrew more and more into the domain of the Christian Dogma, as formulated by the Tridentine Council. Judaism, too, retired more and more into the realm of Halakhah. It still tried for a time to cultivate the super-rational element in the Kabbalah, which reminds us of a somewhat analogous attempt made within the Catholic Church by Pascal and later by the Romanticists to release religion from all rationalistic bounds. But the Jewish leaders soon recognized that if this mystical lore was somehow to serve as a bridge to the external world, Jews would use it only to walk out (Shabbetai Zevi and Jacob Frank) while nobody would use it to come in.

So the Jews returned more and more exclusively to their old firm basis, the four ells of the Halakhah, ignoring, as far as possible, all the changes in the external world. Thus the majority of the Jews who lived in Catholic countries (Poland, southern Germany and Italy) were in many ways nearer to the time of the Saboraim and the early Geonim than to the immediate past of the later Middle

Ages. Only in little Protestant Holland was the small Jewish minority able to persevere for a time in its endeavor to reconcile religion and modern thought.

As a matter of fact, however, the line of development was broken. Only a much later age, originating (and not by mere chance) in equally Protestant Prussia, was destined to accomplish what the Italian Renaissance had failed to do. But when Leopold Zunz, in more than one respect spiritually related to Azariah (whose life and works he recounted to a later and attentive Jewish world), resumed the old effort of his Italian predecessor to harmonize the two aspects of culture, he had to start anew.

9

Azariah de' Rossi's
Historical Method*

THE SIXTEENTH CENTURY REPRESENTS one of the high points in Jewish historiography. In contrast to its ancestors' imposing productions during the biblical and Hellenistic antiquity, medieval Jewry failed to bring forth any major historical work in the true sense of that term. Next to *Yosippon,* which was but an abridged semi-folkloristic paraphrase of Josephus, the main historical works consisted of chronicles, or pious exhortations in the form of chronicles, which, invaluable as historical sources, cannot by any stretch of imagination be considered historiographic works.

Even the Spanish-Muslim period, despite Ibn Daud, did not produce any genuine historian. This is the more surprising, since the Arabic literature of the period included a series of major historical writings, some of which can stand comparison with modern works in this field. True, the greatest Arabic historian, Ibn Khaldun, wrote at a time and in an area where he could no longer exert any creative influence upon Jewish authors. But in the preceding centuries, writers of the Jewish "golden age" in Spain had before them not only their ancient letters, but also more than one remarkable Arabic model which they could imitate in developing an historical literature of their own, written in a more or less modern vein.

Be this as it may, it was only the great migrations of the fifteenth and sixteenth centuries which reawakened the historic interest among Jews. Was it their great disappointment over the

---

* Revised translation of *"La méthode historique d'Azaria de' Rossi,"* *REJ,* LXXXVI (1928), 151-75; LXXXVII (1929), 43-78; also reprint, Paris, 1929.

present, manifesting itself in part in stormy Messianic movements, which also turned many eyes toward the past? Was it nostalgia for their beloved Peninsular fatherlands and the ancestral tombs which inspired their lively concern for matters of the past? Or was it simply the very migratory movements, with all the portentous changes they entailed, which offered the Jews direct familiarity with new countries and peoples and made them better understand the relativity of history? Whatever the cause, the sixteenth century suddenly witnessed the appearance among Jews, during two or three generations, of a whole array of historians approaching the European level of that period.

It is generally conceded that the first place among them is held by Azariah de' Rossi, long celebrated as the "founder of historical criticism" among Jews. His work was particularly influential during the renaissance of Jewish historical studies in the nineteenth century. However, if we wish to go beyond a mere comparison between him and other Jewish historians and place him within the framework of the historiography of the Italian Renaissance, to which he truly belongs, our evaluation of his work may become more tempered, but it will also be more just.[1]

I

From the outset we detect a fundamental difference between Azariah and most of his Christian contemporaries with respect to the *aim* of history. While Renaissance historiography considered history an eminently practical, one might almost say applied, science, it remained pure theory to Azariah. He had none of the pretentiousness of those Italian historians-publicists who believed that from their towering seats of judgment they could confer distinctions or censures, honors or blame on past and present generations.[2] He barely believed that in his specialized domain of Jewish history one could apply to history the designation of a teacher of life. We recall how, with respect to Jews, he expressly rejected Livy's adage, which saw the function of history as teaching man to search for the useful and to avoid the harmful.[3] Azariah believed that the Jews had always lived under the Lord's immediate guidance and that they possessed in their own divine law an assured teacher prescribing for them the precise road to follow under all of life's exigencies, collective as well as personal.[4] Here Azariah adopted in an amazing fashion the regnant view of the Jewish Middle Ages, and time and again he excused himself for spending so much time on history, since, in fact, "what was, was."[5] Clearly, one could not draw important historical conclusions for the religious law as such which, according to the dominant opinion of halakhic Judaism, alone merited intensive study. Azariah agreed, and professed to see the sole justification for historical research in the contributions it might make to the understanding of the ancient sources of tradition. It is sad to think that a people who had once played a most magnificent creative role in the domain of history should have come to such an impasse!

Faithful to this principle, Azariah concerned himself but little with contemporary or recent history. Once, to be sure, he wrote a description of an event which had profoundly influenced the course of his life, the Ferrara earthquake of 1570. But even this little tract was written as a sort of introduction explaining his subsequent literary activity. Otherwise Azariah's dissertations, which one might call "Essays and Studies," are principally devoted to ancient Jewish history.

One cannot attribute this self-imposed limitation to the general penchant of the Renaissance to return to classical antiquity. For most of the distinguished Renaissance historians had concentrated on more recent periods. The Florentines, Bruni, Machiavelli, and Guicciardini, almost exclusively treated the modern history of their extraordinary republic.[6] In other parts of Italy, as well as in other countries, the more recent past likewise constituted the principal subject of historic research, the older periods often being disposed of in brief introductions.

Undoubtedly one reason for this concentration was that many Italian histories were written on a government's initiative, the latter being, of course, interested most in the description of recent events in a light favorable to it. Most of the Italian historians, moreover, had come from some active occupations and thus, both through previous experience and personal interest, had become particularly concerned about recent events.[7] From the scholarly viewpoint, too, the closer their work was to contemporary life, the more records they had at their disposal. The humanists may have looked down upon many sources written in barbaric Latin, but they recognized the value of their data on important facts. Indeed, the more barbaric the style of these sources, the easier it was for a Renaissance historian to display his skill in elegantly retelling the old story. Antiquity, on the contrary, had long been presented by master historians with whom few Renaissance men dared to compete.

In Azariah's case the opposite was true. He was neither a statesman with personal experience in public affairs nor even an active rabbi who, through his ministerial functions, could acquire practical insights. History for him necessarily was but a theoretical science. Nor could he count on any rewarding commissions, but in fact he had to exert much effort to see his book printed.[8] The paucity of medieval Jewish sources was likewise discouraging.[9]

Among the noteworthy Renaissance historians, Flavius Blondus is the one most akin to Azariah, although in his principal work, *Decades,* he, too, treated almost exclusively of medieval developments. He himself declared that after the great historians down to Orosius, ancient history required no further investigation.[10] Azariah was in the more favorable position of being free from this respect for higher authority. While holding Josephus in high esteem, he did not regard him as a canonical source. The truly authoritative talmudic and rabbinic sources, on the other hand, contained but few historical expositions with which he might have to disagree. At the same time he could not always avoid discussing subjects having a bearing on the history of his own time. His detailed studies of the Jewish chronology, in particular, could have practical repercussions among his Jewish contemporaries despite his disclaimers.

An examination of the histories emanating from the school of Blondus will easily reveal that the closer they approach the mid-sixteenth century, the greater an interest they evince in ancient history, so that Azariah is by no means a unique phenomenon among his immediate contemporaries. He himself felt the effects of the Counter-Reformation at the end of his life. Because of the introduction of a strict ecclesiastical censorship, many writers no longer dared to describe contemporary or even medieval events with the same freedom as before, for their descriptions might conflict with the accepted views of the Church. This fear of censorship also played a role in Azariah's approach.

Another effect of the Counter-Reformation was even more decisive.[11] The deep and overwhelming respect for antiquity which had theretofore prevented any attempt to compete with the classical authors greatly diminished. The intervening two centuries since Blondus had also posed new problems, uncovered new points of view and offered new solutions. The keen mind of Machiavelli, in particular, had opened the historians' eyes to some intrinsic relationships between diverse historical developments which could not possibly be satisfied with the historiographic tools of a Livy. Moreover, through his solid archeological and medieval works, Blondus had achieved totally unexpected results even for ancient *realia*. To the school of Blondus belonged especially historians like Panvinio (1529-68), Sigonio (1523/4-84) and Robortello (1516-67), all more or less contemporaries of Azariah. Next to medieval and contemporary history, it was the ancient institutions which attracted the attention of these scholars, Sigonio even writing a *De republica Hebraeorum*. In more than one respect Azariah belongs to this group of polyhistors. He is not as prolific as Panvinio who, despite his premature death, left behind almost an entire library.[12] But one must not forget that de' Rossi had waited almost sixty years before starting to write. For the few years of his advanced age which remained to him, his is a truly prodigious production both in quantity and variety.

II

Although Azariah entered his literary career without much practical experience and did not pursue any utilitarian goals, he never completely lost contact with actual life. He pictures his readers—and this is another point he had in common with Renaissance writers—as a group actively interested in his work; he never loses sight of them and frequently addresses them directly.[13] True, his original optimism concerning their kindly disposition toward him was greatly toned down as a result of the attacks which followed the publication of his work. In his defense he writes resignedly that the sympathy of readers for any author and their desire to avoid misunderstandings ultimately depend on "heavenly assistance."[14] But in his main work he confidently expects a benevolent reception and he begs his audience to weigh his intention equitably even wherever it disagrees with them.[15] He hopes that his book will be well received both by men of culture and the masses.[16] Only while excusing an opinion which might appear unorthodox, does he add that it is really addressed to the superior intellectual class.[17]

For the benefit of his readers, Azariah claims, he wrote his book in the form of disparate studies on more or less important questions of detail. After a lengthy discussion of the methodological advantages and disadvantages of expositions entirely dedicated to single problems as against those forming series of "essays," he decides in favor of the latter approach for it offers something "resembling a garden in which each visitor can choose the flower or fruit which appeals to him most.[18]

Another important consideration was the prevalence in contemporary Italian historiography since Bruni of the annalistic form of presentation, borrowed from Livy and other ancient historians. As a result, one could not treat matters extending beyond a single year before completing the story of the other unconnected events of the same year, thus covering a variety of subjects within a relatively short space.[19] Azariah was sufficiently independent to free himself from these annalistic shackles, whereas Joseph ha-

Kohen, for example, was unable to do so.[20] But Azariah may indeed have preferred not to subject the patience of his readers, spoiled by this type of exposition, to the trying "monotony" of a single subject.

Such disconnected essays were not altogether rare in the contemporary Italian literature. Here again antiquity furnished a model. Imitating the *Noctes Atticae* by Aulus Gellius, a second-century collection of literary and historical essays widely read in the Middle Ages and early modern times,[21] a number of Humanists published similar works. Allessandro d'Alessandro called his book, published in Rome in 1522, quite simply *Dies geniales.* Azariah may also have been influenced by Rhodiginus (Lodovico Celio Ricchieri da Rovigo, 1460-1525) and his *Antiquae lectiones,* for he cites both him and Gellius twice.[22]

De' Rossi doubtless realized that this method would entail many repetitions. He also sensed that he was often citing too many sources duplicating one another with but minor modifications. Here again he advanced the pedagogic excuse that such repetition would make the reader comprehend the subject more easily.[23] In his polemical tract *Maṣref,* where he was more than usually redundant, he declared that his opponents' hostility forced him to make his points doubly clear.[24] Are these reasons sufficiently valid or could at least some repetitions have been avoided by the author's greater literary skill? It is difficult for us to judge. Like the other Renaissance authors, Azariah appears more verbose in certain areas and more concise in others than writers of our times. On the other hand, this method allows him to avoid extensive digressions, an advantage of which he is fully cognizant.[25]

His essayistic form does not prevent Azariah from occasionally presenting lengthy dissertations. Not only is his translation of the *Letter of Aristeas,* placed outside the main work, rather lengthy, but he also devotes four large chapters of his *Imre binah* to the relationships between Philo and traditional Judaism, five to the shape of the priestly vestments, six to the Hebrew language, alphabet and poetry, and the entire third section to researches pertaining to Jewish chronology. The latter section occupies such a focal position in Azariah's entire work that it has often made students forget his other scholarly contributions.

Another intrinsic connection linking these detached studies consists in their clearly apologetic aim. Azariah may constantly affirm his objective quest for truth above everything else[26]—and he possibly believes it—but his work is no less permeated with the desire to defend the Jewish tradition before the Gentile world at all costs.

Not that he was ever prepared to commit outright forgeries of the kind then perpetrated by Annius de Viterbo. Nor was he capable of making conscious textual alterations, a practice so insidiously indulged in by Jovius. But his point of departure was that the Bible in its traditional form, being of divine origin, could not be affected by any human reasoning and that the Jewish tradition, too, in so far as it went back to Moses, was no less sacred and unshakable. Hence arose his basic difficulty of reconciling these sources with other records he considered trustworthy. How often was he, therefore, obliged to present forced, even untenable solutions! This was also the case when two traditional sources controverted each other. A purely historical critique could simply recognize such contradictions and explain them by differences in time or personal preference. But, adhering to his principle that both conflicting statements contained the whole truth, Azariah resorted to daring speculations. At the same time he had to admit that, if he were compared with the distinguished halakhists of the period, his talmudic education would leave something to be desired. Nevertheless, he advanced many a risky opinion which pursued no other aim than to save the honor of all documents sanctified by tradition.

Apart from such dogmatic restraints, Azariah displays great honesty in his researches. He not only refuses to resort to some subterfuge which might prove untenable elsewhere,[27] but he also considers it one of the sages' wisest teachings that "there is nothing more honorable for a man than to correct his earlier contentions even where he does not run the risk of being proved mistaken by someone else."[28] In fact, on more than one occasion he himself withdrew opinions previously stated.[29]

In general, his method of exposition is judicious and calm. Despite the prolixity of his style and the personal tone then generally in use, the tenor of his works is quite reserved. Only exceptionally, when deeply hurt by personal attacks, does he lose his equanimity. The *Maṣref,* in particular, an outright polemical tract, includes many a passage devoted to a sharp repudiation of his adversaries.[30] On occasion he even uses strong language in his polemics.[31]

Compared with the invectives current among the contemporary Italian historians, however—not to speak of that clever blackmailer, Pietro Aretino—Azariah's style was both dignified and restrained. One illustration may suffice. When Joseph Karo had completed his *Commentary* on Maimonides, Azariah actively collaborated in the collection of funds to cover the cost of printing.[32] Nevertheless, after the publication of the *Me'or 'Eynaim,* Karo arrayed himself with Azariah's opponents and, according to later testimony, wished to excommunicate his book. Azariah must have heard something about that hostile plan.[33] Yet even while combating an interpretation by Karo in his *Maṣref,* he did it in very dignified terms, appropriate for a purely objective analysis.[34] It was only when an attack was aimed not at his person but at Judaism or the Jewish tradition, particularly by Karaites, that Azariah lost all his composure and sometimes resorted to outright maledictions.[35] Incidentally, he compensated for these few malevolent outbursts by benedictions and other pious liturgical formulas which he added, particularly at the end of chapters.

Azariah employs a rich and tense language which is quite in consonance with the tastes of his Italian contemporaries, and appears quite irreproachable to us. Strongly influenced by biblical Hebrew, his style approximates most that of the Mishnah, but it is enriched by many more recent Hebrew and even Aramaic words borrowed from the Talmud and medieval literature. It expresses the author's ideas fluently and in a manner easily understood by the readers even when he treats of extremely complicated problems.[36] For Azariah Hebrew is his true literary medium. He not only masters it with ease but contributes some fundamental theoretical observations to its knowledge at the end of his work and in numerous detailed philological comments scattered through many chapters. Italian, which doubtless was his spoken mother tongue, was much less familiar to him, as is evidenced by his letter to the Abbot of Monte Cassino.[37] In addition, like most cultivated men of his time, he understood Latin well and even had some smattering of Greek.[38] But when, in a noteworthy passage, he alludes to Hebrew as a spoken language, one need not take him literally.[39]

De' Rossi's style has another pleasing feature: it is not excessively sophisticated. In their puristic zeal the Humanists were often induced to abandon scholarly precision and to replace medieval Latin terms by "classical" designations drawn from an entirely different environment. Among Jewish historians Joseph ha-Kohen, in particular, in his almost exclusively biblical style, imitated that mannerism and used biblical phrases to describe wholly unrelated medieval realities.[40] Azariah, who, as we have seen, generally adopted the language of the Mishnah, was in a much better position to reconcile his form with the content.

Azariah's mode of exposition reveals another superior feature when compared with the majority of his Jewish and Christian predecessors. The most distinguished Humanists, particularly of the Florentine school, following Livy (and Thucydides) interlaced their stories with speeches which had evidently never been delivered but which were intended to convey to the reader the motives behind the described actions and to keep him interested. In Jewish historiography this mannerism was adopted by Joseph ha-Kohen, while Ibn Verga laid his main emphasis upon the dialogue. Azariah was able to avoid that pitfall, perhaps because of his particular non-activist conception of the aim of history. Not so greatly concerned with setting historical examples for action, Azariah could easily dispense with this expedient and limit himself to the examination of sources which—and this was his main historical objective —would enable the students better to comprehend the great literary monuments of the past. Needless to say he is not alone in this approach; quite a few Italian polyhistors who compiled and criticized documents were less skillful littérateurs than they were erudites.

Azariah's general restraint also made him sparing in his use of the literary device so successfully cultivated by Ibn Verga and many Italian historians, who enlivened their narratives by inserting from time to time a sort of platonic dialogue. Azariah wrote only one chapter in the form of a dialogue, which was intended to justify his chronological theories.[41] In his study of Philo he resorted to the somewhat related procedure of first enumerating all the virtues of the Alexandrine philosopher, and then turning around and becoming an accuser reciting an entire repertory of Philo's faults. He blamed Philo, in particular, for his ignorance of the Hebrew Bible and his deviations from the Palestinian Halakhah. At the end he went over the same subject point by point and advanced a whole series of replies, in part quite forced, to his most decisive charges.[42] In any case, this rather judicious argument pro and con will hardly annoy the modern reader.

Notwithstanding his avowed desire to captivate the readers' interest, Azariah refrained from any extensive use of pleasant anecdotes, as was often done by Ibn Verga, Ibn Yaḥya and most Christian Renaissance historians. When on one occasion he felt impelled to inject a little story into a special note, he offered an excuse for it.[43] At the same time he did not hesitate to illumine a problem under discussion by referring to certain facts or usages known to the reader.[44] But since he principally dealt with ancient problems, such parallels, too, were reduced to a minimum.

In contrast to the rather haphazard mode of presentation by Ibn Verga,[45] Azariah follows a fairly well-organized plan of composition and description.[46] His division into "books" has nothing of the artificiality which often encumbers the works of even the more eminent Renaissance historians; his "books" have a rather natural sequence, following with a certain continuity the subjects, or groups of subjects, treated in them. Only the transition from the first to the second book of his main work is somewhat blurred. His division into chapters is likewise, for the most part, justified by content. Within each chapter, to be sure, he often interrupts his investigation with digressions, heaping proofs in one place and being too succinct in another, or referring to earlier or later discussions when there is no necessity to do so. But in this matter, too, his Jewish predecessors and even his Italian contemporaries did not do much better.

Another feature merits consideration. Azariah is a pious Jew, believing with his whole soul in miracles generally, and in those described in the Bible in particular. Nor does he entertain the slightest doubts concerning Israel's forthcoming miraculous delivery by God.[47] Nevertheless, he carefully refrains from inserting miraculous stories into his exposition. The absence of this element, which so greatly overloads the narratives of most medieval chroniclers, is one of the principal achievements of Renaissance historiography. If a historian like Platina, writing on papal orders (he is occasionally quoted by Azariah[48]), is able to set aside the legendary embellishments so important in the ecclesiastical tradition without shocking his patrons, our author reveals an equal discretion in the area of Jewish history. In this respect he is clearly distinguished not only from the medieval chroniclers but also in particular from Zacuto, Ibn Verga[49] and Ibn Yaḥya.

III

Whatever merits de' Rossi attained in the art of composition, they were not his main claim to fame. What made him the leading Jewish historian of his time was his critical examination of sources. To be sure, his achievements in this domain do not quite deserve the paeans of praise of his nineteenth-century admirers. We shall presently see the limits and defects of his critique, even if measured against the standards of his own time. Nonetheless his work constitutes a tremendous advance in the Jewish historical literature.

He is indubitably strongest in his textual criticism. To begin with, the Renaissance historians had taught him not to be content with readily available source editions. Being a bibliophile by nature, he always sought out older editions and manuscripts. Although he does not seem to have been wealthy at any period of his life,[50] we occasionally learn from his casual references that his library contained a number of relatively rare editions as well as manuscripts precious by virtue of both age and quality. He cites, for example, two three-centuries old manuscripts of the *Yelamdenu* which he had in his possession.[51] Nor did he spare efforts to collate the best texts available in other libraries, public or private. He mentions the manuscript of R. Meir ha-Levi's *Decisions* on the tractate Baba Batra, dating from 1307, which was the property of his brother-in-law;[52] also a beautiful manuscript of Rashi on the entire Bible written in 1312,[53] as well as two vocalized manuscripts going back to the middle of the eleventh century.[54] He consulted all manuscripts, editions and translations to which he had access,[55] in order critically to examine doubtful texts. He was even able to distinguish groups within different editions of the same work. He contrasts, for example, the *Yosippon* of the Turkish edition with the edition printed in Venice which was derived from the former and with the independent German and the two Conat editions.[56]

Azariah does not limit himself to printed books and manuscripts. True, he did not have at his disposal inscriptions similar to those copiously utilized by the entire Blondus school and particularly by Panvinio. Wherever he could, as in the study of the ancient Hebrew script, he made use of ancient Hebrew coins and, on two occasions, he rejoiced over that opportunity.[57] Here he was putting to good use the more refined methods of contemporary experts. Italian numismatics made tremendous strides during the sixteenth century.[58]

If his collector's tastes and his zeal for studies make Azariah a child of his age,[59] the Renaissance had also taught him that the oldest editions were not necessarily the best. That age of awakening criticism had produced new editions of ancient authors which offered far more reliable vehicles for research because of the utilization of original texts (particularly in Greek) and fairly careful source criticism. Azariah himself thus recognized from the outset that, in order to translate the *Letter of Aristeas,* he would have to secure the most authentic texts available.[60] In general he sought to assemble the best possible sources for the investigation of his special subject of inquiry, even if the results thus obtained might ultimately prove erroneous. By acquainting the readers with his sources and his ultimate decisions as to their respective merits, he felt, students would be in a better position to check him.[61]

Going beyond research into all available texts, Azariah quite frequently subjected them to a philosophical critique which strikes us as being almost modern. He seeks to explain some terms by their Greek etymology, although he is not always successful.[62] In studying the permutations in the pronunciation of *he* and *het,*[63] he takes into account the geographic differences in pronunciation.[64] He does not even seem to be disturbed by having to suggest etymologies from languages with which he was not fully familiar.[65] Explanations of words were important to him not only for the clarification of specific texts, but also for their own sake. When he tries, for example, to elucidate the etymology of the term Essenes, which, incidentally, still is under debate today,[66] he derives from it conclusions concerning the nature of that movement.[67]

With this equipment Azariah was able ocassionally to emend the texts of given editions. From time to time he postulates copyists' errors even in the Talmud, Septuagint and Josephus.[68] He believes that he can explain away an erroneous term in Maimonides by assuming that it was a scribe's mistake.[69] He is not altogether circumspect, however, in these textual criticisms. He ventures to correct "Jannaeus" into "Agrippa," although he cannot possibly attribute it to an error in transcription.[70] In another connection, however, he advances the more plausible reason that the text had been copied from a poorly preserved old manuscript.[71] If, on one occasion, he refrains from emending the figure of 180 to 140, he does it not because he is afraid of daring corrections, but because the former number is the subject of a lengthy discussion in the Talmud which, if the figure were changed, would become meaningless.[72]

In any case, the extant talmudic texts seem to him above criticism.[73] Even if he proposes some correction, as in the aforementioned example, he does it with extreme caution and only after very careful consideration. Nowhere does he concede the existence of interpolated passages in the Talmud while he postulates them in almost all other texts dating from approximately the same period. With respect to the Bible, including the book of Chronicles, he refuses energetically and firmly to admit any foreign accretions, although he is familiar with the theory intimated by Ibn Ezra at the beginning of his *Commentary* on Deuteronomy.[74]

Such conservatism toward the literature sanctified by tradition sharply contrasts with his ideas about the rights and duties of editors of more recent and less authoritative documents. Azariah believes that, if an editor finds in an ancient manuscript a reading which appears both more correct and in full consonance with the dogmatic principles of Judaism, he is justified, even obliged, to enter the better text into his edition without further ado.[75] Even where an established text seems to him faulty for dogmatic reasons only, Azariah urges the editor not to limit himself to a correction in a note but rather simply to suppress the incriminated phrases.[76] It is evident that like most of his contemporaries, Azariah did not hesitate to give preference to dogma when it conflicted with science.

IV

In source criticism Azariah's works are far less impressive. Not that he lacked understanding for it, but one must take account of the generally slow advances of the critical schools in that period, and the special limitations on Azariah's freedom to criticize his sources. Renaissance historiography made here, too, sufficient progress to overshadow anything of that type done in the Middle Ages. Names like Bruni, Blondus, and particularly Lorenzo Valla, prove the extent to which foundations had already been laid for the modern type of source criticism. But naturally we cannot apply our own criteria to these men and we may do it even less in the case of Azariah.

From the outset Azariah started from premises which necessarily excluded any detached scholarly criticism. He happened to be working on historical periods, the main sources for which he approached with particular restraint. Above all, he admitted no critique in the case of the Bible. He himself stated expressly that anything found in the Pentateuch and the later biblical books "must not be the subject of critical research because it is absolutely beyond any doubt, for who is the man who would allow himself to cross the path of our king, our God?"[77] He so firmly believed in the sacrosanct position of the Bible's masoretic text that he viewed any assertion contradicting the Masorah as wholly nonsensical.[78] He also unquestioningly followed tradition with respect to the authors of biblical books. He considers Moses the inventor of the dialogue, for he attributes to him, though not with complete confidence, the authorship of the book of Job.[79] For him Ecclesiastes is the work of Solomon,[80] just as Chronicles are that of Ezra. Nevertheless he allows himself transparent doubts concerning the relationships between Chronicles and Ezra, doubts echoed also by modern biblical criticism, though more with respect to the book of Ezra than to his personality.[81]

Azariah also shared his contemporaries' views about the ancient Bible versions. He never expressed doubts about the origin of the Septuagint from a translation of seventy or seventy-two elders made at the invitation of an Egyptian king, as told in the *Letter of Aristeas* which he had translated from the Latin into Hebrew. It is doubly remarkable, therefore, that sometimes he spoke of the version "attributed" to the seventy elders.[82] On the other hand, he belonged to the few men of his time who clearly sensed the difference between Onkelos and 'Aqilas. He actually devoted an entire chapter (XLV) to the analysis of these differences. He confused, however, Jonathan (whose rendition of the Prophets was accessible to him in print, while he knew the Pentateuch version only in manuscript) with the Tanna Jonathan ben 'Uziel in accordance with the traditional interpretation. Hence he made of him a predecessor of both Onkelos and 'Aqilas.[83] He even believed that 'Aqilas had prepared his Greek version under the combined influence of both Jonathan and Onkelos. True, his critical perspicacity could not overlook passages in "Jonathan" which could not possibly date back to the ancient period. But he got out of this difficulty with the aid of the old expedient of declaring such passages later interpolations.[84] Also of interest are his views on the mutual relationship between Jonathan and the Jerusalem Targum.[85] He is also familiar with other ancient versions.[86] Quite frequently he refers to Theodotion, Symmachus, Jerome and the Vulgate. He also knows of the existence of the Hexapla.[87] He even refers to Saadia's Arabic translation as well as to a Persian version.[88] However, with the exception of the Vulgate, he knows the latter versions only from second hand.

Not yet satisfied with these numerous versions, Azariah develops the theory that, during the exilic and post-exilic periods when Aramaic had gradually supplanted Hebrew as the spoken language of Palestine, there existed also an old Aramaic translation which later gave birth to the Greek Septuagint. In his opinion, this ancient Aramaic *Vorlage* helps to explain in part the Septuagint's numerous deviations from the masoretic text.[89] It may well have existed as late as the days of Rab but has since been lost.[90]

However, de' Rossi does not attach too much authority to any of these versions, censuring in particular the Septuagint's wrong readings and its frequent agreement with both the Gospels and the Karaites.[91] He attaches more weight to the Aramaic renditions, as well as to that of 'Aqilas, for he assumes that all of them had been written either by Tannaim or under their influence and supervision.[92]

Azariah's attitude toward talmudic literature is of even more decisive importance. On the one hand, he firmly believes in the existence of an Oral Law which, like Scripture, is ancient and of divine origin, and hence contains only infallible truths. On the other hand, he sees clearly that one cannot ascribe everything written in the Talmud to that oral tradition hailing from Sinai. His critical sense convinced him time and again that the Talmud includes many contradictory statements and that some others are clearly controverted by indubitable historical and scientific facts. In answer, Azariah resorts to the old explanation that, apart from Sinaitic traditions, the Talmud embraces personal opinions of the respective sages which are naturally subject to human error. If the scientific world outlook of the Talmud had clearly become antiquated, this was owing only to the inadequate information of some talmudic teachers or of entire generations, in addition to the Jews' loss of national independence and their consequent inability to develop their outlook freely under the yoke of foreign nations. In this connection Azariah subscribes to the opinion held by Jewish apologists since the Hellenistic age that all human knowledge was essentially of Jewish origin. Since the Exile, however, when their scientific works had been taken away from the Jews, other nations were able to achieve clear superiority.[93]

In practice, however, serious difficulties arose. How was one to distinguish a sage's personal opinion from the old tradition? With his usual apologetic tendency, Azariah was induced to defend even very debatable talmudic statements and to search, contrary to his own protestations, for means of escape hardly reconcilable with historic truth. In this fashion the gate was wide open for arbitrary decisions. Despite his general scholarly conscientiousness, Azariah saw himself forced to apply his criticisms to talmudic sources in a rather haphazard fashion. In many cases the older Spanish-Jewish literature came to his support. For a long time past the great masters of Spanish Jewry, without going much beyond the last geonim, had established the principle that only the Halakhah, the religious law of Judaism, was binding and immutable, whereas one could treat the aggadic element in the Talmud with much greater freedom.

With such an attitude toward the Talmud it is small wonder that Azariah entertains no doubts that the *Seder 'Olam* was a tannaitic work composed by R. Yose,[94] the *Yelamdenu* was written by R. Tanḥuma, and the *Pirqe* were rightly attributed to R. Eliezer b. Hyrcanus.[95]

Far more critical is Azariah's treatment of the Hellenistic literature. Several chapters (III-VI) discuss the extent to which one may confide in Philo's writings and whether one has the right to make use of them. This decision depends, in Azariah's view, on the measure of agreement existing between the Alexandrine philosopher and the talmudic tradition. After a lengthy debate, which includes many a sharp censure of Philo's "errors," he essentially leaves the problem open.[96] The fact that he devotes so much space and energy to the Philonic problem stems from the great popularity which that author was enjoying at the time among the Italian Jews after a long period of oblivion.[97]

Nor is Azariah's attitude toward Josephus more consistent. Although he does not devote any special investigation to Josephus' writings, he must have realized that Josephus was a more important historical source than Philo. There was the additional incentive that, at least among his compatriots, Josephus enjoyed an even more incontestable authority. Moreover, the ancient Palestinian historian, who had himself belonged to the Pharisaic movement, offered fewer divergences from the Talmud.[98] More importantly, it was generally assumed then that the Hebrew *Yosippon* was likewise a work by Josephus, its differences from the Graeco-Latin texts being explained by the different audiences to which the two versions were addressed. The Hebrew book certainly appeared irreproachable to the majority of conforming Jews. Although his critical sense could not always conceal his misgivings, Azariah believed that he could overcome obvious disparities between the two works by the old routine of postulating later interpolations and copyists' errors.[99]

In contrast to his attitude toward Josephus and *Yosippon*, de' Rossi appears quite reserved toward the Geonim. He actually draws a clear line of demarcation between the Talmud and the geonic literature by stating that the transmission of genuine traditions had stopped with the Amoraim.[100] However, he personally so highly esteems these Babylonian continuators of the Talmud that he does not dare to contradict a gaon unless he finds support in some other authorities,[101] even if they are of a lower rank in the hierarchy of the traditional Jewish literature. He discards, for instance, an opinion by Saadia on the basis of his own reasoning with no further support than that of Ibn Ezra.[102]

He behaves with even greater freedom toward later authors. He freely criticizes Maimonides whom he otherwise profoundly respects.[103] He often rejects Ibn Ezra's theories, declares that Gersonides is "too clever," accuses Abravanel of plagiarism,[104] all of which does not prevent him from frequently citing all three writers as outstanding authorities.[105] He indulges in endless polemics with the Tosafists, Ibn Daud, Qimḥi, Israeli, Baḥya, Jacob b. Asher, Arama, Karo, Isserles, and many others.[106] Yet he does not altogether reject their high rank in Jewish learning. When he is forced to express doubts concerning a text in *Kuzari,* he attributes the error to the translator's lack of understanding. But he tries to exonerate the authoritative translator, Samuel ibn Tibbon, and places the onus on the less renowned Yehudah ibn Tibbon.[107] In general, he states his opposing views in a moderate and respectful tone. Even in cases when he clearly must repudiate an opinion voiced by a contemporary or near-contemporary author, he goes out of his way to express his appreciation of the latter's learning and good intentions.[108]

No less significant is his attitude toward the Kabbalah. Personally, he is a rationalist and averse to all mysticism. But in that climactic period of the Jewish "secret lore," he was affected by the dominant tendencies among his contemporaries. He could not even, we recall, discount the practical Kabbalah. Since, together with the majority of his contemporaries, he considered the kabbalistic classics to be of indubitably ancient origin,[109] he had to give them preference even over Maimonides.[110] Only in the case of a conflict between Kabbalah and Talmud, is the latter for him the superior authority.[111] Nevertheless, he recognizes that the *Zohar* contains many interpolations from much later periods than that of its purported author, R. Simon b. Yoḥai.[112] And he has few compunctions about assuming his usual critical posture toward the stories, primarily non-mystical, told by Eldad the Danite.[113]

In this connection we must note how little Azariah cares for most of his predecessors or contemporaries in the field of Jewish historiography. He never cites directly the works by Joseph ha-Kohen or Ibn Verga, although both men had written many years before him.[114] On the single occasion when he quotes Ibn Verga, he does it by referring to a passage in Zacuto.[115] Apparently he never saw the *Shebeṭ Yehudah.* Even the *Yuḥasin* seems to have been inaccessible to him during the first writing of his book, although its Constantinople edition had appeared some five years before his. He himself remarks in a special note[116] that that book had been brought to Italy only a short time before. Hence the citations from Zacuto are all later additions.[117] Incidentally, it appears that Joseph ha-Kohen never saw either Zacuto's or Ibn Verga's work.[118]

Next to the *Seder 'Olam* and Josephus, Azariah holds the *Epistle* of Sherira Gaon in high esteem. He knew it at first only from a manuscript;[119] but he later had access to its printed edition together with that of the *Yuḥasin*.[120] He thinks much less of Ibn Daud. Although he cites him frequently enough, he occasionally accuses him of serious inexactitudes and misinterpretations.[121] Characteristically, he feels the need of warning his reader that that historian is not to be confused with Maimonides' famous halakhic adversary. This aversion is the less astonishing, since Ibn Daud is cited by neither Usque nor Ha-Kohen and, besides Azariah, he is mentioned only by Zacuto and once by Ibn Verga. Even more remarkable is the neglect of Benjamin of Tudela who, except for a brief reference in Zacuto, is mentioned by none of these men, including Azariah.[122] Of more recent authors our historian quotes only Don Isaac Abravanel frequently, but he, however, cannot be considered an historical writer.

On the whole, Azariah's work did not mark so great a progress over that of his predecessors as is sometimes assumed. True, he no longer considers the Aggadah in its totality an irreproachable source, but rather treats some of its statements as mere figures of speech or legends, and on other occasions compares them to the "symbolic" genre of ancient letters.[123] As a rule he does not allow himself to be distracted by them from following the ordinary meaning of the biblical text.[124] Yet this position can by no means be called revolutionary in Jewish literature. On the contrary, he himself attaches great significance to proving that he was in no way an innovator but that he merely reproduced opinions held by the great authorities of the geonic period.

If we have any reason at all to speak of Azariah's originality in the field of source criticism, it relates not to his form or method but rather to the broad foundation upon which he tries to build it. He utilizes literary works of different periods and peoples to an extent which far surpasses anything known in Hebrew literature before. In principle, he was merely responding to the syncretistic tendency of the early Renaissance, which, starting from the assumption of the unity of the human spirit, insisted upon the equal value of all historic sources belonging to whatever language, religion or country. Despite his own strong Jewish convictions, Azariah could no more escape the impact of that trend than did most of his non-Jewish compatriots. From this standpoint there was nothing unusual in his attempt to synthesize the *Abot de-Rabbi Nathan* and Epiphanius; Philo, Josephus and Eusebius; Rashi and Berossus; the Talmud and Plutarch; Onkelos, 'Aqilas, Jonathan, the Jerusalem Targum, R. Eliezer, R. Joshua, Symmachus, Theodotion and many others.[125] Of interest also is his contrast between Philo, some teachers of the Talmud, Augustine, Maimonides and Gersonides, on the one hand, and certain other talmudic sages and Thomas Aquinas, on the other hand.[126] In the same way he speaks of the "theologians of the two religions," whose opinion controverts in a certain point the doctrines of scholars.[127] This comparative method was facilitated for him by his conviction that all the science of foreign nations was to be attributed to Jewish origins. In the same way he demonstrated, this time correctly, that Jerome had written under the influence of the Aggadah.[128] Needless to say, he did not place the non-Jewish sources on the same plane with Jewish traditions. He expressly states that he would never reject any ancient tradition because of conflicting non-Jewish sources, however reliable they were otherwise. Only when later authors, after proper consideration, had admitted that a particular personal opinion of an ancient Jewish authority had been controverted by dependable foreign sources, is he ready to give the latter the right of way.[129]

We might be better able to understand the import of these subtle distinctions if we compare them with the conceptions of Abraham Zacuto, one of De' Rossi's most enlightened immediate predecessors. Zacuto, too, quotes many non-Jewish authors in the sixth chapter of *Yuḥasin* and elsewhere. But he observes in his introduction[130] that he does this mainly to provide Jews living in a

Christian environment with a means of defending their faith and that he otherwise does not consider the writings of non-Jewish scholars in any way equivalent to Jewish sources. This is not only a more definitive formula than anything Azariah had to say on this subject, but in citing St. Augustine, St. Isidore or any other Christian author, Zacuto cannot refrain from adding the phrase, *Yimah shemo* (may his memory be obliterated). Azariah, on the contrary, voices great respect for Augustine, whom he considers the outstanding Church Father. One cannot explain this difference by Azariah's fear of ecclesiastical censorship; it is rather owing to his personal experiences, since all his life he had maintained close contact with Christian scholars and counted many friends among them.[131] Zacuto, on the other hand, could not shake off the memory of the great catastrophe of the expulsion from Spain, to which he had fallen victim shortly before the composition of his book.[132] Although the scientific conscience of this distinguished savant did not permit him to ignore the Christian sources completely, he could not speak of them with any affection. Azariah, on the contrary, did not even reproach a Christian author for an incorrect statement so long as the error stemmed from that writer's laudable aim at strengthening the faith of his readers.[133] On one occasion he followed the non-Jewish sources for purely esthetic reasons. It was not surprising, however, for a disciple of the Renaissance, with its classical criteria of beauty, to apply esthetic standards even to historical facts.[134]

On closer examination of the non-Jewish sources used by Azariah, one is doubly astonished by their vast range and variety.[135] Among the approximately one hundred non-Jewish authors cited by him, no less than fifty belong to the Graeco-Roman period, another facet of his Renaissance heritage which viewed classical literature as the acme of human achievement. Included in that long list are poets from Homer and Aesop to Terence, Virgil, Horace, Ovid and Quintilian. Among the philosophers appear Pythagoras, Plato, Aristotle, Cicero, Seneca and Themistius.[136] The natural sciences are represented by Euclid and Pliny, geography by Strabo, Ptolemy and Solinus, medicine by Hippocrates, Dioscorides and Galen. Even the jurist Modestinus is mentioned. Understandably, the historical literature occupies a most prominent place. Next to the great names, such as Herodotus and Xenophon, Livy and Tacitus, Plutarch and Caesar, the list also includes Dionysius of Halicarnassus, Diodorus Siculus, Suetonius, Dio Cassius, Justin (Pompeius Trogus) and Eutropius. For the history of Alexander the Great, Azariah cites Arrian and Quintus Curtius; for literary history Aulus Gellius and Macrobius; and for the history of philosophy Diogenes Laërtius and Philostratus. Nor does he disregard ancient works proved spurious by later researches, such as the fragments published by Annius da Viterbo, Berossus, Metastenus, and Hermes Trismegistus. Though some of his contemporaries dared to cast doubts on the authenticity of these fragments,[137] Azariah follows the majority opinion which accepted them uncritically.

Such extensive utilization of classical literature is wholly comprehensible. But the use of Church Fathers by a sixteenth-century Jewish writer marks an important step toward a rapprochement with the Christian world. True, other Jewish authors before Azariah had already alluded to patristic writings. But none had done it so extensively and with so much freedom. His frequent quotations from the New Testament, including the Gospels and, more frequently, the Acts and the Pauline Epistles, must have shocked many an Orthodox Jew, especially if he lived outside Italy. It is less surprising that our historian made extensive use of works by Eusebius, Jerome and Augustine. But he also frequently cited authors of the first centuries of the Christian era, such as Justin Martyr, Irenaeus, Clement of Alexandria, Origen, Lactantius, Epiphanius, Rufinus, Orosius and Theodoret. Add to these men a series of medieval authors, beginning with Isidore of Seville and Suidas, and including less well known non-Italian writers like Hugo of St. Victor and Honorius Augustodunensis, both of the twelfth century; Hermannus Contractus, John de Sacrobosco as well as the Spanish king, Alphonso the Wise, sponsor of the Alphonsine Tables, all of the thirteenth century. From Italy one encounters the names of Thomas Aquinas, Dante, Petrarch and Pietro d'Abano. Nor are even the official papal decretals neglected.

Among Muslim writers he occasionally cites scientists and philosophers like Al-Farghani (ninth century), Al-Battani (beginning of tenth century), Al-Kabitius (twelfth century) and above all, Avicenna and Averroës.

Azariah also studied contemporary and near-contemporary publications extensively, the writers of the fifteenth and sixteenth centuries occupying the second place with a total of thirty-five names. Among them we find, indeed, the most eminent writers of many nations, but particularly of Spain and, of course, Italy. Among the Germans he quotes Sebastian Münster and Georg Reisch; from the Low Countries, Gerardus Mercator, Abraham Ortelius and Otto of Bruges; from France, Symphorien Champier (Camperius), and Fernellius. Among the Spaniards, John Luis Vives, Antonio de Guevara, Alphonso Tostadus, Ulloa Mexica, Xantes Pagninus and Gregory of Valencia make frequent appearances. Italy is represented by its theologians Eugubinus, Imola, Cajetan, Gelenius, Lipomanus, Samotheus, Gaspar Canterinus and Rhodiginus. After them appear geographers like Ruscelli and Ludovico Guicciardini, astronomers like Molethius, medical men like Buono, littérateurs and philologists like Ludovico Dolce, Theseus Pavisius and, finally, the celebrated philosophers Marsilio Ficino and Pico della Mirandola. Most remarkably, however, few historians appear in that list. There is no mention, for instance, of Bartolomeo Sacchi Platina. While Ludovico Guicciardini is cited, his much more renowned grandfather, Francesco, is no more mentioned than are Machiavelli, Bruni or Blondus. However, this is explainable in the light of the concentration of most of them on the history of recent periods, which could be of little immediate use for Azariah's researches into the ancient past.

When one reviews this list with care, one is struck by the vastness of Azariah's erudition and its up-to-dateness. He knows, for example, the *Theatrum mundi* by Ortelius, the description of the Netherlands by Guicciardini, and quite a few other works which had been published but a few years before the composition of his book.[138] Curiously, the same Azariah who, as we have seen, does not know the *Yuḥasin* by Zacuto until after the completion of his major work, and completely ignores Joseph ha-Kohen and Ibn Verga, although these men did not live far from him and had written on Jewish history, is perfectly familiar with the general scholarly movement even in the distant Low Countries. It is likewise interesting to note that, while abundantly citing the classical and patristic literatures, he almost totally neglects the medieval scholastics, except for Thomas Aquinas. He does not quote Albertus Magnus, Duns Scotus, Ockham, or even Marsilio of Padua who had lived in his immediate vicinity.

V

It may be of interest briefly to review Azariah's *method* in examing these variegated sources. Notwithstanding his dogmatic limitations, he generally tried to pursue rational principles in their utilization.

To begin with, he always sought to base his information on primary sources.[139] On one occasion he refused to discuss a contradiction in Isaac Israeli merely because he no longer had the work in question before his eyes.[140] In general, he knows that many an author fails to tell the truth because of personal sympathies or antipathies.[141] Hence he tries to learn as much as possible about an author and his objectives.[142] At the same time, he insists that the mere silence of certain sources is not sufficient reason for controverting statements by other authors.[143] However, under certain circumstances silence may indeed be very significant, and he often tries to advance logical reasons for it.[144]

De' Rossi attaches great importance to the context of each source and its stylistic peculiarities. More than once he relies upon his feeling for language and style, believing that he can thus easily recognize, for instance, that the Septuagint translator of the Pentateuch was not the same person who translated the other biblical books.[145] However, these common-sense approaches did not induce Azariah to attribute excessive importance to subjective criteria. Apart from his habitual skepticism toward human cognition, as compared with the divine word transmitted through Scripture or tradition, he places a higher value on any non-suspect primary source than on later speculations, however ingenious. On one occasion, he expressly contests the right to doubt facts affirmed by five reliable witnesses on the basis of personal feelings, as others had done.[146] He admits, however, that sometimes even apparently dependable sources contradict one another. In such cases the student may have to resort to some hazardous harmonization, or else to state expressly on which specific points the sources agree or disagree.[147] But he is forced to concede the purely fictitious character of some narratives, particularly in the Aggadah, merely adding that while untrue in point of fact, they are no less welcome because of the profound moral lessons concealed in them.[148]

These are his principles. But did he observe them in practice? He must have found it very difficult to fix the precise limits where his esthetic and philological penchants had to stop, and the dependability of the source began. Above all, how was one to reconcile in practice these critical principles with fundamental traditionalist convictions absolutely opposed to any criticism?

He, himself, is not quite unaware of that weakness. This is undoubtedly the cause of a certain feeling of *insecurity* which frequently betrays itself in his study of sources. If he runs counter to some authoritative opinions, he often employs all sorts of ambiguous expressions to pacify the reader.[149] Hence stems his reluctance to contradict a gaon, except when he has the support of some other authorities.[150] Wherever he has to take an independent stand, as in the case of Philo, his conclusions are quite indecisive. For this reason, he frequently[151] uses the expression, "be this as it may," or he "leaves it to others to decide whether his hypothesis is correct or completely false."[152] At times he withdraws behind the screen of a person's unknown motives.[153] He also declares himself ever ready to retract when confronted by opposing authority, or if his opinion should fail to meet with the approval of Jewish and Christian scholars.[154]

This general insecurity is mitigated, even wholly effaced, when he is forced to take a firm stand. With rare confidence in the validity of his own arguments at these times, he hopes that they will serve to reinforce the views held by Ibn Daud or Qimḥi.[155] Quite exceptionally, he sometimes even displays an astonishing independence, as when he unwaveringly adheres to his interpretation of the talmudic legend relating to the insect which had caused the death of Titus.[156] But all these are merely exceptions to the rule of his pervasive sense of insecurity.

Nor must we overlook the fact that, notwithstanding his honesty and conscientiousness, Azariah did not sufficiently check the quotations which occupied so prominent a place in all his writings. Occasionally at the time of his writing he no longer had before him the book he had previously consulted; in part because it had in the meantime been suppressed by the censorship which had become particularly strict during the last twenty years of his life. Although endowed with a phenomenal memory, fully attested to by the vast array of sources he quotes despite the almost total absence of reference works, he could rarely remember the verbatim text.[157] On occasions he may even have intentionally altered a quotation in order to avoid an inescapable conflict with the censor. At other times he merely may have hesitated to antagonize his non-Jewish readers by texts expressing undisguised hostility to strangers.[158]

There was also another consideration of great importance. Following the medieval example, the Renaissance viewed literary property from a different angle than we do: it placed the subject matter above the man who expressed it. That is why sources were frequently quoted without acknowledgment of their authorship, Azariah being an exception in carefully noting the authors' names. That is also why most writers took great liberties with the texts they reproduced. When their dogmatic interests were at stake, they felt quite free to alter objectionable readings. Azariah himself reproached Samuel Sulam, editor of the *Yuḥasin,* for not suppressing Zacuto's observations on the *Zohar.*[159] In fact, however, Sulam had not only reproduced a weakened version of Zacuto's statement, if compared with that of the Filipowski edition,[160] but he had also inserted a forceful *caveat* against it, as Azariah had to admit. Thus consideration for the author's text counted little when weighed against the possible damage to readers. Moreover, Azariah knew perfectly well that some of his assertions would evoke numerous objections. Long before the completion of his book he must have heard that some of his theories, interveningly circulated by word of mouth, had aroused a lively opposition. He took cognizance, therefore, even in his *magnum opus,* of his adversaries' strictures.[161] This feeling was necessarily heightened by numerous attacks after the publication of his work. His subsequent pamphlets, *Maṣref* and *Ṣedeq 'olamim,* were essentially devoted to polemics and apologias. One may understand, therefore, his constant preoccupation with forestalling unnecessary conflicts by citing at length those texts which, in his opinion, supported his theses. On the whole, however, these minor imprecisions have little bearing on the theories he espouses.

One of the pillars of Azariah's historical method is *chronology.* He not only devotes the entire third book and many paragraphs in other books to the chronological problems of the traditional computation, but he considers the confrontation of dates an essential element of all historical investigations. Not without reason has posterity considered him primarily a critic of chronology. True, chronological researches were no longer a total innovation in Azariah's time, although chronology had not yet become an independent science into which it was to develop since Joseph Justus Scaliger. Yet Azariah's contemporaries already had before them a number of comprehensive works containing relatively significant contributions to the solution of chronological problems. Pertinent researches by Panvinio and Carlo Sigonio had marked major progress over the confusion which had existed in this respect in medieval chronicles.

The related method of chronologically linking unrelated events and persons appearing at the same time also had its predecessors among the Renaissance annalists. They necessarily had to employ this method in their expositions of universal history,[162] since events taking place in diverse localities had to be treated in the context of each year. In Hebrew literature, too, one need but consult the last paragraph of Zacuto's work to note to what exaggerations this procedure might lead. In his very moderation, Azariah reveals the native talent of a true historian.

In this field, too, he evinced concern about his opponents. He allotted so much space to his chronological studies because he anticipated violent opposition on this score. He indulged in constant repetitions in order to remove any obscurity in his presentation, and cited his sources, however diverse, at excessive lengths in order to buttress his opinions, at least in principle, by those of recognized older authorities.[163] He even ventured to assert that his chronological discussions would protect the public from dangerous practical illusions.[164] The ultimate attacks of his adversaries stimulated him to even more extended and exacting chronological researches which, understandably, led him to certain exaggerations.

Believing in the existence of Atalantus and Prometheus, the ancient Egyptian physician and philosopher, Azariah treated them as contemporaries of Moses while placing Hermes Trismegistus, whom he highly valued, in the fourth generation after Moses.[165] An illustration of his generation's great gullibility, this example merely betrays Azariah's general tendency to connect great non-Jewish with outstanding Jewish personalities with respect to both time and spiritual concerns. Because of the recorded events under Caligula, he dates Philo more or less correctly some twenty-five years before the destruction of the Temple, thus working him into the framework of Jewish history.[166] He considers Justin Martyr a contemporary of "Antoninus" and Judah the Patriarch without analyzing the problem, still insufficiently resolved today, of that Antoninus' identity.[167] We have seen that he dates 'Aqilas after Onkelos and Jonathan. Mar Samuel appears as a contemporary of Antoninus Pius and of the Persian Shabur, the latter, as we shall see, representing in his opinion a title and not a proper name.[168]

Occasionally he commits more serious errors. When he once mentions that Caesar Augustus had pursued Pompey,[169] he evidently employs that name in lieu of Julius Caesar.[170] But when he confuses the similar-sounding names of Lulianus and Julianus and concludes that there must have existed two Rabbis Joshua and two Trajans who were contemporaries of these two men, he is guilty, of course, of a gross error.[171] When he synchronizes the conquest of Persia by the Muslim armies with the Hejira of 622, and places R. Ashi's teachings "around the same period," his mistake stems from his identifying two Persian Yezdegerds as one and the same person.[172] Of interest also are his explanations about the beginning of the Seleucid era. Though he does not give an exact date, he attributes its inception to events occurring six years after the death of Alexander the Great; he thus came far closer to the truth than any of his Jewish predecessors and contemporaries, who ascribed it to the first year of Alexander's reign.[173] Yet even this more correct assumption is derived from the misunderstanding of a passage in Josephus; some of his Christian contemporaries had reached a more exact chronological date on the basis of other events which had taken place at the beginning of the Hellenistic period.

Azariah's dogmatic point of view is also responsible for some chronological errors. He rejects, for instance, a chronology of Josephus, whom he otherwise considers immune from attack, only because it seemingly contradicts data supplied by Scripture. He expressly states as assured historical facts both the four hundred and eighty years which had allegedly elapsed between the Exodus from Egypt and the construction of the First Temple, and the seventy years separating that destruction from the rebuilding of the Second Temple.[174] Occasionally his chronological computations are more conservative than those by Ibn Daud.[175] All of these reservations were not to save him, however, from his opponents' violent criticisms.

If this emphasis on chronological details, together with the careful critique of sources and texts, represented genuine progress in Jewish historiography, Azariah did not entirely bridle his *intuition*, an indispensable tool to any truly original historian for proposing solutions wherever the sources yield only few answers. Intuition, however, is not a perfectly reliable guide. While like a flash of lightning, it sometimes helped him to illumine a centuries-old darkness, at other times it obscured from Azariah information already arrived at by his predecessors. If, faithful to his comparative method, he linked the medieval Karaites with the ancient Sadducees, he was prone to overlook the fundamental differences between the two sects.[176] These differences are undeniable, despite the persistence of certain underground currents from the ancient opposition to the Oral Law to that of 'Anan and Nahawendi. Azariah's interesting identification of the Boethosians with the Essenes is also noteworthy; this hypothesis found defenders even in the nineteenth century.[177] He was certainly correct in claiming that Christian monasticism bears traces of profound Essenian influences.[178] His other hypothesis that Philo was not a Sadducee but that he had affinities to the Boethosian-Essenian sect, though untenable as such, is based on the Alexandrine philosopher's glowing descriptions of the life and doctrines of that sect.[179] At the same time, notwithstanding his personal sympathy for some Essenian doctrines and practices, Azariah bluntly declares that wherever the latter are incompatible with official Pharisaic Judaism, we must treat the Essenes not as Jews but as strangers.[180]

Orthodox preconceptions of this kind did not save him from suspicions. Convinced that the traditional computation had proved untenable, he necessarily concluded that it could not be based upon true tradition, a conclusion which appeared subversive to many of his contemporaries. The latter frowned also upon his denial of the divine origin of the law governing the *molad,* which plays such a tremendous role in the Jewish calendar, and upon his attempt to prove his point by the mere fact that that cycle was also used by other nations employing the lunar calendar, such as the Arabs. Neither could they agree with his contention that the system of *'ibbur* (intercalation of months in certain years in the solilunar Jewish calendar) was likewise a means invented by Jewish sages rather than an integral part of the Mosaic tradition.[181] Though by no means the expression of an iconoclast, since he could invoke in his support certain specific opinions expressed by predecessors, in its totality his approach was both new and daring.

He further defied public opinion by declaring that the world had been created on the first of Nissan. He necessarily deduced from this that the accepted Rosh ha-Shanah prayers, reflecting the popular opinion that the creation took place on the first of Tishre, were merely a later rabbinic concession concomitant with the relatively late introduction of the standard liturgy.[182] This contention, too, though supported by the well-known controversy between R. Eliezer and R. Joshua, antagonized many people in the sixteenth century. If these discussions, largely included in his *Maṣref,* were not published until some three centuries after Azariah's demise, this certainly was not part of his design.

Also related to his historical method are his explanations of the Hebrew language and script. Starting from the premise that the Hebrew language is the world's mother-language synchronous with Creation or even antedating it (according to a well-known aggadah), he concluded that the square characters represent the original script in which it had been written,[183] although some Jewish scholars, particularly Joseph Albo, had admitted that the most ancient script was the one called "Old Hebrew" or, to use the talmudic expression, "the Transjordanian" alphabet. It may seem strange that he felt obligated to supply proof that the Torah had originally been written in the Hebrew language by pointing out that all translations have maintained the Hebrew form of biblical proper names.[184] Also worthy of mention is his theory that Ezra, the redactor of holy Scripture, would not have included in his canon books in any other language. That is why he was prepared to discard the Apocrypha, largely extant in Greek, some of which had become known in his period.[185] How was he to explain, then, the presence in the Bible of Aramaic sections in Ezra and Daniel, as well as the exclusion from the canon of the Hebrew book composed, in his opinion, by Baruch, Jeremiah's disciple? He left these questions unanswered.

In any case he believed that all other peoples had imitated the Hebrew language. Not only were Arabic and Aramaic corrupted forms of Hebrew, but all other languages and dialects had constantly borrowed from the Hebrew, which alone was of divine origin and as such holy and eternal. In this, as in many other respects, Azariah remained faithful to the folkloristic opinions of the Aggadah; he also never wavered from his adherence to the talmudic assumption of a total of seventy peoples and languages in the world.[186] And that almost two centuries after Marco Polo!

Another characteristic feature is Azariah's tendency toward oversimplification. Referring to various currencies whose exact value he did not know, he cuts the discussion short by declaring that the *zuz, drachme, adarkemon, dinar,* etc., all represented the same value.[187] If the Bible mentions the country of Parvaim, it is "without any doubt" Peru.[188] When he is embarrassed by several kings of the same name, he treats the name as a title frequently recurring in different periods. Thus Abimelech and Shabur are, in his opinion, royal titles, not proper names; they, like the Pharaohs in Egypt, designate chiefs of state.[189] Facing difficulties in dating, he does not hesitate to postulate the existence of two tannaim or two amoraim by the same name; for instance, two Joshua ben Levis.[190] Sometimes he claims very unlikely parallels without much ado, as when he finds merely a reminiscence of the Babylonian Semiramis in the dove worshiped in Samaria.[191] With a great deal of oversimplification he draws analogies between Jewish pre-history and his own time, often demonstrating an unexpected naiveté.[192] Such examples can easily be multiplied.[193]

De' Rossi's studies of the rhythm of Hebrew poetry, on the other hand, testify to an amazing erudition and intuitive comprehension.[194] He rejects both the Greek and Arabic meters as totally foreign to the Hebrew language. At the same time he finds in such ancient authorities as Josephus and Jerome allusions to a definite meter employed in ancient Hebrew poetry. Impressionistically assuming that many paragraphs in the Bible were written in verse form, he espouses a theory about the existence of a special Hebrew meter, emphasizing not the number of syllables, as do the Greek and Arabic meters, but rather the subject matter.[195] He thus finds in the Canticle of Moses and in *Ha'azinu* (Give ear, ye heavens; Deut. 32) a meter of 2:2 or 3:3. He is also led to an intuitive recognition of the characteristic *qinah* rhythm. He even reproaches the contemporary Hebrew poets for dealing with most varied subjects in the same rhythm, and for trying to impose Arabic meters upon Hebrew poetry, which runs counter to the genius of its language. But he fully realizes that his few suggestions can achieve no more than to open the gate to further research which, by an intensive study of all pertinent biblical texts, might ultimately resolve the numerous specific difficulties.[196]

Azariah combines with this exposé a very remarkable discussion about the funerary inscriptions used in his time. He condemns as totally absurd the prevalent habit of heaping praises upon a deceased person, and suggests instead merely a brief mention of that person's good deeds and a reference to his or her future resurrection.[197] He prepared his own tombstone inscription in this vein. Inconsistently, however, he failed to use in this poem, or in others he had composed, the Hebrew meter he had postulated, and he rather tacitly followed the literary fashion of his time.[198]

Taken as a whole, Azariah's historiographic contribution was indeed important. He laid the foundations for a major evolution of Jewish historic criticism. If his successors had worked along these paths without interruption, Jewish scholarship might have maintained itself on the level of European historiography. However, by a tragic concatenation, the newly expanding Counter-Reformation barred the Jews from the intellectual life of their environment, especially in Italy. Azariah himself lived to see the inception of the new era of the Italian ghetto. His work not only found no successors, but from the outset had been limited to a small circle of readers. It subsequently went into almost total oblivion among Jews. It was only nineteenth-century scholarship which rediscovered his signal contributions and resumed his constructive quest.

IO

I. M. Jost the Historian*

WE SHALL NOT SAY VERY MUCH ABOUT THE LIFE OF ISAAK MARKUS JOST.
His was the average life of a school-teacher in Berlin and Frankfort,
quiet and without outstanding events. In a certain sense Graetz
was right in saying that Jost equally disliked storms in life and in
history. The really important aspect of that life is the man's background rather than his individual experiences. Born in surroundings
very reminiscent of the medieval ghetto, Jost grew up in a period
of profound transformation in German Jewry. From 1793 to 1860
he witnessed the Revolution and the Restoration and lived to see
the accomplishment, after 1848, of the great emancipation movement in most states of Germany. In his time the storms of the
Jewish Reformation were shaking the foundations of established
Judaism. The period, therefore, is far more interesting than the
man, and the occurrences of his life engage our attention as illustrations of the history of the time much more than as revelations
of his individual character.

Nor shall we discuss at length his pedagogic and linguistic
works of various kinds. Neither his English grammar for school
use, nor his glossary of Shakespeare, nor his many other similar
works are of interest to us today. Not even his achievements as a
journalist and publicist of distinction will be the topic of our consideration at present. Although the Hebrew periodical *Zion,* which
he edited together with Michael Creizenach, and his *Israelitische
Annalen* are among the best of their time, neither they nor his
defense of Judaism and the Jews against opponents like Chiarini
or Streckfuss, are of vital importance in the life-work of Jost. His

* Paper read at the public meeting of the American Academy for Jewish
Research, New York, December 26, 1928. Reprinted from its *Proceedings* [I]
(1928-30), 7-32.

real achievement was in the field of history and in that field alone. In particular, his great *History of the Israelites,* nine volumes of which, dealing with the history of the Jews from the Maccabean period to his own time, appeared from 1820 to 1828, represents the beginning of modern Jewish historiography. Thus, exactly a hundred years ago was completed the first Jewish history written by a Jew, dealing with the life of the Jewish people from antiquity to the modern age. Surely it is appropriate now (1928), on the hundreth anniversary of its publication, to consider its place in the development of Jewish historical literature. This work was supplemented by the tenth volume in three parts which appeared in 1846 and narrated the events of the author's own time starting with 1815. An abridged edition in two volumes, published in 1850, and the three volumes of the *History of Judaism and its Sects,* written towards the end of his life (1857-59), are the outstanding landmarks in the later historical achievements of Jost. Only his general history, however, is of fundamental importance, for here he made his real contribution as founder and pioneer.

It is never easy to be a pioneer. But in most instances, at least, the reward comes in the form of recognition. In the case of Jost even recognition was lacking. In the interval of more than a century between him and his immediate predecessor, Basnage, very few contributions had been made to the knowledge of Jewish history. Unfortunately for Jost, however, simultaneously with him several other pioneers equal and even superior to him were working in different fields of Jewish history. In the South, Luzzatto and Reggio, in the East, Krochmal and Rapoport, and in his own country Zunz, Geiger and many others were thoroughly clarifying the facts of the past and establishing their mutual interdependence. Soon after this titanic work came the time for the new synthesizing endeavor which was accomplished so successfully by Graetz. That severe competition was indeed unfortunate for Jost. Science is cruel. Each new truth supercedes the old one almost completely. And so in the period of that collective pioneering, of that turmoil of creation, the work of the founder could not be duly appreciated. But now after a hundred years we should be able to judge his achievements as well as his shortcomings more objectively and to give him his true place in the history of Jewish historiography.

We shall not understand the work of Jost or of any of his German-Jewish co-workers without considering the great underlying movements in contemporary Germany. It was an historical-minded century or at least half-century, that followed the period of Enlightenment in Central Europe. The disillusioning failure of the glorious revolutionary aspirations seemed to prove beyond doubt that human institutions are too deeply rooted to be overthrown by a purely conscious effort of human reason. Thereupon, European and especially German thinkers started to teach by a process of generalization that all human institutions grow like plants during the long period of their history and that no sudden changes, however rational, can take place. The historical attitude toward every aspect of the life of the individual as well as of society found expression in the convictions of the followers of the Hegelian philosophy; in the minds of great jurists like Savigny and Eichhorn, who represent the so-called historical school in jurisprudence; in the romantic longing for the Middle Ages and their institutions, as voiced by the most representative men in literature and in art, in the study of languages and religions. Of course, the highest expression of this historical state of mind was necessarily to be found in history itself. The foundations of modern historiography were laid in this period. From Niebuhr, the historian of Rome, who is often called the father of modern historical writing, to Ranke and Mommsen, Germany produced a greater number of distinguished historians and made a more profound and diversified attempt to find out the truth about all aspects of the human past than any other single country before or since, in any such brief period.

Such a movement could not but exercise a profound influence upon the young German-Jewish intellectuals for whom the destruction of the intellectual ghetto-walls and full participation in Germany's cultural life were no longer a mere claim or desire. Even outwardly there is one striking similarity. The general movement found its external expression in an organization, the famous German Historical Association, which was sponsored in 1819 by the great Prussian statesman and German patriot Freiherr vom Stein. It soon counted among its members, to mention only a few names, Niebuhr who was then in Rome, Savigny, Dahlmann, the brothers Grimm, Eichhorn, Pertz, the brothers Schlegel, Schlosser, Raumer and Görres. Similarly the early scholarly endeavors in German-Jewish circles were centered around an organization founded exactly two years later. The Verein für Kultur und Wissenschaft der Juden attempted to unite the forces of the young movement of Jewish historical studies toward a common end. A specific incentive was given the Jews by the continual denunciations of Jewish character and morals, and the repeated assertions that they were intellectually degenerate and had the base economic standing of peddlers and *Schacherer*. These arguments, they felt, could best be met by the reasoning that, even if they were true, the situation was the natural result of a specific historical development, the result of persecutions and restrictions for which the responsibility lay not upon the oppressed but upon the oppressor. Apologetics in the higher form, whether conscious or unconscious, was the vital force in all that widely spread historical movement.

We shall see that Jost, too, was a son of his age. But he was less so in many ways than most of his contemporaries, and for this very reason he appeared to be cold, detached and without a fighting spirit. In general, we shall see that even in his method and in his convictions he belongs only partly to his own age, and that in many respects he represents the stage of historiography (as regards both method of research and outlook on life) which had already been reached by the European world in the period of Enlightenment. Jost is indeed between the two periods. By virtue of his frame of mind, his character and interests, he is a belated offspring of the Enlightenment, while in his aims and tasks, in his connection with the surrounding world, he shares in certain aspects of the new movement in history. We shall understand this better if we see that Jost's peculiar position as the real founder of Jewish history imposed upon him the performance of the functions achieved for the world at large both by the Enlightenment and by the historiography of the nineteenth century. Like the Enlightenment he had to destroy traditional forces by rational criticism; like romanticism he had to refashion those scattered fragments into a new comprehensive structure. If he had been a much greater man, he would have been able to utilize those complex forces for the accomplishment of a unique achievement in the evolution of human historical writing. As he was little more than a fine school-teacher, a man with much commonsense but with little vision, with solidity and reliability rather than with real creative genius, he remained between the two. Instead of becoming a source of strength and of creative reconciliation, this double task and this position between two periods resulted in a series of contradictions and hesitations, in weakness and sometimes even in confusion.

We shall best be able to judge the merits and the shortcomings of Jost as a historian by comparing him with two prominent contemporaries, Niebuhr, the leading historian of the age, and Neander, whose field was church history. This is, of course, the subject most closely related to a history of the Jewish people, quite apart from the fact that Neander himself was born a Jew and did not embrace Christianity until the age of seventeen.[1] As a matter of fact, even these two did not represent the most advanced stages that historical research and writing had then reached. On the one hand, Hegel and his school undertook the gigantic task of explaining the history of the world as the outward expression of the workings of the spirit. This view was soon applied with a certain degree of success to the history of law by a Jew, Edward Gans, the president of the Verein für Kultur, and to the history of the church by Baur in his admirable, though essentially faulty work. But perhaps the greatest promise of all was revealed in a little essay published in 1822, at the beginning of Jost's historical career, by Wilhelm von Humboldt, the statesman and poet, the philosopher of art and of language as well as of history. This short essay, entitled "On the Task of the Historian," had a tremendous influence on the future development of historical science in Germany and abroad. It was a clear formulation of that famous *Ideenlehre* of Humboldt, which through its application by Ranke and his school, and by Graetz in Jewish history, became the dominant theory in historical literature about the middle of the century. It should suffice in this connection to quote one passage in this essay which contains both a kind of summary of achievements in historical method up to the author's time and the formulation of the new postulate demanded by him. Humboldt says:

> The number of creative forces in history is by no means exhausted by those manifesting themselves immediately in the events. Even if historiography succeeds in unraveling them all, severally or in their combination, and ascertains *the shape of, and transformations taking place in, the earth, the changes of climate, the intellectual capacity and character of nations, as well as the even more peculiar ones of individual person-alities, the impact of arts and sciences, the deep imprint of social institutions,* there will still remain an even more power-ful principle to be detected. Although not immediately visible, this principle lends impetus to those forces and gives them direction. We are referring to *ideas* which, by their very nature, exist beyond the circle of finality, and yet they imbue and dominate world history in all its parts.

How far did Jost go in the application of these principles? Of course, we cannot expect to find in him the *Ideenlehre*. He has no notion whatever of the existence of certain leading ideas and ten-dencies peculiar to every period such as Ranke emphasized later. To him history seems a straight line of development which he judges very much from the point of view of his own age. In general, Jost's philosophy of history is very simple; he is not even a theo-logian like most of the other Jewish historians of the nineteenth century. It is perhaps one of his essential weaknesses that, treating a subject like the history of the Jewish people, he had no definite view as to what this Jewish people really was. Personally almost an agnostic, a man who boasted of not having gone to a synagogue for more than twenty years, because, as he said, he "did not go to theater,"[2] he could hardly feel deep sympathy with Jewry as a purely religious group. On the other hand, in his eyes the Jewish people was no longer a nationality. The movement for emancipation was so closely connected with assimilation in the Germany of that day, that no advocate of equal rights—and Jost undoubtedly was one—could conceivably assert the existence of a Jewish nation within the German nation. That was an argument used often and with much success by the opponents of Jewish emancipation. Since he was neither a religious nor a national Jew, Jost would have been much confused if he had had to face the task of defining Judaism. Although his work was description rather than definition, this weakness and the resultant inner contradiction could never be fully overcome.[3]

Jost, it can thus be seen, is very far from Neander, throughout whose historical investigations the theological view is dominant, and who, as he says himself in the Preface to his chief work *General History of the Christian Religion and Church,* wrote it as an "eloquent proof of the divine power of Christianity, as a school of Christian experience," and who used to declare that he would "never recognize the difference between the Church history that is edifying and that which is instructive." Jost differs equally in this respect from a secular historian like Niebuhr whose romantic spirit exalted him to the highest regions of belief, and made him declare that only that for which a man is ready to die is a creed. Indeed, he asserted, he would always be prepared to lay his head on the block for the divinity of Jesus. Nevertheless, we have reason to assume that if Niebuhr had lived long enough, he might have applied his philologico-historical method of criticism to the New Testament as thoroughly as he had to Livy and the other Roman sources which he used. In comparison with his treatment of the Latin works, Jost's criticism of the Holy Scriptures, as we shall see, appears almost immature.

Jost's conception of history, untheological as it is, is yet characterized by a kind of theism. He completely excludes miracles but is perfectly convinced that there is a uniform divine rule behind the appearances of the world.[4] But that is almost all. We never find either the teleology of Hegel, or the leading ideas of Humboldt, or the theology of Neander.

What shall we say regarding the other elements mentioned in

that passage of Humboldt? As for the first two, the nature and metamorphoses of the soil and the changes in climate considered as highly influential factors in the growth of civilization—we know that this postulate was not an achievement of the study of history in the nineteenth century, but that the historiography of the Enlightenment had already made full use of these environmental influences. Of course, compared with the *théorie du milieu* of a Taine and Renan in the second half of the nineteenth century, or with the extreme views concerning the climatic and geographical influences on the history of mankind in a Buckle, these views, even in Voltaire or Montesquieu, appear rather shallow and superficial. In this respect too, Jost was a disciple of the Enlightenment. In his first volume he devotes a large chapter of more than one hundred pages to Palestine, its topographic, hydrographic and climatic conditions, because, as he says, "these influences leave a more lasting impression than the endeavors of powerful but mortal heroes."[5] But how little use he makes of that general conception! How insipid his reflections seem to us when compared with the really ingenious and for his time strikingly novel description of the land and the peoples of Italy in the first hundred pages of Niebuhr's work! There is hardly any connection between Jost's long introduction and the other chapters of his book. If occasionally he attempts to explain a certain phenomenon by the influence of nature, he does little more than betray his complete naiveté.[6] Sometimes this element is used to rationalize the phenomena of sacred history. Again, quite in the manner of skeptical enlightenment, he tries to explain (though implicitly and not in so many words), prophecy, religious ecstasy and all those unusual creative movements in the religious history of the country, by a kind of medical abnormality caused by the air of Palestine.[7] On the other hand, he is extremely critical concerning extraordinary facts in nature. For instance, many of the real characteristics of the Dead Sea seem hardly credible to him.[8] Because he refused to believe in supernatural miracles, he did not believe in any of the ordinary miracles of nature. It is highly characteristic of the man that he seems to have abandoned this viewpoint during the "progress" of historical science in the following decades. Because these natural theories of the Enlightenment were somewhat discredited among historians of the nineteenth century, he too gave them up even when they were justified. In his short two-volume history of 1850 he did not include any description of Palestine. One wonders if Graetz, who reproached him with not having learned anything after his early contributions, would have praised him on account of this achievement?

As for the elements next mentioned by Humboldt, namely "the intellectual capacity and character of nations, as well as the even more peculiar ones of individual personalities," we find both of them in Jost in a relatively small degree. Romanticism emphasized the national and racial spirit more and more, and Niebuhr, in particular, succeeded in solving many of the most complicated riddles in ancient Roman history by explaining the dissensions between the Patricians and Plebeians not only as a class and social struggle, but as a clash between two different races. But we find nothing of this kind in Jost, although in the history of the Jews during the dispersion, the racial and national element obviously played a much larger part. Perhaps just because it was so obvious, he tried to conceal it, for he would probably have seen in a racial or national treatment of Jewish history a support for the fervent denunciations, so common at the time, of the alien spirit of the Jews in Germany.

Nor did he adopt the opposite principle, that of emphasizing the importance of great men in history. It is true that that tendency had yet to grow in historical literature. Even Neander, who deals so much with the individual Fathers and Teachers of the Church, and tries to give definite and clean-cut characterizations of these leading personalities, succeeds only in presenting them to us—as Harnack points out—"like stars which immersed in the same light mist are hardly discernible from one other." Neander may have been too little of an artist to have the full desire for it, but Niebuhr's artistic spirit would certainly have created distinctive shapes had he been as gifted a writer as he was an investigator. German historiography, therefore, had to wait until Ranke erected his beautiful "picture gallery," and Jewish historiography until Graetz did the same thing for Jewish history. Jost not only lacked the artist's desire and ability to breathe life into the people of his story, but also seems to have had a preconceived notion that he ought not even attempt to do it. In one remarkable passage he declares expressly that even the culture of a people cannot be judged by the opinions and expressions of individual men.[9] Such a view must have been despised in the following generation of Ranke and Graetz, Carlyle and Renan, but it will undoubtedly be much more appreciated today, when our eyes are turning again to underlying currents, social movements and institutions as opposed to the individual deeds of a few heroes whose lives and accomplishments, however interesting and important, we are banishing more and more to the field of biography. Occasionally Jost does attempt to sketch the profile of an important historical personality, but even when he tries his utmost, as in the case of Herod, his characters are too conventional to be true, too lame and ordinary to be stirring. His was anything but the insight of the great psychologist, anything but the vision of the great artist. Least of all could he understand a personality like Herod's, so complex and so unlike his own. Perhaps in recognition of these limitations of his, and of the fact that in most cases the biographical material at his disposal was not sufficient to enable him to paint a living picture, he gave up any further attempts at full biographical reconstruction. In this respect, Graetz certainly was superior to him. Graetz had much more and much better sifted material. Graetz also had excellent predecessors to imitate and was a much more plastic writer. Jost deserves to be praised only for his realization of his own weakness and for limiting, whether by principle or by opportunistic considerations, his description of most of the active individuals to the mere collection of facts as recorded in the sources.

However, if we find him lacking in the description of geographic or climatic influences, if he knows little about national characteristics as motivations of history, if he pays little attention to the dynamic power of personalities and heroes, he does devote most of his attention to the two remaining elements on Humboldt's list.

Of course, what Humboldt calls the influence of art and science, took in Jost's history rather the form of religion, law and philosophic thought. In the history of the Jewish people, the intellectual element undoubtedly played the most important part. This was so obvious that many historians tended entirely to neglect the other aspects of life in the Jewish past. To be sure, Jost's mind was not of the type best fitted to deal with the complicated and obscure problem of Jewish intellectual history, particularly at a time when the sources were so widely scattered and so little investigated. Being of a rather skeptical and rationalistic trend of mind, he could hardly grasp the vital forces in any purely religious movement; for him, as for most writers of the Enlightenment, religions were often created by individuals in pursuit of worldly ends. Like Voltaire, he assumed that this personal, secular element was predominant throughout the history of churches and religions. He goes so far as to declare that Moses himself "gave his people not a religion but a political constitution"[10]—a statement often made about Muhammed, but not fully justified even in his case. We cannot then be surprised to find him explaining the great movements of the Second Commonwealth and later periods in a more than rationalistic way. Particularly in regard to the great sectarian movements in the period of the Maccabees, he can give us very little beyond such "enlightened platitudes."[11] His chief addition to that trivial explanation is the attempt to discover influences of Greek philosophy on the minds of Palestinian Jews. He declares that the Pharisees obviously followed the *"Schwärmerei und Geheimniskrämerei"* of Pythagoras without, however, fully accepting his ideas; that the Sadducees were more in favor of the teachings of the liberal Epicurus, and that the Essenes were extremely close to the serious-minded Stoics.[12] In the case of the Sadducees, he may have been led astray by the Talmud's interchangeable use of the terms "Zedoki" and "Epicuros," but the other two relationships are entirely his own uncritical amplifications of the well-known statements of Josephus. They are the result of that syncretistic age of Enlightenment, which thought in terms of universal rather than of national history and tried to establish the idea of a uniform development throughout the world, instead of searching for the distinctive peculiarities of each age and people.

Obviously, the secret lore of the Kabbalah could hardly be attractive to Jost's rationalistic mind. He believes in its ancient origin. Indeed he considers the Kabbalistic, Massoretic and Philosophic schools of thought (as he terms them), the three chief factors in the spiritual development of the Second Commonwealth.[13] But regardless of this antiquity he condemns the influences of the Kabbalah as utterly pernicious. "More than two thousand years," he declares, "have already passed and a large number of years have yet to pass before its damaging influences will be felt and recognized by all Jews."[14] But even the more rationalistic movements in Jewish philosophy do not find him a properly sympathetic interpreter. He was not a great original thinker, and all the philosophy he knew was under the predominant influence of the Kantian and post-Kantian systems. What appeal could be made to such a mind by the speculations of the medieval Jewish philosophers who tried so hard to reconcile Judaism and Greek philosophy? The most he could do was to render stereotyped opinions and to furnish some biographical data on individual philosophers. However, even towards that element of Jewish thought which seemed to lie closest to his comprehension, namely Jewish law, he was far from sympathetic. This otherwise quiet and cool-headed man occasionally loses his temper when he speaks of the Talmud and its laws. He has not quite the fervor of the French iconoclasts of the eighteenth century, but he is ready to denounce the Talmud as the source of many evils throughout Jewish history. His condemnation is mitigated only by the assertion that, after all, the study of the Talmud may prove useful from the point of view of a historical, linguistic and philosophic interpretation.[15]

In general, however, he resigns himself to the facts of history without assuming the right to judge. He tries to be impartial even about rabbinism, which he does not like,[16] and about primitive Christianity of which he speaks with a certain degree of sympathy, rather objectionable to many of his Jewish readers.[17]

Perhaps the most remarkable feature, from the methodological point of view, is that he regards all intellectual history or what he calls *"Kulturgeschichte"* as merely secondary in the treatment of Jewish history. He writes it chiefly, he says, only because it helps to attain a better understanding of general Jewish history. "An absolute cultural history of the Jews would have diverted us too greatly from our main task."[18] How different he is in this regard from Graetz and the others, for whom this *Kulturgeschichte* reigns supreme over all parts of the history of the Jews!

Accordingly, we can understand that the final element in Humboldt's list, namely social institutions, plays a considerable part in Jost's conception of history. Of course, he is far from the standards of the last decades of the nineteenth century, with their thorough investigations into the typical as well as the peculiar forms of human institutions in different ages, and into their mutual relations and their influence over history in general. But Jost's treatment of this aspect of history was considerably influenced by whatever the historiography of the Renaissance and the Enlightenment had accomplished on the subject. As a matter of fact, if he had had a keener mind, if he had been a Machiavelli or a Montesquieu (the latter, he, in common with most of his contemporaries, deeply reveres[19]), he would have laid the foundations for the real knowledge of Jewish social institutions. His investigations are more a postulate than an actuality. None the less some of his descriptions, and particularly his collections of sources, surpass much of the work done by his greater successors on these problems. For instance, his remarks concerning the institution of *servi cameratus* in Germany, his attempt to find out the facts about Jewish usury in the Middle Ages, his list of the recorded settlements of Jews in medieval Germany[20] represent endeavors which, however limited in scope and possibilities, however inadequate, let us say, in comparison with those of Stobbe, are better than Graetz's, though Graetz wrote partly after Stobbe had done his great work. To a certain extent Jost had a dim feeling that institutions are stronger than persons, although he could not liberate himself fully from the ordinary explanations of the Enlightenment which considered institutions the result of individual actions and reactions. Of course, when he declares that even rulers do not usually do things which do not correspond to the wishes of the population,[21] he is merely voicing the sentiments of his own age in which the legitimistic theories of monarchy tried to emphasize the benefits derived by the public at large from the monarchical system. Occasionally he goes a step further and recognizes that the general conditions prevailing in certain ages influenced the growth of institutions much more than the individual activities of a few outstanding men. So when he speaks about the development of rabbinism during the Second Commonwealth, he declares that "this was not done by one man, by one school, but rabbinism grew as if by itself through the uniform consent of the disciples of the great schools."[22] But even in such a statement, and even though he often uses the expression, then so popular, of a *Begriff des Rabbinismus,* he is naturally far from the Hegelian philosophy with its intrinsic development of the *Begriffe.*

It is needless to say that he cannot be compared even in regard to this study of institutions and other social factors with Niebuhr. As a son of the famous Danish traveler and landowner, Carsten Niebuhr, the historian of Rome, had, from childhood on, enjoyed opportunities to learn about practical life which Jost never had. In mature life, Niebuhr had an unusual public and financial career as the head of the national banks of Denmark and Prussia, and as Prussian ambassador to Rome and other states. Such activities were not congenial to his romantic, essentially impractical mind with which a real man of action like Baron Stein often grew impatient; but it is only in the light of these experiences that we can understand his deep insight into the fundamental economic and social processes in history. We shall expect in vain to find in Jost anything comparable to Niebuhr's deep understanding of the agrarian problems of ancient Rome. This was an intuitive grasp, to be sure, but based upon practical experience, and, as such, it has been of invaluable assistance to all succeeding investigators, down to Max Weber and Rostovtzeff. But for all of Jost's limited field of experience in his schoolrooms and offices of philanthropic societies, from his desk as editor of periodicals and as fighter for the rights of his people, he could see much more than, for instance, the other historian to whom we are comparing him, Neander. Neander, in his seclusion, knew nothing of life but what was reflected in books. Awkward and sometimes ridiculous in the simplest affairs of everyday life, he betrays in many of his views and opinions an extreme ignorance of everything practical. Jost is somewhere between Neander and Niebuhr. His explanations are sometimes conventionally "enlightened," his treatment of social factors is often entirely detached from that of the other sides of life, but in several cases he makes remarkable attempts to deal with problems neglected by most of his predecessors and successors almost till the end of the nineteenth century.

As a matter of fact he got very little help from his predecessors. There was a great deal of earlier literature on the Jewish past, but it was utterly inadequate in its treatment of most aspects of history. The non-Jewish world then, as later, was much more interested in the history of the Jews before the rise of Christianity than in the following ages. But even those periods were treated for the most part by theologians or philologians. It is interesting to hear from Jost himself how little help he could expect from either his Gentile or Jewish forerunners.[23] The result was that he had to deal with a vast literature from which he received but little valuable information. In some cases he found out with deep and justifiable regret that after many years of intensive work in order to control the abundant literature in this or that field, he was not getting anything worth while out of it. In fact, he himself states that he had been gathering the material for his history fully six years before he started to publish his book. He added nine more years of hard labor while it was in the process of publication. But even this labor did not suffice to cover all the accumulated writings of centuries, and he confesses that in many cases he could not manage to read half of what he knew was written on a subject.[24]

He had one very important predecessor—Basnage. It is typically human that Jost overlooks the important progress in the study of Jewish history made by this pioneer of the early eighteenth century and often proves very harsh and unfair in criticizing his shortcomings. In one general sentence he depreciates the achievements of the French historian and declares them to have been almost useless for himself.[25] So he often calls him *leichtfertig* in his etymologies, speaks about the *Geschwätz des Basnage,* and so on.[26] Nevertheless he is really much indebted to the Frenchman, whose synthesizing endeavor represents a real milestone in Jewish historical literature and whose very shortcomings acted as an incentive towards improvement and progress.

But in Jost's own time there was a strong awakening of interest in the Jewish past among Jews and Gentiles alike. Parallel with the revival of Jewish studies and the foundation of the Wissenschaft des Judentums by great Jewish scholars in different countries, interest among Christian historians was steadily growing. Jost could make use to a large extent of the literature which appeared while his own work was still in progress. For instance, he could utilize for his third volume, published in 1822, a monograph of J. J. Bellermann on the Essenes and another of Bishop Münter on the wars under Trajan and Hadrian, both of which appeared in 1821. In his later volumes dealing with medieval history he was helped considerably by publications inspired by the French Academy, which in 1823 arranged a prize contest for essays dealing with the following question: "To examine the status of Jews in France, Spain and Italy from the beginning of the fifth to the end of the sixteenth centuries of the Common Era, under the different aspects of civil law, commerce and literature."[27] Beugnot's essay proved particularly helpful in Jost's investigations.

However, all this literature could not clear up the most obscure points in the sources themselves. For this purpose Jost had to use his own judgment and in particular the new standards of *criticism*. In this respect, too, he is only partly a son of his own age. Compared with Niebuhr's, his achievements appear to be on a rather limited scale. The historian of Rome could boast of a philological criticism so precise that he "dissected words as the anatomist dissects bodies," and of a historical criticism that penetrated into the very spirit and essence of the sources before him, and, in many cases, found behind the apparent and obvious, the hidden, underlying sources that had been obscured for centuries. We shall look in vain for any such thorough philologico-historical criticism in Jost. However, nobody can be blamed for not utilizing the methods just introduced by a greater mind than his own. Niebuhr's philologico-historical criticism in the investigation of sources proved to be perhaps the most influential element in the development of historical research throughout the century. In comparison, however, with the other historians of his age and particularly with his predecessors, Jost's critical standards are not at all to be despised. Never a distinguished philologian, he yet tries to examine the meaning of words and to find out by analogies and comparisons what their essence is. His historical criticism is superior to his philology. He tries to place every source in its natural surrounding and in its own period. The most interesting in this respect is his biblical criticism. Though he was not an extreme innovator and merely quoted his predecessors, Michaelis, Eichhorn, Tychsen and others with approval, he often corrected them and made a remarkable attempt, on the whole, to surpass the achievements of those before him. Particularly among the Jews, his views must have appeared quite revolutionary. He knows that when he declares that the Holy Scriptures represent a series of fragments written at different times by different authors and collected much later by a redactor without reference to their historical connection, he is adopting Eichhorn's general theory of fragments and his critical application of it to the poetical parts of the Bible. But he regards all this only as a successful beginning. He goes a step further and wants to break up the Holy Scriptures into their components, to extract the different fragments and to rearrange them in their historical order. The means he suggests to achieve this are mainly philological, since he attempts to identify the common authorship of different fragments only by applying the test of style. Style and philology in general must help reconstruct the historical sequence. To illustrate his theory, he tries to show in the case of the Pentateuch how such a reconstruction can be made, but limits himself in regard to the other books of the Hebrew Bible to a few general and occasional remarks. But even in his rearrangement of the Pentateuch fragments he is truly aware that this is merely a beginning which has to be followed by more thorough investigations. He himself promises to deal with it at some future time.[28]

This one example, however inadequate in details, shows us what Jost regarded as important from the point of view of philologico-historical criticism, and what he tried to do wherever a certain amount of work had been done before. Concerning talmudic and post-talmudic literature, there was so little preparatory criticism that Jost, with his limited resources, could only indicate certain general desiderata. He would have been unable to go through this vast literature himself with the sharp "surgeon's knife" of a Niebuhr, even if he had been as exact a philologian and as intuitive a thinker as Niebuhr. The state of Jewish literary and other sources, particularly of the post-biblical period, could not even be compared with the tremendous amount of sifting and clearing already done for the Latin literature by the great minds of the Renaissance. We must count it a great achievement that Jost, guided much more by his own feeling than by the slight remarks of Zacuto and others, declared that most of the Kabbalistic writings must be posterior to their alleged antiquity.[29]

Jost's attitude towards the Jewish prayerbook is also interesting. Although he feels that this book represents "one of the most important documents of ancient culture and at the same time an artistic collection of the most audacious interpolations," he does not undertake the difficult task of classifying the portions of the book historically, because he has learned that this task was being done by another man. But even without Zunz' work we may be quite certain that Jost's critical work would not have much resembled the great achievement of the man whom Jost himself calls the "most erudite in the field of neo-rabbinic literature in the century."[30]

Notwithstanding some daring utterances, Jost may be regarded as a rather conservative critic. He himself knows that he is not "a friend of conjectures," and he emends texts only on rare occasions. He also has a principle of retaining sources as long as he has no conclusive proofs of their unreliability.[31] In general he is as far from the undiscriminating, destructive criticism based on dogmatic prejudices of the Enlightenment as he is from the scientific radicalism of the later nineteenth century with its contempt for traditional sources. In this regard, too, in accordance with his inner nature, he is quiet and rather objective, and much more bellicose in general statements than in their practical application.

Indeed he could not easily make this practical application in such a general work of synthesis. It is an utter injustice to demand from Jost a thorough criticism and compilation of sources like that of Rapoport. To compare a monograph of Rapoport on one single personality like R. Hai Gaon, or R. Nathan of Rome, with corresponding passages in Jost and to declare Jost's narrative "superficial talk," as Graetz does, is anything but fair. The author of a broad synthesis cannot be as accurate on individual points as the investigator of a narrow field. This is particularly true in the case of Jost, whose synthesis is based on so little previous work. Jost himself was quite aware that it needed courage to undertake what he undertook. Zunz, undoubtedly a more gifted man, faced the same problem and withdrew. As is often the case, a certain degree of temerity helped the one to accomplish his task, while full consciousness of the obstacles made the other man renounce the enterprise altogether. Jost partly foresaw the difficulties and with the progress of time felt them more and more keenly.[32] Neither did he overlook the various technical obstacles, like obtaining the necessary books under the then primitive conditions of libraries, and other major and minor handicaps. It is enough to mention that during the publication of the first volumes, the printer had not even enough type to print the final forms of some Hebrew letters. We can only be glad that Jost was not wise enough to see his difficulties fully and to withdraw too early from the field.

However, he felt that he was bound to do the work. Although he was of quite a reserved nature, he regarded it almost as a civic duty, for the sake of the Jews as well as of the world at large, to try to make the past of the Jewish people better understood by Jews and Gentiles alike. It was as much a public service as it was a scientific undertaking in his own eyes. Therefore, he made up his mind from the very beginning to write in as popular a style as possible, without lowering his scholarly standards. This aim imposed upon him limitations which were not quite welcome to him. He felt that he had to give up some of the most brilliant features of contemporary historical literature for the sake of clarity.[33] For the same reason he avoided, as far as possible, discussions of a scientific character in the text itself. At first he removed all references and digressions to the appendix but changed this procedure later, after much urging, by putting brief references under the line for the benefit of the scholar. Even when he chose to insert long quotations from sources into his narrative—some of them cover several pages each—he tried to give a fluent German translation and selected topics which would not bore the general public.

He is in this regard much more orderly than Niebuhr, whose discussions and digressions encumber his historical narrative in a manner hardly palatable to the ordinary reader. But Niebuhr, even though his aspirations exceeded his achievements, was an artist. Jost was just a simple unimaginative narrator. His style has none of the brilliancy, picturesqueness and virility of the great later historians, of a Ranke, a Treitschke, a Renan and, among the Jews, of a Graetz. It is, however, clearer and less involved than the style of Niebuhr, and less monotonous than that of Neander. Much briefer periods and sentences than those of these contemporaries make his German far more comprehensible to the ordinary reader, and that, after all, was his chief aim.

We must not infer, however, that he intended any kind of propaganda in writing his Jewish history. Notwithstanding everything said against his purposes by Graetz in his moralizing manner, we may fully believe that Jost tried to avoid apologetics wherever he could. It may be true that his announcement at the beginning of his work[34] reflected only his intentions at the time, and that they underwent certain changes with the progress of his work. Doubtless his optimism regarding the stage reached in the discussions of the Jewish problem did not last until the end of his historical activities. Had he not himself been obliged to take up arms in defense of Judaism against a new wave of accusations, whether intellectual like those of the Italian-Polish Chiarini, or political like those of the Prussian Streckfuss? But essentially we believe in his sincerity, and his desire to state matters as they were, regardless of any particular ends. Things should be changed only if, after thorough investigation, it is found that improvement is needed. But these practical ends are not to be allowed to interfere with the historical truth as it reveals itself to the inquiring eye of the historian. Impartiality seems to him the most vital element in every real historical work and he asserts his own objectivity so often that he almost arouses suspicion. As a matter of fact, he is not always quite so detached as he would have us believe. Occasionally he finds words of severe condemnation for the lack of enthusiasm of other historians. So he accuses the historians of the Crusades along with the rulers of that period of coolness in dealing with "the horrible fanaticism of the Crusaders."[35] Indeed, he himself is led quite often to use harsher expressions than are absolutely necessary in his denunciations of the Kabbalists within, and the enemies of Judaism without. But these are all only occasional slips and deviations from the general highway of straightforward objective scholarship.

This very objectivity and impartiality may have done him more harm in the eyes of some of his contemporaries than any of the real shortcomings of his work. If Geiger does not detect in him "any character or spirit" or if he regards "the whole man with all his reservations and assertions about lack of tendency and principles, as merely foolish;"[36] and if Graetz declares sharply that "he gave to Jewish history, undeniably heroic, a dry Philistine character, despoiling it of the brightness with which it was endowed even in the eyes of the unprejudiced Christian observers;"[37] it was because they were irritated, most of all, by his lack of enthusiasm and his impartiality both in style and treatment. Luzzatto, again, objects sharply to his criticism of the Bible and his somewhat hostile attitude to the Talmud and its teachers.[38] The young Heine, in his own realm, condemns Jost's manner of writing, and says in a letter to Zunz that Jost "might have purposely written his earlier volumes so poorly, in order to make the later ones appear the more brilliant." In all these denunciations we find very little of that objective and constructive criticism of which Graetz speaks, while accusing Jost of not having learned from it in his later years, as he should have. This kind of criticism was occasionally published in the shape of reviews, usually by Christian scholars, on the volumes of his book as they appeared. Some of them Jost acknowledges; some others, particularly those written in general terms, he rejects. He is in general honest enough to accept the truth from anybody who is ready to give it to him, and time and again he repeats his request to all readers to correct him wherever he may be wrong. But the criticism of Jewish scholars had little of that impartial character. It was too much a period of inner and outward struggle, a period of the severe fight for emancipation and of profound conflicts about the necessity and the extent of the Jewish Reformation, as well as about the problems of assimilation and absorption of the Jewish group by the native majority. In such a period of strong clashes and struggles, scholarship too became a means and a weapon. Consciously or unconsciously most of the scientific contributions became more or less eloquent, more or less ardent, pleas for the views of their authors concerning actual affairs in contemporary life. In such a period impartiality could hardly be tolerated. A non-partisan was almost an enemy, and a man who tried to satisfy everybody, satisfied nobody.

These struggles are over now. The turmoil of those dissensions and quarrels and vicissitudes has quieted down, and although new conflicts have arisen, the old ones are so far from ours that we are not prevented from getting the right perspective for historical judgment. Now we can restore Jost to his rightful position in the historical literature of the Jewish people. Although not a great spirit, he was certainly a pioneer. Although not a man of genius and high aspirations, he was a solid, quiet worker who tried to lay solid, reliable foundations for the development of Jewish historical knowledge, and succeeded in doing so to a large extent. Now, when the mist of depreciation and underestimation, arising from the quarrels of the moment, has been cleared away, now on the hundredth anniversary of the completion of his chief work, we can recognize the real, although not unqualified value of Jost the historian, of Jost who has so greatly influenced both historical research and the writing of Jewish history in the hundred years which have elapsed. Furthermore, some portions of his work are not yet—perhaps we should deplore this fact—as fully antiquated as they appear to be. In particular the tenth volume, or his *Modern History 1815-46,* has the merits of a source, since it was written by a contemporary who witnessed and even took an active part in some of the events described in it. Moreover, it contains so much valuable material, put together with such impartial and often sound judgment, that it has not been replaced by any of the later publications, including those of Graetz, Philippson and Dubnow.

II

Heinrich (Hirsch) Graetz, 1817-1891

*A Biographical Sketch**

GRAETZ'S EARLY YEARS REVEALED some extraordinary features, but they can be only briefly summarized here. Born October 31, 1817, in Xions, Posen, he spent his first years there and in Zerkow. In 1831, he came to Wollstein to study under the direction of the local rabbi, S. S. Munk, who five years later conferred upon him the title, *Ḥaber*. At the same time he taught himself French and Latin and read secular books of all kinds. Having gone through a religious crisis, the future historian was brought back to Orthodox Judaism by reading the then newly published *Nineteen Letters of Ben Uziel*. Its author, Samson Raphael Hirsch, invited him to Oldenburg (Graetz included the correspondence with Hirsch in his *Diary*),[1] where Graetz spent the years 1837-40 as Hirsch's pupil and companion. Subsequently, Graetz accepted a tutorial position in Ostrowo. Beginning in 1842, he was enabled by a special permit from the Ministry of Cults to study in Breslau, but he later (1845) secured his Ph.D. degree in Jena. His dissertation, entitled *Gnostizismus und Judentum,* appeared in Krotoschin in 1846.

Other youthful writings are mentioned by Graetz in his *Diary,* but the literary essays of his Oldenburg period are totally lost. While in Breslau in 1843-45, Graetz sent regular reports to Julius Fürst's *Orient* about the then raging controversy between the Rabbis Abraham Geiger and Gedaliah Tiktin; his accounts definitely opposed Geiger. His first scholarly publication likewise revealed his anti-Geiger animus; it consisted of a sharp review of the latter's important handbook on the language of the Mishnah,

* Abridged translation of the German article in *Encyclopaedia Judaica,* VII (1931), 645-52, where many additional bibliographical data are available.

to which Geiger replied in kind.[2] In August, 1845, Graetz submitted an address of thanks, provided with many signatures, to Zacharias Frankel on the occasion of the latter's demonstrative exodus from the Frankfort Rabbinical Assembly.[3] Soon afterwards he became a collaborator of Frankel's *Zeitschrift für die religiösen Interessen des Judentums*. In 1846 his *Die Konstruktion der jüdischen Geschichte* appeared, a significantly early formulation of his later philosophy of history.[4]

In 1845, Graetz abandoned his original plan to become a rabbi. After passing a teacher's examination, he became the principal of a religious school then newly founded by the Orthodox group of the Breslau community. This school lasted only till 1848. After serving for a while as correspondent of the Breslau *Oder-Zeitung*, he came, on Hirsch's recommendation, to Lundenburg, where he served as principal of the Jewish school (1850). Here he married Marie, daughter of Ber Monasch, a well-known printer and publisher in Krotoschin (Marie's nephew, Sir John Monash, was later to play an historic role as commanding general of the Australian expeditionary force on the western front during World War I). Graetz fell victim, however, to intrigues and denunciations by personal enemies, and was forced in 1852 to give up his position.[5]

From Lundenburg, Graetz moved to Berlin where, at the community's invitation, he delivered lectures on Jewish history before students, sharing this semi-academic position with Leopold Zunz and Michael Sachs. Encouraged by this mark of recognition he began, in 1853, to publish his *Geschichte der Juden von den ältesten Zeiten bis zur Gegenwart*. The first to appear was volume IV, devoted to the period after the destruction of the Second Temple; it was issued by Veit & Co., in Berlin. In that very year Frankel invited him to serve as *Dozent* of Jewish history in the newly founded Jewish Theological Seminary in Breslau, whose small but distinguished faculty also included Frankel himself, Jacob Bernays and Manuel Joel.

Apart from teaching Jewish history and literature, Graetz was able now to devote much time to his extensive scholarly activities which established his international reputation. Yet, on Frankel's demise in 1875, he was not appointed director of the Seminary owing to the statutory provision that this position was to be held by an ordained rabbi. On the other hand, in 1869, the University of Breslau appointed him honorary professor. He was a frequent contributor to the Seminary's journal, the *Monatsschrift für Geschichte und Wissenschaft des Judentums* which, after Frankel's retirement from the editorship in 1869, he took over until 1888 (in 1882-86 he shared the editorial responsibilities with P. F. Frankl). All during this time Graetz was also active as a publicist and communal leader. One of his essays discussing "The Rejuvenation of the Jewish People," in particular, stimulated a lively discussion in the Austrian and German press and had a curious aftermath.[6] The *Wiener Kirchenzeitung* had denounced his implied denial of a personal Messiah, and his interpretation of the Isaianic prophecies as referring to the sufferings of the people of Israel; the Church periodical considered his views as tantamount to heaping ridicule on the belief in the personal Messiah by both Orthodox Jews and Christians. Consequently, Leopold Kompert, editor of the *Jahrbuch*, in which the essay had appeared, was condemned by the Vienna authorities to the payment of a fine.

In 1869, Graetz founded the Jewish Theological Society in Breslau, which he viewed as a nucleus for a middle-of-the-road party between Orthodoxy and Reform. It also was to serve as an agency for the promotion of the science of Judaism. But the Society lasted only one year.[7] For many years Graetz also served as member of the Board of the Alliance Israélite Universelle in Paris, and he probably participated in the founding of the Société des Études Juives. In 1872 he visited Palestine and, together with his associates, published a *Memorandum* on the shortcomings of the then existing system of relief distribution, the so-called *Halukkah,* which evoked a storm of protest from the Palestinian communities.[8] On this occasion, he was also instrumental in establishing an orphanage in Jerusalem under European direction. Upon his return he evinced great interest in the establishment of a Jewish academy of higher learning.[9] Nor was Graetz unaware of the general political developments in his country and abroad, although, in contrast to his early outspoken journalistic correspondence, he now refrained from stating his views publicly. It is only by chance that we learn about his meeting Karl Marx and the latter's daughter during their vacation in Carlsbad. The Jewish historian seems to have sufficiently impressed the great socialist thinker, who was otherwise indifferent, even averse to Judaism; for upon his return to London, Marx sent Graetz his *Kapital* and several other writings, as well as a work by his prospective son-in-law, P. S. Lissagaray. The very fact that the betrothal of Marx's daughter, which was largely kept secret by the family, was divulged to Graetz, shows the impression the historian had made upon the Marx family. In his reply Graetz expressed his opinions on the international situation, the shortcomings of the German Socialist Party, and so forth, with his usual vigor and clarity. He also offered Marx, as a token of his appreciation, his book on *Kohelet*, which, he felt, would possibly be of interest to Marx because of its strongly secular views.[10]

In essence Graetz displayed a Jewish national orientation with some proto-Zionist leanings, in so far as one can speak of Zionism before the foundation of the Zionist movement. This is attested to, in particular, by his "Letters of an English Lady about Judaism and Semitism," as well as by his essay on "The Significance of Judaism for the Present and Future."[11] His *History* made a great impression on, among others, Moses Hess, who translated the third volume into French. After the Kattowitz Conference, in 1884, Graetz joined the Lovers of Zion movement, but withdrew from it because of its growing nationalist extremism.[12] However, like most of his German contemporaries, he repudiated Yiddish as a "ridiculous gibberish" (*lachenerregendes Kauderwelsch*).[13] On the other hand, he had a deep love for the Hebrew language, although his own Hebrew style left much to be desired. Nor is the treatment of modern Hebrew literature in his *History* altogether satisfactory.

Graetz's main achievements lie in the scholarly field, however. Above all one must mention his historical work, which appeared under the title, *Geschichte der Juden von den ältesten Zeiten bis auf die Gegenwart* (that is, up until 1848), over a period of twenty-three years (1853-76). This large work was followed in 1888 by his popular but somewhat more up-to-date three volume *Volkstümliche Geschichte*. In addition, he published a considerable number of historical books and essays, particularly in the annual reports of the Breslau Seminary and in the *Monatsschrift*.[14]

Graetz's historical outlook reveals many influences of the dominant Hegelian philosophy, but it also shows traces of the doctrine of historic ideas expounded by Wilhelm von Humboldt and Leopold von Ranke. At the same time (and this is his peculiarity), Graetz pursued an exclusively national theory of history which caused him to overlook some of the most important connections with world history. In his analytical treatment of the sources, he followed the philological-critical method which had become regnant in German historiography since the days of Barthold Georg Niebuhr, but he did not draw from his source studies widely enough, neglecting, in particular, archival material. He also paid relatively little attention to large areas of Jewish history, including the history of the Jews in Poland, Russia and Turkey. In general, he interpreted the history of the Jews in the Diaspora almost exclusively in terms of a "history of sufferings and scholars" and hence paid little attention to economic and social history.[15] Even political and legal developments were treated mainly as a background for his description of persecutions and the achievements of individual leaders. His treatment is, therefore, predominantly biographical. With extreme subjectivism, he indulged in sharp condemnations of movements within and outside Judaism which he disliked, such as later Christianity, German nationalist trends, Kabbalah, Hasidism, and the Reform movement. The eleventh volume, in particular, dealing with the history of the late eighteenth and nineteenth centuries, often gives the impression of a publicist's indictment or defense, rather than an objective historical treatment.

As a student of the Bible, Graetz insisted upon the unity and pre-exilic origin of the entire Pentateuch.[16] But he was quite radical with respect to Prophets and Hagiographa, accepting without hesitation, for instance, the theory of two Hoseas and three Zechariahs, and placing Kohelet in the days of Herod. His approach was particularly valuable because of his extensive use of the ancient versions and his frequently felicitous utilization of the linguistic materials in talmudic and later Hebrew letters.

At first Graetz's *History* enjoyed little recognition. His old friend Samson Raphael Hirsch published in *Jeschurun* (1855-56) a series of sharp attacks on the fourth volume, which he described as "a piece of fantasy derived from superficial combinatory mannerisms." Less surprisingly, Abraham Geiger assailed the work as containing "stories but no history." Moritz Steinschneider, too, criticized it sharply and even accused Graetz of constant plagiarism.[17] Graetz replied in various periodicals, as well as in later volumes of his *History,* adding many critical asides on his predecessors, Isaac Markus Jost and Leopold Zunz.

While these scholarly polemics were of primary interest only to the Jewish public, Heinrich von Treitschke's sharp attack on Graetz in 1879 (reprinted in the following year in a widely-read pamphlet entitled *Ein Wort über unser Judentum*) created a stir in all German-speaking countries, which were then in the throes of a strong anti-Semitic revival. In the course of that controversy many Jewish and non-Jewish authors published pamphlets of their own. Almost all those who repudiated Treitschke more or less expressly disavowed Graetz as well. The name of Ludwig Philippson stands out among the few who entered the ranks on Graetz's side.[18]

One result of that controversy was that when, in 1885, the Deutsch-Israelitisher-Gemeindebund founded an "Historical Commission for the History of the Jews in Germany," Graetz was not invited to join the Board. In the rest of the Jewish world, however, the historian enjoyed ever greater acceptance. On his seventieth birthday in 1887, he received many signs of recognition, including the publication of a *Jubelschrift* in his honor. That same year he was invited to deliver the opening address at the Anglo-Jewish Historical Exhibition. A year later the Historical Section of the Madrid Academy appointed him its honorary member. His popularity increased after the publication of his "Popular History" and the numerous editions and translations of his magnum opus. At his death on September 7, 1891, he was widely recognized as one of the most representative spokesmen of the science of Judaism of his day.

Graetz and Ranke: A Methodological Study*

IF ONE WISHES TO EVALUATE CORRECTLY Graetz's importance as an historian, one must go back to his own period and milieu. We need but consider the state of Jewish historiography in the 1840's and 1850's, when Graetz began publishing his works, to appreciate the remarkable progress made since, as well as Graetz's own share in this progress.

It was, indeed, in Graetz's lifetime that the great upsurge began. The large historical work of Isaac Marcus Jost appeared in 1820-29; its achievement will remain memorable despite all defects in the author's research and presentation. At the same time, an enormous amount of work was done in special fields of investigation by men of the rank of Leopold Zunz and Abraham Geiger in Germany, Nachman Krochmal and Salomon J. L. Rapoport in Galicia, and Samuel David Luzzatto in Italy. These scholars and their associates had assembled a vast array of new data and critically examined them with the more advanced scholarly techniques of their generation.

Only after all these preliminary studies was it possible to venture a new attempt at synthesis. Although Graetz frequently lacked understanding for the great merits of these predecessors, and although he censured with particular severity the work of Jost, to whose pioneering efforts he owed so much, we must not overlook the essential similarities between the two historians, which far transcended their dissimilarities. Without these forerunners, Graetz would no more have attained his high achievement than would Jost, were he writing forty years later, have remained in the early pioneering stage of Jewish historiography.

---

* Revised translation from the German essay, "Graetzens Geschichtsschreibung," *MGWJ*, LXII (1918), 5-15.

However, forty years had passed, and Graetz represented, indeed, a significant step forward not only because of the greater richness of materials available to him, but also because of his novel method of source investigation and his magnificent presentation. These innovations kept pace with the changes which had, in the meantime, taken place in the European, especially German, historiography—changes to a large extent associated with the name of Leopold von Ranke. Although he was not directly Graetz's teacher (he served as professor in Berlin while Graetz studied at Breslau), Ranke exerted a considerable influence on most German historians of the period, particularly through his works on the popes and on German history during the Reformation.[1] He must have doubly appealed to the like-minded Graetz. Their similarities are so great, their points of contact so numerous, that a comparison between the greatest historian of the German people and the main founder of the Jewish historical science is likely to shed much light on the latter's historical method and general approaches.[2]

Above all, both historians shared the basic doctrine of *historic ideas,* first introduced by Wilhelm von Humboldt. According to this doctrine, every historic period reveals certain dominant trends which determine the evolution of states and nations, and exert considerable influence on the lives of individuals. This theory greatly differs from the Hegelian teleological doctrine of ideas, which sees everywhere in history the progressive evolution of the absolute spirit. Both historians, Graetz and Ranke, thus embarked on the search for the deeper connections concealed behind the innumerable details. As early as 1839, Ranke had obliquely formulated his program by stating in an academic address: "History must try to present the sequence of events as sharply and concisely as possible and lend each of them its particular coloring and shape. Yet it must not rest at this point, but it must also try to penetrate the deepest and most secret motivations of life which is lived by the human kind." We find the same attitude, perhaps to an even greater extent, in the historian of the Jews. David Kaufmann perceptively observed:

Without trying to see in history a mere movement of ideas, according to a prejudiced Hegelianism, nor wishing to impose upon the events a pragmatic interpretation which is as remote from the facts of life as is the imaginary realism of imaginative poets with respect to all the true realities of this world, he [Graetz] untiringly sought to proclaim with emphasis the inner spiritual evolution which forced itself upon him during his investigation of the Jewish past.[3]

Both historians accepted these ideas, however, as existing entities without trying to unravel their deeper origins. Even the Berlin professor of history who, despite his religious bent of mind, rigidly separated the field of theology from that of history, merely attributed these ideas to the divine guidance of history. He himself expressed it bluntly: "Here, too, it is theology."[4] A similar inclination may readily be observed in the case of the professor at the Breslau Theological Seminary, who was often reproached for being more of a theologian than an historian.

Yet even here we find a fundamental difference between the two men: Ranke denied all *national* theories of history, whereas Graetz was their enthusiastic spokesman. Ranke sought the dominant ideas not within any single nation or culture, but in the large international concatenation of the Germanic-Latin civilization, a position which, notwithstanding its intrinsic merits, was, largely for external reasons, abandoned by most of his own disciples and successors. Graetz, on the contrary, was not only the historian of a single people, but he also wished to explain its evolution mainly through internal factors. The dominant trends determining the Jewish developments originate and disappear, according to him, only within the Jewish people as a separate entity. As if it were possible completely to isolate any community or individual from the rest of the world and deny any external influences upon it!

One may still forgive Graetz this self-imposed limitation because of the enormous multitude and variety of the previously inadequately explored Jewish sources. However, most of his successors, even those who were important scholars in their own right, adhered to this one-sided interpretation of the past of the Jewish people, though the insufficiency of this interpretation had become doubly obvious, since as Graetz himself had stated, the Jews had "felt, thought, talked, sung in the tongues of all peoples."

Another significant parallel between Ranke and Graetz lay in their use of *historical psychology,* that is, in their attempt to illumine the far-reaching changes within a country or community by a description of the actions and attitudes of its leading personalities. Rarely had an historian succeeded in so deeply penetrating the innermost thoughts of historic personalities as did Ranke and, in part, also Graetz. Primarily by sketching the lives and works of individual leaders, they succeeded in making entire historic periods come alive before the eyes of the enthralled reader. Obviously, such a treatment frequently led to the neglect of other, more basic elements. But even if they sometimes fell short in the thoroughness of their investigation, these two highly attractive writers more than made it up by the brilliance and human aspects of their presentation.

In this connection Ranke and Graetz reveal another common feature. Both of them present characters congenial to their own personalities in a masterly fashion. Few characterizations by Ranke have rivaled the brilliance of his classic sketches of several Roman popes akin to his own temperament and outlook. On the other hand, he was rather helpless when confronted by earthy and crude personalities; the workings of their minds almost entirely escaped his penetrating eye. The same thing is true of Graetz, who was first and foremost a believer in human reason. That is why his character sketches of great halakhists appear so real and truthful, so graphic and lively. But he is totally unable to probe the inner, highly complicated souls of a kabbalist and a Ḥasid. However, while Ranke, with his general effort at objectivity, tries hard to understand strange phenomena, Graetz, so much more subjective and a sworn enemy of all mystic movements, makes no effort whatsoever to solve such riddles. We may thus understand why so many misfits appear in the otherwise magnificent portrait gallery of the Jewish historian.

The philological-critical examination of sources, rightly considered one of the main virtues of Ranke's historical method, is also employed by Graetz in an extraordinary degree. He was the first to exploit intensively the manifold sources for the treatment of Jewish historical problems from ancient to modern times, examine them critically with philological exactitude, compare them carefully with one another, and only then build upon these firm foundations his imposing structure. He always went back to the original sources, however numerous and resistant to analysis, and scrutinized them in detail. However, even here, we must not judge him by our contemporary standards. As is well known, Ranke leaned excessively, for example, on the reports of the Venetian ambassadors. Graetz, to be sure, did not and could not thus rely upon a single type of source material. Even after the utilization of all available sources there remained too many lacunae which he was able to fill only with his truly creative historical intuition. But he remained alien to archival research, which is now considered a prime requisite in all historical investigation of modern history. One might excuse Graetz, though not the majority of his successors, by the enormous quantity of source material, whether printed or available in a few libraries, which he had at his disposal.

Also connected with this type of source investigation is Graetz's one-sidedness in the field of his historical treatment. Just as Ranke's work shows a reciprocal relationship between his almost exclusive emphasis on political history and his pre-eminent use of political sources, Graetz stresses sources bearing mainly on the story of Jewish sufferings and scholars. Neither historian took cognizance of economic history. Graetz treated even the legal and political history of the Jewish people chiefly as a background for the history of persecutions and scholarship.

A final and most important parallel between the two historians may be found in their style and method of presentation. As a writer, too, Ranke represents a combination of the dry, matter-of-fact historiography of the Enlightenment era, and the lively, colorful narratives of romanticism. Graetz is an unmitigated romantic. His descriptions are more picturesque, his style is richer and more differentiated. He is every inch a writer; indeed, often more writer than objective investigator. In his criticism of the Italian historian, Arrigo Caterino Davila, Ranke wrote:

> If a poetic work combines intellectual content with pure form, everyone is satisfied. If a scholarly work penetrates its materials and explains them in a novel fashion, nothing else is expected. The task of the historian, on the contrary, is simultaneously literary and scholarly; history is both art and science. It has to meet all the postulates of criticism and scholarship like any philological work. But at the same time it must give the intelligent reader the same pleasure as the most excellent literary production.[5]

This double aim was also before Graetz's eyes. In fact, the pleasure offered to the intelligent general reader appeared to him more important than the thoroughgoing review of all available details. Out of this aspiration came the division in his presentation between the narrative sections and the appended large excursuses, which David Kaufmann colorfully compared with basements of banks of issue, where cash and gold buillion is kept ever ready to back up the notes in circulation.

At the same time, one must not overlook another element in Graetz's method of presentation, namely his excessive subjectivity.[6] Ranke, on the other hand, considered objectivity a major virtue or, as he formulated it at the very beginning of his scholarly career, he wished to show how things had really been. While the passionless Ranke objected to the burning passions of his forerunner, B. G. Niebuhr, passionate Graetz viewed his predecessor I. M. Jost's lack of passion as the latter's greatest weakness. For Graetz the reconstruction of the history of his people had become a personal experience fraught with deep emotion. In every line of his *History*, we sense his pulsating heart which cries out over the sufferings of his people, just as it rejoices at the description of its few happy days. This subjectivity, of which the subsequent Jewish historiography was unable to rid itself sufficiently, is a major weakness of Graetz the historian, but one of the strongest aspects of Graetz the writer. In the midst of the difficult struggle to establish the new science of Judaism on firm foundations, and to win for it the minds of a generation partly estranged from the Jewish faith and culture, such subjectivity proved to be more advantageous than harmful. Just as Macaulay (who in this respect shows remarkable affinities with Graetz), undertook the publication of his masterly *History of England* "cheerfully bearing the reproach of having descended below the dignity of history, if I can succeed in placing before the English of the nineteenth century a true picture of the life of their ancestors,"[7] so Graetz succeeded in persuading German Jewish youth, who had increasingly become alienated from Judaism, to put aside for weeks or months at a time the reading of some non-Jewish literature in favor of his presentation of the life of their ancestors. He was able to awaken or to reinforce the interest of the entire Jewish world in its own past. This was a national achievement which, despite minor defects in detail, ultimately accrued to the immeasurable advantage of Jewish historical studies as well.

In this way Graetz had really shown his mastery. Through his *History* and, to a far lesser extent, through his biblical studies, he made lasting contributions to the knowledge of Judaism. Not unexpectedly, many members of the scholarly guild were prepared to overlook his major general achievements because of some minor flaws in detail. It suffices here to quote only Moritz Steinschneider's sharp rejection of "the literary dishonesty and lack of judgment of that historical compiler."[8] But the people as a whole expressed its gratitude to Graetz during his lifetime. Before long the scholars, too, followed suit. Hardly any work of the science of Judaism achieved the success of Graetz's *History*. Published in the original in four or five editions, translated into six languages (Hebrew, English, French, Russian, Hungarian and Yiddish), this voluminous work had become a genuine people's book; it furnished intellectual sustenance to generations of readers without losing its extraordinary scholarly reputation.

12

Moritz Steinschneider's Contributions
to Jewish Historiography*

STEINSCHNEIDER WAS NOT AN HISTORIAN; not even an historian of literature or science, to the history of which he has made such signal contributions. He was primarily a bibliographer who, through a stupendous familiarity with manuscripts and rare books, was able to elucidate an endless array of details pertaining to a great variety of subjects in the history of Jewish and cognate cultures. Yet he happens to be the author of the *Geschichtsliteratur der Juden* which, published in 1905, is thus far the only comprehensive work covering a large area of Jewish historiography. Although this volume, too, is not really a history of Jewish historians, but rather a bibliography of Jewish historical sources, Steinschneider's contributions to medieval and early modern Jewish historiography here and elsewhere are so significant that, in many respects, he has no peer in that much-neglected discipline.[1]

Moreover, for more than a quarter of a century (1858-65, 1869-85) with a brief three-year interruption, he served as editor of the *Hebräische Bibliographie* or as author of the annual review of the literature pertaining to post-biblical Jewish history for the *Jahresberichte der Geschichtswissenschaft*. He also wrote a great many book reviews, particularly in the *Deutsche Literaturzeitung* (1881-96). In all these capacities he critically appraised most of the current Jewish historical publications. In fact, he considered himself a sort of watchdog for their reliability and worthwhileness. "We shall not let ourselves," he declared, "be confounded

* Reprinted from *Alexander Marx Jubilee Volume*, New York, 1950.

in our belief that faithful gardeners must first of all carefully weed their gardens and that he who plucks nettles must be prepared for stings."[2]

Never discouraged by the proven futility of his warnings, he went on pointing out the shoddiness of many pretentious works of scholarship and, less frequently, placing his stamp of approval on worthwhile studies. By the very nature of this type of work, his own contributions have become extremely diffuse, as may be noted by a mere glance at Kohut's bibliography of his writings and the subsequent supplements in *ZHB*. Nor can one expect real consistency in numberless casual remarks uttered over a period of nearly seven decades. If two of Steinschneider's most faithful and best informed disciples found themselves discouraged after years of labor by the complexity of mastering his widely scattered publications and his never-ending corrections and comments on his previous notes,[3] we must necessarily limit ourselves in the present essay to a few more or less summary observations. It is hoped that serious students of Steinschneider's works will go beyond the quest of further documentation and additional illustration—the present writer himself has suppressed many data which appeared to him of secondary importance—and pursue independent explorations in the numerous ramifications of this significant phase in the work of the great polyhistor.

General Approaches

Steinschneider's interpretation of history was in many ways superior to that of his contemporaries. More sharply than others he drew the distinction between "history" in the political sphere and what he called the history of culture and that of literature. In fact, in one of his periodic attacks on Graetz, he raised objections to the fifth volume of the latter's *Geschichte* as being devoted too much to literature and too little to history proper. Similarly, when Kayserling's *Sephardim*, dedicated to biographical and literary studies of Spanish Jewry, was followed by the first volume

of his *Geschichte der Juden in Spanien und Portugal,* Steinschneider
nodded approval with respect to this extension of his friend's
interest into the domain of history as such.[4]

To be sure, he clearly realized the complementary nature of
the two disciplines as illustrated, for example, in the evolution of
Hebrew printing. He also admitted that Jewish political history
in the dispersion had many peculiar features. It "substitutes,"
he declared, "sufferings for deeds, martyrs for heroes, narrow
communal needs and petty personalities for lofty state interests.
However, the status and treatment of Jews mirrors the entire
culture of states and peoples, for whose history they have transmitted testimony of a contemporary, often unique character."[5] By
thus narrowing the concept of political history, he came close to
justifying Graetz's well-known rationalization of the prevailing
excessive emphasis upon "the history of scholars and sufferings."
Yet, by underscoring this weakness in other writers, he counteracted to some extent the widespread desire to obscure this fundamental issue.

Like no other Jewish scholar of his day, Steinschneider also
stressed the importance of comprehensive knowledge of the non-
Jewish environment and background. In contrast to the prevailing
"isolationist" treatment of Jewish history, he tirelessly emphasized
that "Jewish science and literature can properly be understood and
evaluated only in their interrelations with non-Jewish sciences
and literatures." Even in medieval Christendom, he contended,
despite the concerted efforts of State and Church, segregation never
was water-tight. This was evidenced not only by the constant
use of languages other than Hebrew by the Jews, their "linguisti-
cally amphibian life," but also by the impact of Maimonidean
philosophy on Albertus Magnus and Thomas Aquinas, the unexpectedly large number of Hebrew translations from the Latin
and the extensive personal relations between Christian and Jewish
intellectuals. "The spirit knows no ghetto!" Most intimate were,
however, the interrelations in areas where a modicum of freedom
existed and particularly in the two world literatures, the Arabic
and the German.

Among Arabs and Germans Judaism was "integrated" [*aufgegangen*] but not destroyed. With its own specific approaches it recognized the unity of mankind's great and universal ideas and, thereby, broke through the walls of isolation . . . . Judaism's position within these literatures is one of the noblest tasks of our historiography, equally significant for the evolution of Jewish and world letters.[6]

So conceived, the understanding of the Jewish past required arduous study of the various disciplines and countries. Not sweeping generalizations, but an endless series of monographs was indicated. This was, in his opinion, the keynote of all of Zunz's writings directed at the "redemption of the science of Judaism from the ghetto."[7] Steinschneider himself, evidently under the impact of his early studies in Vienna and Leipzig, particularly under the renowned Leipzig Arabist, Heinrich Leberecht Fleischer, whom he greatly admired, devoted his primary attention to the Jewish role in Arabian culture. Already in 1845 he spoke of the Arab expansion of the seventh century as a great turning point in Jewish as well as general history. At that time he undertook to compile a general survey of Arabic Jewish letters under the title of *Bibliotheca Judaeo-Arabica*. After numerous detailed contributions over a period of six decades, he finally carried out his intention in his "Introduction to the Arabic Literature of the Jews" (*JQR*, 1897-1901) and his *Arabische Literatur der Juden* (1901). If, as early as 1846, Frankel cautioned him against his excessive "Arabomania," Steinschneider retorted sixteen years later that he was still confident of finding in Maimonides certain elements of the Koran and Al-Ghazzali much rather than of Plutarch.[8]

Curiously, this great student of medieval Judaism, of its institutions, leadership and intellectual achievements, had very little use for the medieval period as such, "which the Jews outgrew, much later than the Christians." Like that entire post-Napoleonic generation of Jewish scholars, he was greatly affected by the romantically inspired historical schools of Germany. But like Zunz, Geiger and the others he nevertheless revealed the indestructible impact of European enlightenment in his outlook on life and, particularly, in his political and intellectual liberalism. He glorified, for instance, the impact of modern chemistry on breaking down the walls of separation between the classes and thereby destroying the medieval corporate divisions "with all their moral shortcomings." Few eighteenth-century historians found sharper words of condemnation for the Christian Middle Ages than he did in contrasting them with the evolution under Islam.

> What are the most outstanding features in the totality of the two cultures? [he inquired]. Here segregation in political, economic and social life, extortion, expulsion and Inquisition, incitement, persecution, arson and pillage, false accusations of poisoning of wells and ritual murder. On the Jewish side intimate family life, trust in other-worldly re-wards and national restoration, combined with rigid adher-ence to tradition—religious persecution, like an anvil, steels resistance to the point of martyrdom—a plethora of intel-lectual acumen, wasted on casuistic and hermeneutic min-utiae, the Siamese twins of belief and superstition, the eye always turning from the valley of tears toward Heaven.

What pained him most was that his beloved country of adoption, Germany, had been the major culprit. Explaining his failure to include in the *Hebräische Uebersetzungen* many translations by medieval German Jews, he wrote: "The German Middle Ages offered the Jews torture, stakes for men and books, double toll for emperor and feudal lords at the turnpike and cemetery, remission of penalties and premiums for the desertion of the paternal faith and law, superstition for all happenings in life, also pity and compassion with individuals—all these matters on a par with the southern countries—but no science or enlightenment."[9]

As a liberal and a Jew, Steinschneider was ready to fight for the ideals of the Revolution of 1848. He doubly resented Germany's slow progression toward Jewish equality, as he felt that modern Jewry had immeasurably enriched German culture and, through Hebrew translations, helped spread it to other lands. Upon publication, in 1862, of a German translation of Macaulay's well-known address which "with a truly classical precision and brevity disposes of the so-called Jewish emancipation problem," he wondered whether one ought to regret more the delay of thirty years in its appearance or the fact that it was still needed. Notwithstanding his general contempt for publicist efforts, he greatly admired Gabriel Riesser's consistent championship of Jewish equality, while he resented the debates at the Prussian Diet of 1860 with their purely utilitarian approach to the Jewish question, rather than the simple adherence to the principle of human equality. He believed that there was but one remedy for religious persecution, i.e., free science and humanitarianism. For this reason he published with full approval Geiger's exhortation to his coreligionists that, while the struggle for emancipation "is legitimate and must be carried through to success, the confidence in ultimate victory finds its full support only in the reliance on one's innermost spirit, in the conviction that Judaism is a spiritual power whose full influence on the historic evolution of mankind must not be curtailed." Strongly convinced that the fate of Judaism and that of humanity were deeply interlocked, he uttered the truly prophetic warning, "The history of the daughter religions is a constant series of attempts to murder their own mother. Should one ever succeed, the guilty will share the fate of their victim."[10]

His ardent championship of Jewish emancipation did not make him an anti-nationalist, however. He realized the extraordinary peculiarities of the Jewish national feeling and national history "which confronts the historian with a wholly unparalleled problem" and accepted Zunz's definition of the Jews being "a nation *in partibus.*" While emphasizing that Jewish history in the dispersion should be treated only by countries and regions and that it could be understood only in terms of its environment, he was also convinced that these often disparate strains must be brought into a single focus of the people's own evolution.

The Jews are a nation in the original meaning of that word. Other nations have emerged from racial units into peoplehood by virtue of their fatherland and language and the ensuing common interest and easy exchange of ideas. The Jews, on their part, have been united, at least thus far, by an ideal fatherland and Scripture reaching back into their remotest antiquity as well as the liturgical and scholarly languages associated with it. They have neither sufficient reason for denying their race nor for being ashamed of their intimate ideal unity . . . . We affirm, in fact, that the concept "Jewish" cannot be understood merely in terms of dogmas and rituals, but that the entire Jewish cultural evolution must be viewed as a mirror of the underlying religious and moral ideas and national convictions.

This strongly idealistic, almost Hegelian, interpretation did not blind him to dangers to Jewish survival inherent in Jewish emancipation and assimilation. "Perhaps the true flow of Jewish history," he once opined with a shrug, "will dry up with the complete indenization of the Jewish citizens." But such future possibilities must not affect the treatment of the past of which, for example, born Jews, even if converted to another faith, were part and parcel.[11]

At the same time he gradually lost his youthful interest in the Zionist solution. In the early 1840's he had belonged to a group organized in Vienna by Abraham Benisch to promote "the liberation of our Jewish fellow-countrymen from the galling yoke of intolerance and oppression."[12] In the following two years he often summarized for the *Orient* reports from his friends in England about the progress of Benisch's negotiations with the Foreign Office and the general reaction of the British public to the Jewish aspects of the Eastern Question. In one particularly noteworthy correspondence he took issue with the religious impulses of the British movement for Jewish restoration and declared with his characteristic vigor,

> For those, however, who, like ourselves, allow more room to secular rather than to divine elements in their specula-tions concerning the future fate of Syria, it does not appear

to be one of the most improbable suppositions that the restoration and nationalization of the Jewish people, though unlikely at present, should ultimately become the means of reconciling the conflict of interests [*Prätentionen*] and of establishing a new focus of civilization in that interesting region.

He merely doubted the immediate efficacy of a Jewish petition to the Great Powers.[13]

Later on, however, he became ever more skeptical. Increasingly averse to "sentimentality," he had absolutely no understanding for the emotional outpourings of a Judah Alkalai or Moses Hess. He seconded his associate, Kayserling, in his condemnation of Hess's *Rom und Jerusalem* because of its *Prinzipienreiterei* in calling for the return to the ancient synagogue and, on his own, voiced the hope "that this book will not be used *against* prudent endeavors to ameliorate the sad conditions of the Jews in Palestine." He condemned even more sharply Pinsker's *Autoemancipation* and similar ideas voiced in the *Ha-Maggid*. "This type of propaganda for the colonization of Palestine," he declared, "is more dangerous than anti-Semitism and it is high time that we protest against all such endeavors." With reference to Herzl's political Zionism, finally, he wrote in a private letter (Nov. 24, 1898),

> Already in 1840 I was convinced that our ideas emanating from Austrian conditions were unrealizable. Since that time Zionism appears to me to be a fit subject for folk psychiatry such as can only be cured slowly by continuous education. For a Messiah mankind requires perhaps the whole span of its life on our globe.[14]

Nor were his religious moorings any too deep. Although in his youth a serious candidate for rabbinic office and often serving as a preacher, he gradually drifted away from all organized religion. He continued to praise Judaism's historic ideals. He explained, for example, East European Jewry's preference for translations from Schiller rather than Goethe by the former's enthusiasm for freedom, justice and virtue. His alleged "Arabo-mania" did not prevent him from contrasting the serious-minded-ness of medieval Hebrew poetry with the prevalence, among the Arabs, of satirical and amorous poems. He also believed that unlike Islam's and Christendom's quest for secular power, "Judaism had the higher task of teaching the power of an oppressed faith." At the same time he contended "that in our civilized world one can no longer draw any line of demarcation between the various faiths on the basis of general moral concepts and that, within each religion, a constant struggle is carried on between belief, superstition and disbelief, barbarity and humanity." For this reason he objected, in particular, to the idea of Jewish "mission," propa-gated by Geiger and other reformers. He finally came to the con-clusion that "religion is not science in the narrower sense, but rather an opposing principle; the latter is characterized by absence of preconceptions, the former by authority; the latter by law of nature, the former by miracles." He amplified this rare profession of faith by stating,

> The Haggadah tells us that God created many worlds and destroyed them; Arabian theologians teach us that God's creation is a continuous process; history shows that man never ceases to create his God in his own image. God's peace, the messianic prophecy concerning the beating of the swords into plowshares (Micah 4.3), will not come true until man stops his haggling about God and for God.[15]

Under these circumstances he could view with considerable detachment the heated religious controversies of the day. His attempted "impartiality" often reflected merely his indifference, indeed impatience with people who were ready to shed copious ink, if not blood, in a struggle over theological minutiae or com-munal control. While he deeply appreciated the historic significance of talmudic Judaism, he had little use for the militant Orthodoxy of his time. He was fair enough to appreciate the validity of certain arguments advanced by the Orthodox against the dangers of modern enlightenment, but he sharply condemned Ignatz Deutsch, the unscrupulous wealthy leader of the Orthodox party in Vienna. "The freedom of movement," he commented acidly, "has flooded the big cities with a wealthy mob, while the old intelligentsia has remained indifferent." He dismissed curtly certain particularly extremist pamphlets attributed to the Hungarian Rabbi Hillel of Szikszo as a "true offshoot of insanity."[16]

Even from the historical point of view he had little appreciation for both Halakhah and Kabbalah, the two mainstays of medieval Jewry's intellectual creativity. As a conscientious bibliographer he duly registered works written in these fields, especially by such great masters as Saadia, Maimonides or Naḥmanides. He even published special bibliographical studies of kabbalistic writings. But he could not conceal his general indifference to the Halakhah and his outright hostility to all mystic movements. At times he spoke openly of the "mind-splitting" Halakhah and the "degenerated study of the Talmud" in his day. He denied that there was any need or possibility of an exact translation of the Talmud into a western language. All forms of mysticism, on the other hand, were to him but variations of superstitious beliefs, largely borrowed by Judaism from the surrounding civilizations. Their very secrecy was but a scheme for maintaining control over the masses akin to the methods of "secret diplomacy" in the political sphere. Shabbetai Zevi was, of course, nothing but "an infamous sectarian and renegade." As to "curative Hasidism," itself "a malady of Judaism," he admitted on more than one occasion that he was unfamiliar with its literature, an admission doubly significant in the case of this born bibliographer endowed with insatiable curiosity for the smallest leaflet written in Hebrew on any subject. Most fundamentally he considered historical studies consistent with the theory of evolution, because of its essential optimism, but not with any genuine belief in tradition which is necessarily pessimistic and must look forward to some Messianic irruption in order to put an end to the tragedy of existence.[17]

At the same time, he was anything but an adherent of Reform Judaism. He greatly admired Abraham Geiger, "one of the most learned theologians," to whom he devoted a full-length appreciative obituary. He also spoke highly of Gotthold Salomon whom he considered "a model preacher, whose printed and unprinted sermons deserve a complete edition both on account of their importance for the history of culture and because they are to be recommended even today as a corrective for the manifold aberrations of Jewish homiletics." On the other hand, he often spoke deprecatingly of Holdheim's intellectual somersaults and could not refrain even from inserting into the obituary notice a sarcastic remark concerning the Berlin preacher's "alleged" age. He also mentioned without regret the "complete breakdown of the Reform synod." We recall his sharp criticisms of the two basic ideas of the Reform movement, viz., that of a peculiar Jewish "ethical monotheism" and Judaism's "mission" to propagate that faith. More generally he counselled "that all who treat of Reform problems should submit objective arguments in support of their opinions, consistent or modified, of whatever orientation, without blending with them heterogeneous material and present current history with the same scrupulous accuracy which they require in the treatment of ancient times." Such remarks betray his utter lack of understanding for the emotional intensity of these struggles.[18]

It is small wonder that he was taken aback by publications like Israel Hildesheimer's "Open Letter" to Leopold Löw, in which the inadequacy of a "scientific approach" was contrasted with the basic truths of tradition. He did not know how to treat Hildesheimer's exclamation, "Woe unto those who consider intelligence the ultimate aim of religion; woe unto those whose ideal consists in cool objectivity on the basis of history." The complex personality of "the unparalleled" Michael Sachs likewise baffled him completely. In his obituary of Sachs he commented, with an almost audible sigh,

> With his thorough classical education and his personal genius for beauty, strict scientific form or discipline was for him rather a criterion of lack of genius. Insofar as it related to theological subjects, it also was a criterion of lack of conviction, if not altogether of character. For this reason

286

he never clearly defined his orientation, nor worked in its behalf as direct teacher .... Sachs was ingenious [*geistreich*] to excess and paid due homage only to men of similar capacity and orientation—characteristics truly dangerous for a teacher and historian.[19]

Steinschneider himself often lost his scientific composure, however, in discussing Christian conversionist efforts among Jews. Highlighted in his day by the international repercussions of the Mortara Affair, the ceaseless agitation of the Berlin and London missionary societies, Geiger's pamphlet, *Ueber den Austritt,* etc., this aspect of Judeo-Christian relations appeared to him of focal contemporary as well as historic importance. In his general appreciation of the Muslim rather than the Christian Middle Ages, he pointed out that, despite the fairly extensive literature of Judeo-Muslim polemics (to which he devoted a comprehensive monograph), the Muslims entertained close social contacts with Jews, but made few efforts at converting them (*"man verkehrte viel und bekehrte wenig"*). In the Christian world, on the other hand, the history of enforced and voluntary baptisms was so rich and complex that a comprehensive study—in his opinion, a major desideratum—would require detailed familiarity with a vast literature of eighteen centuries. As a Jew and liberal he rejoiced over the failure of the Berlin mission, whose contributions to the knowledge of the Jewish past he considered negligible. At the same time he resented exaggerations of Jewish apologists (e.g., Rev. David Marks of London) concerning Judaism's traditional forbearance of opposing religious convictions. "The Jews," he declared, "could and can not reasonably respect such religious convictions in the name of which many godless and inhuman acts have been committed."[20]

Steinschneider was little appreciative of the existing leadership of the Jewish community, both lay and ecclesiastical. He held in high esteem such rabbis as Isak Noah Mannheimer; in commenting on G. Wolf's biography of that distinguished preacher, he said, "Men of Mannheimer's occupation may be divided into three groups: 1) such as pursue principally their own interests under the guise of the common weal; 2) such as identify the two; 3) such as subordinate their own to the general interests. Mannheimer, in whose proximity the writer had lived in the years 1836-39, never belonged to the first, not seldom to the last group." But on the whole he felt that ever since the rabbinate had in the Middle Ages deteriorated into a salaried communal office and, hence, begun to concentrate exclusively on "ritualistic practice and unbridled homiletics," it had become a fit object of choice irony and superior condescension by philosophically trained writers. In modern times the "rabbinic bureaucracy" had become too much engrossed in communal politics and the quest for power. It is not astonishing, therefore, that "nowadays men of comprehensive liberal education but reluctantly assume the many-sided yoke of rabbinism." The latter's excessive preoccupation with theological problems also prevents the members of that calling from furnishing unbiased trained workers for the science of Judaism which, as he untiringly emphasized, must be first and foremost *streng wissenschaftlich*. Lay leadership, on the other hand, which found almost inexhaustible funds for all sorts of communal undertakings, had little to spare for searching scholarly investigations—a familiar theme song among Jewish scholars for the last century.[21]

For these reasons he, like Geiger, Zunz, Ludwig Philippson and others advocated the establishment of Jewish chairs or faculties at general universities, rather than of separate Jewish theological seminaries. Time and again he reverted to that idea, often deploring the fact that Germany had done even less than other countries in securing independent seats for Jewish learning. In a semi-programmatic statement on contemporary Jewish historiography, he explained some of its weaknesses by the fact that "the history of the Jews finds no natural point of contact in general schools of learning, has no independent representatives at universities and is encouraged by no prize contests at academies." For himself, he was happy not to be associated with any denominational seminary. Referring to the first publication of the *Wissenschaftliche Blätter aus der Veitel-Heine-Ephraimschen Lehranstalt*, at which institution he had been lecturing for many years, he

288

described the vicissitudes of that foundation since its establishment in 1774 as a center for the promotion of the study of the Talmud. In the subsequent period the founder's family had become so deeply estranged from Judaism that the foundation's income was at times used, with governmental permission, for stipends for students of Christian theology. In Steinschneider's time, however, the institution was "dedicated to the science of Judaism without regard to practical tendencies. For this reason it is even freer than a Jewish faculty attached to a university. It is attended by students of all faiths and orientations and extends the advantages of education and a growing library, free of charge and without strings attached."[22]

"Practical tendencies" of any kind were to Steinschneider the bane of Jewish studies. "History," he declared, "even literary history, is the more just and truthful, the less it is forced to reflect present and future conditions, the less its purpose to give instruction is beclouded by the wish to reform." Devoted as he was to the promotion of Jewish learning, he was deeply averse to spreading it among the masses of the population by any form of propaganda and popularization. Personally, he was always prepared to aid young men desirous of engaging in a thoroughgoing study of any phase of Judaism. Pathetically, the then almost nonagenarian Nestor of Jewish studies asked the editors of the *Zeitschrift für hebräische Bibliographie* to publish his request: "If I fail to reply to inquiries from candidates for the doctorate and others concerning manuscripts or dissertation topics, I ask them to assume that I am not in a position to reply." But the number of those to whom he did reply was legion. His correspondence, preserved in the Jewish Theological Seminary of America, embraces letters addressed to him by more than a thousand persons. Unfortunately few of his own letters are preserved, but we have the testimony of Joseph Jacobs and others about the enormous amount of learning which went into some of his postcards.[23]

Somewhat inconsistently he favored publications designed to spread culture among the "backward" East European Jews. He praised the Galician writer, Isaac Erter, not as a poet and stylist, but because "he strove to exercise a moral influence on the culture of his backward compatriots." Even the Hebrew translations of Eugene Sue's *Mystères de Paris* were considered by him "unnatural" only because they revealed to their readers the corruption of the overcivilized metropolis and thus counteracted the beneficial influence of enlightened efforts. But for Germany he condemned all attempts at popularization. He resented the program of such an organization as the Institute for the Promotion of Israelitic Literature which, under the leadership of Philippson and Jost, tried to propagate Jewish learning by publishing books of a semipopular character. He saw in its program an unhealthy acceleration of the progress of Jewish studies which must ultimately lead not only to the lowering of standards of scholarship, but also to the elimination of whatever residue of reverence for learning still existed among the Jewish populace. He was even averse to the prevailing trend of utilizing Jewish history as a major subject of instruction in Jewish religious schools. While wishing to discuss merely a lecture on Jewish physicians, he went out of his way to assail not only the growing practice of public lectures for laymen, but also the fact that

> since approximately half a century the real instruction about Judaism and its adherents, particularly in previous ages, has found centers of cultivation outside the synagogue under the firm name of "history." Youth is to learn, in religious schools, to appreciate justly its ancestors, to admire the martyrs, to revere the scholars . . . . The concepts of religion and nation in their old indissoluble combination underly this instruction, in addition to apologetics against anti-Semitism which lurk in the background. We find here in the elementary instruction not only an analogy to "church history," which in Christian schools is reserved for higher grades, but early youth is being burdened here with a segment of the history of scholars, for the understanding and appreciation of which it has not the slightest preparation.[24]

Understandably, he heartily disliked contemporary Jewish journalism. His attacks were not so much aimed at the mendacity of the press and abuse of its powers—arguments then frequently heard from such radicals as Ferdinand Lassalle—as at the relative insignificance and ephemerality of its contents. Personally he devoted little time to reading newspapers and magazines. Once he excused himself for declining an offer of a free copy of a periodical. He made no effort to secure issues of even such prominent a journal as the *Archives Israélites*. Referring to the history of the Jews in England, he readily confessed that "the Jewish journals in London which very likely contain some data [in this field] are not accessible to the reviewer." The *Jewish Chronicle* certainly did not endear itself to him when, on one occasion, it contended that no copy of the Ferrara edition of the Spanish Bible existed in either of the two major British libraries "without even looking up" his *Bodleian Catalogue*. In any case, he deeply deplored the dispersal of Jewish historical materials in periodicals, jubilee volumes, etc., pointing out that a list compiled in 1878 revealed the existence of some fifty specific Jewish journals, for the most part weeklies, each of which from time to time carried items of genuine historical interest.[25]

He had a special axe to grind in regard to Hebrew periodicals. While he admitted their limited educational value in uncivilized countries (*Länder der Unkultur*), he did not consider Hebrew as an aim in itself, but as a mere instrumentality of ritualistic and scholarly efforts. On learning that Russian Jewry had launched two new Hebrew and one Russian periodicals (the *Ha-Karmel*, *Ha-Meliṣ* and *Razsviet*), he inquired as to "how much space they intended to assign to the ever-expanding patriotic reports on condescending acts of toleration, petty personalities and local developments or on ritualistic and religious controversies, how much to outbreaks of unskilled poetry and rhetoric, amateurish accumulation of notes, etc., and how much space and care they intended to lavish on the correct reproduction of strictly scholarly studies, so that each may cling to his own flag?" Defending himself against moderately phrased, but all the more effective, criticisms of a defender of the existing Hebrew press in Vienna, he exclaimed, "The science of Judaism with its limited resources and personnel can progress but very, very slowly. It is aided least by those who wish to rush up to the pinnacle by lowering its height." For himself, he announced at the completion of the third year of his *Hebräische Bibliographie,* that the journal had reached the optimum of its expansion and that it looked for neither more collaborators nor subscribers.[26]

Critical Standards

This attitude colored all of Steinschneider's remarks on recent scholarly investigations. In the program of his bibliographical journal he announced his intention of making the review section more descriptive than critical, for "no one devoid of a frivolous approach to criticism would expect from us searching reviews of recent publications in so vast a field." But, pointing out the strengths and, more frequently, the weaknesses of contemporary scholars had already become a passionate habit with him at the age of forty-one when he started the journal. He held too strong convictions on the nature and quality of Jewish scholarship to impose upon himself verbal restraints in voicing them on all suitable and unsuitable occasions. He was not completely blind to the value of studies undertaken by dilettantes out of the sheer "zest for learning rooted in Judaism." But wherever he scented the slightest ulterior motives, he went after the culprit with the sharpest weapons in his well-accoutred armory.[27]

He was particularly impatient with any incompetent piece of text editing. "We are long accustomed," he complained, "to find in the 'editor' of a Hebrew manuscript the first best unqualified printer, beggar, speculator and the like." In analytical studies, too, he was a firm believer in the precise inductive method and suspicious of all generalizations. Convinced that "one must gather from all corners the stones needed for the construction of Jewish history," he commented, for instance, on Kayserling's *Geschichte,* "The way from the specific to the general of itself leads to a more objective presentation." Of course, where such generalization, as in the case of Ernest Renan, ran counter to his own point of view, he was doubly aroused. He objected, especially, to Renan's characterization of the Semitic peoples and wholeheartedly approved of H. Steinthal's outspoken reply. "The more Renan's brilliant dialectical and stylistic talent carries the readers away," he declared, "the more necessary is it to reveal the consequences, or rather the inconsistencies of his anti-Semitic prejudices." He praised, in particular, Steinthal's "solid moral tone which is far more appropriate to scientific earnestness than scintillating phrases."[28]

Clearly, he could evince little sympathy for such efforts at historic synthesis as were brilliantly represented in his day by the work of Heinrich Graetz. As many other writers before and after him, he complained of the "overhastiness of Jewish historiography" and felt that the time had not yet come for the comprehensive treatment of the entire evolution of the Jewish people by an individual scholar. "He who, like Graetz, has false illusions about it, becomes ever less historical, and hence less honest." With genuine satisfaction he commented on the publications of 1881, "Little has been written, thank God, in the field of general Jewish history. For brilliant aperçus [like James Darmesteter's *Coup d'oeuil sur l'histoire du peuple juif*] we shall have no firm foundation for a long time to come."[29]

Not that he resented most the unavoidable individual mistakes in these broad presentations. He realized, of course, that detailed corrections and additions can be made as readily in specialized monographs as in comprehensive works of synthesis. In fact, he spent a substantial portion of his life correcting statements in his earlier writings. His comment on Clemens Huart's *History of Arabic Literature,* published in 1903 in a series of *Short Histories* intended for popular use, is typical of his general point of view. He criticized certain mistakes, even "boners," but added, "It would be unjust to evaluate or to condemn on this score the entire work. The reply to the question: For whom do such writings appear?—for the bookseller. Who buys them? This would depend on general considerations for which we have no space here."[30]

He was often inconsistent, however. When asked by the Ersch and Gruber encyclopedia to write a general article on the history of Jewish literature, he knew that both Zunz and Lebrecht had declined the invitation, and yet—we dare say, fortunately —he had enough "temerity" to undertake this comprehensive summary. His essay, grown into seven times its allotted size[31] and later translated into English and Hebrew, became a classic in its field. Although less of a real history than a long array of notes thereon, it was obviously subject to endless corrections. Soon after its compilation Steinschneider himself toiled for a dozen years over his great *Bodleian Catalogue,* which gave him the opportunity of revising many of his earlier assertions. But he was deeply chagrined when someone else, e.g., Jost, censured a large number of these detailed errors. To the good fortune of Jewish scholarship, however, his pique over this and similar experiences did not deter him from publishing later several other broad compositions.

What is more, on frequent occasions he cited approvingly Selig (later Paulus) Cassel's article "Juden," prepared for the same encyclopedia after he himself had declined to write it. Cassel's fine summary of Jewish history has, indeed, merited the universal acclaim it received in the nineteenth century, but Steinschneider's praise of it as "one of the best works in the field of Jewish history by compass, content and interpretation" shows that he was not really opposed to all legitimate generalizations. He was not even seriously disturbed by Cassel's later conversion from neo-Orthodoxy to Christianity. Despite his opposition to Christian missionary activities, he treated such genuine converts with comparative complacency. In fact, he did not even dismiss Cassel's short essay on *Die Juden in der Weltgeschichte* as one of those "brilliant aperçus," but expected it to be an "adumbration of future penetrating studies."[32]

Similarly, the Russian-Jewish convert, Daniel Chwolson, was treated with considerable friendliness. Steinschneider, who usually reacted violently to criticisms, went out of his way to compliment the compiler of the *Corpus Inscriptionum Hebraicarum.* He who had spent many years in collecting data on medieval Jewish manuscripts—which he later utilized in his *Vorlesungen über die Kunde der hebräischen Handschriften*—admitted here that Chwolson's chapters dealing with the difficult problems of epigraphy and the square Hebrew script have "practically exhausted the existing materials." More, even in the controversy among Chwolson, Harkavy and Strack over the "fanatical forger," Abraham Firkovitch, he emphasized that "his personal relations with all these protagonists are almost equally friendly and hence he feels safeguarded against the suspicion of having taken sides unduly."[33]

At times he took sharp issue with Christian scholars, too. We shall see that he rejected, in particular, many of the regnant theories concerning the ancient Semites and biblical criticism. Only occasionally he admitted, as he did in one of his attacks on Ewald, that he wrote "as a Jew." Similarly, in his extraordinarily warm necrology of Alexander von Humboldt, who had "died not to one, but to all science," he pointed out that a very interesting volume could be written about Humboldt's attitude to the Jews.[34]

On the other hand, he censured Paul de Lagarde (who attended some of his lectures), not because of the latter's numerous anti-Semitic essays, but chiefly because, in editing Al-Ḥarizi, Lagarde had "failed to acquaint himself sufficiently with the necessary textual aids and available literature." When he found a Christian apologist for Judaism, like M. J. Schleiden, discussing the role of medieval Jews in the revival of sciences or the "romanticism" of their martyrdom with more zest than knowledge, he lost his temper. "An objective treatment," he declared, "would have served the defended cause much better and would have been more appropriate for a layman." Under these circumstances, he felt, "the martyrdom of the science and history of Judaism will last very long yet, for it finds its torturers among the Jews themselves and their ill-advised friends." He also bitterly complained of the disrespect shown to Jewish studies by those distinguished Christian savants who indiscriminately provided with letters of recommendation such alleged Jewish scholars as were "for the most part men devoid of general education, ignoramuses, charlatans, itinerant beggars and the like."[35]

The only Jewish scholar whom he unreservedly admired was Leopold Zunz. Although never technically Zunz's disciple, he always looked upon the older man as his master. In dedicating his early book, *Die fremdsprachlichen Elemente im Neuhebräischen* (1854), to Zunz (and Fleischer) as "a slight token of deeply felt reverence and gratitude," he emphasized, "Through your classical writings, written and oral communications, you have pointed out to me, too, the road to the 'science of Judaism' and have guided and supported my few attempts so far in this field." Unsparing with superlatives in describing Zunz's works, he compared a chapter in Zunz's *Zur Geschichte und Literatur* with its "extremely ingenious construction" to that of Schiller's *Glocke*. He called Zunz's *Ritus* to the particular attention of those who "know Zunz merely as a scholar and not as a critic." His summary here of Zunz's general attitude in many respects is the best description of his own scholarly ideals.

> Zunz possesses [he declared] that piety and sacrificial attitude to research which is indispensable to strict scientific investigation. He combines with it steadfastness in his convictions which resists all temptations of supposed popularity and the bowing before regnant systems. The motto under his picture is, "Thought is powerful enough without pretension and injustice to prove victorious over pretension and injustice." Such approaches are particularly necessary for Jewish literature, especially in the field of tradition and its derivatives in the Franco-German school. There the task is to detect the organism of history in a large, apparently inorganic and blurred mass. There one must pursue unfailingly a middle course of prudent criticism between the saga and legend, pious self-deception and pietistic obfuscation, between exaggeration and rejection.
>
> For this reason his works were always epoch-making, basic, comprehensive, although the great mob here, as elsewhere, knows how to praise only those happy ones who march on the broad highway and pluck flowers on the paths where

Zunz had blasted rocks, weeded out thistles and strewn seeds. For this entire generation belongs to Zunz's grateful—or ungrateful—pupils.

Before long he came to the conclusion that "praise of Zunz's writings would be an insult to our readers."[36]

Steinschneider showed considerably less attachment to the other great scholars of that "Sturm and Drang" generation in Jewish scholarship. He spoke feelingly of Rapoport's seventieth birthday, advocated an inexpensive edition of the Prague rabbi's collected works and later devoted to him a fairly long, sympathetic obituary, as he also did for Lebrecht and Zedner. When Luzzatto began editing Yehudah Halevi's *Diwan,* Steinschneider emphasized that the great medieval poet had "the rare luck in Hebrew literature of having found a most qualified editor" and hoped that the projected Bible translation would not divert Luzzatto's attention from the continuation of this work. While he sometimes gave vent to critical remarks on Luzzatto's theological views and once even resented the publication in a Hebrew journal of the Italian scholar's youthful "dreams," he was nevertheless deeply moved when the latter passed away. The news had affected him so profoundly, he declared, "that we cannot bring ourselves to say here a few words about the achievements of this remarkable man."[37]

Abraham Geiger likewise stood very high in his esteem. Despite their basic disagreements on Reform Judaism and totally different temperaments, Steinschneider appreciated the wide range and brilliance of Geiger's researches. Even when he criticized the "tendenciousness" of one or another study and objected, for example, to Geiger's obsession with the "Zadokites," he emphasized that "the objective scholar will resent only—lack of thoroughness." On other occasions he emphasized, "We honor in Geiger the spirit, which he knew how to detect everywhere" and, paradoxically, even praised him for belonging "to those productive savants who in their scholarly investigations of ancient letters do not lose sight of the present and its trends, indeed frequently find in the latter the mainspring and standard for the former." He constantly welcomed Geiger's collaboration with him in his bibliographical journal and relished in particular Geiger's measured, but sustained, attacks on Graetz's historical approaches. On Geiger's passing in his early sixties, he wrote two highly appreciative obituaries.[38]

He also greatly appreciated the work of Solomon Munk, whom he slightly envied for his independent scholarly position on the pay-roll of the French government. Although he disliked Munk's election to membership of the Paris Academy as a result of a rumored pro-Jewish demonstration in connection with the Mortara Affair, and resented Renan's replacement by Munk at the Collège de France because of the former's religious liberalism, he was convinced that, were it not for anti-Jewish discrimination, Munk would have had a prior claim on the chair at the Collège.[39] Steinschneider also wrote appreciatively of a number of other contemporaries.[40]

On the whole, however, he was far more outspoken in his condemnation than in his praise. He hated scholarly lack of discipline and unreliability above everything else. He knew that "the struggle of earnest scientific endeavor against a misleading profession which strives after appearances is, in its essentials, the same everywhere and at all times, much as the particular facts and motivations may differ from one another according to periods and localities, varying stages of culture or individual disciplines."[41] In "charlatanry" he saw, indeed, the major menace to Jewish scholarship.

For this reason he was deeply incensed at a personality like Israel Joseph (or Israel ben Joseph), styled Benjamin II. A Rumanian Jew of the old type, Israel Joseph undertook extended journeys through Asia and Africa in the years 1846-55 and later spent several years in America. He recorded these journeys in successive volumes under the picturesque name of Benjamin II, in memory of the great medieval traveller from Tudela. At first Steinschneider was prepared to withhold judgment, since he had not seen the first volume and was awaiting publication of the second. But he protested against the casual remark in R. Gosche's review (in the *Zeitschrift für allgemeine Erdkunde*) that Benjamin

II was "equipped with that happy gift of observation which, in the case of travellers, can replace the lack of strictly scholarly equipment." In his opinion a genuine travelogue presupposed fine scholastic and critical abilities. After familiarizing himself with Benjamin II's publications he decided to take a stand, however uncharitable his attack may have appeared even to those who saw in Benjamin but a poor deserving mendicant. "We believe," he exclaimed, "that today we must demand for the science of Judaism as much—even more—exactitude as for any other science. We do not believe that Jewish literature is an orthopedic institution, a *charité* or hospital for cripples, disabled and unemployed persons." He was doubly irked, therefore, by Benjamin's growing popularity among princes and populace alike and by his securing many letters of recommendation from reputable Christian scholars. "If Nicbuhr and Seetzen," he exclaimed, "had appeared as 'Marco Polo' or 'Mandeville II,' they probably would have received *Laufpässe,* rather than letters of recommendation." He was completely startled by the "American humbug" of the *Pacific Messenger* of San Francisco welcoming Benjamin as one of the greatest living scholarly travellers, the world-renowned colleague of Alexander von Humboldt. Unrelentingly he wrote in his obituary notice, "The man's death cannot change our opinion about his publications. Their content has absolutely no scientific, critical value, for he completely lacked scholarly or writing ability and all his books were prepared by others."[42]

The latter accusation, that of plagiarizing, almost became Steinschneider's life-long obsession. He even denied the fact that in the Middle Ages literary property was treated with considerable latitude by Jewish, Christian and Muslim authors alike. "The notion of literary honesty," he contended, "has always been interpreted subjectively from one or another extreme point of view, and one must hold individuals, rather than periods or classes responsible for it." He also, with almost visible glee, cited Azulai's safeguards for literary property.[43]

Eliakim Carmoly became a recurrent target of these accusations. A complete record of Steinschneider's polemical references to Carmoly's works would doubtless fill a sizable pamphlet. He followed therein Zunz's lead. In two letters addressed to him in 1853, the revered master had referred to someone as a faker whose name was perhaps Eliakim, and then asked Steinschneider how he could inquire "why a falsarius should be called Eliakim." In this life-long feud, Carmoly hit back time and again. For example, in the "Annalen der hebräischem Typographie von Riva di Trento" (*Ben Chananja,* 1864; 2nd ed., Frankfort, 1868), Carmoly not only vigorously assailed the "disreputable fabricator of catalogues," but what hurt most, pointed out numerous serious mistakes in Steinschneider's early essay on Jewish typography. The latter could only expostulate by claiming that most of these errors had already been corrected in his *Bodleian Catalogue* and complain that "ever since 1840 Carmoly practices the art of correcting older writings on the basis of their authors' later publications." So certain was he of Carmoly's wrongdoings that he repudiated all possible excuses. When a writer (*MGWJ*, IV, 106) tried to apologize for Carmoly's work on Eldad the Danite, Steinschneider declared him to be "no judge of forgeries by so great a master." Even thirty years after Carmoly's death (1905) he declared that "to try to defend the *Histoire* [*des médécins*] is a downright sin against criticism."[44]

Only slightly less irate and persistent were Steinschneider's attacks on Julius Fürst. At first, during his brief sojourn in Leipzig, he seems to have been on friendly terms with the editor of the *Orient* with whom he collaborated for several years. The relationship cooled off perceptibly, however, and Steinschneider viewed with growing disapproval Fürst's bibliographical and historical and, to a lesser extent, also philological efforts. Typical is his comment of 1879, "Schorr's and Steinschneider's criticisms have not prevented Julius Fürst from expanding his history of Karaism into three volumes by virtue of repetitions, the dragging in of alien materials and other inappropriate procedures (1862-69) . . . . Of independent research there is no evidence whatsoever, not even in the crude errors which he commits on the aforementioned half-cited writings." On another occasion he rejoiced that the work had not been provided with an index. "It is quite good," he said, "that not every uninformed person should be able readily to copy from such a book."[45]

Somewhat more measured, if no less venomous, were his attacks on the two great historians, Jost and Graetz. Steinschneider who, in his early essay on Jewish literature, had to reject various views expressed by the father of modern Jewish historiography, was touched to the quick when Jost counter-attacked sharply. Both in an article and in the *Geschichte des Judentums,* Jost pointed out numerous cases of "over-hastiness" and "hundreds of instances of mistaken names and wholly incorrect numbers" which had crept into that essay. Steinschneider also resented Jost's praise of Carmoly as "one of the most exact and careful experts." He inserted, therefore, a lengthy excursus on Jost, rather out of context, into the Introduction to his *Bibliographisches Handbuch.* It must be shown, he declared, "how far the writer, Jost, had already travelled away from the otherwise honorable man, Jost." His criticisms included such acute observations as,

> Some forty years ago Jost had the courage to write a history of the Jews, but he had generally the honorable "courage of an opinion," were it only of the then-prevailing prejudiced opinion against everything Jewish. Jewish *literature* had not yet been investigated by Zunz and others, and Jost derived his information chiefly from Christian, sometimes from bad tertiary sources, so long as they saved him the trouble of gathering the material by himself . . . . To write German at that time was in itself a meritorious task and Jost's negligent, incorrect style was good enough for a Jewish historian.

Now, however, Jost's work had greatly deteriorated. If his *Geschichte des Judentums* was supposed to have been written free of prejudice, it was indeed free, not only of any pre-judgment, but of any judgment whatsoever, Jost trying to mediate between opposing extremes and evading any decisive discussions. Shortly after this attack Jost died, and in his brief obituary, Steinschneider proved implacable: "He himself now belongs to history, which some forty years ago he had begun to cultivate, not without merit. His literary activity in the last years, however, was, unfortunately, such that we do not wish to combine the death notice with a criticism of these writings."[46]

No less outspoken was Steinschneider's condemnation of Graetz. For a while their relations were fairly amicable, Steinschneider claiming that he had provided Graetz with some information which the latter abused. But their two temperaments and, especially, their approaches to Jewish history were wholly incompatible. The publication of the fifth volume of Graetz's *Geschichte,* which spoke disparagingly of "Dr. Zunz's more confusing than illuminating heap of notes and dry nomenclatures," greatly antagonized the large Zunz following. Graetz often took direct issue with such "note chasers" (*Notizenjäger*) like Steinschneider, who was therefore not only glad to publish in 1860 Geiger's corrections to Graetz's fifth volume, but to add a sharp comment of his own:

> The author assigns to literature undue emphasis. He contends in his preface that he adheres only to the *primary sources.* This statement is to be understood as saying that in entire sections of his work he ignores the real source books, not casually but systematically. Our ordinary prose designates such proceedings as downright literary *dishonesty.*[47]

Three years later, on the publication of Graetz's seventh volume, Steinschneider lost all self-control. He found that this volume confirmed his dire predictions and that Graetz had gone so far "as to steal from his own master, Carmoly." With reference to M. Wiener's criticisms of Graetz in *Ben Chananja,* he declared that their perusal will give the reader "an impression of the book's literary immorality, but not yet of the plagiarist's ignorance which comes most to the fore where Graetz makes a lot of noise about the alleged errors of unnamed authors and his own supposed discoveries in a style over which not only Klio must blush." The particular instances of these grave shortcomings, quoted by Steinschneider, fail to bear out these high-sounding denunciations, while Graetz's remark about Steinschneider's work here quoted, namely, that it was "thorough-going, though chaotic," squares far more precisely with the facts. It is even less forgivable when Steinschneider coupled here, as well as on other occasions, his attacks on Graetz as a writer with insinuations of a personal nature. He concluded his review by saying, "One must, indeed, congratulate the students of the Breslau Seminary for such a scrupulous guide on the road of history, whose oral lectures probably do not greatly differ from his writings."[48]

Steinschneider did not carry his ill-will to Graetz's pupils, however.[49] He praised, for example, Güdemann's *Geschichte des Erziehungswesens* on account of its "systematic order, fullness and partial novelty of the material . . . [which] lend the study permanent value." If he added the reservation that "in the interpretation of facts the apologist and conservative rabbi struggles with the dispassionate historian," this is indubitably a fair criticism of Güdemann's general approach. He also lauded Güdemann's history of the Jews in Magdeburg which at first appeared in *MGWJ* (1866). "Not enough of such monographs," he commented, "can appear for the time being." Although on occasion he warned the reader to check back the original passages quoted by Güdemann and once even attacked him outright, his comments were for the most part rather friendly.[50] He was also friendly and encouraging to David Kauffmann, Joseph Perles, and others.[51]

Most remarkable is his admiration of the work of such a relatively minor historian as Gerson Wolf. Since Wolf's researches were based on archival studies, such opening up of new sources of Jewish learning caused Steinschneider readily to overlook other shortcomings. Although he published M. Wiener's strictures on the reliability of Wolf as a copyist, which concluded with the condescending hope that Wiener might soon have the opportunity of praising not only Wolf's zeal but also his care and thoroughness, Steinschneider continued to praise "the diligent and conscientious author [who] continues to exploit archival materials for the benefit of Jewish history."[52] He also commended, more or less warmly, other new source studies by Jewish and non-Jewish scholars.[53]

These numerous criticisms of contemporary writers were not only the effect of Steinschneider's bad temper. He felt that the science of Judaism was still too young and that it had become the prey of ambitious, unscrupulous and unlearned students who were much too complacently treated by the leaders and encouraged by their great popularity with the uninformed public. He considered it his duty to stand guard over his chosen fields of study and to keep out all trespassers.[54]

Unfortunately, partly because of this expenditure of verbiage on polemics—to our mind mostly exaggerated and often unnecessary polemics—he tried to save space by excessive brevity in language and by the use of abbreviations. He did not even heed Zunz's early warning. "When you review Dukes," the master had written him on June 9, 1843, "please write somewhat more explicitly for us outsiders than you have done in the evaluation of the Cuzari—so that 'our people' should not obtain further excuses when one denounces their indifference toward Jewish literature."[55] Although he himself complained that abbreviations were "a particularly serious plague in neo-Hebrew literature," his own writings are filled with home-made abbreviations not always consistent and certainly not uniform from one publication to another. Some of these devices cannot even pretend to having saved much space. The writing, for example, of "Zz." for Zunz can hardly be justified on any ground, except the author's minor convenience.[56]

Contributions

Directly and indirectly Steinschneider greatly enriched our knowledge of Jewish historiography. In the field of Jewish bibliography, perhaps history's most significant auxiliary science, he was the undisputed master. By discovering and describing ever new source material of all kinds, especially insofar as it still was hidden away in manuscripts or rare editions, he constantly increased the store of information available to students of all Jewish letters including the specific area of Jewish historical literature.

His magnificent contributions to the history of Jewish scientists also had a great indirect bearing on Jewish historiography. He himself contended,

> The history of the Jews, i.e., of Jewry, may be divided into political and cultural; the cultural into literary, scientific, and religious history. The latter includes dogmatic, ritualistic and halakhic aspects. The blending of these abstract fields into one another in their actual manifestation is particularly characteristic of Jewish history and is explainable only through its own criteria.

To be sure, he realized that he was not a scientist and that he lacked the specialized knowledge of a mathematician, astronomer or physician. His excuse was that "the number of those who combine the necessary substantive and linguistic knowledge is extremely limited in our days. Hence it is a constant task for philologists and bibliographers to place the material at the disposal of experts." He was even more seriously concerned about the legitimacy of designating any savant as a "Jewish" scientist, indeed about the existence of any truly "national" science. He quoted with relish Prof. Seyerlen's statement that "as modern philosophy had been introduced by a Jew [Spinoza] so had the great scientific movement of the Christian Middle Ages been initiated by another Jew [Ibn Gabirol]," and added, on his own, that still another Jew, Abraham bar Ḥiyya (Savasorda) had laid the foundation for Christian Europe's study of geometry. But he immediately qualified his statement, "The more one penetrates into the details of all exact and empirical sciences, one increasingly realizes the importance of the individual, as against the undeniable influences of birth (nationality, language and fatherland)." With reference to Jewish medicine, in particular, he admitted that the direct connection among the Jewish physicians of various countries had practically ceased, and expressed doubt whether the religious and legal provisions of the Bible and Talmud had anything to do with hygiene or any other science.[57]

Despite these hesitations he spent a lifetime in collecting data on Jewish mathematicians, astronomers, medical men, etc. When, upon the completion of his magnum opus, the *Hebräische Uebersetzungen,* he pathetically wrote that taking leave of a lifetime's work is almost like taking leave of life itself, but he had the great comfort of feeling that he had made signal contributions to every phase of medieval Jewish cultural history. In all his works, moreover, he included converted Jews, insofar as there was reason to believe that they had received their early education within the Jewish community. Somewhat inconsistently, he also tried to explain the large number of Jewish mathematicians by the peculiarities of the Jewish mind. Arguing against the facile assumption that the concentration of Jews on commerce and usury had stimulated their interest in mathematical sciences, he pointed out the relative absence of Jewish writings on the subject of mechanics and added, "People excluded from public life and, to a certain extent (owing in part to their ceremonial law) also from social life, will naturally turn to more *abstract* objectives. Even today Russian Jews delight in inventing counting machines. The profitless art of chess playing, i.e., of abstract combination, has produced a number of Jewish champions even in modern times." On the other hand, mathematics, astronomy and astrology have penetrated the Jewish ritual and liturgy, and hence become historical forces shaping Jewish life far beyond the narrow sphere of scientific research. Even in the stricter confines of Jewish historiography, Steinschneider might have added, contributions by such scientists as Abraham bar Ḥiyya or Zacuto were far from accidental. Certainly in the borderline area of Jewish chronology, where legal and ritualistic interests impinged upon those of both history and astronomy, the interlocking of science and historiography was often perfectly evident.[58]

The Middle Ages were Steinschneider's main area of specialization. In the *Geschichtsliteratur* and other writings he paid relatively little attention to the ancient world. He had very little to say, for instance, about the achievements of biblical historiography, not even mentioning the Chronicler's work to which Zunz had devoted a detailed and truly searching investigation. Occasionally he would drop a remark like that referring to Prof. Fausto Lasinio's address on the study of the Bible text, which he hailed as a sign of Italian liberalism. In commenting on Nöldeke's *Ueber die Amalekiter* he found therein mainly the proof that one ought to place little reliance on Arabic records concerning biblical subjects.[59]

Apart from his relatively unfamiliarity with the controversial literature on the Bible, he had objective scientific reservations concerning biblical criticism as practiced in his day. Fully recognizing its importance, in fact emphasizing that the main challenge to modern theology was not materialism but modern criticism, he felt, nevertheless, that there was something basically wrong with these contemporary approaches to Scripture. Not only Renan but also "sound" German scholars seemed to him to be arguing in circles. In a private letter to him, Zunz had indulged in an unbridled attack on Ewald. Following Zunz's example, he too took issue with Ewald's theories both as a Jew and as a scholar. Commenting on R. Dozy's *Israeliten in Mekka,* in which the author had utilized Geiger's theory concerning the conscious alterations of the biblical text, he stated,

> I do not doubt for a moment that Geiger himself would object to the consequences drawn here from his theory of the "internal historical evolution." . . . Here one finds in addition that stark positivism with which Ewald, Hitzig and others publicly offer their hypotheses as history . . . . Even if the old textual forgeries were proved, one would have the more carefully to examine the new texts produced on the basis of "internal history," as that alleged history itself is largely produced in turn by these texts.

We have seen that Geiger himself did not escape the brunt of Steinschneider's accusation that, once having adopted a theory, all facts of ancient history had to be pressed into its mold.[60]

For these reasons he was reluctant to discuss ancient inscriptions which contained valuable historical data. He felt that he had to explain his refusal to include medieval tombstone inscriptions in his major historiographic work by the fact that he had already listed elsewhere the large relevant literature. He also realized the need "of a complete collection of ancient Jewish epigraphic sources." But when it came to individual inscriptions, he found the Mesha stone too unreliable to justify conclusions for Hebrew palaeography. The Shiloam inscription he dismissed by reference to the numerous grammatical errors discovered by Nöldeke in Sayce's reconstruction. The publication of an Eshmunaziride inscription merely elicited his remark that it required a lengthy commentary. "I confess," he added, "that this kind of Hebrew appears to me more remote than the assumption that we deal here with a non-Hebrew vocabulary."[61]

He was only slightly less hesitant about voicing opinions on the early post-biblical period. He knew well enough how important the study of the Talmud was in the whole structure of Jewish learning. In his second annual survey prepared for the *JBGW* he declared that "one cannot study the history of the Jews on the basis of sources without due consideration of this remarkable work of literature [the Talmud]." It had also been, he stated, up to recent times the very foundation of Jewish life. For this reason he felt impelled to give a cursory review of the scholarly investigations of the Talmud in the course of the preceding thirty or forty years. One cannot help feeling, however, that this review, though not completely devoid of merit, clings to the surface. There are only occasional fine "asides," as when he criticized Emanuel Deutsch for having "insinuated modern concepts into the Talmud." He constantly belabored modern talmudists like Frankel and Fassel for showing little understanding for a truly historical approach. He also took issue with the statement by a reviewer of Bacher's *Agada* that, if subjected to an historical analysis, "the talmudic literature loses completely its peculiar character." Steinschneider retorted that history was not called upon to conserve the peculiar character of its sources.[62]

When he tried, however, to summarize, on his own, the historic outlook of the talmudic sages, his presentation became "chaotic," as Israel Lévi called it. He must have been as much at a loss in reconstructing the talmudic outlook on history, as he professedly was in trying to recapture the scientific contributions of that period. He disliked the usual generalization that the "Talmud" held such and such views, since these views were, as a rule, expressed by hundreds of different sages, acting under different impulses over a period of a millennium. But he saw no practicable alternative to this "geological" treatment of an entire historical stratum in Jewish thinking. At the same time he sharply denied the legitimacy of discussing talmudic ideas in terms of a "system" and contended that, for example, the Talmud's linguistic material belonged, in fact, to "the pre-history of grammar." In general, he was never too successful in broad "geological" reconstructions.[63]

The great importance of the vast extra-talmudic literature, too, was freely admitted, but he never subjected it to critical examination. For example, he found Raffaele Garucci's *Cimitero degli antichi Ebrei* very interesting, but admitted that the book "moves in a sphere and presupposes the knowledge of a literature which are completely alien to me." This unfamiliarity did not prevent him, however, from unkindly commenting on Graetz's brief study of Jewish catacomb inscriptions in southern Italy. Schürer's monograph on the Jewish communal organization in ancient Rome elicited but the timid suggestion that a comparison with talmudic and medieval data might have rendered the author's conclusions somewhat more certain. He dismissed rather curtly Freudenthal's still basic investigation of the Hellenistic Jewish historians preserved by Alexander Polyhistor, finding it "of more general interest" to examine the same author's theory concerning the influence of an alleged "Hellenistic midrash" on the Palestinian and Babylonian exegesis. More explicitly he commended the volume, *Eran,* by F. Spiegel. "The outward relations of the science of Judaism," he declared, "are so many and varied that it is impossible for anyone to pursue even a significant part thereof, particularly in monographs devoted to lesser, as yet unfinished researches. The more welcome, therefore, is every comprehensive survey of recent results." Without arrogating to himself any judgment concerning the sources, he merely wished to emphasize Spiegel's "praiseworthy care" in the use of documents.[64]

Curiously, despite his constant awareness of the great historic significance of Judeo-Christian theological controversies, he maintained almost complete silence in regard to their origin in the New Testament period. Occasionally, as with respect to Friedländer's essay on Melchizedeck and the Epistle to the Hebrews, he pleaded unfamiliarity with the sources. He protested against Renan's and Strauss's studies of the life of Jesus because he sensed in their racial antipathy "a more or less conscious tendency to punish the mother for the daughter one wishes to cast away." In fact, he saw therein a valuable object lesson against the "recent belief that one performed a service to the science of Judaism by recommending it as a source for the history of Christianity." He censured even his great friend, Franz Delitzsch, on the publication of the latter's excellent Hebrew translation of the *Epistle to the Romans,* for "wasting his erudition on so fruitless and, from the strictly scholarly viewpoint, senseless an undertaking."[65]

Steinschneider's comments on Josephus are equally unrevealing. He considers this basic source of ancient Jewish history more as a background to its medieval paraphrase, the *Yosippon,* than as the work of the greatest Jewish historian before the nineteenth century. His failure to treat of Josephus in his *Geschichtsliteratur,* where he deals with a great many ephemeral chroniclers, may be explained by his exclusive concern in this volume with Hebrew sources. But even here the problem of the Aramaic original of the *Jewish War* would have merited some attention, as would the modern Hebrew translations of Josephus' works. In fact, in his critical comment on Kalman Schulman's translation of Josephus' *Life,* he himself mentioned that *Against Apion* had first been translated into Hebrew before 1566.[66]

His interest in modern history was likewise very limited. It was typical of his other publications when, in his history of Jewish mathematicians, he decided to relegate the period of

1801-40 to the Appendix, "for I am not sufficiently familiar with the literature." His lectures on Jewish historiography, too, usually ended with a brief sketch of modern writings to the days of Mendelssohn or the end of the eighteenth century. Only occasionally did he venture to extend it to 1840 or even 1900, although here he certainly could not profess equal unfamiliarity with the sources. In fact, while inserting in 1858 a column, "Die Vergangenheit," into his journal, he declared, "For us this [part] goes up to 1857." With all his opposition to apologetics he also emphasized time and again the virtue of making investigations relevant for contemporary life. We have seen that Geiger's work was, in his opinion, enhanced in its value because it was oriented to contemporary problems. As a matter of record, however, he did not consider much of the research devoted to the nineteenth century as being of a really scholarly nature. He believed, for instance, that France was a happy country because it no longer had a Jewish question of practical significance. Hence, its scholars did not have to justify the previous restrictions and could devote themselves to an impartial investigation of the Jewish past in their country. On the other hand, Germany's flood of anti-Semitic or pro-Jewish writings had produced nothing of scholarly significance. What is more, with his acute sense for detail, he dimly realized that he could not possibly hope to master the vast amount of information available for the modern period with the same degree of precise knowledge he commanded with respect to the more limited survivals of medieval letters. Once he expressed almost pained surprise on the publication in the *REJ* of archival studies pertaining to the Revolutionary period. "Our lengthy report," he concluded, "shall prove that even in regard to the most recent period there are still large treasures dormant in archives." He had an uncomfortable suspicion of the paucity of medieval manuscript collections when compared with the mountains of manuscripts assembled in modern archives.[67]

As a result of this dichotomy he limited his work in this field to such occasional bibliographical summaries as those concerned with anti-Semitic publications during certain years, pamphlets on the blood libel kept alive by the controversy over August Rohling's writings and the Tisza-Eszlar affair, or selections from bibliographical works referring to Russian-Jewish history.[68] He could caustically comment on the trial of Sebastian Brunner vs. Ignatz Kuranda or on Heine-Am-Rhyn's *Kulturgeschichte des Judentums*. Pointing out that author's ignorance of Hebrew, he asked, "In what other field would one dare to write a history of culture without knowing the main language?" He evinced particular interest in the oath *more judaico*, since for nine years he had been professionally engaged in its administration. Despite the customary contempt for the backward East European Jews he sympathetically recorded the grievances of Polish Jewry under Alexander II and condemned, in particular, the anti-Jewish abuse of governmental statistics. Discussing I. Loeb's *La situation des Israélites en Turquie, en Serbie et en Romanie,* he expressed regret that the book "has not yet become of mere historic interest."[69]

On the other hand, he listed a compilation of Prussian laws concerning Jews not only because of its practical aspects, but also because "it will retain its value as material for history." He even mentioned such reports as those of the newly formed Anglo-Jewish Association and inquired about its future relations with the Board of Deputies, "whose task has all but ended with Jewish equality." He was much disturbed by George Eliot's Zionism and Disraeli's racism, declaring that *"Coningsby, Daniel Deronda* and the like are products of the split between the Englishman's high appreciation of Judaism and his previous contempt for the Jews. Justice, even of an historical character, and humanity require different approaches under the modern outlook on nature and the world."* These examples, which could be multiplied indefinitely, show that he was deeply puzzled by the cross-currents of modern life. Convinced liberal though he was, he was not too confident of history's ultimate verdict on his own period and merely hoped that some day it might find a future Kompert, who would weave around it as romantic a halo as that adorning the bygone days of the ghetto era in the writings of the contemporary novelist.[70] For himself, he often escaped from the perplexities of modern life and the confusion of the overwhelming torrent of modern letters to the relative security and quiet of medieval Jewish bibliography. Here lay, indeed, his main strength. Despite his general recognition of the interrelations between Jewish and general history, he focused his attention only on materials available in Jewish sources. In a characteristic remark inserted in a reply to a subscriber, he declared with respect to the legend of the Wandering Jew, "This is a subject so totally ignored by the Jews that I have had no occasion to deal with it."[71]

This remark sounds the keynote of his *Geschichtsliteratur* and the incidental comments referring to medieval Jewish historiography scattered in his various writings. In fact, the title, *Geschichtsliteratur,* is somewhat misleading. Although he thus called his course of lectures given twelve times during the years 1865-99, the more correct designation of the book was *Bibliographie der Geschichte bei den Juden,* which title it bore long after it had been sent to the printer.[72]

The first volume dealing with the Hebrew sources was in the press from 1901 to 1905, and although the material had been ready for many years, Steinschneider gradually lost interest in it. Beginning with §100 he transferred the editorial work to his pupil, Alexander Marx, who carried it up to §123. From then on, owing to Marx's departure for America, the undertaking was continued by another disciple, Aron Freimann. Of course both pupils worked on the basis of Steinschneider's manuscript, but put in a great deal of their own effort and learning and, at times, applied somewhat different methods. Upon completion Marx had a considerable number of significant corrections and additions, which he published in his review of the volume as well as in a special essay. Other pupils, particularly Poznanski and Malter, added numerous corrections of their own. The manuscript of a second volume devoted to Jewish historical literature in languages other than Hebrew consisted almost exclusively of titles. This bibliography of some 2,000 entries was prepared for the press by Felix Kaufmann but, unfortunately, never saw the light of day.[73]

In his prefatory statement he made clear that Jewish historical literature was not identical with the literature of Jewish history. The former includes also Jewish records concerning events and developments outside the Jewish community. That is why he felt free to discuss, for instance, Joseph Ha-Kohen's general historical work, *Dibre ha-yamim le-malkhe ṣarfath u-beth ottoman ha-togar*, or Abraham Zacuto's concluding section on world chronology in the same detail as their statements on the history of their people.[74]

On the other hand, he excluded, as a matter of principle, what he considered mere "materials" for Jewish history. The latter, he stated, "consists in proving the connection between sequences (the *propter hoc* in the *post hoc*). Documents, statutes, treaties, negotiations, controversies, electoral announcements and promulgations of bans (about which the positive religions must not throw stones upon one another from their respective glass houses), all these are material for, but not history as such." This line of demarcation is, of course, somewhat arbitrary. Steinschneider himself decided to include in his treatment, for example, the various medieval "memor books." In his other writings he showed keen awareness of the importance of a *codex diplomaticus* for medieval Jewish history, extensively listed and commented upon communal statutes even in far-off countries, and collected references to such communal records for the use of future historians.[75] Had he merely summarized his own widely scattered notes on these records, he would have greatly facilitated the task of social historians in recent decades.

After all, his work on Jewish historiography really consisted of just such strings of notes on various sources of Jewish history. Unmindful of the dictum quoted by himself that matters of this kind are "not counted but weighed," he did little weighing of the individual sources against one another. For example, Azariah de' Rossi, next to Josephus indubitably the outstanding Jewish historian of the pre-Emancipation era, is disposed of in a brief paragraph, probably because the bibliographical problems connected with his works had already been largely disposed of by Zunz, Rapoport, the editorial notes of Cassel and Benjacob, and in Steinschneider's own summary in the *Bodleian Catalogue*. There is not the slightest intimation of the major historiographic problems such as have been discussed by the present writer. On the other hand, Azariah's lesser contemporaries were given far more elaborate treatment.[76]

Similarly, after devoting six crowded pages to *Yosippon* (including attacks on Carmoly, Wellhausen and others), he briefly dismissed the *Chronicle of Ahimaaz,* cavalierly disposing of Kaufmann's fine analysis. We have seen that Abraham bar Ḥiyya's major historical work was relegated to a brief note in the Appendix as were most travelogues, except those of Benjamin and Petaḥiah which were assigned brief paragraphs in the main treatment.[77]

His interest in *Yosippon* is justified, in part, by the importance he rightly attributed to legends which had overgrown the historic traditions. "Legends and sagas," he declared, "in their peculiar course through various periods, countries and nations, are of considerable interest to the investigator. Their relations to literary and cultural history, to philology and archaeology are often manifest, but in other cases can be ascertained only through more searching inquiries and comparisons." Rather inconsistently, however, he mentioned Gedaliah ibn Yaḥya, the other Jewish historian who preserved for posterity a vast amount of Jewish folklore, chiefly as a target for attack. With full approval he quoted Joseph Solomon del Medigo's pun on the title of Ibn Yaḥya's book as the *Shalshelet ha-Shekarim* (Chain of Lies instead of Chain of Tradition). Referring to Kaufmann's essay on a source of one of Gedaliah's statements, he emphasized,

> Gedaliah remains not only a plagiarist (e.g., from Azariah de' Rossi) but also an uncritical compiler. The fact that he sometimes copies texts literally and sometimes omits miracle tales while indulging in them with relish on other occasions is a part of it all. The word 'tradition' applied to stories written down later has menacing implications for history. One should not deny, however, the value of detecting sources, be they merely sources of errors.[78]

At the same time he brought together much valuable information pertaining to such classics of Jewish historiography as the *Seder Olam rabba,* Sherira's *Epistle,* Ibn Daud's chronicle and the historic apologia by Ibn Verga. He called attention to such theretofore neglected historians as Meiri and Capsali. He also frequently spoke with great admiration of Yeḥiel Heilprin's *Seder ha-Dorot.* "Heilprin's investigations about Jewish chronology," he declared on the occasion of a new edition of the work, "enjoy a deserved reputation, especially his detailed investigations about the talmudic sages. Entire sections thereof have been taken over into modern publications without their source having been betrayed by more than the usual 'cf.' "[79]

Far more restrained was his praise of Azulai's *Shem ha-Gedolim.* He was not only discouraged by what he considered Azulai's gullibility, as revealed particularly in the latter's itinerary, but also by the disorder in the original presentation, corrected only by Benjacob's alphabetical arrangement. That is why he was doubly irked by an unauthorized reprint of Benjacob's edition, which he considered a serious infringement upon the copyright then owned by Banjacob's impecunious widow. On the other hand, he was sharply critical of Aaron Walden's *Shem ha-gedolim he-ḥadash,* which dealt largely with the biographies of modern East European rabbis and Ḥasidic leaders and which, in his opinion, "lacked the comprehensive erudition of Azulai but greatly exceeded the latter in blind gullibility and timid superstition." He felt constrained to add, however, that "if the data supplied in this work, apart from the miracle tales, should prove reliable, we would have to be grateful to the author. Only one of his ilk is familiar with this unsavory sort of literature which, after all, had become a portion of the history of unculture [*Unkulturgeschichte*]."[80]

Next to these more or less major works of Jewish historiography, however, the various chronicles and even minor temporary records occupied much space in his presentation. The more obscure an author, and hence the less known in scholarly literature, the more opportunity he gave to Steinschneider to display his unmatched erudition and skill in detecting data in inaccessible books and manuscripts. He must have realized, for one example, that he was not really competent to deal with a problem like "Chmielnicki's March and the Number of Jews (1648)" without the knowledge of Polish and Russian sources and secondary literature, and yet he wrote an article under this title on the basis of Samuel ben Nathan's *Tiṭ ha-yaven*. "I give here," he declared in 1864, "as raw material the names of the cities together with the number of the heads of families in the sequence of the source, as I have excerpted it in Oxford in 1851. I have been careful only in exactly reproducing the names and figures as written in my excerpts. . . . One will take it for granted that Polish names of localities are not likely to have left a Venetian press without serious injury."[81]

Mastery of Details

We thus see Steinschneider making a number of significant contributions to certain phases of Jewish historiography, rather than offering, in any way, a general history of Jewish historical literature. Here, as in most other works, he might have echoed Leclerc's introductory announcement to the *Histoire de la médécine arabe,* which he quoted in his review of that work. "Our history," Leclerc had written, "will be principally what one might call external, or bio-bibliographical history of Arab medicine. We believe that one must begin in this fashion when one deals with an almost completely new subject." And, as Steinschneider pointed out, Leclerc by virtue of his training as a medical man, Orientalist and literary historian was exceptionally well equipped to write the more important internal history as well.[82]

He himself fully realized the limitations of the bio-bibliographical method, particularly in Jewish studies. "Biographical data concerning the authors," he once wrote ruefully, "are very scarce, except in a few cases, for Jewish writers have, as a rule, lived a quiet cloistered life unless persecution or poverty drove them out of their seclusion." For this reason Jewish biographical treatments usually furnish "shadows rather than pictures." But being natively a pioneer in search of uncharted paths and byways rather than of the highways of scholarship, he felt that his primary responsibility was reliably to assemble those preliminary data on the life and work of the Jewish men of letters, without which all more searching analytical inquiries would resemble castles in the air.[83] Wherever possible, he refrained from discussing basic principles. Even the intriguing question as to why ancient and medieval Jews ever since the fall of Jerusalem revealed little historical interest and why, particularly under the Arab domination, they failed to emulate the vast historical literature of the Arab world, is dismissed in a few casual remarks.

> Now that [he wrote in an early essay], through the Dispersion, a national history properly so-called had ceased to exist, this feeling [of national pride] was necessarily confined to a pride in the intellectual powers of individuals. . . . Here the example of the Arabs could have but little influence; as their historical literature must have remained, for the most part, unknown to the Jews and there could have been no opportunity for imitation.

He failed to explain, however, why that literature remained unknown to the Jews, while, according to his own often stressed opinion, Saadia, Hai and others had studied even the Koran. He offered no reason, for example, as to why Saadia should not have known anything about the historical interests of Al-Mas'udi whom he had met personally. Neither is his other explanation more plausible, namely, that the Jews of Muslim lands, having sustained few persecutions, felt little urge to describe their own history. In another connection, he himself admitted that the records concerning the Jewish *Leidensgeschichte* in Christian countries hardly qualify for inclusion in the category of historical literature. Here he resorted to another argument by saying that "feeling for and interest in developing history stem, as a rule, like imperialism, from the love of one's country." But he failed to explain why the love of one's people—and, as we have seen, he himself constantly harped on the theme of Jewish peoplehood—should not have served as an equally powerful incentive.[84]

This strict adherence to details and aversion to more general discussions induced Frankel, as early as 1846, to warn him against his "proneness in dubious cases to give more credence to dead codices than to the [testimony of] the clear living spirit." With more animus, Jakob Goldenthal later disparagingly referred to "such superficial literary activities which easily established one's scholarly reputation." Steinschneider replied by stressing Frankel's theologically restricted unhistorical approach and by sharply attacking the "ingenious chatter and fabrication of hypotheses" by Goldenthal and his like. For himself he definitely preferred the arduous road of "honest studies."[85]

Although highly sensitive to criticism, he did not budge from his chosen road. By endless labor and toil he produced work after work, knowing well enough that "the pain in giving birth to a book is greater than that of giving birth to a child." He certainly had definite ideas as to how history ought to be written. In a characteristic passage, written in the last years of his long life, he declared,

> The history of culture is the true aim of world history, for it is the aim of all intellectual endeavor. History is neither philosophic schematism (Hegel), nor political pragmatism (Rotteck); — how history of culture is to be written was shown us by Buckle (who has worked himself to death, however), as well as by Macaulay in a few chapters of his first volume.

In contrast to these excellent writers, he must have sensed, as Alexander Marx puts it, his own congenital inability to suppress a note. But what he wrote about his *Hebräische Uebersetzungen* holds true of most of his works.

> I have first begun my investigations [he declared] for myself. There have always been men who have considered research an objective in itself, just as other men indulge in

319

other pleasures. I write first of all for such readers, I mean persons who will look up here particular data. These readers I could call "recurrent" [*fortlaufende*]. This book has not been written for continuous readers.

To produce a useful reference work was, indeed, for him the epitome of scholarly attainment. When he wanted to praise to the sky Zunz's *Synagogale Poesie,* he felt that he could say no more than that "the book is not intended for reading, but for study and reference." In his endeavor to supply much-needed reference works he felt that he could appeal only to small selected groups of experts. More than once he expressed the wish that his books (e.g., the Leyden catalogue) should reach only those readers for whom they were written. We remember that he sharply condemned attempts at "confusing different circles of readers" via popularization. "There are areas," he reiterated, "which are never popular, because an understanding of them presupposes a certain type of training and an interest in them depends on a peculiar bent of mind." So sure was he, on the other hand, that the specialist in need of some specific information would overcome all obstacles, that he did not even care to facilitate this task of consultation. Through some of his writings lurks an almost irrepressible contempt for the reader.[86]

Certainly, he has attained his major objective. His formidable array of books and articles, which earned him Harnack's comparison with the "brazen-bowelled" Didymus of ancient times, has been consulted for many decades by legions of specialists in various fields. Few indeed are the nineteenth-century authors whose technical works have been so urgently needed in recent years as to find publishers ready to reprint them and a public eager to acquire and collect them. Not only was the *Bodleian Catalogue* reproduced in a photo-offset edition after three-quarters of a century, but some of Steinschneider's early writings of the 1840's and 1850's saw the light of day again in Jerusalem shortly before World War II. With all their deficiencies in the light of our present knowledge, the prodigious notes of the great polyhistor on almost every phase of cultural, literary and scientific history of medieval Jewry have been an endless source of valuable information for several generations of scholars. Of course, as he sometimes said, he left to his successors much מקום להתגדר בו (room for further work). But if in some areas Jewish scholarship has advanced far beyond anything envisaged by the founder, his contented reply would have been: *In magnis rebus voluisse sat est.*[87]

13

Levi Herzfeld
The First Jewish Economic Historian*

LEVI HERZFELD is one of the forgotten men of Jewish historiography. It is not astonishing for a pioneer to be little appreciated in his own day. The mere choice of subjects which were in the focus of neither scholarly nor popular attention was enough to discourage public recognition. It is more astounding that posterity, too, failed to appreciate the signal services rendered by the quiet and retiring *Landesrabbiner* of Brunswick to Jewish scholarship along many an untrodden path. What is more, despite the constant growth of sociological and economic interpretations of Jewish history and the vast accumulation of both new sources and new specialized monographs, Herzfeld's *Handelsgeschichte der Juden des Altertums* has not yet been superseded by any other comprehensive work of this type. Following an old Jewish custom, otherwise abandoned in modern scholarship, the book still is far better remembered than its author. It may not be amiss, therefore, to review Herzfeld's inner motivations, historical approaches and methods; and to offer this analysis as a minor tribute to the work of a man whose ramified contributions to rabbinic learning have included new and illuminating insights into the deeper interrelations between the Halakhah and ancient Jewish economy, and who, on various occasions, has written with understanding and appreciation of the nineteenth-century Jewish savants.

* Reprinted from *Louis Ginzberg Jubilee Volume,* New York, 1945.

I

Herzfeld was neither an economist nor a sociologist. His training followed the usual line of Jewish studies under rabbinic teachers
and of philosophic-philological studies under university professors.
Among his courses at the University of Berlin only the few devoted
to science and especially to anthropology, psychology, mathematical
geography and history of recent travels were outside the range of
the customary line of instruction in classical and Oriental languages
and literatures and in systematic and historical philosophy. To be
sure, among his teachers were men of such broad and diversified
interests as Böckh, Ritter, Gans, Ideler, Trendelenburg, Bopp,
Steffens, Raumer, Hengstenberg and, on the Jewish side, Leopold
Zunz.[1] Any but the most inert mind would have received deep
stimuli from such a brilliant array of teachers. But none of them
evinced any particular interest in economics as such. To be sure,
the great geographer, Carl Ritter, emphasized, long before Buckle,
the vital geographic factors in all historic evolution and naturally
also paid considerable attention to trade routes. We shall see that
Herzfeld, who later often quoted Ritter's authoritative *Erdkunde*,
also had a keen awareness of the significance of these and other
aspects of economic geography. Friedrich von Raumer, who had
started his scholarly career with his anonymous *Sechs Dialoge über
Krieg und Handel* (1806) must, on more than one occasion, have
stressed the economic and fiscal aspects of political history to
which he had devoted a large part of his main work on the
Hohenstaufen published in 1823-25. Eduard Gans, the well-known
Hegelian convert from Judaism, taught Herzfeld philosophy of
law and had much to say about legal ethics and especially the laws
of inheritance among various nations. In his lectures he may often
have referred to some phases of Jewish social ethics as well. Zunz,
too, although concentrating on the history of Jewish literature,
had pointed the way to a better understanding of the *realia* of
Jewish life in his early essay on the "statistics" of the Jews, though
he used this term in a meaning different from our own in his
Zur Geschichte und Literatur which appeared in 1845, only a

few years after Herzfeld's intimate association with him, and in other writings.[2] However, all these were but indirect stimuli. August Böckh alone may have exercised a more direct influence and even served as a model. His works on the "public economy" and seafaring of the Athenians, his studies in ancient chronology and his *Metrologische Untersuchungen über Gewichte, Münzfüsse und Maasse des Altertums,* published in 1838—all derived from a principally philological approach—are reflections of the universal interests of the famous classicist which evidently left a permanent imprint upon the mind of his pupil.[3] Nonetheless, Herzfeld was rightly conscious of his pioneering interests in the Jewish field. Decades thereafter, in discounting the well-known apologetic passage in Josephus' *Contra Apionem* (I, 12) which had denied any commercial activities of Palestinian Jewry, he emphasized the evident neglect of all economic aspects by that ancient historian and added, with a slightly bitter overtone:

> As a matter of fact one may observe a similar insensitivity toward these and other facets of popular life or the conviction that such matters do not belong to historical writings among practically all historians of ancient and modern times. It is only in recent years that some progress has been made and these matters have been given attention in historical works.[4]

Nor was he altogether wrong in complaining that he had to do all the spadework himself, having found no *Vorarbeiten* whatsoever in the field of ancient Jewish commerce.[5]

Professionally, too, he had but remote contacts with economic activity. Immediately upon his graduation in 1836 he became assistant to his teacher, Samuel L. Eger, Chief Rabbi of the province of Brunswick, from whom he had received his rabbinic ordination,[6] and whom he succeeded six years later at the age of thirty-two. Thenceforth he occupied the provincial chief-rabbinate for the remainder of his life. While Brunswick as a whole participated in the marvellous capitalistic transformation of northern Germany during the half-century of Herzfeld's ministry (1836-84), its Jewish communities felt the impact of the new era far less keenly than did the Jewries of the larger communities of Berlin, Hamburg or Frankfort. Their rabbi, who despite his manifold communal duties remained a fairly typical cloistered scholar, must have sensed but remotely the turbulence of the new economic clashes.

Nevertheless Herzfeld became the founder of the new discipline of Jewish economic history. He was inspired to this historic achievement by his activities in behalf of Jewish religious reform and his awareness of the latter's interrelations with the dominant political trend of the age, the struggle for Jewish emancipation.[7] In his early years he attended the three rabbinical conferences which met at Brunswick, Frankfort and Breslau in 1844-46, playing host to the first and serving as secretary at the last Conference. The very selection of the location for the first gathering was a compliment to the young rabbi, whose opening remarks as well as sermons delivered on that occasion were included in the published protocols.[8]

From the outset steering a middle course, he became ever more intrigued by the historic origin of various Jewish doctrines and observances which, he believed, had met the needs of their age but were also subject to change and adjustment to meet the requirements of the new era. On more than one occasion he ran counter to popular conceptions concerning the alleged sanctity or unimportance of certain ceremonies by uncovering their respective historic roots.[9] As a member of the Conference committee charged with the preparation of reforms in Jewish marriage observances, he became deeply interested in their historical background. He was soon puzzled by the absence of direct biblical references to religious wedding rites in ancient Israel and took great pains in detecting some traces of such a ritual at least in the literature of the Second Commonwealth. "Marriage was invested with religious forms by the most worldly peoples of antiquity," he once asked with deep concern, "but why should the Jewish people alone have refrained from lending religious meaning to wedding rites even in that period of great religious creativity? If nothing else its acquaintance with the religions of the Magi and the Greeks ought to have induced it to do so."[10] Perplexities of this type made him ever more conscious of the historic interrelations between Jewish social and religious life, the realization of which permeated also his practical "proposals" for the reform of Jewish marriage laws.[11]

From the beginning, moreover, he evinced special interest in assembling as exact information as he could on the more obscure phases of ancient Jewish history. Even in his sermons he was more of a lecturer imparting knowledge than a preacher stirring up emotions.[12] Similarly in his scholarly researches he was more interested in gathering and analyzing all extant reliable data on the more obscure periods and byways of ancient Jewish life than in again and again dramatizing the highlights of Jewish intellectual and spiritual achievement. His doctoral dissertation was devoted to the elucidation of biblical chronology; his first essays in Frankel's *Monatsschrift* discussed the chronological sequence of the early rabbis and of the occupation of Jerusalem by Pompey and Herod.[13] Throughout his work he revealed a keen sense for *realia* and especially for such measurable factors as money and currency, weights and measures, prices and costs of living, population trends and public finance. Even his major historical work, the three-volume history of the Jews from the fall of Jerusalem to the beginning of the Maccabean monarchy, though principally devoted to the more orthodox phases of political, literary and religious history, is replete with information of this kind, highly unusual in the Jewish historiography of the period.[14] He finally decided to institute special investigations in this much-neglected area and in 1863-65 published two studies which he modestly designated as "preliminary metrological investigations" to the history of ancient Jewish commerce.[15] These were followed in 1879 by the full-fledged history.

The ultimate stimulus to these publications, however, was Herzfeld's desire to defend the Jewish people against unjust accusations and to describe its major contributions to civilization. Apologetics were the keynote of all Jewish historiography of that time. Herzfeld may not have been fully aware of the new economic trends, but he certainly was familiar with the new anti-Semitic accusations which, after the crisis of 1873, reached an unprecedented fury. The German press and pamphlet literature were increasingly filled with denunciations of the Jew as a middleman who, sterile and unproductive in both economics and culture, was living a parasitic existence at the expense of his neighbors. This was true, the anti-Semitic chorus asserted, not only of the contemporary Jew, but was an essential characteristic of the Jewish people from its early days in Palestine. Herzfeld was impelled to reply. In addressing the local art club in 1863 he chose as his subject "the artistic achievements" of ancient Jewry.[16] He pointed out that the Hebrews had reached unparalleled heights in the fields of poetry and religious oratory, contributed significantly to the development of architecture and its allied arts, and—answering numerous forerunners of Wagner—created music "equal to the best attained by any other ancient people." Their neglect of plastic arts, on the other hand, and their belated entry into the theatrical field had been entirely due to "their religious views, not to lack of understanding or talent."[17] This line of argumentation has hardly been improved upon by Jewish apologists in the intervening decades.

The main anti-Semitic argument, however, aimed at the Jews as the allegedly innate commercial exploiters of humanity from ancient times to the present, could be effectively answered only by a solid factual history of Jewish commerce. Overcoming a feeling of "shyness" because he ventured to devote a whole volume to purely worldly aspects of ancient Jewish history, Herzfeld expressed the hope that henceforth

> everyone willing to see will be able to see that: Firstly the commercial spirit of which the Jews are accused has been imposed upon them by imperative historical developments. Secondly that practically all of the denunciations incessantly heaped upon their mercantile methods are wholly unfounded. And finally that—apart from their religious and ethical mission and other achievements of their spirit—they have, by establishing, developing and intensifying large-scale and petty

trade, bestowed great benefits upon so many nations by foster-
ing the sale of their products, the rise of their industries, their
general well-being and even their culture.[18]

He admitted that his volume marked merely a beginning and
that an equally solid and impartial history of medieval and modern
Jewish commerce "would be even more instructive from this and
other angles." He repeatedly urged younger men to carry on.[19]
But, despite evident shortcomings, he could legitimately take pride
in his own pioneering effort which served as but another vivid
illustration of the widespread experience in both Jewish and non-
Jewish literatures that apologetics often served as the mainspring
for a new historic discipline.

II

Herzfeld's whole work is colored by his fundamental conviction that political and religious history are deeply interrelated.
Even in writing his voluminous history of the Exile and early
Second Commonwealth, on which he spent the better part of
eighteen years and the "main purpose" of which was the presentation of the religious history of that period, he consistently "recognized the political history of the Jews as the foundation and
background of their religious evolution."[20] In fact, he considered
it as his "chief task to demonstrate the emergence of Judaism
out of Hebraism," which could be accomplished only by describing the history of the people first and then that of its religion.[21]
That is why he felt justified, for instance, in devoting a disproportionate amount of space to the Maccabean revolt. The re-estab-
lishment of the throne of David under the scepter of high priests
"may have turned out to be but a passing dream. But this would
not deter the historian, accustomed as he must be to place many
a decade above centuries, from acknowledging that it marked the
beginning of a new epoch."[22]

Of course, he was by no means an extremist. He realized that
among the Jews the political element "has time and again been

deeply intertwined with the religious element" and that "this is the characteristic feature of Jewish history at all times: Israel, as the 'people of the book' or rather as the people of religion, is of universal historical significance; in all other respects, it is of but secondary interest."[23] True to his general identification of politics with statehood, he was also ready to concede that the correlation between the political and the religious history of the Jews was greatly weakened through the loss of their national independence after the first fall of Jerusalem.

> This [direct correlation] can take place only where a people has retained sufficient independence for its inner, moral forces at least to help shape its external status; and where, on the other hand, it feels entitled to regard the divine spirit pervading it as perfectly autonomous and hence unrestrictedly to allow free rein to its own changed opinions and novel conditions.

The Jews of the Second Commonwealth, although permitting themselves far more latitude than is ascribed to them by modern orthodoxy, had nevertheless imposed upon their further religious evolution the shackles of an accepted immutability of the Divine Law. At the same time their external status was determined by foreign, often brutal powers. That is why "their worldly and religious history will have to be more frequently described *side by side,* than explained through *one another.* The later the period, the more often will this be the case."[24] We may perhaps discount some of these programmatic utterances as a rationalization of the author's inability to penetrate more deeply into the more hidden forms of that interrelation and of his taking the line of least resistance in describing first the political and then the religious evolution as two separate entities. But the mere fact that Herzfeld sensed the weakness of such disparate treatment and sought a rationale for it, is in itself highly revealing. Careful scholar that he was, he also consistently refused to apply modern criteria to ancient times.[25] In any case, however, his clear realization that religious history cannot be fully understood without its political background lent him a unique distinction among the predominantly theological-ly-minded Jewish historians of his time. Since he used, moreover, the term "political history" very broadly and included in it many socio-economic developments as well, he came very close to adumbrating the sociological approaches to history so characteristic of our generation.

His major concern, however, was religious rather than social. Just as in his reformatory activities he thought only of changes in obsolete rituals and of purification of beliefs from superannuated accretions, but paid little attention to social or communal reforms,[26] so he was anything but a social radical in his interpretation of the past. He certainly had little in common with Karl Marx, his close contemporary,[27] whose passion for social justice had inspired the extremist economic interpretation of history, the echo of which, however remote and indirect, may well have reached in some subtle way the hidden recesses of Herzfeld's mind. If anything he was socially a conservative, fully approving of the existing social order, extolling the merits of the monarchy as a promoter of fine arts[28] and looking down upon the masses of the people. In describing, for example, the sectarian controversies of the Second Commonwealth, he was ready, before Geiger and Wellhausen, to be fair to the Sadducees who "as religious conservatives are entitled to their religious, and as the aristocratic group, to their political opposition." Essenes and Therapeutai were "an unhealthy growth, but in itself one of the most noble kind." The Pharisees, too, and their popular following, were "ritualistically minded [werkheilig], but in general not hypocritical [scheinheilig] and still less immoral." But he had nothing to say about the masses of the people who belonged to none of these groups. He dismissed them in a parenthetical remark, "In a survey of this kind we must the more readily disregard the rest of the people, crude, intellectually inert and, hence, rather irresponsible, as unfortunately no nation has ever been found to be free of such dregs."[29] Apart from thus uncritically accepting the ancient rabbinic denunciations of the 'am ha-areş, Herzfeld evidently was no democrat, but rather followed the trend of his age in looking down on the uncultured multitude.[30]

The two passions of Herzfeld's life were religious reform and a good Jewish reputation among the nations. As a reformer he belonged to the more moderate wing. On one occasion he invoked his "positive-historical standpoint,"[31] a term which was at the same time applied by Frankel as a justification of his own even more conservative attitudes. Herzfeld believed that reforms should not be introduced arbitrarily to suit the whims of every individual or group, but that they should be the outgrowth of really deep-felt needs of any new generation. In a sermon delivered in 1843, the period of his greatest reformatory zeal, he well described his point of view:

> We thus have . . . found a rule for arranging Jewish life in our time. The religion of our forefathers must be the foundation of it all, so to say the first nourishment of our children. Otherwise everything else will prove to be without endurance, indeed without any genuine advantage. The same is true of religious life in adult age. For we must not merely have some religion, *too,* but religion must be our beginning and end, it must permeate everything that we do, think and feel. Only thus shall we be true children of old Israel. At the same time, however, we must face a world become more friendly with a more cheerful heart and recognize its tasks as our own. In the religious domain we must cautiously, but fearlessly, carry out everything in accordance with the demands of our conscience, so that light may be reconciled with piety, beauty with inwardness. Only thus shall we be at the same time true children of the new Israel.[32]

For this reason well-considered comprehensive adjustments should be made at once, to be followed by a long period in which no changes should be allowed at all. In other words, reforms should take place only at long historic intervals to meet the genuine and imperative requirements of a new age.[33] Only a thorough examination, therefore, of the many-sided historic backgrounds of the various critical stages in the evolution of Judaism would furnish the necessary objective criteria both for the understanding of past adjustments and for the historically accepted methods of reshaping the religious life of the future.

Precisely because of his unstinted recognition that the basic formulations of pre-emancipatory Judaism had their deep roots far back in the exilic and post-exilic periods, Herzfeld decided to devote the best years of his life to their elucidation. He anticipated that opposition to Reform would sooner or later convert that vital, but obscure, epoch of Jewish history into a major battleground. He wished, therefore, by calm and dispassionate marshalling of all available evidence to lay the foundations for a more penetrating understanding of both the historic essence and the historic limitations of the great exilic transition from Hebraism to Judaism and especially of the vitally significant work of Ezra and his disciples.[34] He was perfectly ready to concede the great historic achievements of Jewish law and its immeasurable contribution to Jewish survival.

> The question as to whether Jewish law has materially contributed to the marvellous preservation of our race [he admitted] can best be solved by a simple historic observation. The later, namely, certain groups of Jews emigrated from Palestine or any other center established by them, and hence the more thoroughly Jewish law had been observed at the time of separation and been carried with them by the emigrants, the more enduringly have the latter maintained themselves among the nations. The correctness of this statement is borne out by every chapter of our history; it is a testimony of greatest vitality.[35]

Despite these undeniable achievements and a variety of other mitigating circumstances, Herzfeld believed that Ezra and his confrères had missed a great historic chance to reach out for a still higher stage in religious accomplishment. "This is for me the deeper meaning of our period for Judaism: the evolution begun by Ezra lies behind us, our conscience has broken with its very principle."[36]

Torn between a deep emotional attachment to tradition and a rational conviction that profound changes were overdue, he was not altogether happy to witness the abandonment of many cherished customs and rituals. He advocated the introduction of German prayers into the synagogue, although insisting upon the preservation of a minimum of Hebrew in the liturgy and the continued reading of the scriptural lessons in the original—all this despite his conviction that "there is no language in the world in which one can pray with such inwardness as in Hebrew."[37] He accepted the elimination of the *Kol nidre* prayer not because of any serious intrinsic objections to its content, but merely out of consideration for the ineradicably mistaken notions about it among the non-Jews. With much pain he anticipated the ultimate breakdown of the Sabbath commandments, especially those conflicting with the untrammeled economic activities of Jewish businessmen in an era of diminished willingness for sacrifice, although he was not prepared to vote for any substantial relaxation of the ancient requirement of a full-fledged day of rest. He was prepared to make all these concessions to the new era not because of their intrinsic merits, but because "we are in *Golus*"—a remarkable admission from the lips of a German reformer. In short, he realized that "a new Israel will arise, but old Israel also had its beautiful aspects which may some day be found wanting in the new."[88] However, in the spirit of the prevailing historical determinism, he believed in the irresistible force of the new historic trends. Therefore, the sooner Jewish leadership comprehended their real import and the sooner it helped adjust the life of the people and its religion to them, the better it would meet the new challenge. That is why one had to make doubly sure that these adjustments be fruitfully and enduringly performed from the broad historic perspective of both the past and the present.

Similarly equivocal was Herzfeld's attitude to Jewish commerce. On the one hand, he was a true son of the new capitalist era and a firm believer in private enterprise. In discussing, for instance, King Solomon's promotion of commerce as a state monopoly he declared that "according to our experiences this was not good national economic policy, but under the then existing circumstances it probably was the best conscious or unintentional means of gradually familiarizing private traders with commerce." At the same time, however, he emphasized that the king's recognition of the

333

"blessings of agriculture," his high intellectual attainments, his great love for building and his maintaining a large army in peacetime "testifies to any but a Phoenician spirit."[39] In general he felt that large-scale participation of Jews in commercial endeavors "required no further justification from the cultural-historical or ethical stand-point before the enlightened opinion of our time," and had no patience with those of his fellow scholars who, prompted by apologetic considerations, failed to discuss this subject with the necessary scholarly detachment.[40] He nevertheless constantly took pains to prove that it was not "native predisposition" but historic circum-stances which induced the Jewish people to engage in commerce, merely admitting that "as far back as the biblical period [Israel] possessed the intellectual alertness and willingness to devote itself to it under propitious circumstances" and rather sharply denying that Moses himself ever betrayed an anti-commercial animus.[41] His greatest concern, however, was to stress on each and every occasion that the Jews' trade morals were on the whole equal or superior to those of their neighbors,[42] and that throughout their history they had served "simultaneously as merchants and as genuine bearers of the Jewish conception of God."[43]

In all these approaches Herzfeld revealed keen sensitivity for the Jewish position in the world at large and, what is more important, for the interrelations between Jewish and general history. In this respect he occupies a unique position among the Jewish historians of the period, most of whom—even men of the distinction and breadth of vision of a Graetz—were treating the history of their people as a rather isolated phenomenon. In his examination of the general historical background of Jewish antiquity Herzfeld went so far as to devote whole sections of his *History* to its clarification. In several chapters, some a score of pages each, he discussed the history of Israel's immediate neighbors, of Achaemenide Persia and of the early Hellenistic empires, supplementing them by numerous notes and lengthy chronological excursuses.[44] He must have realized that he was entering here fields for which he could not claim sufficient competence and that he would expose himself to the objec-tion of arbitrarily combining data of unrelated general and Jewish sources.[45] He also knew perfectly well that such lengthy descriptions of what must basically be considered introductory material was not very satisfactory for the integrated understanding of a historic totality. He was glad when he could relinquish this method during the treatment of the Maccabean era.

The history of the Jews from the Exile to this period [he wrote in explanation] was highly dependent on foreign developments, while reacting back on them only on very rare occasions. That is why its description had to be prefaced by several chapters dealing with the external history. This shortcoming is now removed. During the Maccabean struggles it [Jewish history] impinged with sufficient strength upon Syrian and Egyptian history for all three to be fully combined in a single narrative.[46]

This sensitivity to general developments is also clearly noticeable in Herzfeld's treatment of economic history. His metrological investigations are essentially comparative studies of ancient Jewish coins, weights and measures with those of the Egyptians, Babylonians, Persians, Greeks and Romans.[47] Even in regard to Palestinian commerce, he contended, "we shall find that Jewish trade in all periods of antiquity depended to a very large extent on the mercantile conditions in the neighboring countries." He believed that ancient trade generally revealed "more pronounced international traits" than modern trade. It was indeed this conception which led him to a fuller understanding of the interdependence of Jewish migrations and the expansion of Jewish commerce.[48]

III

The outstanding characteristics of Herzfeld's historical method are his objectivity and the comprehensive treatment of his subjects. Despite his apologetical stimuli he always tried to be as objective and impartial as he could. Unlike Graetz or Geiger he avoided all attempts at eloquence and rhetoric. True, for this reason, his presentation often tended to become dull and pedestrian, and it was totally devoid of those sudden flashes of imagination and insight which lent his two colleagues their genuine distinction. But few of his contemporaries could lay claim to greater patience and soundness in their handling of ancient sources.

The great prolixity of his presentation is partly connected with his objectivity. To make sure of his contentions he usually quoted his sources in full or summarized them at great length—sometimes to the point of ridicule. Before discussing, for example, the period of Xerxes he devoted nearly five pages to a summary of the Book of Esther, familiarity with which could readily be presupposed with readers of such a technical volume.[49] He was not quite un-aware of this shortcoming. "The main difficulties of the present work" (the *Handelsgeschichte*), he once wrote, "and the reason for my overloading it with citations and other bits of evidence consisted in that very fact that I have entered therein a hitherto wholly uncultivated field."[50] He "willingly accepted" a reviewer's criticism that he, as well as Ewald, had "made history a handmaid of exegesis rather than its mistress." He took as the motto for his entire work Alexander von Humboldt's remark that "by contact with very gifted men I have early come to realize that without a serious interest and knowledge of details, each great and general conception of the world must needs remain a castle in the air." For added justification Herzfeld pleaded that "a most careful analysis of details is the greatest need during the present stage of research in Jewish history."[51]

This was with him more than an excuse. At all times scholars lacking the ability and power of historic synthesis have readily taken refuge behind the alleged backwardness of contemporary historical research. Herzfeld certainly could not justly claim that the period of Exile and the early Second Commonwealth had not been widely studied. While he and his predecessors naturally had to wrestle with the extreme paucity of extant sources—a handicap little alleviated since by new archeological finds—these sources had been subjected to ever reiterated careful analysis and minute exegesis. For us today Herzfeld's own researches appear as but a link in a long chain. This is not to say that he leaned heavily on the shoulders of his predecessors or that his work was speedily superseded by that of his contemporaries, Jewish or non-Jewish. In fact, one of his great regrets was that so few Jewish scholars cultivated the field of biblical research and that he frequently sensed the absense of stimuli which would have come to him from novel Jewish interpretations.[52] How often has that complaint been heard since from Jewish historians! Nor was he in any way unjustified, while preparing a revised edition of the second and third volumes of his *History* after a lapse of many years, to insert but six pages of corrections and additions, largely consisting of passages previously overlooked rather than of new scholarly findings.[53] Similarly, when in 1870 he issued a popular edition of all three volumes he felt that, apart from eliminating the scholarly apparatus and somewhat simplifying the narrative, "he merely had to incorporate the sound results of more recent investigations by himself or by others." Otherwise he felt that he could leave the general presentation materially unchanged.[54]

Herzfeld's proclivities towards excessive documentation appeared less awkward when he dealt with a subject as little known and as fundamentally controversial as the history of ancient Jewish commerce. There, indeed, he was more justified in his attempt "to gather in the first place all available material and to make it secure by a full citation of sources," for thus alone could he expect to combat the widespread prejudices, based upon ignorance.[55] Even here, however, had he been a more gifted writer, he would have overcome this inherent difficulty and presented a more consecutive and better proportioned narrative.

His literary skill was subjected to the additional strain of trying to satisfy simultaneously a scholarly and a general audience. The result was an extremely tiresome fourfold division of his *History* into a text, brief footnotes, longer notes at the end of each chapter or issue (*Lieferung,* a method of distribution chosen by the publisher for commercial reasons) and still longer excursuses (with a new set of footnotes) at the end of each volume. Of course, there unavoidably was much repetition. In his *Handelsgeschichte* he did little better by omitting footnotes and including instead long quotations in the text and by combining the lengthy notes and excursuses, except for two appendices devoted to a significant analysis of Palestinian currency, weights and measures and prices.[56]

Despite his extreme care in detail, Herzfeld could not avoid speculation. The nature of the available evidence was such that even the least imaginative historian could not stick closely to the letter of the sources. Their very chronological setting usually required a considerable amount of reasoning. Once the date was determined its frequently obscure or equivocal utterances had to be combined with other similarly obscure and equivocal sources, in order to reach certain hypothetical findings which, if converging with other hypotheses, seemed to yield as good scholarly results as could reasonably be secured.[57] Nor did he hesitate, if necessary, to obtain evidence in other roundabout ways. In order to ascertain, for instance, the extent of ancient Palestinian commerce rarely referred to expressly in the sources, he assembled in an extensive chapter, supplemented by several lengthy notes, all the broader evidence concerning "products of nature and industry which at that time were traded in Palestine and partly exported abroad."[58] Since these products, moreover, included also some writing materials Herzfeld felt justified to amplify the data assembled in the text by a long note. He seems to have felt some misgivings about this procedure, so he rationalized:

> The investigations concerning writing materials used by ancient Jews are far from concluded even after [Leopold] Löw's estimable work. I do not wish to continue them here; this note is intended merely to furnish the evidence for my presentation in the text. . . . As I have entered into the discussion of ancient writing materials only because of the trade in them, I consider it advisable, in order to ascertain the compass of that trade, once and for all to assemble all the data relating to what used to be written at that time. Ultimately, we shall be able to draw therefrom many a conclusion concerning trade, too, and incidentally such a collection of data may perhaps also prove to be of interest to the general history of culture.[59]

But we shall quarrel the less with this circuitous method, as the volume approximates a general economic history of ancient Jewry much more than a commercial history as such.

Like many historians of his time, Herzfeld occasionally betrayed undue proneness to accept some current generalization or even cliché which oddly contrasted with his general critical exactitude. Confronted by the old difficulty of having to derive almost all his information concerning the early Israelites from biblical sources written centuries after the events, he sought refuge in the widespread fallacy concerning the alleged "stability of Oriental institutions and conditions at all times, but quite especially in remote antiquity." Explaining the reasons for Diaspora Jewry's entry into the field of commerce, he argued that it had few other economic opportunities. "One need compare only the great difficulties which, as late as fifty years ago, a Jewish boy had to overcome when he sought employment with a Christian master artisan."[60] It did not occur to him that the ancient economy might have been less controlled by exclusive craft guilds than was early nineteenth century Prussia. He was at his weakest when he ventured into the field of economic theory, as when he argued against his teacher, Böckh, that one could not apply to antiquity any general standard of monetary values.[61] On such occasions his lack of economic training came sadly to the fore. But he was neither the first nor the last Jewish or non-Jewish historian to believe that in dealing with ancient history one could dispense with all specialized knowledge provided one mastered the art of reading the sources in the original. Inadvertently he made that curious admission when he apologized for his inability to treat of the far more significant medieval and modern economic history. "A theme of such enormous scope," he stated, "would transcend my powers. Moreover, to present correctly the commercial activities of the Jews in modern times one would require considerable expert knowledge."[62] He had learned from Ritter, however, certain aspects of economic geography and particularly appreciated the significance of trade routes. "In general, I shall carefully deal with trade routes in this work," he wrote with reference to Sidon's commercial activities in the days of Solomon, "since these were of perhaps even greater mercantile importance in antiquity than are the railways today."[63]

Another feature of Herzfeld's method, rather unusual at that time, was his general "aversion for all kinds of polemics."[64] He also considered it more economical merely to state his opinion and to refer to dissenting views only if they were either widely held or backed by some outstanding authority. "May such scholars," he expostulated, "consider the objection raised as a sign of my respect, indeed reverence for them."[65] Quite exceptionally he once called Graetz's acceptance of certain legends in preference to statements in the books of Maccabees an "irresponsible" action. On another occasion he attacked both Frankel and Graetz because of their doubts in the genuineness of two Philonic works. "Either of them would hardly have considered his proofs worthy of serious consideration had not these two works run counter to their preconceived opinions. Does not the science of Judaism become compromised through such proceedings?"[66] More frequently he quoted both Graetz and Frankel with approval, or whenever he presented a divergent point of view he did it with much circumspection and dignity. The same was true in regard to such other scholars as Zunz, Geiger, Philippson, Rapoport, Jost, Luzzatto,[67] his own teacher Hengstenberg and others.[68]

His conservative bent concerning the antiquity of biblical writings often brought him into open conflict with more radical Christian critics. In his very first work on the chronology of the ancient "judges" he had from the outset to dispose of the objection raised against the historicity of that entire period by Ziegler and other critics.[69] In his excursus on the Book of Esther he likewise had to answer doubts concerning its value as an historical source. He then enunciated his general rule that "since the book itself pretends to be historical we have to regard it as such as long as we do not have sufficient proof to the contrary."[70] But whether he differed from coworkers in the field in fundamentals or merely in the interpretation of details, his tone always remained friendly and dispassionate.

IV

Herzfeld's critics did not always reciprocate. On the whole, he had a fairly good press. But some of his reviewers proved to be highly unsympathetic, not only on scholarly grounds, but on the basis of differing biases. Herzfeld realized in advance that his moderately conservative attitude towards the Bible and his general leanings toward moderate Reform would bring upon him the wrath of both extreme parties.[71] What irked him most, however, was his evidently slight popular appeal. In the Preface to the second edition of his *History*, we recall, he argued that the Jewish public, except for a few rabbis and teachers, was not interested in acquiring Jewish books. The other three reasons adduced by him for the slow sale of the first edition are likewise illuminating:

> 2) From the aforementioned Preface to the last volume, one will notice with sufficient clarity that this work has been systematically ignored by influential circles. This happened not because of its intrinsic unworthiness, but because I follow an unwelcome trend in the field of religion.
>
> 3) Possibly it is indeed more thorough and hence more difficult to read, perhaps also more comprehensive than is pleasing to most readers in this blessed age of steam power.
>
> 4) Most Christian scholars on principle read no letters of Jewish authorship.[72]

One need not take such utterances of a disgruntled author at their face value. They nevertheless contained a kernel of truth. His greatest popular shortcoming, of course, unavowed and perhaps unbeknown to himself, was his undramatic and artless presentation, bordering on dullness.

This was, indeed, the import of the criticism voiced by Ludwig Philippson. When Philippson wrote that Herzfeld was the first Jew to undertake a thorough, critical investigation of this period, but that he had generally pursued "more the critical elucidation of specialties" and did not possess "the gift of reproducing for us the past as a living entity with its personalities appearing in well-delineated sketches,"[73] Philippson did not merely object, as Herzfeld thought, to extreme concentration on exegetical detail. Herzfeld's works resembled, indeed, collections of disjointed studies rather than consecutive narratives. That Philippson also had in mind the absence of extensive biographical characterizations such as adorned, for example, Graetz's history need not be considered today an equally grave shortcoming. We have long drifted away from the anecdotal, biographical type of historiography which, it may readily be admitted, effectively helped to dramatize Jewish history.

Perhaps the most balanced criticism of Herzfeld's work stems from Jost. Though a personal friend and fellow reformer—they both collaborated at the three rabbinical assemblies—the founder of modern Jewish historiography was not blind to Herzfeld's faults, but neither did he maliciously magnify them. He wrote in his review of the second volume of Herzfeld's *History*:

> The present continuation [of vol. I] is the result of excellent research, able circumspection and genuine love for truth . . . . The author treats of an exceedingly complicated subject with rare calm and prudence. He dissolves the sources into their tiniest particles, gives us a very complete, often highly circumstantial account of all his findings and keeps himself free of all preconceived notions and imitation . . . . Every one familiar with the enormous difficulties involved . . . will be grateful to Mr. Herzfeld for his courage in pursuing these researches and his refusal to be deterred by the numerous obstacles.[74]

An anonymous reviewer in Frankel's *Monatsschrift,* however, though admitting the author's industry and familiarity with the sources, sharply attacked Herzfeld's alleged "superior contempt for tradition" and particularly objected to the use of the divine name, *Jawe* by a provincial rabbi.[75] Even a Steinschneider had no word of comment on the *Handelsgeschichte,* while in regard to the *Metrologische Voruntersuchungen* he merely offered a caustic observation on its publication as a first installment of a larger monograph rather than as a reprint from the *Jahrbuch*.[76]

No less prejudiced was the bulk of Christian criticism. Hengstenberg's *Allgemeine Kirchenzeitung* spoke in generally favorable terms, but remarked that "this work demonstrates anew the fact that the enlightenment of modern Judaism by no means paves for Christianity the way to the Jewish people."[77] Ewald was downright abusive. Among other gems of literary criticism his review included a condemnation of Herzfeld's work for "clearly showing how much contemporary Judaism is permeated not only by an ungrateful and malicious, but also in general by a gloomy and mean state of mind." He wanted also "therewith once and for all kindly to advise contemporary Jews of all shades that, if they accept Christian scholarship, they should also accept the Christian, i.e., a sublime and noble spirit."[78] These theologically prejudiced criticisms were surpassed in literary venom during the period of rising modern anti-Semitism in the turbulent 1870's. When, shortly before his death, Herzfeld published a philological treatise on the etymology of Hebrew roots,[79] a southern German scholar (E. N.) published a scurrilous review in the influential *Literarisches Centralblatt*.[80] He not only denied Herzfeld's knowledge of Semitic languages and even of Hebrew, but declared the volume to be "a symptom of that widespread Semitic insolence which does not hesitate to throw the most inferior products on the book market with a magnificent gesture."

Herzfeld thus experienced the usual frustrations of a Jewish apologist, but he also had the satisfaction of learning that the greatest German historian of antiquity, Theodor Mommsen, considered him "the foremost and most reliable of all Jewish historians."[81] Although somewhat harsh on Herzfeld's Jewish confrères, this judgment may well serve as a memento of the pioneering services rendered by one of the outstanding leaders of the much-neglected second generation among the nineteenth-century modern Jewish scholars.

Notes

WORLD DIMENSIONS OF JEWISH HISTORY

1. English trans. by Koppel S. Pinson in his *Nationalism and History, Essays on Old and New Judaism by Simon Dubnow* (Philadelphia, 1958, and Cleveland, 1961, paperback), p. 336.

2. *Seder Eliyahu rabba* XX, ed. by Meir Friedmann (Vienna, 1902), p. 54. On the date of that midrash, see the opposing theories cited in my *A Social and Religious History of the Jews*, 2nd ed., VI, pp. 401 f., no. 7. The latter work, in both editions, will supply fuller documentation for many facts and views expressed in this essay.

3. "Yehudah Halevi: an Answer to an Historic Challenge," *Jewish Social Studies*, III (1941), 243-72.

4. "American Jewish Communal Pioneering," *Publications of the American Jewish Historical Society*, XLIII (1954), 133-50.

5. Julius Aronius *et al.*, eds., *Regesten zur Geschichte der Juden im fränkischen und deutschen Reiche* (Berlin, 1897-1902), pp. 123, no. 280, 139 ff., no. 314a; Eugen Täubler, "Urkundliche Beiträge zur Geschichte der Juden in Deutschland," *Mitteilungen* of the Gesamtarchiv der deutschen Juden, IV (1913), 32 f., 44 f.

6. "'Plenitude of Apostolic Powers' and Medieval 'Jewish Serfdom'" (Hebrew), *Sefer Yobel le-Yitzhak Baer* (Y. F. Baer Jubilee volume) (Jerusalem, 1960), pp. 102-24. See also my "Medieval Nationalism and Jewish Serfdom," in *Studies and Essays in Honor of Abraham A. Neuman* (Leiden, 1962), pp. 17-48.

7. Matthias Döring in his continuation of Theodore Engelhaus' chronicle, cited by Johannes E. Scherer in *Die Rechtsverhältnisse der Juden in den deutsch-österreichischen Ländern* (Leipzig, 1901), pp. 42 f., no. 2.

EMPHASES IN JEWISH HISTORY

1. See S. M. Dubnow, *Weltgeschichte*, I, xxiii-xxviii. It is a curious historical irony that Dubnow, in a review of the author's *Social and Religious History*, found himself placed in the position of taking issue with the general chronological latitude employed in this work. See *Die Zukunft*, XLII (1937), 765-68.

2. *Systematische Bibliographie der Palästina-Literatur* (Leipzig, 1908-38).
3. A. Neubauer, *La Géographie du Talmud* (Paris, 1868); J. Obermeyer, *Die Landschaft Babylonien im Zeitalter des Talmuds und des Gaonats* (Frankfort, 1929); H. Gross, *Gallia Judaica: Dictionnaire géographique de la France d'après les sources rabbiniques* (Paris, 1897); M. Brann, I. Elbogen, and others, *Germania Judaica,* 2 vols. (Frankfort, 1917 and Breslau, 1934); E. Natali, *Il ghetto di Roma* (Rome, 1887); I. Schwarz, *Das Wiener Ghetto, seine Häuser und seine Bewohner* (Vienna, 1909); M. Balaban, *Die Judenstadt von Lublin* (Berlin, 1919); A. Pinthus, "Studien über die bauliche Entwicklung der Judengassen in den deutschen Städten," *Zeitschrift für die Geschichte der Juden in Deutschland,* II (1930-31), 101-30, 197-217, 284-300; D. Philipson, *Old European Jewries* (Philadelphia, 1894).

4. The idea of the "negation of the *galuth*" has long had theoretical champions among the extremist Zionist thinkers. More recently it has been applied to the interpretation of the Jewish past by two eloquent and competent protagonists, Jecheskel Kaufmann and Yitzhak (Fritz) Baer. See especially Kaufmann's *Golah ve-nekar* (Tel Aviv, 1929-32) and Baer's *Galut* (Berlin, 1937) and his review of the author's *Social and Religious History of the Jews,* in *Zion,* III (1938), 277-99.

5. Karl Marx, "On the Jewish Question," in *Selected Essays* (London, 1926), pp. 40-97; Karl Kautsky, *Are the Jews a Race?* 2nd English ed. (New York, 1926), and *Foundations of Christianity,* English translation from the 13th German ed. (New York, 1925); Otto Heller, *Der Untergang des Judentums. Die Judenfrage, ihre Lösung durch den Sozialismus* (Vienna, 1931). The influence of Marx's essays on the subsequent Socialist attitudes to the Jewish question is treated by Gustav Mayer in his "Early German Socialism and Jewish Emancipation," *Jewish Social Studies,* I (1939), 409-422. See also *infra,* p. 447, n. 10.

6. The paucity of the material on this subject is so great that Prof. Baer, in his above-mentioned review, questioned the wisdom of offering any such summary of the social philosophy of the rabbis. It has been our feeling, however, that a beginning, inadequate as it may be, must be made now, so as to stimulate more extensive and intensive researches in detail. By writing a comprehensive monograph on the "economic teachings" of Maimonides—which together with a previously published essay on the "historical outlook" and another, yet to be written, on the "political theory" of that philosopher-jurist is to analyze in detail the main social teachings of one of the chief intellectual spokesmen of medieval Jewry—the present author hopes to help fill one of the major lacunae in our knowledge of the medieval Jewish economic outlook. The monograph appeared in *Essays on Maimonides,* ed. by the author (New York, 1941), pp. 127-264. See below, pp. 265 f.

7. Hegel, *Die Wissenschaft der Logik,* in *Werke,* VI, 2nd ed. (Berlin, 1843), p. 382.

8. *Geschichte der Juden,* IV, 4th ed., p. xv. Not rendered in the English translation of Graetz's *History.*

9. For further brief observations on the communal approach, see the present author's "Historical Critique of the Jewish Community," in *Jewish Social Service Quarterly,* XI (1935), 44-49 and "Socio-Religious Research in Jewish History" (Yiddish), in *Die Zukunft,* XLIII (1938), 341-47.

10. *Rektoratsrede* (Berlin, 1874), reprinted in his *Reden und Aufsätze* (Berlin, 1905), p. 11.

NEWER EMPHASES IN JEWISH HISTORY

1. *Jewish Social Studies,* I (1939), 15-38. Subsequently I discussed some further aspects of that problem in "New Horizons in Jewish History," *Freedom and Reason: Studies in Philosophy and Jewish Culture in Memory of Morris Raphael Cohen* (Glencoe, Ill., 1951), pp. 337-53. This publication too, was sponsored by the Conference on Jewish Social Studies.

2. Most of these monographs are listed in the comprehensive bibliographical series edited by Philip Friedman and Jacob Robinson, the publication of which is now nearing completion. See especially their *Guide to Jewish History under Nazi Impact* (New York, 1960).

3. Suffice it to mention here the important monographs on the Jews of New York by Hyman B. Grinstein and the De Sola Pools; of Rochester by Stuart Rosenberg; of Buffalo by Selig Adler; of Utica by S. Joshua Kohn; of Charleston by Charles Resnikoff and U. Z. Engleman; of Minnesota by W. Gunther Plaut; of nineteenth-century California by Rudolph Glanz; and of Milwaukee by Louis J. Swichkow and Lloyd P. Gartner. The pioneering work on American-Jewish demography, edited by Sophia Robison and Joshua Starr, was followed by numerous local and regional surveys. Other aspects of Jewish sociology also made considerable advances in the works of Marshall Sklare, Nathan Glazer and others. See also my comments on "American Jewish History: Problems and Methods," *Publications of the American Jewish Historical Society,* XXXIX (1950), 207-66.

4. Yitzhak Ben-Zvi, *Nidhe Yisrael* (The Dispersed of Israel) (Tel Aviv, 1953); in the English trans. by Isaac A. Abbady, entitled *The Exiled and the Redeemed* (Philadelphia, 1957; 2nd edition, 1961).

5. See the list of publications in the *Studies and Reports* of the Ben-Zvi Institute for Research on Jewish Communities in the East at the Hebrew University in Jerusalem since 1953; and the recent pamphlet *Publications of the Ben-Zvi Institute* (Jerusalem, 1963).

6. See, for instance, the "Papers and Proceedings on the Emergence of New African States and World Jewry, Presented at the Annual Meeting of the Conference on Jewish Social Studies . . . June 7, 1961," published in *Jewish Social Studies,* vol. XXIV (1962), 67-107.

7. Yehudah b. Samuel Halevi, *Kitab al-Khazari* (Sepher ha-Kuzari), iv, 22, translated from the Arabic with an Introduction by Hartwig Hirschfeld, 2d ed. (New York, 1927).

8. On the various theories advanced concerning the identity of that town see my *A Social and Religious History of the Jews,* 2d ed., vol. IV, pp. 103, 291 n. 17.

9. Isaiah Sonne, ed., *Mi-Pavlo ha-rebi'i 'ad Pius ha-hamishi* (From Paul IV to Pius V; a Hebrew chronicle of the sixteenth century), (Jerusalem, 1954), pp. 24 f.; Joseph ha-Kohen, *'Emeq ha-bakha* (The Valley of Tears; a History of the Persecutions of Jews from 70 to 1575), ed. by Meir Letteris (Vienna, 1852), pp. 117 ff.

10. Joshua Soncino, *She'elot u-teshubot* (Responsa), fol. 39 b.

11. See *supra,* "World Dimensions of Jewish History."

12. See Robert H. McNeal, "Soviet Historiography on the October Revolution: a Review of Forty Years," *American Slavic and East-European Review,* XVII (1958), 269-81; Matthew P. Gallagher, *The Soviet History of World War II: Myths, Memoirs and Realities* (New York, 1963).

13. S. Dimenshtain, ed., "Evrei," *Bolshaia sovetskaia entsiklopedia,* 1st ed., (Moscow, 1932), XXIV, 13-121 (with other pertinent articles, *ibid.,* pp. 122-65), contrasted with the same title in the new edition, XV (1952), 377-79 (also 379-82). Soon after the publication of the latter edition a Polish-Jewish communist, Michael Mirsky, courageously criticized that article in the Warsaw Yiddish paper, *Folks Shtime* of January 24-26, 1957. A comprehensive analysis of the difference in the treatment of Jewish entries in the two editions of that encyclopedia is offered by Marc Jarblum in *Le problème juif dans la theorie et la pratique du communisme* (Paris, 1953), pp. 29 ff., 43 ff.

14. See *supra,* "World Dimensions of Jewish History."

15. Samuel David Luzzatto, *Iggerot* (Letters), (Przemysl, 1882), p. 1367.

16. See my brief observations on "The Problem of Teaching Religion," *Columbia College Today,* Spring-Summer 1963, 25-27.

THE HISTORICAL OUTLOOK OF MAIMONIDES

1. It is noteworthy that, although the doctrine of the Torah's pre-existence has found a counterpart in the orthodox Muslim's belief in the primordial nature of the Koran, Maimuni maintains silence on the subject.

The works of Maimonides will be cited in the following abbreviations: C.M. = Commentary on the Mishna (in the usual Hebrew translations, unless a special Arabic edition is indicated). *C.M. Intro.* = Introduction to Zera'im; *I.S.* = אגרת השמד in חמדה גנוזה ed. Z. H. Edelman (Königsberg, 1856), ff. 6-13; *I.T.* = אגרת תימן ed. D. Holub (Vienna, 1875), and *Kobeṣ* II (I had at my disposal also an English translation from the Arabic original prepared by B.

Cohen, to whom I am also indebted for the two references therefrom in nn. 50 and 162; (This translation has since been published in Abraham S. Halkin's critical edition of the *Iggeret Teman* [Epistle to Yemen], New York, 1952). *Kobeṣ* = קובץ תשובות חרמב"ם ואגרותיו ed. A. L. Lichtenberg, 3 parts, (Leipzig, 1859); *M.N.* = מורה נבוכים (the English quotations are usually variations of the Friedlaender translation); *M.T.* = משנה תורה; *Resp.* = תשובות הרמב"ם ed. A. H. Freimann (Jerusalem, 1934); *S.M.* = ספר המצוות Hebrew transl. ed. Ch. Heller (Petrokow, 1914) (unless Arabic original ed. by M. Bloch [Paris, 1888], is indicated). Among modern works the following will be quoted in abbreviated form: *BB* = W. Bacher, "Die Bibelexegese Moses Maimuni," *Jahresbericht* . . . Budapest 1895-96 (Budapest, 1896); *GL* = L. Ginzberg, *The Legends of the Jews*, 6 vols. (Philadelphia, 1909-27) and *MbM* = *Moses ben Maimon* by J. Guttmann and others, 2 vols. (Leipzig, 1908-14).

2. The reticence of even the modern Jewish theologians to discuss the problem of "creed versus history" vividly contrasts with the extended Protestant discussions under the leadership of R. Seeberg and others, and clearly shows how little germane this subject is to Jewish theology. A. Weiser's *Glaube und Geschichte im Alten Testament* (Stuttgart, 1931), is a typical endeavor to treat the Old Testament under the aspect of New Testament difficulties.

3. This lack of "originality" in Maimuni's historical approach explains also the total absence of studies on this subject in the vast literature on the medieval sage. A few general remarks and more or less incidental references will be found, especially, in *BB* and Bacher, "Die Agada in Maimunis Werken" in *MbM*, II, 131-97.

4. *C.M.* to Sanh. X, 1: אבוד הזמן בהבל כגון אלו הספרים הנמצאים אצל הערב מספור דברי הימים והנהגת המלכים ויחוסי הערבים וספרי הנגון וכיוצא בהן מן הספרים שאין בהן חכמה ולא תועלת גופני אלא אבוד הזמן בלבד. This juxtaposition of history, public law, government, genealogy and poetry is truly characteristic of the Arabic letters of the period. For Maimuni's sharp antagonism even to Hebrew poetry modeled after Arabic patterns, cf. especially his *Resp.* No. 370. He also rebuked the superficiality of a reader who, in his opinion, glanced over the contents of Scripture as if he "were reading an historical work or some poetic composition." *M.N.* I, 2. Cf. also *ibid.*, III, 8 and 39.

5. Among recent surveys cf. especially D. S. Margoliouth, *Lectures on Arabic Historians* (Calcutta, 1930), and the stimulating methodological discussion in M. K. Ayad, *Geschichts- und Gesellschaftslehre Ibn Halduns* (Stuttgart, 1930). Unfortunately our knowledge of Maimuni's Arabic readings is extremely limited. His direct citations are even fewer than those from Jewish sources. The available investigations, moreover, of the affinities of Maimonidean philosophy to that of the Kalam, Avicenna, Alfarabi or Averroës, however meritorious in themselves, throw little light on the question of Maimuni's direct indebtedness to the works of his predecessors. The literary output of the Arabs had become so enormous that Samau'al ibn Yaḥya rightly asserted that it was impossible

for a man to master all that was written in a single branch of science. Cf. M. Schreiner, "Samau'al ben Yaḥya al-Magribî und seine Schrift, 'Ifhâm al-Yahûd,'" *MGWJ*, XLII (1898), p. 172. In view also of the far-reaching specialization, one may readily assume that Maimuni, like every other educated person in his day, read not only the famous classics, but many less substantial writings (cf. e.g., his statement quoted in note 14), of which only a small part has come down to us. Only a minute expert examination of the few direct and the many indirect references in his works may yield valuable clues to his intellectual background.

6. Maimonides' familiarity with Abraham bar Hiyya's *Megillat ha-Megalle* was deduced from a reference to a Messianic computation in *I.T.* by A. Geiger, *Moses ben Maimon*, I (Breslau, 1850) (=*Nachgel. Schriften* III, 34-96), note 53 and Jacob Guttmann, "Über Abraham bar Chijas, 'Buch der Enthüllung,'" *MGWJ*, XLVII (1903), p. 453. This reference as well as the similarity of the Maimonidean doctrine concerning the degrees in prophecy with that of Bar Hiyya may be inconclusive, as pointed out by Jul. Guttmann in his introduction to the edition of the *Megillat ha-Megalle*, pp. xxiii ff., but one may perhaps find more convincing evidence in another passage. In *I.T.* pp. 18 ff. (*Kobeṣ* II, 2a), Maimuni sketches the history of three religions which arose after Judaism, namely, Christianity, Manicheism and Islam, in a fashion strikingly similar to that of Bar Hiyya. The singling out of these three creeds (although Mani is not mentioned by name in *I.T.*) as representing three important historical movements; the interpretation of Dan. 11.14 as referring to Jesus (*Meg. ha-Meg.*, p. 136); the acceptance of Jesus' execution as a fact and the explanation that it was merely the result of his transgressions (*ibid.*: כי הוא מת בחטאו ובעונו); the emphasis upon the inefficacy of Mani's preachment (*ibid.*, p. 145: אשר לא נאמנו דבריו ולא ארכו ימיו) and that upon Muhammed's seizure of power through lies and the force of arms (*ibid.*: המשוגע הנבזה אשר החזיק את המלכות בהלקלקות כזב ובכח חרב ומלחמה)—are all resemblances too close to be merely accidental. Cf. also note 8.

7. Cf. especially his justification of that method, *ibid.*, p. 115. Apart from Muslim historians and astrologers, such as Yaḳubi and Abu Maashar (the likely influence of the latter on Bar Hiyya is emphasized by M. Steinschneider, *Hebräische Übersetzungen*, p. 572), a curious Latin epistle, apparently written in Spain by Bar Hiyya's contemporary, John Avendeath, the famous translator (a professing or baptized Jew), offers interesting parallels. Cf. F. Baer, "Eine jüdische Messiasprophetie auf das Jahr 1186 und der dritte Kreuzzug," *MGWJ*, LXX (1926), pp. 113-22 and 155-65.

8. For Maimonides' views on astrology, cf. especially A. Marx, "The Correspondence between the Rabbis of Southern France and Maimonides about Astrology," *HUC Annual*, III (1926), pp. 311-58. In *I.T.*, pp. 39 ff. (*Kobeṣ* II, 5b) he specifically repudiated astral influences on history, as assumed by his Yemenite correspondents. It is not impossible, however, that he also had Bar Hiyya in mind.

9. Cf. Schreiner, *op. cit.*, pp. 127 and 412.

10. It is needless to say that only the significant references in Maimuni's works to a person or event in the past will be listed here. In checking up the sources of his information attention will be paid primarily to the Babylonian Talmud which had for him great, almost "canonical," authority. On the other hand, it has long been recognized that Maimuni had greater familiarity with and appreciated more deeply the older tannaitic sources and the Palestinian Talmud than the majority of his halakhic contemporaries and successors. Cf. now, especially, L. Finkelstein, "Maimonides and the Tannaitic Midrashim," *JQR*, N.S., XXV (1935), pp. 469-517 and J. N. Epstein, "Mechilta and Sifre in the Works of Maimonides" (Hebrew), *Tarbiz*, VI (1934-5), pp. 99-138.

11. *M.T.* Sanhedrin 12, 3, closely following the texts in M. Sanh. IV, 5. Maimuni, however, not only characteristically omits the other purposes enumerated in the Mishnah, but also changes: לפיכך כל אחד ואחד חייב לומר בשבילי נברא העולם into יכול לומר which lends it a different emphasis. It is possible that he stresses נפש אחת מן העולם in order to oppose certain texts limiting it to: מישראל. Cf. דקדוקי סופרים, p. 100 n. 'ב. The chronological basis of Maimuni's date will be discussed later on. For various Arab computations of the period which elapsed between Noah and Abraham, cf., e.g., Maqdasi, *Le Livre de la Création et de l'Histoire*, ed. and transl. by Cl. Huart, 6 vols. (Paris, 1899-1919), III, 47.

12. *M.T.* Bet ha-Beḥirah 2, 2. The general source is Pesikta r. 31 and Palestinian Targum to Gen. 22.9. Cf. also Pirke R. Eliezer, 12. The last quotation is from Gen. r. 14, 9 (ed. Theodor-Albeck, p. 132) based upon the Aggadah in j. Nazir VII, 2, 56b.

13. Cf. the long list in *GL*, V, 92 n. 55.

14. דעו רבותי שאני חפשתי בדברים אלו הרבה ותחילת מה שלמדתי היא חכמה זו שקורין גזרת הכוכבים כלומר שידע ממנה האדם מה עתיד להיות בעולם או במדינה או במלכות זו או מה יארע לאיש זה כל ימיו. וגם קראתי בכל עניני עבודה זרה כולה כדומה לי שלא נשאר חבור בעולם בענין זה בלשון ערבי שהעתיקו אותו משאר לשונות עד שקראתי אותו והבנתי ענינו וירדתי עד סוף דעתו. Marx, *op. cit.*, p. 351 (with slight variations *Kobeṣ* II, 25ab). The juxtaposition of astrology with idolatry is characteristic of Maimuni's views on the history of religion. If the works quoted in *M.N.* III, 29 ff. should serve as a sample of these readings, he seems to have been rather uncritical in the selection of authentic documents revealing the early growth of pagan cults. There is a real need for a fresh re-examination of the influence of works such as the *Nabatean Agriculture* and the *Book Tomtom* on Maimuni in the light of our present-day knowledge, to supplement the investigations of D. Chwolson, *Die Ssabier und der Ssabismus*, 2 vols. (St. Petersburg, 1856). Cf. also notes 5 and 20.

15. Cf. especially *C.M.* to 'Abodah Zarah IV, 7; *M.T.* 'Abodat Kokabim 1, 1.2; *M.N.* III, 29-49.

16. This date is obviously derived from the numerous aggadic interpretations of Gen. 4.26. Maimuni insists, however, that חיה השועים מן עצמו ואנוש against the prevalent exoneration of Enosh himself. *GL*, V, 151 assumes that Maimonides referred to some older sources, although Hekalot 6, 173 and Shab. 118b: כאנוש (rather than אנוש כדור; cf. דקדוקי סופרים) are somewhat dubious. Cf. also *ibid.*, p. 153. It is not unlikely, however, that this emphasis was due to an intentional rejection of the theory of the hereditary transfer of the prophetic soul. This theory, evolved by the Shiya to legitimize the Alides' dynastic aspirations, contended that Enosh received the light from Seth and bequeathed it to a prophet or *imam* of each subsequent generation until Muhammed. Cf. Mas'udi, *Les prairies d'or*, 2 vols. (Paris, 1861-63), I, 69-71. Although rejected by most other Muslim schools (Tabari, for example, emphasizes in his *Chronique*, French transl. H. Zotenberg, I [Paris, 1867], p. 88, "Know ye that both Enosh and Kenan were kings of the whole earth, but were not prophets"), this doctrine found its way into Jewish philosophy through Bar Hiyya and Halevi (*Meg. ha-Meg*. p. 72: נתגלגלה הזה העניין ועל הנשמה השהורה משת לאנוש ומאנוש לקינן; Al-Khazari I, 95, etc. Cf. B. Ziemlich "Abr. b. Chija und Jehuda Halevi," *MGWJ*, XXIX (1880), pp. 366-74; Jac. Guttmann, *op. cit.*, pp. 465 f. and Jul. Guttmann, Introduction to *Meg. ha-Meg.*, pp. XXI f.), but had no place in the comprehensive Maimonidean theory of prophecy. Maimuni also ridicules the "Sabean" assumption that it was Seth who began worshiping the moon against the wish of his father, Adam (*M.N.* III, 29). Cf. also further on note 19. The general interpretation, however, that the images were the second stage evolved out of the wish plastically to represent the stars and the rest of the theory concerning the rise of the astral cults, appears to be largely his own.

17. This identification of stars with spheres and angels (for the meaning of this term, cf. especially *M.N.* II, 6) is here, of course, an anachronism.

18. Maimonides rationalistically insists that Enoch's ascension, like that of Elijah later, meant death (*Kobeṣ* II, 34c; cf. n. 29). Whether the brevity of the assertion concerning Enoch in contrast to the full discussion about Elijah was accidental or had a polemical slant against the Sabean glorification of Enoch-Hermes, is an open question.

19. *M.N.* III, 39. Here, as often throughout his writings Maimuni anachronistically ascribes a Beth Din or Midrash to these and other ancient leaders to reconcile history with his legal requirement of collegiate action for certain legislative measures. Cf. Bacher in *MbM*, II, 145. This insistence upon the infinite supremacy of Moses as a prophet is incidentally also in line with his rejection of continuous prophetic leadership in the pre-Mosaic age.

20. *C.M.* to 'Ab. Zarah, IV, 7; *M.N.* III, 37 and *Kobeṣ* II, 25 ab. The name Sabeans is frequently used by Maimuni in a wider sense, i.e., the entire pagan world before Abraham; but, when placed along with the names of other nations, it represents a specific ethnic-religious group (Munk, III, 217, n. 1

fails to draw this distinction). It is questionable, however, whether Maimuni had at all in mind the pre-Islamic inhabitants of southern Arabia, of whose history and religion the Muslim world (except for a few natives, such as Hamdani) had very faint notions. For him the Sabeans were a distinct religio-philosophical trend which, tolerated by the successive Muslim governments, combined crude and primitive with advanced philosophical ideas. This unhistorical estimate of the Sabean religion was shared even by such Arab experts as Shahrastani, Cf. vol. II part I and the remarks of the translator, Haarbruecker, in his preface to Shahrastani's *Religionspartheien und Philosophen-Schulen*, 2 vols. (Halle a.S., 1850-51). Cf. also Al-Biruni, *The Chronology of Ancient Nations*, Eng. transl. E. Sachau (London, 1879), pp. 186 ff., where among the queer etymologies of that name appears the identifi-cation of this sect with alleged descendants of Sabi, son of Methuselah. That is why Maimuni's Hebrew translators were justified in retaining the Arabic form צאב"ה instead of the biblical שבא.

21. *M.N.* III, 29 starts with the sweeping assertion מעולם אן אברהם, אבינו עא"ס נשא פי מלה אלצאבה ומדהבהם.

22. *M.T.* 'Abodat Kokabim 12, 7; *M.N.* III, 37 and 45. Of course, Maimuni takes it for granted that every reader would be familiar with the talmudic interpretation of Num. 25.3 (Sanh. 64a, etc.).

23. They stressed the impurity of blood to the extreme of isolating completely a menstruating woman and declaring impure any person that spoke to her or was touched by a wind that passed over her. For their sacrifices of wild animals and their ritualistic consumption of blood Maimuni quotes as his source the allegedly Indian book *Tomtom*. Cf. *M.N.* III, 41 and 46 and Munk, III, 240 n. 1. *BB*, p. 137, n. 1. points out that this interpretation of Lev. 3.26 is found already in Ibn Ezra and that Maimuni himself in his halakic writings prefers to follow the hermeneutic application of this verse to a rebellious son. Cf. *S.M.*, Prohibition 165 and *M.T.* Mamrim 7, 1.

24. *M.N.* III, 48. The only substantiation he offers is the propinquity of two of the three verses prohibiting the seething of a kid in its mother's milk with those enjoining the three annual pilgrimages to Jerusalem.

25. *M.N.* III, 49. Like everybody else at that time Maimuni believed in the early spread of writing, although he did not mention the legends current among the Arabs (e.g., Mas'udi, *op. cit.*, p. 73) concerning the thirty-one, twenty-nine and thirty leaves handed by God to Adam, Seth and Enoch respectively. Tabari (*Chronique*, p. 86) records a tradition going back to Muhammed that God sent down altogether 114 books: 50 to Adam and Seth, 30 to Noah, 20 to Abraham and 10 to various other prophets. Among these 10 books were the Pentateuch, the Gospels, the Psalms and the Koran. Maimuni may have seen therein a reflection on the uniqueness of the Torah which was given in full to Moses (see further on, note 75), although some Arabs were ready to concede that, in contrast to those stray leaves, the Penta-

teuch was the first real book. Cf. e.g., Shahrastani-Haarbruecker, *op. cit.*, I, 48. He admits, however, in speaking of Abraham וחבר בו ספרים *M.T.* 'Abodat Kokabim 1, 3. He probably refers to the book on idolatry which according to 'Ab. Zarah 14b was written by Abraham and consisted of 400 chapters.

26. *M.T. ibid.; M.N.* III, 29. Cf. also Bacher's comments, *MbM* II, 148 ff. The alleged Sabean tradition that Abraham was born in Kutha = Ur is found also in B.B. 91a and in non-Sabean Arabic sources. Cf. Munk III, 219, n. 6 and *GL,* V, 211 n. 20. Maqdasi, *op. cit.* III, 53 calls it Kutha Rabba in the cultivated territory of Kufa. Cf. also Huart, *ibid.*, n. 1. The non-committal, כיון שנגמל, is evidently due to the contradictory rabbinic legends, listed by Ginzberg, p. 209 n. 13 which seem to have escaped the attention of RABD *ad loc.* The date of forty years instead of the forty-eight given in Gen. r. 30, 8 which greatly troubled the medieval commentators (*Maimuni Glosses* and *Kesef Mishneh;* cf. Zacuto, *Yuḥasin* 5a: שלקח גרסא משבשת) seems to have been Maimonides' own correction perhaps on the basis of בן ארבעים לבינה (Abot V), as suggested by Bacher, p. 149 n. 1. Maqdasi III, 49 speaks of fifteen years as the age at which Abraham left the cave and, coming among men, began to reflect on religious problems. Ṭabari (*Chronique, pp.* 128 ff.) asserts that Abraham at the age of fifteen months was as tall as a boy of fifteen, and that in his day the whole world was steeped in astrology.

27. *Resp.* No. 42: ועיקר הדבר שאברהם אבינו הוא שלמד כל העם והשכילם והודיעם דת האמת וייחודו של הקב"ה ובעט בע"ז וחפר עבודתה והכניס רבים תחת כנפי השכינה ולמדם ולמדם והורם . . . This historical summary, adduced by Maimonides in justification of his insistence that a proselyte recite in his prayers ואלוחי אבותינו, is in essential agreement with both the Aggadah and modern biblical research. Cf. *GL,* V, 215 n. 42-3 and 220 n. 61 and Fr. M. Th. Boehl, *Das Zeitalter Abrahams* (Leipzig, 1930), pp. 41 f.

28. *M.N.* III, 45. Cf. Munk III, 468 f. The Muslims, too, generally believed that Abraham, after the "sacrifice" of Isaac, built the Temple on that mountain. Cf. Koran II, 121; Mas'udi, *op. cit.*, I, 87, etc. Only few preferred to leave the question open as to whether Ishmael or Isaac was the "sacrifice." Cf. Ṭabari, *Chronique,* p. 171. According to Abraham Maimuni, his father rejected the computation of the Aggadah (cf. the passages listed in Theodor-Albeck, *op. cit.,* pp. 587 f. note), that Isaac was then thirty-seven years old, because this would have shifted the burden of the sacrifice from Abraham to him. Cf. S. Eppenstein, "Beiträge zur Pentateuchexegese Maimunis," in *MbM* I, 414.

29. *Kobeṣ,* II, 34a. For a defense of the authenticity of the *Pirqe ha-haṣlaḥah* written in the late years of Maimuni's life, cf. Bacher, "The Treatise of Eternal Bliss attributed to Moses Maimuni," *JQR,* IX (1896-97), pp. 270-89.

30. M.N. III, 29. While Maimuni allows here for certain exceptions, Maqdasi, *op. cit.,* III, 51, recklessly asserts that "there is now no one of whatever creed who denies Abraham (may peace rest upon him) and who does not follow him in his prayers." It is characteristic that Maimuni calls here Abraham

Notes   (119)

עמודו של עולם and איתן but not ידיד ח', although the latter appellation is much more frequent in the Aggadah and even has scriptural backing in II Chr. 20.7. Cf. GL, V, 207 n. 4. In the Arabic S.M. Comm. 3, however, perhaps under the impact of prevalent Muslim usage, he uses the term אוהב rendered by the Hebrew translator by אוהב השם of the Chronicles, but he quotes Isa. 41.8. C.M. to Abot V, 3 enumerates the ten "trials" of Abraham. Discarding all the supernatural features of the well-known ancient legends (for their variations cf. Schechter's note to his edition of Ab. R.N. 34, 94 f. and GL, V, 218 n. 52), Maimuni gives a full list of human tribulations, all recorded in Scripture.

31. M.N. III, 8, quoting a variation of the statement of Yeb. 76a; Gen. r. 98, 4 and 99, 3 (Theodor-Albeck, pp. 1253 and 1257); Aggadat Bereschit 82, etc. Another example is adduced from Elisha, in accordance with the homiletical explanation of קדוש in II Kings 4.9 Ber. 10b, etc.

32. C.M. to Abot Introd. (=The Eight Chapters) 7; M.N. II, 36, based upon the homiletical interpretations of Gen. 45.27 in Targum Jonathan and Rashi ad loc.; Pirke R. Eliezer, 38, etc. For the meaning of the passage in M.N. cf. the opposing views of Z. Diesendruck, "Maimonides' Lehre von der Prophetie," in Jewish Studies in Memory of I. Abrahams (Vienna, 1927), p. 111 n. 139 and H. A. Wolfson, "Maimonides on the Internal Senses," JQR, N.S. XXV (1935), p. 456, n. 66.

33. M.T. Sekirut 13, 7 based upon Gen. 31.6. The reward for such behavior is intimated in Gen. 30.43.

34. I.S., p. 9a. Both Esau's immorality and his filial piety are a commonplace of the Aggadah. For a recent discussion of the identification of Esau-Edom with Rome and the Catholic Church cf. S. Krauss, "Die hebräischen Benennungen der fremden Völker," Jewish Studies in Memory of G. A. Kohut (N. Y., 1935), pp. 379-412. This identification, although denied by Saadia (Saadia's Polemic against Hivvi al-Balkhi, ed. by I. Davidson [N. Y., 1915], p. 76), was widely accepted in medieval Jewry and penetrated even the Muslim world. Cf. e.g., Mas'udi, op. cit., I, 89 f., where the 550 years of Roman domination over the Jews (approximately 70-620 C. E.) are explained as the result of Jacob's fear of Esau. Also the belief that Esau-Rome will be given dominion until the days of the Messiah is widespread in the Aggadah. Cf. e.g., Pesikta r., ed. Friedmann p. 50a and the editor's remarks and Bacher, Pal. Amoräer, I, 525, n. 7. Cf. also GL, V, 272 n. 19, 278 n. 51, 304 n. 246, etc. That this admission comes also from Maimuni, however, despite his considerable anti-Christian animus, is quite remarkable.

35. M.N. III, 50. This is a variation of the reason given by Saadia ס. הגלוי. Cf. BB, p. 117 n. 1. For the use of סתרי תורה in this connection which means the moral lessons hidden in a biblical narrative, cf. ibid. p. 13 n. 4. For the aggadic source cf. Munk, III, 428 n. 1 and GL, V, 323 n. 323 and 372 n. 424. Curiously, Abraham Maimuni offers the same interpretation of Gen. 36,

355

without referring to his father. Cf. S. Eppenstein, *Abraham Maimuni* (Berlin, 1914), p. 52.

36. *M.T.* Melakim 5, 11, based on Ket. 111a. For the numerous legends concerning the burial of Jacob and Joseph cf. *GL* V, 317 n. 415 ff. and 375 f. nn. 437-8. Maimuni *M.T.* Naḥlot 6, 13 finds in the story of Jacob's favoritism in regard to Joseph the moral lesson that such discrimination among children necessarily leads to endless quarrels. צוו חכמים evidently refers to Shab. 10b and Meg. 16ab.

37. *M.T.* Melakim 9, 14 in connection with *ibid.* 6, 1 and 9, 9. Maimuni seems to attempt here a new historical justification, unsupported by the Aggadah, incidentally provoking also Naḥmanides' opposition on juridical grounds. Cf. the latter's *Commentary* on Gen. 34.13.

38. *M.N.* III, 49, following the old interpretation of Gen. 12.11 (Pal. Targum, B. B. 16a, etc.) concerning Abraham's chastity. (In *C.M.* to Abot V, 19 he renders against the general view the נפש שפלה of the Mishnah by זהירות = sexual self-control and declares it to have been along with moderation and humility the outstanding virtue of the patriarch, while the opposite was true of Balaam). The theory concerning the purpose of circumcision, however, seems to be Maimonides' own contribution, since he scarcely had any knowledge of Philo's similar assumption, quoted by Munk, III, 417 n. 4. It is of interest to note that the theory combatted here is found not only in Saadia (see Munk, n. 2), but also in the Aggadah. Cf. e.g., Gen. r. 43, 7 (Theodor-Albeck, p. 420) about Melchizedek מלך שלם ר' יצחק הבבלי אומר שנולד מהול and Gen. r. 46, 1 (p. 458) concerning Abraham himself. With respect to the exclusion of Ishmael and Esau and the inclusion of the children of Keturah *M.T.* Melakim 10, 8 follows Sanh. 59b, but in contrast to Rashi, Maimuni interprets לרבות בני קטורה as extending also to their descendants. That the children of Keturah lived, at least in part, on the Arabian Peninsula is a widely accepted tradition in the Aggadah. Cf. the numerous, often contradictory views expressed in the sources, listed in *GL,* V, 264 f., n. 309 ff. The Arabs themselves, although generally claiming descent from Ishmael, conceded a certain relationship to the sons of Keturah. Cf. e.g., Mas'udi, *op. cit.,* I, 80. They also contended that they ought to follow Ishmael's example and perform the rite of circumcision at the age of thirteen. It is partly against such claims that Maimuni somewhat forcedly interprets Gen. 21.13 in *I.T. Kobeṣ* II, 3d (ed. Holub, p. 29 mutilated).

39. *M.T.* Melakim 9, 1, primarily based upon Ber. 16b. For the other sources cf. Bacher, *MbM,* II, 150 n. 7. The pleasing symmetry in Maimuni's arrangements evoked the opposition of RABD who, on the basis of Gen. 14.20, ascribed the introduction of tithes to Abraham rather than Isaac. But it was easy for the commentators to point out the different aggadic sources.

40. *M.T.* Keri'at Shema' 1, 4, on the basis of Pes. 56a. As pointed out by Karo, **Maimuni changed** ביקש יעקב לגלות לבניו קץ הימין into ח' על ייחוד ח' ציום וזרום על ייחוד ח'.

He evidently resented the inclusion of Jacob among the "computers of the end." He had, however, sufficient rabbinic backing for his statement not only in the context, but also in Sifre Deut. 32, Gen. r. 98, 4, etc. For other sources cf. *GL*, V, 366 nn. 382-3.

41. *M.T.* 'Abodat Kokabim 1, 3: ויעקב אבינו לימד בניו כולם וחבדיל לוי ומינהו ראש וחושיבו בישיבה ללמד דרך ח' ולשמור מצות אברהם. The idea that there were academies in the patriarchal age is very common in the Aggadah. For statements concerning the teachers of the law from the house of Levi cf. *GL*, V, 367 n. 387. Cf also next note.

42. *I.S.* 7a; *M.T.* 'Abodat Kokabim 1, 3 and Melakim 9, 1; *M.N.* III, 46. While the relapse of the Israelitic majority is a commonplace in the Aggadah and familiar even to Muslim writers (e.g., Maqdasi, *op. cit.*, III, 85), the source of the statement ובמצרים נצטווה עמרם במצות יתירות has puzzled the commentators, such as Karo. Bacher, *MbM*, II 150 n. 7 suggests that Maimuni had in mind Sotah 12a where Amram is called גדול הדור (in the parallel passages Ex. r. 1, 13 and 19 this title is used interchangeably with ראש סנהדרין; cf. also *GL*, V, 394 n. 27 and 396 n. 37) which seems to intimate that he was the recipient of divine commandments concerning marriage and divorce. Apart from the arbitrariness of this assumption, it is wholly disproved by Maimonides' views concerning the great freedom of sex relationships before the Mosaic legislation. Cf. further on note 64.

43. *M.T.* Bet ha-Beḥirah 6, 11: ומשה רבנו מלך חיה. Similarly *C.M.* to Shebuot II, 2, following the obvious implication of the Talmud (Shebuot 14b), as understood by R. Hananel and Rashi. Maimuni points to the source in Deut. 33.5.

44. Especially *C.M.* to Sanh. X, Introd.; *M.T.* Yesode ha-Torah 7, 6; *M.N.* II, 31. For the terms מבחר המין האנושי and אדון כל הנביאים הראשונים והאחרונים (*I.T.*, p. 17 and 40 = *Kobeṣ* II, 1d and 5b) cf. *BB*, p. 78 and *GL*, VI, 44 n. 242.

45. *M.N.* II, 35. Maimuni uses the expression פי תבאת צו אלשמס (Tibbon: מעמידת אור השמש) for Joshua's miracle, which strikingly resembles the rationalization of Ibn Chiquitilla to Joshua 10.12. Cf. S. Poznanski, *Moses b. Sam. Hakkohen Ibn Chiquitilla* (Leipzig, 1895), pp. 98 and 132 f. We also know that Maimuni highly esteemed this commentator as one of the אנשי תבונה מן המפרשים (*Kobeṣ* II, 9d). Cf. also Poznanski, pp. 59 and 140. Nevertheless, the burden of the present argument is not the inferiority of Joshua's feat, but its performance לעיני ישראל rather than לעיני כל ישראל. The impression left by the public Sinaitic revelation was so profound and enduring that Moses needed no miraculous signs thereafter to convince Israel of his mission, as he had needed before it. *M.T.* Yesode ha-Torah 8, 2.

46. *I.T.* p. 46 (*Kobeṣ* II, 6c).—*Kobeṣ* II, 23c. סוף נבואה is perhaps borrowed from the Muslim appellative of Muhammed.

47. *S.M.* Commandment 7 seems to refer to a custom prevalent in Maimuni's day to swear חי משה which he takes pains to explain as referring to the God

357

of Moses or to the One who sent Moses. I have thus far failed, however, to secure confirmation from the sources of that period.

48. *M.T.* Sanh. 2, 7 and Melakim 2, 6 referring to Ex. 16.7 for which both the Palestinian Targum and Targum Jonathan offer the translation: ואנחנו מה אנן חשיבין. Similarly Rashi and Naḥmanides against the less moralistic interpretation of Ibn Ezra. *M.T.* Deot 2, 3 on the basis of Num. 12.3 and M. Abot IV, 4. Cf. also the extensive discussion in *C.M.* to that Mishnah.

49. *M.T.* Sanhedrin 25, 2 referring to Ex. 6.13 and the aggadic comment thereto in Ex. r. 6, 2 and *I.S.*, p. 7b, on the basis of Ex. 4.1; Nu. 20.12 and the homily Shab. 97a. The emphasis ונענש לאלתר may have been intended to counteract those aggadic statements which denied Moses' affliction with leprosy. Cf. *GL*, V, 421 n. 132. He may also have considered the Muslim tradition that the Israelites suspected Moses of having been stricken with leprosy, but that God speedily rehabilitated him. Cf. Al-Bukhari, *Les traditions islamiques*, French transl. II (Paris, 1906), p. 482. In another connection (*C.M.* Eight Chapters 4) Maimuni explains Moses' transgression at the waters of Meribah with his impatience in scolding the Israelite "rebels" (Num. 20.10). For the midrashic sources cf. the notes to *GL*, III, 311 ff.

50. *M.T.* Issure Biah 13, 1-3; *I.S.* p. 7b on the basis of Sifre Num. 9, 5; Ker. 9a; Ex. r. 19, 5; Shir r. 1, 12 and 3, 7. The entire period of Egyptian bondage lasted, in Maimuni's opinion, 210 years. Some Israelites mistook, however, the original calculation of the 400 years and, anxious to leave Egypt, began marching ahead of time. This attempt ended disastrously. *I.T.*, p. 36 (*Kobeṣ* II, 5a) with reference to Sanh. 92b. Cf. Holub's note and *GL*, V, 420 n. 126.—*C.M.* to Abot V, 4 identifies the "ten miracles" which occurred to Israel in Egypt with the ten plagues which miraculously spared the Jews. Maimuni argues that even in the case of the plague of lice, where such escape is not intimated in the biblical narrative, it is self-evident that the Jews were not afflicted: אבל היו נמצאים אצלם ולא היו מצערים אותם וכן באו החכמים. This statement, evidently repeated from Maimuni, in Meiri on Abot and Shu'aib on Va-era, seems, notwithstanding Meiri's assertion, not to be found in our texts of the Talmud. Cf. *GL*, V, 429 n. 183. Maimuni's החכמים (in Arabic, ed. E. Baneth [Berlin, 1905]: אלחכמים) may like the החו"ל or רבותינו of *I.T.*, p. 49 (*Kobeṣ* II, 7b; two extant Arabic Mss. read likewise: אלחכמים ז"ל) concerning the homiletical exposition of Gen. 25.15 refer to the sages under Islam rather than under Rome and Persia.

51. *M.T.* Genebah 7, 12; Malveh ve-Loveh on the basis of B.M. 61a. The first passage is in part a quotation from Sifra Kedoshim 8, 10. *M.N.* II, 31 stresses the two functions of the Sabbath, with the exclusion of the social function emphasized in Deut. 5.14. Ibn Ezra *ad loc.* knows of the two views affirming and denying this function. (Maimuni's familiarity with Ibn Ezra's commentary has been conclusively proven in *BB*, p. 172). Cf. also Naḥmanides *ad loc.* who rejects the interpretations of both Ibn Ezra and Maimuni.—

C.M. to Abot V, 4 describes in great detail the "ten miracles" during the cross-ing of the Red Sea, and states that the Egyptians suffered there many more plagues than in Egypt proper, but that all these plagues belonged to the same ten kinds as those originally inflicted. For the rabbinic sources cf. *GL,* VI, 6 f. Although insisting that our knowledge of these events is based merely upon tradition, Maimuni tries to furnish from frequently very far-fetched passages biblical substantiation for all of them.

52. *M.T.* Melakim 5, 7-8; *S.M.* Prohib. 46 referring to j. Sukkah V, 1, 55b. (Cf. the significant reservation in Targum Jonathan לא תוספון למיחמי יתהון עוד עד עלמא בשעבור). That Alexandria was included in the prohibition is stated b. Sukkah 51b. Temporary sojourn in Egypt or passing through it to other lands is permitted, according to j. Sanh. X, 8, 29d. It is characteristic that Maimuni changes the talmudic לכבוש את הארץ ולפרקמטיא ולסחורה את הוזר into לעבור לארץ אחרת (*S.M.*) or into לכבוש ארצות אחרות (*M.T.*). The medi-eval codifiers differed on this subject. Cf. Geiger, *op. cit.,* notes 21-25. Maimuni (as after him Naḥmanides on Ex. 14.13: שהיא מצוה באמת לא הבטחה) made no attempt to explain the obvious conflict between theory and practice. Among his successors, Elijah Mizraḥi suggested that the biblical prohibition referred exclusively to reimmigration from Palestine, but not from other countries. Cf. *Glosses on Maimuni M.T., l. c.* The geographic boundaries are specifically given as bordering on Ethiopia and the desert. The size of 160,000 square parasangs is naturally not exact.

53. *C.M.* to Kelim I, 8 referring to Num. 1.50. This idea is amplified in Num. r. 1, 12 end. *M.N.* III, 50 gives the reason for the detailed biblical descriptions of Israel's journeys before they reached the Holy Land. The Torah thereby anticipated the incredulity of subsequent generations (as sug-gested by Munk, IV, 431, n. 1, this is perhaps a dig at Hivi al-Balkhi whose rationalist explanation of the *Manna* is attacked by Ibn Ezra to Ex. 16.13; unfortunately the extant fragment of *Saadia's Polemic* does not contain queries on Exodus) and forewarned that the legends concerning Jewish aim-less wanderings in the desert were altogether baseless. Cf. *BB,* p. 118. Maimuni does not hesitate, however, to declare that the "forty years" of the desert migration, Num. 32.13, were in fact only thirty-eight years (Eppenstein, *MbM,* I, 416: there is an apparent contradiction in the figures: 38 and ל"מ). If this text is authentic, one may perceive Maimuni's compunction to count the first year which preceded the sending of spies and the last year which followed after Aaron's death. He may well have been familiar with the com-ments of not only Ibn Ezra but also R. Moses ha-Darshan quoted by Rashi to Num. 33.1.

54. *M.T.* Bet ha-Beḥirah 1, 1 emphasizing the temporary character of the Tabernacle, according to Deut. 12.9 as explained in Sifre Deut. 66, Megillah 10a, etc. Cf. also Rashi *ad loc.* The idea that Moses introduced the *Kibla* (*M.T.* Tefillah 1, 3) is derived, according to Karo, from a statement in the

Baraita of R. Eliezer son of R. Jose the Galilean (possibly referring to *The Mishnah of R. Eliezer*, ed. H. G. Enelow [N. Y., 1933], p. 150, interpreting Ex. 20.18). However, Karo's reference to *S.M.* (probably Commandment 21) has no bearing on this subject. Neither is his doubt as ·to whether the בכל מקום שיחיה refers to the various locations of the sanctuary or to the place of the worshipers justified in view of the singular form.

55. *M.N.* III, 45-46. This much debated theory seems to be Maimonides' original contribution to the "rational" explanation of biblical ceremonies. That the argument is essentially historical makes it doubly relevant to our discussion.

56. *M.T.* Kle ha-Mikdash 1, 1-12, based primarily on Ker. 5; Hor. 11b; Shebuot 15a; Yoma 12b. Cf. also *GL*, VI, 72 n. 371. The explanation of המור הוא הדם הצרור בחיה שבהודו הידוע לכל שמתבשמין בה בני אדם בכל מקום has evoked an irate comment of RABD. But neither he nor Maimuni (nor for that matter Saadia from whom this identification of מור with musk is taken) has any hesitation concerning the availability of this and other Indian articles (to which Maimuni refers in this connection) in the Palestinian desert. Cf. also I. Loew, *Die Flora der Juden*, I, 310.

57. *C.M.* to Middot III, 1; *M.T.* Bet ha-Behirah 2, 5 on the basis of the prevalent opinion (of R. Jose) in Zeb. 59b. The explanation of the meaning of the cherubim (*M.N.* III, 45) discounts the numerous anthropomorphic features of the Aggadah. Maimuni also declines to consider seriously the legend concerning the magic influence of the tables placed in north and south. Cf. *GL*, III, 158-60.

58. *C.M.* to Sanh. I, 6 and *M.T.* Sanh. 1, 3. The eternality of that institution is derived from לו: Num. 11.16 in Sifre Num. 92.

59. *M.T.* Melakim 6, 6-7 evidently on the basis of Sifre Num. 157 (apparently assuming that R. Nathan interpreted rather than opposed the majority opinion; cf. Friedmann's note כ"ג and Finkelstein, *op. cit.*, pp. 496 ff.) and of Targum Jonathan to Num. 31.7.

60. *S.M.* Comm. 189-90 and Prohib. 49, 56 and 59 (Ar. original: 48, 55, 58) with reference to Sifre Deut. 296 and Sifra Behukotai Introd. 3 (like Nahmanides to Deut. 25.17 he cites the latter passage also under the name Sifre, probably referring to Midrash Tannaim to Deut. *ibid.* [ed. Hoffmann p. 169]; cf. editor's note פ' and Heller's note to his edition of *S.M.* Comm. 189. In this case we have here another instance of his use of Mekilta on Deut.; cf. Finkelstein, *op. cit.*) as well as Sifre Deut. 200. In Prohib. 56 he quotes also Sifre Deut. 251. In *M.T.* Melakim 6, 1-6 these laws are repeated with the significant reservation: אבל שבעת עממין ועמלק שלא השלימו אין מניחין מהם נשמה which seems to imply that if they had surrendered they would have been saved. This evokes a sharp rebuke from RABD, which the medieval commentators are hardly able to mitigate. Heller in his note on *S.M.* Comm. 190 attempts in vain to interpret *M.T.* as referring merely to an historical fact,

that they actually refused to surrender. This theory appears untenable in the face of the tense of מניחין and the very inclusion of this statement in the Code. It is more plausible that Maimuni again gave preference to the Mekilta on Deut. over the Sifre, as suggested by Finkelstein, *op. cit.*, p. 492. This contravention of the most authoritative halakhic sources is apparently due to Maimuni's views concerning the reasons for his harsh treatment. In *M.T. l. c.* and still more in *M.N.* III, 41 he transforms the historic hatred of the Israelites and the natives (including Amalek) into an ethical-religious safeguard to prevent contamination through idolatry. It is evident that this aim could be fully accomplished through the surrender of these nations and their acceptance of the Noahide commandments, the first of which enjoins abstention from pagan beliefs and observances.

61. *C.M.* to Abot IV, 2 emphasizing that even a man so greatly endowed with pious achievement as Moses did not disdain to fulfill half a commandment, when the opportunity afforded itself. Maimuni quotes to this effect a statement in Makkot 10a. Cf. also *ibid.* 9b; Sifre Num. 160; Tos. Makkot II, 1 and j. Makkot II, 7, 31d. *M.T.* Roṣeaḥ u-Shemirat Nefesh 8, 2-4 adds the information that in the days of the Messiah nine cities of refuge will be allotted in the territory of the Kenizite, the Kenite and the Kadmoni which had been promised to Abraham, but were never incorporated into ancient Palestine. This is derived from j. Makkot II, 6, 32a. Cf. also Rashi to Deut. 19.8.

62. *S.M.* Introd. 3 and Comm. 1; *M.N.* II, 33. The number 613 for the commandments, although perhaps not of tannaitic origin, was widely accepted in the talmudic and geonic period. The entire *S.M.* referring to the statement in Makkot 23b was devoted to their detailed enumeration. That only two of the Ten Commandments were heard by the entire people has the backing of some aggadic sources, as against others which maintain that all the nations could hear their annunciation on Sinai. Cf. *GL*, VI, 30 n. 181 and 45 n. 243. In general, however, Maimuni extols the מעמד הר סיני (so used also in the Arabic context of *M.N.* II, 33) as a unique event in history, because of the participation in it of an entire nation as witnessed by friend and enemy. Especially in *I.T.* he waxes enthusiastic in the description of that glorious event. He pacified his philosophic conscience by the assumption of a "created voice" (*Kobeṣ* II. 23d and *M.N.* I, 65; cf. Munk I, 290 n. 2). That there was a qualitative difference between Moses and the people even in the perception of this voice appears to Maimuni clearly indicated in the nuance of Onkelos' version, which for him has the indirect authority of a tannaitic source.

63. *C.M.* Introd.; *M.T.* Introd. and Sanh. 4, 1. For details of this historic development underlying all Pharisaic and Rabbanite Judaism cf. further on.

64. *S.M.* Prohib. 365; *M.T.* Ishut 1, 1-4 and *M.N.* III, 49. Cf. also the extensive discussion in *C.M.* to Sanh. VII, 4. The primary source for the pre-Mosaic situation is the story of Judah and Tamar, from which Maimuni derives the moral lessons that one should be reticent in divulging sex relationships and

also keep his financial pledges to his wife in the same degree as an indebtedness for wages to an employee. The expression קודם מתן תורה חיה אדם פוגע אשה בשוק has a quaint anachronistic sound, especially when applied to Tamar. Cf. also Eppenstein, *MbM* I, 415.

65. *M.T.* Issure Biah 22, 18 with reference to the homiletical interpretation of Num. 11.10 in Sifre Num. 90, Yoma 75a, etc. Cf. also Targum Jonathan and Rashi *ad loc.* Maimonides gives it the wider range to include both incest and free sexual relationships.

66. *S.M.* Prohib. 52; *M.T.* Issure Biah 12, 1-10, on the basis of Sanh. 81b f.; 'Ab. Zarah 36b, etc. *M.T.* 12, 4 states concerning the law of lynching ודבר זה הלם"ט הלא ראיה לדבר זה מעשה פנחס בזמרי. In accordance with the talmudic interpretation, however, Maimuni limits this procedure to immediate action against the shameless transgressors who perform their intercourse in the presence of at least ten Israelites and thus duplicate the sin of Zimri. RABD wishes to add even the requirement of a preceding warning which reflects the wavering attitudes of the rabbis in b. and j. Cf. *Migdal 'Oz, ad loc.* The historicity of such a public performance, however, is doubted by neither scholar in view of its numerous descriptions in the Aggadah. Cf. the notes to *GL*, III, 380 ff. The laws concerning the prisoners of war are discussed *S.M.* Prohib. 263-4 and *M.T.* Melakim 8, 2 ff. with reference to Sifre Deut. 214 and Ḳid. 21b f.

67. *M.T.* Shebuot 6, 2. This is an interesting attempt at reconciling the contradictory opinions of M. Ḥag. I, 8 (Maimuni accentuates it even more: אין לו עקר כלל) and the other Tannaim and Amoraim who try to find a biblical foundation (Ḥag. 10a). Cf. also Targum Jonathan to Num. 30.3. Other historically significant examples of oral traditions going back to Moses are: 1) The offering of the 'Omer which, according to an unwritten Mosaic ordinance, is to be a measure of barley. *M.T.* Temidin u-Musafin 7, 11; *S.M.* Comm. 44, referring to Mekilta, Jethro, Baḥodesh ch. XI, Sifra Lev. section 13, 2.4 and Men. 68b. The quotation of the full verse Lev. 2.14 may imply the acceptance of R. Eliezer's motivations. Cf. Rashi *ad loc.* Also the date of the sixteenth of Nisan is Mosaic: מפי השמועה למדו . . . וכן ראו תמיד הנביאים והסנהדרין בכל דור ודור, and Maimuni describes at great length the anti-Sadducean ceremony in accordance with M. Men. VI, 3 and b. 65a. 2) The segregation of the high priest seven days before the Day of Atonement. *M.T.* 'Abodat Yom ha-Kippurim 1, 3. In *C.M.* to Yoma I, 1 the scriptural backing is adduced from Lev. 8. 33-4, according to R. Ishmael's interpretation Yoma 3b. Cf. also Mekilta Ṣav, end; Rashi, *ad loc.* 3) The institution of seven days of mourning for a deceased relative and seven days of feasting a bridegroom *M.T.* 'Ebel 1, 1: ומשה רבנו תקן תקן לחם לישראל evidently referring to j. Ket. I, 1, 25a. In regard to mourning he merely renewed an older custom (Gen. 50.10) which was abolished by the Torah. (This is perhaps a harmonization of b. M.Ḳ. 21a and j. M.Ḳ. III, 5, 82c which appears to favor the obligatory biblical

character of seven day mourning). In *S.M.* Comm. 37, Maimuni quotes many indirect sources, including the historical illustration by the case of Joseph ha-Kohen. Cf. Zeb. 100a and M. Higger, *Treatise Semaḥot* (N. Y., 1931), pp. 30 f., 117 and 126. The wedding week, too, had pre-Mosaic antecedents. In regard to Jacob cf. Pirke R. Eliezer 36 and the Pal. Targum to Gen. 29.27. For Samson cf. Jud. 14.17 and Yalkut Shim'oni 70.

68. Although not stated in as many words this distinction is clearly implied in *M.T.* Mamrim 1, 2-3, referring to the homiletical interpretation of Deut. 17.10-11, which offers a characteristic variation of the prevalent rabbinic expositions, such as given Sanh. 97a. In *S.M.* Prohib. 312 contravention of traditional law is briefly outlawed with reference to Sifre Deut. 154 interpreting the same verse. Cf. also *C.M.* Introd.

69. *S.M.* Introd., Root 3 with numerous illustrations but no detailed enumeration.

70. *C.M.* to Sanh. X, 2 and Introd. §2; *M.T.* Melakim 11, 1; *M.N.* II, 45. The latter passage stressing כאן פי האל צלאחת (Tibbon: בעת שהיה טוב) obviously refers to Balaam's deterioration from prophet to sorcerer as emphasized, e.g., Sanh. 106a. The Davidic-messianic interpretation of Num. 24.17-18 is very common in the Aggadah. Cf. *GL*, VI, 125 n. 727 and 133 n. 782. Ibn Ezra *ad loc.* accepts the Davidic, but rejects the messianic implications, qualifying this statement וחסירי דעת יחשבו כי המפרש דרך כוכב על דוד הוא יחשב ביאת המשיח חלילה חלילה. Maimuni agrees with him in the interpretation of this particular phrase, but finds messianic forebodings in the parallel passage. Cf. also *BB*, p. 139 n. 16. Among the other adversaries of Israel in the Mosaic age, Sihon and Og engage Maimuni's special attention, because of the difficulty of reconciling the biblical narrative with his own philosophic views. That God should have hardened the spirit of Sihon (Deut. 2.30) had puzzled "many commentators" who saw therein a contradiction to the doctrine of free will. But as in the case of Pharaoh and the Israelite transgressors in the days of Elijah, Maimuni asserts, such affliction connotes only Sihon's deserved punishment on account of his previous sins and his inability to repent. *C.M.* Eight Chapters, 8 and *M.T.* Teshubah 6, 3. For still less deterministic explanations cf. e.g., Ibn Ezra and Seforno to Ex. 4.21 and Albo, *Ikkarim* IV, 25 (ed. Husik, IV, 230 f.).—In *M.N.* II, 47 he insists that Deut. 3.11 speaks only of Og's bed, while Og himself was but slightly more than six ells tall. Against the well-known exaggerations of the Aggadah as well as against the interpretation of both the Pal. Targum and Rashi of באמת איש, he accepts Ibn Ezra's equation with באמת כל אדם. Since the ancient Hebrew ell was about 50 cm. (the small ells = 45-49.5 cm., the king's ells 52.5-55 cm.; cf. Benzinger *Hebrä-ische Archäologie* [Leipzig, 1927], pp. 191 f.; Onkelos translates here: באמת מלך)· his approximate size of ten feet would be extraordinarily large, but not in itself disproportionate. Cf. also *BB*, pp. 94 f. and 140 and C. H. Becker, *Islamstudien* I, 181 f.

71. *I.T.* pp. 45 f. (*Kobeṣ* II, 6b f.). The date in the Arabic manuscript and the Hebrew translations varies between 1210, 1212 and 1216. Since Azariah de' Rossi the origin of that family tradition has been traced back to j. Shab. VI, 9, 8d (Ed. Cassel, pp. 375 f. making much of R. Ḥanina's נראין חדברים which is not included in our text). Cf. also D. Frænkel's commentary *Korban ha-'Edah, ad loc.;* Geiger, *op. cit.,* n. 54; *BB,* p. 138 n. 5 and A. H. Silver, *Messianic Speculation in Israel* (N. Y., 1927), p. 75 n. 71. The authenticity of this Maimonidean utterance, impugned by D. Kauffmann, M. Friedlaender and others, was convincingly defended by W. Bacher, "Le passage relatif au Messie dans la lettre de Maimonide aux Juifs de Yémen," *REJ,* XXXIV (1897), pp. 101-5. Cf. also A. Marx in הצופה, V (1921), p. 195 and n. 199.

72. In *C.M.* Introd. Maimuni picturesquely describes the successive stages in the instruction given by Moses to Aaron, Eleazar, Ittamar, the seventy elders and the rest of the people which allowed everyone to hear the lesson four times; he slightly amplifies the tannaitic story narrated in 'Er. 54b. In *M.T.* Introd. and Sanh. 4, 1 he speaks briefly of the instruction given to the elders, Eleazar and Phinehas, but stresses the transmission to Joshua above all others. *S.M.* Introd. Root 3 and Commandment 34 emphasizes on the basis of numerous biblical passages the temporary nature of Num. 7.9, thus evoking the protest of, e.g., Naḥmanides. *M.T.* Kle ha-Mikdash 4, 3 chooses from among the conflicting traditions in Ta'anit 27a that contained in the Baraita beginning with מיתיבי. The reason for this rather dubious selection (cf. the note to H. Malter's critical edition of the treatise p. 128) evidently is the wish to fit it into the theory that for every such major change in the constitution the coöperation of a king, prophet and seventy elders is necessary. Cf. e.g., *M.T.* Bet ha-Beḥirah 6, 11 concerning the extension of the city of Jerusalem and the Temple precincts.

73. *S.M.* Comm. 209, Prohib. 45, referring to Sanh. 109b f. and the homiletical interpretations of Num. 21.5, etc. in Num r. 18,20. The story of Korah (Qarun) has found its way also into the Koran and Arabian historical literature. Cf. e.g., Maqdasi III, 88 f.

74. *C.M.* to Abot I, 12 referring to the legend in Ab. R.N., *ibid.,* ed. Schechter, pp. 48 ff. Maimuni also tries to explain the "golden calf" with the contagious influence of astrology at that time which induced many Israelites to worship therein a symbol of the constellation, under which they had been delivered from Egypt. Eppenstein, *MbM* I, 418.

75. *C.M.* Introd.; *M.T.* Introd. There is no real contradiction between these two statements with respect to the destination of the thirteenth scroll according to Deut. 31.26. Cf. also Num. r. 4, 20. The emphasis that the scrolls contained the Pentateuch to the very end is in agreement with R. Simon, B.B. 15a, etc.; the story of the *thirteen scrolls* is evidently taken from Deut. r. 9, 9 (cf. the interesting note of Z. W. Einhorn). *C.M.* Eight Chapters 8 adds that Moses wrote the entire Torah at God's dictation and that is why he was called

מחוקק: Deut. 33.21 (cf. Targum Onkelos *ad loc.,* perhaps in connection with the statement of R. Eliezer: Sotah 13b), but insists that the way in which the divine will was communicated to Moses was known to the lawgiver only. Cf. also *Kobeṣ* II, 1a. In his epistle to Joseph ibn Gabir in Bagdad (*Kobeṣ* II, 15c ff.) Maimuni rigorously defends the Mosaic origin of the entire Torah against the "great foolishness" of those who think that Moses merely reproduced those laws which had been previously given, e.g., circumcision. Even today their binding force is derived from God's revelation to Moses and not from that to Abraham, etc. In *Resp.* No. 5 he follows the opinion of Eleazar of Modi'in and Judah the Patriarch, against that of the others in Sanh. 21b f. (also Tos. Sanh. IV, 7; j. Meg. I, 11, 71b), that the square script served as the divine medium in giving the Torah (he adds also: the two tables of the Covenant). Of historical interest is the remark: ולכך תמצא חרות תמיר על שקלי הקדש דברים של חול בכתב עברי, which raises the question whether Maimuni actually saw many Maccabean coins. Cf., also the editor's notes pp. 5 f. and Pseudo-Hai's comments on M. Yadaim IV, 5 (ed. J. N. Epstein [Berlin, 1924], p. 135). In *C.M.* to IV, 6 Maimuni glorifies the square script on account of the diversity of its letters and discontinuity of writing and applies to it homiletically Gen. 30.13.

76. *C.M.* Introd. Maimuni graphically describes the scenes before Moses' death, how on the first day of Shebat Moses gathered the entire people and day after day elucidated to them the obscure points in law, quoting Sifre Deut. 4 in reference to Deut. 1.3-5. For the date he quotes the well-known tradition Tos. Sotah XI, 2; Ḳid. 38a; Meg. 13b, etc. That it was at noon is quoted from Sifre Deut. 337. He finally quotes the tradition (Sotah 13b; more succinctly Sifre Deut. 357) that Moses, like Elijah, did not die a normal human death.

77. *M.T.* Melakim 6, 5 (for the text cf. *Kesef Mishneh*) on the basis of j. Sheb. VI, 1, 36c and Giṭ. 46a. Cf. also *GL,* VI, 177 f. nn. 33-35. While Maimuni derives from that story the moral that all wars must be preceded by an exhortation to surrender, RABD interprets literally the עד שלא יכנס לארץ in j. *l. c.* So do Tosafot Giṭ. 46a s.v. כיון, although the talmudic text there obviously favors Maimuni's explanation.

78. *M.T.* Issure Biah 12, 22-24, on the basis of Kid. 78b f.; Yeb. 79a; j. Ḳid. IV, 1, 65c; Ex. r. 8, 4, etc. For other references cf. *GL,* VI, 178 n. 36 and 269 n. 114. Instead of j.'s quotation from Neh. 3.20, Maimuni cites Ezra 8.20 which helps him explain the different nature of Joshua's and David's punitive measures.

79. *S.M.* Comm. 187. This view which, on its face, appears quite modern is evidently based upon the biblical narrative, especially that concerning the Jebusites whose territory was conquered by David. Among the events during the war the conquest of Jericho looms large in Maimonides' mind, especially since, according to tradition, it took place on a Sabbath, thus proving that in

war the Sabbath rest commandment may be violated. Cf. *M.T.* Shabbat 2, 25 on the basis of j. Shab. I, 3, 4a f.; Seder 'Olam 11, etc. Maimuni ignores here completely the Christian and Karaite polemics which had prompted Saadia to deny the capture of Jericho on Sabbath. Cf. *GL,* VI, 174 n. 22.

80. *C.M.* to B.B. VIII, 3 in the light of the Talmud's explanation 117a f.

81. *M.T.* Nizke Mamon 5, 3, on the basis of B.Ḳ. 80 b ff. Cf. also Tos. B.M. XI, 32; j. B.B. V, 1, 15a (see remarks in *Yefeh Eynaim* to b. *ad loc.*). Like Alfasi, Maimuni regards only these ten ordinances as having been issued by Joshua, but not the others mentioned in the talmudic discussion on that Baraita. He interprets some of these ordinances in his own fashion. ומעין חיוצא בתחילה בני העיר מסתפקים ממנו evidently wishes to emphasize communal use of a spring against the exclusive rights of the landowner. The Talmud adds, against the opinion of Rabbah b. R. Huna, that the land-owner cannot even demand compensation. Cf. also Asheri *ad loc.* The reason for Maimuni's preference for the limitation of the rights of the neighboring community to which the main source of the water might be traced back, is not clear. Neither does he explain whether the local landowner is entitled to a compensation by his own community. The text ומחכין בימה של מבריא ובלבד שלא יפרום קלע ויעמיד את הספינה, particularly if combined with the Baraita בראשונה etc., quoted here by b. from Tos. VIII, 17-18, likewise carries the connotation that not even the rightful owners of the shores were allowed to spread out nets hindering traffic on the lake, but could make use exclusively of small fishing nets. Cf. Tosafot s.v. ומחכין, Asheri, etc. Maimuni wishes to see the right of the neighboring landowners extended much further. It is likely, moreover, that his ויעמיד ספינה שם has the meaning of sending out rather than hindering the boats (cf. e.g., יעמיד לו חמור אחר, B.Ḳ. 116b), thus allowing the fishermen on the shore to send out boats into the lake for fishing purposes, a right withheld from strangers. This interpretation, evidently supported by the text of the Tosefta *l. c.*: אין אדם פורש חרמו ומעמיד ספינתו, undoubtedly squares closely with the historical situation and Maimuni, while in Palestine, might have himself observed such practice. Maimuni's explanation of יתידות הדרכים as equivalent to soft mud is likewise both more logical and in closer accordance with M. Miḳvaot IX, 2 than that of Rashi *ad loc.* The inversion of the order of ordinances 8 and 9 by Maimuni was perhaps intended to add emphasis to the elimination of the preceding ומהלכין בשבילי הרשות עד שתרד רביעה שניה from the list of Joshua's enactments. In accord-ance with the Talmud and Alfasi (on the basis of Prov. 3.27), he regards this enactment as superimposed by King Solomon. *Ibid.* §4. The talmudic source of Maimonides escaped Zacuto, *Yuḥasin,* p. 8 (finding a contrast between the Talmud and Maimuni) and, at first, Zevi Chajes. Cf. the latter's gloss to b. *ad loc.* This permission is given from the end of the harvest to Marḥeshvan 17, 23, or Kislev 1, depending on the beginning of the rainy season in Palestine. *C.M.* to Peah VIII, 1 and to Sheb. IX, 6 (cf. J. Landau's

note *ibid.* in the Vilna Talmud edition); *M.T.* Matnot 'Aniyim 1, 11, cf. *Kesef Mishneh, ibid.* Cf. also *GL*, IV, 16, where the ninth ordinance is omitted, and M. A. Bloch, *Sha'are Torat ha-Takkanot* I (Vienna, 1879), pp. 54-64 and 76-8.

82. *M.T.* Shemiṭṭah ve-Yobel 12, 15-16, on the basis of the lengthy discussions in Mishnah and Gemara 'Ar. 32a ff., Shebu. 16a and Meg. 3b f. The inconsistency in the Maimonidean interpretation was immediately pointed out by RABD and Karo. If one were to accept the latter's strained explanation, it would merely furnish a striking illustration for Maimuni's method of postulating, without further evidence, certain historical situations, in order to straighten out halakhic contradictions.

83. This ramified semi-historical and semi-halakhic problem looms very large in Maimuni's writings. Following the talmudic sources he tries to furnish historical reasons for often contradictory customs and observances, which had developed in the period and around the second fall of Jerusalem. The amplest discussion is to be found in *M.T.* Terumot 1, 1-9, where the following five geographic divisions are established, each of which has a distinctive position in Jewish law: 1) Palestine of the early Second Commonwealth; 2) The remainder of the Holy Land; 3) Syria; 4) Ammon, Moab, Egypt and Babylonia; 5) the rest of the world. Cf. also *C.M.* to Demai VI, 11; Hal. II, 11; Bik. II, 10; *M.T.* Bikkurim 2, 1; Shemiṭṭah ve-Yobel 4, 25-8 and 13, 11; Bet ha-Beḥirah 6, 16; Tum'at Met 11, 6; Sanhedrin 4, 6; Melakim 5, 6 and *Resp.* 136, quoting Sifre Deut. 51, the Mishnahs commented upon, etc. Of greatest interest from the historical point of view is the distinction drawn in *M.T.* Bet ha-Beḥirah 6, 16 between Joshua and Ezra. Because the latter לא קדשה אלא בכבוש אלא בחזקה שהחזיקו בה the sanctity thus established had permanent force. This theory ran counter to the ideas of not only those who, like RABD, denied the eternality of the Temple's own sanctity, but even of those who tried to defend the Maimonidean position. Cf. *Kesef Mishnah, ibid.*, who asks אמאי מי עדיפא חזקה בלא כבוש מחזקה עם כבוש. The basis of this distinction is obviously the statement in *Seder 'Olam* 30 (with the homiletical interpretation of Deut. 30.5), quoted Yeb. 82b and Niddah 46b. But while Rashi on the latter passages declares it to be a גזרת הכתוב, Maimuni looks for a rational explanation. What he had in mind was most likely the difference between military conquest which can be nullified by another military act (Nebuchadnezzar against Joshua), whereas pacific occupation and *usucapio,* which establish civil law ownership and cannot be abolished by a victory in war, wherefore Titus' warlike exploits could not abrogate the effects of Ezra's pacific penetration. Cf. also *SeMaG* Commandment 163. Maimuni's personal opinion (יראה לי) that, in contrast to the Palestinian conquest, the priests and Levites are entitled to a share in the land and the booty during warfare in other lands (*M.T.* Shemiṭṭah ve-Yobel 13, 11), is likewise of considerable historical interest. This decision can hardly be defended on the basis of the sources, as

pointed out by RABD, but appears justifiable on the ground of the assumed motivation of the law (*ibid.* §12), since in foreign lands neither the priests nor the Levites would have to perform any particular sanctuary functions. Characteristically, Maimuni fails to mention, as does, e.g., Moses of Coucy who quotes him (*SeMaG* Prohib. 266-7), that in the messianic age both priests and Levites will be eligible for a share even in Palestine. Cf. B.B. 122a. The author's failure, here as well as in other instances, to indicate the law of the messianic era militates against the assumption that *M.T.* "was prepared as a Jewish Constitution for a future Jewish State" (S. Zeitlin, *Maimonides* [N. Y., 1935], p. 88).

84. *C.M.* to Sanh. VI, 2 and *M.T.* Sanh. 18, 6. There are characteristic differences between the two statements: In *C.M.* the emergency character is exclusively stressed, while the evidence is declared insufficient, when based on either confession or prophecy. In *M.T.* the element of prophecy is disregarded as not pertinent to the subject, but the alternative given: דין מלכות היה. This is in line with the Maimonidean theory concerning the royal power over the life of the subject, as developed in *S.M.* Commandment 173 and *M.T.* Melakim 3, 8.10. It is noteworthy that, although twice stressing גזירת מלך היא, and גזירת הכתוב היא, Maimuni nevertheless tries to rationalize this principle. Gersonides in his *Commentary* to II Sam. 1.16 is satisfied with Maimuni's explanation of the emergency, but to Josh. 7, 15 ff. advances a more venturesome reason.

85. *S.M.* Introd. Root 2, quoting Tem. 16a. Cf. also *GL,* VI, 185 n. 23.

86. *C.M.* to Zeb. XIV, 6-7 and *M.T.* Bet ha-Beḥirah 1, 2 on the basis of the generally accepted chronology of *Seder 'Olam* 11-15; Zeb. 118b, etc. Cf. also further on pp. 96 ff.

87. *M.T.* Melakim 5, 9 evidently on the basis of B.B. 91a. Maimuni's omission of Elimelech (Tos. 'Ab. Zarah IV [V], 4 has only אלימלך) may be due to the consideration of the type of punishment: while Elimelech died leaving behind him sons, the נתחייבו כלייה למקום (cf. Ruth r. 2, 5: מחלון שנמחו מן העולם, וכליון שכלו מן העולם). It is also possible that Maimuni considered the different reason of Elimelech's death, advanced in Ruth r. 1, 4.—*I.S.* p. 9a is based on Ruth r. 2, 9 (cf. also Seder 'Olam 12). It is noteworthy that Maimuni chooses this illustration rather than that frequently referred to in the Talmud (Nazir 23b which Maimuni seems to quote; Sotah 47a; Sanh. 105b and Hor. 10b) that Ruth's distinguished progeny was really a reward for the reverent act of Balak, the supposed grandfather of Eglon. In these sources the texts vary as to whether Ruth was the daughter or the granddaughter of Eglon.

88. *M.T.* Issure Biah 13, 14-16. Maimuni makes use of the talmudic defense of Solomon (cf. Yeb. 76a f., 24b and Shab. 56b) to exonerate also Samson "who saved Israel" (reference to Jud. 13.5). The mere fact that he married the Gentile women only after their conversion to Judaism is indicated in the

reply to one of them: גיורת אני, as reported in Sotah 10a. This view is also shared by various commentators on Jud. 14.2, such as Gersonides. In j. Sotah I, 8, 17b even this excuse is dropped. In *C.M.* to Sotah I, 8 Maimuni makes no pertinent observation. Cf. also *GL*, VI, 208 n. 121.

89. *C.M.* to Nazir I, 2 and IX, 5 and *M.T.* Nezirut 3, 12-13 and 16, on the basis of the two Mishnahs and the discussion in the Gemara Nazir 4a ff. The halakhic difficulty of Maimuni's decision is discussed in *Kesef Mishneh*, *ad loc.* and *Tosefot Yom Tob* to Nazir I, 2. *C.M.* to Abot IV, 5 stresses Samuel's incorruptibility to the extent of his never accepting the hospitality of other people even on his journeys. This is evidently based upon the statement (variously attributed to R. Johanan and Raba): שכל מקום שהלך שם ביתו עמו Ber. 10b; Ned. 38a, etc. The exoneration of Samuel's sons. *M.T.* Sanh. 23, 3 follows the talmudic legends Shab. 56a; Tos. Sotah XIV, 5-6, etc. Cf. also *GL*, VI, 208 n. 121; 228 f. nn. 43-44; 266 n. 98.

90. *M.T.* Melakim 1, 1-2 and *S.M.* Commandment 173 quoting Sifre 67 and 157. Cf. also *ibid.* 156, Midrash Tannaim to Deut. 17.14 and Sanh. 20b as well as *GL*, VI, 230 n. 47. Modern biblical scholarship generally finds in I Sam. a compilation of pro- and anti-monarchical sources, due to divergent attitudes, which found their counterparts in the tannaitic age. That Maimuni adopts only those talmudic interpretations which favor monarchy is fully in line with his general political theory advocating strong monarchical government. This attitude could but be fostered by the realities of the Muslim state (especially the Egypt of Saladin) and the prevalent political doctrines under Islam. *M.N.* III, 45 adds the logical reason for the precedence of the establishment of monarchy to the building of the Temple, namely, that a strong centralized power was needed to prevent quarrels between the tribes as to the place where the structure should be erected.

91. *C.M.* to Abot IV, gives this general characteristic, in order to emphasize the great humility of the poet-king, so eloquently expressed in Ps. 51.19. For the Davidic interpretation of Num. 24.17 cf. n. 70 above. As a prophet David belonged only to those endowed with this gift in the first (the lowest) degree. *M.N.* II, 45, quoting I Sam. 16.13 in accordance with the interpretation of the Targum. Kimhi *ad loc.* is obviously influenced by Maimuni. Some time before David's death, the spirit of prophecy left him, as it also left Jeremiah and the other prophets. *M.N. l. c.,* quoting II Sam. 23.1, in the meaning implied in M.K 16b. Cf. also Bacher, *MbM* II, 146 n. 2 and *GL*, VI, 249 n. 24. For David as teacher and halakhist cf. further on. In *M.T.* Dehot 5, 11 Maimuni commends the exemplarily circumspect behavior of David, thus interpreting the word משכיל in I Sam. 18.14.

92. *M.T.* Teshubah 8, 7 referring to Ps. 27.13 and *I.T.*, p. 22 (*Kobeṣ* II, 2c) referring to Ps. 129.2. Even more prophetic were the forebodings that the Jews were to suffer most severe persecutions at the hands of the Arabs. *I.T.*, pp. 49 f. (*Kobeṣ* II, 6b) referring to Ps. 120.5;7. Neither here nor in any

other connection does Maimuni voice the slightest doubt in the Davidic authorship of all the Psalms. He also specifically names David as the author of the *hallel* (Ps. 113-8) in *S.M.* Introd. Root 1.

93. *Resp.* No. 351, contrasting it with the impious armies of Jeroboam I and Ahab. This responsum was written with the aim of explaining an obscure passage in Ket. 9a f., which implied an exoneration of David for his relationship with Bathsheba. Cf. also Shab. 56a.

94. *M.T.* Sanh. 4, 7 on the basis of j. Sanh. X, 2, 29a: תשעים אלף זקנים מינה דוד ביום אחד (cf. also Num. r. 4, 20 and Midrash Samuel 25). Although the context does not warrant it, Maimuni assumes as a matter of course that this was a regular ordination of the kind practiced in the tannaitic age. He seems, however, to have some compunction with regard to the large number. His reduction to 30,000 is hardly due to a different text of j., as suggested by *Kesef Mishneh* and *Lehem Mishneh, ad loc.,* since that would nullify the entire exposition of II Sam. 6.1. It is more likely that he preferred to adopt the biblical figure, abandoning the strained homily of וייסף עוד. He obviates the physical difficulty of one man's conferring an ordination upon such a multitude in the short span of a day by stating that every ordained teacher may simultaneously ordain an unlimited number of persons by uttering a brief formula. The placing of one's hand upon the head of the ordained man, although frequently practiced, is not required by law. *M.T. l. c.* §2, on the basis of R. Ashi's decision in Sanh. 13b. The religious disputations of David are deduced in *M.T.* Me'ilah 8, 8 from Ps. 119.69; 86. Few legislative acts, however, are recorded as associated with David. Maimuni mentions specifically David's and his court's extension of the biblical prohibition of *Yihud* (privacy between man and woman) to apply not only to near relatives and married women but also to all unmarried Jewesses. *M.T.* Issure Biah 22, 3 on the basis of Sanh. 21a f. and 'Ab. Zarah 36b. The statement דוד ובית דינו is a combination of דוד in the latter and גזרו in the former source, and is fully in line with Maimuni's general assumption that from the earliest days regular sanhedrins coöperated with Israel's leaders in issuing ordinances. In *C.M.* to Sanh. I, 5 he emphasizes that David never engaged in a "war from choice" without first consulting his sanhedrin, כמו שהוא מפורסם אצלנו ממנהגו עליו השלום (for the text cf. the Arabic original ed. M. Weisz [Halle, 1893], p. 7), evidently referring to Ber. 3b, without the pietistic motivation of Rashi s.v. ונמלכים. The Davidic decree, Maimuni asserts, was occasioned by the Amnon and Tamar affair, implying that Tamar was not Amnon's full-fledged sister, because she had been born while her mother was a prisoner of war, as is asserted in Sanh. *l. c.* Cf. also GL, VI, 276 n. 143.

95. *M.T.* Kle ha-Mikdash 3, 9. Cf. above n. 72.

96. The exclusive right to sit in the *'azarah* is stressed *S.M.* Comm. 21 and *M.T.* Sanhedrin 14, 12, on the basis of an oft-quoted statement Sanh. 101b, etc. More complicated is the problem of jurisdiction and testimony. *C.M.* to

Sanh. II, 3; *M.T.* Sanhedrin 2, 5; Edut 11, 9; Melakim 3, 7 simply accept R. Joseph's distinction between the two dynasties in Sanh. 19a f. In contrast to e.g., the Tosafists, *ibid.* s.v. אבל, Maimuni extends the jurisdiction of the Davidic dynasty also to capital crimes. Karo to Mel. 3, 7 raises a number of pertinent historical as well as legal objections. Although his answer is quite unsatisfactory (cf. also *Mishneh le-Melek, ad. loc.*), the responsibility for the historical inconsistency rests with the redactor of the Talmud rather than with Maimuni, who cautiously avoids referring to the trial of Alexander Jannaeus. For him most likely this trial merely revealed the weakness of the court in the face of a lawless ruler, and he needed no further proofs for the frequent lawlessness of the North Israelitic kings. It may be mentioned that the phrase מלכי ישראל, here contrasted with בית דוד, has in Maimuni's writings the more inclusive connotation embracing both the northern and the southern kings. Cf. e.g., *M.T.* 'Ebel 3, 14, where he quotes almost verbatim the Baraita Ber. 19b; Melakim 1, 9-10: מלך משאר ישראל and מלך ישראל מזרע דוד.—In Mel. 1, 9 as well as *S.M.* Prohib. 362 the perpetuity of the Davidic dynasty is stressed with reference to biblical (II Sam. 7.16 contrasted with I Kings 11.30) and talmudic quotations (e.g., Meg. 14a). In *S.M.* he even insists that it is an integral part of the Mosaic creed to believe in a Jewish king coming only from among the descendants of David and Solomon. For the latter cf. Ch. Heller's note ד' *ad loc.*

97. *C.M.* to Ker. I, 1; *M.T.* Melakim 1, 7-12 and Kle ha-Miḳdash 1, 7-11, on the basis of Ker. 5b, Hor. 11b f., etc. Cf. also above n. 56.

98. *M.N.* III, 51, referring to I Chr. 28.9. Cf. also W. Bacher, *Die Bibel-exegese der jüdischen Religionsphilosophen* (Strassburg, 1892), p. 107. In *C.M.* to Ḥul. I, 2 Maimuni cites in accordance with numerous rabbinic legends, Doeg, Ahitophel, Gehazi (Elisha's servant) and Elisha Aḥer as outstanding agnostics.

99. Although he frequently extols Solomon's wisdom, Maimuni quotes *M.N.* III, 54 the significant rabbinic qualification of I Kings 5.11 that he was not wiser than Moses (R.H. 21b) and adds, on his own part, that the biblical narrator merely wanted to indicate that Solomon was wiser than any man in his generation, which included a number of celebrated sages, as is, indeed, the ordinary meaning of the biblical verse. He does not mention I Kings 3.12, but there is hardly any doubt that he could dismiss this objection as arising merely from a dream. Cf. *M.N.* II, 36. True to his general exaltation of Moses as the greatest of all men, he takes cognizance neither of the Aggadot which equated Heman in I Kings 5.11 with Moses (Pesikta r. 14, 60a; Num. r. 19, 3, etc.) nor of the controversy between Rab and Samuel in R.H. 21b. For Solomon, the author cf. *C.M.* to Sanh. X Introd.; *M.T.* Deot 2, 7 and Talmud Torah 5, 4; *M.N.* II, 28 (also a defense of Solomon against the assumption that he believed in the eternity of the world) and III, 8; *I.T.*, pp. 25 f., etc., on the basis of the well-known rabbinic theories in Shir r. 1, 1.10, etc. Cf. also

GL, VI, 282 ff. nn. 18-25. *M.T.* Yesode ha-Torah 6, 9 repeats, as a matter of law, the talmudic assertion (Shebuot 35b) that with the exception of 8.12 every "Shlomo" mentioned in the Song of Songs is a surname of God. He ignores, however, the other version in the Talmud declaring Shir 3.7 as profane, evidently because he dislikes its magic implications. Cf. Rashi *s.v.* הנה referring to Giṭ. 68b.

100. *S.M.* Introd. Root 1; *M.T.* Erubin 1, 2-4; Abot ha-Tum'ot 8, 2.8 and Nizke Mamon 5, 4. In the first source Maimuni quotes 'Er. 21b. Cf. also Shab. 14b f., where the distinction is drawn between the sacred objects, for which alone Solomon disqualified such impure hands, and the heave offering to which the disqualification was extended by subsequent legislators. (To the discussion of RABD, Karo, etc., cf. also R. Nissim's comments to Ber. 52a). For the permission of trespassing cf. above n. 81. It is noteworthy that neither in *S.M. l. c.,* nor in *C.M.* to Yeb. II, 4 nor, finally in *M.T.* Ishut I, 6 does Maimuni expressly attribute to Solomon the extension of the prohibited marriages to certain categories of relatives—he counts twenty of them— although in *M.T.* he comes close to naming the great king by using the strange formula ויש נשים אחרות שהן אסורות מפי הקבלה ואיסורן מדברי סופרים. He evidently uses here the expression Kabbalah in the talmudic sense of דברי קבלה which, if contrasted with דברי תורה, has the meaning of biblical, but post-mosaic, traditions. Cf. W. Bacher, *Die exegetische Terminologie der Traditionsliteratur* I (1899), pp. 155 f., 165 f.; II (1905), p. 185. That such traditions are דברי סופרים is stressed in our connection by Maimuni in *S.M. l. c.* as well as M.T. 'Er. I, 2 and Abot ha-Tum'ot 8, 2 (cf. also *M.T.* Kelim 17, 12) which answers the dissenting view of the problem raised by Karo to *M.T.* Ishut 1, 6. Cf. also *Zera' Abraham,* quoted in *Kelale ha-Rambam* No. 8 and Ch. Tschernowitz, *Toledoth ha-Halaḳah* (N.Y., 1934), p. 18 n. 1. Maimuni's failure here to mention the king is, under these circumstances, probably due to his source Yeb. 21a, where Solomon's authorship of this ordinance, postulated (by implication) by R. Judah, is controverted by the opinion of Raba. *M.T.* Berakot 2, 1: David and Solomon jointly introduced the third benediction into the *Birḳat ha-Mazon* following the example of Moses, the author of the first, and of Joshua who had been responsible for the second benediction. Cf. Ber. 48b. Cf. in general also Bloch *op. cit.* I, 9-27 and 72-8, where the שניות לעריות are likewise omitted.

101. *Kobeṣ* II, 23d, on the basis of Pesikta r. 14, 58b and Num. r. 19, 3 referring to Koh. 7.23.

102. *C.M.* to Zeb. XIV, 8; *S.M.* Comm. 20-21; *M.T.* Bet ha-Beḥirah 1, 3-4 and 2, 2.5; *M.N.* III, 45, on the basis of numerous utterances of the rabbis. Cf. especially Zeb. 119a f. In *C.M.* to Abot V, 5 Maimuni tries to explain rationally two of the ten "miracles" which, according to that Mishnah, made the worship in the Temple such an extraordinary blessing. Cf. also above notes 12, 28 and 90.

103. *M.T.* Bet ha-Beḥirah 4, 1 on the basis of Tos. Yoma III [II], 6-7; b. Yoma 52b, etc. Maimuni's omission of the chest sent by the Philistines which is mentioned here and in the parallel passages Tos. Soṭah XIII, 1; Hor. 12a; Ker. 5b, is probably due to the consideration that it was not an integral part of the Temple utensils. Neither is it mentioned in Ab. R.N. 41, 135. None of these sources, however, ascribe to Solomon the foresight to prepare an underground passage, but this legend is clearly implied in II Chr. 35.3 which Maimuni quotes. Cf. also Melekct ha-Mishkan VII (Eisenstein, *Oẓar Midrashim* I, 301). Kimḥi to I Kings 6.19 and II Chr. 35.3 evidently follows Maimuni. Correct accordingly *GL,* VI, 377 n. 118.

104. *C.M.* to Sanh. I, 5 and *M.T.* Sanhedrin 5, 1, the former supplying the reason, *viz.* the different degrees of sanctity of the land included in the Temple area, elsewhere in Jerusalem or Palestine. He quotes the Mishnah Tohorot (= Kelim) I, 8 and the homiletical derivation from Ex. 25.9 in Sanh. 16b.

105. *M.T.* Melakim 1, 8-9, evidently on the basis of Seder 'Olam 15-16 which emphasizes that originally the dynasty was to last only for thirty-six years of the reign of Jeroboam and his son. Cf. also Tos. Soṭah XII, 1-2. This is perhaps the reason for Maimuni's cautious formulation מלך מבניו ויהיה. RABD, apparently unaware of these sources, contends that Jeroboam's dynasty might have occupied permanently a semi-royal position: כגון קיסר ופלגי קיסר. In writing this RABD not only betrays his residence in feudalistic Provence, but also refers to the dim recollections of the situation under the Roman Empire after the reform of Diocletian, which found their way into the Talmud Sanh. 98b. It was easy for Maimuni's commentators to defend his position, *Migdal 'Oz* specifically referring to a *M.T.* text revised by the author himself.

106. *I.T.* p. 27 (*Kobeṣ* II, 3c), evidently referring to I Kings 12.32-3. In *I.S.,* p. 6b Jeroboam's voluntary apostasy is contrasted with the forced conversions of later ages.

107. *I.S.,* pp. 7b and 9a; *M.T.* Roṣeah u-Shemirat Nefesh 4, 9, on the basis of I Kings 19.18; 22.21-2 (in the homiletical interpretation of Sanh. 89a) and Ta'anit 25b. Cf. also *M.T.* Gezelah va-'Abedah 1, 11.

108. *M.T.* Melakim 2, 5 on the basis of Ket. 102b and Mak. 24a. The general etiquette, however, was that even a prophet should stand up in the presence of the king, as exemplified by Nathan, when he addressed David; I Kings 1.23.

109. *C.M.* to Pes. IV, 8 (9) and *M.N.* III, 37, on the basis of Pes. 56a, Ber. 10b, etc. Maimuni's text followed that of the Talmud rather than the Mishnah, inasmuch as he specifically expostulates for his commentary on a "Tosefta." His assault on those who believed that Solomon had been the author of this medical treatise (which is not stated explicitly in any of the rabbinic sources; cf. *GL,* VI, 369 n. 90) and that Hezekiah suppressed it only because people had placed all their reliance on it and neglected to pray to God for help (cf. *e.g.,* Rashi *ad loc.*) is wholly in line with Maimuni's rational attitude toward medicine. His own explanation that it has contained magical

formulae and that "undoubtedly" it had been written by Sabeans is likewise in keeping with his general Sabean bogey. Cf. also Munk, III, 292 n. 1. It is interesting to note that *M.T.* 'Abodat Kokabim 2, 10 speaks of Rabshakeh, the Assyrian chief who assaulted Hezekiah, as of a renegade Jew, which is in accordance with Sanh. 60a.

110. *C.M.* to Sanh. X Introd., on the basis of Sanh. 99b. Cf. also above nn. 36 and 53. Uzziah is mentioned *S.M.* Prohib. 45 as an illustration of the punishment meted out to rebels against the established priesthood, a punishment different from that of Korah. This evidently refers to a widespread legend. Cf. *GL,* VI, 357 f. nn. 29-31.

111. *I.S.,* p. 7b quoting Midrash Ḥazit 1, 6 and Sanh. 103c; *M.N.* II, 36; *C.M* to Abot IV, 5 which tries to interpret away the statement in Ber. 10b in order to fit it into his own, more rigid ethical standards. For Isaiah, whom Maimuni calls "the nation's bearer of good tidings" (*I.T.,* pp. 26 and 44 = *Kobeṣ* II, 3b and 6c: מבשר האומה) and his martyrdom, cf. *GL,* VI, 374 n. 103.

112. *C.M.* Introd. and *M.T.* Yesode ha-Torah 9, 3 with reference to I Kings 18.30 ff. in the interpretation of Sanh. 89b, etc. (cf. also *GL,* VI, 319 n. 13) and II Kings 3.19, where Maimuni, however, does not accept the explanation of the Aggadah concerning the special wickedness of Moab (cf. e.g., Yalḳut *ad loc.*), but advances his own explanation by placing it on a par with the temporary innovation of Elijah. In this reasoning he is followed by both Kimḥi and Gersonides *ad. loc.* (Cf. also the latter's long discussion in his *Commentary* on Deut. 18). Of particular interest is Maimuni's dating of a prophecy of Habakkuk after Nebuchadnezzar's massacres (*M.N.* III, 17) which contradicts the prevailing rabbinic chronology placing that prophet under the reign of Manasseh. Cf. e.g., Seder 'Olam 20. Maimuni must have been familiar with the legend, taken over by Yosippon (ed. Günzburg, pp. 25 f.) from the Apocrypha, that Habakkuk was transferred from Palestine to Babylonia to feed and comfort Daniel in the lion's den. The Hebrew original of the apocryphal work *Bel and the Dragon,* where this story first appears— if such an original ever existed— was no longer known to Origen and the Church Fathers, but the story itself was known to many medieval rabbis, such as the author of Yeraḥmeel (72, 220 f.), Moses ha-Darshan (cf. the excerpts of his Bereshit Rabbati, quoted by Raymond Martini in *Pugio Fidei,* [Leipzig, 1687], p. 957 and A. Epstein *Magazin f. Gesch. u. Lit.* XV [1888], pp. 78 f.) and Eleazar of Worms (cf. his *Rimze ha-Haftarot* [Warsaw, 1875], p. 13 and Brüll *Jahrbücher* VIII [1887], p. 29 n. 1). Cf. also A. Neubauer, *The Book Tobit. A Chaldee Text* (Oxf., 1878), p. 42 (I am indebted to Prof. A. Marx for the latter references) and *GL,* VI, 432-4 nn. 6 and 8. Harmonistically one may perhaps stretch the lifetime of the prophet from Manasseh to Daniel. Cf., however, another Aggadah which identifies Habakkuk with the son of the Shunammite woman in *Zohar* I, 7b, etc.

113. *M.N.* III, 40. Cf. also *BB,* p. 81.

114. This prohibition was deduced by Maimuni from the כמני in Deut. 18.15, cf. Eppenstein *MbM* I, 480. With respect to Job and his associates we may pursue the following development: In *I.T.* p. 33 (*Kobes* II, 4c) he declares that, although heathens, they are generally recognized by Jews as true prophets. In *C.M.* to Sanh. X Introd. he reports the opinion of some rabbis that the book of Job was merely an allegory (cf. B.B. 15a, etc.). In *M.N.* III, 22 he expounds this view as his own and characteristically argues in its defense by pointing out the divergences in the Aggadah concerning the period of their activity.

115. *C.M.* Yadaim IV, 4 and *M.T.* Issure Biah 12, 25 on the basis of that Mishnah and Tos. Ḳid. V, 4. He disregards completely the historical evidence for the time of Nebuchadnezzar, such as troubled later, for instance, R. Simon of Sens in his comments on Yadaim *l. c.* Maimuni follows blindly the talmudic confusion of the permanent effects of the upheaval under Alexander with the fairly superficial changes under Sennacherib.

116. *C.M.* to Ber. VIII, 4, quoting b. 47a and Ḥul. 6a and warning the reader that this lengthy discussion is to define the meaning of "Cutheans" as used in the subsequent references to them. This is a typical instance of Maimuni's attempt at harmonization of contradictory utterances due to contradictory biases and changing historical situations. His hypothesis that all pro-Cuthean statements antedated the so-called investigation cannot, of course, stand the test of a critical examination of the sources.

117. *S.M.* Commandment 9; *I.S.,* p. 8a. Instead of: ואולם החרש והמסגר read ואולי as it reads in *I.S.* ed. Geiger (Appendix to *Moses ben Maimon*), p. 2b. The enforced conversion under Nebuchadnezzar is frequently mentioned in the Aggadah (cf. *GL,* VI, 416 n. 84). For the identification of החרש והמסגר with learned men cf. Giṭ. 88a and, in different versions, Yalḳut and Rashi to II Kings 24.14.

118. *M.T.* Roṣeaḥ u-Shemirat Nefesh 12, 15 on the basis of B.B. 4a.

119. *I.S.,* p. 9a and *C.M.* to Abot IV, 22 quoting Sanh. 96a. Cf. also Lev. r. 20, 1, etc. listed in *GL,* VI, 427 n. 114. It is interesting that he disregards the detailed chronology (of 45 years) given in Meg. 11b and most texts of Seder 'Olam 28 and that he prefers the equation with Solomon's forty years rather than with David's which is homiletically supported by Scripture.

120. *C.M.* to Ḳid. IV, 1 referring to the discussion b. 69b ff. Maimuni's general pro-Palestinian orientation prevents him, however, from fully accepting the Babylonian biases concerning Palestine's inferiority in family purity, as have come to the fore in that talmudic discussion. For this reason he introduces a new element: the supervision by the Palestinian supreme court.

121. *M.T.* Matnot 'Aniyim 6, 5 on the basis of M. Yadaim IV, 3, Yeb. 16a, etc. Cf. also note 83. Curiously *C.M.* to Yadaim *l. c.* Maimuni defines Ammon and Moab as identical with the cities of Sihon and Og. By this historical inexactitude he probably wished to indicate that all of Transjordan, insofar as it

was not reoccupied by the Jews, was free from the Sabbatical observance, but subjected to the poor man's tithe. Maimuni, following the Mishnaic phraseology, calls this regulation a Sinaitic tradition—which has annoyed his commentators, such as Karo. But he evidently did not mean to convey the idea that this actually was Mosaic law. In another connection, *M.T.* Terumot 1, 26 he states expressly that even in the days of Ezra in the Jerusalem district the very *terumah* was no longer a biblical obligation, because the latter was contingent upon the settlement of *all* Jewry in Palestine. Such a condition prevailed under the First Commonwealth and would recur in the Messianic era, but failed to materialize under the Second Temple. Cf. Yeb. 82a, RABD and the commentaries. Karo's explanation that Maimuni's usage of הלמ״מ was inaccurate (Simon of Sens uses the same phrase לאו דוקא with respect to the Mishnah) is controverted by Maimuni's citation of this passage among the Sinaitic traditions in his Introd. to *C.M.* Karo simply overlooked Maimuni's distinction between biblical law and Sinaitic tradition. Cf. also Tchernowitz, *op. cit.,* pp. 29 ff.

122. *C.M.* to Middot III, 1 and *M.T.* Bet ha-Behirah 2, 4 on the basis of Zeb. 62a. Like Rashi and Tosafot, Maimuni interprets: אחד שהעיד עליהם על המזבח as referring to the altar's dimensions and, in *M.T.,* logically reverses the order of both the Baraita and R. Johanan's utterance. He does not mention, however, the names of the three prophets, although he must have accepted the general understanding that those were Haggai, Zechariah and Malachi whom, in another connection, he calls the "latter prophets" in contrast to the נביאים ראשונים that included all those who appeared under the first Temple. *C.M.* to Sotah IX, 12. Cf. also *GL,* VI, 69 n. 358.

123. *C.M.* to Middot and Tamid *passim* and *M.T.* Bet ha-Behirah *passim,* where he describes the architecture of the Temple with a wealth of detail. The reference to Susa is in *C.M.* to Middot I, 3, on the basis of that Mishnah and Men. 98a.—Maimuni mentions in another connection the eastern entrance to the Temple court, the so-called Gate of Nicanor, and explains the name by relating the well-known legend, only stripping it of some of its supernatural accretions. *C.M.* to Yoma III, 10 on the basis of Tos. Yoma II, 4; b. 38a, etc. It is characteristic that, in contrast to his sources, he regards Nicanor as a Palestinian Jew, who proceeded to Alexandria in order to obtain there the sacred gate, rather than as the Temple's Egyptian Jewish benefactor.— *C.M.* to Middot V, 3 explains the name לשכת הפרוה as given on account of a Persian (מגוסי), Parva, who was apprehended while attempting to bore through the wall in order to see the high priest officiating. His source is the venturesome explanation of R. Joseph in Yoma 35a which has given rise to various comments. Cf. *Arukh, s.v.* (similar to Maimuni's), Rashi on Yoma *l. c.,* Bartenora on Middot *l. c.*—*M.T.* Parah 'Adumah 2, 7 repeats the venturesome story of M. Parah III, 2-3 concerning the houses built in Jerusalem upon overhanging rocks, where children were born and brought up and thus safeguarded against

impurity attached to living in quarters possibly built upon a human grave, and that also the entire Temple mountain and the *'Azarah* had such an underground empty space. As in *C.M.* to those Mishnahs, he decides the controversy in the first case against, in the second for R. Jose.

124. *C.M.* to Ma'aser Sheni V, 15 (repeated by the translator in *C.M.* to Sotah IX,10) on the basis of the discussion in Yeb. 86b which quotes Ezra 8.15.

125. *C.M.* Introd. and *M.T.* Introd. on the basis of various talmudic and geonic sources discussed in *GL,* VI, 447 n. 56. Maimonides did neither hesitate to include in the list practically all the prophets and leaders of the early post-exilic age, mentioned anywhere in the Bible, nor to place them all in a single generation. This was in agreement with his acceptance of the talmudic chronology concerning the short duration of the Persian period. He omits, however, Joshua, the high priest, probably because he regards Ezra as his successor in office, which is in accordance with the Aggadah in Cant. r. 5, 5. On the other hand, when *C.M.* to Shek I, 1 accepts the Mishnah's identification of one of the Temple's supervisors, Petahiah, with the returning exile, Mordecai-Bilshan, it is with the understanding that these supervisors were the most distinguished men in their particular function irrespective of the period of their activity. Nevertheless Maimuni apparently did not hesitate to place the story told in j. Shek. I, 1 48d in the name of Petahiah and in b. Men. 64b in the name of Mordecai in the Maccabean age, some two centuries after Ezra. Cf. Rashi on Men. *l. c., s.v.* מרדכי, Tosafot *ibid., s.v.* אמר and *Yuhasin,* p. 10b. —Descent from Ezra naturally was a special reason for pride and Maimonides reiterates almost on all occasions that R. Eleazar b. Azariah was Ezra's descendant in the tenth generation. *C.M.* Introd. ch. III and *Resp.* No. 135, on the basis of Ber. 27b, j. Yeb. 1, 1, 3d, etc. Maimuni's relative reticence in extolling Ezra in his Arabic *C.M.* as against the Hebrew *M.T.* may perhaps be due to apprehension, lest Muslim readers find therein confirmation, however far-fetched, for the widespread accusation that the Jews worshiped Ezra as a son of God. This accusation, originating with Muhammed, achieved canonical authority by its inclusion in the Koran (9.30) and was reinforced by tradition. Cf. Al-Bukhari, *Les traditions islamiques,* French transl. IV (Paris, 1914), 97, 24.4, p. 601 and A. Geiger, *Was hat Mohammed aus dem Judentum aufgenommen?* (Bonn, 1833), pp. 194 ff.

126. For the prohibition of intermarriage, as including the members of all nations, and not only of the seven Palestinian tribes, Maimuni invokes the testimony of Neh. 10.31. *M.T.* Issure Biah 12, 1.— The final formulation of all benedictions by "Ezra and his court" (*M.T.* Berakot 1, 5) is the equivalent of R. Johanan's well known statement: אנשי כנסת הגדולה תקנו להם וכו' Ber. 33a.—The institution of the interpreter (*M.T.* Tefillah 12, 10) became necesssary, as did the fixation of the Eighteen Benedictions, because the Jews, as a result of Nebuchadnezzar's Exile, mixed with "the Persians, the Greeks and other nations" and began speaking a jargon of many linguistic components.

Ibid., 1, 4.—The regulation of the *sinar* was one of the ten ordinances ascribed to Ezra in B.Ḳ. 82a (cf. also j. Meg. IV, 1, 75a) most of which Maimuni records. His omissions are likewise significant. 1) The Torah reading on Sabbath afternoon: *M.T.* Tefillah 12, 1.—2) The Torah readings on Monday and Thursday, originally instituted by Moses (in view of the quotation from Ex. 15.22 Maimuni identifies the נביאים שביניהם with the lawgiver himself), were definitely arranged on the basis of three readers reciting ten verses. *Ibid.*—3) The public sessions of the courts on Monday and Thursday are not recorded as a matter of law by Maimuni. Seeing the court's functioning on all week days in his own time, he reverses even the talmudic phrase אי איכא ב"ד דקבועין האידנא, Ket. 3a into the complementary assumption מקום שאין ב"ד יושבין בו אלא בב' וח': *M.T.* Ishut 10, 15 and *C.M.* to Ket. I, 1.—4) Thursday as a family wash day: *M.T.* Shabbat, 30, 3.—5). The recommendation to eat garlic on Friday is omitted (in *C.M.* to Ned. III, 10 he mentions it merely as a custom of bygone days), because it militated against his medical conscience. In fact, in *M.T.* Deot 4, 9 he enumerates garlic among the bad foodstuffs which ought to be taken very rarely and only in winter.—6) The early hour for baking bread for the benefit of the poor is mentioned *M.T.* Ishut 21, 5 in connection with the wife's duty to perform that service personally, if the family is poor. But there is no reason to believe that Maimuni wished to exclude the application of this ordinance to servants baking the bread for well-to-do families.— 7) The sinar (probably $= \zeta \omega v \acute{\alpha} \varrho \iota o v$). *Ibid.,* 24, 13.—8) The combing of hair before taking a ritual bath: *M.T.* Mikvaot 2, 16.—9) The right of peddlers to sell merchandise in various towns so that the women be supplied with ornaments: *M.T.* Shekenim 6, 9. In the light of B.B. 22a, Maimuni qualifies this right to peddling, but not to permanent shopkeeping which may cause detriment to local merchants.—10) The obligatory ritual bath after a nocturnal pollution extended to all who wish to study the Torah is mentioned *M.T.* Keri'at Shema' 4, 8 negatively as having fallen into desuetude, because the mass of the people could not stand the strain. This is based upon Ber. 22a, reformulated so as to fit into the Maimonidean theory of the mode of abrogation of ordinances. Cf. *Kesef Mishneh, ad. loc.* Cf. also M. Bloch, *op. cit.* I, 107-38; S. Zeitlin, "Takkanot Ezra," *JQR,* N.S. VIII (1917-18), pp. 161-74, and *GL,* VI, 444 f., nn. 46-9.

127. *M.T.* Gerushin 1, 27 וכבר נהגו כל ישראל למנות בגיטין או ליצירה או למלכות אלכסנדרוס מוקדון שהוא מנין שטרות follows the general misconception of the ancient Jewish chronologers.—Apart from his silence on the subject of the hellenistic diaspora, there are several references in his writings which unmistakably point to his unawareness of its existence. That he regarded Nicanor as a Palestinian, has already been mentioned. The vagueness of the stories concerning the origin and spread of the Septuagint and the erection of the Onias Temple, discussed later on, seems sufficiently conclusive.

128. *C.M.* to Meg. II, 1 generally on the basis of the talmudic discussion

Meg. 8b ff. and 18a. However, dissatisfied with the talmudic homily in support of Simon ben Gamaliel's preferential treatment of Greek, Maimuni adds his *historical* explanation.—*C.M.* to Sotah I, 14 on the basis of the talmudic discussion Sotah 49b, etc. Incidentally, this passage with its queer etymology of פולמוס as well as other such etymologies (cf. e.g., *C.M.* to Yadaim IV, 6: כספרי המירם) confirm the otherwise well-known fact that Maimuni himself —like the overwhelming majority of his Jewish and non-Jewish contemporaries under both Islam and Western Christendom—had not the slightest knowledge of Greek. *M.T.* Tefillin u-Mezuzah 1, 19 he remarks: וכבר נשקע יוני מן העולם ונשתבש ואבד. (Cf., however, n. 194). That is very likely why he fails to mention the Greek Bible among the Scriptures which are to be saved from fire. Cf. *Kesef Mishneh* on *M.T.* Shabbat 23, 26. He may have known, however, of Ibn Isḥak's Arabic translation of the Septuagint for use in Christian churches which certainly did not enhance in his eyes the necessity of continuing the exceptional protection granted to it by talmudic law. More significantly, the numerous textual divergences between LXX and the masoretic text lent themselves to polemical exploitation (e.g., by Ibn Hazm) as proofs of the alleged "forgeries" of Scripture by the Jews. Cf. G. Vajda, "La version des Septante dans la littérature musulmane," *REJ*, XC (1931), pp. 65-70.

129. *M.T.* Megillah ve-Ḥanukkah 3, 1; *I.T.* pp. 22 f. (*Kobes* II, 2c; here quoted from B. Cohen's unpublished translation; with slight variations in the more recent edition by A. S. Halkin, p. v) and *I.S.* p. 8b. Cf. also next note. Maimuni's description of the Syrian persecutions is evidently based upon aggadic sources and, especially, the Megillat Ta'anit, but has also many new and perplexing features. The enforced engraving of a denial of Judaism is a commonplace in the Aggadah. Cf. Meg. Ta'an. 2, 7, 11, 12; Gen. r. 2, 4 (Theodor, pp. 16f.; see further references there). Whether Maimuni had a reading which included the inscription upon a garment is doubtful. He may merely have amplified the aggadic statement by a reference to the reality of a Jewish badge under Islam and the undoubtedly still vivid recollection of Caliph Hakim bi'Amr-Illah's excesses in tenth century Egypt. The prohibition of closing the doors, mentioned only in the generally hasty and frequently ill-considered *I.S.*, may have been a misreading of Meg. Ta'an. 2 and 7: ולא היו ישראל יכולין לצאת ולבוא ביום אלא בלילה. The period of about fifty-two years appears likewise dubious. The terminus ad quem probably is 141 B.C., the usual basis for the rabbinic computation of the establishment of the Hasmonean dynasty. Cf. e.g., S. Zeitlin, *Megillat Ta'anit* (Phila., 1922), p. 84 n. 235. But why should the persecution have started in 193 B.C.? It is possible that he knew the correct date of Antiochus' spoliation of the Jerusalem temple in 170 B.C. and that he followed the chronology recorded, e.g., in *Megillat Antiochos* that this event took place in the twenty-third year of the Syrian king's reign.

130. *M.T. ibid.*, §1-3.14 on the basis of the well-known discussions in Shab. 21 ff. Maimuni's equivocal מפני זה allows him to leave the choice open between the historical fact and the miracle.—*C.M.* to Middot I, 6 identifies on the basis of Yoma 15b f. the compartment where the Hasmoneans deposited the stones of the altar defiled by the Syrians with the "compartment of seals" mentioned in M. Tamid III, 3.

131. *C.M.* to Men. XIII, 10 on the basis of Men. 109b, trying to reconcile in part the contradictory traditions of R. Meir and R. Judah. But according to the Halakhah he follows chiefly the latter. Of course, he shares the confusion of the talmudic sources concerning Onias II, III and IV and aggravates it further by referring back to his Introduction where he had bluntly declared that Simon the Pious, although the youngest, was a member of the original Great Synagogue of one hundred and twenty. Cf. also *M.T.* Introd. He also stresses that the Onias temple was built for a special sect which he calls קבצר and that Egyptians (evidently non-Jews) worshiped there the God of Israel. He may have heard of certain confused Coptic traditions claiming descent from Egyptian Jewish ancestry originally associated with the worship at that temple.

132. *M.T.* Ma'aser 9, 1-2. Cf. also *C.M.* to Ma'aser Sheni V, 15 (repeated by the translator to Sotah IX, 10). These two Mishnahs and the discussion Sotah 48a are the main sources. Maimuni's historical qualification: שהיה אחר שמעון הצדיק was hardly intended to draw a distinction between this Johanan the high priest and his heretical namesake John Hyrcanus, as suggested by Karo *ad loc.* Evidently both lived after Simon the Pious who, according to Maimuni, succeeded Ezra and, even as Onias' father, died at least two hundred years before the fall of Jerusalem. This characterization evidently was to convey to the reader the notion that this measure, like that concerning the abolition of the declaration of tithe by the same high priest (see n. 124), was enacted in the early days of the Second Commonwealth in modification of Ezra's reform of the entire system of tithes.—In *C.M.* Introd. ch. IV and VI, however, Johanan the High Priest is identified as "Johanan, son of Matatiah mentioned in the prayers in connection with the wars against the Greek kings" and placed in the fourth generation after Ezra alongside Joshua b. Perahia and Nittai of Arbela.

133. *C.M.* to Bik. III, 4 and to Sotah VII, 6 on the basis of the talmudic reversal of the friendly attitude of the Mishnah in Sotah 41b (= Tos. VII, 16) and B.B. 3b. The reading ולא היתה לו אם מוישראל rather than אב is more in keeping with the Halakhah, as restated *M.T.* 1, 4. Cf. also Rashi's comment on the Mishnah (Sotah 41a *s.v.* אחינו) and the objection raised by the Tosafists (B.B. 3b *s.v.* כל). It is questionable, nevertheless, whether Maimuni assumed that Agrippa's mother was Glaphyra, a non-Jewess. His partial Jewish descent through his grandmother, the Hasmonean Mariamne, if at all legally significant, could be disregarded in the light of B.B. 3b.

134. *C.M.* to Yoma I, 3, generalizing the statement concerning Joshua ben Gamala, Yoma 18a and Yeb. 61a.

135. *M.T.* Sanh. 24, 4 and *C.M.* to Sanh. VI, 4 on the basis of that Mishnah, b. Sanh. 46a and Yeb. 90b. Maimuni names sorcery as the ground of Simon b. Shetaḥ's stern measure and emphasizes that both the large number of executed and the unusual method of hanging had an emergency character. Whether he realized the connection with the sectarian trends—in which case he would admit with the majority in the Mishnah the regularity of hanging at least one male criminal—is an open question. To justify the related right of the court to condemn any property it may deem necessary, he invokes the threat in Ezra 10.8, *M.T.* Sanh. 24, 6 on the basis of Git. 36b, etc.

136. *C.M.* to Abot I, 3, on the basis of the well-known Aggadah in Abot de-R. Nathan V. Maimuni's description is partly colored by his knowledge of contemporary Karaism, with which he fully identifies that ancient sect. When he speaks of its numerous divisions and of the tendency to arbitrary interpretation of Scripture he reflects Karaite realities and their insistence, since the days of Anan, on "search well in the Torah." Notwithstanding the equivocal statement in *Resp.* No. 46 concerning the Karaites: אבל יקראו אותם צדוקים ובית ומין הם הסמרה it is likely that Malmuni knew the difference between the Samaritans and the Saducees and Karaites.—The Pharisees, on the other hand, are for him, as they usually are in the Aggadah, not a sect, but a group of exceedingly pious Jews who go beyond the letter of the law in fulfilling certain commandments. They eat, for example, even ordinary food in a state of purity. *C.M.* to Ḥag. II, 7 and Tohorot IV, 12, on the basis of the latter Mishnah.

137. The following doctrinal and legal deviations of the Sadducees are mentioned in Maimuni's writings: 1) The denial of a world to come, *C.M.* to Abot I, 3; Ber. IX, 1, etc.—2) The repudiation of tradition, *ibid.; M.T.* Teshubah 3, 8, etc.—3) The date of the Feast of Weeks, *M.T.* Temidin u-Musafin 7, 11 on the basis of Men. 65 f. Although not mentioned by name the המועים שיצאו מכלל ישראל בבית שני are easily identified.—4) The place of burning the incense, *C.M.* to Yoma I, 5 and *M.T.* 'Abodat Yom ha-Kippurim, 1, 7 on the basis of Yoma 19b and 53a.—5) The insistence that the priest burning the red heifer be "one who becomes clean at sunset," *M.T.* Parah 'Adumah 1, 14 on the basis of M. Parah III, 7; Yoma 2a, etc. In *C.M.* to Parah *ibid.* he mentions briefly this opinion of קצת צדוקין, a qualification which was probably due to his knowledge of Karaite opinion on the subject.—6) The prostration before an idol need not be performed by the stretching of arms and legs in order to fall under that biblical prohibition, *C.M.* to Hor. I, 3 (includes the two other illustrations of the Mishnah); *M.T.* Shegagot 14, 2 (without naming the Sadducees); *Resp.* No. 365 on the basis of Hor. 4a. Cf. also *M.T.* Sanh. 10, 9.—7) Differences in the method of slaughtering animals, so that an Israelite must not partake of their meat, *C.M.* to Ḥul. I, 2

(referring primarily to Karaites). Maimuni seems to have been ignorant, however, of the controversy concerning free will, because it was not mentioned in the sources accessible to him. Otherwise he most likely would have mentioned it at least in *C.M.* to Ber. IX, 1.

138. *C.M.* to Niddah IV, 2 in the light of the Gemara 33b.

139. *I.T.* in the Arabic original. Due to Christian censorship this passage is mutilated in the three Hebrew translations. The legal point of his Jewishness is decided according to Yeb. 23a, etc. Cf. *M.T.* Issure Biah 15, 3.—Maimuni frequently refers to Christians in his writings. He mentions their belief in the abrogation of the old dispensation, *M.T.* Teshubah 3, 8; discusses their well-known homiletical derivation of the trinitarian creed from אלהינו ה' ה' in the Shema' (*Kobeṣ* II, 7c, cf. also *M.N.* I, 50); accepts the Christian tradition that the rabbis were instrumental in the crucifixion of Jesus, *I.T., l. c.;* and declares that even if one were to believe in Jesus' miracles, there would still be a thousand proofs from Scripture even from the Christian point of view that Jesus was not the Messiah, *ibid.,* p. 48 (*Kobeṣ* II, 7a). Nevertheless, Maimuni's information concerning early Christianity seems to have come exclusively from Jewish and Muslim sources. His unfamiliarity with the gospels is also attested by his assumption that the paraclete mentioned in John 14.26; 16.7, etc. was the equivalent of the Arabic Aḥmed rather than Muhammed, *I.T.* p. 30 (*Kobeṣ* II, 4a). Otherwise he does not seem to oppose the strange *gematria,* apparently first advanced by Ali aṭ-Ṭabari, that *paraclet* numerically equals *Muhammad bin 'Abdallah an-Nabbiyul-Hadi* (M. son of Abd., the rightly guiding prophet) or in the Syriac form *paracleta* = M. *Rasulun Ḥabibun Tayyibun* (M. is a beloved and good apostle). Cf. his *The Book of Religion and Empire,* Eng. transl. A. Mingana (Manchester, 1922), pp. 140-42. —Maimuni knows that the Minim in the Talmud are not Sadducees (cf. *Resp.* No. 46), but he also fails to identify them with the Christians. He comes close to such identification, however, when with reference to Sanh. 99a, Ber. 12a and j. Ber. I, 8, 3c he mentions that some Minim acknowledged the divine authority of the Decalogue alone and that therefore the sages discontinued its daily recitation, or when in discussing the new benediction instituted in the days of R. Gamaliel, he says, רבו האפיקורסין בישראל והיו מצרים לישראל ומסיתין אותו לשוב מאחרי ה', *M.T.* Tefillah 2, 1 on the basis of Ber. 28b. *C.M.* to Ḥul. I, 2 gives a somewhat confused definition of Minim, which includes diverse characteristics of what *M.T.* Teshubah 3, 7 assigns to five classes of sectarians. Historically, Maimuni identifies them with the heretics of various ages, such as the disciples of Doeg, Aḥitophel, Gehazi and Elisha Aḥer. Cf. also n. 152.

140. *M.T.* 'Abodat Kokabim 9, 4 and *C.M.* to 'Ab. Zarah I, 3 referring to the talmudic discussion A.Z. 8a ff. The rabbis in Christian lands naturally had to find excuses for trading with Christians on Sunday. Cf. e.g., *Maimuni Glosses, ad. loc.* quoting R. Samuel b. Meir and R. Baruch b. Isaac.—For the

permission of instruction cf. *Resp.* No. 364, with reference to Sanh. 59a. Cf.
also Abraham Maimuni's remark quoted by Eppenstein, *MbM* II, 87.
    141. *I.T.,* p. 19 (*Kobeṣ* II, 2a). It has long been suggested that Maimuni
refers here to Mani. Although his statements are so vague that no definite
conclusion may be drawn, it appears that he accepted the usual succession of
religious reformers as found among his Jewish predecessors and successors.
For Abraham bar Hiyya, for example, cf. above n. 6. The major difficulty consists in Maimuni's characterization: מבני עשו (which incidentally is omitted
in Nahum Ma'arabi's translation), while the most reliable sources agree that
he was a Babylonian (of Persian origin). It seems, however, that among the
Jews the notion was current that Mani had first been a Christian, and Barhe-
braeus' statement to this effect (*Historia compendiosa dynastiarum,* ed.
Pococke [Oxford, 1663], p. 82) a few decades later may well have been derived
from his Jewish ancestors. That Jews contributed to his execution, however,
is nowhere recorded. The more common story of his death, such as reported
by Bar Hiyya, is essentially related by Al-Biruni, *Chronology,* pp. 207-9
(Engl. transl., pp. 189-92) and others.
    142. *M.T.* Sanh. 1 and 2 on the basis of the well-known discussions in h
Sanh., etc. With respect to the selection of candidates in the provinces Maimuni
follows the reading of Tos. Sanh. VII, 1; Ḥag. II, 9 etc.: ומשם שולחין ובודקין
rather than that of Sanh. 88b: משם כותבין ושולחין which seems to indicate
appointment by correspondence. Following strictly the talmudic sources Maimuni is not even aware of the problem, which has puzzled modern scholars,
as to whether the high priest or the rabbinic *nasi* was the presiding officer,
the former being intimated by extra-talmudic sources, such as Josephus and
the New Testament. Cf. e.g., Z. Taubes, *Ha-Nasi ba-Sanhedrin ha-Gedolah,*
Vienna, 1925. In describing the seating arrangement (1, 3) Maimuni follows
Tos. Sanh. VIII, 1. He reads with certain Mss. in the testimony of R. Eleazar
b. R. Zadok: אבא מימינו omitting ואחר. Cf. also *Kesef Mishneh, ad. loc.* In
C.M. Introd., however, in describing Moses' instruction of the seventy elders
he places Aaron and one of his sons to Moses' right.
    143. *M.T.* Issure Biah 20, 2 and *C.M.* to Ḳid. IV, 5, on the basis of that
Mishnah; b. Ḳid. 76b; Sanh. 36b. In *C.M.* he refers to M. Middot V, 4,
where the Sanhedrin's function in probing priestly lineage is described. He
also promises more extensive comments on the subject in *C.M.* to Sanh., but
none are found in our editions, not even to IV, 2 where the Talmud 36b
repeats its remarks of Ḳid. 76b with the citation of Num. 11.16 which Maimuni
likewise quotes.
    144. *M.T.* Sanh. 14, 12 and *C.M.* to Ket. IV, 6 and Middot V, 3. In the
latter he emphasizes that the compartment Gazit had two doors, one leading
to the holy chambers, one open to the outside, so that one half of the compartment could be assigned to the meetings of the Sanhedrin with its numerous non-priestly members. Maimuni follows the source concerning the ten

migrations in R.H. 31, including the messianic prediction that Tiberias will also be the starting point at the end of days. By using the term high court rather than Sanhedrin, he avoids the difficulties inherent in the often contradictory use of the latter designation in the talmudic sources. He stresses, however, specifically: ומשם לא עמד ב"ד גדול עד עתה. This has a decidedly polemical sound, probably directed against the use of this high-sounding title by the Academy in Bagdad. Cf. the passages listed by V. Aptowitzer, "Formularies of Decrees and Documents from a Gaonic Court," *JQR,* N.S. IV (1913-4), pp. 35 ff. and J. Mann, "The Responsa of the Babylonian Geonim as a Source of Jewish History," *ibid.,* VII (1916-7), pp. 468 ff.

145. *M.T.* Mamrim 1, 4 and 2, 2, on the basis of Tos. Sanh. VII, 1; b. 88b; M. 'Eduyot I, 5 and Beṣah 5a. The interpretation of the latter passage is impugned by RABD and defended by Maimuni's commentators. *Migdal 'Oz, ad. loc.* suggests j. Makkot as the source for the decision by public opinion, but I have not been able to locate any such passage in our text of j.

146. *M.T.* Sanh. 14, 11-14 combining the two talmudic prerequisites for capital jurisdiction: the existence of an officiating priest and the functioning of the Sanhedrin in its own original location in the Temple, on the basis of Sanh. 52b and 'Ab. Zarah 8b. Once these two prerequisites were met, a little sanhedrin consisting of members ordained in Jerusalem could and did exercise capital jurisdiction even in the diaspora. Cf. Tos. Sanh. III, 10-11; b. 7a. On the basis of these sources *M.T.* Sanh. 13, 8 states that a sentence of a court abroad was annulled if a criminal succeeded in escaping to Palestine. The formula סותרין את דינו על כל פנים combines the סותרין את דינו in the two Talmudim and נידונין כתחילה in Tos. Maimuni does not seem to object, nonetheless, to the infliction of capital punishment on informers as practiced already in his day in Spain. Cf. n. 170. *M.T.* 1, 2: אבל בחו"ל אינן חייבין להעמיד ב"ד בכל פלך ופלך runs counter to all these three sources to such an extent that many commentators (Karo and Rosanes *ad. loc.* and Moses Margulis in *Mar'eh ha-Panim* on j. Makkot I, 8, 31b) have emended the text by adding אלא before בכל. Such emendation is supported by neither manuscripts nor editions. Cf. e.g., [J. Feigenbaum] שנויי נוסחאות וגירסאות לס' משנה תורה (Frankfort, 1889), p. 140. Maimuni seems to have given preference to the interpretation in Midrash Tannaim on Deut. 16.18, ed. Hoffman, p. 197, and that is why he quotes the entire verse, deriving his interpretation from נותן לך rather than from בשעריך. Cf. also Naḥmanides on Deut., *ibid.*

147. *M.T.* Introd. and *C.M.* Introd. (for a more detailed examination of the chronological succession of the bearers of tradition cf. later on), on the basis of the well-known M. Abot I. In *C.M.* to Peah II, 6 explaining the word זוגות, he enumerates only the more familiar three generations of Judah b. Ṭabbai to Hillel. He seems to accept R. Meir's opinion, supported by M. Ḥag. II, 2 and Abot I, 8 that Judah b. Ṭabbai was the *nasi* and Simon b. Shetaḥ the *ab bet din.*

148. *C.M.* to Shab. I, 4 on the basis of Shab. 13b, Ḥag. 13ab. The assumption that all the scholars of the generation were present is necessary in order
to explain the meaning of the majority in such an accidental gathering. This
assumption seems to underlie the venturesome narrative about the use of
brutal force by the Shammaites in j. Shab. I, 4, 3b, which is otherwise
ignored by Maimuni. His enumeration of the eighteen enactments conflicts
in part with both b. and j. Cf. Zeraḥiah ha-Levi, *Ha-Maor ha-Gadol* on Alfasi's
reproduction of M. Shab. I, 4 and *Korban ha-Edah* on j. *l. c. s.v.* חשש and
שמונה עשר. Cf. also H. Graetz, *Geschichte,* III⁴ note 26 and I. Halevy,
Dorot ha Rishonim, I, 3, 580-602.

149. *C.M.* Introd.: Hillel descended from Shephatiah, the son of Abital,
king David's wife (II Sam. 3.4), on the basis of Ket. 62b as against j.
Ta'anit IV, 2, 68a and Gen. r. 98, 10; Maimuni follows the geonic interpretation in *Teshubot ha-Geonim,* ed. Harkavy, No. 349. Cf. also Albeck's
note 4 to Gen. r. *l. c.* For a full discussion of these sources cf. I. Levi,
"L'origine davidique de Hillel," *REJ,* XXXI (1895), pp. 202-11; XXXII (1896),
pp. 143 f. *M.T.* Sanh. 4, 5 concerning ordination seems to be based upon j.
Sanh. I, 2, 19a, although the historical description of R. Ba evidently places
the reform in the period after R. Akiba (and the Bar Kokeba revolt).
Maimuni possibly understood the חזרו וחלקו כבוד לבית זה which obviously
refers to the house of Hillel as implying the restoration of a procedure
prevalent in the years between Hillel and Joḥanan b. Zakkai. He also assumes
that the second rather than the first change restored fully the original
prerogative and that אלא מדעת ב"ד meant the coöperation of the vice-
president.—*C.M.* to Sheb. X, 3 and *M.T.* Shemiṭṭa ve-Yobel 9, 16-17 referring
to Giṭ. 35a ff. In *C.M.* he enjoins the courts to protect a poor debtor by
accepting his claim that the Sabbatical year had annulled his debt and to
advance this argument for the sake of the debtor's heirs, while in *M.T.* he
stresses that only a high tribunal, such as that headed by R. Ammi and R. Assi,
was entitled to issue a prosbol. In other words, the prosbol is a necessary
evil, enacted for social reasons, and should be dispensed with wherever
possible. That it was, nevertheless, a necessity under the advanced economy
of early Islam, may be seen in the inclusion of the writ in the formularies
of R. Judah al-Barceloni. Cf. his *Sefer ha-Shetarot,* ed. Halberstam (Berlin,
1898), No. 48. The absence of this document in Hai's similar collection is
undoubtedly due to its general incompleteness. Cf. S. Assaf's remarks in the
introduction to his edition of this work (Jerusalem, 1930), p. 8. Indeed, even
in the more backward Franco-German regions a prosbol is recorded to have
been issued by R. Jacob Tam. Cf. Tosafot Giṭ. 36b, *s.v.* דאלימו.

150. *C.M.* to Sotah IX, 15 on the basis of Meg. 21a.

151. *C.M.* to Ket. IV, 6, referring to Isa. 27.2. This refers to the somewhat
later period of R. Eleazar b. Azariah whom he mentions as a descendant of
Ezra in the tenth generation. The source for both is j. Ber. IV, 1, 7d, although

the Talmud does not refer to Isaiah. Cf. also n. 125.—*C.M.* to Suk. III, 12 and *M.T.* Sukkah 7, 15. Although he emphasizes *C.M.* to Men. X, 6 that R. Johanan merely explained an older tradition, as is intimated in דרש והתקין Suk. 41b, he feels prompted to emphasize that in the messianic age all these *takkanot* will expire.—*M.T.* Metam'ei Mishkab 10, 3 he reports on the basis of Bek. 30b that after the destruction of the Temple overcautious priests refused to give information concerning certain laws of purity even to scholars. Cf. also *C.M.* to Demai II, 3 and to Sanh. V, 2.

152. *I.S.* p. 8a, referring to the well-known story concerning R. Eliezer's trial. Cf. esp. B. Z. Bokser, *Pharisaic Judaism in Transition* (N. Y., 1935), p. 16. It is remarkable that Maimuni quotes Koh. r. (I, 32 to I, 8) rather than Tos. Ḥul. II, 24 or, in a somewhat abbreviated form, 'Ab. Zarah 16b f. In keeping with the purpose of his pamphlet, he does not try to explain away the שנתפס לשם מינות as does, e.g., Rashi the כשנתפס למינות in A.Z. *l. c.* According to his definition here: זה שהמינים יכריתם האל יתלוצצו בדתות ויאמרו אויל המתעסק בהם משוגע הלמד אותם ויבטלו הנבואה לגמרי, Minim were militant atheists rather than Christian or other heretics. He has evidently in mind certain Muslim schools of thought, such as the *Dahriya,* and places them in the period of R. Eliezer, thus motivating their talmudic repudiation as worse than idolatry (probably referring to R. Tarfon's anti-Christian exclamation, Shab. 116a). In *M.T.* Teshubah 3, 7 atheists appear only as the first of five classes of Minim.—R. Eliezer, as the author of *Pirke,* is frequently quoted in *M.N.* Cf. I, 61 and 70 and, especially, II, 26, where he admits his inability to explain the anthropomorphic passages in *Pirke* III and quotes a passage from Gen. r. 12, 11 where R. Eliezer has "repeated the same thing expressing himself more clearly."

153. That R. Akiba was mainly R. Eliezer's disciple is emphasized *C.M.* Introd.; to Sheb. VIII, 9 and *M.T.* Introd., although in the first passage the testimony of the Talmud (Ket. 84b) is invoked, according to which he had received some instruction also from R. Tarfon. Maimuni does not mention, however, his study under R. Joshua (from whom he received his ordination) and Nahum of Gimzo. Cf. Ab. R.N. VI (ed. Schechter, p' 29); j. Sanh. I, 3, 19a; Ber. 22a. Cf. also Zacuto, *Yuḥasin,* p. 37b. In *C.M.* to Sotah V, 2 he denies specifically any direct instruction by R. Joḥanan b. Zakkai. *M.T.* Melakim II, 3 cites on the basis of j. Ta'anit IV, 8, 68d R. Akiba's support of Bar Kokhba as an illustration for the doctrine that no outward signs or miracles are necessary to identify the Messiah. Maimuni overstates the case not only when he calls R. Akiba נושא כליו של בן כוזיבא המלך (cf. the objections of Zacuto, *l. c.* and Karo *ad. loc.*), but he says that all the scholars of the generation saw in Bar Kokhba a king-messiah. (Cf. also *M.T.* Ta'aniot 5, 3 on the basis of Ta'an. 26b, 29a, etc.). He may have discarded the legend of the execution of the pretender by the rabbis themselves (Sanh. 93b, cited by RABD *al. loc.*), because it was controverted by the legally and

historically more defendable tradition of his death at the hands of the enemy (Lam. r. 2, 2; cf. *Migdal 'Oz* and *Kesef Mishneh ad. loc.*). He should have thought, however, of the opposition of R. Eleazar of Modi'in, Bar Kokhba's uncle, and R. Joḥanan b. Toreta, recorded in j. Ta'anit *l. c.* The martyrdom of R. Akiba and his associates as well as of the martyrs of Lydda is cited *I.S.*, p. 11a quoting Pes. 50a as one which vouchsafes the world to come to the victim, regardless of other merits.—*S.M.* Commandment 153 refers to R. Akiba's proclamation of a leap year in Nehardea, recorded in M. Yeb. XVI, 7. Maimuni explains this as having occurred during the absence of authorized scholars in Palestine, which can only mean to say, during some sort of upheaval. Modern scholars, however, usually date R. Akiba's journey around 110 C.E., i.e., even before the outbreak of the revolt against Trajan which caused minor disturbances in Palestine.

154. *M.T.* Ḳiddush ha-Ḥodesh 5, 3, on the basis of R.H. 21a, etc. It refers to the well-known calendar reform of Hillel II, the date of which was usually given by medieval chronologers as 670 Seleucid era (358-9 C.E.), or about 16 years after Raba's death. Cf. Abraham bar Hiyya, *Sefer ha-'Ibbur* (London, 1851), p. 97 citing a tradition of R. Hai Gaon. E. Mahler, *Handbuch der jüdischen Chronologie* (Leipzig, 1916), p. 462, however, prefers the date of 344 C.E.

155. *C.M.* to Neg. XIV, 13 quoting Sifra. *I.S.* p. 8a referring to 'Ab. Zarah 18a f.—As in the case of R. Akiba *M.T.* Introd. emphasizes R. Meir's descent from a proselyte father, but refrains from relating his extraction to Emperor Nero. For a defense of the latter legend in Giṭ. 56a cf. Zacuto, *Yuḥasin*, p. 42b.

156. See later on n. 191.

157. *M.T.* Terumot 1, 5 on the basis of Ḥul. 6b. In contrast to Rashi, Tosafot and RABD, Maimuni regards this liberation from tithes as extending over all grains and not only vegetables, since he regards the entire system of tithes after the Restoration under Ezra as based upon a rabbinic regulation rather than binding Mosaic law. Cf. *M.T. ibid.*, §26.—On the basis of j. Sheb. VI, 1, 36c and Yeb. VII, 3, 8a, Maimuni ascribes to R. Judah also the liberation of Ascalon. Both texts contain the name Rabbi, against *Kesef Mishneh ad. loc.* (Cf. also Tos. Ohalot XVIII, 18.) The latter's query why Maimuni failed to mention the three other cities included by j. Demai II, 1, 22c in the patriarch's reform, may perhaps be answered by the example set to this effect in b. Ḥul. 6b. Although realizing that R. Akiba and R. Ishmael had already composed their respective Mekiltas, Maimuni states, almost in the same breath, that from the days of Moses to those of R. Judah the Patriarch no work was written to instruct the public in oral law and that the leaders of the intervening generations wrote down notes of what they had heard from their teachers for their own use, but gave only oral instruction to others. *M.T.* Introd. Perhaps he regarded the two Mekiltas as such personal

notes. As to the other Tannaitic collections, he states that they were assembled in the generation following R. Judah's by R. Ḥiyya (Tosefta); R. Hoshaya (a tannaitic collection on Genesis = Gen. r.) and Abba Arika (various Baraitot, such as Sifra and Sifre). *Ibid.* and *C.M.* Introd. Notwithstanding the well-known statement in Sanh. 86a, 'Er. 96b, etc. concerning the major trend in Sifra and Sifre (סתם ספרא), the name *debe-Rab* and the citation of authorities later than R. Judah has induced many medieval and modern scholars to ascribe their redaction to Rab. Maimuni is also a great admirer of R. Judah's style. Not only does he praise the expert knowledge of all shades of the Hebrew language manifested by the compiler of the Mishnah (*C.M.* Introd.: even R. Judah's servants were frequently consulted in linguistic matters; cf. R.H. 26b), but wishes to emulate this style in his own great legal compilation. Cf. *S.M.* Introd.

158. *Resp.* No. 58, quoting R. Nissim's *Mafteaḥ* (cf. his *Commentary* on Shab. 105b). As illustrations he cites the Mishnah of Bar Kappara or R. Hoshaya, evidently neither of which he had seen. Cf. I. Halevy, *Dorot ha-Rishonim* II, 123-5. Cf. also n. 157.

159. *M.T.* Introd. The chronology is, of course, not very exact. He has probably in mind the large midrashic collections, such as the Rabbot. He must have known of many younger aggadic compilations, since this type of literary creativity was continued long beyond his own day.

160. *Resp.* No. 349 commenting on an uncomplimentary utterance of R. Jeremiah on the subject of Babylonian scholarship in Yoma 57a. He quotes another similar utterance of R. Jeremiah from Sanh. 24a and an anecdote concerning R. Ze'era's attempt to forget his Babylonian training from B.M. 85a, but explains them all as referring to the temporary decline of Jewish learning there on account of severe persecutions which occurred during the two generations of Rabbah, R. Joseph, Abaye and Raba. He quotes B.M. 86a and Ḥul. 46a. Soon afterwards, however, and especially in the days of R. Ashi, Babylonian learning reached a high degree of fruition, as is seen Giṭ. 59a and Sanh. 36a.

161. *C.M.* to Bek. IV, 4 and *M.T.* Sanh. 4, 12-13 and 6, 2, on the basis of the Babylonian orientation of Sanh. 5a, etc. However, in *C.M. ibid* IV, 3, referring back to *C.M.* to Hor. (especially I, 5 on the basis of Hor. 5a ff.) and in *M.T.* Bek. 3, 1 he admits, as does his talmudic source, that an authorization of the Palestinian partiarch and not one of the exilarch enabled a scholar to declare a first-born animal as being without blemish. More significantly *M.T.* Sanh. 5, 8 admits, on the basis of B.Ḳ. 84af., etc., that the very foundation of Jewish administration of justice in the dispersion rests upon a general mandate of the only legitimate Palestinian court, to which alone the title *Elohim* of Ex. 22.7-8 may be applied.—*M.T.* To'en ve-Niṭ'an 13, 2.10 classifies on the basis of B.B. 36a the talmudic exilarchs on a par with robbers and Gentiles as men of violence. Out of deference to the contemporary

exilarchs Maimuni stresses in both passages: ראשי גליות של אותו זמן and שהיו בימי חכמים.

162. *I.T.* p. 28 (*Kobeṣ* II, 3d). In his defense against the accusation of Jewish forgeries of Scripture, Maimuni adduces the existence of several ancient translations for the Gentile public. The Syriac version refers obviously to the Peshiṭṭa, as the Greek refers to the Septuagint. The לעז of the Hebrew translations of *I.T.* (in the Arabic Mss no equivalent is found) can hardly refer to an Arabic version existent *before* Muhammed. It is much rather the equivalent of Latin. Cf. *BB* p. 175. Nothing is known of the existence of an ancient or medieval Persian version of the Bible.—Onkelos is frequently referred to in Maimonides' writings. Cf. especially *M.N.* II, 33 quoting Meg. 3a; *C.M.* Eight Chapters 7; *S.M.* Prohib. 128; *M.T.* Ishut 8, 4 and Issure Biah 12, 13. In the latter passage he invokes the translation of Deut. 23.18 as testimony of the severity of the sin committed by cohabiting with a slave, but in the face of contradictory biblical and talmudic evidence he refuses to follow the translator in declaring it a direct legal prohibition. See also A. S. Halkin's remarks in his ed. of *I.T.*, pp. 38 f. nn. 55-56; and my *A Social and Religious History of the Jews*, 2nd ed., VI, 263 f., 457 f. n. 39

163. *I.T.*, pp. 19 f. (*Kobeṣ* II, 2a) and *I.S.*, p. 8b, where the figure of victims quoted by Maimuni from his opponent without contradiction is given as 52,000. The lower figure is found in ed. Geiger, *op. cit.*, p. 3a and *Kobeṣ* II, 13b. The bloody suppression of the Jews of Yathrib and Khaibar (some twenty tribes are recorded) by Muhammed and Omar I is a well-known historical fact, but the two figures seem, nonetheless, decidedly exaggerated. They are undoubtedly based upon old Muslim traditions, such as that concerning the 10,000 Jewish warriors in Khaibar. The Jews themselves were interested in overemphasizing their strength so as to discourage attacks. Cf. R. Leszynsky, *Die Juden in Arabien zur Zeit Mohammeds* (Berlin, 1910), pp. 86 ff. The epithet משוגע for Muhammed is used also by R. Sherira Gaon and others.—Maimuni argues against the veracity of Muhammed's preachment or that of Omar and Zeid on objective rather than national grounds. He specifically stresses in this connection *I.T.*, p. 33 (*Kobeṣ* II, 4c), as he does more elaborately in his theories of prophecy, *C.M.* Introd. and *M.N.* II, that non-Jews, such as Job and his friends, may be true prophets just as born Jews may turn out to be false prophets.—Maimuni's effort comprehensively to disprove alleged biblical forebodings of the appearance of Muhammed (*I.T.* pp. 27 ff.; *Kobeṣ* II, 3c ff.) is understandable in view of the great weight carried by such arguments at that time. Even a Christian apologist like 'Ali aṭ-Ṭabari actually quotes Deut. 18.15; 33.2-3 as early biblical references to the founder of Islam, curiously arguing from the text of 18.15 that it cannot refer to Jesus. Cf. his *The Book of Religion and Empire* (Eng. transl., London, 1922), pp. 85 ff. Cf. also H. Hirschfeld, "Mohammedan Criticism of the Bible," *JQR*, O.S., XIII (1901), pp. 222-40. Maimuni in disputing these and similar inter-

pretations is right in saying that they had long "been controverted after having gained widespread popularity" and that the enlightened Muslims themselves no longer believed in such "proofs."

164. *I.S. passim* and *I.T. passim*. The danger which threatened Maimuni on account of an Arab's accusation in Egypt that he, previously a convert to Islam, had relapsed into Judaism, recorded in Al-Kifti, ed. Lipper, p. 113) is referred to in his remark to Jephet ben Elijah: גם ארעוני צרות רבות גלויות בארץ מצרים מחלאים והפסד ממון ועמירת מוסרים עלי לחרגני (ed. Geiger, *op. cit.,* p. 6b and *Kobeṣ* II, 37d). That this remark should refer to his Jewish opponents, as suggested by Eppenstein, *MbM* II, 39 n. 3, is not supported by any evidence. On what other grounds than alleged apostasy, moreover, could even Jewish informers expect to bring about the condemnation to death of a highly esteemed physician and rabbi? This leaves, of course, in abeyance the moot question as to whether Maimon's family outwardly professed Islam under the Almohades or merely refrained from publicly adhering to Judaism. Cf. the literature cited in A. Berliner, *MbM* II, 104-30. In any case it would have been merely lip service, as stressed in *I.S.*—The stauncher resistance of the Christians to the Almohade persecutions, partly attested also through Arabic sources (cf. S. Munk, *Notice sur Joseph Ben-Iehouda,* pp. 44 f.), need not have had any further stimulus, but the greater dependance of the Catholic Church upon *public* worship than that of Judaism.—It also appears that the persecutions were much less severe in Morocco than in Spain, which may have been the reason for Maimon's family emigrating to Africa. We hear that at least in 1170 Yakub Almanzur, while still intolerant in his European possessions, permitted some of his "mozarab" subjects to erect churches in Morocco. Cf. Fr. Javier Simonet, *Historia de los Mozárabes de España* (Madrid, 1897-1903), p. 770.

165. Cf. *I.T.,* p. 28 (*Kobeṣ* II, 3d) and, especially, *Resp.* No. 369. The identification of certain elements of Islamic ritual (a continuation of pre-Islamic Arab practices) with the heathen worship of Pe'or, Kemosh and Mercury as described in 'Ab. Zarah 64a, belongs to the class of those facile identifications so prevalent in Greek and Arabian historiography. Maimuni stresses that the Arabs themselves were clearly aware of their pagan origin. For his attitude to Christianity, cf. above, nn. 139-40.

166. *M.T.* Mamrim 3, 3, *Resp.* No. 371, which quotes numerous talmudic passages, as well as R. Judah and R. Hai Gaon (for the identity of the former cf. the references in the editor's note to p. 341). It refers specifically to the Karaites of Egypt, Damascus and the other Muslim countries. The friendly attitude of both Hai and Maimuni may perhaps have come from their apprehension that otherwise many of these sectarians would adopt Islam. At least, Ibn Yaḥya reports such mass desertion from Karaism to the dominant creed. Cf. Schreiner, *MGWJ,* XLII, 260. That Maimuni's friendliness bore

fruit in helping induce numerous Karaites in 1213 to embrace rabbanite Judaism is suggested by Eppenstein, *MbM* II, 44.

167. *Resp*. Nos. 14 and 162. The attempt to impugn the authenticity of the latter responsum (cf. *Ohole Ya'aḳob* quoted in the editor's note), is altogether baseless. The non-validity of Karaite acts in all cases where they do not acknowledge rabbanite law is frequently stressed by Maimuni. *C.M.* to 'Er. VI, 2 (quoting 'Er. 68b f.) and *M.T.* Erubin 2, 16 prohibits association with "Sadducees, Boethuseans and all who deny the oral law" in erecting an *'Erub*. כללו של דבר כל מי שאינו מודה במצות עירוב אין מערבין עמו is the same motivation as that offered in the two responsa. *C.M.* to Ḥul. I, 2 goes further and not only excludes these heretics from the class of מומרים whose slaughtering is declared valid by the Talmud (3a and 17a), but postulates their complete annihilation, in order to prevent the contamination of rabbanite Jewry. "Know ye, that we have a tradition from our teachers" (this term, at least in the Hebrew usage of *M.T.*, may also refer to a single teacher; cf. כללי הרמב"ם No. 13 and A. Schwarz, *Der Mishneh Torah, ein System der mosaisch-talm. Gesetzeslehre* [Vienna, 1905], p. 137), that the discontinuation of capital jurisdiction in the diaspora applies only to Jews committing a capital crime, but not to Epicureans, Sadducees and Boethuseans who should be given no quarter. "Numerous legal precedents to this effect have been established in the western lands." It is possible that this harsh animosity carried over from Spain, where Karaism had been ruthlessly suppressed in the Jewish communities, was later toned down in the light of Egyptian realities. Cf. J. Mann, *Jews in Egypt and Palestine under the Fatimid Caliphs* (London, 1920-22), *passim*. Maimuni's enactments in his adopted country, if animated by anti-Karaite bias as interpreted by Eppenstein, *MbM* II, 40 ff. (cf. *Resp*. No. 99: אבל אנשי מצרים מצינו אותם נוטים לדברי מינות וחולכים אחר סדור הקראים), are of a purely defensive character. Neither are his brief references to Kalam's influence on Karaite (and also rabbanite) thinkers (*M.N.* I, 71) or, for that matter, to the individualistic divergences of Karaite Bible commentators (implied in *C.M.* to Abot I, 3) more than mildly polemical. It is to be regretted that Maimuni (*Resp*. No. 14) has refrained from answering the broader question concerning the differences between rabbanism and Karaism submitted to him by his inquirers. Cf. *ibid.*, p. 43 n. 4. Cf. also Assaf, *op. cit.*, p. 58 and above nn. 136-7.

168. *M.T.* Introd. — *M.T.* Malveh ve-Loveh, 2, 2-4 we have together: כשראו הגאונים הראשונים . . . וכן חורו רבותי . . . ותקנת אחרונים היא (cf. n. 170).—Here is not the place to discuss the relations between the "Geonim" and Maimuni, whom one enthusiastic admirer called עטרת הגאונים (Jedaiah of Beziers, *Ketab ha-Hitnaṣlut*, in Adret, *Responsa* [Venice, 1545], p. 72b). A. Schwarz, "Das Verhältnis Maimuni's zu den Geonen," *MbM* I, 332-410 has assembled sixty-eight passages in *M.T.* where Maimuni expressly quotes the geonim, frequently (in 22 cases) rejecting their opinion. (It is to

be noted that no less than 27 of these passages are to be found in those two sections of M.T. [books XII and XIII] which deal with civil law, thus illustrating the numerous adjustments of the law necessitated by the commercial civilization during the "Renaissance of Islam"). A similar number could easily be culled from *Resp.* and his other writings. But far more numerous are his tacit acceptances or rejections of geonic interpretations. Sometimes he even changes his mind and, after having followed the interpretation of a geonic predecessor, he reconsiders it after a more searching inquiry. Cf. especially, *Resp.* No. 240, where he explains on this score a contradiction between an early edition of *C.M.* and *M.T.* His basic attitudes are well formulated in his reiterated statement, וכל דבר שימצא לאחד מן הגאונים ולא נדע סבתו ראוי לומר בו לא מקרע תקרעוניה ולא מגמר תגמרון מוניה אולי יש להם בזה עיקר (*Resp.* No. 3; cf. also No. 69 cont. p. 364 and No. 345; *M.T.* Introd.). Such benefit of doubt must not extend to a practical decision, however.—Among his numerous references to individual predecessors are especially noteworthy: 1) His exoneration of Saadia's Messianic computation on the ground of the exceptional dangers threatening Judaism in his time. Were it not for his deeds and writings the heretical trends would almost have submerged the Torah. *I.T.,* p. 39 (*Kobeṣ* II, 5b). 2) His reference to Hai's phylacteries, *Resp.* No. 7, in defense of the order of biblical passages as taught in *M.T.* Tefillin 3, 6. In the same connection Maimuni relates a story of how Moses Dar'ai, after arriving in Palestine from Morocco, discarded his phylacteries, because he recognized the validity of the proofs produced by the elder geonim. 3) Hefeṣ b. Yaṣliaḥ is quoted very rarely. In *Resp.* No. 240 he is cited merely to explain Maimuni's own erroneous interpretation. Nevertheless, B. Z. Halper, *A Volume of the Book of Precepts of Ḥ. b. Y.* (Phila., 1915), pp. 59-88, has demonstrated that that work exerted a decisive influence on the early halakhic writings of Maimuni. 4) Alfasi looms large in Maimuni's mind. In *C.M.* Introd. he asserts that one may object only to few of the RIF's legal decisions, the total of such passages by no means exceeding ten. In a later *Resp.* (No. 353) he raises the number to thirty or more. This figure seems to be more or less accurate, since Maimuni, according to that communication, happened to be engaged at that time in the preparation of special scholia to Alfasi's *Halakhot.* He also says that in part he followed Alfasi's own student Ibn Migash, and that in some cases he succeeded in tracing the error back to R. Ḥananel.

169. Cf. e.g., *M.T.* Introd. וכל אלו הגאונים בא"י ובארץ שנער ובספרד ובצרפת *M.T.* Ma'akalot Asurot: הורו גאוני המערב. *Kobeṣ* II, 16d (epistle to Joseph ibn Gabir): ורוב גאונינו מן המערב על דעתנו (quoting later specifically Ibn Gasus, a student of R. Ḥananel). Cf. also his sarcastic remarks concerning the anarchical use of various high-sounding titles in *C.M.* to Bek. IV, 4. For Samuel b. Ali cf. especially *Resp.* No. 67-9 (with cont. pp. 363 ff.) and Eppenstein, *MbM* II, 88 ff. His profound respect for Franco-Jewish learning

comes clearly to the fore in his correspondence with the sages of Lunel. Cf. especially, *Resp.* No. 57, where in answering certain objections to decisions in *M.T.* he mentions that also the Babylonian scholars had attacked a certain passage (Shabbat 20, 7) "with minor matters which would hardly have appeared dubious to you, while they failed to penetrate the depth of your inquiries."—The very uncomplimentary remarks concerning the French scholars in *Kobeṣ* II, 40a are evidently spurious, as is the entire "ethical will," *ibid.,* pp. 38 ff.

170. *Resp.* No. 7 (cf. also p. 356). The following illustrations are particularly interesting: *M.T.* Tefillah 4, 6: מנהג פשוט בשנער ובספרד; *M.T.* Sheḥitah 11, 15: ומעולם לא נהגו זה לא בצרפת ולא בספרד ולא נשמע זה במערב, ואין ראוי; *Resp.* No. 99: לנהוג כמנהג זה . . . וזה מנהגינו המפורסם בכל ארצותינו ובכל ארצות צרפת והוא דין התלמוד ועליו מצינו בני ארץ ישראל כולם בעת שחיינו ביניהם אבל אנשי מצרים מצינו אותם נושים בזה לדברי מינות (the plural in ארצות צרפת evidently refers not only to the feudal subdivisions of contemporary France, but to all western Europe; cf. also Ibn Tibbon's transl. of *M.N.* III, 48, and Munk III, 396 n. 5). *Resp.* No. 97: אבל ברוב ערי מצרים שכחו דיני תורתנו—. In discussing the geonic innovation, imposed by the highly developed credit system of the caliphate, which allowed creditors to collect also from the movable part of the deceased debtor's estate, *M.T.* Malveh ve-Loveh 11, 11 acknowledges that "this is the practice in all Jewish courts in the world." Maimuni adds, nevertheless, that in the West special clauses in loan contracts provide that the creditor may obtain payment from the movable and immovable property both in the lifetime and after the death of the debtor, and highly commends this usage (וסייג גדול עשו בדבר) which obviates the frequent necessity of collecting from orphaned minors in the defiance of talmudic law. Although less specific, some such clauses appear in a few extant early Spanish contracts. Cf. e.g., U. Gonzalez Palencia, *Los Mozárabes de Toledo,* III (Madrid, 1927), No. 1145 which, although concerning a gift, is referred to as חוב גמור בשטר, in which the donor pledges all her present and future fortune. They are not included in the loan contract published in Meir Abulafia's responsum in *'Or la-Ṣaddiḳim* (Salonica, 1799), No. 262, nor in No. 3 of the early Spanish Shetarot, published by R. J. H. Gottheil, *JQR,* O.S. XVI (1903-4), p. 706. Cf. in general also F. Baer, *Die Juden im christlichen Spanien,* I (Berlin, 1929), pp. 1044 ff. It is remarkable, however, that Maimuni seems to ignore a similar practice in Babylonia which must have been prevalent enough to warrant Hai's inclusion in his formula for a *usual* loan contract: ואחריות שטר חוב דנן עלי . . . ועל ירתאי בתראי על כל שפר ארג נכסין וקנין וממון דאית לי . . . בין ממקרקעי ובין מן מטלטלי . . . ed. Assaf, *op. cit.,* p. 21. Cf. also Schwarz, *MbM* I, 346, 372 ff. and 391 ff. It seems that by גאונים האחרונים here Maimuni wishes to accentuate that this was not an enactment of the גאונים הראשונים (*M.T. ibid.* 2, 2), evidently referring to the Saboraim. Cf. *Maimuni Glosses, ibid., SeMaG* Commandment

93 and Zacuto, *Yuḥasin,* p. 204a (against Schwarz, pp. 386 f.). It is possible that גאונים קדמונים in *Resp.* No. 7 likewise refers to the Saboraim (cf. n. 168).—
M.T. Ḥobel u-Mazzik 8, 11 discusses the punishment of hardened informers and states ומעשים בכל זמן בערי המערב להרוג המוסרים שהוחזקו למסור ממון
... להרגם . ולמסור המוסרים ביד העכו"ם ישראל. This passage is equivocal in two crucial points: 1) Is the capital punishment of informers, here intimated, directly executed or at least pronounced by Jewish courts (as is possibly intimated also in *C.M.* to Ḥul. I, 2), or do the Jews merely hand over the criminal to the general courts for both condemnation and execution? 2) Do the ערי המערב include, as is usual, both Muslim Spain and Morocco, or do they refer here exclusively to Christian Spain, where at least in the later middle ages capital jurisdiction over informers was well established. More information about the Jewish judicial autonomy in Muslim Spain is needed before a definite answer to these questions may be given. J. Mann's theory (סקירה היסטורית על "דיני נפשות בזמן הזה" in *Dissertations hebraicae* in honor of L. Blau, pp. 200-208), that the Muslim conquerors after 712 extended this right to the Jews in recognition of their assistance, is thus far admittedly based upon very slender evidence.—In certain cases Maimuni explains regional differences on meteorological grounds. Cf. e.g., *Resp.* No. 363.

171. *S.M.* Introd. Already David ibn Zimra (*Responsa* III, No. 645) recognized that Maimuni had particularly Ibn Gabirol in mind. For his opposition to the *Piyyutim* cf. especially *Resp.* No. 360.— He holds in much higher esteem the exegetical literature. He not only quotes with approval commentators, such as Chiquitilla, Ibn Balaam and Ibn Ezra (cf. *Kobeṣ* II, 9d and 27a and n. 45), but specifically includes Jewish Bible commentaries in the general prohibition of burning or destroying Scriptures. *M.T.* Yesode ha-Torah 6, 8. Cf. *BB,* p. 174.

172. *Resp.* No. 373 (cf. the literature cited there). The דרשינן אלרום in the Arabic text of Geiger-Heilberg, *Nit'e Ne'emanim* (Breslau, 1847), p. 17b are cited likewise in this Hebrew term in the Arabic of *C.M.* to Sanh. X Introd. and *M.N.* II, 29. Cf. Bacher, *MbM* II, 141.

173. *M.T.* Megillah ve-Ḥanukkah 3, 14; Matnot 'Aniyim 9, 3; *Resp.* No. 202; *C.M.* to Giṭ. V, 8; *M.T.* Sanh. 6, 9.—Of special historical interest is also *C.M.* to Meg. I,1 and *M.T.* Megillah ve-Ḥanukkah 1, 4-9. Commenting on the talmudic law which allowed the reading of the Book of Esther between the 11th and 15th of Adar and stated that the people of Susa used to read it on the fifteenth in commemoration of their own miracle, he insists that this applied only "to the time when we were powerful enough to observe the commandments in their fullness, but nowadays, i.e., from the redaction of the Talmud to the coming of the Messiah (speedily in our days), one reads it only in the regular days of the 14th and 15th." The reading on the fifteenth is restricted to the inhabitants of those Palestinian cities which had been walled in in the days of Joshua (cf. n. 82) and of Susa. Did he refer to con-

temporary Palestinians and Baghdadians?—*C.M.* to 'Ab. Zarah I, 9 stresses the difference between the talmudic age when leasing a bathhouse to a Gentile, because infrequent, was prohibited, lest the Jewish owner be suspected of breaking the Sabbath (cf. Tos. 'Ab. Zarah II, 9 and b. 21b), and "our" days when such leaseholds were similar in nature to those of land. *M.T.* Shabbat 6, 15 is non-committal on the subject and the German *Maimuni Glosses*, evidently reflecting German realities, where the bathhouse usually was a communal enterprise, once more quote bathhouses as an illustration of forbidden, because rare, leaseholds.—For Maimuni's insistence on the continued obligation to observe the Sabbatical year cf. especially *Resp.* No. 233, and of the Levitical tithes, *ibid.*, No. 133, where the general principle is repeated that "all the commandments are valid anywhere and anytime unless it is specifically stated that they apply only to Palestine or only during the existence of a Temple." Cf. also *S.H.* Introd. Root 8.—In *Resp.* No. 5 Maimuni records that he had combated a custom prevalent in Egypt to place on the necks of children silver or gold boards inscribed with the "Song of Afflictions" (Ps. 91.1-9). Cf. Shebuot 15b.

174. *M.T.* Nizke Mamon 8, 5. Maimuni substitutes this rational and relatively humane motivation for the rigidly nationalistic ones given in B.Ḳ. 38a. Cf. also *Mishneh le-Melek, ad. loc.* In *C.M.* to B.Ḳ. IV, 3 he had followed the anti-Gentile orientation of the two talmudic sages and stated that, in cases of damages, the Jew has the choice to apply either the Jewish or the Gentile law in question, dependent on which is more favorable to himself. "You need not be astounded by that as you are not perturbed over the slaughtering of innocent animals, because he who does not possess the full measure of human qualities is not really a full-fledged man, but the purpose of his existence is to satisfy the needs of real men. A discussion of this subject would require special treatment, however." In offering the argument of reciprocity, on the other hand, Maimuni pays no attention to the *historical* aspect of whether such practice existed in the Roman law of the time of R Johanan and R. Abahu. As to Muslim law it may suffice to state here that even homicide and mayhem committed by a Muslim on a *dhimmi* was not punished by full retaliation. For the opinion of the Shiyites, e.g., cf. the thirteenth-century compilation of Al-Muhakkik, transl. by A. Querry, *Recueil des lois concernant les Musulmans schyites* III, 11.137; 317-21 in Vol. II (Paris, 1872), pp. 565 ff. and in general W. Heffening, *Das islamische Fremdenrecht* (Hanover, 1925), pp. 37-44. It is little wonder that *RABD*, no less unhistorically, generalizes what apparently was Provençal usage in his time, and states that Gentile courts in such cases seized the animal in question. This in turn evoked the humorous reply of Vidal of Tolosa who pointed out that Spanish (probably = Catalan) law gave the right to the guilty man to remove his animal and thus escape punishment. Cf. *Migdal 'Oz, ad. loc.* Notwithstanding the possibility, however, that Maimuni spent some time in Christian Almeria (cf.

Lebrecht-Berliner, *MbM* II, 114), his familiarity with the Christian law of Spain is rather dubious.

175. *M.N.* III, 48.—Of historical interest are also the numerous references in Maimuni's writings to extended commercial travels of Jews to India. Cf. especially, *Resp.* Nos. 214, 265, 267, 272, 275, 331, 335. This movement which had apparently begun in the Persian age, had assumed such proportions under the Caliphate, that in tenth-century Sura it became proverbial that "he who goes to India gets rich." Cf. Saadia, *Beliefs and Opinions,* Introd. Characteristically, *I.T.,* p. 48 (*Kobeṣ* II, 7a) explains Isa. 18.2 as referring to the tidings of Israel's restoration which will penetrate distant India.

176. *M.N.* III, 51. While these אלתרך and אלסודאן are supposed to have no religion, *M.N.* III, 29 speaks of תרך and אלהנוד (Turks in the North and Hindus in the South) where are to be found remnants of ancient Sabean heathendom. In *M.N.* III, 46 Hindus are quoted once more as preservers of ancient paganism. Cf. also Munk, III, 221 n. 4; 362 n. 4 and 434 n. 1 and Al-Biruni, *Chronology,* Engl. transl., p. 191. Ethnologically even more remarkable is Maimuni's repetition without comment of the talmudic injunction that he who sees a Kushite or other people different in physiognomy from the mass of the population should recite a special benediction. *M.T.* Berakot 10, 12, on the basis of Ber. 58b. The existence of numerous Negro slaves in all Muslim lands must have made such legal observance much more cumbersome than in Roman Palestine, where it had first been enacted.

177. This material has been first published in Hebrew translation and interpreted by J. Mann at the end of his comprehensive Hebrew study of the "Messianic Movements during the First Crusades," in *Hatekufah,* XXIII (1925), pp. 243-61 and XXIV (1928), pp. 335-58.

178. Interest in chronology was generally very vivid under Islam, where the accuracy of a tradition was frequently checked by chronological details. This applied not only to controversial literary and theological problems, but also to political and economic privileges claimed by various groups in the population. It is reported, for example, that a document produced by a Jew of Khaibar, in which allegedly 'Ali b. Abi Talib at Muhammed's order granted the Jews of that region a remission of the poll tax, was proved to be forged by certain anachronisms in the names of witnesses: one had died two years before the taking of Khaibar, another became a Muslim a year later. Cf. Margoliouth, *Arabic Historians,* p. 149. Some Arabs took pains to establish even the chronologies of the unbelievers. For a contemporary of Saadia cf. M. Steinschneider, "Die jüdische Chronik nach Hamza el-Isfahani," in *Zeitschrift für die religiösen Interessen des Judentums,* II (1845), pp. 271-78 and 321-28. With the work of Al-Biruni, particularly, chronology in the mathematical as well as historical sense, became a highly developed science.—For the mathematical aspects of Maimuni's chronological work, especially important where he discusses the Jewish calendar, cf. E. Baneth, "Maimonides

als Chronologe und Astronom," *MbM* II, 243-79.—Maimuni's chronological sense is frequently revealed by such incidental remarks as when, after enumerating the Tannaim quoted as the bearers of one or more traditions in the Mishnah, he states, "We have not followed the chronological order in this list of names." *C.M.* Introd. ch. I.

179. There are two detailed chronological statements of Maimuni which are in many ways complementary, especially since they were written only one year apart (1175-6): *Resp.* No. 234 and *M.T.* Shemiṭṭah ve-Yobel 10, 2-8. Schwarz, *MbM* I, 369 ff. commenting on the latter failed to take sufficient account of the responsum. The figure in *M.T.* §2: נמצאת אומר בשנת שלש וחמש מאות ואלפים ליצירה ליצירה מראש השנה מאחר מולד אדם הראשון שנה שניה ליצירה becomes plain when the first ליצירה is deleted as an obvious insertion of a copyist. It is, indeed, lacking in Ms. Trivulzio. Cf. *Shinnuye Nushaot, ad. loc.* This date (more exact than the round number of 2500 years which were supposed to have elapsed between Adam and Moses, *M.N.* III, 50), is in accordance with the chronology of *Seder 'Olam,* etc.

180. *Ibid.,* on the basis of 'Ar. 12 f.

101. *M.T.* 88, on the basis of 'Ar. 32b.

182. *Resp., l. c.,* based upon the well-known rabbinic chronology of 'Ab. Zarah 9a: מלכות פרס בפני הבית שלשים וארבע שנה and that the Seleucid era began with the first year of Alexander's conquest. Whether or not this was the original meaning of that passage (cf. A. Z. Lauterbach, "Misunderstood Chronological Statements in the Talmudic Literature," *Proceedings of the American Academy for Jewish Research,* V, 77-84), Maimuni and all medieval rabbis so understood it. Cf. above n. 127. Adding the first seven years of the Temple until Ezra one obtains the forty-one years. It is evident, therefore, that לפי שבשנת אחד וארבעים לחרבן התחילו למנות לשטרות, although apparently found in all Mss. and editions, should read: לבנין הבית, since otherwise there is no room left for the seventy years of Babylonian Exile, stressed also in *M.T.* §3.

183. Cf. R. Hai Gaon's responsum in *Teshubot ha-Geonim,* ed. Harkavy, No. 45, where the chronological data are generally more exact. The divergence between his and Maimuni's interpretation is explainable in view of contradictory talmudic sources, many passages in which clearly bear the marks of afterthoughts. Cf. also Schwarz *l. c.* The geonic "tradition" dating back to the talmudic age is borne out also by recent excavations which show that, long after the fall of Jerusalem, the era of destruction was combined with that of Sabbatical cycles. On the other hand, the tombstone inscription of Kasr et-Tuba dated "on the first day of Marḥeshvan of the first year of the shemiṭṭah in the year 364 since the destruction of the Temple" (cf. L. H. Vincent, "Une colonie juive oubliée," *Révue biblique,* LXXXV [1927], pp. 401-7 and Th. Reinach, "Inscriptions de Touba," *REJ,* LXXXV [1928], pp. 1-10) is inconclusive with respect to our main controversy as to whether the jubilee

cycles continue to count in 50 or only in 49 year ranges. 364 happens to be either $7 \times 50 + 14$ or $7 \times 49 + 21$. In any case, it confirms the talmudic-Maimonidean statement that the destruction took place in the first year of the cycle or at least that the computation לחרבן began in such a year. Cf. also, in general, H. J. Bornstein, תאריכי ישראל, *Haṭekufah*, VIII (1920), pp. 281-338 and IX (1921), pp. 202-64 and E. Mahler, *Handbuch der jüdischen Chronologie* [Leipzig, 1916], pp. 149 ff. and 409.

184. *Resp.* No. 239 referring to the year 1196 (not 1198) which had just passed. It is only remarkable that Maimuni's solemn injunctions *M.T., l. c.* §6: ועל זה אנו סומכין וכפי החשבון הזה אנו מורין ... שהקבלה והמעשה עמודים גדולים בהוראה ובהן ראוי להתלות had so little effect upon some of his enthusiastic disciples.

185. While *C.M.* Introd. is limited to the series of Abot: Joshua—elders—prophets—men of the Great Synagogue, *M.T.* Introd. enumerates nineteen names between Joshua and Ezra. Eleazar as Moses' student is mentioned 'Er. 54b. (Incidentally, *C.M.'s* preference for R. Judah's theory concerning Aaron's seat to the right rather than the left of Moses evidently comes from the later seating order in the Sanhedrin, where the vice-chairman is placed to the right of the president; cf. above n. 142). Both Eleazar and Phinehas are mentioned as authors of the final section of the book Joshua in B.B. 15a, whence may be inferred that both survived the great conqueror. Among the other "elders" Maimuni undoubtedly counted Othniel, the son of Kenaz. Since he accepted the period of 369 years for the tabernacle at Shiloh, whose transfer there after fourteen years in Gilgal must have more or less coincided with the death of Joshua, and allowing for Eli's pontificate of forty years (cf. *Seder 'Olam* 13 and Zacuto, *Yuḥasin*, p. 7a), he had to accept Phinehas' longevity, although he nowhere refers to the well-known identification of Phinehas with Elijah, accepted, e.g., by Gersonides. Cf. *GL*, VI, 138 n. 803; 214 n. 140; 220 n. 25; 316 n. 3 and *Yuḥasin*, p. 9a. In fact, they appear as the third and the eighth members of the group respectively. Cf. next note.

186. For David's prophetic gifts cf. above n. 91. The assumption that Ahijah was among those redeemed from Egypt and that he had lived through the 40 years of the desert migration, the 400 years that elapsed between the settlement and the building of the Solomonian Temple and the remainder of Solomon's reign (36 years) until the anointment of Jeroboam I (cf. n. 105) seems to Maimuni no more impossible than Phinehas' long life. He uncritically takes over the statement of B.B. 121b (like Rashi *s.v.* אחיה, he may have seen therein a refusal to accept the equation of Phinehas and Elijah) and *Seder 'Olam* 1. He refrains from mentioning, however, Ahijah's birth 60 years before the Exodus and his martyr's death under Abijah. The purpose of this historical excursus which evoked the opposition of RABD (this seems to be the meaning of his note rather than the difference between David and David's

court, as suggested by Karo *ad. loc.*) was perhaps to forestall the more orthodox objection that Ahijah might appear as a direct continuator of Moses.
187. For Elijah as Ahijah's successor see 'Er. *l. c.* His disciple was Elisha,
which ruled out Obadiah, the prophet, whom the Aggadah identified with
king Ahab's official bearing that name and made one of Elijah's prominent
pupils. Besides, his allegedly Edomite descent, although far from preventing
him from becoming a prophet of doom for Edom, certainly did not enhance
his eligibility in the eyes of Maimuni. Cf. Sanh. 39b and other sources listed
in *GL*, VI, 34 f. nn. 6-7. Elisha's successor was Jehoiada rather than Jonah,
very likely in view of the glowing description of the former's restoration of
the worship in Jerusalem in II Chr. 23.16 ff. Incidentally when *M.T.* Kle
ha-Mikdash 5, 10 somewhat modifies the rigid prohibition for the high priest
to marry two wives, stated in *M.T.* Issure Biah 17, 13, by giving him the
choice of divorcing one wife before the Day of Atonement, Maimuni may have
had compunctions over II Chr. 24.3, although he might have interpreted it,
as did Josephus and the Vulgate, as referring to Joash or, like Vidal of Tolosa,
as meaning two wives succeeding one another. Cf. *RABD* and *Maggid
Mishneh* Issure Biah *l. c.* and *GL*, VI, 354 n. 11. Jonah was discarded because
of his preachment to a foreign city only, the frequently unfavorable comments
of the Aggadah and, perhaps, because after leaving the country he had no
direct successor. Zechariah lent himself to serve as another link because of
the characterization כהן ונביא ודיין in j. Ta'anit IV, 5, 69a. The chronological
difficulty that Jehoiada and his son were southern contemporaries of the
Northern Israelite, Elisha, if it came at all to Maimuni's mind, would have
troubled him little, since contemporaries may well serve as successive transmitters to later generations. Cf. e.g., Zacuto, *Yuḥasin,* p. 9a who following
closely Maimuni's list, nevertheless, admits the possibility that Jehoiada died
before Elisha and Zechariah only two years after him.—A similar succession
of contemporaries, due to seniority, is the following group of Hosea, Amos,
Isaiah and Micah. Cf. *Seder 'Olam* 20; Pes. 87a, etc. Hosea's precedence
before Amos is based upon the arrangement of the redactor of the Minor
Prophets and, perhaps, also upon Hos. 1.2 בהושע תחלת דבר ה', quoted to this
effect in *Yuḥasin,* p. 9b.—In the date of Joel, Nahum and Habakkuk Maimuni
follows *Seder 'Olam* 20, where they are all placed under the reign of Manasseh, as against other rabbinic chronologies. Cf. *GL*, VI, 314 f. n. 98 and above
n. 112. Their relative position is indicated by the redactor of Minor Prophets.
Cf. also *Yuḥasin, l. c.*—Zephaniah is the natural transition to Jeremiah and
his disciple Baruch. The failure to mention Ezekiel is due not only to the
precedence given to Baruch who was both a student of Jeremiah and a teacher
of Ezra, as suggested by Bacher, *MbM* II, 147, but, possibly, also because of
certain dubious points in the exilic prophet's Halakhah. Cf. also his quotation
of the somewhat uncomplimentary remark in Mekilta Beshalaḥ (to Ex. 15.2)
in *C.M.* to Abot Eight Chapters 4 end.

188. M. Abot I. Cf. above nn. 125 and 147.

189. This list of two Gamaliels and three Simons is stated in the main section of *M.T.* Introd. and *C.M.* Introd. ch. III, but is shortened in the subsequent summary of forty generations in *M.T.* and the general survey in *C.M.*, both of which speak only of one Gamaliel and two Simons. Although partly supported by M. Abot I (where, however, the first Simon is missing), the latter reading is evidently a copyist's mistake, because it would furnish thirty-eight instead of forty generations. In *C.M.* ch. IV he fails to mention R. Gamaliel of Yabneh and his son, Simon, in the second and third generation after the fall of Jerusalem, but he must have realized that there was a gap between R. Simon b. Gamaliel of the first and R. Judah of the fourth generation. The historical situation is too obvious, the sources too outspoken for Maimuni to have overlooked them completely. The listing of R. Johanan b. Zakkai directly after Hillel is due to the well-known Aggadah that he was his youngest disciple. Cf. j. Ned. V, 6, 39b. But apparently Maimuni agreed that he did not serve as *nasi* until after Gamliel the Elder. Cf. Zacuto, *Yuhasin,* p. 19b. Zacuto's attempt (p. 21a) to explain Maimonides enumeration as substituting 30) R. Johanan; 31) R. Eliezer and R. Joshua; 32) R. Akiba for the three Hillelites is untenable. His objections, however, to Maimuni's artificial classification, that the greatest Tannaim, such as Hillel, Shammai, Shemaiah and Abtalion, were cited without a prefix by the redactor of the Mishnah, the next greatest quoted with the title "Rabban," and all the others with that of "Rabbi" (*C.M.* Introd. ch. VII) are undoubtedly valid. Cf. p. 20a, etc.

190. That Palestine's amoraic scholarship was discontinued after R. Johanan is in accordance with Maimuni's conviction that R. Johanan was the redactor of the Palestinian Talmud, although the date of three hundred years after the destruction is obviously an overstatement. It is even more clearly so, when one realizes that Maimuni assigns only one hundred years more for the compilation of the Babylonian Talmud under R. Ashi four generations later. Had Maimuni interpreted the statement in Kid. 72b to mean that R. Ashi was not born until after Raba's death, he would have had to insert another generation of R. Papa. But he evidently read with Alfasi: עד שלא מת רבא נולד ר' אשי which not only emphasizes the workings of Providence much better, but also corresponds more closely to the parallel of Eli and Samuel. Cf. *Yuhasin,* pp. 117b and 203b.—Maimuni realizes, however, that R. Ashi did not complete the redaction of the Babylonian Talmud. He qualifies his אשי הוא שחיבר הגמרא הבבלית ור' by adding not only Rabina, but also R. Ashi's son to the list of transmitters, sums up אשי ור' רבינא נמצא and adds ואחר ב"ד וחבריהם סוף גדולי חכמי ישראל חמעתיקים תורה שבעל פה של ר' אשי שחבר הגמרא וגמרו בימי בנו.

191. It would transcend the bounds of the present paper to enumerate all the "contemporaries," although a fresh reëxamination of Maimuni's selection

and dating in the light of present day knowledge would undoubtedly clarify certain details in his historical approach.

192. The entire period of forty generations covered some 1780 years. It included: 40 years of desert migration, 440 years from the settlement to the building of the Temple, 410 under the first Temple = 890 years; 70 years of the Babylonian Exile, 420 of the Second Commonwealth and 400 between the destruction and R. Ashi — 890 years. It is this sense of symmetry very likely which influenced his late dating of R. Ashi, as compared with Sherira's 738 Sel. era = 359 after the destruction.—This average of 45 years is also borne out by the ten generations from Ezra to R. Eleazar b. Azariah over a period of approximately 450 years.

193. *M.T.* 'Abodat Kokabim 1, 1. A similar thought had been expressed by Ibn Gabirol, "Yet is not Thy glory diminished by reason of those that worship aught besides Thee, for the yearning of them all is to draw nigh Thee" (*Keter Malkut* in *Selected Religious Poems,* ed. by I. Davidson and transl. by I. Zangwill, p. 86).

194. *Pirke Mosheh* in *Kobeṣ* II, 22d f. and Epistle to Samuel ibn Tibbon, *ibid.,* p. 27c. For Maimuni's general theory of the conventional origin of languages cf. *M.N.* II, 30 and the comments as well as parallels in *BB,* pp. 163 f. It appears likely that Maimuni's racial theory is based on the assumption of Al-Maqdasi (*op. cit.* III, 33) and others that the Persians as well as the Greeks were descendants of Shem, although the Jews generally associated the Greeks with the Japhethite group. For the Semitic origin of the Persians, cf. also Mas'udi, *op. cit.,* I, 78.—It is interesting that in that discussion of human cultures both China and India completely escape Maimuni's vision. He does not seem to know anything about China, although among his Arab predecessors and contemporaries some travellers' reports concerning the great eastern civilization were fairly current. Even Benjamin of Tudela has a faint notion of it. India is frequently referred to in Maimonides' writings (cf. n. 175), but he fails to draw it into the orbit of the general history of civilization, probably because its influence upon Arabian thought was rather indirect. Shahrastani (*op. cit.,* I, 3), on the other hand, counts the Indians, along with the Arabs, Persians and Greeks among the four leading nations of history.— It is also noteworthy that on all occasions he paraphrases "the seventy languages" of the Talmud by "most languages," thus revealing the enormous impact of Arabic in his day. *C.M.* to Sotah VII and *M.T.* Sanh. 2, 6. For practical purposes, he decides in *Resp.* No. 102, it is sufficient when a judge understands the language of the parties concerned, without having a speaking knowledge of it. Notwithstanding his admiration for Hebrew, Maimuni insists, against the opinion of his "teachers" (probably Ibn Migash), that an oath administered in the courts may be sworn in any language known to the party or witness and that, although the general practice is to recite the oath in Hebrew, the person concerned should at least be made to understand the

content of the oath in his own language. *M.T.* Shebuot 11, 14. Cf also Schwarz, *MbM* I, 363 f.

195. Cf. above nn. 180-82.

196. *I.T.*, pp. 22 ff. (*Kobeṣ* II, 1d and 2d), *M.N.* II, 29 and *M.T.* Issure Biah 14, 4-5.—Of course, Jewish sufferings have been intensified through the dispersion. *I.S.*, p. 12b written in the defense of forcible converts appropriately lends a most moving expression to that idea of eternal suffering ומיום שגלינו מארצנו לא פסק ממנו שמד כי מנעורינו גדלנו כאב ומבטן אמנו ינחנו. The homiletical interpretation of Gen. 14.14 is a variation of the two given in Gen. r. 69, 5: מה עפר הארץ מבלה את כלי מתכות והוא קיים לעולם כך בניך מבלים מה פלטיה זו מבלה את העוברים והשבים והיא and את כל או"ה והן קיימים לעולם קיימת לעולם כך וכו'. Cf. also Theodor-Albeck, pp. 395 f. and 794 f. The formula in *M.T.* is a characteristic Maimonidean variation of הוי יודע שהעולם חבא אינו עשוי אלא לצדיקים וישראל בזמן הזה אינם יכולים לקבל לא רוב טובה ומודיעין אותו עיקרי ולא רוב פורעניות in Bar. Yeb. 47ab. So is the addition הדת שהוא יחוד השם ואיסור עכו"ם and the generally greater sympathy for proselytism. Israel is nevertheless bound to praise God for his manifold benefactions, especially in the various benedictions, such as were recited during the first offerings or still are being read when one sees a place where miracles were once performed for Jews. Cf. e.g., *S.H.* Commandment 132 and *M.T.* Berakot 10, 9.

197. *I.T.*, p. 22 (*Kobeṣ* II, 2c) referring to Ps. 129.1-2; Maimuni's interpretation of Ex. 19.6, as quoted by his son Abraham, in Eppenstein *MbM* I, 117 f. and *I.S.*, p. 7b. Cf. nn. 49 and 111. According to Bahya b. Asher, Maimuni stressed, with reference to Deut. 7.7, that God in choosing Israel disregarded its small number, whereas an earthly king normally prefers a large retinue. Cf. Eppenstein, pp. 119 ff.

198. *M.N.* I, 71 beg., repeating a contention widespread among Maimuni's Jewish and non-Jewish predecessors and contemporaries. Cf. Munk I, 332 n. 3.—For Ibn Yaḥya cf. n. 5. That many Jews were so impressed by the power of Islam and the political impotence of Jewry as to abandon their ancestral creed is intimated by Maimuni himself, I. T. p. 16 (*Kobeṣ* II, 1c).

199. *I.T.*, especially pp. 21 and 44 ff. (*Kobeṣ* II, 1d f. and 6b), supporting the Messianic implications of Dan. 7.17 ff. by many other Scriptural passages. The interpretation of Daniel's vision, which naturally varied with the ages, was under Islam usually given in an historic succession of empires with Islam as the fourth or last, to be superseded by the advent of the Messiah. The Arab view, on the other hand, is best expressed in the following passage of Ṭabari (*Book of Religion and Empire*, p. 136): "The fourth beast . . . is the image of this Arab kingdom, about which God said that it shall be the greatest and the highest of all kingdoms, and that it shall dominate all the earth, tread it down under its feet and devour it completely. It is also the latest

kingdom; and this testifies to the fact that the Prophet . . . is the last prophet; that all prophecies were realized through him, ended with him and did not go beyond him. To this all the preceding prophecies pointed and referred." Maimuni appears, however, to combine the idea of succession with that of simultaneity, inasmuch as he sees in the Arabian expansion the victory of the fourth Empire over the preceding three of Greece (Byzantium), Rome—Edom (western Europe) and Sassanian Persia. For various older interpretations cf. e.g., the sources listed in *GL*, VI, 63 n. 323. The basis of the family tradition evidently was Balaam's date and the statement in j. Shab. VI, 9, 8d כבחצי ימיו של עולם היה אותו רשע עומד. Cf. n. 71. Characteristically, Maimuni makes no use of the date in Dan. 12.12, utilized by most other Jewish and non Jewish "computers of the end." Christians and Muslims had to use the suspicious method of *gematria* to find in 1335 the equivalent of either Jesus or Muhammed. E.g. in Ṭabari, pp. 137 ff. it is equal to the numerical value of the Arabic letters of "Muhammed, the last prophet, the Mahdi, the illustrious."

200. Here is not the place to discuss the full implications of Maimuni's messianic doctrine, as laid down, especially, in C.M. to Sanh. X Introd. and Principle 12; *M.T.* Melakim 11-12 and *I.T. passim*. It suffices for us to realize that the messianic hope was the true culmination of Maimuni's historical outlook. It was a humanitarian, pacifist and intellectual hope, best characterized in the concluding sentences of his code, "The sages and prophets did not yearn for the days of the Messiah, in order to rule the world, tyrannize the heathens and receive homage from the nations, nor in order to eat and drink and enjoy life, but that they be free to devote themselves to the study of the Torah and its wisdom without oppression and interference, and that they gain the world to come. . . . At that time, there will be neither hunger, nor war, nor envy and rivalry, because there will be an abundance of everything, and everybody's concern will only be to know God, so that the Jews will be great sages, who will understand the hidden things and achieve the knowledge of their Creator to the limit of human capacity." Cf. also *M.T.* Teshubah 9, 3 and, for the reërection of the Sanhedrin, *C.M.* to Sanh. I, 3 and *M.T.* Sanh. 4, 11. Maimuni's theory that an agreement of all Palestinian rabbis to ordain a group of scholars would reinstall the chain of ordination led to the well-known controversy between Jacob Berab and Levi ibn Ḥabib in the sixteenth century.

201. *C.M.* Introd. and *M.N.* Introd.

202. *M.N.* III, 50 and *C.M.* to Sanh. X Principle 8. Cf. also above nn. 35 and 110.

203. *M.N.* I, 71 in his polemic with the early Mutakallimun, Syriac as well as Arabic.—II, 15 argument against majority opinion is paralleled by similar utterances of Halevi, Albo, etc., as pointed out by Schreiner, *MGWJ*, XLII, 132 n. 1. The likely influence of the Muslim *ijma'* upon the reiterated Mai-

monidean emphasis upon ישראל כל עליהם הסכימו ,הסכימו ישראל בכל ופשטו, *M.T.*
Introd., etc., has been pointed out by L. Blau, *MbM* II, 351 ff. It must be
realized, however, that this method of reconciling a general binding law
with divergent local customs and social needs became such an urgent necessity
in both the vast caliphate and the still vaster Jewish dispersion that it undoubtedly would have been invented in full independence of one another.

204. In his epistle to Ibn Aknin, 1190, Maimuni defines the task of the
conscientious man as one "who does not want to state anything which he
cannot support by argument and without knowing where it has been said
and how it can be demonstrated." (Munk, *Notice*, p. 31). For his basic
acceptance of Christian and Muslim traditions cf., in particular, his polemic
against both in *I.T.* His rejection of the authority of the Aggadah, when it
contradicts his logical or theological convictions, is well illustrated by his
defense of his own doctrine of free will and retribution., "He who sets aside
our statements built upon authoritative foundations and searches in some
Aggadah, Midrash or utterance of one of the geonim until he finds there a
passage to impugn our words, which are words of knowledge and wisdom, is
but committing intellectual suicide." *Resp.* No. 345. His historical outlook,
however, is wholly determined by the aggadic elaborations of past events.
Here, too, he rejects all legends which appear rationally impossible, but not
those which lack confirmation in the original sources. Only occasionally
he shelves the responsibility by a cautious remark, such as רב על עליו אמרו
that he had never been seen going four ells without Torah, show-fringes
and philacteries. *M.T.* Tefillin u-Mezuzah 4, 25 on the basis of Meg. 28a
where, however, our texts read R. Ze'era. As to the minutiae of textual criticism one need refer merely to his ceaseless efforts to secure reliable manuscripts,
his numerous textual emendations and his objections to hasty conclusions
from a passage without considering its context (cf. *I.T.*, p. 32; *Kobeṣ* II, 4b)
to see how "modern" in many ways was his scientific approach. So is the
remark in his narrative at the end of *I.T.* concerning his "verification" of a
Messianic incident which had occurred not long before.

205. *I.T.*, pp. 39 f. (*Kobeṣ* II, 5b f.), where the futility of astrological predictions is demonstrated by the example of the Egyptian and Chaldean
astrologers in the days of Moses and the Exile who foretold the perpetual
prosperity of their nations and the eternal subjection of Israel. Similarly
God will disprove the contention of more recent enemies, that the Jewish
people would never be redeemed, by speedily sending the Messiah.

206. Cf. above nn. 50, 84, 88, 91, 103, 112, and 187 ff. The influence of
Maimuni's historical views on the subsequent writers deserves special monographic treatment.

AZARIAH DE' ROSSI: A BIOGRAPHICAL SKETCH

1. Isaiah Sonne, "Contributions to the History of the Jews in Bologna at the Beginning of the Sixteenth Century" (Hebrew), *HUCA,* XVI (1941), 38 n. 4.

2. This translation was appended to the first edition of the Greek original printed by Schardius in Basel, 1561.

3. In the two best editions by Isaac Benjacob and David Cassel the entire fourth section of Azariah's *magnum opus* is erroneously included under that heading. This designation runs counter to the author's expressed statements at the beginnings of chapters xxix and xlii, as well as to the first edition which appeared in his own lifetime.

4. De' Rossi, *Me'or 'Eynaim,* XXVIII, ed. by Benjacob, I; ed. by Cassel, pp. 269 f.

5. David Kaufmann, "Contributions à l'histoire des luttes d'Azaria de Rossi," *REJ,* XXXIII (1896), 77-87 (appeared later in its German original in Kaufmann's *Gesammelte Schriften,* ed. by Marcus Brann, 3 vols. [Frankfort, 1908-15], III, 83-95).

6. A communication by Elisha Galico and the testimony of Meir Alshech cited by Hayyim Joseph David Azulai in his *Mahziq berakhah* (Conveying Blessings), on *Orah Hayyim,* Supplements no. 315 (Leghorn, 1785), fol. 133b; Jacob Emden, *She'elat Ya'avits.* See also S. Z. H. Halberstam, "Three Letters about the Book Me'or 'Eynaim, etc." (Hebrew), *Festschrift Moritz Steinschneider* (Leipzig, 1896), p. 4; and Giuseppe Jaré, "Excerpts from the Writings of Hananel Neppi" (Hebrew), *Festschrift A. Harkavy* (St. Petersburg, 1908), Hebrew section, pp. 466 ff.

7. This eternal dualism between God and the world is one of the most tions: Mantua, 1573-75, new ed. by Isaac Satanov, Berlin, 1794; Vienna, 1829-30; Vilna, 1865 (ed. by Isaac Benjacob); Vilna, 1864-66 (ed. by David Cassel). Published almost at the same time, the latter two editions are far superior to the earlier ones, and that by Cassel is also provided by the editor with excellent notes and an Index. A subsequent edition with notes by Z. H. Jaffe appeared in Warsaw, 1899. De' Rossi's book, *Masref le-khesef* was first edited by Hirsch Filipowski in Edinburgh, 1854, and was later reproduced in the aforementioned Benjacob and Cassel editions.

The following additional literature is also noteworthy: Leopold Zunz, "The Life of Azariah de' Rossi" (with additions by him and S. J. L. Rapoport; Hebrew), *Kerem Chemed,* V, VII (reprinted with minor changes in Benjacob's ed.); L. Modona, "Une lettre d'Azaria de Rossi," *REJ,* XXX (1895), 313-16 (dated March 14, 1576); Eliezer Landshut, *'Ammude ha-'Abodah,* p. 301; Zunz, *Synagogale Poesie,* p. 419; J. Bergmann, "Gedichte Asarja de Rossi's," *Zeitschrift für hebräische Bibliographie,* III (1899), 53-58.

AZARIAH DE' ROSSI'S ATTITUDE TO LIFE

1. See above, Essay no. 7. The following references to Azariah's opinions are quoted from the two best and most popular editions of Benjacob and D. Cassel. מצרף לכסף = מ"ל, צדק עולמים = צ"ע.

2. I, 18 (C. 19): העולם אשר הוא אדם גדול . . . לאדם שהוא עולם קטן. This notion was stressed again among the Jews not long before Azariah by Leone Ebreo in the second of his *Dialoghi di Amore,* known and highly appreciated by Azariah who called them פילון וסופיאה. Cf. I, 9 (C. 10) and also H. Pflaum, *Die Idee der Liebe. Leone Ebreo* (Tübingen, 1926), p. 104.

3. I, 84 (C. 100): שע"כ נאמין בו ית' אחדות גמורה בהרחקת כל צדי גשמות. .בכל בני ישראל תמומי דרך.

4. Cf. especially his sharp polemics against Philo's admission of a primordial matter (I, 96 ff.; C. 112 ff.): אך שוב נשוב אל ידידיה ואל דבריו בחומר, אין ספק כפי הנראה מהם כי בן הכות הוא בגללם על הלחי, וזו אינה צריכה לפנים שכבר נודע כי כל תופשי התורה איבעית אימא קרא ואי בעית אימא קבלה יעידון .יגידון איך חבריאה היתה כולה חדוש משולח בלי קדמות כל חומר. This harshness is understandable in view of the fact that Philo was very popular in Italian Jewry, as we learn from Azariah himself (I, 112; C. 129); his own opinion about the Sage of Alexandria, after a long discussion (ch. 3-6), being rather equivocal. Cf. also I, 106 n. (C. 123 n.).

5. II, 118 (C. 389 ff.): האמנה לכל הפנים אחרי שזוג החכמים . . . פתרו מלות. תהו ובהו הבל ואין כאמור . . . לך אמור להם למפרשים אותם חומר וצורה במשכם דברי אלהים חיים לדמיוני היונים בחיולי וצורותיו המתחלפות כי במחילה מכבוד תורתם לא יבינו בזה אל פעולות אלהינו. Azariah here rejects the Aristotelian conception of primordial matter and form as he had rejected before the Platonic theory of the primordial Hyle, introduced again into Jewish philosophy by Leone Ebreo (in his third Dialogue). Cf. also Pflaum, *op. cit.,* pp. 123 ff. As to Azariah's own different interpretation of Plato, based upon Marsilio Ficino, the other authoritative Platonist, cf. I, 105 ff. (C. 123).

6. II, 195 (C. 462): ואדרבא קודם לכן (לששת ימי בראשית) אילו יונח מן האפשר . . . אך אין ספק שהנאות הוא להאמין בו רמז נסתר כי לכל יודעי בינה .הזמן אשר בלעדיו אין קדימה ואחור הוא מכלל הנבראות ככל צבאות השמים והארץ. Cf. also I, 84 (C. 100).

7. This eternal dualism between God and the world is one of the most fundamental views in Azariah's philosophy. It is true that we find passages like this (I, 5): עד אמרו דבר ראוי להסתכלות והוא שלהיות האלהיות נראה בכל .נמצא הנה העולם כולו שמותיו ית' . . . Yet Azariah is very far from any really pantheistic conception, although pantheism had received already in his time a very articulate formulation in the works of Giordano Bruno (whose chief activity was indeed after the death of Azariah), and earlier to a lesser extent in the Dialogues of Leone. Cf. B. Zimmels, *Leo Hebraeus* (Leipzig,

1886), pp. 59 ff. On the other hand, we miss in Azariah's conception of the guidance of the world by God any mediator, such as the Philonic Logos or even the Aristotelian-medieval "Active Intelligence." Cf. also II, 99 (C. 371). For him the relation between Creator and Created was quite immediate. The old fundamental question of how this imperfect world could have been created directly by an absolutely perfect Creator, seems not to have seriously troubled him.

8. Cf. especially I, 12-14 (C. 13-15).

9. I, 12 (C. 13): המשתמש גם כן בסבות הטבעיות במדרגת הכלי. See also II, 100 (C. 379). Cf. Coluccio Salutati (*De nobil. leg. et med.,* c. 31); Est natura, sunt et homines Dei cuncta facientis indubitaliter instrumenta.

10. The eclectic method of Azariah is apparent further in sentences like these: (I, 85; C. 100): העולם האמת חכמי יקרואוהו לדעתי אשר) העולם השכלי; (I, 86; C.101): האצילות והספירות) . . . הלא על קריאת השמות אם בן הוא או אצילות ואור וספירה ואידיאה כדבר אפלטון . . . בהסכים החכמים על הענינים לא נחוש אם בכנוייהם איש מרעהו יפרדו. The mention of the light in this connection was due perhaps to the teachings of Leone Ebreo and Patritius (1529-1597).

11. I, 13: או לפחות נסור משתי הקצוות אל האמצע ונאמר . . . סבותיהם לא אל האלהים תמיד ולא אל הטבע תמיד, אבל פעמים יבואו ממנו ית' ופעמים כיתר הפעולות הטבעיות מדרך הקרי.

12. Cf. C. 14 n.

13. Nevertheless, this whole discussion greatly impressed R. David Gans. Cf. his צמח דוד on the year של"א (1571): דברים נפלאים מדבר הרעשים.

14. Here Azariah remains on the long-established ground of Aristotelian-medieval physics. Even when he mentions some existing doubts on this point he merely quotes Maimonides and other medieval authorities (I, 163; C. 179), not taking any notice of the theory of his contemporary, Cardanus (1501-1571), then so much discussed. The latter reduced the number of elements to three, declaring fire to be not a substance but an accident. On the other hand, when we find Azariah distinguishing between the four elements only according to their weight, without any reference to the other common medieval distinction of temperature, this was due perhaps to his tacit opposition to the theories of this philosopher or to those of another contemporary, Telesius (1508-1588), who declared that heat is the chief universal principle in nature. Also the new elements introduced by the alchemists have no place in his physical conception. It seems that this occult science did not exercise upon him the sort of attraction that it did upon many of his contemporaries, notably among the Gentiles. But cf. his views upon the practical Kabbalah below.

15. I, 145 (C. 161): כי תפקח עיניך על הכדור המקשה שבו יצוירו האקלמים עם הימים והנחלים וכל יותר החלקים המתיחסים אל יסוד העפר והמים אשר לכובד חמרם ברצון הבורא ירדו מטה מטה.

16. He says about the heavens (I, 149; C. 165): בהתאמת אצלם דעת החוקר
(Aristotle) שאינם רק גשם חמשי. In I, 164 (C. 179) he speaks merely about:
.המונת המפורסם מהרכבת ארבעה היסודות בכל נמצא תחת הירח

17. I, 183 (C. 194): הכלל המתוקן והמקובל אל כל חכמי לב שהדבר יכונה על
שם החלק הגובר במחברת, כמו שכנוי האדם הוא מן האדמה המרובה על יתר היסודות
.במתכונת . . .

18. He quotes Philo (I, 84; C. 99): גם הספק . . . בצבא השמים אם הם בעלי
נפש משכלת אם אין, הנה . . . הוכיח כי כן . . . Cf. also II, 60 (C. 332).

19. Besides the seven planets Azariah also mentions the: גלגל המזלות or
הגלגל היומי המקיף בכל and the הכוכבים העומדים.

20. Cf. P. Duhem, *Le système du Monde,* I (Paris, 1914), pp. 125 ff. Azariah
thus appears to have had some appreciation of the epicycloidic theory of the
Ptolemaic astronomy, notwithstanding the then widespread ignorance of this
complicated theory—cf. S. Oppenheim, *Das astronomische Weltbild im
Wandel der Zeiten,* 2nd ed. (Leipzig, 1912), p. 64— and regardless of the
opposition of some Arab astronomers and of Gersonides (I, 163, C. 179).
(The Arab opposition was known to Azariah from Isaac Israeli's יסוד עולם,
I, himself concurring in the ruling theory. Cf. י"ע ed. Berlin, 1848, pp. 15
and 25 ff.) Cf. also *Moreh,* II, ch. 29; M. Delambre, *Histoire de l'astronomie
du moyen-âge* (Paris, 1819), p. 171 ff. and Duhem, *op. cit.,* p. 130 ff.

21. Cf. I, 150 ff. and 140 (C. 166 and 156).

22. Cf. the interesting note מ"ל, pp. 113 ff. (C. 117 ff.). Also his underestimate of the size of the sun as being only 166⅔ times larger than the earth
(I, 263; C. 273) is only a repetition of an erroneous hypothesis by Ptolemy,
due to the latter's miscalculation that the distance between the sun and the
earth is equivalent to 1,210 radii of earth. Today we measure 23,300 radii on
the average. Cf. Duhem, *op. cit.,* II, 34.

23. Cf. I, 158 (C. 173 ff.).

24. The fact that he kept aloof from alchemy does not prove anything as
regards his attitude to astrology. Leone Ebreo rejected every kind of magic
and yet he, too, developed a whole astrological theory in his second Dialogue.
Cf. also Zimmels, *op. cit.,* p. 56. On the other hand, Azariah most likely knew
the distinction made shortly before him by Pomponatius, who admitted signs
given for extraordinary events like the birth of Jesus, but denied the ordinary
individual astrology. Cf. M. Carrière, *Die philosophische Weltanschauung der
Reformationszeit,* 2nd ed. (Leipzig, 1887), p. 84.

25. II, 174 (C. 445): ולא בלבד המקרים היוצאים ממסודר הטבע כאותם שזכרנו
יחשבו בהראותם למופתים על עתידות גוראות אבל גם החוים בנוחג שבעולם יתוארו
על ככה, כמו לקות המאורות אשר סבתן היא התמצע הירח בן השמש לארץ או הארץ
בין השמש לירח וכו'. See also the passages quoted in note 60. Cf. however,
II, 76 n. (C. 348 n.).

26. מ"ל, p. 33 (C. 35): איך באמת ובתמים נשחק להמון המשוררים כגוי אובד
עצות לימים קדמונים על הזיונתיהם שאילן תות התאדם מדם חללי זוג העוגבים

חבבליים . . . וכיוצא באלה מן הטעמים של תחו אשר דמו על פעולות הטבע.

27. Cf. I, 154 (C. 170): הרי לפנינו הסכמת האלהיים בשתי האומות נגד מה
שהתבאר אל החוקרים הנזכרים לא בלבד מן המופת כי גם מן החוש וכלי
האסטרולאביאו . . . . Still, a man like Coluccio Salutati held the opposite
medieval view. Cf. A. Martin, *Mittelalterliche Welt- und Lebensanschauung
im Spiegel der Schriften Col. Sal.* (München and Berlin, 1913), p. 96.

28. I, 165 n. (C, 178 ff.): והרי זה כלו עוות כי אין בחקות השמים מדע ארושי
אשר תאמר כי הוא ואין זולתו זולתו אמתי בשלוח. Cf. also I, 19, 149 (C. 20, 165).
This epistemological skepticism of Azariah has as little to do with the widespread philosophical skepticism of his age (the first two parts of Montaigne's
Essays appeared 1580, only five years after the מ"ע) as his empirical view
has to do with the future development of Francis Bacon's (born 1561) empirical philosophy. It was, on the contrary, a belittlement of human reason,
as was then emphasized by the leading men both of the Reformation and
Counter-Reformation in order to prove the superiority of the divine revelation.
It may be, however, that Azariah was influenced in this kind of skepticism as
well as in his empiricism by that "founder of the modern empirical psychology" (Lange and Höffding), Johannes Ludovicus Vives (1492—ca. 1540),
whose commentary on Augustine he quotes twice.

29. As is well known this was even a matter of serious halakhic codification
in the days of Azariah and afterwards, cf. *Yoreh Deah* 179, esp. (19). On the
other hand, among the Christians of that time, even such an independent
and usually unprejudiced thinker as Jean Bodin was firmly convinced of the
existence of demons and he devoted to this subject a special treatise, his
Démonomanie (1581), not to speak of Giordano Bruno (cf. his *De magia*)
and others.

30. מ"ל, p. 101 n. (C. 107 n.): אשר לבד מהיותו הלק רע ושמאלי נמצא בו
ג"כ הבכנה לכשפים אצל הנפשות אשר בשקידתן על רשומם תתפעלנה מהמה. Cf. also
I, 80 (C. 95): מסטרא דמסאבא.

31. I, 19 and II, 157 ff. (C. 20, 428 ff.). Cf. the interesting argumentation
of Ficino, who had a great influence upon Azariah (cf. מ"ל, p. 15 n.; C.
17 n.) in his *De christiana religione*, ch. 10: Noli . . . mirari, quod Marsilius
Ficinus, philosophiae studiosus miracula introducat . . . Sunt autem propria
rerum naturalium rationes, quae secundum naturam sunt; divinarum vero,
quae super naturam huiusmodi sunt, tum metaphysicae probationes, tum vel
maxime miracula etc. Cf. also Fr. Olgiati, *L'anima dell'umanesimo e dell'-
rinascimento* (Milan, 1924), p. 591.

32. I, 83 (C. 98): דברו (Philo's) הטוב כי הנפש בלי ספק נשארת אחר המות.
Thus he does not even think worthy of discussion the controversy between
the Averroists and Alexandrists about immortality, which had stirred all the
leading spirits in Italy a few decades earlier and which was indeed the "chief
problem of the philosophy of the Renaissance" (E. Gothein, *Schriften zur
Kulturgeschichte der Renaissance, Reformation und Konterreformation,* II

[Berlin, 1924], 106). Neither does he allude to the theory of Pomponatius in his then very famous *Tractatus de immortalitate animae* (1516), which, as Fiorentino says, was rather a treatise "De mortalitate" that immortality is a religious but not a scientific truth. Azariah was thus in agreement with the official view of the Church which in 1513 had restated the dogma of individual immortality and always rejected any duality of Truth.

33. I, 111 ff. n. (C. missing) אל הגוף (חנפש) אל הגוף וידעת קבלתנו בתחיה שתשוב אשר היה שם אהלה עם היות מחלוקת אם תחיה אף לרשעים או לצדיקים בלבד שהוא הנראה קרוב אליה ביותר. Cf. also I, 18 ff. (C. 92 ff.).

34. Cf. II, 106 ff. (C. 358) and I, 99 (C. 115 ff.).

35. It is worth mentioning that Azariah himself quotes (I, 145; C. 160) the very remarkable sentence of R. Hamnuna (*Zohar* III, 10ª) רהא כל ישובא מתגלגלא כעגולא דבדור which, notwithstanding the opposite endeavors of Duhem (*op. cit.*, V, pp. 143 ff.), cannot be understood in its original Aramaic except as implying the earth's rotation round its axis. Azariah, however, makes use of it only as evidence of the earth's rotundity. This is the more characteristic, as Azariah certainly knew from the *Praeparatio Evangelica* of Eusebius (1.XV, c. 58), a book quoted by him many times, that some of the Greek philosophers had taught that the earth rotates round its own axis. Cf. also Duhem, *op. cit.*, I, 25 and 404 ff.

36. His chief work, *Astronomiae instauratae progymnasmata,* appeared in 1589.

37. Azariah is here reflecting the habit of his age, which regarded every ancient source as authentic beyond doubt. And if the great Humanists themselves did not criticize the antique Greek sources (cf. G. Voight, *Die Wiederbelebung des klassischen Altertums,* 3rd ed. [Berlin, 1893], pp. 365 ff.); how much more reverent was the attitude toward the Holy Scriptures, every letter of which was of divine origin. Even Jean Bodin says (*Methodus* c. 8): "Ac tanti est apud me Mosis unius auctoritas, ut omnibus omnium philosophorum scriptis ac sententiis longe anteponam." Cf. also J. Guttmann in *MGWJ*, XLIX (1905), 315 ff. and 459 ff. Lorenzo Valla, with his relatively radical criticism of Livy and of the Vulgate, is merely an exception which proves the rule. And even he was ready to recant quickly everything he had said.

38. Cf. especially ch. XI which is thus summarized by Azariah: כבוד חכמינו לעולם ינחלו עם המצא לעת כיום אנשי התבונה והנסיון נוטים מקצת דבריהם אשר כתבו על עצמי קצת נמצאות ומקריהן, כי הנה לא דברו בם כמו כמו בדיני התורה על פי מסורת מסיני וקבלה נבואית אשר לה בודאי בלתי הרהור ומחקר תכרע כל ברך, אבל כפי חכמת האדם והשערתו, והיא היתה המפורסמת למעיינים בימים או בגלילות ההמה, לבד מחיות גם כן אפשר כי דבריהם בכל או בקצת יוטיבו מאלה.

39. In Azariah's polemics against this work of the great Polish Halakhist, we detect an unusually sharp note. Referring to its title he writes (I, 166; C. 180): ואמרתי עליו אם תעלה עולה לה' אל אמת תעלינה, כי הנה טוב מאד להחריש מהצדיק צדיקים בטענות לא יתכנו.

40. Azariah's description of this voyage (I, 145 ff.; C. 161 ff.), based upon a secondary source (Ulloa's biography of Charles V), contains numerous inaccuracies. He does not tell us that the ship "Victoria" of Del Cano was only one of the five which left San Lucar under the command of Magellan (whose name does not figure at all in his account), and he gives the number of the crew on it כד' מאות איש, while the boat with its 85 tons could not have carried such a number. In fact, 237 men left Spain with Magellan and only 18 came back with Del Cano. The journey covered the period from September 20, 1519 to September 8, 1522, not just שלש שנים כשני שכיר. The words: "Primus circumdedisti me" were not chosen by Del Cano himself, but were engraved on a crest, given him by Charles V. Also his return route was around Africa and not through the Mediterranean Sea, as supposed by Azariah. Cf. the minute description of the voyage by Antonio Pigafetta, one of the surviving members of the expedition (Engl. transl. in *The Earliest Voyages Around the World*, ed. by P. F. Alexander [Cambridge, 1916], pp. 1, 5, 84, 206). We shall see later how Azariah supposed a ship could travel from the Red Sea to the Mediterranean.

41. I, 149 (C. 164)· הרי נוטל כוח שזכרנו בענין זה כי אנית שלמה הנזכרת וזו היא היתה נוסעת על האופן האמור מן הפאה ואל הפאה של מטע האניה ויטוריאה, ובכן העולם הנזכר איננו חדש כי אם אצלנו, ומאמר רב החובל אתח ראשון סבבתני לא צדק כי אם אחרי שוב הארצות ההנה להתגלות ביום הזה, אמנם בבחינת האמת כבר נמצא מי שקדם אליו בימי שלמה. It is worth mentioning that 30 years later a well known Christian geographer in Germany, E. Schmidt, declared, that the New World was known to Homer, Plato, Aristotle, Virgil, Seneca and especially to King Solomon as the land of Ophir. Cf. S. Günther, "Der Humanismus in seinem Einfluss auf die Entwicklung der Erdkunde," *Geographische Zeitschrift*, VI (1900), p. 69.

42. Cf. I, 152 (C. 167).

43. Cf. I, 146 ff. and 155 (C. 162 ff. and 171).

44. Cf. O. Peschel, *Geschichte der Erdkunde* (München, 1865), pp. 50 ff.

45. So the famous maps of Jacopo Gastaldi (1543) and Girolamo Ruscelli (1561).

46. E.g. Alkhwarizmi (9th century) with his 51½ degrees maximum distance. Cf. S. Günther, *Geschichte der Erdkunde* (Leipzig und Wien, 1914), p. 49.

47. Cf. C. A. Beazley, *The Dawn of Modern Geography*, III (Oxford, 1906), 501 n. 3. The Alphonsine Tables were reprinted very often in the sixteenth century. Cf. Delambre, *op. cit.*, p. 249. Azariah himself quotes them twice in his works. Furthermore, it is remarkable that Azariah took no notice of Israeli's *Yesod Olam* (*loc. cit.*, f. 19) which gives the longitude of Jerusalem as 66° 30′ and that of Toledo as 28° (instead of 11° as in the Ptolemaic *Geography*), so that the difference in longitude between the two points would be 38° 30′, a figure nearer the truth than any of the others.

48. Azariah's measure (I, 263; C. 273) of 5,650 German or 22,600 Italian miles (probably equal to nautical miles today) would result in more than 41,900 km for the Equator, while it is in fact, slightly less than 40,000 km. At the same time Ptolemy's 180,000 stadia (cf. his *Geography* I, 11, 2) if multiplied by 210, the number of meters in a stadium, makes only 37,800 km. Cf. Günther, *Geschichte der Erdkunde,* pp. 23 ff.; Duhem, *op. cit.,* II, 6-8; Wright, *The Geographical Lore of the Time of the Crusades* (New York, 1925), p. 17. Notwithstanding the almost universal agreement that Ptolemy had underestimated the size of the circumference, we may venture to remark that if we take as a basis for the stadium of Eratosthenes (total 252,000) and of Poseidonios (total 240,000) not 157.5 or 158, but 168 meters, as assumed by Thalamas, then Eratosthenes' measure would be too great and Poseidonios' (= 40,320 km) nearly correct. The same would then be the case with Ptolemy's computation, because his 180,000 stadia are merely a reduction of Poseidonios' 240,000, as a result of an increase of ⅓ on each stadium. Consequently, Azariah's acceptance of Rava's שיתא אלפי פרסי הוה עלמא (b. Pes. 94a.) against the decision of the Gemara, while assuming that those 6,000 parasangs are equal to 6,000 German or 24,000 Italian miles, means nothing else but a further increase in the wrong direction. The opinion of Rava, however, also has found advocates in more recent times. Cf. Günther, *Studien zur mathematischen und physikalischen Geographie* (Halle a. d. S., 1877), p. 102.

49. Cf. I, 145 and 152 ff. (C. 161 and 197 ff.).

50. Cf. I, 152 ff. (C. 167 ff.).

51. Thus the first climate covered 8½' lat., the 24th only 3'. Cf. J. Hann, *Handbook of Climatology,* I (Engl. transl., New York, 1903), 91 ff. and Pauly-Wissowa-Kroll, *Realencyclopädie,* XI (1922), 838 ff. Cf. also *Yesod Olam,* f. 18. The remark of Cassel (p. 168) is erroneous.

52. I, 161 (C. 176): ועוד לחבב א"י על בעליה ולתת כבוד לשמה וטעם אל מעלתה אמרו היותה באמצע, עם כי לא במחוגה או בחבל תמדוד ממנה אל סביבותיה יספיק לנו שהיא באקלים הרביעי ואמצעי לכל השבעה, אשר על כן אוירו מחכים כשוה המזג. Here Azariah is probably following Estori ha-Parḥi's כפתור ופרח, quoted by him several times in other conections. Cf. ed. Berlin (1852) f. 18a.; ed. Jerusalem (1897), pp. 102-105. But Estori's conceptions are based upon the older theory which only divided the northern hemisphere into seven climates, the first beginning at the Equator. On the other hand, Azariah, who accepts the differences of half an hour in the length of the day, must necessarily approve the medieval division into twenty-four climates. In fact, however, neither Ptolemy's (Agathodemon's) fourth climate beginning at 36° lat. nor even that of Sacrobosco (well known to Azariah) at 43° 40' lat. includes Jerusalem, which is situated, as mentioned above, at about 32°. Cf. Wright, *op. cit.,* pp. 454 ff.

53. Cf. e.g., the curious explanations of Rashi and R. Tam to מטרא במערבא סהדא רבה פרח (b. Sabb. 65a.).

54. I, 146 (C. 162): וארץ אופיר ופרוים אשר ממנה אנית תרשיש אחת לשלש
שנים . . . היתה מביאה אליו זהב וכסף . . . אין ספק שהיא מדינת הפי"רו הנמצאת
בעולם חדש. Cf. Cassel's note *ibid.* and also II, 149 (C. 420). I, 147 (C. 163):
כי חרשי העץ אשר בעציון היו קרובים אל הים הנזכר או יושבים על נהרות הולכים
אליו וחיתה להם הכנת עצים (כי אולי על כן נקראה עציון) ואומנות יתרה לעשות
אניות טובות לצורך מהלכי תרשיש.

55. Cf. I, 181 and II, 203 (C. 192 and 474). As to the identification of the
anonymous author quoted with Sebastian Münster, and the reasons why
Azariah does not mention his name, cf. Cassel's Register, p. 170 and J. Perles,
Beiträge zur Geschichte der hebräischen und aramäischen Studien (München,
1884), pp. 40 ff. The widespread belief in Prester John was even supported by
apparent facts, as the sailors of Vasco da Gama's famous expedition had
brought home not long before what seemed to be reliable narratives from the
natives of Mozambique about numerous cities founded by Prester John along
the coast and his vast realm inland. Cf. R. H. Major, *The Discoveries of
Prince Henry the Navigator* (London, 1877), pp. 547 ff. This realm was then
already identified with Abyssinia, which corresponds to the frontier given by
Azariah. Cf. the chapters on Africa and Abyssinia in the then very popular
Theatrum mundi by Abraham Ortellius, published not long before but already
quoted by Azariah. Cf. further, S. Günther, *Geschichte der Erdkunde,* pp. 57,
n. 5 and 72, n. 2 and Wright, *op. cit.,* 283 ff. As to the Italian Jews, besides
the narratives well known to them of David Reubeni, cf. Zunz, *GS,* I, 175,
no. 60.

56. Cf. his interesting discussion I, 181 ff. (C. 193 ff.).

57. Cf. J. Burckhardt, *The Civilization of the Renaissance in Italy* (Engl.
transl. of the 3rd ed., London, 1890), pp. 298 and 47.

58. As an illustration of the extent to which his knowledge of nature was
for him a *Bildungserlebnis* rather than an *Urerlebnis* (Gundolf), we may give
the following (I, 204; C. 215): ובחולין פ"ג (נ"ח א) בהדיא אמרו כל בריח שאין
לה עצם אינה חיה (צ"ל: מתקיימת) י"ב חדש. Cf. also in the same connection
his deduction about the anatomical position of the nose relative to the brain,
and the origin of metals. Cf., however, what he writes I, 161 (C. 176) about
the situation of the face of a new-born child: ותאמרנה המילדות העבריות.

59. I, 154 ff. (C. 160 ff.). Cf. further H. Eicken, *Geschichte und System der
mittelalterlichen Weltanschauung* (Stuttgart, 1887), p. 622 and Wright, *op.
cit.,* pp. 259 ff.

60. II, 175 (C. 446): והנה ישמח לבנו ותגל נפשנו עדת בני ישראל כי עם אשר
בחיותנו מרבים לחטוא בכל הגוים אותות השמים ויתר הסימנים אפשר להם שיורו
בשוה על כלנו, הלא בעשותנו רצון אבינו שבשמים אשר לסגולתו האמירנו לא ימשול
ולא יורה עלינו לא נחש ולא קסם כדבר בלעם באומות העולם והנביא בעל לשון
הלמודים בישראל(ירמ' י' ב') מאותות השמים אל תחתו. Cf. also I, 16, 19, II,
98 (C. 16, 20, 370).

61. II, 182 (C. 453): אומר כי אם תמצא בעדת חכמינו הראשונים . . . מי שחשב

כי שבעים הלשון כלם היו גם לפני דור הפלגה, הנה הדעת הגובר ואשר בפי כל
ישרים יתרומם הוא כי רק בימי פלג נתחדשו ברצון האלהים, ועד העת ההיא לא היה
בעולם רק לשון הקדש. Among the arguments which Azariah gathers to prove
this opinion perhaps the most interesting is that which he learned from his
friend Leone Muscato: היות מן הראוי נתינת חשלם לשלם ובפרט מאת השלם שהוא
החבורא . . . כן נצדק בדברנו שהבורא ית', אשר לא חסר בעולמו רבר מן הגאות לא
נמנע מהשפיע על אדם הראשון השלם במינו . . . את הלשון הזה אשר הוא היותר
ואני לחדוש יקר הגני: (C. 464) שלם לכמה סגולות שבו וכו'. Cf. further II, 192
מוסיף . . . טעם נכון בחתיחם תאר קדוש אל לשוננו, והוא כי לתיותו בריאה אלהית
באדם הראשון מעת ימי בראשית . . . ולא מוסכם מבני האדם כיתר הלשונות עם
שנלוה להם בם עזר האלוהי הנה הם כלם נכונים אל ההפסד ככל מעשי אנוש . . . והוא
לבדו יעמוד עם יתר הנבראות . . . ובכן יצדק בו מאד תאר קדוש המורה קיים ונצחי.
That Azariah lays so much stress upon this assertion is due perhaps to the
fact that the general opinion among the Gentiles was bent toward the opposite
view. Even Giannozzo Manetti (1396-1459), notwithstanding all his high
respect for the Hebrew language and his relatively expert knowledge (cf. U.
Cassuto, *Gli Ebrei à Firenze nell'età di rinascimento* [Firenze, 1918], pp. 275 ff.),
professed that all languages as well as scripts were invented by man when he
first felt the need to communicate with his fellow-men. Cf. G. Gentile in his
Giordano Bruno e il pensiero di rinascimento (Firenze, 1920), p. 176.

62. Cf. the long discussion in II, 193 ff. (C. 464 ff.). As to the antiquity
as well as the eternal future of the Torah, cf. his quotations from Philo and
Josephus I, 86 (C. 102).

63. II, 204 (C. 476): כל דברי החכמים . . . יצדקו יחדיו שהנקודות נתנו מסיני
ובימי עזרא ואחר חתימת הגמרא היינו שנראו בהתחדשם אז אחרי השתכחם או
התבלבלם ביד ההמון כאילו היום ההוא נתנו וגם יצדק עמהם מה שנראה לנו היותן
מסודרות עם אותיות הכתב מימי בראשית והכל תמיד ע"ד שכחום וחזרו ויסדום.

64. Azariah is quite aware that Aramaic was the common language of the
Jews in Palestine throughout the period of the Second Temple. He even
develops a theory that the Torah was then in general use only in an Aramaic
translation, the Hebrew original being accessible exclusively to the educated
classes. Cf. I, 126 ff. (C. 142 ff.).

65. II, 202 (C. 473): כלשון העברי תחלה והערבי והארמי אחריו אשר נשתבשו
חימנו.

66. I, 3.

67. II, 193 (C. 464).

68. When Azariah tells us once (מ"ל, p. 102; C. 107 n.): ונהי דהמון העם
בבית שני היו מדברים בלשון ארמי . . . הלא אנחנו כיום עם היות שפתנו אתנו
ללועזות בלעז משכילי עם אשר רבו למעלה יביעו ידברו ויכתבו בלשון הקדש,
we must assume that this use of a spoken Hebrew language was most likely
confined—like the contemporary Latin conversation—to exceptional occasions
in the high educated circles. Another similarity to the humanistic customs

may be found in a kind of a modern linguistic purism of Azariah, even in the reshaping of proper names as in the case of Philo (I, 76; C. 90): אשר לרדוף את דרך קצת יחידי סגולה הנמצאים בדורנו החילותי מראש לכנותו קרוב לחוראת שמו הנזכר : ידידיה. This tendency corresponds to the mannerism, then very popular, of appropriating the most astounding classical names, even for ordinary use. Cf. Burckhardt, *op. cit.*, pp. 250-256.

69.   I, 73 (C. 87): ועוד מה לחם לדרך מצרים לבקש תורה מפי גוי כרתים, ומקרב אחינו היה לנו המלך שלמה אשר דבר על הארז ועד האזוב . . . או יונח כדבר חרב המורה . . . שעקר ידיעתם יצא ראשונה מבני עמנו. Azariah even supposes that all true knowledge of every age is included in the Bible. He says (I, 255; C. 264): ואם בתענית פ״ק (ט׳ א׳) אמרו מי איכא מידי בכתובי דלא רמיזא באוריתא כ״ש שתאמר מי איכי מידי דברי הבאי (in the Talmud with slight variations) של חולין דליתיה בתורת משה והגלוח אליה מכתבי הקדש. Cf. also Jacob Provençali in his ש״ות בדבר למוד החכמות (1490, see later on) p. 67. Plato in particular was regarded by many Jews and Gentiles (Pico, Leone Ebreo, etc.) as a disciple of Moses. Azariah rejects sharply the opinion held by some Jews of that time that Aristotle himself in his old age became converted to Judaism. Cf. I, 236 ff. (C. 246 ff.).

70.   I, 74 (C. 87): הלא אחרי בוא ספרי הסגולה ליד חנכרים אשר משלו בנו אח חכל למדנו מהם בהכרח.

71.   Cf. מ״ל, p. 55 (C. 58).

72.   Cf. e.g., his arguments in favor of discussing problems which, as וזאת סבה הלכתא למשיחא, have no immediate importance (II, 2; C. 276): שליש׳ה אל הדרוש הזה ובלתי ריקנית כי מתוך הויכוח תתברר הלכתא למשיחא באמת אשר לדעת רבים ונכבדים קרוב לבוא עתה. Cf. also II, 127 and 146 (C. 399 and 417).

73.   Cf. the ingenious deliberations, quoted in ch. 43 and based chiefly on a book published a few years before: מגדל דוד by Mordecai Dato (1525—after 1591; cf. C. Roth, *REJ*, LXXX [1925], 71 ff.).

74.   Azariah had special reasons for this attitude. For only so could he meet the attacks against his own innovations in Jewish chronology. According to his computation the time passed since the creation of the world was about a hundred years more than the official Jewish מנין לבריאת העולם. Thus at the time of the composition of the מ״ע, it was already certain that the real year 5335 was not the year of the redemption. He tries, therefore, to prove that his theory, far from weakening the popular hope in the coming of the Messiah, is, on the contrary, promoting it by preventing disillusionment. II, 103 (C. 374): ואולם לבד מכל האמור אשאל את החכמים הנזכרים ובחסדם יודיעונו אם בוא יבוא הזמן ההוא של״ה . . . ואנחנו ח״ו לא גושענו מה יענו מלאכי גוי ומה ישיבו אל לבם המון עניי הדעת נכאי לבב וקשי רוח ואנה נעזוב את כבודנו, כי על כל אלה נכון הדבר בעיני ואחשבהו לי מעשה צדקה לפני אלהינו להקדים וכו׳.

75.   Cf. I, 209 (C. 220).

76. After quoting (II, 106 ff.; C. 378) from Naḥmanides' ספר הגאולה :
כי הנה אין תכלית גמולנו ימות המשיח ולאכול מפרי הארץ והתרחץ בחמי טבריא
וכיוצא בהם מן התענוגים, וגם לא הקרבנות ועבודת בית המקדש הם תכלית חפצו
ממנו, אבל גמולנו ומבטנו הוא חיי העולם והתענג הנפש התענוג הנכרא גן עדן והנצל
מעונש הגיהנם. ואנחנו עם זה מקוים את דבר הגאולה וכו'. Azariah adds:
אפס נפלאתי כי לפי דעתו יכול היה להוסיף בסבות תאותנו אל הגאולה אחת רשומה
מאד והיא שמרנו אז את המצות במקום עיקר חיובן שהוא הארץ. As to this last
point cf. also I, 162 (C. 177). The quotation from Naḥmanides differs in
many points from the original (ed. Lipschitz, London, 1909, pp. 206 ff.). The
most characteristic changes and omissions are those made by Azariah, in
order to avoid hurting the Christians. Thus he changes לחשיג היום בגלות עם
חיום מלאים into העמים המחטיאים אותנו ועם מה שאנחנו מן הטומאה והשקוץ
לא מאשר נחיה פוסחים. He omits entirely: חמת הצרות והמקרים המעיקים אותנו
or: על אמונות נכריות אולי הן אמת כאשר יחשבו חסרי הדעת הדעת באומתנו . . .
שכינה . . . אנשי הדתות הזרות כי רוח זרעו וסופתה וקצורו. Cf. further Solomon
Schechter, *Studies*, pp. 105 ff., where the passage is not rendered exactly.
77. II, 175 (C. 446): למען דעת כל עמי הארץ כי אנחנו שארית הפלטה כל ימי
היותנו גרים ותושבים בארץ לא לנו, חייבים על פי נביאי האמת וכפי מנהג האבות
שהוא תורה, להתפלל בשלומה של המלכות המושלת בנו, וכי לעת כזאת בפרט אשר
עוניגו הפיצונו בארבע רוחות השמים יש לנו לשחר את אל על על שלום בני תבל כלם
לבל ישא גוי אל גוי חרב. Cf. also the last passage in ch. 55.
78. Cf. also his characteristic expectation (II, 116; C. 387): גם קרוב אלי
הדבר מאד ולדעתי ייטב אצל משכילי הנוצרים ונבוני עמנו . . .
79. Cf. *REJ*, XXX (1895), 315 ff.
80. Cf. his treatment of certain Jewish prayers (II, 177; C. 448): ומעתה
קורא משכיל לשם קדמונינו תתן כבוד על מה שתקנו בתפלות מראשית השנה על כלה
מלוך על כל העולם כלו וכו . . . גם מה שכתוב בקצת התפלות להעביר ממשלת הזדון
ולעקור מלכותו . . . עלינו באמת לשבח אותו כשיובנו הדברים על הנכון הזה והוא
שנבקש תקומת החולה בהסרת החולי כו'. Characteristic of Azariah's caution in
not hurting the feelings of his Gentile readers is also his conscious alteration
of biblical passages as quoted in the Talmud (I, 210; C. 221): בשר חמורים בשרם
(Ez. 23, 20) into: בשר אבירים ב' and אשר פיהם דבר שוא (Ps. 144, 11) into:
אשר פיה של אותה ריבה ד"ש.
81. So when he speaks about the faction of Judah the Zealot which rejected
the earthly kingdom, he adds in a special note (I, 77; C. 91): נגד דעת תוה"ק
ודעת כל חכמי הפרושים שהחזיקו במלכות והזהירו לסור למשמעתה ולשמור חקיה
כנודע.
82. I, 90 (C. 106): אבל נשער כי תכליות המלוכה שנים, האחד לשפוט את העם
כי יריבון אנשים, והשני להושיעם מכף אויביהם אם יגברו צרימו, והנה על דבר
המשפט מלוכת הרבים היא הנאותה מאד כי לא יסכימו בעול, אכן על אודות המלחמה
האות מלוכת היחיד כי בתחבולות יעשנה בלתי הפר מחשבות מאין סוד. His own
view may be best defined in the words which he had quoted previously from
Plato: מלוכת היחיד אשר יתנהג על פי התורות היא המעולה על כלן כאשר בלעדי

התורות אין כמות לרוע. Notwithstanding his זו"ל, these words are not to be regarded as a literal quotation from Plato. In fact, Plato, after finishing a long discussion about the forms of government, reached the conclusion (Resp. IX, 6 580 c) that the best one is to be seen in a King, whom he calls βασιλικωτατον καὶ βασιλεύοντα αὐτοῦ. This differs greatly from the formulation of Azariah. But Azariah's words actually reproduce the Platonic theory of government, if not in the ideal state of the "Republic" at least in the second best state of the "Laws." Cf. IV, 710 E. In fact, however, Plato's detailed deliberations about the content of such a monarchical constitution (βασιλικὴ πολιτεία) in his third (693 D ff.) and sixth book (756 E) suggest rather a mixed constitution whose components are oligarchy (rather than monarchy) and democracy, as had been pointed out already by Aristotle in his "Politics" (1266 a). On the other hand, this criticism of Aristotle could no longer overshadow in the period of the Renaissance the Platonic classification of governments into two chief divisions only (μητέρες πολιτικῶν III, 693 D): monarchy and democracy. Thus we find in the very beginning of Machiavelli's *Principe* the following statement: "Tutti gli stati, tutti i dominij, che hanno avuto, et hanno imperio sopra gli uomini, sono stati e sono o republiche o principati." With or without knowledge of the great Florentine, Azariah followed the same line, reaching, however, quite different conclusions. It might be of considerable interest to compare these political theories of Azariah with those of other rabbis, particularly Maimonides and Abravanel, but this is not the place for it. See for the time being: Erwin Rosenthal, "Maimonides' Conception of State and Society," in *Moses Maimonides,* ed. by Isidore Epstein (London, 1936), pp. 189-214; Yitzhak Fritz Baer, "Don Isaac Abravanel and His Attitude toward Historical and Political Problems" (Hebrew), *Tarbiz,* VIII (1936-37), 241-59; Ephraim E. Urbach, "Die Staatsauffassung des Don Isaak Abravanel," *MGWJ,* LXXXI (1937), 257-70.

83. Cf. e.g., his *Six livres de la République* which appeared only one year after the ע"מ, 1. II c. III (3rd ed., Paris, 1578, p. 205) beginning with: "Le Monarque Royal est celui qui se rend aussi obéissant aux loix de nature, comme il désire les sujets estre enuers luy . . ."

84. מ"ע *ibid.*: אמנה ישראל הנושעים מאויביהם בה' אלהינו אין להם שום סבה לבקש ממלכת היחיד . . . אך לכל הפנים אין לשומו למען שפוט על דברי הריבות כי המשפטים כבר הושמו לפנינו מאדון כל הארץ.

85. II, 178 (C. 448): וכן המנהג אשר לתוספת חזוק נמצא בקצת הקהלות לברך את שריהם וכל אבזריהו, הוא באמת מנהג ותיקין למצא בעיני אלהים ואדם חן ושכל.

86. As to Azariah's own personal relations with Christian scholars cf. I, 21 (C. 22): in Ferrara; I, 130 (C. 146): near Mantua; *REJ, loc. cit.*: at Monte Cassino.

87. Cf. I, 86, 121 (C. 100, 137), etc.

88. Cf. II, 75 ff. (C. 347 ff.). Cf., however, צ"ע, p. 130 (C. 134).

89. Cf. I, 85 (C. 100 ff.).

90. I, 86 (C. 101): ‫ובאמת אצל חישרים בלבותם נאוה לחם על זה תהלה, כי כל‬
‫המרבה לחפך בזכות דתו הרי זה משובח‬. Cf. also I, 101 and 133 ff. (C. 117 ff., 149).

91. Published under the title ‫שו"ת בדבר למוד החכמות‬ in the collection
‫דברי חכמים‬ by Eliezer Ashkenazi (Metz, 1849), pp. 63 ff.

92. Although he himself confesses (p. 73) that he suffered much from the numerous advocates of philosophy, this is only one of a series of complaints about his own lack of financial success, and not to be taken literally. Also his origin from Marseilles does not in itself explain his utterly hostile attitude towards philosophy. Cf. further (Vogelstein) Rieger, *Geschichte der Juden in Rom* (Berlin, 1895), II, 66.

93. Cf. I, 189, 261; II, 30 (C. 202, 271 and 303).

94. I, 75 (C. 89): ‫ובכלל בהא סלקינן ובהא נחתינן כי כל מקום שאין בו כפירה‬
‫לא לתורה שבכתב ולא לתורה שעל פה לא דבר רק הוא בעיני ללמור הסתום לנו מן‬
‫המפורש לחכמי האומות‬.

95. II, 53 (C. 325): ‫האמנה מהצטרך לסמוך בכלן על דברי נכרים בלי ראית‬
‫כתבי קדש, יהיו כאין ולא נשית עליהם לבנו‬. Although he must have known how difficult it would be in practice to bring this into agreement with another principle accepted by him from Maimonides (I, 75; C. 89): ‫שאם הדברים אשר‬
‫לצורך השעה אבקש יהי מטבעם להמצא בכתבי הקדש, בלי ספק קראתי בפנים מאירות‬
‫למאהבי מבני עמי, וכעת לא הבאתי ילדי נכרים אל שערינו‬.

96. II, 4 (C. 278): ‫הנה עם שנתרצה כראוי לנו לחלוק מכבוד אלהינו ליראו‬
‫ולומר שאם יהיו כל חכמי א"ה בכף מאזנים ואחד מהם בכף שניה מכריע הוא את כלם‬. The reason for that we find in another interesting discussion of A. (I, 257 ff.; C. 267 ff.) about the difference between the ‫נביא‬ and the ‫חכם‬, in which he reaches the conclusion: ‫ואין לך צעיר בנביאים אשר לא יעלה גם עלה על כל‬
‫החכמים שנמצאו מני שים אדם עלי ארץ, כי רוח יתירא ביה . . .‬. Cf. also a statement of Coluccio Salutati about questions in natural science (quoted by Martin, *op. cit.*, p. 104): Augustino teste, cui tum intellectus acumine, tum profunditate scientiae, tum manifesta sancti spiritus in eo loquentio auctoritate, plus quam physicis credo.

97. I, 185 (C. 196): ‫שככה יעוז אנוש לגמגם על תורת משה עצמה חלילה שהם‬
‫גם כן מסרוה לנו . . .‬.

98. Gothein, *op. cit.*, p. 98. Cf. e.g., *De verbo Dei* 1. IV, c. 4th ed. (Rome, 1832), I, 152 ff.

99. I, 74 (C. 88): ‫והנה המעיין דברינו בפרקים הבאים ימצא כי כל הגוים אשר‬
‫קראנו פה בשם לאיזה גלויי מילתא תרויהו איתנהו בהו, היינו שהם משיחים לתומם‬
‫ולא שייכי בגופא דעובדא כל מאומה . . . הכא נמי כל כותבי הזכרונות שיחיו נקראים‬
‫בדברינו אלה אשר כלם אשר הקפידו על כבודם שלא יחיה לבוז בדברם כזב, ובקשו לעשות‬
‫להם בקולמוסם המתוקן ומקובל שם תפארת עם מלכים ויועצי ארץ, הוו לחו כנוטרין‬
‫אשר נאמנו‬. We feel in this description how much Azariah had before his eyes actual conditions in Italy, that is, the widespread search for glory and for some rich Maecenas from among the dukes and courtiers. He overlooked, however, how much these very motives might actually have had the opposite

result and shaken the reliability of men like Annius de Viterbo, Pietro Aretino and Giovio.

100. He is, of course, bound to explain away many hostile utterances of the Talmud against the חכמת יונית and the ספרים חצונים. About the latter he declares (I, 69; C. 82 ff.): שכונתם באסור קריאת הספרים החצונים איננה רק כשהיא קבע לא של עראי וקרי שהקורא כמשתקע בהם וחושב אותם ספרים מסולאים לשתות בצמא את דבריהם הרי זה ודאי חומס נפשו . . . אכן על הקריאה לרגעים וכל שכן לבקש הגוכל להתעורר מהם על ברור איזה דבר מתיחס בצד מה לדרושי תורתנו אין ספק שלא יקפידו מאומה... But it is certainly more than doubtful that Azariah himself was able to acquire his profound erudition in the non-Jewish literature by such a קריאה לרגעים, notwithstanding his גם בקצת מעתות הפנאי עברתי ... (I, 205; C. 216).

101. The fact of his signing an Italian letter to the abbot of Monte Cassino with the Italian name Buon'aiuto for עזריה does not mean much for that time, except perhaps that it is another illustration of his puristic inclinations. The same name occurs before Azariah in Rome (cf. Rieger, *op. cit.*, p. 175) and (for עזריאל) in Florence (cf. Cassuto, *op. cit.*, p. 235).

102. Cf. I, 259 (C, 269).

103. *Ibid.*: וכפי מה שכתב הרב הגדול רמב"ם ז"ל . . . שבכל הדבר בקטן כגדול הנמסר לגו מהם באמרם שכך נתקבל ממשה רבינו, וכן כל מה שלמדוהו באחת ממדות התורה, או שהם עשוהו סיג אליה, לא נהרהר ח"ו אחריו מאומה לדרוש ולתור ולבוא אתם עליו במשפט כאילו עדותם לא נאמנו מאד, או שגבהו מדרכיהם דרכינו וכדעתם נדע גם אנחנו, חלילה לנו מעשות זאת. והאיש זד יחיר אשר יעוז על ככה, לא יראה כי יבוא טוב, והיה כערער בערבה עשן מארובה ומוק לפני רוח. Cf. the whole ch. 28. In fact, all laws are equally important and all sins equally grave. Cf. his quotation from Cicero II, 34 (C. 307).

104. כי האמנה כן ראוי תמיד לקיים את אשר נתפשט בהמון p. 88 (C. 94): מ"ל כל עוד שלא יהיה בו נזק תורני חלילה, בשגם לא בכל זאת תגעל הדלת בפני כל הבא לחקור בסוד חכמים את האמת... Cf. also *ibid.*, p. 66 (C. 71), where he mentions a number of customs in actual force although their original reason had vanished. II, 92 (C. 364): מלבד כי יש לי עדי אמונה להביא תנאים אמוראים וגאונים שחכמינו לא יקפידו בגלוי הדבר אשר כסוהו אלא בשיתגלה בדרשות על פה כי אז נחוש על ההמון השומע, אבל לא בהכתבו אל המשכילים על ספר... Cf. also his first תשובה in צ"ע, p. 119 (C.123).

105. Cf. Burckhardt, *op. cit.*

106. מ"ל, p. 66 (C. 71): ובבחינת האמת הכלל המועיל וקיים הוא כי כל אשר יעשה ב"ד של מטה בכל המתיחס למקראי קדש הוא לבדו נרצה בב"ד של מעלה... Cf. also ע"צ, p. 130 (C. 134).

107. After quoting (מ"ל, p. 26 n.; C. 27 n.) Christian authorities (Origen and Rhodiginus) to show that even the Gentiles believed that Moses also received from God an oral Law which he taught to the Jews, and which, later forgotten, had been restored by Ezra, he adds: ועתה יראה כל מבין עם תלמיד, עד מה הקראים אנשי בוגדות ראוים לתוכחת מגולה, כי גם אשר לא מבני ישראל

הֹמֵה יקיימוה בידינו ... Cf. also I, 102 n. (C. 119 n.): אנשי רשע, צ"ע *loc. cit.*
יאבד זכרם :(C. 125) 121 .p ,צ"ע and חורשי און

108. I, 243 (C. 253): (כרס"ג) הלא ידענו כי בנוהג שבעולם גברא רבה כותיה
דאמר מלתא ובפרט בלתי מתיחסת רק לידיעת העתים אין כל גופה צריכה בדיקה
ואחריו כל אדם ימשוך. ולכל הפנים בשגם אפשר כי נתעלמה הלכה זו מן הנכבדים
שזכרנו הנה התגצלותם נגלה כי הטרודים בגופי תורה אין מדקדקין בטעיות כאלה ...
Cf. also מ"ל, p. 42 (C. 74).

109. II, 2 (C. 275 ff.): האמנה מביט אני מראשית כי תאמר בלבבך קורא נעים
הלא זאת החקירה (ע"ד המנין ליצירה) היא כהלכתא למשיחא וגרועה עוד הימנה,
כי מה לנו ולה ומאי דהוה הוה זה אלפי שנים או כהנה שבעתים, אף אתה תשיב
אמריך לך כי תתבונן ראשונה איך האמת בעצמו הנדרש ג"כ מאלפי חכמים בחקירות
יותר רחוקות מזאת, הלא הוא כחוט אלהי אמת סגולת הנפש היפה וטוב שהכל
יכספוהו, ושגיח לה העולה ביותר כי במשך הדרוש הזה תראה שיזדמן לנו להבין
טעמי קצת דברים אשר בכתבי הקדש ... וזאת סבה שלישיה אל הדרוש הזה ובלתי
ריקנית כי מתוך הויכוח תתברר הלכתא למשיחא באמת ... While discussing the
different talmudic sources about the assaults on the Jews in Alexandria, he
remarks (I, 167 ff.; C. 182): ומאשר הואלנו עתה לחקור על קשט הדברים האלה
לא בעד גופא דעובדא דמאי דהוה הוה זה רק למאי דאיכפת לן שלא ימצאו דברי חכמינו
זה את זה סותרים ומפורסמות מאורעות של בספורים. Cf. also I, 175 (C. 189). This
repeated emphasis upon the מאי דהוה הוה goes back to b. Ketub. 3a. Cf. I,
256 (C. 266). The other passage from b. Ḥag. 16 a. is not only wrongly
quoted by Azariah, but has in fact quite the opposite meaning.

110. I, 254 (C. 264): אשר לפניו ואחריו עד היום לא קם באומות העולם כמוהו...

111. *Ibid.*: ואמנם לא שקר מליו בבחינת העמים אשר לא ראו אור התורה התמימה
עם יתר כתבי הקדש ובחשכת הלמודים האנושיים יתהלכו, כי הם הם בזעת אפם וטורח
שכלם יצטרכו לזרות ולחבר את כל אשר תוציא האדמה ממקרי בני האדם עד מקרי
הבהמה ולהתבונן מה יעשו לטוב להם מספר ימי צבאם תחת השמש, אבל אנחנו עם
אלהי אברהם וזרע יעבדנו ... כבר יצאנו חפשים וקוממיות מן העבודה הזאת עד
בלתי השאיר לנו כשרון שנעמול בה לרוח, כי הלא בתורתו ומצותיו שם כל מחשך
לפנינו לאור ויפתח לנו שערי צדק אל הדרך אשר יעלה בה איש ואיש או המונים
המונים להתרחק מכל הצר הצורר ולקרבה אל ההצלחה ככל אות נפשנו.

112. Cf. I, 126, 157, 176 (C. 142, 173, 190) and the passage quoted n. 113.

113. Since the days of Lionardo Bruni Aretinus (1369-1444). Cf. E. Fueter,
Geschichte der neueren Historiographie (Leipzig, 1911), pp. 12 and 17.

114. I, 198 (C. 211): מתאמת דבר הספרי הנזכר רצונך להכיר את יוצר הכל עסוק
באגדה, כי בודאי המשתדל במשליו ובמליצת דבריו למשוך את לב ההמון להכרתו
ית' הלא לבו ממש הוא הנמשך מקדם.

115. II, 45 (C. 318): וזה עני אשר על אף אויבינו ורודפינו צוה שיבנה הבית
בימי זרובבל בהנחות ונדבות כפי הידוע ... באופן שעל ידו ובעזרו נבנתה העיר
על תלה וארמון הקדש על משפטו, איככה נוכל לחשוב, כי אלהי משפט ה' סר מעליו
פתאם ויהי ערהו להסגירו ביד צר בשצף קצף, אלה המצות וזה שכרן.

116. After discussing *Sifre* (II, 39 ff.; C. 312 ff.): בשביל שהיו מוכרים את
הרי כי על ששת הדורות he concludes: הכהונה בדמים התחילו שנותיהן מתקצרות
הראשונים שלא עשו כאלה יש לנו לחשוב כי ימותם רבו לא שעשו להם כנפים ...

420

117. Cf. I, 14.

118. Although the term Kabbalah had been current for the occult science in Judaism during more than three centuries (occurring already in 1233 as a technical term in this sense in a Jewish-Arabic book quoted by Harkavy in his annotations to גרץ-שפ"ר, די"י V, 47), and although it was common in this sense also in the Italian literature of his day, Azariah never uses it. He either applies the word to the old talmudic antithesis of דברי תורח and דברי קבלה (cf. Bacher, *Die älteste Terminologie* ... [Leipzig, 1899], pp. 165 ff.), or he uses it, like other medieval writers, with regard to the oral tradition. Cf. however, I, 104 (C. 121): מקבלי האמת.

119. II, 110 (C. 380 ff.): אחר כן אומר שיסלח לנו הרב המורה לנזכר אם לא נקשיב בזה אל דבריו, כי ... הנה עיניגו רואות חכמי האמת מחזיקים בדעת ...

120. II, 201 (C. 472): כל הבהיר והזוהר והתקונין ומערכת האלהות (אשר יצאו החוצה מפעולות ר' נחוניה בן הקנה רש"בי וסיעתו לפני חבור המשנה) המפיקים ... אל זן אמרות טהורות. It is true, however, that in Halakhic questions he gives preference to the Talmud over the *Zohar* (cf. מ"ל, p. 40; C. 42), thus following the example of the chief Halakhic authorities, even those who, like R. Joseph Karo (Azariah quotes him in one such instance), were themselves extreme partisans of the secret lore.

121. I, 223 ff. (C. 232 ff.) footnote: וכן בזוהר עצמו ... נמצאו אמוראים לא מעט ... וכבר דברתי מזה עם כמה חכמי לב אשר גם המה ראו כן תמהו, והקרוב לכלם כי איזה תלמיד אשר תשוקתו גדלה מהשגתו מצא הגהות בגליונים והבליען בספר ... וחנה בס' יוחסין לחר"רא זכות ... תמצא כי בחגיע חמחבר לזכור בין האחרונים הר"ר משה דיליאון ... כתב בשם דיין עכו דברי שקר על קצת דברי אמת לומר כי זה רבי משה בכח שם הכותב בדא אל תוכם מלבו להג הרבה...כי על כן שבח אני את המדפיס הנזכר (ed. Constantinople, 1566) אשר הוסיף בשולי חסדור ההוא הגהה אלו דבריה, הנך רואה סכלות הדוברים על צדיק עתק לא ידעו ולא יבינו התופכים ללענה דברים שהם כבשוגו של עולם והספר ההתום לזר יחשבוהו וישימו לאל מלתן וראיותם וטענגותם הבל ואין בם מועיל, עד כאן לשוגו המכפר בעד הואיל והסכים להדפים הספור ההוא, אשר אמנה יותר היה רתוי לו ההלל בדלוג, דאי מלת הגהתו בסלע משתוקת הספור כלו בתרין ...

122. Cf. *ibid.*, the end of the note.

123. I, 16 (C. 17): ... ספרים יקרי הערך ... חכם גדול לנוצרים. Cf. also I, 89, 123, 237 (C. 104, 139, 247).

124. Cf. Burckhardt, *op. cit.*, pp. 183 ff. No wonder, therefore, that the Renaissance also took over from the Middle Ages their chief social principle—aristocracy by birth—to such an extent that many prominent Italians prided themselves on their descent from some celebrated family of antiquity, e.g., Ahenobarbus in Rome or Plato himself. This reminds us how Azariah does not fail to mention (II, 212; C. 483): על משפחתי מן האדומים אשר קבלנו מקדמוגיגו היותה אחת מן הארבע היקרות שהגגלה טיטוס לרומי ...

125. Azariah too uses the phrase almost stereotyped in all times and languages (מ"ל, p. 3; C. 56): יחירות הדורות הולך וגדול.

421

126. I, 209 (C. 220). Cf., however, I, 216 (C. 226).

127. After pointing out that the actual calendar, if it were of divine origin, would be superior to the ancient קדוש ע"פי הראיה that depended on a decision of an earthly court, he adds (מ"ל, p. 87; C. 93): עד שתאמר כי חימים הראשונים לא חיו טובים מאלה ואדרבא טוב לנו מאז עתה כי ה' מחוקקנו. As to the date cf. II, 56 (C. 328).

128. Azariah writes a special chapter (14) on the question: מחלוקות אשר נמצאו לרבים ממפרשינו האחרונים ז"ל על דברי החכמים בבאור קצת מכתבי הקדש ואיככה ידומה... I, 190 (C. 201): ויקשה כי הלא אין לחשוב שראו יותר מחמה שאנחנו העטלפים ראינו יותר מחמה. Cf. also his reference to the demonstration from the *Kuzari, ibid.,* and I, 261, II, 94 (C. 271 and 366).

129. Cf. his quotation from Ptolemy about geographic questions (I, 149; C. 164): כי כל דרוש כזה טוב להודות עליו לאחרונים אשר לכמה סבות יעמדו מיום אל יום על האמת ביותר.

130. Cf. I, 3. Azariah states even the following as a rule (II, 14; C. 287): וכבר ידעת גם כן מהעתקת ספר אריסטיאו של מעלה כי את אחרונים אני הוא כחביבים ביותר.

131. After quoting many talmudic sentences about the superiority of the ancients, he adds (I, 185 ff.; C. 196): האמנה אחרי הגיע אל האחרונים מה שהשיגו הראשונים לבד מהשגתם עצמה נראה דהוה ליה כמשל הננם הרוכב על הענק שזכר בעל שבולי הלקט בהקדמתו על שם אחד מחכמי קדם, באופן שיאות להאמר כי היתרון אשר אמנה נמצא לקדמון על האחרון בדברים הנתלים בנבואה מצד היותו יותר קרוב לבעליה הגו לאחרון על הקדמון בדברים אשר חטרם יצא מגזע העיון והנסיון, יען היותו תמיד הולך ומוסיף חבל לחבל ומשיחה למשיחה עד כי בעזר הראשונים עצמם אשר נלאו סביבות היאורים להוציא להם מים אמור יאמר הכורה ... אחר כורה אני קרתי ושתיתי. Azariah is not aware that by this formulation he is giving up most of what he had said previously on the same page and elsewhere.

132. In his *Il carattere dell'umanesimo e del rinascimento,* p. 252. Cf. already Burckhardt, *op. cit.,* pp. 1 ff.

AZARIAH DE' ROSSI'S HISTORICAL METHOD

1. The present study bears only upon De Rossi's scholarly method. The bibliographical and critical problems of the vast array of sources used by him can merely be referred to here incidentally; their fuller analysis must be reserved for a later, more detailed treatment. Azariah's own works are cited in the Benjacob edition (and parenthetically also in that of D. Cassel). *M.L.* = *Maṣref le-Khesef; S.O.* = *Ṣedeq 'Olamim.*

2. This consideration explains why, for example, Machiavelli considered it a sufficient motive for historians of the rank of Bruni and Poggio to neglect the internal history of their native cities out of fear that they might hurt the feelings of the descendants of personalities who, in their day, had taken part

in domestic struggles. If Machiavelli himself believed such fears were unfounded, his explanation is no less characteristic: "E se quelli nobilissimi Scrittori furono ritenuti per no offendere la memoria di coloro, di chi eglino avevano a ragionare, se ne ignannarono, e mostrarono di coggnoscere poco l'ambizione degli uomini, e il desiderio che egli hanno di perpetuare il nome de' loro antichi e di loro." *Istorie fiorentine,* Introduction.

3. As an example of Azariah's method of translating from the Latin we may compare Livy's text with his Hebrew version: Hoc illud est praecipue in cognitione rerum salubre et frugiferum, omnis te exempli documenta in inlustri posita monumento intueri; inde tibi tuaeque rei publicae quod imitere capias, inde foedum inceptu, foedum exitu, quod vites (*ab urbe condita,* Preface), which is freely translated (I, 254; C. 264): הנה ידיעת מח שהיה
לעולמים על פי ספרי הזכרונות תתן לנו פריה זה אשר עד מאד יועילנו, כי ממנה
נקח הלמודים הטמונים בכל מיני חדוגמות, ובהם נכיר את הטוב בעדנו ובעד
עמנו להרחיק המזיק ולקרב התועלת.

4. See Azariah's conclusion, *ibid.*: "Our perfect Law and the books of the Prophets contain many reports of experiences and observations on matters which preceded or followed the promulgation of the Law. In this fashion we are able to penetrate the truth of everything useful to us through our reason and our senses, 'manifestly, and not in dark speeches' [Num. 12.8]. We have no need of expending our physical and literary energies on matters which, among the other nations, constantly lead to conflicting interpretations. Among us everything is regulated by divine justice." Here is what Machiavelli writes (*loc. cit.*) in the opposite sense: "Perché se niuna cosa diletta o *insegna* nella istoria, è quella che particolarmente si descrive; se niuna lezione è utile a'cittadini che governano le Repubbliche, è quella che dimostra le cagioni degli odj e delle divisioni della città, acciocché possano, con il pericolo d'altri diventati savj, mantenersi uniti. E se ogni esempio di Repubblica muove, quelli che si leggono della propria, muovono molto più, e molto più sono utili." See the Introduction to Guicciardini's *Storia d'Italia* (in the excellent ed. by A. Gherardi, Florence, 1919, I, 3): "Dalla cognizione de' quali casi, tanto varii e tanto gravi, potrà ciascuno, e per sé proprio e per bene publico prendere molti salutiferi documenti . . ." See also Flavius Blondus' introduction to his *Italia illustrata* (in his *Opera,* Basel, 1531, I, 293). In contrast to Azariah, most of his Jewish confreres, too, sought to teach, move or fortify the reader. Joseph ha-Kohen explains the title of his book, the *Valley of Tears,* by his intention to make the reader feel desolate and moved so that his eyes would shed many tears and, while wringing his hands, he would exclaim: "How long, O Lord!" Ibn Verga, too, defines the aim of his work in his Introduction by saying that by believing and understanding the stories and dialogues presented by him, Jews will be induced to repent and will implore the merciful Lord to forgive their sins on account of what had befallen them.

5. See the passages cited, *supra,* p. 420 n. 109. See also De' Rossi, II, 128 (C. 399).

6. We know that Machiavelli wished to start his history of Florence in 1434. Even in its present form the last four books, half of the whole work, relate only to the period of 1434-92. Book IX which remained incomplete was supposed to continue the story to 1503.

7. See Eduard Fueter's correct remarks against Georg Voight, who believed that Renaissance historiography had been principally concerned with antiquity. See Fueter's *Geschichte der neueren Historiographie* (Leipzig, 1911), p. 16. But Fueter seems to attach too much importance to its semi-official character. Bruni, Poggio, Scala, Guicciardini and many others wrote the histories of their cities on their own initiative and from their personal knowledge. See, in fact, what Fueter himself says (p. 26). Another Florentine chancellor, Accolti (1415-66), was inspired to write a detailed history of the First Crusade and the Turkish peril which menaced all of Christendom.

8. I, 218 ff. (C. 229).

9. All of this did not prevent Joseph ha-Kohen or Ibn Verga from following the humanistic tendency regnant in both Italy and Spain and from almost exclusively describing the history of recent generations.

10. See his *Historiarum romanorum decades tres,* XXXI *(loc. cit.,* II, 3): "Romanorum Imperi originem incrementaque cognoscere facillimum facit scriptorum copia, quam illius ad summum usque culmen erecti tempora maxima habuerunt."

11. That censorship alone cannot explain this new trend, as suggested by Fueter *(op. cit.,* pp. 130 f.), is evidenced by the continued interest of later historians in the Midle Ages. The true progress consisted more in the extension of their researches into antiquity than in their turning their backs on the medieval period.

12. Girolamo Tiraboschi, *Storia della letteratura italiana,* 2d ed., 9 vols., VII, Part 3 (Florence, 1805-13), pp. 813 ff.

13. See, for example, how the author expressly refers to the "readers" (without any further *epitheton*) four times in the first chapter alone.

14. See *S.O.,* p. 125 (C. 129).

15. I, 68 (C. 81): "It is possible that in this work I shall overlook errors equally shocking to me and to the reader. I announce in advance, therefore, to any intelligent, kindly and sympathetic person that he will give me great pleasure in criticizing me and in pointing out my faults with judicious reasons, so that all obstacles may be removed from our road. If he be generous, he will not fail to judge me with indulgence, a proper thing for all of us, and the Lord will reward him." See also I, 75 (C. 89 f.), the final poem, II, 215 (C. 485), and his self-asssured affirmation in *M.L.,* p. 6.

16. See the aforementioned final poem.

17. See *supra,* p. 419, especially n. 104.

18. I, 63 (C. 78).

19. Leopold von Ranke in his *Zur Kritik der neuen Geschichtsschreiber* (in his *Sämmtliche Werke*, XXXIII-IV, 6 f.), reproaches Guicciardini for interrupting the description of the same campaign because Imola was taken in December, 1499, while Forlì did not fall until January, 1500. Another interruption was occasioned by a certain act of Cesare Borgia of December 31, 1502 which was not followed by a similar action on the part of his father until January 3, 1503. These excesses appear even more blatantly among lesser historians.

20. As a consequence, the *Valley of Tears*, for one example, contains on a single page (Vienna, 1852 ed., p. 35) the end of a description of Jewish persecutions in Europe, notes on the literary works by Ibn Ezra and Ibn Daud and, finally, the beginning of the story of David Alroy. The shortcomings of the annalistic method are somewhat less glaring here, only because the historian's condensed narration of events extending over several centuries allowed little room for the happenings of a single year. This is unlike the effect of the annalistic method on a large work extending over a short period such as Guicciardini's *History of Florence*, which mainly describes the events of 1492-1509, or his *History of Italy*, whose main bearing is upon the years 1492-1534.

21. Aulus Gellius' popularity is attested to by the numerous medieval manuscripts still extant today and by the first edition of his work printed as early as 1469 in Rome. See Pauly-Wissowa-Kroll, *Realencyclopädie der classischen Altertumswissenschaft*, VII (1912), 992 f.

22. I, 123, 236, 244 (C. 139, 246, 253), and *M.L.*, p. 25 n. (C. 27 n.).

23. I, 111; II, 78 f. (C. 127, 350 f.). Occasionally Azariah offers the additional explanation that, if one ventures to correct an opinion held by a high authority, one must present all possible evidence even if it be superfluous. See *M.L.*, p. 63 (C. 66).

24. *M.L.*, pp. 31 f. (C. 33). See also *ibid.*, pp. 34, 78 (C. 36, 84).

25. Here is how he excuses his long delay in dealing with a question (II, 173; C. 444): "It did not appear appropriate to inject here any subject which, if dealt with briefly, would remain inadequately analyzed, and if extensively treated, would make the reader forget the bearing of the entire chapter."

26. See I, 256 (C. 266); *M.L.*, p. 126 (C. 128); and the text cited *supra*, n. 15. Of course, one need not take literally such assertions of unflinching veracity as may be seen in the example of Paulus Jovius (Giovio) who is famed for his conscious subjectivity (to use a mild term) and who nevertheless does not hesitate to declare in the Introduction to his *Historiae sui temporis*, Venice, 1553-60, "Quae amore vel odio nunquam distracti fideli literarum memoriae mandavimus"; and again in his *Elogia virorum literis illustrium*, (Basel, 1577), with even greater emphasis: "Religiosa fide, freti, conscienta

integri pudoris cum vivis ad oblectationem, tum posteris ad exemplum historicis edidimus." Obviously, Azariah hewed more closely to his professed intention.

27. See I, 244 (C. 263).

28. II, 109 f. (C. *M.L.*, 140).

29. *M.L.*, p. 3: "So long as the author adheres to his general purpose, the errors which had crept into some points of detail must accrue to his credit if he retracts and replaces them by more correct statements. I may consider myself fortunate, therefore, that I have been pressed by my objectors to become wiser in the end. This is not meant to be a retraction of my essential purpose, which appears to me as clear as the sun and which, I swear, I should have abandoned if I considered it wrong, but because in this fashion my propositions may be in fuller consonance with the truth."

30. See, for example, *M.L.*, p. 21 (C. 22).

31. *M.L.*, p. 123 (C. 127): "Not like the grievous mistake which, I am told, you have committed in your letter of recrimination . . . as well as the other statements full of vanity."

32. I, 242 (C. 251 f.).

33. See the interesting passage explaining why in Muslim countries, esp. in Safed, secular sciences were peremptorily rejected (*M.L.*, p. 116; C. 119 f.).

34. *M.L.*, pp. 25, 46 (C. 27, 49).

35. See *supra*, p. 419 n. 107. See also *M.L.*, p. 22 (C. 23): "Karaite books which ought to be burned"; and *ibid.*, C. 70 (it is missing in the Benjacob ed.) where, after citing the Karaite Aaron ben Joseph, Azariah adds: "May the souls of the father, as well as that of the son, descend to Hell." He follows here the example set by Abraham ibn Daud and others. See the list of anti-Karaite diatribes cited by Ismar Elbogen in his "Abraham ibn Daud als Geschichtsschreiber," *Festschrift Jakob Guttmann*, pp. 192 f. Among the Jews it is Joseph ha-Kohen who most extensively competes in this point with the contemporary non-Jewish historians. When he exclaims, for example, "Give him O Lord! according to his evil deeds" (*Valley of Tears*, p. 5), this is a relatively mild curse. He is more outspoken (on p. 17) where he assumes a *qinah* cadence and expresses his sorrowful anger in behalf of martyrs: "Take up, O Lord! the cause of their souls, adjudicate their case and avenge the blood of thy servants, as Scripture says 'I will hold as innocent their blood' [Joel 4.21]." We even find entire pages (for instance, pp. 23 f.) written in that vein. We must not forget, to be sure, that Azariah had to restrain himself, at least with respect to Christendom, out of fear of censorship (this is undoubtedly also why Joseph ha-Kohen's works other than his *World History* remained unpublished for a long time). But it stands to reason that even without such apprehensions Azariah's personal temperament and his attitude toward Christianity would not have inspired in him the desire to attack it. In another context he formally protested against the idea of considering all

non-Jewish writers enemies of Judaism, "which indeed they are not." (*M.L.*, p. 116; C. 120).

36. The employment of such phrases does not lend Azariah's style any real baroque flavor of the kind injected by the biblical *melisah* into the literature of the *Haskalah*. We need but consider a few characteristic illustrations: he often felicitously applies halakhic formulas such as: לא יראה ולא ימצא בשום פעם (II, 66; C. 338). While wishing to excuse the errors of certain ancient and more recent authorities, he explains (I, 256; C. 266): כי הרי זה חוליין; בחוץ לא קדשים בעזרת הקודש. Sometimes he borrows a phrase from the Italian, as when he says about Rashi (II, 23; C. 296): שחוא טורח לעשות „(כמשל החדיוט) הרגל אל המנעל". He also successfully resorts to puns, for instance, when he asserts about the High-Priest Jaddua (I, 236; C. 246): מידוע שב לבלתי ידוע. Similarly, when Isaac Israeli the Younger, referring to the sages' knowledge of the first *molad* (nativity of a new moon), had contended that נתגלה להם במחקרם או מדרך הנבואה, Azariah expanded that statement in the following terms (II, 68; C. 339): ואם לחגדיל החכמה ולהאדירה חוסיף לומר או מדרך הנבואה אין לו אלה אלא דברי נביאות. Another felicitous use of puns, which were very popular among the contemporary writers, is seen in Azariah's employment of the very title of his opponent's work as a point of departure for his rejoinder. See *S.O.*, p. 120 (C. 123).

37. Published by L. Modona in "Une lettre d'Azaria de Rossi," *REJ*, XXX (1895), 313-16.

38. See I, 11 (C. 3), as well as his occasional etymologies derived from the Greek. Cf., however, his very important admission while discussing Aristobulos (I, 130; C. 146): "I have heard that a large Greek treatise by him is found in the magnificent library of the city of Florence and also among the distinguished fathers of the Benedictine order in the district of Mantua. . . . I wish I could understand it or that God should induce one of the learned men to translate it into Latin or Italian."

39. See *supra*, p. 414 n. 68.

40. When he writes, for example, ויבנו במות בעל (*Valley*, p. 5) he does not even remotely suggest that the Romans offered sacrifices to Baal. He merely repeats a stereotyped biblical phrase.

41. Chap. XLII, which contains "Exchanges between the author and his friend relating to doubts about the Jewish era of Creation," may possibly reflect a real debate. But it is more likely a wholly imaginary means of self-justification.

42. See the sequence of Chapters IV-VI which follow the more general introduction in Chapter III.

43. II, 15 n. (C. 387 n.).

44. At times Azariah delights in mentioning facts first revealed through the great voyages of discovery. On one occasion he cites Magellan's journey of half a century before (I, 145; C. 161). He likes to refer to maps (I, 156; C.

172) and to argue from the apparent direction of the river Po (I, 158; C. 173). He borrows from direct observation proofs for Italian Jewry's orientation during prayers (I, 159; C. 174), and mentions the local usage of crowning a "king" on Purim (II, 40 f.; C. 313). Such examples could easily be multiplied.

45. Fritz Baer has made remarkable although not wholly successful attempts to introduce order into Ibn Verga's chaos (see his *Untersuchungen über Quellen und Komposition des Schebet Jehuda* [Berlin, 1923], pp. 78 ff.).

46. This is more applicable to the *Me'or 'Eynaim* as such than to the *Maṣref*, the composition of which betrays signs of haste. Azariah realizes it and refers to his indifferent health and advanced age as an excuse (I, 116 f.; C. 121).

47. See *supra*, p. 409, n. 31.

48. See Cassel's Index *s.v.*

49. See especially Isidore Loeb, "Le folklore Juif dans la chronique du 'Schebet Iehouda' d'Ibn Verga," *REJ*, XXIV (1892), 7 ff.

50. See, for example, Azariah's poem (no. 13) published by J. Bergmann in his "Gedichte Asarja de Rossi's," *Zeitschrift für hebräische Bibliographie,* III (1899), 57.

51. I, 122 (C. 231). See also I, 78 n. (C. 93 n. 2).

52. I, 200 (C. 212 n.).

53. I, 229 (C. 239). This manuscript, which belonged to Moses Shalit of Mantua, was so beautifully illustrated that Azariah could not restrain his joy.

54. II, 204 (C. 475). His function as corrector, or as Jewish precensor before the official ecclesiastical censorship (see Rapoport's note on Zunz's biography of Azariah in Benjacob's ed., p. 25; and Cassel's note 5 on that passage by Azariah), may well have permitted him to handle many books. On his use of rare manuscripts and prints, see also I, 102 n. (C. 119 n.) for Venice; I, 127 and II, 179 (C. 143, 449 f.) for Mantua; I, 135, 217, 284 (C. 150, 388, 455) for Ferrara. On another occasion, he rejoiced over being able to consult a manuscript of the Maimonidean *Guide* once used by R. Baruch of Posquières and enriched by him with autograph notes. See I, 245 (C. 255).

55. Azariah cites three different translations of the Maimonidean *Sefer ha-Miṣvot* (which he always cites as SMQ = *Sefer ha-miṣvot ha-qatan* in contrast to SMG = *Sefer ha-miṣvot ha-gadol* by Moses of Coucy), adding that by good fortune he possessed all three. See *M.L.,* p. 55 (C. 58).

56. I, 225 (C. 254). Azariah also distinguishes between the ordinary edition and the "correct texts" of the *Sifra*. See I, 228 (C. 238). In contrast, Zacuto had at his disposal only a small collection of books (see his *Yuḥasin,* ed. by H. Filipowski, p. 22), which explains some of his weaknesses.

57. II, 180, 188 (C. 451, 460).

58. During the first half of the sixteenth century the works by Budeus (*De asse*) and Portius (*De re pecuniaria antiquorum*) had made their appearance. But it was Azariah's generation which pursued numismatic researches with particular zest, and especially two scholars whom he might have met in

Ferrara: Ennea Vico (died in Ferrara after 1564), whose *Discorsi sopre le medaglie degli antichi* were published in Venice in 1555, and Costanzo Landi, who frequently visited Ferrara about 1550 and whose *Selectionum numismatum praecipue Romanorum Expositiones* appeared in Lyons in 1559. See Tiraboschi, *op. cit.,* VII, part 3, pp. 347 f., 850 ff.

59. See, for example, I, 223 (C. 233), where he informs us that another Ferrara Jew, Ahtalion di Modena, had announced in the local Bet ha-Midrash a more correct reading of Alfasi by referring to ancient manuscripts.

60. I, 11 (C. 3). In general, Azariah considers it a great advantage for his generation that it could familiarize itself with ancient historians and other writers hitherto ignored by Jews because they had written in Greek (II, 128; C. 399). In another passage he explains why, in his citations from Josephus, he constantly referred to the new Latin translation by Sigismundus Gelenius, whose superiority over his predecessors had long been recognized by Christian scholars (II, 13 f.; C. 287).

61. II, 145 (C. 416).

62. See I, 70, 142 (C. 84, 158) as well as the entire Chap. XLV. Conversely, Azariah sometimes falls back on old fallacies when he tries to explain some excellent Greek terms through Hebrew. He reports, for example (II, 5 f.; C. 457), that a society of Jewish scholars in Ferrara assumed the name of Academy. When a member expressed amazement that a Jewish society should adopt a Greek name, Azariah reassured him that that term might have a Hebrew etymology (from *'eqed* and *adam!*). However, one must take into account the syncretistic spirit of the age and the general apologetic proclivities of his Jewish contemporaries. It suffices to quote his compatriot, David Provençali, who had written an entire volume entitled *Dor haflagah,* listing more than two thousand words in Latin, Greek, Italian and other languages, all of which had allegedly been borrowed from the Hebrew (II, 185; C. 456). See also Cassel's observation on p. 457 n.

63. II, 115 (C. 386 f.).

64. *Ibid.*: "This is neither an error nor a variant . . . but rather a defect of local pronunciation; in some localities they pronounce *he* like *ḥet* and vice versa, as did (in the talmudic period) the inhabitants of Haifa, Bet-Shan and Tabun. . . . I have indeed observed an old man, native of Apulia, who, when questioned about this phenomenon, attributed it to local usage."

65. See *supra,* n. 39. Curiously, he had only learned from Theseus Pavisius that when Ibn Ezra called Saadiah's language Ishmaelite he referred to Arabic, not Turkish (I, 104 n.; C. 122 n.).

66. See I, 79 (C. 94 n.): the name ὅσιοι, employed by Philo and Eusebius, signifies "saints" (Ἐσσαῖοι). This explanation replaces another, in which Azariah had attributed to Philo an Aramaic etymology (from *asiya*) of the term *Therapeutai* (healers of the soul). But he changed his mind, accepted the etymology of "saint" even for Philo, and referred to a personal

experience. Very likely he was induced to do it when, after first citing from Philo's *Quod omnis probus liber*, xii (ed. by Mangey, II, 457; ed. by Cohn and Wendland, VI, 22, 2), he took fuller cognizance of two more clearly formulated texts, namely that of Philo, *ibid.*, xiii, and that of Eusebius in his *Praeparatio evangelica*, viii.11 (see Mangey's ed. II, 632). Probably also in order to harmonize the contradiction between the numbers 4,000 and 10,000 Essenes cited in the two respective passages by Philo, Azariah first mentions the total number of 4,000 Essenes, but he immediately adds that "although many of them lived in cities, their élite consisting of approximately 4,000 souls dwelt in Greek cities, of which Alexandria was the metropolis."

67. See *ibid.*, I, 231 n. (C. 240 n.): according to Samotheus, the name of "Maccabees" is derived from the Greek and means the same thing as *paladino* in Italian; others explain the name as forming initials of the watchword, *Mi ka-mokha ba-elim YHWH*, which was inscribed on their flag. However, according to that second explanation one would not understand Josephus' calling the martyrs Eleazar, Hannah and the seven children by the name Maccabees at a time when the Hasmoneans had not yet made themselves known. Since these martyrs, too, had been heroes, the first explanation appeared to be more plausible.

68. I, 92; II, 112, 171 (C. 108, 383, 442). It is noteworthy that in the first of these texts he refers to St. Augustine.

69. See I, 79 n. (C. 93 n.): A statement included in an old manuscript of Maimonides' *Commentary* on the Mishnah was a later addition by the author used for self-justification in lieu of the simple term, "as we have already explained it," which he had put in the first recension and which was subsequently retained in the ordinary editions. After discussing this hypothesis Azariah adds: "It appears to me most probable that the words 'as we have already explained it,' represent a copyist's error, for this explanation is found nowhere else and that author is not a man to mislead us. If we had before us the Arabic original, I believe that we would find therein the equivalent of 'as it is self-explanatory.' " This special note shows how little Azariah hesitated, on a remote possibility, to declare a traditional text faulty by referring to a language which he did not know. Cf. Cassel's comment on this passage.

70. I, 234 (C. 244).

71. I, 88 (C. 104).

72. I, 251 f. (C. 261).

73. It is only in regard to the so-called "small tractates" that he shows himself more critical. He observes, for instance, about a text of the tractate *Soferim* "that it is certainly inexact and that this tractate in general does not vouchsafe the same degree of correctness as do the other books of our ancient sages" (I, 120; C. 136). But in this case he could cite the authority of an outstanding rabbi like Asher ben Yeḥiel. See also *M.L.*, p. 40 (C. 42).

74. See II, 52 (C. 324): "Far be it from us to follow even a great man of extraordinary ingenuity if he permits himself to impinge upon Scripture as did Ibn Ezra when he dared to write at the beginning of Deuteronomy ['if you understand the mystery of the twelve verses'] against men more righteous and better than himself. May God keep me from phantasy of this kind!" Azariah also categorically rejected the hypothesis that the redactor of the Bible had modified some texts. "The supposition that Ezra might have arrogated to himself the power of adding to, or deleting anything from, God's Scripture, is neither appropriate for him nor for us!" (I, 223; C. 232).

75. See *supra,* n. 69, also insisting that "he who will reprint this [Maimonidean] text will perform a pious act by using the emended language."

76. See below.

77. II, 3 (C. 277).

78. I, 102 (C. 119): "All these are but stupidities contrary to the Masorah."

79. I, 190 f. (C. 201 f.).

80. *Ibid.*

81. See II, 23 (C. 297): "The other prophet who wrote the book of Chronicles." Contrast this statement with II, 50 (C. 322): "It is thus quite evident that Ezra, who composed the Chronicles, as our sages assert in the first chapter of Baba Batra, and particularly its first pages here discussed, did it under the Persian domination before the arrival of the Greek kings." See also II, 52 (C. 323). In *M.L.,* p. 14 (C. 15 f.), he expresses himself even more guardedly.

82. *M.L.,* pp. 41 f. (C. 44): "And this is what I saw in the Greek translation *attributed* to the seventy elders."

83. I, 126 f.; II, 118 (C. 143, 389).

84. *M.L.,* p. 42 (C. 44).

85. I, 127 (C. 143), where he reaches the conclusion that "although there exist numerous parallels, the differences force us to assume the presence of two distinct authors, unless a single author had translated it in two different fashions . . . and the copyists had called one Jonathan ben 'Uziel and the other the Jerusalem Targum."

86. See his interesting exposition of the history of the ancient versions, I, 120 f.; II, 117 (C. 136 f., 388). We are not at all surprised that he considers Theodotion and Symmachus "Greek Jews." Even today we are not sufficiently informed about their biographies. See the marginal gloss on I, 120.

87. II, 117 (C. 388) and other passages listed in Cassel's Index.

88. I, 104 (C. 121).

89. I, 92 f. (C. 108 f.). Because of its length we cannot reproduce here fully Azariah's very informative exposition. See also I, 128, 133 (C. 142 f., 147).

90. II, 118 (C. 389).

91. I, 132 (C. 148) and *S.O.,* p. 121 (C. 125).

92. These discussions are also noteworthy for the state of critical studies in his time.

93. See *supra*, p. 415 n. 70. See also II, 209 (C. 481) where, in order to confirm a hypothesis by his friend Judah Provençali, he cites the Maimonidean *Guide* and the author of *Derekh emunah*: "Originally the numerous sciences belonged to Israel, but when the nations subjugated us, these passed into their hands; when we now learn anything from them, it appears as if they had priority, whereas the contrary is true." The following passage in Zacuto shows how widely that opinion was shared by Azariah's contemporaries: "Many things of which the nations boast they may have found in the ancient books of the Sages of Israel which, in retribution for our sins, have been lost during our long Exile and on account of our numerous sufferings. Among these are the astronomic works composed by the sons of Issachar, as well as books of medicine and natural sciences which King Solomon wrote on the subject of trees, stones, herbs, the power of stars; also the books on ancient history and so forth." (*Yuḥasin*, pp. 231 f.).

94. I, 187, 214; *M.L.*, p. 41, etc.; Cassel's Index *s.v.* Yose ben Ḥalafta.

95. I, 142, 203, 222 (C. 158, 214, 231).

96. I, 113 (C. 129): "For all matters relating to this chapter I say to the children of Israel: I do not wish to decide whether this Yedidiah or Philo, according to his Greek name, is pure or impure; I shall call him neither master nor sage, nor a heretic and Epicurean, but simply Yedidiah, the Alexandrine. By citing him in my book I do not propose to enter him into the intimate circle of my people. We shall merely listen to his words, as to those of any of the world's sages, concerning matters in which he has no axe to grind. It is up to any reader to pass judgment on his merits, to reject his errors, but to utilize him if he adds to the truth. As far as I am concerned I shall neither combat him, nor shall I lean upon him."

97. I, 111 (C. 129).

98. This does not prevent Zacuto from refusing to accept Josephus for dogmatic reasons. See *Yuḥasin*, p. 531: "All the [non-Jewish] authors trust Joseph b. Gorion but I do not rely upon him. He is hyperbolical, permits himself many exaggerations, and implies things which do not agree with the clear meaning of the Torah."

99. I, 224 f. (C. 234): "This statement by no means stems from Yosippon himself; it is but an idea which is introduced in order to make a certain impression upon the reader. It is, indeed, not found in the Latin Josephus.... Similarly, the story of the Torah translation, as reported in the Hebrew *Yosippon*, Book III, chapter 17, is certainly false and it differs from all other versions I have seen. Anyone examining the matter with care will note that Josephus himself writes differently for the Hebrews in chapter 14 than for the Romans in Book 12, chapter 2." See also I, 80, 118; II, 171 (C. 95, 134, 442), as well as the Index in Cassel, II, *s.v.* Yosippon.

100. *M.L.*, p. 79 (C. 85).

101. *Ibid.,* p. 84 (C. 90): "I know that it is inappropriate for me to contradict a gaon. Yet in the higher interests of truth, I humbly lean upon those numerous authorities who differ from him."

102. *Ibid.,* p. 94 (C. 100).

103. I, 150 f. (C. 166): "Notwithstanding all the respect due to his [Maimonides'] high dignity, he is clearly controverted by chapter VI of *Genesis rabbah.* . . . But this is an error preferable to another far more serious which one cannot justify at all. . . . A false opinion. . . . If he only could have kept silent! And this is not all. . . ." See also II, 110 (C. 380); *M.L.,* pp. 34, 62 (C. 35 f., 65) as well as his interesting objection to Gersonides *ibid.,* p. 69 (C. 75): "I shall not quarrel with him for God is the right judge. But it is clear as day to me that no true scholar could speak in this fashion against Moses and still be held in high esteem in our generation."

104. Against Ibn Ezra, II, 52 (C. 324): "A daring contention"; *M.L.,* p. 41: "troublesome words."—Against Gersonides, II, 74 (C. 346): "In any case we need not pay any attention to him because he tries to be too clever."—Against both, II, 125 f. (C. 397): "I believe that one need not waste time in reading them, for on this subject their words are like the wind."—Against Abravanel, I, 175 (C. 189): "In my opinion Don Isaac lacks good sense on this point"; II, 49 (C. 321): "It appears that he has stolen this idea from the Christian translator [Jerome]." Elsewhere, however, Azariah tries to justify Ibn Ezra by suggesting the possibility of an interpolation; *M.L.,* p. 97 (C. 103).

105. See, in particular, concerning Gersonides, *M.L.,* pp. 67, 72 f. (C. 73, 78).

106. See I, 141, 165 f., 239 f.; II, 66, 119 (C. 157, 179 f., 249 f., 338, 390); *M.L.,* pp. 25, 35 f., 46, 69, 83 (C. 25, 37 f., 49, 75, 89) and many other passages.

107. II, 35 (C. 308): "I suspect that the translator of *Kuzari* was not quite faithful to the author's intention. If it be Ibn Tibbon, it could not be Samuel who always preserves the meaning of the text without mixing in any invention of his own." See also Cassel's note, *ibid.*

108. Against Isserles: I, 165 f. (C. 180): "I have heard that he was a man of God, saintly and for our period a great talmudist . . . a great man . . . in any case his intentions were good and his lot now is eternal blessed life." With regard to Abravanel he writes (*ibid.* and p. 298; C. 369 f.): "The sage and great statesman that Don Isaac was." Azariah had composed an entire poem in honor of Abravanel which is reproduced in the Appendix to Cassel's ed. of *M.L.,* p. 139.

109. See *supra,* p. 421, nn. 119 ff. See also especially II, 201 f. (C. 473).

110. II, 66, 110 (C. 338, 380 f.).

111. See the interesting discussion in *M.L.,* p. 40 (C. 42): "The *Midrash rabbah* is, according to Rashi, a Palestinian Aggadah which the Babylonian Talmud undoubtedly considered inferior to the *Yerushalmi.* Similarly the *Zohar* to which the same reasoning applies. That is why we are in the habit

of eating meat after cheese, contrary to the *Zohar* on the Sabbatical lesson *Mishpaṭim,* because the Talmud permitted it in its chapter *Kol ha-Basar.* For the same reason we recite two benedictions over the phylacteries, and also wear them on half-holidays, contrary to the *Zohar* on the lesson *Pinḥas."*

112. See chap. xix; and particularly I, 223 f. n. (C. 232 f. n.).

113. II, 188 (C. 460): "In some cases we may trust the book by Eldad the Danite, who had come to us from the Ten Tribes, despite everything Ibn Ezra has written thereon in his *Commentary* on *Shemot."*

114. The *Shebeṭ Yehudah* appeared in print for the first time approximtely in 1550 (1554?) and it was reprinted in Sabionetta *ca.* 1570. The *'Emeq ha-baḵha* remained unpublished long after Azariah's death. Yet its first recension had been completed in 1553 and a number of manuscript copies were available in several Italian cities. See Samuel David Luzzatto's Introduction to Meir Letteris's edition thereof, p. x. But it evidently remained unknown to Azariah.

115. *M.L.,* p. 48 (C. 51).

116. I, 2 n. (C. 2): "The *Yuḥasin* printed in Constantinople and recently introduced into Italy."

117. Cassel's Index, *s.v.* Abraham Zacut.

118. See Isidore Loeb, "Joseph Hacohen et les chroniqueurs juifs," *REJ,* XVII (1888), 269.

119. I, 244 (C. 254): "I was very happy that God provided me with the text of the *Epistle* sent by Sherira Gaon to the holy community of Kairowan, not the one mentioned in the *'Aruḵh* under the entry, "Abbaye," but another more than seven times its size."

120. See *M.L.,* p. 8.

121. I, 114 (C. 131): "In his *Sefer ha-Qabbalah,* Ibn Daud cites the text of the Talmud with commentaries of his own invention; I believe that one need not attach too much importance to that work which does not always conform with the thought of our sages, but mixes in elements borrowed from the Hebrew *Yosippon.* You will find further criticism on him in our chapter xix." —I, 235 (C. 245): "Consciously or not Ibn Daud has confused this issue in his book." See also especially, I, 231; II, 19 (C. 241, 292).

122. See also Loeb in *REJ,* XVII, 269 f. On Ibn Verga, cf. Graetz's *Geschichte,* VIII, 397; and Baer, *op. cit.,* p. 14. While writing his major work Azariah did not know Zacuto's note in *Yuḥasin,* p. 219, referring to "R. Benjamin of Navarre [Tudela] who had traversed the world in sixty stages in the year 4938." Nor is it astonishing that the brief reference in Abravanel escaped Azariah. See Elie Carmoly, *Notice historique sur Benjamin de Tudèle* (Paris, 1852), pp. 7 f. It is more surprising that De' Rossi did not know of the Constantinople 1543 edition of Benjamin or that of Ferrara in 1556, which had appeared in his own city. Otherwise he certainly would have had more than one occasion to utilize Benjamin's travelogue, particularly in connection with his geographic analyses.

123. *M.L.,* p. 33 (C. 35): "Not everything our sages say is to be taken literally; many of these nice statements are made in order to induce a good state of mind among the readers."—I, 179 (C. 179): "There are two answers: one, that this sentence belongs to the domain of the *Aggadah* and hence is not conclusive; as Sherira Goan says, this is an opinion not a tradition. . . . Moreover, we declare: if this be a tradition we shall accept it, but if it is a personal decision it is open to debate." II, 67 (C. 339): "You will learn therefore that the truth in these matters is . . . that one ought to understand such words of the sages and their enigmas as parables and metaphors, similar to those of the ancient pagan sages who, while treating philosophic problems, alluded to imaginary stories of actions by demi-gods, men, and all sorts of animals, whether in order to make them inaccessible to the masses or to humor the listener, to make him remember them, or for some other reason . . . this is a way of speaking by analogy and allusion which is called symbolic. We find the same genre . . . in a multitude of pleasant sayings by our rabbis."

124. I, 180 (C. 192): "In brief, these *aggadot* and forced interpretations should not turn our hearts away from the simple sacred texts and sayings which are as clear as the day." See also I, 223 (C. 232).

125. I, 78 f., 136 f., 214; II, 118 (C. 92, 94, 152 f., 224, 389 f.).

126. *M.L.,* pp. 68 f. (C. 74).

127. I, 154 (C. 170).

128. II, 116 (C. 387): "I consider it equally probable and I shall undoubtedly be in agreement with both Jewish and Christian scholars, that this is the origin of the interpretation of their learned translator of עד כי יבא שילה [Gen. 49:10] although the Septuagint, which generally serves as his guide reads: שלו, scil.: to whom the scepter belongs."

129. See *supra,* p. 418, n. 96. See also II, 139 (C. 410).

130. *Yuḥasin,* p. 231: "This will be useful for Jews living among Christians while discussing their respective religions. For this reason I cite writers not belonging to our faith, even though I should not have cited them, since they had been elevated into saints. Our holy Torah, too, mentions evildoers, who do not deserve to be recorded, except that it is done for our benefit. However, you ought to be aware that not all that is written in their books of history from which I happen to quote some pasages is entirely truthful in the way the books of our holy Torah are, may God keep us from such a thought!"

131. See *supra,* p. 417 n. 86 as well as I, 21 f., 225; II, 26, 30, 204 (C. 22, 234, 300, 303, 475 f.); *M.L.* pp. 15, 114 (C. 17, 118 n.).

132. In his Introduction Zacuto pathetically justifies certain imperfections in his story: "Because of my sins and the persecutions, the exile and poverty, I have neither the strength nor the knowledge; my scholarship has not been maintained, my judgment has been weakened."

133. I, 208 (C. 218): "Even if one admits that it could not have happened as they tell it . . . one ought to be grateful to them, for their intention was to

persuade men...." See also *supra,* p. 418, n. 90. For this reason Azariah prefers pagan creeds, in whatever form, to atheism which he condemns as antisocial and subversive. II, 149 f. (C. 420 f.).

134. Cf. II, 139 (C. 410), where he explains his surprising preference for data derived from non-Jewish authors: "The more so since esthetic considerations prove that [the priestly vestments] described by these authors are superior in beauty to those depicted by some of our commentators. . . . I am obliged to state that in the eyes of a polished person [the garb attributed by the latter to the high-priest] is not an attire appropriate for a servant of God and the chief of our nation. Certainly, if it were clearly prescribed by the Law that the high priest should wear hobnailed sandals and place old rags upon his vestments, these would be for him a source of pride and glory. But wherever it is possible to explain a regulation in a way agreeable to both God and man this is a good thing to do."

135. For the references in the following list, which is by no means complete, one should consult the Indices in Cassel's edition, sections II and III. The use of these names undoubtedly requires further detailed analysis, but such a broad study would far transcend the bounds of this chapter and must be reserved for a special monograph on Azariah's sources.

136. That Azariah knew Themistius' "paraphrases" of Aristotle (I, 126; C. 142), was undoubtedly owing to the appearance of its Latin version prepared from the only extant Hebrew renditions by two Italian Jews. The translation by Moses Finzi of the paraphrase of Aristotle's *Metaphysics* Book Lambda made its appearance in 1558. See the new edition, with the Hebrew introduction, by Samuel Landauer (Berlin, 1903), p. 7 n. 1, against Moritz Steinschneider's *Hebräische Uebersetzungen,* p. 177. See also the latter's "Metaphysik Aristoteles" in his *Jüdische Bearbeitungen,* pp. 24 f. The paraphrase of Aristotle's *De coelo* appeared almost simultaneously with Azariah's work in 1574. But Moses Alatino had much earlier discovered a Hebrew manuscript in Perugia, and, since 1568, had been translating that work which "since the days of Averroës until today had always remained shrouded in darkness." Azariah may well have known about it, since Alatino lived at that time in Ferrara, as is indicated in the preface which bears the date: "Ferrariae Calendis Sextilis MDLXXII." See Landauer's edition (Berlin, 1902), p. xiii. See also the privilege issued in 1592 by Pope Clement VIII in favor of Alatino and his son, Bonajuto ('Azriel), in *REJ,* XIX (1889), 134 f., as well as Steinschneider's remark in his *Catalogus librorum hebraeorum in Bibliotheca Bodleiana,* col. 1767; and his *Hebräische Uebersetzungen,* p. 126 n. 128. Incidentally, the younger Alatino's Italian name parallels that occasionally used by Azariah. See *supra,* p. 419 n. 101.

137. Particularly Merula in his book, *De Gallorum Cisalpinorum antiquitate ac origine,* published in 1536.

138. Guicciardini's *La Descrizione de' Paesi Bassi,* and Ortelius' *Theatrum orbis terrarum,* first appeared in Antwerp, 1567 and 1570 respectively. Azariah knew the latter work in its later edition of 1572. Cf. I, 181 (C. 193). A work by Mercator of 1569 is cited in the appendix, II, 90 n. (C. 361 n.).

139. I, 115 (C. 132): "Everyone knows that fluids poured from one vessel to another do not retain their flavor."

140. *M.L.,* p. 60 (C. 62).

141. II, 98 (C. 369). With reference to the numerous Messianic computations of the past, Azariah declares here: "With all due respect to the aforementioned authorities it appears that their bias had gained the upper hand and, in some cases, their human reason had made them err and caused them to assign its [mistaken] findings an inappropriate place in a sacred location," namely, in the context of the Prophets' Messianic predictions. See also with reference to Plutarch and Maimonides, I, 115 (C. 132).

142. On this subject cf. the citation from Averroës in *M.L.,* pp. 94 f. (C. 101).

143. I, 252 (C. 262).

144. *M.L.,* p. 14 (C. 15): "On reflection, it becomes clear that if he had known it, he would not have passed it over in silence." See *ibid.,* pp. 34 f., 54 (C. 36, 57).

145. I, 118 (C. 134): "In any case . . . he who appreciates it will easily recognize that the style and language of the Septuagint Pentateuch is not the same as that of the translator of the rest of the Bible."—I, 223 (C. 232): "He who has the taste for it will realize that in certain places it is not the author's style." See also what Azariah says about the language of the book of Daniel (II, 189; C. 460), and phrases like the following: "If one has an intimate knowledge of the Talmud one notices clearly that this manner of speech indicates an individual opinion" (*M.L.,* p. 39; C. 41).

146. I, 228 (C. 238).

147. II, 156 (C. 428): "In these accounts we need not attach too much significance to divergencies in detail so long as they agree on essential points."

148. *M.L.,* p. 66 (C. 71).

149. *M.L.,* p. 98 (C. 105 n.): "When I decided to record these matters in writing I had compunctions lest the faithful servants of the Torah be displeased. Therefore I stipulate in advance that no one pass judgment on them before listening to the numerous scholars who confirm them one by one."

150. II, 22 f. (C. 394): "Fearing that I might have erred while taxing others with error, I was delighted to find the gaon Karo. . . ."

151. I, 75, 88, 127, 160, 243; II, 210, 226 (C. 92, 104, 143, 174, 252, 481, 499); *M.L.,* pp. 29, 46, 54, 108, 115 (C. 31, 49, 57, 113, 119 n.), etc.

152. I, 82 (C. 99).

153. I, 104 (C. 121): "Or for some other reason unknown to me."

154. I, 126 (C. 142): "I consider this opinion correct under the condition that Jewish and Christian scholars agree with it; otherwise may it be null and

void."—I, 144 (C. 160): "But if my words . . . should not meet with the agreement of the literati, I am prepared to give them up."

155. II, 32 (C. 305): "However, I do not hide behind them, but on the contrary it is my opinion which, with God's help, will serve to support them."

156. I, 209 (C. 219): "I shall not conceal from you, dear reader, that when our scholars learned what I had written on the subject of Titus' insect they assailed me and asserted that I had wronged the holy words of our sages and that God's hand was not too weak to chastize enemies like Titus according to their merits. But I have not retreated and renounced what I had written." See also the justification of this unexpected fortitude which follows this passage.

157. See, for example, the two faulty quotations, in a single paragraph, from Pesaḥim, 94b and from the Baraitha and Rashi in Baba Batra, 25ab (I, 140-42; C. 156-57).

158. See *supra*, pp. 170 f. Despite his precautions Azariah's work did not escape censorship altogether. In the *Purgatio aliquorum librorum hebraicorum* (which I have seen in the probably unique seventeenth-century manuscript of the Municipal Library of Ferrara, no. 290; it is also briefly mentioned by Gustave Sacerdote in his "Deux index expurgatoires des livres hébreux," *REJ*, XXX, 1895, 260) which had been started in Mantua by Azariah's friend Abraham Provençali and had subsequently been revised and completed in 1584 by the Minorite monk, Hippolyte of Ferrara, one finds the following correction on page 161: "Maor Enaim i. Luminare oculorum. In hora qua Deus meminit filios suos positos in tribulatione inter nationes mundi, duas lacrimas in mare magnum emittit et vox ejus auditur usque ad extremum mundi. Mag. r Chatina dicit: manus suas ad inuicem (?) colligat, ut habet Et etiam ego percutiam manus meas super manus meas. Mag. r Jochanan d.: Anxius ero et suspirabo. Mag. r Acha dicit: impellit pedes suas sub solio Glorie. Aliqui dicunt, Deus rugire voce sua, et terram facit tremere. p. 6." The Church simply did not wish to tolerate even the slightest derogation which one might have read into such passages.

159. I, 224 n. (C. 233).

160. See *Yuḥasin*, pp. 45, 88 f., 95 f.

161. I, 189, 260 f. (C. 200, 270 f.).

162. Cf., for example, Marco Guazzo, *La Chronica dal principio del mondo fino a questi tempi* (Venice, 1553).

163. I, 189, 260 f. (C. 200, 270 f.).

164. II, 105 (C. 376): "He [the reader] will thus see that the correction suggested by me . . . is by no means susceptible to causing prejudice; on the contrary, there is room for hope that such researches will enable us to preserve people from pitfalls."

165. I, 85 (C. 100 f.): "Since in Moses' generation there lived in Egypt the greatest astronomer, Atalantus, and his brother Prometheus, first among the physicians, it is possible that, because of their scientific achievements and those

of other sages of that period, God had chosen Egypt for his experiment with 'the iron furnace.' This is also why it is written: 'And Solomon's wisdom excelled the wisdom of all the children of the east, and all the wisdom of Egypt' [I Kings 5.10]. . . . Four generations after Prometheus there appeared an extraordinary sage called by the Greeks Hermes and by the Latins Mercury with a surname of Trismegistus, which means three times great, because he was a great philosopher and, because of it, also a great priest and a great king." —See the chonological divergences in *Yuḥasin,* pp. 234 f.

166. I, 86 (C. 102).

167. I, 116 (C. 132): "He [Justin] lived in the period of Antoninus and Rabbi, for the printed collection of his writings includes a beautiful book against idolatry addressed to the said Antoninus. Perhaps on account of this and Rabbi's teaching, Antoninus converted to Judaism, as is reported in the Palestinian Talmud." See also *Yuḥasin,* pp. 244 f. which, despite its brevity, is more explicit.

168. *M.L.,* p. 28 n. (C. 29 n.).

169. I, 123 (C. 139).

170. Earlier, too, he had briefly cited Caesar's *Gallic Wars* under the name of Caesar Augustus. See also I, 169; II, 153 (C. 188, 424 f.); *M.L.,* p. 30 (C. 32). This is the more surprising, as Renaissance historiography generally distinguished between uncle and nephew and knew that the title "Augustus" was not conferred on Octavius by the Senate until January 27th of the year 27. See, for example, Blondus, *op. cit.,* I, 99, 293. Incidentally, Azariah attributes the calendar reform to Julius Caesar, but dates it forty-five years before its actual computation. See II, 76 f. (C. 347 f.).

171. I, 207 (C. 218).

172. See *M.L.,* p. 28 n. (C. 29 n.).

173. See chap. XXIII and Cassel's note thereon, p. 253.

174. II, 22 (C. 295): "The four hundred and eighty years which elapsed from the Exodus from Egypt to the construction of the Temple and the seventy years which separated the First from the Second Temple offer no obscurity whatsoever. They are clearly indicated in the holy Scripture without leaving any doubt and without allowing for any increase or reduction."—Zacuto adopts a similarly critical attitude toward the figures given by Josephus, but he often gives a chronology different from that of Azariah.

175. II, 87 f. (C. 358 f.).

176. I, 81, f. (C. 96 f.). It may be mentioned that some Karaites like the seventeenth-century writer, Mordecai ben Nissan, distinguished between the sectarian Sadducees and another sect designated by the name of *Ṣedoqim,* because they had pursued justice (*ṣedeq*), by quoting our author, chap. iii. See Ben-Zion Halper's Hebrew review of Mordecai ben Joseph Sultanski's *Zekher Ṣaddiqim* (Memory of the Righteous: a brief survey of Karaism), ed. by Samuel Abraham Poznanski (Warsaw, 1920), in *Miqlaṭ,* IV (1920), 456.

177. See I, 81 f. (C. 96 f.). What he says in order to explain the etymology of these two names has merely a methodological interest: "I have also thought of the affinity of the words Boethosians and Essenes, ... because of the junction of the two words בית and איסיא, originated the word ביתוסים.

178. I, 79 (C. 94): "Similarly the monastic orders which we see today forming among Christians in all sections of their establishment are sustained by them because they have followed their [the Essenes'] example and learned from them." This was by no means a discovery for Church historians.

179. I, 182 (C. 190).

180. I, 113 (C. 129): "I shall not take the trouble now to explain my statement concerning the four thousand Greeks; I wrote it with the idea that, like the Sadducees, they followed Judaism with certain modifications. From the moment, however, when another spirit reigned among them, they had nothing more in common with us."

181. *M. L.,* pp. 79, 92 (C. 84 f., 98 f.).

182. *Ibid.,* pp. 40 f. (C. 43 f.): "Today our prayers are arranged according to a fixed order common to all, which was not the case in the past. From Moses until that period, the command 'to serve the Lord thy God with all thy heart [Deut. 11:12], that is prayer' was observed in the sense that anyone enjoys the freedom of singing a song to our God, be it in supplication or in thanks, in response to the sorrow or the joy of his own heart."

183. See *supra,* p. 429, n. 62.

184. II, 183 (C. 454): "Since these narratives have been translated into all languages, we may see that the proper names have not been modified but are reproduced by all peoples in the sacred language itself: Adam, Cain, Noah, etc. This is a strong demonstration and certain testimony which all peoples offer to us that they trace their origins back to the Hebrew language."

185. II, 190 (C. 461): "Ezra was interested only in books written by prophets under divine inspiration and in the Hebrew language. Our sages, too, in their profound wisdom, have preserved only the books approved by him."

186. II, 184 (C. 455): "In any case, we shall not discard the opinion of our sages, which sets the number of languages, peoples and their [protective] angels at the number of seventy."

187. II, 182 (C. 453).

188. I, 146 (C. 162).

189. II, 170 (C. 441): "The result of which is that Monobaz is merely the title of a monarch, similar to that of Pharaoh for the Egyptians and Abimelech for the Philistines."

190. I, 196 (C. 209) and *supra,* pp. 181 ff. This method was frequently employed by medieval commentators on the Talmud, particularly the Tosafists. Another method of resolving the difficulties of this kind consisted in postulating an extremely long life of the person in question. See Zacuto's analysis (in

his *Yuḥasin,* p. 17) of the problem of R. Yehudah ben Batira about whom
we are still uncertain today as to whether there were two or three tannaim
by that name. Zacuto's answer is simply: "He lived in Babylonian Nisibis while
the Temple was still in existence as is mentioned in the Talmud at the beginning of the tractate Pesaḥim. . . . He did not participate in the pilgrimage to
Jerusalem, for he was old, and as such, freed from that duty. Nonetheless he
lived long thereafter, since we find him still [a century and a half later] in
the days of Rab and Samuel." In order to harmonize several passages in the
Talmud, Azariah also makes Onkelos live from the period of Hillel to that
of R. Eliezer and R. Joshua, but he reduces this century-long interval by
attributing to Hillel a life-time of one hundred and twenty years. See II, 121
(C. 392).

191. I, 232 f. (C. 242). This hypothesis is buttressed by his curious etymology
of the name of Semiramis: ולדעתי הוא מלשון עת הזמיר הגיע בחילוף הזי"ין
בס"מך . . .

192. See, for instance, II, 119 (C. 390): According to the Bible Joseph was
a child of Jacob's old age which Azariah interprets to mean that he was "a
wise child and prudent like an old man," and adds: "It is because his father
made for him a long tunic, as is customary with persons dedicated to studies
and showing signs of a reflective mind and as is still the usage today among
the high classes of the renowned city of Venice where it is worn with a belt.
Joseph undoubtedly wore it while he was en route. And I was happy to find
the same interpretation in *Genesis rabbah,* chap. LXXXIV פסים שהיתה מגעת
עד פס ידו."

193. See Zunz's biography of Azariah in Benjacob's edition, pp. 14 f.

194. See the very interesting discussions in the concluding chapter (lx).

195. See II, 208 (C. 469), where we are told how he happened to arrive at
these conclusions. Azariah adds: "Moreover, I have consulted several scholars
of our time and no one was able to identify any particular rhythm or meter,
but they all recognized that the mere reading of it gives the impression of
poetic harmony; also that there is a difference between such passages and the
rest of the Bible, though no one was able exactly to put his finger on that
variation. After constant efforts to clarify this matter and to secure some
satisfactory result, I became convinced that the sacred poetry follows certain
measurements but that these are not derived from the play of long and short
vowels as do modern poems. The *Kuzari* teaches us that the latter rule applies
also to Arabic poetry which is but a corruption of our Hebrew. The [Hebrew]
rhythm, on the contrary, corresponds to the content." For greater reassurance
he submitted that theory to a friend, Judah Provençali, an expert on Hebrew
poetry, and rejoiced over his approval.

196. II, 209 (C. 480): "I recognize that there remain many verses which I
cannot fit into the indicated rules. Perhaps the exceptions are more numerous
than the rule. But unquestionably, with the aid of the preceding, students

ought to carry on this task and to find what I myself was unable to detect."—
Similarly, II, 211 (C. 482): "I know that my words mean very little and that
they are a mere drop in the bucket, but an understanding person will comprehend them and sagaciously fill in what is lacking."

197. II, 211 f. (C. 482).

198. See Cassel's edition which reproduces all of Azariah's poetic creations.

I. M. JOST THE HISTORIAN

1. Cf. in general E. Fueter, *Geschichte der neueren Historiographie,* 1912
and A. Guilland, *Modern Germany and her Historians,* 1915. It is worthwhile to remark that David Mendel (this was the name of Neander as long
as he was a Jew) at the age of sixteen, when he entered the *Akademisches
Gymnasium* in Goettingen, delivered an address "De Judaeis optima conditone
in civitatem recipiendis" which was soon thereafter (1805) published with
annotations by the director of that institution. However, Harnack in his "Rede
auf August Neander" (*Reden u. Aufsätze,* I, 195ff), delivered on the hundreth
birthday of his great predecessor in the Berlin chair for Church History, may
have been right in assuming that this speech of Mendel concerning the emancipation of the Jews reflected the opinions of the director far more than those
of the student himself.

2. Cf. H. Zirndorf, *Isaak Markus Jost und seine Freunde* (Cincinnati,
1886), p. 130.

3. Even in the title of his book there is apparent the essential contrast
between pure theory and those demands which grew out of life. While calling
his book *Geschichte der Israeliten,* he knows very well that that term can
hardly be applied to a period beginning with the Maccabees. On the other
hand "Juden" was not a respectable name in his time and the Jews themselves
tried to avoid it whenever they could. So he attempts to justify it in the
following way: "Demnach hätte dies Werk den Namen einer Geschichte der
Juden tragen sollen, denn Israeliten gab es damals eigentlich nicht mehr im
Lande Palästina. Allein da hier auch der schon bei der Zerstörung des ersten
Tempels ausgewanderten eigentlichen Israeliten gedacht werden soll, so schien
der allgemeinere Name schicklicher, besonders da die Juden kurz vor ihrer
gänzlichen Zerstreuung ohnehin auch jenen Namen trugen." Cf. I, p. XII.
Obviously a weak argument. Only in his last work on the *Geschichte des
Judentums,* does he feel obliged to tell what this "Judentum" means. But
besides such general terms as "Auferstehung des Geistes nach dem Absterben
des Leibes," on acount of the spiritual survival after the loss of political
independence, he has nothing definite to say. Reaching his own period, however, in his classifications he declares blandly: "Das Judentum sucht die Welt
um sich her, um seine eigene Stellung und Aufgabe zu erkennen. . . . Alles
ist noch im Werden begriffen."

442

4. It is interesting to see that almost simultaneously Humboldt in his essay and Jost in his third volume, both of which appeared in 1822, used a similar phraseology. Humboldt says: "Die Weltgeschichte ist nicht ohne eine Weltregierung verständlich," but confesses at the same time that there has not been given to the historian an organ "die Pläne der Weltregierung unmittelbar zu erforschen und jeder Versuch dazu dürfte ihn, wie das Aufsuchen von Endursachen nur auf Abwege führen."

Jost in discussing the possibilities of a critical investigation of the Bible says (III, Anhang, 203): "Der Teil des Bibel-Inhalts, den man einem hohen Wesen zuschreibt, ist nicht der körperliche, sondern nur ein geistiger Ausfluss des Allregierers in die Seele desjenigen, welcher durch eine Schrift ein Organ der Weltregierung wird." It is true that this terminology was widely spread at that time and that the most popular German historian of the previous generation, Schlosser, had applied it extensively in his universal history—which term he used as opposed to world history, and in which the superhuman element played such an important part.

5. Cf. I, 1.

6. To quote only a few of his commonplaces reminiscent of the period of Enlightenment:

"Wenn der Körper keine Übung, der Geist keiner sonderlichen Anstrengung bedarf, so verfällt der Mensch in eine Ruhe und Schlaffheit, die der Gauner zum eigenen Gewinne benutzt, und der Boshafte zur Ausführung heilloser Entwürfe missbraucht" (I, 4 f.).

"Gebirge und Wüsteneien sind von jeher der Sitz des Aberglaubens gewesen, der sich gerne da ansiedelt, wo die Natur sein Reich durch seltsame Wirkungen unterstützt" (I, 5).

"Die Schweiz als ein Gebirgsland ist sehr oft die Wiege fanatischer Gräuel gewesen" (VII, Anhg. 432).

7. Cf. I, 12.

8. Cf. in particular his description, I, 18.

9. "So wie es überhaupt unrichtig ist, die *Bildung eines Volkes* nach den vorherrschenden Ansichten und Äusserungen einzelner bedeutender Männer die gleichzeitig gelebt und sich ausgesprochen haben, zu beurteilen, und von ihrem beschränkten Wirkungskreise auf das Eigentümliche eines ganzen Volkes zu schliessen; so würde dies Verfahren bei der Darstellung der Volksbildung der Juden in Palästina kurz vor ihrem Untergang, dem Blicke durchaus nur schiefe Richtungen gewähren, und keine gehörige Uebersicht des Ganzen verschaffen." III, 165 f.

10. I, 40, he adds to that "alle Völker der damaligen Zeit knüpften die Religion an die Verfassung mit unauflöslichen Banden."

11. I, 67 f.: "Von der Zerrüttung der Meinungen in Religionssachen, rührten die meisten Zwistigkeiten der Juden her, wie bei allen Völkern, die sich selbst nicht kennen, und, Blinden gleich, dem Leitbande Einzelner oder

Mehrerer folgen müssen. Jeder, der sich ins Herz des Schwachen einzuschleichen wusste, unterliess nicht zur Zeit auch dessen Arm in Anspruch zu nehmen, wenn eigene Zwecke es erheischten. So wurden Teile des Volkes gegen einander gereizt, ohne eigentlich zu wissen, warum. Ein heftiger aber dummer Eifer focht für Heiligkeit, während er sie durch Rach-, Raub- und Mordsucht gerade entweihete." Cf. also III, 34.

12. Cf. I, 152.

13. Cf. III, 33-78.

14. Cf. III, 77.

15. Cf. V, pp. XII f.: "Niemand kann die Abgeschmacktheit der talmudischen Scholastik in Abrede stellen, aber niemand wird aus der Betrachtung derselben, ohne mit einer linguistischen und philosophischen Ausbeute, mehr aber noch mit einem historischen Schatz bereichert zu sein, zurückkehren. Der Talmud kann nebenher dazu dienen, über die Ansichten von einzelnen Mosaischen Gesetzen Licht zu verbreiten, aber Methode und Ordnung muss man so wenig darin suchen, wie richtige Erklärung der Mosaischen Gesetze im Allgemeinen."

16. The following utterance is certainly remarkably typical of Jost's whole attitude: "Es ist hier nicht mehr zu erörtern, ob dieses Gesetz in seinem Grundlagen oder in der Art der Ausarbeitung vollständig einem Volke genügend sein könne; ob es der unendlichen Opfer, welche die Juden ihm einmal zu bringen entschlossen waren, und in der Tat brachten, wohl würdig sei; sondern die Kraft der Überzeugung von der Notwendigkeit, von der Unumstösslichkeit dieses Gesetzes, fordert nunmehr unsere Aufmerksamkeit. Lob oder Tadel des Beweggrundes und der Handlungsweise würde der Geschichte keine andere Richtung geben. Wir sehen nur diese Ursache und diesen natürlichen Erfolg." III, 182.

17. Cf. III, 157 ff.

18. Cf. III, p. VII.

19. When he wants to correct a statement of the French thinker he feel that he must apologize. Cf. V, Anhg. 331.

20. Cf. VII, Anhg. 408 ff., 426 ff., 428 f.

21. Cf. V, Anhg. 336: " Nun hatte zwar die Laune und der Eigensinn der Machthaber oder ihrer Gehilfen viel Teil an den Gesetzen, aber man darf noch nicht so weit gehen, sie als den alleinigen Grund anzusehen; denn jeder Herrscher will doch gerne gerecht erscheinen, und giebt seinen Aussprüchen den Anstrich der Gerechtigkeit."

22. Cf. III, 120. However, immediately thereafter he reintroduces the individual element, "Je grösser das Elend ward in welchem das Volk schmachtete, desto wichtiger schien es den Gelehrten, Mittel zu ersinnen, wodurch das Volk Trost in der Ausdauer, Hoffnung in der Vernichtung finden könnte."

Later in his *Neueste Geschichte* he seems to have felt the influence of his age more strongly, and he is led to a formulation which he had never uttered before: "Selbst Könige und Gründer grosser Staaten sind in ihren Unternmungen nicht frei und unabhängig, ihr Charakter selbst ist oft nur das Werk der Geschichte." X, 1, p. 20.

23. He says about the Christian historians: "die Hottinger, die Buxtorffe, Lightfoot und andere, die zugleich die Orakel ihrer Nachfolger wurden, hatten bei ihren philologischen Untersuchungen die Zeiten und den historischen Gang der Jüdischen Cultur nicht überall beobachtet, und nicht beobachten wollen." On the other hand, the Jewish historians were "der Weltgeschichte fremd, von keiner echten Entwickelung einen Begriff hatten. Ihnen ist nur die Sache und der Name etwas wert, gleichviel wann, wo und wodurch etwas entstanden ist und sich fortgebildet hat." III, pp. III f.

24. It is true that sometimes he made things easier for himself than they really were. If, for instance, he declares that nobody would blame him for not having utilized fully the literature on Josephus' well-known definition of the Second Jewish Commonwealth as a theocracy, because "die Sache ist zu einfach um so viel darüber zu studiren. Josephus hat es nie mit seinen Worten sehr genau genommen, er vermischt Theocratie, Monarchie, Aristokratie; er weiss selbst nicht recht was er sagt. Daher ist daraus nichts zu schliesen" (III, Anhg. 115); the matter was really not quite as simple as that.

25. "Niemand wird mir Basnage *Hist. des Juifs* als Hilfsquelle anempfehlen. Der gelehrte Franzose hat freilich viel gelesen, aber weniges in den Urschriften, noch weniger in den Haupt-Quellen aus älterer Zeit. Bald critisirt er zu viel, bald zu wenig, und man muss am Ende einer jeden Periode mühsam die Resultate und ihre Urheber, denen Basnage seinen Beifall zu geben scheint, heraussuchen, so unsicher stellt er Glaubhaftes und Fabelhaftes, Unbezweifeltes mit Bestrittenem, Wirkliches und Mögliches zusammen. Wir werden über seine Fehler im Einzelnen sprechen, welches uns so nötiger ist, als die *Hist. des Juifs* dieses Verfassers fast das Ansehen einer Haupt-Quelle erreicht hat, die man ohne weitere Untersuchung anführen oder compilatorisch abschreiben dürfe." III, Anhg. 165-71.

26. Cf. III, Anhg. 185, VII. Anhg. 398, etc.

27. Cf. V, Anhg. 334 f.

28. Cf. in particular II, Anhg. 120-36, 198-218, *Allgemeine Geschichte*, 12 ff.

29. His statement in this connection: "Im Gegenteil könne man aus der Sprache, dem Inhalte, und den Anspielungen aller jener Zeit beigelegten Cabbalistischen Bücher, den Beweis der Untergeschobenheit derselben führen. Die Wirkungen, die sie notwendiger Weise haben mussten, zeigen sich nirgend, und schon dadurch werden sie bedeutungslos, selbst wenn sie damals, aber nur unbekannt existirt hätten" (III, Anhg. 196), is indicative of his general critical method in which the more philological inner criticism of the sources is connected with their general historical background and influences. But in this case, as in general, Jost limits himself to a few remarks without penetrating into details.

30. Cf. III, Anhg. 192 f., V, Anhg. 339.

31. Cf. III, Anhg. 147-49.

32. Remarkable in this connection is his admission in the preface to the fifth volume dealing with the history of the Jews in the earliest Middle Ages: "Wenn gleich ich das ganze Unternehmen, eine allgemeine Geschichte der Juden zu schreiben, mit geringem Selbstvertrauen begonnen habe, weil mir die Schwierigkeiten der Aufführung eines so weitläufigen Werkes auf einem noch unempfänglichen Boden hinlänglich bekannt waren, und ich deshalb teils im Voraus auf nachsichtsvolle Beurtheilung rechnete, teils immer nur durch die beifälligen Stimmen mancher minder strengen Beurteiler des bereits Geleisteten zur Fortsetzung der begonnenen Arbeit ermuntert worden bin, so kann ich doch nicht umhin, bei Herausgabe dieses fünften Teiles einzugestehen, dass der Inhalt desselben, mehr als der früheren, vielfältigen Urteilen ausgesetzt sein dürfte und dass ich ihn mit einer gewissen Schüchternheit dem gelehrten Leser vorlege."

33. "Um die allgemeine Teilnahme rege zu erhalten wählte der Verfasser eine Sprache und Darstellungsweise die allgemein verständlich und fasslich sei vielleicht auf Kosten der historischen Würde und Lebhaftigkeit, des Enthusiasmus, der den Leser oft mehr fesselt, als Klarheit und Deutlichkeit; allein das Streben, die Wahrheit hier von allen entstellten Gewändern zu entkleiden, und sie nackt ihrem Wesen nach zu offenbaren, möge dies entschuldigen." I, p. XI. Comp. with this his similar statement in the preface to his last work (*Gesch. d. Judentums,* I, p. IX): "Geflissentlich meiden wir Redeprunk und anlockenden Farbenglanz." It looks, however, very much as if the grapes may have been too sour for him.

34. "Es ist Zeit die Akten über den Wert oder Unwert der Juden und des Judentums zu schliessen, und mit der Untersuchung der Erscheinung selbst, ihrer Entstehung und Fortbildung nach, zu beginnen, um ihr Wesen zu erkennen, und sie, wenn es für gut befunden wird, zu ändern." I, pp. VIII f.

35. Cf. VII, 234.

36. Cf. *Nachg. Schr.,* V, 114 and 188.

37. Cf. *History,* V, 595 (Eng. translation).

38. In a series of violent denunciations he goes as far as to call Jost the "hater of God and enemy of the Jews"; cf. in particular his *Iggaroth,* letter 71; however, later on, after 1837, Luzzatto's attitude became much friendlier, cf. letters 172, 249. Finally, in 1839, in a letter to Jost, he assures him, "that among all the Jewish scholars of the generation known to him, he regards Jost as the greatest," cf. letter 263.

HEINRICH (HIRSCH) GRAETZ, 1817-1891: A BIOGRAPHICAL SKETCH

1. Markus Brann, "Aus H. Graetzens Lehr- und Wanderjahren," *MGWJ,* LXII (1918), 260 ff.

2. Graetz's review of Abraham Geiger's *Lehr- und Lesebuch zur Sprache der Mischna* appeared in *Literaturblatt des Orients,* V (1844), 822-27; VI (1845), 13-16, 30-32, 54-59, 75-78, 86-90, 631-35, 643-49, 664-66, 725-30, 771-75, 784-89, 832, 842-46; and Geiger's reply in the *Literaturblatt* of the *Israelit des 19. Jahrhunderts* (1845), pp. 21 ff.

3. See *Orient,* VI (1845), 277 ff.; and Z. Frankel's reply, *ibid.,* pp. 281 f.

4. Graetz, "Die Konstruktion der jüdischen Geschichte," *Zeitschrift für die religiösen Interessen des Judentums,* III (1846), 270-73, 307-12, 349-52. See Nathan Rotenstreich's analysis of "Graetz and the Philosophy of History" (Hebrew), *Zion,* VIII (1942-43), 51-59.

5. See especially Graetz's letter to A. Placzek in Adolf Frankl-Grün's *Geschichte der Juden in Kremsier,* 3 vols., III (Breslau, 1896-1901), 9.

6. See Graetz's letter to Raphael Kirchheim of July 7, 1879, ed . by S. Unna in "Briefe von H. Grätz an Raphael Kirchheim," *JJLG,* XII (1918), 323 f.; and his "Die Verjüngung des jüdischen Stammes" in Joseph Wertheimer and Leopold Kompert's *Jahrbuch für Israeliten,* X (1863), 1-13; reprinted with notes by Theodor Zlocisti in *Jüdischer Volkskalender* (Brünn, 1903); English trans. by Isaac Leeser in *Occident,* 1865, pp. 193 ff.

7. Graetz's letter to S. S. Ch. Halberstam, cited by Ismar Elbogen in "Aus H. Graetz' Briefen an S. J. Halberstam" in *Festskrift . . . David Simonsens* (Copenhagen, 1923), pp. 391 f.

8. Graetz's "Denkschrift über die Zustände der jüdischen Gemeinden in Palaestina und besonders in Jerusalem," reprinted in Josef Meisl's biography, *Heinrich Graetz. Eine Würdigung des Historikers und Juden* (Berlin, 1917), pp. 142 ff.

9. See *Jewish Chronicle* (London), of July 22, 1887.

10. Graetz's letter to Marx, dated February 1, 1877, was found by B. Niko-layevsky in the archives of the German Social-Democratic Party, then in Paris, and was published in facsimile with a Yiddish translation and with an Introduction by Elias Tscherikower in *YIVO Studies in History,* II (1937), 656-65. From among the host of essays dealing with Marx's attitude to Jews and Judaism we need but mention here the judicious analysis by Solomon F. Bloom in his "Karl Marx and the Jews," *Jewish Social Studies,* IV (1942), 3-16; and *supra,* p. 346, n. 5.

11. Graetz's *Briefe einer englischen Dame über Juden und Semitismus,* published anonymously (Stuttgart, 1883), and republished two years later under the title, *Gedanken einer Jüdin über das Judentum in Vergangenheit, Gegenwart und Zukunft* (Stuttgart, 1885); idem, "The Significance of Judaism for the Present and Future," *JQR,* I (1888), 4-13; II (1889), 257-69.

12. Moses Hess's translation of vol. III, entitled *Sinaï et Golgatha ou les Origines du Judaïsme et du Christianisme,* appeared in Paris, 1867. On Graetz's attitude to the Lovers of Zion movement, see Meisl's aforementioned biography, pp. 106 f., 165.

13. Graetz, *Geschichte,* IX, 3rd ed., 445.

14. A full bibliography of these monographs was published by M. Brann in his "Verzeichnis von H. Graetzens Schriften und Abhandlungen," *MGWJ,* LXI (1917), 444-91; supplemented by "Nachträge und Berichtigungen" by Brann, Samuel Poznanski and Bela Bernstein, *ibid.,* LXII (1918), 266-69. See also the more selective list in the German original of this essay in *Encyclopaedia Judaica,* VII, cols. 650 ff.

15. See Graetz's oft-quoted Introduction to his *Geschichte,* vol. V.

16. Graetz, "Die allerneueste Biblekritik Wellhausen-Renan," *MGWJ,* XXXV (1886), 193-204, 233-51.

17. Abraham Geiger, "Aus einem Briefwechsel," *Jüdische Zeitschrift,* IV (1866), 145-50; *idem,* "Berichtigung einiger neuer Behauptungen," *Hebräische Bibliographie,* III (1860), 1-4; Moritz Steinschneider's critical notes on successive volumes of Graetz's *Geschichte, ibid.,* pp. 103 ff.; IV (1861), 84; V (1862), 31; VI (1863), 73 ff. Steinschneider also refers here to Meir Wiener's largely negative "Zur Würdigung des Verfahrens von Graetz bei die Bearbeitung seiner Geschichte," *Ben Chananja* (1863), nos. 22-23.

18. See, for instance, Hermann Cohen's essay "Ein Bekenntnis in der Judenfrage," reproduced in his *Jüdische Schriften,* ed. by Bruno Strauss with an Introduction by Franz Rosenzweig, 3 vols., II (Berlin, 1924), 73-94, esp. p. 86 (see also *ibid.,* pp. 470 ff.); Ludwig Philipson's "Antwort an Professor Dr. v. Treitschke," *Allgemeine Zeitung des Judentums,* XLIII (1879), 785-87; *idem,* "Wider Herrn von Treitschke," *ibid.,* XLIV (1880), 19-21. See also Graetz's letter to Samuel Kristeller of October 16, 1885, reproduced by Meisl in his biography, p. 183.

GRAETZ AND RANKE: A METHODOLOGICAL STUDY

1. Leopold von Ranke, *Die römischen Päpste, ihre Kirche und ihr Staat im 16. und 17. Jahrhundert* (1834-36); *Deutsche Geschichte im Zeitalter der Reformation* (1839-47), both reprinted in his *Sämmtliche Werke,* 54 vols. (Leipzig, 1868-90), vols. I-VI, XXXVII-XXXIX (available also in English translations).

2. On Ranke see the excellent chapter in Eduard Fueter, *Geschichte der neueren Historiographie,* pp. 473 ff.

3. David Kaufmann, "H. Graetz" (1891), reproduced in his *Gesammelte Schriften,* ed. by M. Brann, 3 vols., I (Frankfort, 1908-15), 277. See also Richard Fester, "Humboldt's und Ranke's Ideenlehre," *Deutsche Zeitschrift für Geschichtswissenschaft,* VI (1891), 235-56.

4. Ranke's letter to his son Heinrich of February 26, 1835, with reference to his "hard work" on the completion of his book on the Roman popes, in his *Zur eigenen Lebensgeschichte,* ed. by Alfred Dove (Leipzig, 1890) in *Sämmtliche Werke,* LIII-LIV, 273; A. von Reumont, "Leopold von Ranke,"

Historisches Jahrbuch der Görresgesellschaft, VII (1886), 608-35, esp. 630. It may be noted that the editor of the *Jahrbuch*, Victor Gramich, felt impelled to add a note to this quotation from Ranke, stating his dissenting view of the relation between theology and history. He referred to his earlier review of "L. von Ranke's Weltgeschichte," *Historisches Jahrbuch der Görresgesellschaft*, V (1884), 3-51.

5. Ranke, *Französische Geschichte vornehmlich im sechzehnten und sieb zehnten Jahrhundert*, reproduced in his *Sämmtliche Werke*, XII, 3.

6. What Philip Bloch and B. Rippner say in this matter in their introduction to the second edition of Graetz's *Geschichte*, vol. I, is merely another typical attempt by biographers to discount the faults of the personalities described by them.

7. Thomas Babington Macaulay, *The History of England from the Accession of James II*, I (New York, 1899), 15.

8. Moritz Steinschneider, "Josef (Ibn) Aknin," reprinted in his *Gesammelte Schriften*, ed. by Heinrich Malter and Alexander Marx, I (Berlin, 1925), 76 f. See also *supra*, p. 293.

MORITZ STEINSCHNEIDER'S CONTRIBUTIONS TO JEWISH HISTORIOGRAPHY

1. Cf. below n. 72. Apart from the usual periodical abbreviations, the following shortened forms will be used in our notes: *AL* = Arabische Literatur der Juden, Frankfort, 1901; *BHB* = Bibliographisches Handbuch über die... hebräische Sprachkunde (Leipzig, 1859), 2d ed. (Jerusalem, 1937); *RM* = Bibliotheca mathematica (Stockholm); *CB* = Catalogus librorum hebraeorum in Bibliotheca Bodleiana (Berlin, 1852-60), new impression (Berlin, 1931); *EJB* = Essays in Jewish Biography by Alexander Marx (Philadelphia, 1947); *FE* = Die fremdsprachlichen Elemente im Neuhebräischen (Prague, 1845); *GL* = Die Geschichtsliteratur der Juden (Frankfort, 1905); *GS* = Gesammelte Schriften, I, ed. by H. Malter and A. Marx (Berlin, 1925); *HB* = Hebräische Bibliographie, ed. by Steinschneider (Berlin, 1858-65, 1869-81); *HU* = Die hebräischen Uebersetzungen des Mittelalters (Berlin, 1893); *JBGW* = Jahresberichte der Geschichtswissenschaft, I-VI (Berlin, 1880-88; the page references here are given to the respective first sections of each volume); *JL* = Jewish Literature, English transl. (London, 1857); *PAL* = Polemische und apologetische Literatur in arabischer Sprache (Leipzig, 1877); St. = Steinschneider; *ZHB* = Zeitschrift für hebräische Bibliographie (Berlin and Frankfort, 1896-1920).

The present writer wishes to thank Professor Alexander Marx for generously placing at his disposal transcripts of many manuscript letters received by St. Brief excerpts from these letters in their original spelling (elsewhere modern orthography is preferred) are given below in notes 6, 18, 21, 35, 36, 47, 54, 55,

56, 60, 86. The letters from Cassel and Loeb were collated with the originals. Unfortunately those written by Geiger were not available at the time this essay went to press. Cf. also below n. 23.

2. *HB*, III, 65.

3. Cf. George Alexander Kohut's "Bibliography" in *Festschrift . . . Stein-schneider* (Leipzig, 1896), pp. v-xxxix, successively brought up to date in *ZHB*, V (1901), 189-91; IX (1905), 90-92; XIII (1909), 94-95; and H. Malter and A. Marx's Foreword to their ed. of *GS*, pp. viii f. St. himself often lost track of his publications. Not only are his articles and letters filled with complaints about misplaced manuscripts, inability to consult previous comments, etc., but he, as well as the editors of *ZHB*, overlooked the fact that one of his "Miscellen" had already appeared in that journal three years before. The mistake was detected by Marx after the event. Cf. *ZHB*, VI, 159; IX, 120 f.; X, 92.

4. *HB*, III, 67. In a previous installment he had actually blamed Kayserling for having superimposed upon his earlier strictly literary and bibliographical study an "Aufguss" of history, in order to make it more palatable to the general reader. *Ibid.*, II, 83 f. Cf. also III, 104; IV. 11, 64 f., etc.

5. *JBGW*, I, 38; *HB*, II, 108; V, 110.

6. *FE*, pp. 5 f., 26, 29; *BHB*, p. x; *HU*, p. xxii; *HB*, II, 83; VI, 31 f.; IX, 12 f. St.'s remark (*ibid.*, I, 110) concerning the personal relations seems to have inspired Berliner's pertinent monograph. Cf. also the sharp expression of similar views in his "Robert von Anjou und die jüdische Literatur," *Vierteljahrsschrift für Kultur . . . der Renaissance*, I (1885), 137. They had long been shared by his friend, David Cassel. "Das Judenthum tritt mit allen Wissenschaften," Cassel wrote him on April 13, 1843, in connection with their joint preparations of a comprehensive Jewish encyclopedia, "mit allen Völkern, mit allen Gegenden, in eine bald nähere, bald weitere Berührung, und sobald man aus dem eigentlichen Gebiete jüdischer Wissenschaft herausgetreten ist, wird man durch die unbegrenzte Ausdehnung dessen, was weiter zu durchwandern ist, erschrekt, z. B., jüdische Geschichte."

7. *HB*, VI, 7, 31. From this angle he sharply criticized a number of studies, published in 1883 and devoted to the general characterization of Judaism or the Jewish people, particularly in relation to Christianity, "welche, wenn sie unbefangen und gerecht sein soll, der Gesammtgeschichte, namentlich der Kulturgeschichte, entnommen sein müsste. Die letztere ist kaum angebahnt. Auf diesem Boden, oder richtiger in diesem Luftreiche, lassen sich Schlösser aus gewissen allgemeinen Voraussetzungen bauen; da ist viel Spielraum für geistreiche Kombination, aber auch für kühne Behauptungen." *JBGW*, VI, 38.

8. *FE*, pp. 26 f.; *AL*, pp. xii ff.; xlvi ff.; Z. Frankel, "Allgemeine theologische Bibliographie," *Zeitschrift für die rel. Interessen*, III (1846), 466 (with reference to St.'s introduction and notes to Maimonides' *Sefer ha-Yihud*); *HB*, V,

117 f. In 1845 he also planned to state his views in a comprehensive article, "Araber," in the projected Jewish encyclopedia, *FE, l.c.*

9. *Der Aberglaube* (Hamburg, 1900), p. 5 (= Sammlung gemeinverständlicher Vorträge, XLVI, 347); *AL*, pp. vii f.; *HU*, p. xx; *GL*, pp. 26 ff. Cf. also *IIB*, XVIII, 81: "Obwohl die Geschichte der Juden in Deutschland im Allgemeinen nur Variationen desselben traurigen Themas darbietet. . . ."

10. *HB*, II, 73 f.; III, 48 f.; IV, 26 f.; V, 139; *HU*, p. xxiv. On his views on the interrelations between the science of Judaism, the Reform movement and Jewish Emancipation cf. *HB*, IX, 76 ff. It is also noteworthy that William Wright, though generally corresponding with him only about technical problems of scholarship, felt prompted to add to the letter of May 18, 1857 a reassuring postscript: "I think your coreligionists have a fair chance of being admitted into parliament this time, as government has taken up the measure." Cf. A. Marx, "William Wright's Letters to Moritz Steinschneider," *Gaster Anniversary Volume* (London, 1936), p. 436. St.'s innermost belief in the ultimate triumph of justice through learning found expression even in his concluding remarks on the Passover Haggadah in L. Landshuth's *Maggid Mereshîth* (Berlin, 1856), p. xxix: "In der Tat hat die Bosheit stets ihren besten Helfershelfer an der *Unwissenheit* gefunden! Möge daher das Gebot: 'Du sollst verkünden deinem Sohne' nie vergessen sein in Israel, und den Abend des Erlösungsfests das Licht der Wissenschaft verklären." On his (minor) part in the Revolution of 1848, cf. Marx, *EJB*, p. 131; and Adolph Kober, "Jews in the Revolution of 1848 in Germany," *JSS*, X (1948), 157, 163 f. In 1880, however, while criticizing Henry S. Morais's biographical sketch, St. contended, at least with reference to his Vienna period, that he had "an keinerlei politischer Agitation sich beteiligt," *HB*, XX, 59. Cf. also below notes 67-70.

11. *JBGW*, I, 38; *HB*, II, 81; *AL*, p. xlix. In the programmatic statement introducing his bibliographical journal he likewise declared: "Wir scheuen es nicht für das Schrifttum der Juden in seinem Zusammenhang die Bezeichnung 'national' zu gebrauchen. . . . Die Befürchtung religiöser, politischer und sozialer Folgerungen und Trugschlüsse aus dieser Bezeichnung kann für unser Blatt von gar keiner oder höchst untergeordneter Bedeutung sein, indem wir den Kampf und Sieg auf dem dankbaren Felde religiöser und politischer Kontroverse den hierzu berufenen—und unberufenen—Federn überlassen." *HB*, I, 2. Cf. also the early comment on Ibn Sahula in his *Manna* (Berlin, 1847), p. 113; his *Letteratura italiana degli Giudei* (Rome, 1884), pp. 2 f.; "Die Mathematik bei den Juden," *BM*, 1893, 66; "Allgemeine Einleitung in die jüdische Literatur des Mittelalters," *JQR*, XV (1903), 303 f.; and Marx, *EJB*, p. 181. He sounded a noteworthy warning, however, against the prevailing fashion of treating the Spanish Marranos indiscriminately as a part of Jewish history (*HB*, III, 68; VII, 98); and, finally, entirely repudiated the term, race "mit seinem verworrenen, entweder verherrlichenden oder erniedrigenden

Nebenbedeutungen" *(GL,* p. vi). Cf. also his critical review of "Racenstudien" in *HB,* XIII, 18 ff., 44; *JQR,* XVII, 577 f.; and below notes 60 and 65.

12. From later reminiscences by Albert Löwy, one of the charter members of that secret society, in the *Jewish Chronicle* of Nov. 13, 1891, p. 30. Cf. also S. W. Baron, "Abraham Benisch's Project for Jewish Colonization in Palestine (1842)," *Jewish Studies . . . George A. Kohut* (New York, 1935), pp. 73 ff.

13. *Orient* of Sept. 19, 1940, pp. 290 f. On St.'s authorship of this anony-mous correspondence, cf. Baron, *op. cit.,* p. 75 n. 9.

14. *Ibid.,* p. 85; Marx, *EJB,* p. 132; *HB,* I, 28; V, 137; XXI, 123. In another context he referred, with more detachment, to the renewed interest of many Jews in the colonization of Palestine created in the early 1880's "by the Russian calamities." *JBGW,* IV, 28. Cf. also his cool obituaries of Alkalai, Elijah Gut-macher, Hirsch Kalischer and even Benisch himself in *HB,* XV, 133; XVIII, 135.

15. *HB,* II, 74; VII, 125 f.; *Manna,* pp. 29, 97; *HU,* p. xxii; *AL,* p. ix. Harping on his perennial theme of the interrelations between Jewish culture and those of the environment he declared, in another context, that the so-called peculiarity of the Jews is often but the outgrowth of ignorance of these foreign influences. "Die Grundideen des Judentums, Einheit und Geistigkeit des Weltprinzips, gleiches Recht und Nächstenliebe, haben vieles Fremde zuge-lassen, grösstenteils assimilirt, sogar Giftiges, zur Verwirrung seiner unauf-hörlichen Leichenredner," *HU,* pp. xxiii f. Cf. also his critique of L. Lazarus's essay on talmudic ethics in *HB,* XVII, 31. It is small wonder that Felix Adler's ethical culture movement struck a responsive chord in St. In his review of Adler's *Creed and Deed* (1877) he stated that the latter's "Religion des Ideals," though devoid of mass appeal, should find general approval among the edu-cated members of all denominations, *HB,* XVIII, 10. Cf. also G. A. Kohut, "Steinschneideriana," *Studies in Bibliography . . . Solomon Freidus* (New York, 1929), p. 84.

16. *HB,* VII, 6, 74; VIII, 4. He readily admitted his unfamiliarity with the writings of a leading Orthodox rabbi, Seligmann Beer Bamberger of Würz-burg, *ibid.,* XVII, 89. Cf. also *ibid.,* I, 32; III, 28, etc.

17. *JBGW,* VI, 27 f., 41 f.; *Der Aberglaube,* pp. 23, 29, 32; *HB,* X, 156 ff.; XIV, 332 ff.; XVII, 36 ff.; XVIII, 18 ff., 62; *BM,* 1893, 66; *JQR,* XV, 312 f.; *ZHB,* VIII, 154; *GL,* pp. vii, 52. Apart from its irrationality, the Kabbalah was found objectionable also because "Schwärmer, Betrüger und Buchstaben-deuter wussten Alles unterzubringen, selbst Trinität und die Verspottung des Talmuds, hauptsächlich aber bildeten sie einen *Dualismus* aus, in welchem die Völker die 'andere (dämonische) Seite' *Sitra Aḥara* vertraten." *PAL,* p. 360. Cf. also *MGWJ,* XL, 132 (where he attacked the "Wortschwall" of the compiler of the *Zohar* and declared, "Die eklektischen Lorianer habe ich gar nicht berücksichtigt"); *HB,* X, 156, 161; and other writings listed by G. Scholem in his *Bibliographia Kabbalistica* (Leipzig, 1927), pp. 148 ff. He was

close to thirty when, as he wrote with relish, he had thrown off "the drudgery
of the irksome, large literature of practical and ceremonial law," Marx, *EJB*,
pp. 127 f. Later on he criticized even David Hoffmann's monograph on the
first Mishnah as having been written "with much expert knowledge but with
an Orthodox tendency," *JBGW*, V, 40. Cf. also *ibid.*, IV, 28. Nor could he
repress his anger when he learned from Joseph Halévy's journey that, as in
the days of Maimonides, "in Jemen spukt noch der Messiasschwindel," *HB*,
XIII, 4 f. On one occasion he objected to a liturgical work "of harmless piety"
because it contained prayers of superstitious origin of which most of the
worshipers were completely unaware. "Um so mehr müssen wir den Wunsch
aussprechen, dass fromme aber denkende, und als Gelehrte in allgemeiner
Achtung stehende Männer nicht ihren Namen an die Spitze solcher Unter-
nehmungen stellen," *HB*, II, 24.

18. *GS*, I, 634 ff.; *HB*, III, 73; V, 38, 59, 138; VI, 17; VII, 123 ff.; VIII, 36,
39 f.; XV, 134. Cf. also his non-committal reference to David Einhorn's death
(*HB*, XXI, 124); and his sarcastic remark (*ibid.*, I, 75) on the *Minhag America*
of Wise and Lilienthal (he never forgave the latter for the sloppy list of the
Munich Hebrew manuscripts, cf. *ibid.*, V, 107 ff.), which he knew only from
newspaper reports. On the other hand, he hailed the acquisition of a large
Hebrew library by Temple Emanu-El in New York (*ibid.*, XI, 89 f.) and
praised highly the rare "clarity" with which Isak Mieses discussed the differences between Orthodoxy and Reform in a Hebrew essay published in Kobak's
Jeschurun, III (*ibid.*, III, 5). He also welcomed the Prussian law of 1876,
allowing secession on grounds of "religious scruples." His position on this
controversial subject simply was that "Freiheit gebührt allen; wer sie nicht
gebührend anwendet, wird ohne Zweifel den Schaden zuerst an sich selbst
gewahren," *HB*, XVII, 6. Cf. S. W. Baron, "Freedom and Constraint in the
Jewish Community," *Essays . . . Linda R. Miller* (New York, 1938), pp. 9-22.
This lackadaisical attitude appealed, of course, but little to Geiger's ardent
temperament. In his letter of Dec. 11, 1853 the latter reproached St. for his
lukewarm attitude toward various essays in Schorr's *Hechaluṣ*, II: "Die tüch-
tigen, zu reformatorischen Resultaten führenden kritischen Untersuchungen
über den Talmud und die Rezension über Rapoport's *'Erekh Millin* sind
Ihnen zu reformatorisch, zu wenig voraussetzungslos, das heisst zu wenig mit
der Absicht unternommen, alles zu lassen, wie es ist."

19. *HB*, I, 97; VII, 9 f.; XIII, 66.

20. *HB*, I, 30, 121; II, 2, 33, 53 f.; 80 f., 121; V, 139; *AL*, p. xxi; *JBGW*,
II, 52. Of course, he did not mean to deny altogether Islam's conversionist
pressures. He himself pointed out that among the more than two hundred
ascertainable names of Jewish authors of Arabic works were eight converts
to Islam, *AL*, pp. xxi f. He was right, however, about the comparatively
greater toleration of the Jewish minority in Muslim lands. He was also greatly
impressed by the freedom of religious debates there on which he assembled

extensive data in *PAL* which, in his opinion, had merely demonstrated the ineffectiveness of religious polemics (p. ix).

21. *HB*, I, 52 ff.; VI, 140; VII, 55; *HU*, p. xxiii. Cf. also his sharp attack on M. Duschak's *Umriss des biblisch-talmudischen Synagogenrechts*: "Die Bibel kennt keine Synagoge. Der Verfasser macht sich nach katholischem Muster von Kirche und Kirchenrecht ein Synagogenrecht zurecht, um den Rabbinern Vorrechte der Geistlichkeit zu vindiziren," *JQR*, XV, 311. Knowing his dislike of the rabbinate, Geiger once facetiously wrote him (May 24, 1859): "Uebersehen Sie mir die Niederträchtigkeit, dass ich Rabbiner bin; wenn ich einst zum zweiten Male geboren bin, werde ich es nicht wieder thun." Five years later (April 8, 1864) the great reformer commented in a more serious vein about the "desolate" conditions in Berlin: "Was wollen Sie also von den armen Rabbinern, wenn die Gemeinden und unabhängigen Gelehrten nichts taugen, wenn die ehrlichen und kenntnisreichen Rabbiner naserümpfend betrachtet werden, weil sie das Verbrechen begehen, Rabbiner zu sein?" If, on the other hand, St. objected to Jellinek's appeal (in *Beth-Talmud*, III, 99) for funds for a critical edition of Midrashim, because a just appreciation of Jewish literature would prove more helpful to the Jewish people than the support of Jewish refugees from Russia and their transfer to America, it was not because he disagreed with Jellinek's evaluation of the two endeavors, but because he wished to see Jewish scholarship divorced from all practical considerations, *JBGW*, V, 40. In fact, on another occasion he praised Leon Horowitz for the Hebrew pamphlet, *Rumania we Amerika*, because the latter "will nicht Amerika mit Müssiggängern bevölkern," *HB*, XIV, 8 f. Cf. also *HB*, I, 32; II, 7 f., 82 n. 2; VII, 25 f.

22. *JBGW*, I, 40; *HB*, V, 119 ff.; VI, 15 f.; VII, 61. St. registered with approval such bequests as Isaac Lyon Goldsmith's legacy of £2000 for a Hebrew chair at the University of London and the establishment of an unbiased "Zunz-Stiftung" for the promotion of Jewish learning, *HB*, I, 26; II, 71; VII, 73 f. He also hailed Alexander II's gift of a diamond ring to Adam Ber Lebensohn as a sign of governmental recognition of Jewish scholarly endeavors and welcomed the sponsorship, by the Imperial Academy of Sciences in St. Petersburg, of a Jewish fund for Academy prizes in the field of Hebrew literature, *HB*, I, 65; II, 97. The repercussions of his attack on the newly-founded Berlin *Hochschule*, "the new ghetto for Jewish learning" (1875) and his refusal to accept a call to the Budapest Seminary (1876) are described by Marx in *EJB*, pp. 140, 144. Cf. also *idem* in "Steinschneideriana, II," *Jewish Studies . . . Kohut*, pp. 318 ff. On his part, St. somewhat naively refused to accept the excuse of a student of the Eisenstadt rabbinical academy that the latter's visit to the Berlin Institute would have been bitterly resented by Hildesheimer, *HB*, XIV, 118. Cf. also *ibid.*, IX, 78.

23. *Letteratura italiana*, p. 1; *ZHB*, VII, 160; Marx, *EJB*, p. 168. His readiness to help serious-minded scholars came to the fore not only in his opening

the pages of his journal to legitimate inquiries addressed to any informed reader, but also in his public offer to place his vast accumulated material at the disposal of any scholar (preferably one having access to Italian libraries) who might wish to compile a comprehensive bibliography of Italian-Jewish literature in the *Corriere israelitico*. Cf. *HB*, VI, 2; IX, 25; XI, 142. After several years of waiting he proceeded to the publication of these data in *Il Buonaroti* (1871-76), *Vessillo israelitico* (1877-80) and *MGWJ* (1898-1900). Conversely, he acknowledged without stint help received from such scholars as Zedner, Neubauer, Lasinio and particularly Prince Boncompagni, "ce noble et libéral savant, qui m'a fourni pendant vingt-cinq années tant des matériaux intéressants." Cf. "Une Dédicace d'Abraham de Balmes au Cardinal Dom. Grimani," *REJ*, V (1883), 113. On the other hand, disappointed by the failure of his announcement (in *HB*, I, 5) to elicit sufficient response from contemporary authors, he decided to terminate one of his major bibliographical compilations with the beginning of the century, for "eine Literatur der Gegenwart ist nirgends ohne lebendige Mitwirkung oder ein eigenes Organ ausführbar." Cf. *BHB*, p. xxxi. Unfortunately George Kohut's announcement, several decades ago, of a forthcoming publication of the St. letters by Miss Adeline Goldberg, St.'s devoted secretary, never materialized. Cf. *Studies . . . Freidus*, pp. 86, 118 n. 97.

24. *HB* I, 29, 79 f.; III, 103; *ZHB*, VIII, 151. He also expressed doubts as to the effects of the study of modern Bible criticism and natural sciences upon the religious convictions of Jewish youth in *HB*, XIV, 75. Cf. also *ibid.*, XIX, 4 f. He did not try to repress his gloating over the downfall of the Institute after twenty years of activity which, he believed, had fully justified his reiterated pun of its having promoted Jewish "Makulatur" (waste paper) rather than "Literatur," *ibid.*, p. 132. He evidently forgot that a quarter century earlier he himself had published selected translations from medieval Hebrew writers which, he had hoped, would "das Interesse eines grösseren Publikums für diese Literatur gewinnen." Cf. *Manna*, Preface. In his middle years and ever after, however, he came to believe that "je mehr auf allen Seiten auf eine s. g. praktische Verwendung aller Studien hingedrängt wird, desto dringlicher ist die Mahnung, die Geschichte nicht zur Magd herabzuwürdigen," *HB*, II, 107. Cf. also his *Ueber Sprachkenntnis und Sprachkunde* (Hamburg, 1899), p. 8 (= Sammlung gemeinverst. Vorträge, N. F. XIV, Heft 322, p. 312), which, though itself the transcript of *popular* lectures, began with an attack on popularization. He underwent a similar transformation with respect to the usefulness of a Jewish encyclopedia. In his late twenties he spent endless hours in preparing, jointly with David Cassel, a draft of a *Real-Encyclopädie des Judentums,* exchanging numerous letters, discussing articles with prospective contributors, etc. In 1865, however, he declared, "Der vor 20 Jahren gefasste Plan einer Realencyclopädie über die gesammte Wissenschaft des Judentums wäre noch heute verfrüht." Later on he sneered at the

dilletantism of the American *Jewish Encyclopedia,* ed. by Isidore Singer, calling it the *Singer-Maschine,* and but grudgingly admitted some of its merits. Cf. Marx, *EJB,* p. 125; *HB,* VIII, 134; Kohut in *Studies . . . Freidus,* pp. 108 ff. He also rejoiced when he had occasion for a dig at the "practical Englishmen" or for pointing out, on the example of the allegedly pragmatic science of astrology that "der s. g. 'praktische Sinn'—welchen man oft den leeren fruchtlosen Spekulationen gegenüberstellt—sich bis zum Wahnsinn verirrt, wenn er eben nicht von einer vernünftiger Theorie geleitet wird." Cf. *HB* I, 26; *Der Aberglaube,* p. 7.

25. *HB,* III, 12, 36, 76; V, 95; XVIII, 25, 77; *JBGW,* I, 41; IV, 23; VI, 50. Cf. also his comments on the *Jahrbuch für Israeliten 5619* (in *HB,* II, 22 f.); and on the *Illustrierte Monatshefte (ibid.,* VIII, 131); and his caustic remark, "Eine Uebersicht der sich in unerfreulicher Weise mehrenden Zeitschriften giebt Ch. D. Lippes *Bibliographisches Lexikon" (JBGW,* III, 57). On the other hand, he irately attacked the liberal *Grenzboten* for reproducing, without proper condemnation, the contents of an early Jesuit treatise referring to the affair of the Jewish boy, Simle Abeles in Prague of 1693. Cf. *HB,* I, 121; II, 80 f. (Here St. unnecessarily censured M. Güdemann's failure to quote him in "Jesuiten und Judenkinder," *MGWJ,* VIII, 1859, 365-74).

26. "Hebräische Zeitschriften," *Zeitschrift für die rel. Interessen,* III, (1846), 28-33; *HB,* I, 3, 28, 78, 91; III, 21 f., 101 f.; VIII, 130 (with reference to Keller's *Bikkurim,* II, 194). For a time he himself toyed with the idea of editing a Hebrew periodical. In 1859 he wrote, "Unser eigenes Projekt einer hebräischen Zeitschrift schreitet nur sehr langsam vorwärts, worüber wir durchaus nicht klagen, da wir noch nicht einmal einen Prospectus veröffentlicht, und schon manche Anmeldung erhalten haben," *HB,* II, 2. He was doubtless stimulated to this undertaking by his cherished conviction that, as a result of eighteenth-century German humanism and Mendelssohn's "immortal achievement," German Jewry, even more than the Jewish Hellenists and Arabists before it, faced the historic task, "auf die Gesammtheit ihrer Glaubensgenossen umgestaltend einzuwirken, die jüdische Wissenschaft unter den Juden, wie der Deutsche die Wissenschaft überhaupt, zu vertreten." Nor was he unaware of the necessity of keeping up with the constantly growing output of Jewish monographs and articles for "nirgends gilt das *dies diem docet* mehr als in dem regen Leben der jungen jüdischen Wissenschaft." Cf. *FE,* pp. vi, 29. Nevertheless, this constant look-out for current publications often became so tedious that he decided to discontinue temporarily the *HB* in 1865 and to abandon altogether his annual review of historical literature in *JBGW* after six years. Cf. *HB,* VIII, 129; *JBGW,* VI, 35. After a while he ceased paying attention even to such a valuable scholarly journal as Löwenstein's *Blätter für jüdische Geschichte und Literatur,* published for many years as a supplement to the *Israelit* in Mayence. Cf. *GL,* p. xi.

27. *HB,* I, 2, 94 f. This was, in part, also the reason for his objections to the

excessive stimulation of Jewish studies by popularizing agencies of the community: "Die Wissenschaft will auf einem natürlichen Boden gepflegt sein, in Treibhäusern und Mistbeeten bringt sie nur exotische Gewächse aber keine Früchte," *ibid.,* p. 26.

28. *HB,* I, 95; III, 16; IV, 11; VII, 58 f.; XIII, 18 f., 44; *JBGW,* VI, 38. He encouraged G. Wolf's archival studies: "Möge er auf diesem richtigen Wege vom Einzelnen zum Ganzen verharren," *HB,* VII, 108.

29. *HB,* II, 66; III, 104; XVI, 36; *JBGW,* IV, 25. He also cited, with full approval, Harry Bresslau's remark, likewise aimed at Graetz, "Es ist ein Unglück der jüdischen Historiographie, dass sie sich der Universalgeschichte zugewandt hat, ehe in Spezialdarstellungen der Boden geebnet und der Pfad gebahnt war," *ibid.,* I, 40.

30. *ZHB,* IX, 153 f.

31. Marx, *EJB,* pp. 148 f.

32. *JBGW,* I, 46; II, 56 n. 1; IV, 33 n. 1; *HB,* XIX, 77 n. 1. St. objected here to the studied attempt of Jewish scholars to ignore Cassel's publications on account of the author's conversion. Cf. also *Letteratura italiana,* pp. 11 ff.; "Mathematik bei den Juden," *BM* (1893), 67.

33. *JBGW,* I, 43; V, 36; *HB,* XX, 70. Cf. also his praise of Chwolson's *Die semitischen Völker* in *HB,* III, 44; his comments on the backwardness of Hebrew palaeography, *ibid.,* XXI, 95; and his frequent references to Firkovitch and his forgeries, *ibid.,* VII, 109 ff.; X, 139; XIV, 133 f. (F.'s obituary).

34. *HB,* II, 5 f., 37 ff. He quoted, in this connection, from Humboldt's letter to M. Mortara of Nov. 12, 1853 and from another autograph letter to an unnamed correspondent (Steinschneider himself?) of May 4, 1857. To justify the inclusion of Humboldt's obituary in a journal devoted to Jewish bibliography, St. argued significantly that it belonged to the annals of that discipline, "welche zum Probirstein echter Wissenschaft überhaupt geworden —die des Judentums, die noch immer, mit den Juden selbst, auf ihre Befreiung von den Fesseln harrt, an welchen Geistlichkeit und Theologie seit Jahrhunderten geschmiedet."

35. Marx, *EJB,* p. 141; GL, p. 27 n. 2; *JBGW,* I, 44; VI, 47; *HB,* I, 32; XVII, 34 f. Cf. also his attack on an exaggerating American philo-Semite in "Die Juden und die profanen Wissenschaften," *MWJ,* XX (1893), 229 ff. I. Loeb shared his deprecation of Schleiden's work. Before sending St. a copy of the French transl. published by the Alliance (cf. *HB,* XVII, 85), he wrote confidentially, "Le travail original fourmille de fautes, mais il est fait à bonne intention, il peut avoir quelque effet utile et à ce titre, il a paru bon de la repandre. Nous avons naturellement laissé à l'auteur toute la responsabilité de ses erreurs. Il y en a tant qu'il était impossible de les corriger" (Aug. 17, 1877).

36. *JBGW,* I, 39 n. 4; *HB,* II, 27, 49; XV, 9. Cf. also his admiring review of Zunz's *Zur Geschichte* in *Serapeum,* VII (1846), 38-45; his list of *Die Schriften*

des Dr. L. Zunz des Begründers der jüdischen Wissenschaft, Berlin, 1857 (with numerous attacks on Zunz's detractors); the dedicatory Forewords to his ed. of the *Mischnat ha-Middot* (Berlin, 1864); his *Vite di matematici arabi* (Rome, 1874); and such occasional diatribes as *HB* I, 66 n. 1 ("eine kurze, aber in der bekannten Weise des Meisters gründlich gearbeitete Darstellung"); and VIII, 138 ("wie selten vereinigt sich solche Wärme der Begeisterung mit solcher Schärfe der Kritik und solchem Umfang der Gelehrsamkeit"). He must have been terribly shocked when he read in Geiger's letter to him of July 27, 1864 the following devastating comment, which, incidentally, also implied a condemnation of some of his own best efforts: "Mit Zunz habe ich mich recht gefreut, er war ganz der Alte, und ärgerte mich nur, was aber nicht von heute datirt, dass er seine Kraft den deutsch-französischen . . . zuwendet; ich meine, es sei nachgerade im Kote genug herumgewühlt. Ich für meine Person danke Gott, dass ich höhere Probleme gefunden, und denke, dass zu deren Aufhellung noch genug zu thun sei. Wenn die besten Kräfte der Juden an solch Untergeordnetem sich zerarbeiten, wie kann man verlangen, dass die Christen Respect vor jüdischer Wissenschaft haben sollen?"

37. *CB,* cols. xliv n. 41, 1633 ff., 2131 f.; *BHB,* pp. xiv n. v; xxiv, xxx f.; *HB,* III, 41, 61 f.; VIII, 11, 50 f., 117 f.; XII, 68; XXI, 16; *GS,* I, 216 f., 624 ff.; *Bolletino italiano degli studi orientali,* 1876, 153 f. Not being seriously interested in the philosophy of Jewish History, he mentioned Krochmal only casually, as when he wished to illustrate the impact of Hegelianism on recent Hebrew letters. But he collaborated with Zunz in the preparation of the posthumous edition of the *Moreh nebukhe ha-zeman.* Cf. *FE,* p. 32; *CB,* cols. 1589 f.; and Zunz's introd. to Krochmal's work. Cf. also Simon Rawidowicz's introd. to his ed. (Berlin, 1924), p. 219 n. 1; and his "Zunz's Notes on the Edition of the *Moreh nebukhe ha-zeman"* (Hebrew), *Keneset,* VII (1942), 378 n. 1.

38. *HB,* I, 30, 123; XIV, 133 f.; XVII, 79 f.; and above n. 18. His first reaction after Geiger's death was to publish a complete bibliography of Geiger's works and a brief description of the manuscripts left in the estate (*ibid.,* XIV, 134), but he seems to have left the execution of these plans to Abraham's son, Ludwig, whose appeal for the loan of biographical materials he mentioned in *ibid.,* XV, 52. Unfortunately, Ludwig Geiger, in publishing a volume of his father's letters, omitted, out of consideration for that mythical personality, the "general reader," the "technical" communications to and from Steinschneider. Cf. A. Geiger's *Nachgelassene Schriften* (Berlin, 1875-85), V, p. vi. Cf. also *ZHB,* IX, 119 ff.

39. *HB,* I, 125; VII, 10; IX, 17 f. Strangely St. claimed priority over a suggestion by Munk to Reinaud which the latter published in 1842, while his own statement appeared in 1848 and his preparations had not begun before 1844. Cf. *BM,* 1895, 26.

40. Cf. e.g., *CB,* col. xliv n. 41; *HB,* III, 30 (Almanzi); II, 80 (Beer); VI,

108 f.; VIII, 8; XX, 73; *JBGW*, III, 58 (Benjacob; cf. also his review of Benjacob's *Quntros Debarim 'Attiqim* in *Zeitschrift f. d. rel. Interessen*, III, 196 f., 274 ff., 399 f.; and Moses Schorr, "Aus einem Briefwechsel betreffend Benjacob's Thesaurus," *Jewish Studies . . . Kohut*, pp. 543 ff.); *HB*, XII, 90; XX, 4; XXI, 93 f. (Berliner); *FE*, p. 22; *HB*, XV, 133 (Frankel); *JBGW*, IV, 24 (Halberstamm); *HB*, XIII, 3; XVIII, 18; XX, 55; XXI, 99 (Jellinek); XVIII, 31 (Lazarus); XV, 133, 135 f. (L. Löw); XX, 138 (Malbim); II, 102 f. (Reifmann); XII, 68 (Della Torre); XVI, 98 f. (I. H. Weiss). On his relations to David Cassel, Harkavy and Neubauer, cf. Marx, *EJB*, pp. 172 ff. As an illustration, however, of his early strained relations with Neubauer we need cite but his "Abfertigung" of a passage in the Oxford bibliographer's essay in the *AZJ*: " 'Das Berliner bibliographische Orakel selbst . . . hat diesen neuen פ״סב adoptiert.' Diese Zeilen enthalten eine *unverschämte böswillige Lüge*," *HB*, VIII, 32.

41. "Wissenschaft und Charlatanerie unter den Arabern im neunten Jahrhundert," *Virchows Archiv für pathologische Anatomie*, XXXVI (1867), 570.

42. *HB*, I, 37, 51 f.; II, 12 f.; III, 80; VII, 61; *GL*, pp. 14 f. Benjamin's popularity highlighted, in his opinion, the corruption of contemporary journalism, "indem es den jüdischen Journalen so recht bequem gemacht wird, für die Unterhaltung ihrer Leser zu sorgen, unbekümmert um Wahrheit und Wissenschaft," *HB*, III, 9. Cf. however, his considerably milder critique of Jacob Saphir's travelogue, *ibid.*, XIV, 115.

43. *HB*, IV, 10; VI, 31.

44. Marx in *PAAJR*, V, 136 f.; *JL*, p. 289 n. 2a, 292 n. 42; *CB*, col. 815; *HB*, VII, 113 f.; *JBGW*, III, 61; *ZHB*, IX, 119 ff. He summed up his grievances in his uniquely vindictive obituary notice: "Am 15. Februar kehrte auch zu Frankfurt a. Main in 'die Wahreit' ein der ehemalige Rabbiner in Brüssel, Elijakim Carmoly (ursprünglich Getsch Sulz aus Colmar), nachdem er dieselbe durch Fälschungen aller Art und freche Plagiate in zahlreichen Schriften und Artikeln verläugnet und misshandelt hatte. Obwohl seine, durch Belesenheit und Dreistigkeit unterstützte, alle Kritik verhöhnende Tätigkeit, schon vor einem halben Menschenalter warnende Stimmen (Zunz, Geiger u. A.) wach gerufen, fehlte es doch nicht an Männern (Jost, Fürst, Löw und Andere), welche seinen hebräischen und französischen Artikeln Verbreitung verschafften. . . . Als er den Geist aufgab, hatte letzterer ihn selbst längst aufgegeben. . . . Wenn es aber die Aufgabe der Kritik ist, 'der Wahrheit die Ehre zu geben,' so bleibt dem Andenken Carmoly's kein Segen der Gerechten übrig," *HB*, XV, 134. This notice and similar ones on the death of Fürst and others naturally created widespread resentment, and St. himself felt obliged to explain this behavior to his students. Cf. Marx's testimony in *EJB*, p. 171. Such "exhibitionism" nevertheless alienated many thoughtful young men, e.g., Immanuel Löw. Cf. Kohut's report in *Studies . . . Freidus*, p. 115. I. Löw's distaste must have increased when he read, in St.'s

obituary of his father, Leopold, the censure of "eine sich immer mehr vordrängende polemische Tendenz, deren Ausdruck, namentlich in der von ihm redigierten Zeitschrift *Ben Chananja* (1858-67) die Grenzen des wissenschaftlichen Ernstes nicht einzubehalten wusste," *HB,* XV, 135 f. Cf. also *ibid.,* III, 79; XV, 105 ff.; XVII, 78; *BHB,* p. xxxii n. 3; *Letteratura italiana,* pp. 11 n. 33, 13, 37 n. 150, etc. Cf., on the other hand, his defense of the bookseller, M. W. Schapira in *JBGW,* V, 34.

45. *FE,* pp. 16 n. 33, 27; *CB,* p. xliii; *BHB,* p. xxviii; *JBGW,* II, 59; *HB,* VII, 30; VIII, 51; XX, 70. Fürst's book gave him also a welcome opportunity of attacking its publisher once again: "Mit der Herausgabe dieses, ohne alle eigene Quellenkenntnis und Kritik aus modernen Büchern fabrizierten Machwerks haben die 'Leiter' sich und der Zweckmässigkeit ihres Instituts ein unzweideutiges Denkmal gesetzt," *HB,* V, 134. Cf. also *PAL,* pp. 343 ff.

46. *BHB,* pp. xxxii ff.; *HB,* III, 117. He referred back to that attack on Jost, *ibid.,* II, 99 f.; III, 48. Of course, Jost's joint leadership of the Institute with his former critic, Ludwig Philippson, gave St. the opportunity of attacking both. Cf. *BHB,* pp. xxxiv f.; *HB,* I, 51; II, 98 f.; XIV, 132. Cf. also his incidental sharp remarks in *HB,* III, 60, 80 n. 4, 104, etc.; and, more generally, *supra,* pp. 260 ff.

47. Geiger, "Berichtigung einiger neuen Behauptungen," *HB,* III, 1 ff.; Steinschneider, *ibid.,* II, 28 f.; III, 104 f.; *JL,* p. 290 n. 18. Geiger's dislike of Graetz came to the fore already in his letter to St. of Aug. 29, 1853, in which he reported the receipt of "Jellinek's Sammlung שמות של unter d. T. בית המדרש" and of vol. IV of Graetz's *Geschichte* which was the first to appear. He was certain of St.'s sympathy when he wrote, without giving it much benefit of doubt, that he had not yet opened it. "Die Belehrung, die ich daraus zu schöpfen habe, werden (!) mir noch zeitlich genug kommen." Cf. also St.'s biting remark in *HB,* V, 30: "Ueber Maimonides' offizielle Annerkennung als Rabbiner von *Kahira* (sic) wird man wohl auch noch die genaueren Daten aus HSS. von Carmoly zur Bestättigung der Conjecturen Graetz's abwarten müssen."

48. *Ibid.,* VI, 73 ff. He carried his dislike of Graetz to the extent of frequently quoting criticisms by other scholars and attacking Graetz's magazine articles and biblical studies, which he otherwise shunned. Cf. *HB,* III, 107 f.; V, 50 n. 1; VIII, 10; XI, 53 n. 4; XII, 131; XIV, 1, 77; XIX, 6 f.; XXI, 12; *JBGW,* I, 41; II, 59; III, 66; IV, 24 f.; V, 37; *GL,* pp. 8 f., 18, 22, 25, 58, 60, etc. On one occasion he admitted, however regretfully, that Graetz's major critic, Emanuel Schreiber, was not Graetz's equal, *JBGW,* IV, 25; and even that a conjecture by Graetz had been confirmed by N. Brüll, *ibid.,* II, 60.

49. Personal reasons alone seem, however, to have made him refrain from extensively using the *MGWJ* as an outlet for his publications during the Frankel-Graetz regime. This is evident from both his more frequent appearances in that journal after Graetz's death and his occasional complaints about

the unavailability of sufficient space for his writings. Cf., for instance, his "Occidentalische Uebersetzungen aus dem Arabischen im Mittelalter," *ZDMG*, XXVIII (1874), 453 n. 1, concerning the suspension of the *Serapeum* which caused him to discontinue one of his publications; and his complaint that the *ZDMG* itself did not evince enough interest in Jewish studies, *HB*, II, 6, n. 2. For this reason he could not himself live up to the praise he bestowed upon I. Blumenfeld for exercising so much restraint in the *Oṣar neḥmad*, as not to appear in it at all, *ibid.*, III, 60 f. A mere perusal of *HB* shows how much space (fortunately for us) he appropriated to himself. Cf. also the pathetic remark in *ZDMG*, XXVIII, 456: "Der Stoff [for what was to become the *HU*] ist mir selbst so angewachsen, dass ich für die materiellen Mittel zu einer Veröffentlichung meiner weitausgreifenden Arbeit vorläufig keinen Rat weiss, dennoch für eine sehr zweifelhafte Zukunft fortarbeite." We know that only the prize contest of the Académie des Inscriptions finally determined him to submit a complete ms. (cf. Joseph Derenbourg's letter about it published by Kohut in *Studies . . . Freidus*, pp. 119 f.) and even then he had to publish the German original at his own expense. Cf. *HU*, p. x. Undismayed by this continued lack of facilities, however, he untiringly collected materials for his *AL., GL* and other works over a period of several decades.

50. *JBGW*, III, 60; *HB*, III, 5; VIII, 134. Güdemann's *Religionsgeschichtliche Studien*, 1876, elicited the following comment: "Sinnreiche Kombinationen, mitunter mehr verlockend als überzeugend, und an der Bibel respektvoll stille stehend," *ibid.*, XVI, 124. Cf. also *ibid.*, XIV, 16, 45; XXI, 45, 99, 115, 125; *ZHB*, VII, 118 ff.; *JQR*, V, 312.

51. Cf. *HB*, I, 33 f.; VIII, 136; XVIII, 32, etc. Although he was sometimes impatient with Kaufmann's overflowing enthusiasm, he occasionally admitted that "K. versteht es aber, mit seiner Begeisterung den Leser anzustecken, den ungläubigen mit Neid um den guten Glauben zu erfüllen." Cf. his review of *Die Haggadah von Sarajewo* in *OLZ*, I (1898), 308 ff. Cf. also below notes 77, 83. St. also encouraged such promising young scholars as Ignaz Goldziher and Immanuel Löw. Cf. *ibid.*, X, 111; XXI, 55.

52. *HB*, II, 107; III, 87; IV, 3 ff. (Wiener's criticisms); VI, 139 f.; VII, 108: VIII, 112, 137; XX, 89. At the same time he thought highly of Wiener. Cf. his aforementioned quotation from Wiener's critiques of Graetz and his brief obituary in *HB*, XX, 138.

53. Cf., e.g., *HB*, XVIII, 81 (Barbeck); II, 66 (M. A. Lewy); XVII, 82; XIX, 124 n. 2 (Loeb); XIX, 77 (Löwenstein); I, 110 (Oelsner); XVI, 36, (Osimo); XVIII, 132 (Pesaro); XVIII, 127; XXI, 104 (Saige, with reference to his own article in *REJ*, V, 277 ff.); *JBGW*, VI, 40 (De Soignie); *HB*, XIV, 116; XXI, 45 (J. M. Zunz). Cf. also his remarks on Arsène Darmesteter's family, *ibid.*, XV, 3; and on Ch. D. Lippe's bibliographical lexicon, *ibid.*, XXI, 15. On the other hand, he spoiled his friendship of many years with Meyer Kayserling (cf. above and *HB*, XXI, 126; *JBGW*, II, 52) by an

unbridled attack on Ludwig Philippson, Kayserling's father-in-law and subject of the latter's full-length biography; cf. Marx, *EJB*, p. 174.

54. The following passages may serve as further illustrations of this attitude: *HB*, XXI, 53; *GL*, pp. 41 f. (Gaster); *HB*, III, 66 f. (Goldenthal); *HB*, XXI, 3; *JBGW*, IV, 27 (Ch. M. Horowitz); *HB*, XXI, 15; *JBGW*, IV, 26 (D. Joel); *HB*, XXI, 122 (Luncz); XX, 42 (Picciotto); XX, 74 f. (Schlossberg); XXI 129; *JBGW*, V, 35 (M. Schwab); *JL*, p. 292 n. 37 (Y. Schwarz); *HB*, XXI, 47 (Smolenskin). With reference to his attack on Goldenthal in *CB*, col. 1020 f. (then in the press), he explained to Geiger in his letter of March 25, 1855: "Solche Kerle muss man nur mit Knütteln kritisieren." Cf. on the other hand, his change of mind in regard to Schwab in *ZHB*, X, 184.

55. Marx in *PAAJR*, V, 118. In a letter dated May 16, 1844, Cassel also warned him, in behalf of Zunz, that he should beware of heaping details upon details in his articles for the *Realencyclopädie*, since this was not going to be a "Gelehrtenbuch." Cf. also *GL*, p. xi; his correspondence with Geiger and the authorities of the Bodleian Library who had objected to the lack of "brevity and perspicuity" in *CB*, cited by Marx in *EJB*, pp. 136 f.; and below n. 86.

56. *ZHB*, VII, 91 (with Marx's supplement thereto, *ibid.*, p. vii); "Gab es eine hebräische Kurzschrift?" *Archiv für Stenographie*, 1877, nos. 466-67 (cf. Kohut's note thereon in his "Bibliography," p. xvi); "Talmid" in *HB*, VII, 16 ff. Even with respect to his private correspondence D. Cassel in a letter dated May 10, 1844, not unjustly called him "Papiergeizig."

57. *GL*, p. v; *Virchow's Archiv*, XXXVI, 573; LII, 341; "Arabische Mathematiker mit Einschluss der Astronomen," *OLZ*, IV (1901), 91; *ZHB*, VIII, 152 ff. Cf. also his review of Lucien Leclerc's *Histoire de la médécine arabe* in *Deutsches Archiv f. Geschichte der Medicin*, I (1878), 356 ("Ref. muss von vornherein seine Unfähigkeit betonen über eigentliche Geschichte der Medizin ein Urteil abzugeben"); his somewhat bolder declaration in his study of "Die Metaphysik des Aristoteles in jüdischen Bearbeitungen," *Jubelschrift . . . Zunz* (Berlin, 1884), p. 1 ("Wir müssen hier der Versuchung widerstehen, in das Gebiet der Geschichte der Philosophie selbst abzuschweifen, zu welcher unser Versuch gelegentlich einiges weniger bekanntes Material liefern wird"); and his obituary of Olry Terquem (Zarfati) whose expert knowledge of the history of mathematics was, in his opinion, greatly vitiated by the "ignorance of Hebrew palaeography," *HB*, V, 95. Understandably he was even more skeptical about the connection between the achievements of modern Jewish scientists and the evolution of Judaism. Cf. his caustic remarks in *ZHB*, X, 187. One can readily imagine, therefore, his wrath over the uncalled-for editorial note accompanying an essay on Maimonides in the same *Deutsches Archiv*, II (1879), 463 ff. The influence of all Semitic peoples, including the Arabs, the editors wrote, "in den Wissenschaften und Künsten im Allgemeinen bloss ein conservativer, conservierender und weiterbildender, aber kein productiver [ist], indem das Erfindungs- und Entdeckungstalent, sowie der

Geist der Initiative ihnen abgeht." Cf. *HB*, XX, 37. St.'s interest in the history of science evidently emerged from his bibliographical preoccupations. During their joint preparation of the *Realencyclopädie* it occurred to neither Cassel nor himself that he be entrusted with any of the projected articles in this field. Cf. also St.'s reminiscences half a century later concerning the difficulties he had had in preparing *JL* to secure significant information about the scientific branches of Jewish literature. Cf. *BM*, 1893, 65.

58. *HU*, p. xxiv; *BM*, 1893, 68 ff.; 1894, 99; 1895, 19; "Schach bei den Juden" in Van der Linde's *Geschichte . . . des Schachspiels* (Berlin, 1873), pp. 155-201. Cf. his review of G. Wertheim's *Die Arithmetik des Elia Misrachi* in *MGWJ*, XLI (1897), 96. Cf. also F. H. Garrison, "Moritz Steinschneider as a Contributor to the History and Bibliography of Medical Literature," *Contributions . . . Emanuel Libman* (New York, 1932). Although on more than one occasion St. professed his belief in the unity of the human mind, he made little effort at integrating Bar Ḥiyya's and Zacuto's scientific outlook and method with their historical works. In the *Megillat ha-megalleh* the former had advanced what we may call an outright "astrological conception" of Jewish and general history. Nevertheless St. disposed of his work in a brief paragraph inserted in the "Appendix" to his *GL*, p. 81. He should at least have been alerted to its importance by his own discovery of the great influence this book had exercised on the outlook of Don Isaac Abravanel, however much he disliked that "uncritical eclectic" and "fine plagiarist." Cf. his "Apocalypsen mit polemischer Tendenz," *ZDMG*, XXVIII (1874), 633; *PAL*, pp. 375 ff. Cf. also *ibid.*, pp. 307, 341, 350; *GS*, I, 327 ff., 333 f. Only his utter aversion to all astrologers, "deren Anschauungen wohl mit Recht der Vergangenheit übergegeben werden" (*ZDMG*, XXVIII, 631), was at the root of this conspicuous neglect. Zacuto, to be sure, was treated extensively (*GL*, pp. 88 ff.), but his scientific achievements were merely mentioned here in passing. At the same time, St. greatly regretted that interest in chronology, long kept alive by its halakhic relevance, had steadily declined until it was completely shoved aside in Joseph Karo's legal code. Cf. *BM*, 1896, 109. Cf. also *CB*, cols. xiv ff., xxxvii ff., 706 ff.

59. *HB*, V, 57 ff.; VII, 31. It is doubtful whether he would have mentioned Lasinio's address, were it not for his personal appreciation of the Florentine librarian to whom he later dedicated his *PAL*. Cf. also his "Anfragen und Bemerkungen über einige Handschriften der *Medicea* zu Florence an Herrn Prof. Lasinio in Pisa gerichtet," Kobak's *Jeschurun*, VI (1868), 92-102; and *ibid.* (Hebrew), VIII (1895), 66 ff. Even in his fine terminological study of the term "scale" (*ibid.*, IX [German], 87 f.) he used the book of Job merely as a background for its medieval commentators. Similarly, notwithstanding his clear realization that the book of Daniel was the fountainhead of the whole medieval apocalyptic literature and Messianic speculation, he was more interested in its subsequent exegesis, "which may be considered a segment of

463

world history," than in the book itself. Cf. *ZDMG*, XXVIII, 628. It is not astonishing, therefore, that, when approached by Delitzsch for some information in connection with a new edition of the Septuagint, he concentrated mainly on supplying data concerning the use of Greek by the Jews of medieval Greece. Cf. *HB*, XV, 37.

60. *HB*, II, 5; VII, 105, 124; Marx in *PAAJR*, V, 125. His dislike of Ewald must have been reinforced by Geiger's comments. In an undated letter received by St. on Sept. 23, 1860, Geiger wrote: "Ich denke, dass die זלזולים, welche ich mir von Ewald zuziehe, mir zu כפרה dienen werden; aber ich werde ihn doch immer weiter streicheln." On June 13, 1862, Geiger added, "Dass sich Ewald blamiert, so oft er eine jüdische Schrift bespricht, versteht sich von selbst." Cf. also Geiger's "Das Studium der nachbiblischen Literatur unter den Christen," *HB*, III (1860), 77 ff. St. objected, especially, to lower criticism on account of its extreme subjectivity, pointing to Graetz's commentaries on the books of Ecclesiastes and Song of Songs as a particularly "abhorrent example." Even Geiger's reconstructed *Urschrift* was based, in his opinion, on the far-fetched assumption that "der ängstlichen Masora eine lange Periode willkürlicher Entstellungen vorangegangen, wie sie wohl an keinem anderen Buch historisch nachgewiesen ist," *HB*, XII, 131; XVII, 79 f. Higher criticism, on the other hand, seemed to him undermined not only by the vicious circle of its argumentation, but also by the total inability of the critics to agree on any fundamental issue. In his various, though on the whole rather restrained, criticisms of Wellhausen he sharply rejected the latter's admission that certain hypotheses must be postulated without direct evidence. On another occasion, refering to Wellhausen's (and Kuenen's) brief survey of the major trends in the criticism of the Pentateuch since Bleek, he inquired: "Wie steht es nun mit jenen positiven Resultaten, zu welchen die kritische Schule so viel Aufwand von Fleiss und Scharfsinn verwendet hat? Kaum in wenigen Hypothesen über die Grundquellen und deren Bearbeitung sind die Hauptvertreter einverstanden und ihren ersten Ansichten treu geblieben, selbst über die Methode wird scharf gestritten . . .," *HB*, XV, 30 f.; XVIII, 82 f. Cf. also *ibid.*, XIX, 56 f.; "An Introduction to the Arabic Literature of the Jews," *JQR*, IX (1896-97), 235 f. Of course, he was least impressed by theories focused on the allegedly peculiar traits of the ancient Semites, which were called upon to explain certain crucial difficulties in biblical literature. Cf. *HB*, III, 44; XI, 55; XV, 60 and above n. 11. On the other hand, he also disagreed with such fundamentalist evasions as when Güdemann called Eve "a biblical personality." Cf. *ibid.*, XVI, 124. On occasion, he attacked a Jewish scholar like Bacher for failing to indicate the composite nature, e.g., of Psalm 119. Cf. *JQR*, XVII, 559.

61. *GL*, p. vii n. 2; *HB*, XVI, 56; XIX, 79; XXI, 95, 104 f. Cf. also *ibid.*, p. 122. To medieval tombstone inscriptions, however, he devoted an interesting, though brief summary in his "Allgemeine Einleitung," *JQR*, XVI, 374 ff.,

followed by a lengthy bibliographical list (*ibid.*, XVII, 564 ff.), which includes a few other items. Similarly, his attack on M. A. Lewy's *Geschichte der jüdischen Münzkunde* (*HB*, V, 134), was not the result of his disparagement of numismatics as history's auxiliary science (cf. his brief remarks in *JQR*, XV, 328 f.), but of his dislike of the Institute's popularizing efforts: "Hat es denn aber irgend einen vernünftigen Zweck, dass sich Kreti und Pleti für Münzkunde interessiere und etwas davon zu verstehen sich einbilde?" He was somewhat more skeptical, at least in his earlier years, about the value of comparative linguistic studies, for, unlike that of the postbiblical literature, the language of the Bible seemed to him to show few outside influences. Cf. *FE*, pp. 1 f.; *BHB*, p. ix; and his comments on M. A. Lewy's *Phönizische Studien* in *HB*, VII, 7. On the other hand, he conceded the value of popular and pedagogic presentations of biblical history, provided they preserved the vigor of the original texts. Cf. *HB*, II, 27 (with reference to the Bunsen Bible); III, 13 f.

62. *HB*, I, 5; X, 166 f.; XVIII, 78; *JBGW*, II, 53 ff. Cf. his somewhat inconsistent criticisms of Hamburger's *Real-Encyclopädie für Bibel und Talmud* and his apprehensions that J. Levy's talmudic dictionary might be attempting to combine the simple task of translation with a far more ambitious encyclopedic array of quotations. Cf. *HB*, XV, 103; XVIII, 32 f.; *JBGW*, VI, 44. On other such critical comments cf. *HB*, VII, 122; XX, 5, 60; XXI, 3. While criticizing, however, Beer's *Leben Abrahams nach der Auffassung der jüdischen Sage* as a "hybrid" of edification and scientific inquiry, he admitted the legitimacy of a free rendition of the Aggadah. Such free translators, he declared, "sind selbst die Haggada und der Midrasch unserer Zeit," *HB*, II, 100.

63. *GL*, pp. 1 ff.; *BM*, 1893, 67 f.; *HB*, X, 165 f.; XX, 4; Lévi's review of *GL* in *REJ*, LIII (1909), 160. Cf. also *FE*, p. 21. At the same time St. realized the focal importance of "tradition" in ancient life and letters, and admired the interpretations given to it by Geiger and, with reference to parallel developments in the Muslim world, by A. Sprenger. Cf. *HB*, V, 66; VI, 125. He was perfectly aware, however, of the non-acceptance of this interpretation in Orthodox circles, both Jewish and Christian. Cf. his remark on Sprenger in *PAL*, p. 9 n. 2.

64. *HB*, VI, 102; VII, 33; XIV, 10; XIX, 79; *JBGW*, III, 66. Even in his special monograph, "Zur Alexandersage," *HB*, IX, 13-19, 44-53, he analyzed *Yosippon* carefully rather than any ancient records. Cf. also his critical comments *ibid.*, I, 123 (Geiger's essay on the Ecclesiasticus); and XIX, 6 f. (Graetz's *Das Königreich Mesene*).

65. *JBGW*, V, 42; VI, 38; *HB*, VII, 59; XIII, 19; XVII, 2. While suspending judgment on M. Rahmer's *Die hebräische Tradition in den Werken des Hieronymus* until its completion, he went off to the more familiar field of Saadiah's and Hai's knowledge of the Koran, *ibid.*, IV, 12. On his relations with Delitzsch, cf. in particular, the latter's remarks on their collaboration in

the edition of Aaron of Nicomedia's *Eş Ḥayyim* (1841); and the letter of recommendation of July 18, 1846, written by Delitzsch in support of St.'s application for Prussian naturalization and published by Marx in *Jewish Studies . . . Kohut*, pp. 512 f. (D. stressed here St.'s "respektvolle Stellung zum christlichen Glauben").

66. *HB*, II, 10 f.; III, 47; IX, 16 f., 44; *GL*, p. 89 (p. 24 erroneously quoted). Cf. also *FE*, pp. 22. Even Frankel's essay on a subject so close to his heart as "Juden und Judentum nach römischer Anschauung," *MGWJ*, IX (1860), 125-42, induced him merely to compile a brief, far from satisfactory bibliographical list of studies on this subject, *HB*, III, 50 f.; V, 81 f.

67. *BM*, 1893, 67; *GL*, pp. viii f.; *HB*, I, 3; *JBGW*, III, 59, 69, 72; IV, 28; VI, 47. His underestimate of the vigor of French anti-Semitism in the 1880's was shared by many complacent observers in France until their rude awakening during the Dreyfus affair. How unjustified this complacency was may be seen from the pertinent recent studies by R. F. Byrnes, E. Silberner and Z. Szajkowski in *JSS*, VIII-X.

68. *HB*, XIV, 20 f., 87; XX, 29, 76; XXI, 11, 47, 126, 130; *JBGW*, VI, 39; *AL*, p. xii n. 1; *ZHB*, IX, 186. He regretted, on the one hand, that the sixty and more German pamphlets and articles published during a year had produced nothing of historical and scholarly value and, on the other hand, felt in regard to such apologetic writings, as Güdemann's *Kinderschlächter*, that "wer nicht belehrt sein will, den werden auch die heutigen Schriften nicht belehren," *JBGW*, II, 53; *HB*, XXI, 125. Cf., however, the more hopeful Foreword to his new edition of Zunz's *Damaskus* (Berlin, 1859); and the note on the events of 1775 in his "Ein Blatt der Geschichte," in Brüll's *Populärwissenschaftliche Monatsblätter*, III (1882-83), 8-10. In mentioning the new impression of Menasseh ben Israel's *Mikveh Yisrael* he underscored the Spanish editor's prefatory remarks. "Die Deutschen müssen 1881 eine Toleranzpredigt aus Madrid zu hören bekommen!" *HB*, XXI, 128.

69. *HB*, II, 15, 86; III, 86; VII, 80; XVI, 115; XVII, 82; XX, 84; "Literatur des Judeneides," *ZHB*, I (1896), 17-22; Marx, *EJB*, p. 139. As a curiosity he quoted fully an excerpt from an African Hebrew manuscript predicting the downfall of the Christian religion in 1832-34. More in the nature of a curiosity, he also compiled jointly with M. Roest a bibliography of Jewish patriotic writings under the title, "Zur loyalen und patriotischen Poesie und Andacht," *Israel. Letterbode*, V (1879-80), 33-39. Cf. *GL*, p. xi n. 5. His own view on these outpourings is best summarized in his sarcastic remark on a Hebrew poem published on the occasion of Radetsky's death, *HB*, II, 44.

70. *HB*, VII, 127; XVI, 77; XXI, 14, 57 f. Cf. also his criticisms of such publicist efforts as M. Auerbach and S. Salant's *Open Letter to Sir Moses Montefiore* which, because of an awkward note by Dr. Loewe, he condemned as a "literary humbug"; and his wish that Picciotto's *Sketches* were "weniger feuilletonartig," *ibid.*, XVI, 123; XX, 44. As late as 1858, when Benjamin

Disraeli had already achieved great eminence as a statesman and writer, he curiously misinterpreted the latter's remark about his father's faith, *ibid.*, I, 132.
71. *HB*, III, 120. He pointed out that in a dissertation on *Die Legende des Judenknaben*, E. Woleter "verfolgt die Ausbildung in allen Verzweigungen mit grosser Genauigkeit; einen historischen Hintergrund wusste er wohl nicht zu finden," *HB*, XX, 120. Cf. also above n. 25.
72. In his *AL*, p. xxi n. 1 (Preface dated September 1902), he complained: "Meine Bibliographie der Geschichte bei den Juden, I. Hebräische Schriften, wird seit 1901 mit langen Unterbrechungen gedruckt, beim Abdruck dieser Zeilen sind 64 Seiten, 62§§, fertig." Cf. also *ZHB*, V (1901), 158: "in einer für den Druck bearbeiteten *Bibliographie* der Geschichte der Juden." As far back as 1878 he wrote, "Mit einer Zusammenstellung der Schriften über, und Quellen für jüdische Geschichte beschäftigt—wozu ich jede Nachweisung unbekannten oder seltenen Materials mit Dank annehmen werde," *HB*, XVIII, 129. Cf., however, *ZHB*, VI (1902), 159: "in meiner Gesch. Lit."
73. Cf. *GL.*, p. x; Marx in *ZHB*, IX, 135-41; X, 149-56; Poznanski in *JQR*, XVIII, 181-90; Malter in *Jewish Comment*, XXII. Cf. also *ZHB*, X, 158. One must not attribute this disorganized form of publication exclusively to St.'s old age (he was eighty-nine years old when *GL* appeared). He had equally bad experiences with such earlier publications as *PAL* which was in the press from 1862 to 1877. Cf. his Foreword thereto and *ZDMG*, XXVIII, 627.
74. *GL*, pp. vi, 93, 102.
75. *GL*, pp. vi f., 36 ff. Cf. especially his "Gemeindestatuten," *HB*, VI, 42 ff.; VIII, 103; XVI, 32 ff., 57 ff.; "Ein Codex diplomaticus judaicus," *ibid.*, XVIII, 129 f. (with comments thereon by S. Löwenfeld, *ibid.*, XX, 13); "Zur Quellenkunde für Geschichte der Juden," *ZGJD*, II (1887), 150-53; and "Statuten," *ZHB*, VIII, 124-26. Cf. also M. Wiener's "Ueber das bisher vernachlässigte Quellenstudium der jüdischen Geschichte," *HB*, IV, 1 ff. (the prominent place given to this article in his journal shows St.'s vivid interest in the subject); and St.'s comments, *ibid.*, XXI, 87 (societies for the support of needy brides); XX, 55 (the Worms memor book, ed. by Jellinek); XXI, 116 (the medieval school ordinance, ed. by Güdemann); XVIII, 81 (urging renewed investigation of the Nuremberg documents); XX, 89 (Moravia); XVI, 40 (Ferrara); XVIII, 136 (Alsace); *Jeschurun*, VII (1871), 44-45 (Prossnitz); *MGWJ*, XXXIX (1895), 238-39 (Mecklenburg); *HB*, III, 48 (Danzig); XVII, 86 (Berlin, 1873-76); XV, 30 (Cleveland); XX, 80 (B'nai-B'rith documents), 117 f. (American Jewish statistics). Even in his studies of medieval Hebrew poetry he was interested in such communal aspects as the existence or absence of literary societies and circles. This was, in fact, the burden of his presentation of the "Zeitgenossen des Moses ibn Esra und Jehuda ha-Levi" in *Festschrift . . . Harkavy* (St. Petersburg, 1908), pp. 126-36. With reference to the statutes of the Vienna society for the support of needy students (1862)

he stated: "Auch dergleichen wird einst als Material für Culturgeschichte dienen; ich erwähne daher die mir zufällig bekannten ähnlichen," *HB*, V, 39. It seems that he originally intended to include this type of documentary material in his compilation of historical records. In his aforementioned early reference to this project (*HB*, XVIII, 129 f.) he wrote that in this connection "hat sich mir das Bedürfnis einer Sammlung alter Urkunden als Grundlage für die Geschichte der politischen, juridischen und sozialen Verhältnisse der Juden als unabweislich herausgestellt." It is to be regretted that he later changed his mind and that not only a full-fledged *corpus*, but even a mere bibliographical listing of all pertinent documents, is still but a scholarly desideratum. Certainly St.'s list of eight (!) entries under "Gemeindewesen," can not be sufficiently excused even by his admission, "dass ich hier nicht das Resultat eigener spezieller Forschung wiedergebe, aber auch die jüdische Geschichtsforschung hat sich mit den jüdischen Gemeindeverhältnissen bis in die neueste Zeit wenig beschäftigt," *JQR*, XV, 311; XVII, 546. Cf., on the other hand, *ibid.*, XV, 314 f.; XVII, 546 f., where, under the curious heading of "socialism," he listed a heterogeneous assortment of writings ranging from a British Museum manuscript on the Mantua Ḥevrat raḥamim of 1579, through various studies of the Jewish family, charities and occupations down to Kayserling's essay on sumptuary laws. Cf. also his somewhat grudging recognition that "in den letzten Jahren hat man die Geschichte der Juden in England mit grossem Eifer, nicht ohne Voreingenommenheit, verfolgt," *BM*, 1896, 82.

76. *GL*, pp. viii, 107; *CB*, col. 747. Cf. also such incidental appreciative remarks as *HB*, III, 17; IX, 19.

77. *GL*, pp. 28 ff., 35 f., 49 ff., 83 f. Cf. *supra*, notes 58 and 64.

78. *HB*, IX, 13; *JBGW*, V, 38. In *CB*, cols. xxxix, 1002, he pointed out that even credulous Azulai did not consider Gedaliah trustworthy. In *GL*, p. 109, he admitted, however, that a new edition of the *Shalshelet*, provided with critical notes, was much to be desired. He also made good use of Ibn Yaḥya's materials, e.g., in *PAL*, pp. 306, 308, 320. Cf. also *JL*, p. 290 n. 22; *HB*, III, 42; VI, 61; "Zur Frauenliteratur," *Isr. Letterbode*, XII (1888), 62 f.

79. *GL*, pp. 7 ff., 23 ff., 45 ff., 55 ff., 76 ff., 93 f., 141 f.; *HB*, II, 9; *JBGW*, II, 51; III, 65. Of course, many of his remarks in *GL* are a repetition or elaboration of data supplied already in *CB* under the respective authors. Cf. also his commendation of ever new efforts to secure a correct Sherira text, even if the author of the new study, J. Wallerstein, happened to be a pupil of Graetz (*HB*, IV, 13; the use of Graetz's copy is not mentioned here, however; cf. *GL*, p. 24); his remarks on Ibn Daud's biography (*HU*, pp. 368 f.); his objection to Kayserling's unconcerned treatment of Ibn Verga as an historical source: "das ist bedenklich" (*HB*, IX, 79); and his extensive use of Capsali's chronicle in his "Candia, Cenni di storia letteraria," *Il Mosé*, II-V (1879-82). Cf. also Kohut's note on the latter essay in his *Bibliography*, p. xxx.

80. *CB*, cols. xli, 758 ff.; *HB*, VIII, 8, 108 f.; *JBGW*, II, 51 f. St. communicated Abraham Berliner's report of 1870, in behalf of the bibliophile, H. Lipschütz, that a manuscript of Azulai's itinerary (since published by Λ. Freimann) had been in the possession of an Italian rabbi, "der es sorgsam bewahrt und es nicht veröffentlichen will, weil darin viele Ausfälle gegen manche Rabbiner und Gelehrte jener Zeit sich befinden," *HB*, X, 82 f.

81. *HB*, VII, 36 ff. Cf. also his irate remarks on the news about the erection of a monument to the Cossack chieftain, *ibid.*, XIII, 16. Once again he was not consistent. He rationalized his failure to make extensive use of the Genizah materials, which had begun to revolutionize the entire outlook on Jewish history under early Islam, by defending his *AL* against Hirschfeld's strictures. "Hier ist zunächst," he wrote, "Geschichte mit Stoff confundiert. . . . Und alle jene bisher unbekannten Fragmente, was beweisen sie gegenüber den zusammengestellten Schriften der Klassiker? . . . Was Anderes, als dass sie meist unbekannt, weil einflusslos blieben," *GL*, p. viii. Cf. also *ZHB*, X, 89 f. The criterion of influence certainly was not St.'s usual standard.

82. Leclerc, *Histoire*, I, 11; Steinschneider in *Deutsches Archiv f. Gesch. der Medicin*, I (1878), 356 f.

83. *BM*, 1893, 110; *JBGW*, I, 39. The peculiar difficulties of Jewish bio-bibliography are stressed, from another angle, in "Pseudo-Juden und zweifelhafte Autoren," *MGWJ*, XXXVIII (1894), 39-48. St. noted, therefore, with particular relish the preservation of such an early autobiographical account as that included in Shabbetai Donnolo's commentary on the *Sefer Yeṣirah*, *BM*, 1896, 44. At the same time he felt that the career of a leading scholar often reflected the destinies of the whole generation, be it only in their common sufferings. He derided, however, David Kaufmann for extolling Jewish scholars as "heroes." At this exaggeration, he declared, "konnte ich mich des komischen Eindrucks nicht erwehren, den die Bilder eines Herkules oder Achilles neben dem eines deutschen oder polnischen Klausrabbi machen müssen," *GL*, pp. vi, viii; *HB*, XVII, 32.

84. *JL*, pp. 75 f.; *PAL*, pp. 313 ff.; *AL*, pp. xx f.; *GL*, pp. vii f.; *HB*, III, 113; Al-Mas'udi, *Kitab at-Tanbih*, ed. by Goeje, pp. 112 f. (in the French transl. by B. Carra de Vaux, Paris, 1896, pp. 159 f.). St. himself vigorously protested against the often-heard assertion that Maimonides "had no understanding for the history of nations and states." Cf. *HB*, XIV, 42 f.; and *supra*, essay no. 6, on "The Historical Outlook of Maimonides."

85. Z. Frankel in *Zeitschrift f. d. rel. Interessen*, III, 465 f.; J. Goldenthal "Ueber einige Benennungen synagogaler Gesänge des Mittelalters," *Sitzungsberichte* of the Vienna Academy, XXXI (1859), 400, 405 ff. (with reference to his earlier essay, "Die neueste historische Schule in der jüdischen Literatur," *ibid.*, IX, 1852, 306-35, in which, however, he had reviewed the works of Dukes rather than St.); Steinschneider in *HB*, I, 5; III, 66 f.; V, 118; XV, 133; *JQR*, XVII, 577. Cf. also *HB*, I, 33 f. ("Es ist freilich in neuerer Zeit sehr viel

vom 'Geist' die Rede, wo höchstens Gespenster spuken. . . . Merkwürdiger
Weise sind diese 'Ritter vom Geiste' nicht selten irrende Ritter—was freilich
nicht die Schuld des Geistes ist,—und noch häufiger ganz gemeine Wege-
lagerer oder ausgewitzte Schmuggler und schlaue Wiederverkäufer"); and
Geiger's review of Frankel's *Entwurf, ibid.*, VIII, 37-39.

86. Hebrew letter to Jacob Benjacob published by Schorr in *Jewish Studies*
. . . *Kohut*, p. 548; *JQR*, XV, 312; *HU*, p. xxiv; *Catalogus* . . . *Bibliothecae* . . .
Lugduno-Batavae (Leyden, 1858), pp. xxiii f.; *HB*, II, 30; VIII, 137. Cf. also
ibid., V, 62; *ZHB*, VI, 182; IX, 157 f.; and above notes 24-26. He was, nevertheless, irked when Loeb explained to him the difficulty of securing a French
edition of *JL* because "für unsere französischen Leser, die in diesem Gegen-
stand gar nicht eingeweiht sind, scheint mir das Buch etwas zu trocken und
algebraisch" (Feb. 22, 1880). St. irately underscored the last four words.
His documentation is generally so integral a part of his work that one may
keenly regret, for instance, his decision to abstain from annotating his "Beiträge zur Palästinakunde aus neueren jüdischen Quellen," *ZDPV*, III (1880),
220-33, under the rather flimsy excuse that he had "bei den Lesern dieser
Blätter vielmehr eine gewisse Kenntnis vorausgesetzt, welche jene überflüssig
macht." Certainly a mere summary of parts of two Hebrew pamphlets,
however rare, which St. had excerpted in Oxford thirty years before, was a
scholarly "contribution" along the lines of least resistance. Cf. also his *Liqqu-
ṭim me-ḥokhmath ha-musiqah* which appeared in the *Bet Oṣar ha-Sifrut*, I
(1887), pp. xxix-xxxii, etc. It may also be noted that, for the sake of precision,
he preferred to write in German or Hebrew, for "man schreibt genau so, wie
man denkt, nur in der Muttersprache," *HU*, p. x. His compilation of *CB* in
Latin was imposed upon him by the authorities of the Bodleian Library; cf.
his comments cited by Marx in *EJB*, pp. 136 f. Curiously, however, he ventured
to write his letters to Boncompagni, *Intorno ad alcuni matematici* (Rome,
1863), in Italian, "già a me dilettissima fra le lingue moderne fino della mia
fanciulezza" (p. 4), and to submit his lengthy "Introduction to the Arabic
Literature of the Jews" to the editors of *JQR* in English (IX, 228). At the
same time he was quite sensitive about whatever editorial operations were
performed on his manuscripts in such journals as the *ZDMG*. Cf. e.g., *HB*,
VII, 81. For this reason he also wrote to George Kohut with reference to the
enclosed essay "Lapidarien" for the Alexander Kohut memorial volume: "Ich
gestatte nur einen unveränderten Abdruck, sonst erbitte ich mir das Ms.
zurück," *Studies . . . Freidus*, p. 87.

87. Harnack's letter on his ninetieth birthday, published by Marx in *Jewish
Studies . . . Kohut*, pp. 526 f.; *Der Aberglaube*, p. 3. St.'s remark in his
"Apocalypsen mit polemischer Tendenz" (*ZDMG*, XXVIII, 627) sounded
the keynote of many other publications as well: "Wenn dieser erste Versuch
weitere Untersuchungen und Mitteilungen hervorruft, so hat er seinen Haupt-
zweck erreicht."

LEVI HERZFELD, THE FIRST JEWISH ECONOMIC HISTORIAN

1. Cf. the survey based on the official University transcripts in Gustav Karpeles's biographical sketch of Herzfeld in the Introd. to the 2nd ed. of the latter's *Handelsgeschichte der Juden des Altertums* (Brunswick, 1894), pp. iv f. Cf. also Herzfeld's brief *Vita* in his dissertation, *Chronologia iudicum et primorum regum hebraeorum* (Berlin, 1836), p. 74.

2. In his autobiographical sketch Herzfeld mentioned Zunz only as his teacher in the "historical interpretation of the Psalms." But in the Preface to his *Metrologische Voruntersuchungen zu einer Geschichte des ibräischen, resp. altjüdischen Handels*, Pt. I (Leipzig, 1863), p. 4, he acknowledged his indebtedness to the chapter on "numismatics" in Zunz's *Zur Geschichte*. Although he rightly emphasized that Zunz's major concern was with the coins used by medieval rather than ancient Jewry, there is an undeniable impact of Zunz's method on all his writings. It was more than a temporary flush of youthful enthusiasm which inspired Herzfeld to dedicate his dissertation to Zunz, *viro de literatura judaica meritissimo*. Cf. also the detailed studies by Fritz Bamberger, "Zunz's Conception of History," *Proceedings of the American Academy for Jewish Research*, XI (1941), 1-25 (especially pp. 14 ff.) and by Luitpold Wallach, "The Scientific and Philosophical Background of Zunz's 'Science of Judaism,'" *Historia Judaica*, IV (1942), 56 f.

3. The encyclopedic nature of Böckh's University lectures delivered over a period of more than half a century is well illustrated by the title chosen by their compiler E. Bratuschek, viz. *Encyclopädie und Methodologie der philologischen Wissenschaften*, 2d ed. (Leipzig, 1886). Vol. I of Böckh's *Staatsleitung der Athener*, published in 1817, was entirely devoted to a discussion of economic and population problems including such subjects as money and its changing value, prices, wages, etc. On December 20, 1836, a short time after Herzfeld completed his studies at the University, Böckh wrote to his colleague Welcker: ". . . Zweitens bin ich auf verzweifelte *Untersuchungen über Mass und Gewicht* gerathen, womit ich mich bald ein halbes Jahr herumschlage." Max Hoffmann, *August Böckh, Lebensbeschreibung und Auswahl aus seinem wissenschaftlichen Briefwechsel* (Leipzig, 1901), p. 185. In the aforementioned Preface to his *Metrologische Voruntersuchungen*, Herzfeld acknowledged at least his literary indebtedness to Böckh's analogous work.

4. *Handelsgeschichte*, pp. 80 f.

5. *Ibid.*, p. xlvii.

6. *Chronologia*, pp. 73 f.

7. In explaining, for instance, the inclusion of a sermon preached in 1848 in his *Predigten* (2d ed., Leipzig, 1863) he wrote (p. v): "als die uns gewährte volle Einbürgerung die Weglassung einiger veralteten Gebetsformeln drin gender als bisher empfahl."

8. *Protocolle der ersten Rabbinerversammlung abgehalten zu Braunschweig* (Brunswick, 1844), Appendix nos. 3-5, pp. 105 ff.

9. Karpeles in *Handelsgeschichte,* p. xxix.

10. Herzfeld, *Geschichte des Volkes Jisrael von Vollendung des zweiten Tempels bis zur Einsetzung des Makkabäers Schimon zum hohen Priester und Fürsten* (Nordhausen, 1857), II [III], 225. This work is but a continuation of his *Geschichte des Volkes Jisrael von der Zerstörung des ersten Tempels bis zur Einsetzung,* etc., vol. I of which appeared in Brunswick, 1847. All three volumes will be quoted as *Geschichte* I, II, or III, viz., those published in 1847, 1854 and 1857 respectively. Vols. II and III appeared also in a second edition in 1863. There also was a briefer, popular edition, issued in a single volume in 1870 by the Institut zur Förderung der israelitischen Literatur, on the board of which Herzfeld had served for many years. But apart from a few corrections the latter work reiterated the author's views in his larger book and merely eliminated the vast scholarly apparatus, which in many ways, however, had been his most significant contribution to scholarship.

11. *Vorschläge zu einer Reform der jüdischen Ehegesetze* (Brunswick, 1846).

12. In the Preface to his *Predigten* (p. iv) he defined his objective: "ich erblicke die Aufgabe des Predigers bloss darin, Religion und Sittlichkeit klar zu lehren und warm ans Herz zu legen." This feature is emphasized also in J[oel]'s generally laudatory review of this collection of sermons in *MGWJ,* VIII (1859), 195 f.

13. "Chronologische Ansetzung der Schriftgelehrten von Antigonus aus Socho bis R. Akiba," *MGWJ,* III (1854), 221-29, 273-77; "Wann war die Eroberung Jerusalems durch Pompejus und wann die durch Herodes?" *ibid.,* IV (1855), 109-15. As a student of chronology Herzfeld had learned much from his teacher Christian Ludwig Ideler, whose well-known *Handbuch der Chronologie* he had called *doctissima computatio* in his *Chronologia iudicum,* p. 5.

14. Cf. e.g., *Geschichte,* II, 13, 61, 67, 75 f., 138 ff., 141 ff., 148, etc. His study, "Zur Geschichte des Bar Kokba," *MGWJ,* V (1856), 101-11 is likewise so principally devoted to the elucidation of the topographical, as well as chronological, aspects of the Bar-Kokhba revolt that, in order to amplify a statement in his final paragraph, he added a special brief article, "Ueber die Lage von Petra," *ibid.,* pp. 186-89. It is a pity that, evidently antagonized by a sharp, indeed unpardonable, review of his history in the following volume of the *Monatsschrift* (see below note 75), Herzfeld discontinued his collaboration with that main organ of Jewish scholarly opinion at that time.

15. *Metrologische Voruntersuchungen,* etc., 2 pts. (Leipzig, 1863-65). Published by the aforementioned "Institute for the Promotion of Jewish Literature."

16. *Zwei Vorträge über die Kunstleistungen der Hebräer und alten Juden* (Leipzig, 1864); likewise an Institute publication.

17. *Ibid.*, pp. 6, 62.

18. *Handelsgeschichte*, p. xlvi. The Preface to his *Metrol. Voruntersuchungen*, I, written in the calmer intellectual atmosphere of the early 1860's, stressed the Jewish contribution to civilization, rather than the Jew-baiting denunciations. It is, in many ways, so illustrative of Herzfeld's general outlook that it deserves to be cited here in a lengthy excerpt: "Man is gewohnt, höchstens auf dem religiösen Gebiete weltgeschichtliche Einwirkungen der Juden anzuerkennen, dagegen von jedem durchgreifenden Einflusse derselben auf die Entwicklung anderer menschheitlicher Potenzen zu schweigen, selbst wo Thatsachen von solcher Evidenz vorliegen, wie dass fast die ganze neuere Philosophie in Spinoza wurzelt, oder dass zu der Entfaltung des Handels, auf welchem in so ausgedehntem Masse die Völkerwohlfahrt beruhet, kein Stamm der Erde nachhaltiger als der jüdische beigetragen hat. . . . Die Juden sind nicht von Hause aus ein Handelsvolk; geschichtliche Einflüsse, die sich grossentheils noch nachweisen lassen, haben ihnen diese Erwerbsthätigkeit aufgezwungen. Aber, sei nun die Anlage dazu eine gleichwohl diesem Stamme angeborene, die nur der Erweckung harrete, oder liege es in dem jüdischen Wesen, jederlei Richtung welche das Geschick ihnen aufnöthigt, mit Talent zu verfolgen, das ist unbestreitbar, dass, wenn einmal eine gute Geschichte des Handels geschrieben werden wird, den Juden ein Hauptabschnitt darin nicht versagt werden kann; desgleichen wenn erst einmal in einer Geschichte der Menschheit die Beschreibungen blutiger Schlachten etwas abgekürzt werden, um für eine gebührende Würdigung auch der friedlichen Bestrebungen der Völker einigen Raum zu gewinnen alsdann, so nur Unpartheilichkeit die Feder führt, der vielgeschmähete jüdische Handelsgeist seine Ehrenrettung und seinen Ehrenplatz finden wird."

19. *Handelsgeschichte*, p. 278.

20. *Geschichte*, I, 1 f.; II, 338; III, 1. This high estimate of political history is connected with Herzfeld's general attitude to politics, colored by the dominant German political theory of the time. In his remarkable plea for certain alleviations in the Sabbath rest commandment to enable Jews to occupy public offices, he exclaimed at the Third Rabbinic Conference of 1846, "Der Staat ist entweder schon die Verkörperung der höchsten Sittlichkeit, oder er muss noch dazu erhoben werden: im ersten Falle sollten wir Juden aus Religiosität uns der Betheiligung an der erhabensten menschlichen Thätigkeit enthalten müssen? im zweite Falle sollten wir aus Religiosität an der Versittlichung des Staates, also an der Herbeiführung der Messias-Reiches nicht mitarbeiten dürfen? Wir sind die ältesten und verpflichteten Arbeiter an diesem Bau, dessen Spitze in den Himmel ragt." *Protokolle*, p. 108.

21. *Geschichte*, II, 219.

22. *Ibid.*, pp. 337 f.

23. *Ibid.*, I, 2; III, 604 f.

24. *Ibid.*, I, 2.

25. He repudiated, for example, Joseph Salvador's explanation of Antiochus Epiphanes' outlawry of Judaism and other subject faiths as a political stratagem designed to strengthen the homogeneity of the Syrian Empire in the face of Roman aggression. Cf. Salvador's *Histoire de la domination romaine en Judée* (Paris, 1846), I, 60. Such designs appeared to Herzfeld as "too much in the style of modern statesmanship." *Geschichte,* II, 233 f. Better insights into the nationalistic ingredients of ancient Greek civilization than were given to Herzfeld's generation (cf. e.g. the recent literature cited in Hans Kohn's *The Idea of Nationalism,* New York, 1944, pp. 586 ff.) may well have persuaded him not to dismiss so lightly here and elsewhere, traces of "modernity" in the ancient world. However, we shall certainly not blame him for exercising even excessive caution against facile modern parallels.

26. This is clearly illustrated by his sermons which, discussing a variety of theological, ethical and ritualistic problems, made little reference to the existing shortcomings in the social order or communal organization. Even when he dealt with Jewish emancipation, a subject close to his heart, he did it timidly and hesitatingly. In a sermon delivered a few weeks after the Brunswick Conference of 1844, he not only referred to his own "happy little country" as giving rise to few legitimate complaints, but declared, also in behalf of his rabbinical colleagues: ". . . weil es unser unverbrüchlicher Vorsatz ist, von jedem Versuche auf den Staat einzuwirken uns durchaus fern zu halten; wir werden uns nicht in Bahnen eindrängen, auf welchen so leicht auszugleiten ist." When on another occasion, he preached a sermon on "Do not Worry" and tried to persuade his congregants to be less calculating and concerned about their future, financially or otherwise, he was principally an apologist trying to defend the Jews against the accusation, "dass wir ein ungemüthliches Volk wären, in welchem der kalte, berechnende Verstand weit mehr vorherrsche, als das Gefühl, und dass namentlich ein heiteres Unbekümmertsein um den morgenden Tag höchst selten oder gar nicht unter uns anzutreffen sei." The catastrophic fire which destroyed a large part of the city of Hamburg with numerous casualties in 1842 inspired him merely to a public speculation over the complexities of Theodicy. In this connection he characteristically defined the tasks of a preacher: "Neben der stetigen Pflicht, die Wahrheiten seiner Religion zu lehren um die widerkehrenden Erscheinungen des Lebens durch sie in das rechte Licht zu setzen, hat der Geistliche die ebenso wichtige, stattgehabte ungewöhnliche Ereignisse vom religiösen Standpunkte aus seiner Gemeinde zu beleuchten." Cf. *Predigten,* pp. 121 ff., 156 ff., 231 ff. Although undoubtedly influenced by the prevailing fashion among German rabbis who, even in recent decades, used to air controversial social problems from the pulpit far less frequently than did their American colleagues, Herzfeld evidently was sufficiently wrought up about them to mention them in passing with some trenchant remark.

27. Herzfeld was born on December 27, 1810, in Elbrich am Harz in the

Prussian province of Saxony; Marx on May 5, 1818, in Prussian Trier. Though far apart in their native endowment, family background and upbringing, they both grew up in the same general atmosphere of emancipatory Prussian Jewry and idealistic German philosophy. This does not mean, of course, that Herzfeld was an adept of the then fashionable dialectical philosophy. Neither his bent of mind nor the influence of his teachers, among whom Henrik Steffens was outspokenly anti-Hegelian, predisposed him for embracing uncritically, as did many of his fellow reformers, Hegelian tenets and methods. During a discussion on Sabbath reforms at the Third Conference at Breslau in 1846, he protested against the injection into the debate of philosophical arguments, "weniger, weil sie dem Volke nicht gut können zugänglich gemacht werden, als weil durch sie unser Lehrer Moscheh zu einem dialektisch gewandten Philosophen gemacht wird. Das war er nicht, er war schlicht und einfach, und ebenso die Lehre, die er uns befahl." Cf. *Protokolle* (Breslau, 1847), p. 103.

28. Cf. his *Kunstleistungen*, p. 8.

29. *Geschichte*, III, 605.

30. There was a bitter personal undertone in his explanation why his *History* had been selling so poorly. Among the reasons mentioned the first and foremost was that "von den Juden, für welche allerdings dasselbe [Werk] zunächst geschrieben ist, kaufen fast bloss die Geistlichen und Lehrer jüdische Bücher: Diese aber sind nicht zahlreich, und auch ziemlich durchgängig so gestellt, dass sie kostspielige Werke nicht anschaffen können." *Ibid.*, II, p. v.

31. *Protokolle und Aktenstücke der zweiten Rabbinerversammlung* (Frankfort, 1845), p. 59.

32. *Predigten*, p. 66.

33. *Ibid.*, p. v.

34. *Geschichte*, I, pp. v f.

35. *Ibid.*, III, 425.

36. *Ibid.*, II, 31 f., 34.

37. *Predigten*, pp. 162 f. In his own booklet, *Das Deutsche in der Liturgie der Braunschweiger Synagoge* (Brunswick, 1844), which superimposed but a few German prayers upon the traditional prayerbook, Herzfeld stressed on the title page the fact that these changes had already been introduced under the regime of his predecessor, Eger [See also *AZdJ* VI (1842) 411-412, 460-461]. He also expressed the conviction that "die Liturgie, welche, so Gott will, aus dem Schoosse der künftigen Rabbiner-Versammlungen hervorgehen wird, muss aus Einem Gusse sein, wenn auch von dem alten Typus jedenfalls beibehalten werden soll, was nur möglich ist zu retten. . . ." *Ibid.*, p. vii. Cf. also his interesting observations, based on more than two decades of both teaching and rabbinical experience, in the Preface to his textbook, מנחת זכרון, 2d ed. (Leipzig, 1866); and his noteworthy votes at the Second Rabbinical Conference in *Protokolle*, pp. 58 f., 125, 319 ff.

38. *Predigten*, pp. 161, 164. Although this particular sermon (one of Herzfeld's best) preached in 1844 was evidently intended to appease an apparently vocal conservative faction in the congregation, there is no reason to doubt its sincerity.

39. *Handelsgeschichte*, pp. 20, 35.

40. *Ibid.*, pp. 81, 274.

41. *Ibid.*, pp. 6 ff., 271.

42. *Ibid.*, p. 8: ". . . der unpartheische Forscher die Juden auch im Handelsverkehr eher über, als unter dem Niveau der allgemeinen Moral, im Judenthum durchweg die lauteste und zuweilen selbst eine ideale Rechtlichkeit auf diesem, wie auf jedem sonstigen Gebiete gefordert finden wird." Cf. also his programmatic statement cited above n. 18.

43. *Ibid.*, p. 278.

44. *Geschichte*, I, 15-21, 148-98, 326-42, 348-56, 370-78, 455-65; II, 86-114, 151-77, 206-10, 397-404, 409-16.

45. This objection was indeed voiced by a critic in *Grenzboten* (1854), 419.

46. *Geschichte*, II, 219.

47. If the data from Graeco-Roman sources far outnumber those from the more closely related Oriental systems, this was obviously due to their ready availability rather than to Herzfeld's own preference.

48. *Handelsgeschichte*, pp. 20 f., 273 f.: "Fortgesetzte Forschungen innerhalb meines Thema's haben mir diese Wechselwirkung immer von neuem bestätigt, und zu einem grossen Theile in Rücksicht auf sie bin ich in diesem Werke so oft den Spuren von Israels Verbreitung nachgegangen."

49. *Geschichte*, II, 3 ff.

50. *Handelsgeschichte*, p. 81.

51. *Geschichte*, II, title-page and p. iii. Humboldt's saying, here twice repeated, was taken from *Kosmos* (Stuttgart, 1845), I, p. vi.

52. *Ibid.*, I, pp. vi ff.: "Vergrössert wurde diese Schwierigkeit [der Datierung biblischer Bücher] noch dadurch, dass wenn die verdienstlichen Anfänge auf diesem Gebiete, früher von Zunz, später von Reggio, Krochmal und Philippson, abgerechnet werden, die neuere Kritik der heiligen Schriften bisher aller jüdischen Einwirkung entbehrte, ein Mangel, dessen Erheblichkeit freilich die Wortführer auf diesem Felde nicht zugestehen werden, den ich aber oft während meiner Arbeit zu bedauern Gelegenheit fand."

53. *Geschichte*, II, pp. vi ff.

54. *Geschichte des Volkes Jisrael von der Zerstörung des ersten Tempels bis zur Einsetzung des Makkabäers Schimon zum Hohenpriester und Fürsten, nach seinem dreibändigen Werke des gleichen Titels kürzer dargestellt und überarbeitet* (Leipzig, 1870), Preface.

55. *Handelsgeschichte*, pp. 89 f.

56. *Ibid.*, pp. 171 ff.

57. *Geschichte*, I, p. ix: "Ich war daher genöthigt in die Darstellung nicht wenige Vermuthungen aufzunehmen und diese in einem Anhange hinläng lich und deshalb oft ausführlich zu begründen."

58. *Handelsgeschichte*, pp. 88 ff.

59. *Ibid.*, pp. 113 ff., 312 f. Curiously, M. Grünwald, an unfriendly and far from penetrating reviewer of this work, censured Herzfeld for his failure to refer to modern literature, "so z.B. bei der Rede vom Schreibmateriale auf L. Löws bedeutende Arbeit." Cf. *MGWJ*, XXVIII (1879), 239.

60. *Handelsgeschichte*, pp. 2, 275.

61. *Ibid.*, p. 140. He admitted such a standard only for modern times: "Die socialen Anschauungen der Neuzeit haben mit sich geführt, dass in Nahrung, Kleidung, Comfort, Vergnügungen und Aehnlichem, die mittleren Stände es den höheren, die untersten den mittleren gleichthun wollen, und bis zu einem gewissen Grade leistet ja die durchbrechende Anerkennung der Menschenwürde und die gewachsene öffentliche Humanität den untersten Volksschichten einigen Vorschub hierin: daraus kann—ausser vielem Guten und Schlimmen—auch ein allgemeiner Geldwerth sich hervorbilden. . . ."

62. *Ibid.*, p. xlvii. He was more specific in the Preface to his *Metrologische Voruntersuchungen* (I, 2 f.). He considered the collaboration of a scientifically trained businessman with a good knowledge of rabbinics as indispensable for a proper study of modern Jewish economic history. In regard to the nineteenth century during which trade in commercial papers of all sorts assumed such enormous significance "[wird] ein anderer als ein Geschäftserfahrener selbst schwerlich befähigt sein."

63. *Handelsgeschichte*, p. 22.

64. *Ibid.*, p. 277.

65. *Geschichte*, I, p. x.

66. *Ibid.*, II, 266 n. 80; III, 382.

67. It was a somewhat misplaced jest when Herzfeld apologized: "Der wahrheitsliebende L. wird es mir verzeihen, dass ich etwas in einem Buche bekämpfe, das er so gütig war mir zum Geschenk zu senden." *Ibid.*, III, 397.

68. Cf. *ibid.*, II, 357, 386 f., 395, 417; III, 61 ff., 178, 210, 217, 268, 287, 334, 340 f., 344 n. 42, 346 n. 45, 351 n. 47, 354, 383, 387, 391 f., 394 ff., 415, 427, 499, 528 n. 65, 532, 535, 541, 548, 552, 554, 556, 606, 610 f., etc.

69. *Chronologia iudicum*, pp. 1 ff.

70. *Geschichte*, II, 357. Cf. on the other hand, his spirited defense of Bible criticism against those conservatives who condemned it indiscriminately as a menace to religion, *ibid.*, I, p. vii.

71. *Ibid.*, pp. xi f.

72. *Ibid.*, II, p. v. Herzfeld may well have had in mind his personal experience with his teacher Hengstenberg. When the latter published in 1839 the third volume of his *Beiträge zur Einleitung ins Alte Testament* in which he

devoted a lengthy chapter to the period of the Judges, he quoted numerous Christian authors but failed to mention Herzfeld's *Chronologia iudicum,* published three years earlier, very likely in part under his own supervision.

73. *AZdJ,* XVIII (1854), 393, 596.

74. *Israelitischer Volkslehrer,* V (1855), 300 ff.

75. *MGWJ,* V (1856), 233-34. This anonymous review is so typical of the relation of certain conservative circles to Herzfeld that it deserves to be quoted here in a few significant excerpts: "Die nicht nur schonungslose, sondern vornehme Verachtung gegen Tradition und frühe Angabe zur Schau tragende, sich selbst überschätzende Kritik des Verfassers muss umso tiefer verletzen, als er auf der anderen Seite manchem Neuern, der noch sprechen kann (die Todten schweigen) unbedingt folgt [a reference to Ewald].... So ist im Munde eines Landesrabbiners das 'Jawe' nicht nur anstössig, sondern auch unwürdig . . . . Eine ausführliche Kritik würde bei dem Reichthume des von H. Gebotenen ein besonderes Werk erfordern; wir hoffen jedoch zu öfteren Malen auf diese Schrift zurückzukommen." Attitude and tone, as well as the concluding passage, seem to point to Frankel, the editor, to whom, indeed, Brann, *MGWJ,* XLV (1901), 345, ascribes the authorship of this unbridled attack. For Herzfeld's dignified reply, cf. his *Geschichte* III, pp. v ff.

76. *Hebräische Bibliographie,* XIX (1879), 7; VI (1863), 130. With reference to this "Lieferung I" being but a reprint from the *Jahrbuch für die Geschichte der Juden,* III, Steinschneider wrote: "Wohl so bezeichnet wegen unveränderten *Sonderabdrucks,* in welchem freilich das Verhältnis zum Jahrbuch mit keiner Silbe verraten ist, als ob dergleichen in keine der Rubriken von Sittlichkeit und Frömmigkeit gehörte, welche zu lehren des Verfassers Beruf ist."

77. *Allgemeine Kirchenzeitung* (in Appendix, *Theolog. Literaturblatt*) of Sept. 5, 1855.

78. Ewald in his *Jahrbücher der biblischen Wissenschaft,* VI (1853-54), 145 f. Cf. also Herzfeld's reply in his Preface to *Geschichte,* III.

79. *Einblicke in das Sprachliche der semitischen Urzeit betreffend die Entstehungsweise der meisten hebräischen Wortstäme* (Hanover, 1883). Cf. *ibid.,* pp. 15 f. for Herzfeld's keen characterization of his main predecessors, Gesenius and Fürst.

80. 1884, No. 3, pp. 88 f.: ". . . Der Kundige hat an diesen Proben genug und der Ref. könnte hiermit schliessen, wenn dieses Buch nur für sich stände und nicht Symptom einer allgemeinen Erscheinung wäre, nämlich einerseits jener weit verbreiteten semitischen Unverfrorenheit, die sich nicht scheut, das elendste Zeug grossartig auf den Büchmarkt zu werfen, und jener ebenso weit verbreiteten Nachgiebigkeit von Seite unserer Universitäten andrerseits, die durch Verleihung des Doctortitels an so manchen vom Osten stammenden

jüdischen Jüngling sich für derartige Dinge mit verantwortlich machen und an dieser semitischen Selbstüberhebung zum grossen Teil mit schuld sind." Herzfeld again replied with great dignity. Cf. *AZdJ*, XLVIII (1884), 152. According to Herzfeld, a friend of his inquired from the editor of the *Centralblatt*, whether a reply would be accepted by the journal. The editor's answer was not only negative, but couched "in terms which were no less anti-Semitic than the review itself."

81. Quoted, without a source, by Karpeles in *Handelsgeschichte*, p. xx.

Index

481

Index

Index

Index

Index

"Lachrymose" conception of Jewish history, 64, 88, 96. *See* Sufferings
de Lagarde, Paul, 295
Land, in ancient Palestinian law, 81; Joshua and, 128-129, 366-367
Langobard kings, 28
Language; *see* Hebrew language
Lasinio, Fausto, 307, 455, 463
Lassalle, Ferdinand, ix, 291
Law, Jewish, and history, 81-86; Herzfeld on, 329, 332; Jost on, 250-252; de' Rossi on, 194-197; 419-420; in Messianic Age, Maimonides on, 158, 403. *See also* Land
Law, Mosaic, 121-127; political, de' Rossi on, 189-190, 417; oral, *see* Oral law
"Law of Return," 5, 19
Laws, Torah, Maimonides on, 117-118; validity of, 125, 363; *see also* Land
Leadership, Jewish communal, 82-85; and Jewish history, 88; Steinschneider on, 288, 453. *See also* Calendar
Leap Year, 144, 387. *See also* Calendar
Learning, and Jewish survival, 55; *see also* Education
Lebrecht, F., 294, 297
Leclerc, Jean, 317, 469
Legend, and history, xv
Leghorn, 83-84
Lenin, Nicolai, 45-46
Leone Ebreo, 202, 406, 407, 408
Leprosy, of Moses, Maimonides on, 122, 358
Letteris, Meir, 348
Levi, 120, 357
Levi ibn Habib, 403
Levites, 126, 137; under Ezra, 139, 376f.; Maimonides on, 122, 359
Lichtenberg, A. L., 349
Lilienthal, Max, 453
Lissagaray, P. S., 266
Literature, and history, Steinschneider on, 277-292, 450-456
Liturgy, Herzfeld on, 333
Litvinoff, Maxim, 18

Livy, 206-207, 209, 210, 214, 246; de' Rossi on, 196, 420
Loans, Maimonides on laws of, 393f.
Loeb, I., 312
Loew ben Bezalel of Prague (MHRL), 174, 194
Loew, Leopold, 286, 338
London, 61
Lost Tribes, de' Rossi on, 184, 413
Louis IX (of France), 40
Lovers of Zion, Graetz and, 266
Lurie, M., 73
Lusitano, Amato, 172
Luther, Martin, 30
Luzzatto, Samuel David, 105, 241, 260, 269, 297, 340, 348, 446
Lynching, Maimonides on, 125, 362

Macaulay, Thomas Babington, xvi, 65, 275, 281, 319
Maccabees, 69, 94, 139, 140, 340; de' Rossi on etymology of, 430; Herzfeld on, 328, 335
Machiavelli, Niccolo, 170, 174, 188, 207, 209, 252, 424
Magellan, F., 181, 182, 411, 427f.
Magic, Maimonides on, 116-117
Mahlon, 130
Mahzor, Roman, 169
Maimonides, Moses, xv, 180, 197, 279, 285, 346, 421, 428, 430; and general history, 154-161, 401-404; historical outlook of, summary, 161-163, 404; de' Rossi on, 223, 433; M. on revelation, 121, 367; on reason, 160
Malachi, Prophet, 138, 376
Malter, Henry, 313, 467
Malthus, Thomas R., 50
Manasseh, 134-135, 374
Manetti, Giannozzo, 414
Mani (Manichaeus), 350; Maimonides on, 383
Mankind, de' Rossi's theory of Man, 177, 407f.; Maimonides on unity of, 154, 401
Manna, 359
Mannheimer, Isak Noah, 287-288

493

Index

Milton, John, xvi
Milwaukee, 347
Minnesota, 347
Minority, Jewish, in Czechoslovakia, 16-17
Minority rights, Jewish, in Soviet Union, 46
Miracles, Jost on, 246f., 443; de' Rossi on, 179, 216, 409; of Moses, Maimonides on, 121
Mirsky, Michael, 348
Mishael, 136, 378
Mishnah, 124, 137, 138, 388; (Ab. Zarah), 352; (Abot), 355; Maimonides and chronology of, 152-154, 398-401; (Sanh.), 351; language of, 213f., 437; Maimonides on, 145; on Samaritans, 136
Mission, Jewish, idea of, 284, 286
Miṣvot, de' Rossi on, 197
Moabites, 124, 136, 138
Modena, Leon da, 172
Modern history, Steinschneider and, 310-311, 466
Mohammed, see Muhammed
Mommsen, Theodor, 86, 242, 343, 347
Monarchy, in ancient Israel, 131, 369; the Bible and, 188f.; and communal life, 83; Jost on, 253, 444f.; Maimonides on, 158, 402f.; de' Rossi on, 188f., 416f.
Monasch, Ber, 264
Monasch, Sir John, 264
Monatsschrift fuer die Wissenschaft des Judentums, 265, 267, 326, 342
Moneylending, 9; and Jewish law, 74f. See also Usury
Monopolies, and the Jews, 61f.
Monotheism, ethical, 286; Maimonides on, 117
Montaigne, Michel E. de, 409
Monte Cassino, 169, 187, 214, 427
Montesquieu, de La Brède, 247, 252f.
Moon worship, 26
Moors, 29
Moravia, 16-17
Mores, Jewish and modern capitalism, 57-62

Moriah, Mt., 118
Morin, Jean, 173
Morocco, 29, 146, 148, 394
Mortality, 80
Mortara Affair, 298, 458
Moses, 114, 117, 132, 143, 352, 383, 415; character of, 121f.; death of, 127, 365; Jost on, 250; law of, Maimonides on, 121-127; as leader, 122f., 126; as prophet, Maimonides on, 121; de' Rossi on, 191
Moses of Cordova, 148
Moses of Coucy, 368
Moses Dar'ai, 392
Moses ha-Darshan, 359, 374
Moses Isserles, 180, 410
Moses de Leon, 197
Moses Provençali, 171
Mt. Gerizim, 136
Muenter, Bishop, 255
Muhammed, ix, 32, 113, 250, 352, 353; Maimonides on, 146, 389f.
Munk, Solomon S., 263, 298, 352, 353, 356, 458
Muscato, Leone, 424
Muscato, Yehudah Leone, 171, 414
Muslims, authors quoted by de' Rossi, 229; claim of superiority, Maimonides on, 157, 402; as persecutors of Jews, Maimonides on, 146
Mutakallimun, Maimonides and, 403
Mysticism, Maimonides on, 148f.
Mysticism, Jewish, and Italian Gentiles, 198, 421; Maimonides on, 148f.; de' Rossi on, 431f.

Nabatean Agriculture, 115, 351
Naboth, 134
Nagid, 84
Nahmanides, 200, 285, 356, 358, 416
Nahum of Gimzo, 386
Naphtali, 128
Napoleonic Wars, divergent descriptions, 38; and historiography, 102
Nasi, Maimonides on, 143, 383
Natali, E., 346

495

Index

on, 119f., 356; and Jewish immigration, 59; Jost on, 247f., 443; as real home of Jews, de' Rossi on, 190, 417; reoccupation under Ezra, 137f.; sanctity of, 129; Steinschneider on, 283, 452

Palestinocentrism, 72

Panvinio, 209, 217, 233

Parnasim, role of, 55

Parochialism, in Jewish historiography, 93f.

Parthia, 12, 27, 28

Partisans, Jewish, 96

Parvaim, as "Peru," de' Rossi on, 183, 238, 440

Passivity, Jewish, 36f.

Patriarchate, Palestinian, 83

Patriarchs, Maimonides on, 118-20

Patritius, 407

Paul IV (Pope), 98, 348

Pavisius, Theseus, 429

Pearl Harbor, 37f.

Peddlers, Jewish, pioneering role of, 33f.

Pentateuch, 353f.; Graetz and, 256f., 267, 448; and laws, 81f., 125, 363

Periodicals, Hebrew, Steinschneider on, 291f.

Perles, Joseph, 303

Persecutions, and Jewish history, 96

Persia(ns), 6-7, 12, 27, 117, 139; language, Maimonides on, 155, 401f.

Pertz, G. H., 243

Pesaro, 97, 98f., 171

Petahiah of Regensburg, 315

Pharaoh, 363

Pharisees, 69, 94, 330; Jost on, 250

Philip Augustus, 40

Philip the Fair, 40

Philipson, D., 346

Philippson, Ludwig, 262, 268, 288, 340, 342

Philo, 8, 169, 176, 188, 340, 356, 406, 415, 429f.; de' Rossi on, 215, 222f., 236, 427, 432

Philo-Semitism, and Jewish history, 37f.

Philology, and historiography, 273

Philosophers, Maimonides on, 117

Philosophy, German idealistic, 76; and Jewish history, Jost and, 250

Phinehas, 125, 126, 362

Phoenicia, 31f.

Phylacteries, 402

Physics, medieval, de' Rossi on, 176-179, 417f.

Pico della Mirandola, Giovanni, 198, 201

Piety, as factor in Jewish survival, 55

Pilgrimages, Jewish, Roman Palestine, 27; to Second Temple, 12

Pinsker, Leo, 283

Pinson, Koppel S., 345

Pinthus, A., 346

Pioneering, as factor in Jewish history, 31-35

Pirque de R. Eliezer, 222

Pius V (Pope), 167, 348

Plagiarism, Steinschneider on, 299-300, 459

Plagues, Ten, 359; Maimonides on, 122, 358

Planets, de' Rossi on, 177-178, 408

Platina, 216

Plato, 189, 415, 417

Plaut, W. Gunther, 347

Pliny, 32

Pluralism, cultural, 21

Plutarch, 279

Poetry, Hebrew, 284; Maimonides on, 148; de' Rossi on, 238

Poggio, G. F., 422, 424

Pogroms, in Poland, 88

Polemics, de' Rossi on, 233

Political history, relation to religious history, Herzfeld on, 328-345; Steinschneider and, 277-292, 450-456

Polygamy, among Jews, 80

Pompey, 326

Pomponatius, 408, 420

Pool, David de Sola, 347

Popes, 9-10, 98, 167, 348; and Frederick II, 41; 16th century, 97f.

Population, Jewish, growth of, 50f.; and Jewish history, 79-81; decline of, 58f.

Sulam, Samuel, 232
Sun worship, Maimonides on, 118
Superiority, of Jews, de' Rossi on, 187
Supernatural, the, de' Rossi on, 178f., 409f.
Survival, Jewish, factors in, 38; Maimonides on, 156f., 402; and modern capitalism, 43-46, 53; will to, 21, 63f., 102; and world power, 27-29
Susa, 138f.
Swichkow, Louis J., 347
Symmachus, 221, 431
Synagogue, Ezra's establishment of, 139, 377; Herzfeld and, 333; and the Jewish community, 54; and Jewish identity, 20; as revolutionary institution, 34
Syncretism, 250; of Jewish and Christian sources, de' Rossi on, 226, 435; in the Renaissance, de' Rossi on, 201
Synods, and Jewish history, 83
Syria, 128f., 138

Tabari, Muhammed, 113, 363, 364, 399
Tabernacle, 126; Maimonides on, 122, 130, 359, 368
Taeubler, Eugen, 345
Taine, H., 247
Talmud, Babylonian, 24, 30, 39, 74, 124; Palestinian, 145
Talmud, Babylonian, and Babylonian geography, 71; as historical source, Maimonides on, 162; and history, 109f.; Jost on, 250f., 260, 444; vs. Kabbalah, de' Rossi on, 197, 421; laws on foreign languages, 139, 378f.; literature of, de' Rossi and, 221f., 432; and natural science, de' Rossi on, 180f.; origin of, 145; and science, de' Rossi on, 200; Steinschneider on, 284-286, 308f., 452f., 465; textual criticism of, de' Rossi, 218f., 430
Talmud, treatises of, 'Abodah Zarah, 354; Berakot, 355, 356; Ketubot, 356; Megillah, 356; Pesaḥim, 356;

Sanhedrin, 351, 353; Shabbat, 352, 356; Yebamot, 355
Tamar, 361f., 370
Tamḥui, 149
Tanḥuma, 222
Tannaim, 221; Maimonides on, 143-145, 153f., 387f., 401f.
Tarfon, 145, 386
Targum, Jerusalem, 221, 421; see also Bible
Taxes, Jewish, communal, and voting rights, 84f.; in Roman Empire, 104
Teachers, computation of generations of, Maimonides on, 152-154, 398-401; see also Sages
Teaching, of Jewish history, Steinschneider on, 288f.
Teilhaber, Felix, 58
Telesius, 407
Television, the Jews and, 34
Temple, Jerusalem, Herodian, 138-140; Maimonides on, 114f., 118, 122f.; rebuilding of, 138, 139, 376f.; utensils, 133-373; Solomonic, 130-133, 369-372; destruction of, 136
Temple Emanuel, New York, 453
Temporary National Economic Committee, 60
Terah, 25
Terumah, 376
Theocracy, 6; and Jewish history, 76; de' Rossi on, 196, 420
Theodicy, Maimonides on, 156
Theodor-Albeck, 354, 355, 356
Theodotion, 221, 431
Theology, and history, 271, 448f.; modern, 106; Jost and, 246, 443
Thirty Years' War, 51
Thomsen, Peter, 70, 346
Thucydides, 214
Tiberias, 128, 143, 384
Tiktin, Gedaliah, 263
Tisza-Eszlar, 312, 466
Tithes, 129, 138, 141, 145, 387f.; under Ezra, 139, 376f.
Titus, Emperor, 103f.; descriptions of, 39-40
Tolerance, and nationalism, 35-36